OXFORD MEDIEVAL TEXTS

General Editors

J. W. BINNS   B. F. HARVEY
M. LAPIDGE   T. REUTER

SYMEON OF DURHAM

*LIBELLVS DE EXORDIO ATQVE PROCVRSV
ISTIVS, HOC EST DVNHELMENSIS,
ECCLESIE*

TRACT ON THE ORIGINS AND PROGRESS
OF THIS THE CHURCH OF DURHAM

Symeon of Durham

LIBELLVS DE EXORDIO ATQVE PROCVRSV ISTIVS, HOC EST DVNHELMENSIS, ECCLESIE

Tract on the Origins and Progress of this the Church of Durham

EDITED AND TRANSLATED BY
DAVID ROLLASON

CLARENDON PRESS · OXFORD

OXFORD
UNIVERSITY PRESS

Great Clarendon Street, Oxford OX2 6DP

Oxford University Press is a department of the University of Oxford.
It furthers the University's aim of excellence in research, scholarship,
and education by publishing worldwide in

Oxford New York

Athens Auckland Bangkok Bogotá Bombay Buenos Aires Calcutta
Cape Town Chennai Dar es Salaam Delhi Florence Hong Kong Istanbul
Karachi Kuala Lumpur Madrid Melbourne Mexico City Mumbai
Nairobi Paris São Paulo Singapore Taipei Tokyo Toronto Warsaw

and associated companies in Berlin Ibadan

Oxford is a registered trade mark of Oxford University Press
in the UK and certain other countries

Published in the United States
by Oxford University Press Inc., New York

British Library Cataloguing in Publication Data

Data available

Library of Congress Cataloging in Publication Data

Data available

ISBN 0-19-820207-5

1 3 5 7 9 10 8 6 4 2

Typeset by Joshua Associates Ltd., Oxford
Printed in Great Britain
on acid-free paper by
Biddles Ltd., Guildford and King's Lynn

In memory of my father

WILLIAM GEORGE GOODALL ROLLASON

(1913–94)

PREFACE

THIS edition has taken longer to prepare than was originally envisaged, but the extra time has made it possible for it to take note of, and to be enriched by, the work of a number of scholars. In the earliest stages, I benefited from the expertise and generosity of my Durham friends Ian Doyle and Alan Piper, without whose intimate knowledge of the manuscripts and history of Durham Cathedral Priory the task would scarcely have been possible. Then in 1993 the Anglo-Norman Durham conference, held in Durham in September of that year, introduced me to the work of Michael Gullick, who was already collaborating with Alan Piper and whose ground-breaking identification of the hand of Symeon of Durham was published in the proceedings of the conference in 1994 (Gullick, 'Scribes'). As things turned out, however, the conference was only a beginning. The spring of 1995 saw a remarkable gathering of palaeographical, historical, linguistic, and art historical specialists in Durham to discuss the manuscripts and work associated with Symeon, and further substantial progress was made (published subsequently as Rollason, *Symeon*). To all these specialists, I am immensely grateful, for their patience, enthusiasm, and generous willingness to allow me to use their work. Just as I argue below that Symeon's work was itself a team effort, so too in a real sense is this edition.

The editors of OMT have been consistently supportive and helpful. My work has benefited greatly from the advice and assistance of the staffs of the British Library, especially Dr Michelle Brown; Cambridge University Library, especially Dr Jayne Ringrose; the Bodleian Library, especially Dr Bruce Barker Benfield; and above all the Dean and Chapter Library and the University Library at Durham, where Roger Norris and Beth Rainey have been towers of strength to me, as well as Alan Piper and Ian Doyle mentioned above. A very considerable debt is also owed to my colleagues and students in the University of Durham history department, for their interest in my work, for their support for it, and for the congenial and stimulating environment in which it has been carried out.

My most valued collaborator, however, will not see this book. My

father, W. G. G. Rollason, who patiently and painstakingly improved the clarity of my thought and the lucidity of my expression over a period of twenty years, assisted me with the translation published here shortly before his death in 1994. What it posssesses of distinction in English style is largely due to him, and I can only hope that I have learned sufficient from him for readers of what I have written subsequently not to be as conscious of his loss as I am.

D.W.R.

Durham
10 May 1999

CONTENTS

ABBREVIATIONS

Aird, *Cuthbert*	W. M. Aird, *St Cuthbert and the Normans: The Church of Durham, 1071–1153* (Woodbridge, 1998)
ALf	Wilhelm Levison, 'Die "Annales Lindisfarnenses et Dunelmenses" kritisch untersucht und neu herausgegeben', *Deutsches Archiv für Erforschung des Mittelalters*, xvii (1961), 447–506
Anderson, *Early Sources*	A. O. Anderson, *Early Sources of Scottish History, AD 500 to 1286* (2 vols.; Edinburgh, 1922)
Anon. *V. Cuth.*	*Vita sancti Cuthberti auctore anonymo*, the anonymous *Life of St Cuthbert*, cited by book and chapter; edn. and trans. in Colgrave, *Two Lives*, pp. 59–139 and 310–40
Arnold, *Sym. Op.*	*Symeonis monachi opera omnia*, ed. T. Arnold (2 vols., RS lxxv; London, 1882–5)
ASC	Anglo-Saxon Chronicle, cited *sub anno* (s.a.) and, where necessary, by the conventional manuscript sigla, A–G; text in *Two of the Saxon Chronicles Parallel*, ed. J. Earle and C. Plummer (2 vols.; Oxford, 1892–9); trans. in *The Anglo-Saxon Chronicle*, ed. D. Whitelock *et al.* (London, 1961), and in *English Historical Documents*, i, *c.500–1042*, ed. D. Whitelock (London, 1979), pp. 145–61
Asser	*Asser's Life of King Alfred together with the Annals of Saint Neot's erroneously ascribed to Asser*, ed. W. H. Stevenson (Oxford, 1904, rev. edn. 1959), pp. 1–96, cited by chapter
Battiscombe, *Relics*	*The Relics of St Cuthbert*, ed. C. F. Battiscombe (Oxford, 1956)
Bede, *HE*	*Bede's Ecclesiastical History of the English People*, ed. B. Colgrave and R. A. B. Mynors (OMT, 1969; rev. edn. 1990)
Bede, *V. Cuth.*	*Vita sancti Cuthberti auctore Beda*, Bede's prose *Life of St Cuthbert*, cited by chapter; edn. and trans. in Colgrave, *Two Lives*, pp. 141–307 and 341–59
BL	London, British Library
Bod. Lib.	Oxford, Bodleian Library
Bonner, *Cuthbert*	*St Cuthbert, his Cult and his Community to AD 1200*,

	ed. G. Bonner, D. Rollason, and C. Stancliffe (Woodbridge, 1989)
Botfield, *Catalogi veteres*	*Catalogi veteres librorum ecclesiae Dunelmensis*, ed. B. Botfield (SS vii; 1838)
CCCC	Cambridge, Corpus Christi College
CCCO 157	Oxford, Corpus Christi College 157
CMD	*Chronicon Monasterii Dunelmensis*, reconstructed by Craster, 'Red book', pp. 523–9, to which references relate
Colgrave, *Two Lives*	Two *Lives of St Cuthbert: A Life by an Anonymous Monk of Lindisfarne and Bede's Prose Life*, ed. and trans. B. Colgrave (Cambridge, 1940; repr. 1985)
Coxe, *Flores*	*Rogeri de Wendover chronica siue flores historiarum*, ed. H. Coxe (4 vols., English Historical Society, iv; London, 1841–2)
Cramp, *Corpus*	R. J. Cramp, *County Durham and Northumberland* (British Academy Corpus of Anglo-Saxon Stone Sculpture in England, i; Oxford, 1984)
Craster, 'Red book'	H. H. E. Craster, 'The red book of Durham', *English Historical Review*, xl (1925), 504–32
DCDCM	Durham Cathedral, Dean and Chapter Muniments
DCL	Durham Cathedral, Dean and Chapter Library
De miraculis	*Capitula (liber) de miraculis et translationibus sancti Cuthberti*, in Arnold, *Sym. Op.* i. 229–61 and ii. 333–62; also edited (under the title *Historia translationum sancti Cuthberti*) in *Symeonis Dunelmensis Opera et Collectanea*, ed. J. Hodgson Hinde (SS li; 1868), pp. 158–201 with different chapter-numbering
Doyle, 'Claxton'	A. I. Doyle, 'William Claxton and the Durham chronicles', *Books and Collectors 1200–1700: Essays presented to Andrew Watson*, ed. J. P. Carley and C. G. C. Tite (London, 1997), pp. 335–55
DPSA	*De primo Saxonum aduentu*, ed. Arnold, *Sym. Op.* ii. 365–84
EEMF	Early English Manuscripts in Facsimile
Freeman, *Norman Conquest*	E. A. Freeman, *The History of the Norman Conquest of England* (6 vols., Oxford, 1873–9)
Freeman, *William Rufus*	E. A. Freeman, *The Reign of William Rufus and the Accession of Henry I* (2 vols.; Oxford, 1882)
Gullick, 'Earliest manuscripts'	M. Gullick, 'The two earliest manuscripts of the *Libellus de exordio*', Rollason, *Symeon*, pp. 106–19
Gullick, 'Hand'	M. Gullick, 'The hand of Symeon of Durham:

further observations on the Durham martyrology
scribe', in Rollason, *Symeon*, pp. 14–31

Gullick, 'Scribes'   M. Gullick, 'The scribes of the Durham cantor's
book (Durham, Dean and Chapter Library B.IV.24)
and the Durham martyrology scribe', in Rollason,
Anglo-Norman Durham, pp. 93–124

Hart, *Early Charters*   C. R. Hart, *Early Charters of Northern England and
the North Midlands* (Leicester, 1975)

Heads of Religious   *The Heads of Religious Houses: England and Wales*
Houses   *940–1216*, eds. D. Knowles, C. N. L. Brooke, and
V. C. M. London (Cambridge, 1972)

HECont   Continuations to Bede, *Historia ecclesiastica gentis
Anglorum*, edn. and trans. in Bede, *HE*, pp. 572–7

HpB   *Historia post Bedam*, edn. in *Chronica Rogeri de
Houedene*, ed. W. Stubbs (4 vols.; RS li; London,
1868–71)

HReg   *Historia regum*, edn. in Arnold, *Sym. Op.* ii. 3–283

HSC   *Historia de sancto Cuthberto*, edn. in Arnold, *Sym.
Op.* i. 196–214

JW i   *The Chronicle of John of Worcester*, vol. i, ed. and
trans. P. McGurk (OMT, forthcoming)

JW ii   *The Chronicle of John of Worcester*, vol. ii, ed. R. R.
Darlington and P. McGurk, trans. J. Bray and
P. McGurk (OMT, 1995)

JW iii   *The Chronicle of John of Worcester*, vol. iii, ed. and
trans P. McGurk (OMT, 1998)

LDE   Symeon of Durham, *Libellus de exordio atque procursu
istius, hoc est Dunelmensis, ecclesie*, formerly known as
Historia Dunelmensis ecclesie

Liber Vitae   BL, Cotton Domitian VII. All references are to *Liber
Vitae Ecclesiae Dunelmensis: A Collotype Facsimile of
the Original Manuscript*, ed. A. Hamilton Thompson
(SS cxxxvi; 1923), using the pencil foliation in
preference to the erroneous ink foliation

Meehan, 'Symeon'   'A Reconsideration of the Historical Works associated with Symeon of Durham: Manuscripts,
Texts, and Influences', Ph.D. thesis (Edinburgh,
1979)

MGH Epp.   *Monumenta Germaniae Historica, Epistolae*

Mynors, *Manuscripts*   R. A. B. Mynors, *Durham Cathedral Manuscripts to
the End of the Twelfth Century* (Durham, 1939)

NMT   Nelson's Medieval Texts

Offler, *DIV*   *De iniusta uexacione Willelmi episcopi primi per Willel-*

mum regem filium Willelmi magni, ed. H. S. Offler, rev. for publication A. J. Piper and A. I. Doyle (Camden Miscellany, xxxiv; 1998), pp. 49–101

Offler, 'Early arch-
deacons'
H. S. Offler, 'The early archdeacons in the diocese of Durham', *Trans. of the Architectural and Archaeo-logical Society of Durham and Northumberland*, xi (1962), 189–207 (repr. Offler, *North of the Tees*, no. III)

Offler, *Episcopal Charters*
Durham Episcopal Charters, 1071–1152, ed. H. S. Offler (SS clxxix; 1968)

Offler, *Medieval His-torians*
H. S. Offler, *Medieval Historians of Durham* (Durham, 1958) (repr. Offler, *North of the Tees*, no. 1)

Offler, *North of the Tees*
H. S. Offler, *North of the Tees: Studies in Medieval British History*, eds. A. J. Piper and A. I. Doyle (Collected Studies; Aldershot, 1996)

OMT
Oxford Medieval Texts

Piper, 'Lists'
A. J. Piper, 'The early lists and obits of the Durham monks', Rollason, *Symeon*, pp. 161–201

Plummer, *Bede*
Venerabilis Baedae Opera Historica, ed. Charles Plummer (2 vols.; Oxford, 1896)

Raine, *Cuth. virt.*
Reginaldi monachi Dunelmensis libellus de admirandis beati Cuthberti virtutibus quae novellis patratae sunt temporibus, ed. J. Raine (SS i; 1835)

Raine, *Scriptores tres*
Historiae Dunelmensis scriptores tres: Gaufridus de Coldingham, Robertus de Greystanes, et Willielmus de Chambre, ed. J. Raine (SS ix; 1839)

Rollason, *Anglo-Norman Durham*
Anglo-Norman Durham, 1093–1193, ed. D. Rollason, M. Harvey, and M. Prestwich (Woodbridge, 1994)

Rollason, 'Erasures'
D. Rollason, 'The making of the *Libellus de exordio*: the evidence of erasures and alterations in the two earliest manuscripts', in Rollason, *Symeon*, pp. 140–56

Rollason, *Sources*
D. Rollason with D. Gower, *Sources for York History before 1100* (Archaeology of York, 1; York, 1998)

Rollason, *Symeon*
Symeon of Durham: Historian of Durham and the North, ed. D. Rollason (Stamford, 1998)

RS
Rolls Series

SS
Surtees Society

VCH Durham
The Victoria History of the County of Durham, ed. W. Page (London, 1905–)

Young, *Cumin*
A. Young, *William Cumin: Border Politics and the Bishopric of Durham 1141–1144* (Borthwick Paper liv; York, 1979)

INTRODUCTION

THE text edited and translated in this volume has often been known as the *Historia Dunelmensis ecclesie* ('History of the Church of Durham'), but is here presented under its original title *Libellus de exordio atque procursu istius, hoc est Dunhelmensis, ecclesie* ('Tract on the Origins and Progress of this the Church of Durham'). In fact, it concerns not only the church of Durham from its foundation in 995 to the year 1096, but also the churches of Lindisfarne and Chester-le-Street which it claimed as its predecessors. The text begins with King Oswald of the Northumbrians and his role, with Bishop Aidan, in founding in 635 a monastery on the island of Lindisfarne off the Northumbrian coast. Alongside the history of that monastery and of the kingdom of Northumbria, the text focuses on Lindisfarne's principal saint, Cuthbert. Drawing heavily on Bede's prose Life, it follows Cuthbert's entry into the monastery of Melrose, his time at Lindisfarne, his subsequent life as a hermit on the island of Inner Farne just to the south, his brief career as bishop of Lindisfarne (685–7), his death, burial on Lindisfarne, and disinterment after eleven years with the discovery that his body had remained undecayed. An account is then given of the bishops who succeeded him and of the kings who ruled after his death, especially King Ceolwulf, to whom Bede dedicated his *Historia ecclesiastica gentis Anglorum*, and who retired to Lindisfarne as a monk. Once arrived at the year 735, the text inserts verbatim Bede's own account of his career and writings and (with some modifications) the letter on the death of Bede by another Cuthbert.

There then follows an account of the kings of the Northumbrians and the bishops of Lindisfarne in the eighth and ninth centuries, with particular emphasis on the Viking attack on Lindisfarne in 793 and the activities of the Viking 'Great Army' which captured York in 867. Not long after this, in the year 875, the religious community of Lindisfarne abandoned its original home, and after an abortive attempt to cross to Ireland, part of it set off with the undecayed body of St Cuthbert and relics of other saints for a period of wandering across northern England, stopping for a while at Crayke just north of York, and settling eventually at Chester-le-Street a few miles north of Durham. There the church was richly endowed by a

Viking king called Guthred, whom the religious community was itself supposed to have helped to the throne, and remained there as the episcopal see of the former diocese of Lindisfarne and the resting-place of the body of St Cuthbert until the year 995. Under that year our text is the first to tell the story of how, faced with the threat of renewed Viking attack, the religious community at Chester-le-Street withdrew for a time with the body of its saint to Ripon. Once the threat had subsided, it set out to return to Chester-le-Street, but on the way St Cuthbert's remains became too heavy to lift. Having held a fast and a vigil to determine the reason for this, the saint revealed that he wished to be taken to Durham. Once the decision to do this had been made, his body became light and easy to move. With the help of Uhtred, future earl of the Northumbrians, the rocky, wooded pensinsula in the bend of the River Wear at Durham was cleared, and it became the site of the cathedral, the shrine of St Cuthbert, and the see which had previously been at Chester-le-Street.

Our text then follows the history of Durham cathedral through the early eleventh century, dwelling chiefly on the careers of the bishops but also making it clear that the religious community of Durham was no longer one of monks as it had been on Lindisfarne but of secular clerks. After the Norman Conquest, Durham's relations with King William I were not good. The first Norman earl of Northumbria was murdered there, and the first Norman-appointed bishop, a Lotharingian called Walcher, was also murdered in 1080, not before he had attempted to turn the secular clerks of his cathedral into regular canons. In 1073–4, however, three monks from the monasteries of Evesham (Worcs.) and Winchcombe (Glos.) arrived in Northumbria, intent on refounding the monasteries which had flourished in Bede's time. With Walcher's support, they established Benedictine communities at Bede's former monasteries of Jarrow and Monkwearmouth. Their sojourn there was to be relatively brief. In 1083, the French bishop of Durham, William of Saint-Calais, himself a monk, replaced the religious community serving his cathedral with Benedictine monks transferred from Jarrow and Monkwearmouth. This was the foundation of Durham Cathedral Priory as it was to subsist until the Dissolution of the Monasteries in the sixteenth century. Our text now follows William of Saint-Calais's career as bishop, his exile from England, his return and the construction of the new cathedral, and his death in 1096 with which it concludes.

1. MANUSCRIPTS

It may be apparent even from the survey above that the *Libellus de exordio* is complex, with marked hagiographical as well as historiographical elements, and that the history it purports to describe is potentially a distorted one, in which the interests of the present have a strong bearing on the perception of the past. Any understanding of it, however, must begin with the manuscripts in which it is preserved, for they are crucial to the question of its date of composition, authorship, title, and indeed even the elements which it originally comprised. As will appear, the *Libellus de exordio* had attached to it various continuations and it was in this way absorbed into a history of the bishops of Durham extending into the sixteenth century. In addition, material was interpolated into the original text to expand and adapt it. An understanding of all this depends on close attention to the surviving manuscripts, and we therefore begin with a description of them, not as full as might be expected in a catalogue, but full enough, it is hoped, for the reader to appreciate the developments and adaptations in the text. The manuscripts in question also cast an interesting light on the texts with which the *Libellus de exordio* was associated, some of which were connected with it either as sources or derivatives. Except where the components of a manuscript were clearly not associated with the *Libellus de exordio* in the Middle Ages, the other contents of the manuscripts are also listed with the place of publication given at the first occurrence of an item.

C   Durham, University Library, Cosin V.II.6
113 parchment leaves with one paper quire   292 mm × 185 mm[1]

1 fos. i–viii   A paper quire containing various notes on the *Libellus de exordio*, including an autograph and fair copy of Thomas Rud's

[1] For accounts of this manuscript, see Gullick, 'Earliest manuscripts', pp. 106–19, at 106–8, 110–18; and A. I. Doyle, 'The original and later structure of Durham University Library, Cosin V.II.6', Rollason, *Symeon*, pp. 120–7. See also Botfield, *Catalogi veteres*, pp. 147–50; Mynors, *Manuscripts*, no. 86 (pp. 60–1); N. R. Ker, *English Manuscripts in the Century after the Norman Conquest* (Oxford, 1960), pp. 24–5 and pl. 8b; and A. I. Doyle and A. J. Piper, *Catalogue of Medieval Manuscripts in Durham University Library* (forthcoming). I am very grateful to the authors for permission to use this last work prior to publication, and also for their help and guidance. The pencil foliation used here replaces the 18th-cent. ink pagination to which reference was made, for example, in Mynors, *Manuscripts*, and Botfield, *Catalogi veteres*. For further plates, see Rollason, *Symeon*, pls. 1a, 2, 3a, 4a, 5a, 6a–b, and Rollason, *Anglo-Norman Durham*, pl. 5a.

discussion of its authorship entitled *Disquisitio de uero auctore huius Historiae Dunelmensis ecclesiæ*.[2]

2 fos. 1ᵛ–4ᵛ A summary of the *Libellus de exordio* beginning 'Regnante apud Northanhymbros'.[3] A hand of the first half of the fourteenth century has entered the heading, 'Libellus de exordio et processu Dunelmensis ecclesie'; and a sixteenth-century heading reads: 'Breue summarium seu descriptio status ecclesie Lindisfernensis et Dunelmi a tempore Aidani usque ad Willelmum Karilephe'.

3 fos. 5ʳ⁻ᵛ *Lindisfernensis insulae discriptio* (*sic*), a compilation derived from Bede's *Historia ecclesiastica gentis Anglorum* and from the *Libellus de exordio* itself.[4]

4(a) fo. 6ʳ A preface to the *Libellus de exordio*, beginning 'Exordium huius hoc est Dunelmensis ecclesie describere'.[5] A sixteenth-century rubric reads: 'Incipit libellus de statu Lindisfarnensis idem (*sic*) Dunelmensis ecclesie secundum uenerabilem Bedam presbiterum. Et postmodum de gestis episcoporum Dunelmensium'.

(b) fo. 6ʳ⁻ᵛ A list of the bishops of Lindisfarne, Chester-le-Street, and Durham running from Aidan to Ranulf Flambard (1099–1128) in one hand,[6] with additions in various hands taking the list down to William Talbot (1721–30).

(c) fos. 7ʳ–8ᵛ A paragraph beginning 'Hic scripta continentur nomina monachorum', introducing a list in various hands of 230 monks of Durham.[7] Fos. 9–10v are ruled as if to receive further names, but have been left blank.

(d) fos. 11ʳ–98ʳ The main body of the text of the *Libellus de exordio*, beginning 'Gloriosi quondam regis Northanhymbrorum', and introduced by a rubric in the hand of the text scribe: 'Incipit libellus de exordio atque procursu istius, hoc est Dunhelmensis, ecclesie'.[8] It lacks chapter headings and contemporary chapter numbers. Fo. 11ʳ has the medieval shelf-mark 'O' and an early fifteenth-century rubric, 'Cronica de exordio et progressu ecclesie Dunelmensis, De registro siue officio Cancellariatus ecclesie Dunelmensis'.

[2] *Symeonis monachi Dunhelmensis, Libellus de exordio atque procursu Dunhelmensis ecclesiæ*, ed. T. Bedford (London, 1732), pp. i–xxxv.

[3] See below, Appendix A, pp. 258–65.

[4] Unpublished.

[5] See below, pp. 2–3.

[6] See below, pp. 4–5.

[7] See below, pp. 4–15.

[8] See below, pp. 16–257.

5 fos. 88^r–98^r A quire, inserted into item 4(d), containing the *De iniusta uexacione Willelmi episcopi primi*, a defence of the actions of Bishop William of Saint-Calais.[9]

6 fos. 98^v–113^r A continuation of the *Libellus de exordio*, beginning 'Tribus dehinc annis ecclesia uacante pastore', and ending 'episcopus sollempniter susceptus est'. It deals with the period from the appointment of Bishop Ranulf Flambard (1099–1128) to the installation of Bishop William of Sainte-Barbe in 1144.[10] Fo. 109 is a sixteenth-century replacement for a leaf, the absence of which was noted in the manuscript in the early fourteenth century.[11]

7 fo. 113^v An extract copied from Durham, Cathedral Library, B.II.35, fo. 277.[12]

The text in C is laid out consistently in single columns, ruled with a drypoint, and with single pricking. The decoration of the initials is also consistent, involving foliage and both human and animal forms (fos. 6^r, 7^r, 11^r, and 77^v), and it has been suggested that the initials are themselves the work of the scribe.[13] There is thus a strong presumption that items 4(a)–(c) always formed prefatory material to item 4(d) in C as they do now.

There are two possible objections to this. First, items 4(a)–(c) occupy a separate quire (fos. 5–10), which is irregular and has, to judge from the evidence of ink offsets, been disordered at some time. A. I. Doyle has shown, however, on the basis of a very detailed codicological study, that the present order of the leaves is likely to have been the original one. The probable cause of the disordering is that two leaves were left blank, one following the list of bishops, one the list of monks. Doyle has suggested convincingly that these leaves, which were intended to receive more names of bishops and monks respectively, were never in fact used, and were therefore removed, causing the damage and disordering noted above.[14]

Secondly, the first folio of item 4(d) (fo. 11) has an early fifteenth-century title and catalogue mark, which corresponds to the 1421 list

[9] Offler, *DIV*.   [10] See below, Appendix B, pp. 266–311.

[11] Doyle, in Rollason, *Symeon*, p. 126.

[12] *Symeonis Libellus*, ed. Bedford, pp. 293–4.

[13] Gullick, 'Earliest manuscripts', p. 112.

[14] Doyle, in Rollason, *Symeon*, pp. 120–6 and figs. 6–7. Doyle notes A. J. Piper's unpublished reconstruction of the structure of this part of C, which postulates that there were two quires, that the original order began with the paragraph beginning 'Hic scripta continentur nomina monachorum', and that the list of monks preceded the list of bishops (Rollason, *Symeon*, fig. 8).

of books in the monastic chancery, as does the reference to the words beginning the second folio there given.[15] At that time, therefore, item 4(d) was separate from items 4(a)–(c), a circumstance further corroborated by the signs of wear on fo. 11^r and by the catalogue letter on fo. 7^r. The 1421 list, however, states that the item corresponding to 4(d) was 'in quaterno', that is, lightly stitched into a membrane wrapper rather than being properly bound in boards. It would seem therefore that the manuscript's binding had at some stage been broken, and this could well account for the separation of items 4(a)–(c). That separation could have been quite recent in 1421; and, in any case, manuscripts of thirteenth- and fourteenth-century date deriving from C, or its exemplar, have much the same sequence of items as in C, but without the list of monks, which was probably superseded soon after C was written by increased use of the *Liber Vitae* as a repository of such lists.

Accepting that all the sections of item 4 were copied at the same time and as components of the same text has important implications for dating. In the list of the monks of Durham (item 4(c)), the name of Turgot is in capitals, suggesting that he was prior of Durham, just as later the names of Lawrence and Absalom were entered in capitals at the periods during which they were respectively prior. Now Turgot was prior from 1087 until probably 1107 when he was elected bishop of St Andrews, although it is possible that he retained the office of prior until 1109 when he took up his bishopric, or even until 1115 when he died.[16] Since there is internal evidence to suggest that the *Libellus de exordio* was composed between 1104 and Turgot's ceasing to be prior, this means that item 4 was copied into C at or very soon after the completion of the text itself, although further names were added to item 4(c) in the course of the twelfth century.[17]

Items 2 and 6 were added at separate times in the twelfth century. Item 2 is on a separate quire. Its use of pencil rather than drypoint for ruling suggests a date later than that of item 4, and its script that it was written in or shortly after the second quarter of the twelfth

[15] Botfield, *Catalogi veteres*, pp. 123–4. The shelfmark on fo. 7^r at the beginning of item 4 appears to be 'R' and to belong to the early 15th-cent., but this cannot be identified in the 1421 catalogue which goes no further than the letter 'Q'.

[16] *Heads of Religious Houses*, p. 43. See further, Piper, 'Lists', p. 162; and cf. K.-U. Jäschke, 'Remarks on datings in the *Libellus de exordio atque procursu istius hoc est Dunhelmensis ecclesie*', Rollason, *Symeon*, pp. 46–60, 52.

[17] Below, p. xlii.

century.[18] Item 6 begins on the five empty pages (fos. 98^v–100^v) left blank by the scribe of item 4(d), and continues on quires which are of stiffer parchment, and are double-pricked and ruled with pencil rather than drypoint as is item 4(c). Although copied either by two scribes or by the same scribe in two campaigns, with a change either of scribe or of campaign on fo. 102^r towards the end of the account of Flambard,[19] the decorated initials are consistent throughout the item. The scribe of the section down to fo. 102^r (and perhaps of the whole) also wrote a section of the list of monks, that which follows the section entered when Prior Absalom (1154–58/9) was in office,[20] while from fo. 102^r the hand (whether of the same scribe or his successor) is the same as that of a Durham charter (DCDCM, 4.2.Spec.34), dateable 1162 × 1174. Item 6 was therefore entered in C in the second half of the twelfth century, with the second half somewhat later than the first.[21]

Item 4 was almost certainly written at Durham because its hand is close to, and its decorated initials similar to, those in the Durham manuscript of Bede's prose *Vita s. Cuthberti*, Oxford, University College 165, and other manuscripts of Durham provenance;[22] and there are strong grounds for thinking that the early corrector, apart from the scribe himself, was Symeon, the author of the *Libellus de exordio*.[23] It seems likely that the other twelfth-century items were added at Durham, and part at least of the manuscript can be shown to have been in the library of Durham Cathedral Priory in the fifteenth century.[24] It seems likely then that C never left Durham. Chapter

---

[18] Doyle, in Rollason, *Symeon*, pp. 120–1; Gullick, 'Hand', p. 116 and n. 25, where it is suggested that the scribe may have been German; cf. Meehan, 'Symeon', p. 40.

[19] Doyle, in Rollason, *Symeon*, p. 126; Gullick, 'Hand', p. 116.

[20] Below, p. 11 n. 45.

[21] Gullick, 'Earliest manuscripts', pp. 116–17; Doyle, in Rollason, *Symeon*, p. 126; and Meehan, 'Symeon', pp. 40–1. The earlier view that item 6 was written into C by two scribes immediately after the last events described in the sections of texts which they copied (respectively 1128 and 1144) must therefore be rejected; for this view, see J. Conway Davies, 'Bishop Cosin's manuscripts', *The Durham Philobiblion*, i (1949–55), 10–16, at p. 11; Mynors, *Manuscripts*, pp. 60–1; and Offler, *Medieval Historians*, p. 22 n. 30.

[22] E. Temple, 'A note on the University College life of St Cuthbert', *Bodleian Library Record*, ix (1973–8), 320–2; Ker, *English Manuscripts*, p. 25; Gullick, 'Hand', pp. 111–12; cf. Meehan, 'Symeon', pp. 42–3. The scribe was a continental, who was probably brought to Durham by Bishop William of Saint-Calais, since he seems to have begun his work in the Durham scriptorium in the early 1090s, the time of the bishop's return from exile. He appears to have been active until about the end of the first decade of the 12th cent. (Gullick, 'Earliest manuscripts', p. 107).   [23] See below, pp. xliii–xliv.

[24] See above. C may be the *Liber de statu Dunelmensis ecclesie* mentioned in a 12th-cent. catalogue (Botfield, *Catalogi veteres*, p. 4).

numbers were added in the margins rather sporadically in the
fourteenth and fifteenth centuries, corresponding to those in other
Durham manuscripts of the work. Items 3 and 5 were added to it in
the sixteenth century, item 5 and the headings on fos. 1ᵛ and 6ʳ
perhaps by William Claxton of Wynyard (d. 1597), who was
associated with other Durham books, including two copies of the
Libellus de exordio, Bod. Lib., Fairfax 6 (Fx), and Laud misc. 700
(L).[25] It was in the library of Bishop John Cosin before 1668, when he
founded the Episcopal Library, entrusted to the University of
Durham in 1937.

F   London, British Library, Cotton Faustina A.V
107 parchment leaves   241 mm × 176 mm[26]

This manuscript, which contains a selection of texts of quite different
character, varying widely in date, script, and layout, and including
sermons, clerical petitions, and the work of Richard Rolle of Ham-
pole, was almost certainly assembled from disparate materials in
modern times, probably by one of its former owners, Henry Savile,
Thomas Allen, or Robert Cotton.[27]

Fos. 25ʳ–97ʳ contain a copy of the *Libellus de exordio* beginning
'Gloriosi quondam regis Northanhymbrorum', and introduced by a
rubric in the hand of the text scribe: 'Incipit libellus de exordio atque
procursu istius hoc est Dunelmensis ecclesiae'. As in C, there are no
contemporary chapter headings or chapter numbers, but divisions in
the text are indicated by the use of minor and major initials. F's copy,

---

[25] Doyle, 'Claxton', p. 344.

[26] For a list of contents, see J. Planta, *A Catalogue of Manuscripts in the Cottonian
Library* (London, 1801), p. 603. The foliation used in what follows is the definitive pencil
foliation established in 1876.

[27] Thomas Allen's signature appears on fo. 25 and there is also inscribed on the flyleaf
(fo. 1): 'Thomas Allen ex dono magistri Henrici Savelli 1589'. It appears that at the time
of this gift Henry Savile the Elder (to whom this note refers) divided a larger miscellaneous
collection, giving the portion embodying F to Allen and retaining the remainder for
himself. The latter portion passed to Ussher who gave it to Trinity College, Dublin, in the
library of which institution it is now MS A.5.2 (114). Allen's portion, which forms the
manuscript with which we are now concerned, was given to Cotton and so came into the
British Library as Cotton Faustina A.V. See A. G. Watson, 'Thomas Allen of Oxford and
his books', in *Medieval Scribes, Manuscripts and Libraries: Essays Presented to N. R. Ker*, ed.
M. B. Parkes and A. G. Watson (London, 1978), pp. 279–314, at 289 and n. 49; and A. G.
Watson, *The Manuscripts of Henry Savile of Bank* (London, 1969), p. 33 (no. 76). Watson
regarded fos. 1–12 of F as outside this sequence of events and presumably saw them as an
addition made perhaps by Cotton. See also N. R. Ker, *Catalogue of Manuscripts Containing
Anglo-Saxon* (Oxford, 1957), no. 152.

however, lacks the prefatory material, the continuation beginning 'Tribus dehinc annis', and the summary beginning 'Regnante apud Northanhymbros', and thus consists only of what is in C item 4(d). Did F once contain the other components of C's item 4 which have now been lost? Fos. 97^v–98^v at the end of the last quire of the *Libellus de exordio* were left blank until the sixteenth century, so it seems unlikely that F ever contained the continuation found in C. F's text of the *Libellus de exordio* begins, however, on the recto of the first leaf of a new quire, so it is possible that a quire of prefatory material such as is found in C (items 4(a)–(c)) has been lost. The appearance of a late twelfth- or early thirteenth-century Fountains *ex libris* inscription on fo. 25^r might suggest either that such a loss occurred very early on, or that no prefatory material existed and that fo. 25 was always the beginning of F's text, or that the prefatory material was kept separate from the main text as seems to have been the case in the fifteenth century with C.[28]

F's copy was made rather less lavishly and meticulously than C's, with slightly less generous use of parchment, but it is very similar to it in script, ruling, and layout, and the decorated initials may even be by the same hand in both manuscripts. It is very likely, therefore, that F's copy too was written in Durham, although the hand has not been identified in other manuscripts.[29] Moreover, it has the same rubric as C's and in the same position relative to the text, and like C's it lacks chapter rubrics or numbers but uses minor and major initials to subdivide the text in exactly the same way. The *ex libris* inscription shows, however, that this section of F was at Fountains Abbey by the late twelfth or early thirteenth century, and that it was there at the beginning of the sixteenth is shown by the occurrence on fo. 98^r of attestations of the probationaries of Fountains relating to the year 1512.[30]

---

[28] See above, pp. xix–xx.

[29] Gullick, 'Earliest manuscripts', pp. 109–12.

[30] Compare the parallel inscription, which has some names in common and also has the date 1512, on fo. ii of the Fountains manuscript BL, Additional 62130. (I owe this reference to Dr Michelle Brown.) A possible complication is the inscription on fo. 97^v which reads: 'Liber sancte Marie de Fontibus ex donis Willelmi de Coutton quondam monachi de Fontibus', repeated in a somewhat later hand immediately below. If the donor in question is William Cowton, prior of Durham (1321–40/1), which is consistent with the date of the script, it can be conjectured that the book returned to Durham with Cowton when he left Fountains to become prior of Durham and was then re-presented to Fountains. See Meehan, 'Symeon', p. 48. The inscription on fo. 98^v which Meehan read as 'hic est liber Willelmi de Coutton' is not now fully legible even under ultra-violet

Ca Cambridge, University Library, Ff. i.27

323 parchment leaves 295 × 212 mm[31]

This manuscript consists of two distinct parts. One is a portion of a fourteenth-century book from Bury St Edmunds which is bound into Ca between pp. 40 and 73, and after p. 252. The remainder, which concerns us here, represents all or part of a manuscript of the later twelfth century and contains the following items:

1 pp. 1–14 Gildas, *De excidio Britanniae*.[32]

2 pp. 14–40 [Nennius], *Historia Brittonum*.[33]

3 pp. 73–120 Bede, *De temporibus*,[34] with the end of the quire filled in with notes from Bede's scientific works and two miracle-stories by William of Malmesbury (*De hospite mutato in asinum* and *De capite statue loquentis*, p. 120).[35]

4(a) p. 122 The preface to the *Libellus de exordio*, beginning 'Exordium huius hoc est Dunelmensis ecclesie describere', identical to C's item 4(a), but with the addition of one sentence at the end. It has rubrics at the beginning and end, respectively: 'Incipit apologia Symeonis monachi' and 'Explicit apologia Symeonis monachi'.

(b) pp. 123–5 The summary beginning 'Regnante apud North-anhymbros', identical to C's item 2, preceded by the rubric: 'Incipit prefatio reuerendi Symeonis monachi et precentoris ecclesie sancti Cuthberti Dunelmi in historia de exordio Christianitatis et religionis tocius Northumbrie de fide et origine sancti Oswaldi regis et martiris et de predicatione sancti Aidani episcopi'.

(c) pp. 125–8 A list of chapter headings for the *Libellus de exordio*, unique to this manuscript.[36]

(d) pp. 128–30 A genealogy of King Æthelwulf; a brief account

---

light beyond the 'd' of 'de'. The letter following may be an 'e' or a 'c' and the word following that seems to begin with a 'd'.

[31] For a description, see *A Catalogue of Manuscripts preserved in the Library of the University of Cambridge* (5 vols.; Cambridge, 1856–67), ii. 318–29. The pagination used there, which is that of Archbishop Parker, has been retained in what follows. The modern pencil foliation is based on a sectionalization of the book and is very confusing.

[32] *Monumenta Germaniae Historica, Auctores antiquissimi* (Berlin, 1894), xiii. 25–85.

[33] Ibid., pp. 111–222.

[34] Bede, *De temporibus liber*, ed. C. W. Jones, in *Bedae Venerabilis Opera, pars vi.3* (Corpus Christianorum, series latina, cxxiiiC, Turnhout, 1980), pp. 579–611.

[35] *Catalogue of Manuscripts in the University of Cambridge*, ii. 322.

[36] See below, Appendix C, pp. 328–33.

of the kings of the Northumbrians and the English from Ida to Henry I; and an account of the sees and shires of England. This seems to be in the same hand as item 4(c).[37]

(e) pp. 129–86   The main body of the text of the *Libellus de exordio*, beginning 'Gloriosi quondam regis Northanhymbrorum'. Rubrics at the beginning and end read respectively: 'Incipit historia sancte et suauis memorie Simeonis monachi sancti Cuthberti Dunelmi de exordio Christianitatis et religionis tocius Northumbrie et de exortu et processu Lindisfarnensis siue Dunelmensis ecclesie', and 'Explicit historia Simeonis'. The first of these rubrics somewhat exceeds the space available and may be a slightly later insertion.[38] The text has contemporary chapter numbers corresponding to item 4(c). A different but near-contemporary hand has filled in the remainder of the last leaf and into the bottom margin with a copy of a purported charter of King Ecgfrith granting Carlisle to St Cuthbert, beginning 'Anno dominice incarnationis .dclxxxv. congregata sinodo iuxta fluuium Alne'.[39]

5   pp. 187–94   On a new quire of four leaves, a continuation of the *Libellus de exordio* beginning, as in C's item 6, 'Tribus dehinc annis ecclesia uacante pastore'. From Geoffrey Rufus's death onwards, however, it offers a quite different text, unique to this manuscript, and it also has a passage on Bishop Hugh of le Puiset.[40]

6   p. 194   A list of Durham relics.[41]

7   pp. 195–201   The *Historia de sancto Cuthberto*[42]

8   pp. 201–2   A list of gifts made by King Æthelstan to the church of St Cuthbert.[43]

p. 202   The Old English poem *De situ Dunelmi*.[44]

9   pp. 203–20   Æthelwulf, *De abbatibus*,[45] with the end of the quire

---

[37] Arnold, *Sym. Op.* ii. 389–93.

[38] Meehan, 'Symeon', pp. 62–3.

[39] For editions and other manuscripts (this one is not noted), see P. H. Sawyer, *Anglo-Saxon Charters: An Annotated List and Bibliography* (London, 1968), no. 66.

[40] See below, Appendix B, pp. 310–23. The hands of item 5 are as follows: a new rather ornate hand begins at 'Quo comperto rex Scotie Dauid ad curiam . . .', perhaps of s. xiii[in] date, and continues to the end of the account of Hugh of le Puiset.

[41] Arnold, *Sym. Op.* i. 168–9.

[42] Arnold, *Sym. Op.* i. 196–214.

[43] As found in *HSC*; pr. Arnold, *Sym. Op.* i. 211.

[44] D. R. Howlett, 'The shape and meaning of the Old English poem "Durham"', Rollason, *Anglo-Norman Durham*, pp. 485–95, at 489.

[45] *Æthelwulf, De abbatibus*, ed. A. Campbell (Oxford, 1967).

filled in with a list of kings and kingdoms and accounts of miracles and visions (pp. 215–20), including cc. 36 and 35 of Alexander of Canterbury, *Liber ex dictis beati Anselmi* (pp. 217–19).[46]

10 pp. 221–36 Richard of Hexham, *De statu et episcopis Hagustaldensis ecclesie.*[47]

11 pp. 237–52 Gilbert of Limerick, *De statu ecclesie,*[48] with historical notes on pp. 243–52.

Item 4(a), containing the preface beginning 'Exordium huius', occupies a single parchment leaf attached to the beginning of a quire of four leaves. The hand, which is probably of the second half of the twelfth century, is similar to that of the scribe of the charter on p. 186 and of the beginning of item 5, and of the corrector of the last seven lines of p. 36 col. b, and also to that of the rubricator of pp. 1–40. The parchment, however, is very thick, much thicker than would normally be used for a book; so that it is possible that it was originally a wrapper, on which the preface beginning 'Exordium huius' was added rather as an afterthought.[49]

Items 4(b)–(c) occupy the quire to which the leaf with item 4(a) is attached. Although they are ruled with double pricking, whereas item 4(d), the main text of the *Libellus de exordio*, is single-pricked, they are nevertheless written in a hand closely similar to that of item 4(d). So items 4(b)–(c) may have been added as a separate quire in front of item 4(d) immediately after it had been copied (there are indications that the chapter-numbers in the text, although contemporary, were inserted shortly after the copying of the text on which they sometimes intrude). The spare parchment following them was then filled up in a somewhat different hand with the miscellaneous items, 4(d).

A fifteenth-century contents list in CCCC 66, now partially erased, and a relict pagination suggest that at least in that period items 1–11 of Ca were bound with the twelfth-century portion of CCCC 66 to form one manuscript; Christopher Norton's recent study of the iconography and arrangement of the two components abundantly

---

[46] See *Memorials of St Anselm*, ed. R. W. Southern and F. S. Schmitt (Auctores Britannici Medii Aevi, i; Oxford, 1969), p. 29.

[47] *The Priory of Hexham*, ed. J. Raine (2 vols.; SS xliv, xlvi; Durham, 1864–5), i. 1–62.

[48] *Patrologiae cursus completus, series latina*, ed. J. P. Migne (221 vols.; Paris, 1844–64), clix, cols. 995–1004.

[49] For help with this manuscript I am very grateful to Dr Jayne Ringrose, and above all to Mr Michael Gullick, whose views are those summarized above.

confirm this suggestion.[50] This manuscript was at one time in the library of Sawley Abbey, as the CCCC 66 portion of it has an *ex libris* inscription of that Cistercian house.[51] It is utterly unlikely, however, that such a manuscript was produced at Sawley, since it is ambitious and lavishly illustrated, and Sawley was a poor abbey lacking the resources necessary for such work.[52] There are, however, strong grounds for assigning a Durham provenance to the manuscript. Its initials are consistent with it having been produced at Durham; and the comparanda for its remarkable series of illustrations are to be found in Durham manuscripts. Moreover, item 11 of Ca was almost certainly copied from a Durham copy of Gilbert of Limerick preserved in DCL B.II.35; and the text of item 1 (Gildas, *De excidio*) is closely related to that in the same manuscript, suggesting that it has been corrected by reference to it. Finally, the fact that Ca contains such items of local Durham interest as a relic-list and the poem on Durham, *De situ Dunelmi*, further suggests a Durham provenance.[53]

Items 1–11 of Ca are all written in hands of the late twelfth century, apart from pp. 41–71, which seem to be a later thirteenth-century replacement for a lost quire. Meehan proposed a dating of 'around the beginning of the last quarter of the twelfth century'.[54] Norton has now demonstrated that the manuscript was conceived and executed as a unity, the most likely date being 1188 (as indicated by the text of an *explicit* on fo. 50ᵛ) or shortly afterwards. He has further suggested that it may have been produced as a gift from the Durham monks to Bishop Hugh of le Puiset.[55]

[50] C. Norton, 'History, wisdom and illumination', Rollason, *Symeon*, pp. 61–105, at 63–71. B. Meehan's doubts about the original unity of the components can now be dismissed ('Durham twelfth-century manuscripts in Cistercian houses', Rollason, *Anglo-Norman Durham*, pp. 439–49, at 442–5).

[51] M. R. James, *A Descriptive Catalogue of the Manuscripts in the Library of Corpus Christi College, Cambridge* (2 vols.; Cambridge, 1912), i. 137–45; and D. N. Dumville, 'The sixteenth-century history of two Cambridge books from Sawley', *Transactions of the Cambridge Bibliographical Society*, vii (1980), 427–44.

[52] D. Baker, 'Scissors and paste: Corpus Christi, Cambridge, MS 139 again', *Studies in Church History*, xi (1975), 83–123, at pp. 103–4; and Norton, in Rollason, *Symeon*, p. 74.

[53] Meehan, in Rollason, *Anglo-Norman Durham*, pp. 445–6; and esp. Norton, in Rollason, *Symeon*, pp. 72–89.

[54] Meehan, 'Symeon', pp. 63–4.

[55] Norton, in Rollason, *Symeon*, pp. 71–2, 89–101.

D Durham, Cathedral Library, A.IV.36
2 paper leaves and 126 parchment leaves   208 mm × 122 mm[56]

1(a) fos. iv^r–v^v A list of 122 chapter-headings, different from that in Ca, and embracing items 1–3.[57]

(b) fos. 1^r–4^r The summary beginning 'Regnante apud North-anhymbros'.

(c) fo. 4^r The preface to the *Libellus de exordio*, beginning 'Exordium huius hoc est Dunelmensis ecclesie describere'.

(d) fo. 4^{r-v} A list of the bishops of Lindisfarne, Chester-le-Street, and Durham down to Philip of Poitou (1195 × 6–1208).

(e) fos. 4^v–90^r The main body of the text of the *Libellus de exordio*, beginning 'Gloriosi quondam regis Northanhymbrorum'.

2 fos. 90^r–107^r The continuation of the *Libellus de exordio*, beginning 'Tribus dehinc annis ecclesia uacante pastore', and ending 'episcopus sollempniter susceptus est'.

3 fos. 107^r–121^v Geoffrey of Coldingham, *Liber de statu ecclesie Dunhelmensis*,[58] which has no rubric and breaks off at the end of c. 112, leaving the rest of fo. 121^v and all of fo. 122 blank.

Apart from item 1(a), script, layout, and decoration are consistent throughout the manuscript; and the writing is a gothic bookhand of the early thirteenth century, with a change of hand between fos. 14 and 15, and possibly on fo. 107^v. All the items overlap the quires, and items 2 and 3 run on from item 1 without rubrics or other dividing marks. Since the last name in the bishop-list is that of Philip of Poitou (1195–1208), and no years of pontificate are given, the manuscript was presumably written either in his pontificate or in the vacancy which followed his death (1208–17), which is consistent with the date of the script.[59] The last event mentioned (in the *Liber de statu* of Geoffrey of Coldingham) is the death of Richard I in 1199, but other versions of this text in H and Y extend to the abortive election of Morgan to the see of Durham in 1213, and it is not clear whether the text in D is an earlier recension or simply an unfinished copy.[60]

---

[56] For a description, see J. Conway Davies, 'A recovered manuscript of Symeon of Durham', *Durham University Journal*, xliv (1950–1), 22–8; and now A. I. Doyle, 'Bede's death song in Durham Cathedral, MS A.IV.36', Rollason, *Symeon*, pp. 157–60. Fo. 25^v is illustrated in Rollason, *Symeon*, pl. 28, and fo. 4^v in *Friends of the National Libraries Annual Report* (1950–1), pl. I.   [57] See below, Appendix C, pp. 324–8.

[58] Raine, *Scriptores tres*, pp. 3–20.   [59] Piper, pers. comm.

[60] Offler implied that it was a version carried down only to 1199, noting that the next

Item 1(a) is written in a script of the late thirteenth or early fourteenth century on a separate quire of quite different parchment from that of the rest of the volume. Moreover, it does not correspond to the text since it gives 122 chapters whereas there are in fact only 113 (the last nine chapters of Coldingham being missing). It may therefore have originally been intended for a copy of the text in another manuscript.[61]

The script and decoration are consistent with D having been produced in Durham. There is an erased Durham *ex libris* of the beginning of the fifteenth century at the top of fo. 1; and in the later middle ages it received annotations by identifiable Durham monks.[62] Although no catalogue marks survive, perhaps because they have been cut away in binding, it is certain that D is the 'Gesta episcoporum, incomplete', listed in the 1395 catalogue of books in the Durham claustral library.[63] There the beginning of the second folio is given as 'prolatum est', whereas in D it is 'perlatum est' (fo. 2^r), but this is probably a slip. The book was in 1568 given to Matthew Parker by Robert Horne, who had been a dean of Durham (1551/3–1559/61). It was possibly at York later on, where it appears in a catalogue of 1697, and was seen there by Thomas Rud. It was in the Sir Thomas Phillipps's Library as MS 9374, and was purchased for the Dean and Chapter Library, Durham, in 1950.[64]

H   Oxford, Bodleian Library, Holkham misc. 25 (formerly Holkham Hall 468)
75 parchment leaves   205 mm × 145mm[65]

1(a) fos. 1–2   A list of chapter-headings, similar to D's but giving 121 rather than 122 chapters up to the end of item 3, because H's c. 91 amalgamates two chapters which are separate in other manu-scripts.[66]

chapter as found in other manuscripts begins with words suggestive of the start of a continuation: 'Hiis adiicere libet que nouorum tumultuum parturiuit incursus' (Offler, *Medieval Historians*, p. 23 n. 32).

[61] A later hand has made some effort to add the appropriate rubrics from the chapter-list to the margins of the text in D.

[62] Doyle, in Rollason, *Symeon*, p. 158.   [63] Botfield, *Catalogi veteres*, p. 56

[64] Offler, *Medieval Historians*, p. 23 n. 32; Doyle, in Rollason, *Symeon*, pp. 159–60; and *Friends of the National Libraries Annual Report* (1950–1), pp. 9–10.

[65] For a description, see the typescript catalogue of 'Additions to the Medieval Manuscripts' in the Selden End, Bodleian Library.

[66] Offler, *Medieval Historians*, p. 23 n. 39. Between cc. 90 and 121 the chapter numbers

(b) fo. 3^r The preface to the the *Libellus de exordio* beginning 'Exordium huius', introduced by the rubric: 'Incipit liber Symonis *(sic)* monachi Dunelmensis de statu Lindisfarnensis et Dunelmensis ecclesie usque ad electionem Hugonis de Puteaco'.

(c) fo. 3^v A list of the bishops of Lindisfarne, Chester-le-Street, and Durham down to Anthony Bek (1283–1311).

(d) fos. 4^r–52^r The main body of the text of the *Libellus de exordio*, beginning 'Gloriosi quondam regis Northanhymbrorum'.

2 fos. 52^r–62^v The continuation of the *Libellus de exordio*, beginning 'Tribus dehinc annis ecclesia uacante pastore', and ending 'episcopus sollempniter est susceptus'.

3 fos. 63^r–74^v An incomplete text of Geoffrey of Coldingham, *Liber de statu ecclesie Dunhelmensis*, preceded by the rubric: 'Incipit liber Gaufridi sacriste de Coldingham de statu ecclesie Dunelmensis. Qui incipit ad obitum Willelmi episcopi de Sancta Barbara'.

Although more than one scribe appears to have been involved in this manuscript—changes of hand may be discernible on fo. 22v and after fo. 70^v, for example—there can be no doubt that it was produced as a unitary book. The script is all of one date, the layout is in single columns, the rubrication and written space are uniform, and there are contemporary catchwords for several quires, notably for that on which item 3 begins. Item 1(a), although occupying a bifolium separate from the first main quire, is in the same hand as that of the succeeding text, apart from corrected chapter numbers between cc. 90 and 121 and some additions to the chapter headings. In most cases chapter headings have been inserted as rubrics at the time of writing at the end of lines.[67] The book seems, however, to have lost a quire, since Geoffrey's *Liber de statu* breaks off at the foot of fo. 74^v and at the end of a quire at 'Iussique sunt ut se in tres partes diuiderent, de nouo electionem', that is, in the chapter here numbered 114.[68]

Item 1(c) is all in the original hand and runs to Anthony Bek (1283–1311). The fact that the length of his pontificate is not given might show that it was written during his lifetime; but lengths of

have been modified by a contemporary hand which has also added chapter numbers in the margin of the text and some marginal chapter headings.

[67] Where they have been omitted, a scribe writing a gothic hand in brown ink has supplied the missing titles throughout and has also added chapter numbers in the margin. The same hand corrected numerals in the list of chapters

[68] Raine, *Scriptores tres*, p. 24.

pontificates are not given for several of his predecessors either so this may simply be an omission, allowing the manuscript to have been written during the pontificate of his successor, Richard Kellawe (1311–16). The script itself could certainly belong to the early fourteenth century.[69] It is not possible to establish H's provenance, although on grounds of content Durham is possible.[70] H entered the collection of Sir Edward Coke at Holkham Hall, Norfolk, in which it was no. 715, and was seen there in 1717 by Petrus le Neve. Thomas William Coke wrote his name on fo. 1[r]. The manuscript appears in De Ricci's handlist as no. 468,[71] and it passed to the Bodleian Library in 1956.

T   London, British Libary, Cotton Titus A.II
162 parchment leaves   225 mm × 149 mm[72]

1(a) fos. 2[r]–4[v]   A chapter-list like D's but for 184 chapters covering items 1(b)-4, and listing five chapters from the *De miraculis*, which are interpolated into the text in some manuscripts but not in this one.

(b) fo. 5[r]   The preface to the *Libellus de exordio*, beginning 'Exordium huius hoc est Dunelmensis ecclesie describere', introduced by the rubric 'Incipit de statu Lindisfarnensis ecclesie, id est Dunelmensis ecclesie, secundum uenerabilem Bedam presbiterum et primorum de gestis episcoporum Dunelmie'.

(c) fo. 5[r–v]   A list of the bishops of Lindisfarne, Chester-le-Street, and Durham down to Anthony Bek (1283–1311) with lengths of their episcopates.

(d) fos. 5[v]–7[v]   The summary beginning 'Regnante apud North-anhymbros'.

---

[69] 'Additions' gives 'first half of the thirteenth century', but this must be too early in view of the list of bishops.

[70] There is no press-mark, and the first words of the second folio of the main text, 'uiuenti claruerint', do not correspond to those noted in the medieval Durham catalogues. There is on fo. 3[r] a 15th-cent. inscription, 'Domino Johanni Barker pertinet iste', but this person is otherwise unknown. In the 17th cent. the book apparently belonged to a certain Richard Topclyffe, an Elizabethan priest-hunter (1532–1604) (*Dictionary of National Biography*, ed. L. Stephen and S. Lee (Oxford, 1917–), xix. 979–80), who wrote his name on fo. 1[r], as also did a certain Smith whose name has been partly cut away.

[71] *A Catalogue of the Library of Sir Edward Coke*, ed. W. O. Hassall (New Haven, 1950), p. 59; and *A Handlist of the Manuscripts in the Library of the Earl of Leicester at Holkham Hall*, ed. S. de Ricci (Oxford, 1932), p. 41.

[72] For a list of contents, see Planta, *Catalogue of Cottonian Library*, p. 511.

(e) fos. 7^v–57^r The main body of the text of the *Libellus de exordio*, beginning 'Gloriosi quondam regis Northanhymbrorum'.

2 fos. 57^r–68^r The continuation of the *Libellus de exordio*, beginning 'Tribus dehinc annis ecclesia uacante pastore'.

3 fos. 68^r–85^v Geoffrey of Coldingham, *Liber de statu ecclesie Dunhelmensis*, preceded by the rubric: 'Incipit liber Gaufridi sacriste de Coldingham de statu ecclesie Dunelmensis. Qui incipit ad obitum Willelmi episcopi de Sancta Barbara usque ad electionem domini Morgani'.

4 fos. 86^r–126^v Robert Greystanes, *Historia de statu ecclesie Dunelmensis*, preceded on fo. 85^v by a note beginning 'Memorandum quod beatus Cuthbertus'.[73]

5 fos. 127^r–132^r Five chapters from the *De miraculis* (cc. 1, 4, 5, 8, 13).[74]

6 fos. 132^r–133^v Lives of Bishop Richard de Bury (1333–45).[75]

7 fos. 134^r–147^v *Libellus de ortu sancti Cuthberti.*[76]

8 fos. 148^r–152^v Bede, *Vita sancti Cuthberti metrice.*[77]

9 fos. 153^r–157^v An apparently unfinished index to the *Libellus de exordio*.

10 fos. 158^r–160^v *Breuis relatio de sancto Cuthberto.*[78]

11 fos. 160^v–161^v *Breuiarium chronice Hagustaldensis ecclesie.*[79]

Items 1(b)–(e), 2, and 3 seem to have been produced as a unity. Layout and script are identical throughout, the latter suggesting a date in the first half of the fourteenth century. This is consistent with the evidence of the bishop-list (item 1(c)) which includes Anthony Bek (1283–1311) with his dates of pontificate in the original hand, and therefore suggests that this copy of the *Libellus* was written in the time of his successor Richard Kellawe (1311–16). Item 4, however, is in a script which, although of broadly similar date, is smaller and less formal, with pen-flourished initials of quite different style from those of the preceding section. The written space, moreover, is different. Further, items 1–3 occupy quires of different size and with larger

[73] Raine, *Scriptores tres*, pp. 35–123.

[74] Arnold, *Sym. Op.* i. 229–34, 240–45; ii. 333–5, 345–7.

[75] Raine, *Scriptores tres*, pp. 127–30.

[76] *Miscellanea biographica: Oswinus, rex Northumbriae; Cuthbertus, episcopus Lindisfarnensis; Eata, episcopus Hagustaldensis*, ed. J. Raine (SS viii; Durham, 1838), pp. 63–87.

[77] *Bedas metrische Vita sancti Cuthberti*, ed. W. Jaager (Palaestra, cxcviii; Leipzig, 1935).

[78] *Symeonis Dunelmensis Opera et Collectanea*, i , ed. J. H. Hinde (SS li; Durham, 1868), pp. 230–3.

[79] *Priory of Hexham*, ed. Raine, i. 219–20.

catchwords than those occupied by item 4. It seems therefore that item 4 was added to the book later. Down to fo. 125^{v}, its script suggests that this copying took place soon after the composition of Greystanes's *Historia* in 1336, but from that point to the end a second hand, perhaps of the second half of the fourteenth century, took over. This hand also wrote items 5 and 1(a). Moreover, having written item 5, the same hand inserted notes into item 1(e) to show to what parts of the text of the *Libellus de exordio* the miracles contained in that item, with the exception of the first, are related. These are the same points at which in Y, Fx, and L the miracle stories themselves have been interpolated into the text. The same hand also added a note about the fate of the canons expelled from Durham in 1083, apparently based on the text at this point in Y.[80] A hand of the late fourteenth or early fifteenth century then added item 6 to the lower margin of fo. 52^{r}, at the end of the quire on which item 5 finishes. The remaining items, 7–11, are written in various hands of the fourteenth and fifteenth centuries but there is nothing to prove that they were originally bound with the preceding items, apart from item 9 (the unfinished index) which was presumably associated with item 1. There are no marks of ownership on the book or any clues to its provenance apart from its contents, which indicate that a Durham provenance is possible.[81] In the sixteenth century, however, it was owned by Christopher Watson (d. 1581), the Durham antiquary, who annotated it and possibly collated it with another manuscript.[82]

V   London, British Library, Cotton Vespasian A.VI
183 parchment leaves   *c.*220 mm × *c.*163 mm[83]

This manuscript is an assemblage of booklets of diverse character and origins, bound together no doubt by or for Robert Cotton. Amongst the booklets, which include material from Ely (fos. 90^{r}–133^{v}), and the miracles of Simon de Montfort (fos. 162^{r}–183^{r}), is one (fos. 61^{r}–89^{v}) chiefly devoted to a fragmentary text of the *Libellus de exordio*.

[80] See below, pp. 230–1 and n. 20.

[81] N. R. Ker, *Medieval Libraries of Great Britain: A List of Surviving Books, Supplement to the Second Edition*, ed. A. G. Watson (London, 1987), p. 30.

[82] Doyle, 'Claxton', p. 345.

[83] For a list of contents, see Planta, *Catalogue of Cottonian Library*, pp. 434–5. The pencil foliation is used throughout. I am grateful to Dr Michelle Brown for help with this manuscript.

1 fos. 61^r–62^v A list of the bishops of Durham from William of Saint-Calais (1080–96) to Walter Skirlaw (1388–1406), and a list of the priors of Durham from Aldwin (1083–7) to a prior called here John of Guisborough, presumably to be identified with John of Hemingbrough (1391–1416). Fo. 61 is a cut-down leaf which formerly contained French prose-verse in a fifteenth-century hand, now partially scraped away, but still legible in part on fo. 61^r.

2 fos. 63^r–86^r The main text of the *Libellus de exordio*, preserved incompletely on three irregular quires. A quire has been lost at the beginning, for the text starts in mid-sentence in the account of Colman's episcopate. A further quire has been lost between fos. 66 and 67, where the text breaks off in the account of Bede's writings about Cuthbert and resumes in the middle of the account of Cynewulf's episcopate.

3 fos. 86^r–89^v An incomplete copy of the continuation of the *Libellus de exordio*, beginning 'Tribus dehinc annis ecclesia uacante pastore', occupying the end of the third quire of the *Libellus de exordio*, and breaking off abruptly in the account of William Cumin's usurpation. Evidently one or more further quires have been lost.

Item 1 is in a hand of the end of the fourteenth or beginning of the fifteenth century. It is roughly written on a separate quire, and there are no grounds for supposing that it was originally bound with items 2–3. The latter are all in the same hand, of the late thirteenth or early fourteenth century, and the layout is consistent throughout. There are chapter rubrics corresponding in most cases to those in D, Fx, L, T, and Y, with no elision of cc. 90 and 91 as found in H. There are no indications of the provenance of this section of the manuscript, but Durham has been suggested on grounds of content.[84]

Y York, Minster Library, XVI.I.12
227 parchment leaves   260 × 173mm[85]

1 fos. 1^r–10^r Richard of Hexham, *Historia Hagustaldensis Ecclesiae*.[86]

---

[84] Ker, *Medieval Libraries, Supplement*, p. 30.

[85] For a description, see N. R. Ker and A. J. Piper, *Medieval Manuscripts in British Libraries*, iv. *Paisley–York* (Oxford, 1992), pp. 720–2. I am indebted to this and also to an unpublished description of the manuscript by Richard Sharpe which he kindly placed at my disposal.

[86] Raine, *Priory of Hexham*, i. 1–62.

2 fos. 10[r]–12[v] *Vita sancti Eate.*[87]

3 fo. 12[v] *Quomodo ecclesia Hagustaldensis ab hostili incursu Scottorum cum suis et cum multis aliis liberata sit.* [88]

4 fos. 13[r]–14[v] A Durham relic-list.[89]

5 fos. 14[v]–15[v] Two stories relating to the Inner Farne, beginning 'In insula quae uocatur Farne' and 'Quidam piscandi gracia Farne uenerat'.[90]

6 fos.16[r]–66[r] Reginald of Durham, *Libellus de admirandis beati Cuthberti uirtutibus.*[91]

7 fos. 67[r]–70[r] An account of the see of Lindisfarne beginning 'Anno ab incarnacione Domini sescentesimo tricesimo quinto Paulinus', possibly to be attributed to Symeon.[92]

8 fos. 71[r]–84[v] *Libellus de ortu sancti Cuthberti.*

9 fos. 85[r]–94[r] Cc. 18–21 from the *De miraculis et translationibus sancti Cuthberti.*[93]

10(a) fos. 96[r]–97[v] A list of chapter-headings like D's, but with 131 embracing items 10(d)-12. The text of these items has corresponding chapter headings in red, generally contemporary and integral with it.

(b) fo. 99[r] The preface to the *Libellus de exordio*, beginning 'Exordium huius hoc est Dunelmensis ecclesie describere', introduced by a rubric with approximately thirty letters erased: 'Incipit *[erasure]* de statu Lindisfarnensis, id est Dunhelmensis ecclesie secundum uenerabilem Bedam presbiterum et postmodum de gestis episcoporum Dunhelmie'.

(c) fos. 99[r–v] A list of the bishops of Lindisfarne, Chester-le-Street, and Durham down to Anthony Bek (1283–1311).

(d) fos. 99[v]–155[r] The main body of the text of the *Libellus de exordio*, beginning 'Gloriosi quondam regis Northanhymbrorum', with red chapter heading rubrics contemporary with the text, and with five chapters from the *De miraculis* inserted into the text.

11 fos. 155[r]–165[v] The continuation of the *Libellus de exordio*, beginning 'Tribus dehinc annis ecclesia uacante pastore', and ending 'episcopus sollempniter susceptus est'.

[87] Raine, *Miscellanea biographica*, pp. 121–5.   [88] Unprinted.

[89] Raine, *Scriptores tres*, app. no. 331 (pp. cccxxvi-xxx).

[90] H. H. E. Craster, 'The miracles of St Cuthbert at Farne', *Analecta Bollandiana*, lxx (1952), 5–19.

[91] Raine, *Cuth. virt.*

[92] R. Sharpe, 'Symeon as pamphleteer', Rollason, *Symeon*, pp. 214–29.

[93] Arnold, *Sym. Op.* i. 229–61; ii. 333–62.

12 fos. 165^v–182^r Geoffrey of Coldingham, *Liber de statu ecclesie Dunhelmensis*, introduced by the rubric 'Incipit liber Gaufridi sacriste de Coldingham de statu ecclesie Dunhelmensis. Qui incipit ad obitum Willelmi episcopi de Sancta Barbara usque ad electionem domini Morgani'.

13 fos. 183^r–225^v Robert Greystanes, *Historia de statu ecclesie Dunelmensis*, preceded on fo. 182^r by the note beginning 'Memorandum quod beatus Cuthbertus'.[94]

14 fos. 225^v–227^r The lives of Richard of Bury.

Y was written in England, probably at Durham Cathedral Priory. Although it is not identifiable in the medieval catalogues, a late fourteenth- or early fifteenth-century inscription at the top of fo. 1^r is legible under ultra-violet light as '[..] Capella prioris D[..]elm', and the word 'Duresmie', also incompletely erased, occurs in fourteenth-century script at the foot of fo. 182. Y was at York in the late seventeenth century, and it was seen there by Rud, who added attributions of authorship on fos. 1^r and 183^r.[95]

Items 10–12 are written in the same or very similar hands of the late thirteenth or early fourteenth century, consistent with the bishop-list which runs in the original hand to Anthony Bek (1283–1311), whose length of pontificate was not originally given but has been added in a different ink and a different hand.[96] This suggests that this copy of the *Libellus* was written in Bek's time.

The last leaf of the quire containing the end of item 12 (fo. 182^r) is occupied by the note beginning 'Memorandum quod beatus Cuthbertus', in a different and probably somewhat later fourteenth-century hand. A new quire then begins with the history of Robert Greystanes without a contemporary rubric and in a different hand, with plain red rather than pen-flourished initials, and chapter rubrics which are frequently written in boxes in the margins rather than inserted into the text as is the case with the preceding material. From fo. 195 (where a new quire begins) to the end of Greystanes the hand changes to a cursive rather than a textura hand of similar date. The last leaves of the final quire were subsequently filled with the lives of

---

[94] The text omits the whole of c. 174 as found in Fx, L, and BL, Additional 24059, fo. 51 (Offler, *Medieval Historians*, p. 23).

[95] Ker and Piper, *Medieval Manuscripts in British Libraries*, iv. 722; and Offler, *Medieval Historians*, p. 23.

[96] There are signs of erasure after Bek's name, but in view of the date assigned to the script it is unlikely that names of bishops in the original hand have been deleted.

Richard of Bury (fos. 225^v–227^r) in a script of the late fourteenth or early fifteenth century.[97]

Fx   Oxford, Bodleian Library, Fairfax 6
vi + 299 parchment leaves   328 mm × 205 mm[98]

1 fos. iv^r-vi^r Lists of the bishops of Lindisfarne, Chester-le-Street, and Durham to Thomas Morton (1632–59) and priors to Hugh Whitehead (1524–39).

2 fo. vi^v List of contents of the manuscript.

3 fos. 1^r–8^r *Libellus de ortu sancti Cuthberti.*

4 fos. 8^r–12^v Bede, *Vita sancti Cuthberti metrice.*

5 fos. 13^r–29^v Bede, *Vita sancti Cuthberti.*[99]

6 fos. 29^v–30^r Bede, *Historia ecclesiastica gentis Anglorum*, iv. 31–2.[100]

7 fos. 30^r–43^v *De miraculis*, with *LDE* iii. 3 added (s. xvi ex) on fo. 43^v.

8 fos. 43^v–135^r Reginald of Durham, *De uirtutibus sancti Cuthberti.*

9 fos. 136^r–163^r Reginald of Durham, *Vita sancti Oswaldi*,[101] followed by extracts from Bede's *Ecclesiastical History* forming *De sancto Aidano*, and then by the *Vita Eatae.*

10 fos. 164^r–173^v Reginald of Durham, *Vita sancte Ebbe.*[102]

11 fos. 174^r–179^r Bede, *Historia abbatum.*[103]

12 fos. 179^r–184^r *Vita Bede.*[104]

13 fos. 184^r–198^r Reginald of Durham, *Vita sancti Godrici.*[105]

14 fos. 199^r–206^r Geoffrey of Coldingham, *Vita sancti Bartholomei.*[106]

15 fos. 207^r–212^r *De iniusta uexacione Willelmi episcopi primi.*

[97] A. I. Doyle, pers. comm.

[98] For a description, see *A Summary Catalogue of Western Manuscripts in the Bodleian Library at Oxford*, ii, pt. 2, ed. F. Madan, H. H. E. Craster, and N. Denholm-Young (Oxford, 1937), pp. 773–5 (no. 3886).

[99] Colgrave, *Two Lives*, pp. 141–307.

[100] Bede, *HE*.

[101] Arnold, *Sym. Op.* i. 326–85.

[102] Abridged version in *Nova Legenda Anglie*, ed. C. Horstman (2 vols.; Oxford, 1901), i. 303–11.

[103] Plummer, *Bede* i. 364–87.

[104] Unprinted.

[105] *Libellus de vita et miraculis s. Godrici, heremitae de Finchale, auctore Reginaldo monacho Dunelmensi*, ed. J. Stevenson (SS xx; London, 1847).

[106] Arnold, *Symeon*, i. 295–325.

16(a) fo. 212^v The summary beginning 'Regnante apud North-anhymbros'.

(b) fo. 213^r The preface to the *Libellus de exordio*, beginning 'Exordium huius hoc est Dunelmensis ecclesie describere'.

(c) fo. 213^r A list of the bishops of Lindisfarne, Chester-le-Street, and Durham running in the original hand to Louis de Beaumont (1317–33), continued in an imitative hand to Cuthbert Tunstall (1530–59), and then in later hands to Toby Matthew (1595–1606).

(d) fo. 213^{r-v} A list of chapter-headings for 184 chapters, embracing items 16–19.

(e) fos. 214^r–242^v The main body of the text of the *Libellus de exordio*, beginning 'Gloriosi quondam regis Northanhym-brorum', with red chapter-heading rubrics contemporary with the text, and with five chapters from the *De miraculis* inserted into the text.[107]

17 fos. 242^v–248^r The continuation of the *Libellus de exordio*, beginning 'Tribus dehinc annis ecclesia uacante pastore' and ending 'solempniter susceptus est'.

18 fos. 248^r–257^r Geoffrey of Coldingham, *Liber de statu ecclesie Dunhelmensis*, introduced by the rubric 'Incipit liber Gaufridi sacriste de Coldingham de statu ecclesie Dunelmensis. Qui incipit ad obitum Willelmi episcopi de Sancta Barbara usque ad electionem domini Morgani'.

19 fos. 257^r–281^v Robert Greystanes, *Historia de statu ecclesie Dunelmensis*.

20 fos. 281^v–282^v The lives of Richard of Bury.

21 fos. 282^v–296^r The 'History of William Chambre'.[108]

With certain exceptions noted below, this manuscript is written throughout in hands of the middle and second half of the fourteenth century.[109] It contains a contemporary contents-list which, although subject to some early correction, corresponds to the present contents, and to contemporary folio numbers and index-tabs.

Items 15–18 were written contemporaneously. These items overlap leaves and quires; all have an identical layout, that is two columns, a written space of 255 × 145 mm, elaborate blue and red pen-

---

[107] See below, p. lx n. 238.

[108] Raine, *Scriptores tres*, pp. 130–56.

[109] The principal scribe's name appears to have been *Petrus Plenus Amoris*, recorded as the *nomen scriptoris* in a contemporary hand on fo. vi^v.

flourished initials often decorated with leaf-and-tile work, and integral chapter-headings with marginal chapter-numbers. The script is consistent with the evidence of the bishop-list which runs in the original hand to Louis de Beaumont and gives the length of his pontificate, suggesting that it was compiled in the time of his successor Richard of Bury (1333–45).

Item 19 may represent a slightly later addition to the book. Its script seems later, its initials are a crude attempt to imitate those in the preceding texts, it lacks chapter-headings, and its chapter-numbers are in a quite different hand from that which added chapter-numbers to items 16–18. Item 19 also seems to have been continued in a different ink and by a different scribe after c. 131. The implication is that items 16–18 were copied in Fx before the composition of Greystanes' history, which was added soon after its appearance in 1336. Item 20 is the work of a fifteenth-century scribe, item 21 the work of the Durham antiquary, William Claxton, who also inserted the chapter of the *Libellus de exordio* on fo. 43ᵛ in a blank space immediately following item 7, added some headings throughout, and added the text of Bede's 'death-song' to item 16(e).[110]

That Fx belonged to Durham from the fourteenth century is shown by a press-mark 'P' on fo. 1ʳ and the beginning of fo. 2ʳ ('ramine et prudencia'), which correspond with an entry in the 1395 cloister catalogue; and by annotations in the hand of the Durham monk Thomas Swalwell (d. 1539). That it remained in Durham in the early modern period is shown by the addition to it (fos. iv–v) of lists of the bishops to 1529 and priors of Durham to 1519 by Thomas Swalwell.[111] The contents suggest that it was commissioned for Durham priory, and it may have been written there, since the text of Bede's *Historia abbatum* derives from, and is possibly a transcript of, the copy of the text in Durham, Cathedral Library, B.II.35 which Bishop William of Saint-Calais presented to the priory.[112]

---

[110] Doyle, 'Claxton', pp. 343–4; and for the relationship between this chronicle and the lives of Richard of Bury, N. Denholm-Young, 'The birth of a chronicle', *Bodleian Quarterly Review*, vii (1933), 326–8.

[111] Botfield, *Catalogi veteres*, p. 55; Doyle, 'Claxton', p. 342.

[112] Plummer, *Bede*, i, p. cxxxviii.

L Oxford, Bodleian Library, Laud misc. 700

164 parchment leaves 235 × 160 mm[113]

1 fos. 1ʳ–9ʳ An alphabetical index to items 7–10, to which it is keyed by chapter numbers and marginal letters.

2 fos. 10ᵛ–12ʳ The summary beginning 'Regnante apud Northanhymbros'.

3 fo. 12ᵛ The preface to the *Libellus de exordio*, beginning 'Exordium huius hoc est Dunelmensis ecclesie describere'.

4 fo. 12ᵛ A list of the bishops of Lindisfarne, Chester-le-Street, and Durham down to Hugh of le Puiset (1153–95) in the original hand, continued to Cuthbert Tunstall (1530–59) by a later hand.

5 fo. 13ʳ *Lindisfernensis insule descriptio.*

6 fo. 13ᵛ *Catalogus episcoporum Dunelmensium quorum corpora inueniuntur sepulta.*[114]

7(a) fo. 14ʳ A second copy of the preface to the *Libellus de exordio*, beginning 'Exordium huius hoc est Dunelmensis ecclesie describere'.

  (b) fo. 14ʳ⁻ᵛ A list of the bishops of Lindisfarne, Chester-le-Street, and Durham down to John Fordham (1381–8).

  (c) fos. 14ᵛ–17ʳ A list of 184 chapter-headings embracing items 7–10 in the original hand, extending to 198 headings and embracing items 11 and part of item 12 in a later hand.

  (d) fos. 17ᵛ–75aʳ The main body of the text of the *Libellus de exordio*, beginning 'Gloriosi quondam regis Northanhymbrorum', incorporating five chapters of the *De miraculis* and the whole of the *De iniusta uexacione Willelmi episcopi primi* (fos. 66ʳ–74ᵛ).

8 fos. 75aʳ–82ᵛ The continuation of the *Libellus de exordio*, beginning 'Tribus dehinc annis ecclesia uacante pastore', and ending 'episcopus sollempniter susceptus est'.

9 fos. 82ᵛ–96ᵛ Geoffrey of Coldingham, *Liber de statu ecclesie Dunhelmensis*, with some Durham documents added on fos. 97ʳ–101ʳ, in the same hand as item 7(c) and the chapter-numbers.

10 fos. 103ʳ–133ᵛ Robert Greystanes, *Historia de statu ecclesie Dunelmensis*.

11 fos. 133ᵛ–135ᵛ Lives of Richard of Bury.

---

[113] For a description, see H. O. Coxe, *Bodleian Library Quarto Catalogues*, ii. *Laudian Manuscripts*, rev. R. W. Hunt (Oxford, 1973), cols. 501–2 and 580. The foliation is imperfect and some folios have had to be numbered 'a' and 'b'. Hence the final folio is in fact numbered 156.

[114] Unprinted.

12 fos. 135ᵛ–156ʳ The 'History of William Chambre', followed by miscellaneous materials.

Items 7–9 seem to have been written at the same time. The layout in single columns (written space approximately 190 × 125 mm) and the crude red initials and chapter-numbers are uniform throughout, and the scripts are all of the middle to second half of the fourteenth century, consistent with the evidence of the bishop-list, which finishes with John Fordham (1381–8). His length of pontificate is given, but it is uncertain whether or not this is an addition. If it is not, the list could have been compiled under his successor, Walter Skirlaw (1388–1406).

The remainder of the last quire of item 9 was originally left blank, permitting the Durham documents to be entered on it. Item 10 begins on a new quire and appears to represent a separate booklet. The initials, although similar, are not identical to those of items 7–9. The parchment is browner and more worn, the hand smaller and less upright, suggesting a date in the mid-fourteenth century. The text has been densely annotated whereas the preceding texts are relatively free of annotation. It seems likely therefore that when the manuscript was put together in the late fourteenth or early fifteenth century a new copy of items 7–9 was made and bound up with an existing copy of Greystanes. A list of chapter headings embraced all the compo-nents, and the rubricator who added the chapter-numbers to the earlier part of the work added them also to Greystanes. The index, which also takes in the whole work, is in a textura script and may be slightly later. Finally a later sixteenth-century hand, that of William Claxton, copied items 11–12 on to the last leaf of the last quire occupied by Greystanes and then on further quires. In view of its early modern initials and rubric and the early modern additions to it, the quire containing items 2–4 may also have been added at this time. It was Claxton who continued the list of bishops (item 4) and wrote in full item 5. He was also responsible for inserting Bede's 'death-song' into item 7(d).[115]

The manuscript preserves no *ex libris* inscriptions or catalogue marks; the beginning of the second folio ('inueniri poterant') does not correspond with any entry in the medieval catalogues of Durham; and there are no annotations by identifiable Durham monks. The fact that it was owned by William Claxton (his name is on fo. 158ᵛ) who was of

---

[115] Doyle, 'Claxton', pp. 339, 344.

Wynyard in County Durham and known to have been associated with other Durham books, including C and Fx, nevertheless makes a Durham provenance very likely, although the book may have been kept at one of the cells of the cathedral priory.[116]

2. DATE AND AUTHORSHIP OF THE *LIBELLUS DE EXORDIO*

It has already been indicated that two manuscripts of the *Libellus de exordio*, C and F, belong to the very early twelfth century, and that C appears to have been written before Turgot ceased to be prior of Durham, that is before 1107, or possibly before 1109, or at the very latest before 1115.[117] As we shall see, confirmation of this is to be found in F, which preserves the text of the original version of the *Libellus de exordio*, and has at the end of its account of Turgot a sentence to the effect that he was prior at the time of writing.[118] The *Libellus de exordio* must therefore have been written before 1107 × 1115. The earliest date at which it could have been written is established by a clear reference in it to the opening of St Cuthbert's tomb immediately prior to his translation into the new cathedral at Durham on 29 August 1104.[119] It must therefore have been written in the period 1104–1107 × 1115.

Discussion of its authorship has until recently been based on the evidence of the rubrics in Ca, belonging to the third quarter of the twelfth century, and the rubric in H, which belongs to the late thirteenth or early fourteenth. These rubrics assign the *Libellus de exordio* to Symeon, whom both call a monk of Durham and Ca calls in addition the cantor (*precentor*) of the church of Durham. Scholars have in the main been content to accept these rubrics and assign the text to Symeon, despite the absence of his name from the rubrics in C and F.[120] The credibility of Ca's rubrics is strengthened by their close similarity in script and wording to the rubrics in CCCC 139, which assign the *Historia regum* to Symeon, an attribution about which scholars have been doubtful but which should probably now be

---

[116] Ibid., pp. 337–8.
[117] See above, p. xx.
[118] See below, p. liv.
[119] See below, pp. 52–3 and n. 67.
[120] For discussion and refutation of Selden's attribution of the work to Turgot, for which the evidence is wholly inadequate, see Arnold, *Sym. Op.* i, pp. xx–xxiii. See also, C, item 1, pr. Bedford, *Symeonis Libellus*, pp. i–xxxv.

upheld.[121] The credibility of H's rubric is weakened by the fact that it attributes accounts of the period down to Bishop Hugh of le Puiset (1153–95) to Symeon, but this is perhaps an understandable mistake in view of the progressive enlargement of the the *Libellus de exordio* by the composition of continuations.

The attribution to Symeon on the basis of the rubrics has been confirmed by a new line of approach developed by Piper and Gullick, beginning from Symeon's role as cantor (or precentor) of the church of Durham.[122] The evidence for this is partly the rubrics in Ca noted above, partly the surviving account of a vision of heaven and hell experienced in Howdenshire (Yorks.) by a thirteen-year old boy called Orm in November 1126. This was written down by his priest and sent through the intermediary of a monk of Durham called Aldred 'to the venerable monk and servant of God and of the most holy bishop Cuthbert, Symeon, cantor (*precentori*) of the church of Durham'.[123] Now, the function of the cantor is laid out clearly in the monastic constitutions of Archbishop Lanfranc, which were almost certainly observed at Durham Cathedral Priory. According to these, the cantor's tasks, aside from supervising the singing in the choir, were as follows: 'It also pertains to his office to supervise the letters sent out to ask for prayers for the dead brethren, and to keep count of the week's and month's mind. He takes care of all the books of the house, and has them in his keeping.'[124] That is to say, the cantor was responsible for recording obits, for the calendar, and for the books of the monastery. This list of tasks suggests strongly that the late eleventh- and twelfth-century Durham Cathedral Priory manuscript now DCL B.IV.24 was the cantor's own book, for it contains items necessary for his work: aside from a copy of Lanfranc's monastic constitutions and Old English and Latin copies of the Rule of St Benedict, it contains a calendar with obits, a martyrology also with obits, and mid-twelfth-century lists of the priory's books.[125] As we have seen, Symeon was cantor in 1126, so it follows that DCL B.IV.24 was Symeon's own book.

[121] See below, pp. xlviii–xlix.
[122] What follows is based on A. J. Piper, 'The Durham cantor's book (Durham, Dean and Chapter Library, MS B.IV.24)'; Rollason, *Anglo-Norman Durham*, pp. 79–92; and Gullick, 'Scribes', pp. 93–124.
[123] H. Farmer, 'The vision of Orm', *Analecta Bollandiana*, lxxv (1957), 72–82.
[124] *The Monastic Constitutions of Lanfranc*, ed. D. Knowles (NMT, 1951), p. 82. See also M. E. Fassler, 'The office of the cantor in early western monastic rules and customaries: a preliminary investigation', *Early Music History*, v (1985), 29–51.
[125] Gullick, 'Scribes', p. 94.

Gullick has noted that one hand wrote the martyrology and pericopes in this book and, between the 1090s and 1128, added to it obits and agreements with other monasteries; given the line of argument set out above, this hand must have been that of Symeon himself.[126] Moreover, the same hand was responsible for most of the early corrections and also for matter entered over erasure in C, much of it of an authorial nature.[127] We have thus arrived at confirmation that Symeon, cantor of the church of Durham, was responsible for the *Libellus de exordio*. This conclusion is further corroborated by the author of the text's implication that he was present at the translation of St Cuthbert in 1104, when compared with Reginald of Durham's list of the monks who were present at that event, which includes Symeon.[128]

Despite the formal anonymity of the two earliest manuscripts, the attribution will be accepted in this edition. That anonymity may of course have been owing to the fact that Symeon was neither the originator nor the sole author of the *Libellus de exordio*. The first words of the preface refer to the author writing at the command of his superiors (presumably Prior Turgot and the sub-prior Algar); while the sentence immediately preceding the list of monks asks readers to pray for the soul of him (singular) who ordered the work to be written and those (plural) who executed it. The meaning must be that one man, presumably Prior Turgot, commissioned the work, and others, no doubt led by Symeon, compiled it.[129] It was thus a team effort.

3 . SYMEON'S CAREER

Aside from its reference to his presence at the 1104 translation of St Cuthbert noted above, the text of the *Libellus de exordio* provides little information about the career of its author. Arnold drew attention to a passage in it in which Symeon states that the clerks who founded Durham in 995 were accustomed to sing the office in the manner of monks, and preserved this custom until the time of Bishop Walcher (1071–80), 'sicut eos sepe canentes audiuimus'. He regarded this as proving either that Symeon was himself a resident of Durham in Walcher's time, or that he was a monk of Jarrow and Monkwear-

---

[126] See also Gullick, 'Hand', pp. 14–31.
[127] See below, p. liii.
[128] See below, pp. 52–3; and Raine, *Cuth. virt.*, c. 60.
[129] Rollason, 'Erasures', pp. 140–2.

mouth under Aldwin in the 1070s, and that he heard the clerks singing when he visited Durham from there. He held the second inference to be strengthened by Symeon's warm portrait of Aldwin, supposedly redolent of the devotion of a follower.[130] The interpretation of the passage about the singing, however, rests on the assumption that the person of the verb *audiuimus* relates to Symeon personally rather than to the whole community of Durham Cathedral Priory, which at the time of writing contained at least one monk, Turgot, who had come to Durham in 1083 from Monkwearmouth and Jarrow.[131] The fact that the name Symeon occurs only thirty-eighth in the list of monks in C, whereas F gives twenty-three (erased in C) as the number of monks who came to Durham in 1083, would seem to destroy any hypothesis that Symeon was among them.[132]

A more solid basis for reconstructing Symeon's career is provided by Gullick's palaeographical researches. Symeon's hand shows that he was from northern France or Normandy, while the chronology of his writing suggests strongly that he came to Durham with William of Saint-Calais on his return from exile in 1091, for his earliest securely datable piece of writing at Durham is a copy in the *Liber Vitae* of the agreement (*conuentio*) between the monks of Durham and Malcolm, king of Scots, his queen Margaret, and their children, made before the deaths of the king and queen in 1093, and there is evidence that he had already been working for Saint-Calais in Normandy before that.[133]

Thanks to Gullick's work, it is also possible to reconstruct Symeon's activity as a scribe. He was responsible for writing or modifying a considerable number of Durham documents and manuscripts, so that Gullick has commented, 'no other contemporary Durham scribe can be compared to the martyrology scribe [i.e. Symeon] in the range and extent of his work'.[134] This work included copying important priory documents, including charters of King Edgar of Scots (1097–1107), writs of Bishop Ranulf Flambard, and

---

[130] Arnold, *Sym. Op.* i. x–xi; see below, pp. 102–5.

[131] Arnold, *Sym. Op.* ii. 202–4. Arnold's use of a similar reminiscence about the pre-1083 Jarrow community in *HReg*, *s.a.* 1121, is open to a similar objection (op. cit., i. x, ii. 260–1).

[132] Below, pp. 8–9, 230–3; Piper, 'Lists', p. 179. Arnold's suggestion that he was a member of the pre-1083 community but as a clerk rather than as a monk, on which argument he would have taken monastic vows after 1083, and so his name would not have appeared amongst those of the first twenty-three in the list, is unconvincing (Arnold, *Sym. Op.* i. xii). [133] Gullick, 'Hand', p. 18; Gullick, 'Scribes', pp. 102, 104.

[134] Gullick, 'Scribes', pp. 97–108.

the same bishop's charters restoring to the monks of Durham their liberties and the property he had taken from them since his accession.[135] Especially interesting is Symeon's role in copying historical and hagiographical texts at Durham Cathedral Priory. He copied Bod. Lib., Digby 175, which contains what may be the oldest version of the characteristically Durham recension of Bede's prose *Vita S. Cuthberti*, as well as extracts from Bede's *Historia ecclesiastica* and the *De miraculis*.[136] He also executed a copy of Bede's prose *Vita S. Cuthberti* now in Bod. Lib., Bodley 596, into which he also copied Bede's metrical life of the saint and the text known as the *Historia de sancto Cuthberto*.[137] All these texts were heavily used as sources for the *Libellus de exordio*, and it is almost as if we are seeing Symeon collecting materials for that work. The *Historia de sancto Cuthberto* is particularly striking in this connection, since it exists in only two other manuscripts: Ca and the fifteenth-century book, London, Lincoln's Inn, Hale 114.[138]

Three of the manuscripts on which Symeon worked show him involved with computistical and annalistic work. In DCL, Hunter 100, a manuscript of shortly after 1100 devoted to computistical and scientific texts, he wrote part of Bishop Robert of Hereford's treatise on Marianus Scotus's era of the Incarnation.[139] In DCL B.IV.22, he wrote a series of annals of English and continental affairs laid out in parallel, on what are now the flyleaves.[140] Finally, in Glasgow, University Library, Hunterian 85 (T.4.2), he added annals for the years 532–1063 to the margins of a set of Easter tables to produce what have since been known as the *Annales Lindisfarnenses et Dunelmenses*.[141] In these manuscripts, we are seeing Symeon developing his studies of history at Durham, and we are being offered

[135] Gullick, 'Scribes', pp. 104–8; and Gullick, 'Hand', pp. 24–31.
[136] Gullick, 'Hand', p. 24; Gullick, 'Scribes', pp. 97–8, pls. 2a–b; W. D. Macray, *Catalogus Codicum manuscriptorum Bibliothecae Bodleianae, Pars IX, Codices a viro clarissimo Kenelm Digby* (Oxford, 1883), p. 187; Colgrave, *Two Lives*, pp. 22, 47–50.
[137] Gullick, 'Hand', p. 24; Gullick, 'Scribes', pp. 97, 98, 101, pl. 3a; Colgrave, *Two Lives*, pp. 24–5. It is just possible that some at least of this manuscript was copied in Normandy, for the version of the prose life contained in it is not connected with Durham but is related to at least one manuscript of French provenance (Gullick, 'Scribes', p. 98).
[138] E. Craster, 'The patrimony of St Cuthbert', *English Historical Review*, xlix (1954), 177–99, at 177.
[139] Gullick, 'Hand', p. 27 and n. 33; cf. Gullick, 'Scribes', p 105.
[140] Gullick, 'Hand', p. 30; Gullick, 'Scribes', p. 105; J. E. Story, 'Symeon as Annalist', Rollason, *Symeon*, pp. 202–13, pls. 32–7.
[141] Gullick, 'Hand', p. 30; Story, in Rollason, *Symeon*, pp. 207–8, pls. 39–41; and *ALf.*

valuable insight into the make-up and historiographical background of the *Libellus de exordio*.

The latest datable examples of Symeon's hand are the charters of Ranulf Flambard of 1128.[142] No manuscripts and documents in which he can be shown to have worked are later than that. Thus Symeon's career at Durham embraced the period from no later than 1093 (the date of the agreement with King Malcom and Queen Margaret) and 1128. The account of the vision of Orm referred to above corroborates this by showing that he was still active in 1126.[143]

Symeon's activity as an author is in the present state of knowledge less easy to reconstruct, but what evidence there is for it is consistent with the chronology of his career derived from palaeographical study. As we have seen, the *Libellus de exordio*, although anonymous in its earliest manuscripts, can confidently be attributed to him, although other writers may well have been involved, and belongs to the period 1104–1107 × 1115.[144] There are, in addition, two works which can be assigned to Symeon because he names himself as author. First, there is a letter on the archbishops of York, addressed to Dean Hugh of York, a dean of which name is attested in 1093, 1108, 1113–14, and 1119–35; the letter may have been composed after 1114, since the list of archbishops of York in the earliest manuscript of the letter ends with Thurstan, who was consecrated in that year.[145] The letter would thus have been composed while, or soon after, work on the *Libellus de exordio* was being carried out.

The second work is a letter to Hildebert of Lavardin (*c.*1056–1133) on Origen. This is undated, but the letter itself shows that it was written after Symeon's prior, Algar, had returned home following a meeting with Hildebert, at which doubts concerning the homilies of Origen had been discussed, and Symeon had been set to resolve them. The date of the meeting cannot be established with certainty, but a council at Reims in October 1119 was certainly attended by Hildebert and Ranulf Flambard, bishop of Durham, and Algar may have accompanied his bishop. If so, it is not unreasonable to suppose that Symeon's letter was composed soon after Algar's return to Durham, perhaps in early 1120.[146]

---

[142] Gullick, 'Hand', p. 30, pls. 7b–c.

[143] See above, p. xliii.   [144] See above, p xlii.

[145] Arnold, *Sym. Op.* i. 10; and R. Sharpe, 'Symeon as pamphleteer', Rollason, *Symeon*, pp. 214–29, at 218–19.

[146] R. Sharpe, 'Symeon, Hildebert, and the errors of Origen', Rollason, *Symeon*, pp. 282–300, esp. 283.

The two sets of annals referred to above may be tentatively attributed to Symeon because his involvement as a scribe, revealed by palaeographical evidence, is such as to suggest that he may also have been the author; and their composition would fit equally well within the proposed time-range for his career. These are: the annals copied by Symeon on the flyleaves of DCL B.IV.22, which terminate in 1125; and the *Annales Lindisfarnenses et Dunelmenses*, copied by Symeon in the manuscript which is now Glasgow Hunterian 85, and which extend to 1127 in what appears to be the first recension.[147]

One further text is assigned to Symeon by means of rubrics. This is the text known as the *Historia regum*, an historical compilation extending from the death of Bede to 1129,[148] the only manuscript of which (CCCC 139) has an *incipit* and an *explicit* referring to Symeon as the author.[149] These rubrics cannot be contemporary with the text, since they state that it extended from the death of Bede in 735 for a period of 429 years, that is to 1164. This is not in fact the case, since the work terminates in 1129, but it may well refer to the compilation of the manuscript as a whole (which contains other texts besides the *Historia regum*) or its exemplar.[150] The authority of the rubrics is enhanced, however, by their similarities to those in Ca's copy of the *Libellus de exordio*, with which they share the words 'historia sancte et suauis memorie Symeonis' and 'Symeonis monachi et precentoris ecclesie sancti Cuthberti Dunelmi'.[151] As noted above, Ca's copy is now shown to have been produced in Durham in the last quarter of the twelfth century, possibly from 1188.[152] These similarities, together with close textual relationships between the twelfth-century contents of Ca and those of CCCC 66 (which once formed

---

[147] See above, p. xlvi.

[148] *HReg.*

[149] The *incipit* on fo. 51ᵛ reads: 'Incipit historia sancte et suauis memorie Simeonis, monachi et precentoris ecclesie sancti Cuthberti Dunelmi, de regibus Anglorum et Dacorum, et creberrimis bellis, rapinis, et incendiis eorum, post obitum uenerabilis Bede presbyteri fere usque ad obitum regis primi Henrici, filii Willelmi Nothi qui Angliam adquisiuit, id est .ccccxxix. annorum et .iv. mensium' (Arnold, *Sym. Op.* ii. 3). The *explicit* on fo. 129ᵛ reads: 'Explicit historia suauis et sancte memorie Symeonis monachi et precentoris ecclesie sancti Cuthberti Dunelmi annorum .ccccxxix. et mensium quattuor' (ibid. ii. 283). See P. Hunter Blair, 'Some observations on the *Historia regum* attributed to Symeon of Durham', *Celt and Saxon: Studies in the Early British Border*, ed. N. K. Chadwick (Cambridge, 1963), pp. 63–118, at 75 (repr. in his *Anglo-Saxon Northumbria*, ed. M. Lapidge and P. Hunter Blair (London, 1984), no. III).

[150] Blair, op. cit., pp. 77–8.

[151] Cf. pp. xxiv–xxv above.

[152] See above, p. xxvii.

part of the same manuscript), and CCCC 139, show that CCCC 139 was also produced at Durham,[153] a conclusion corroborated by Story's discovery that the set of annals which occupies fos. 46ʳ–48ᵛ is derived from the annals copied by Symeon on the flyleaves of DCL B.IV.22.[154] In the last quarter of the twelfth century in Durham, therefore, the *Historia regum* was assigned to Symeon, and this attribution should be taken seriously.

Symeon's role in the compilation of the *Historia regum* was, however, relatively limited. The work is composite, and it is now clear that the first five sections, including a version of the Northern Annals from 732 to 802 and a chronicle from 849 to 887 derived mainly from Asser, were originally a compilation made by Byrhtferth of Ramsey (*c*.970–*c*.1020).[155] To this have been added: a chronicle from 888 to 957,[156] extracts from William of Malmesbury's *De gestis regum*,[157] a chronicle from 848 to 1118, derived from John of Worcester with additional material relating to northern events,[158] and a chronicle from 1119 to 1129.[159] If Symeon compiled the whole work in its present form, he was probably the author only of the last section and the northern material in the penultimate section.[160] There are indications that the work was not complete at Symeon's death and is effectively unfinished. The chronicle from 848 to 1118 overlaps with that from 849 to 887 in the early sections; and there are discrepancies between the work and the *Libellus de exordio*, for example in the account of the capture of the Northumbrian prince Offa in 750, which may reveal unfinished editing of the *Historia regum*.[161] Such an interpretation fits well with the palaeographical

[153] See above, pp. xxvi–xxvii, and Meehan, in Rollason, *Anglo-Norman Durham*, pp. 440–2, and Norton, in Rollason, *Symeon*, p. 87.

[154] Story, in Rollason, *Symeon*, pp. 210–13, with references at p. 211 n. 33 to earlier discussions of CCCC 139's provenance, which have suggested Hexham, Sawley, and Fountains.

[155] For the sections of *HReg*, see Blair, 'Some observations', pp. 77–111. The text of the early sections is pr. Arnold, *Sym. Op.* ii. 3–91; on which, see M. Lapidge, 'Byrhtferth of Ramsey and the early sections of the Historia Regum attributed to Symeon of Durham', *Anglo-Saxon England*, x (1982), 97–122 (repr. in his *Anglo-Latin Literature 900–1066* (London and Ronceverte, 1993), pp. 317–42); and C. Hart, 'Byrhtferth's Northumbrian chronicle', *English Historical Review*, xcvii (1982), 558–82.

[156] Arnold, *Sym. Op.* ii. 91–5.

[157] Ibid. ii. 95–8.

[158] Ibid. ii. 98–253.

[159] Ibid. ii. 253–83.

[160] Blair, 'Some observations', p. 117; and D. Rollason, 'Symeon's contribution to historical writing in northern England', Rollason, *Symeon*, pp. 1–13, at 10.

[161] See below, pp. 79–81, 80 n. 5. Offler was inclined to attribute these discrepancies to Symeon having changed his mind; see Offler, *Medieval Historians*, p. 9.

evidence which suggests that Symeon died in or shortly after 1128;[162] he would thus have completed the annal for 1129, but have left no successor to bring his work to a satisfactory state of completion.

No other texts can with any confidence be assigned to Symeon, although several of those printed by Thomas Arnold under the title *Symeonis monachi opera omnia* are likely to have been produced in Durham in Symeon's time and he may have had a hand in them.[163] The account of the see of Lindisfarne in Y (item 7), which Arnold did not print and which has been attributed to Symeon on the grounds of its subject matter and the preoccupations it reveals, cannot be closely dated, but probably belongs to the same period as the *Libellus de exordio*.[164]

4. The Development of the Text of the *Libellvs de exordio*

(a) The text in C, F, and Ca

The two earliest manuscripts of the *Libellus de exordio*, C and F, have much in common. Their script and decoration are sufficiently similar to suggest that they were produced in the same scriptorium, probably that of Durham, in the early twelfth century. Both are *de luxe* manuscripts. Neither has chapter numbers or rubrics, but both use minor initials to subdivide the text into chapters according to the same scheme established with a list of books and chapter headings by Ca; both have a large decorated initial at the start of the main text (beginning 'Gloriosi quondam') and at the start of what is in Ca book iv (beginning 'Transactis post occisionem').[165] Further, both have the Old English poem known as Bede's 'death-song' written in the same semi-Insular script, although not by the same scribe.[166] Which of these manuscripts is the earlier and what is their

---

[162] See above, p. xlvii.

[163] Arnold, *Sym. Op.*, although he makes clear in his introduction that he did not regard all the texts he printed as being by Symeon. For the *De miraculis et translationibus sancti Cuthberti*, see below, pp. lxxv–lxxvi; for the *De iniusta uexacione*, p. lxxviii; for *DPSA*, below, p. lxxix; for the summary beginning *Regnante apud*, below, pp. lxvi–lxvii; and for the *De obsessione Dunelmi*, below, pp. lxxviii–lxxix.

[164] Sharpe, in Rollason, *Symeon*, pp. 214–29. For the possibility that Symeon may have been the author of *De obsessione Dunelmi*, see below, p. lxxix.

[165] Gullick, 'Hand', pp. 106–19.

[166] A. I. Doyle, pers. comm. See below, pp. xci, 72–3.

relationship to each other? It looks at first sight as if F has been copied
from C, because there are two erasures in C with no corresponding
text in F. Seventeen lines have been erased from an account of Bishop
Eardwulf (854–99), following a sentence describing how Carlisle not
only belonged to the proper jurisdiction of St Cuthbert, but was also
subject to the rule of the see of Durham by virtue of a gift of King
Ecgfrith (d. 685).[167] Twenty full lines and one part-line have been
erased following an account of the expulsion of the canons from the
church of Durham by Bishop William of Saint-Calais in 1083;[168] and
one word (presumably the name *Turgotum*) has been erased after 'hic'
in the phrase 'Hic magistrum de monasterio . . . proficiscentem
secutus'.[169]

There is in addition an erasure of fourteen lines in C, of which the
first twelve have been replaced in a contemporary hand with the text
found at this point in F. This re-written portion concerns the fate of a
rich man's wife who committed suicide after illicitly breaching the
prohibition on women entering the churchyard of Durham.[170] In all
cases the erasure has been very thorough and no trace of the original
text remains; and in all cases the corresponding text in F follows
exactly the erased or altered version in C without any extra space or
other indication that text is missing. On the basis of this evidence
alone therefore, it could be argued that F was copied directly or
indirectly from C, the passages in question having been altered in C
before F was produced.

Consideration of the significant number of textual variants between
C and F, amounting to over 100 in all, however, makes this difficult to
accept. Some can be dismissed as scribal changes: in the spelling of
proper names, and in minor inversions of word order. Some are more
serious, however, involving F's omission of words and phrases found
in C, as for example 'sedes' in 'sedes episcopalis',[171] 'uno anno',[172] 'et
in Gyruum',[173] 'contra Aethelstanum',[174] and 'presulatus'.[175] There
are a number of instances where C's text appears superior to that of F:
for example, the omission of 'sedes' in 'sedes episcopalis' destroys the
sense, and the use in F of 'commune' for 'continue'[176] and of 'ibi' for
'ipsi'[177] seems to be wrong, as does the indicative mood of F's

[167] Fo. 35ʳ; see below, pp. 94–5 n. 38.   [168] Fo. 80ʳ⁻ᵛ; see below, pp. 230–1 n. 20.
[169] Fo. 72ᵛ; see below, p. 208 n. 86.   [170] Fos. 39ᵛ–40ʳ; see below, p. 110 n. 60.
[171] See below, p. 32.   [172] See below, p 58.
[173] See below, p. 64.   [174] See below, p. 138.
[175] See below, p. 210.   [176] See below, p. 178.
[177] See below, p. 204.

'uocabat' in place of C's 'uocaret'.[178] It is especially striking that some of the variants occur in the writings of other authors copied into the *Libellus de exordio* and in these cases F's version is often farther from the original than C's. In passages from Bede's prose *Vita S. Cuthberti*, for example, C agrees with this text in reading 'indui' where F has 'uti'.[179] In passages from Bede's *Historia ecclesiastica*, C agrees with the Durham copy of Bede (DCL B.II.35) in reading 'de capillis' where F has 'capillorum',[180] 'premonstraret' in place of F's 'premonstrauit',[181] and 'cubicula' for F's 'cubilia' in the account of the destruction of Coldingham.[182] The same is true of the *Historia de sancto Cuthberto*, where C's version of the confirmation of laws by King Edmund is closer to the original text than F's.[183] There is also a number of different readings in F in the *Libellus de exordio*'s copy of Cuthbert's letter on the death of Bede, which has caused F's version to be described as 'somewhat eccentric textually'.[184] It therefore seems unlikely that F was copied from C, unless we are to assume that F was hastily and carelessly made. It seems more likely that F was the earlier text, and that C represents a revised and corrected version.

As noted above, both C and F are *de luxe* manuscripts, so that neither can conceivably represent the first setting down on parchment of the *Libellus de exordio*. There must have been a working copy containing the original version now lost, which we shall call O. The most plausible, although certainly not the only, explanation of the variants between C and F can be given in terms of the following sequence of events. F was produced as a copy of Version O. Version O_I was produced subsequently by revising and correcting version O, possibly in the working copy, and by adding to it the now lost passages about Carlisle and the expulsion of the canons, and supplying a new version of the story of the suicidal woman. C was produced as a copy of Version O_I, perhaps taken from the revised working copy.

F's text was thus rapidly superseded by C's, and this may explain

---

[178] See below, p. 246.
[179] See below, p. 50; Colgrave, *Two Lives*, p. 272.
[180] See below, p. 56; Bede, *HE*, iv. 32 (30), p. 448.
[181] See below, p. 48; Bede, *HE*, iv. 28 (26), p. 438.
[182] See below, p. 106; Bede, *HE*, iv. 25 (23), p. 424.
[183] See below, p. 140; *HSC* c. 28.
[184] See below, pp. 70–7; E. van Kirk Dobbie, *The Manuscripts of Caedmon's Hymn and Bede's Death Song* (Columbia, 1937), p. 84.

why F had been given to Fountains Abbey by the end of the twelfth century,[185] perhaps being regarded as an inferior text. It had virtually no influence on the subsequent development of the *Libellus de exordio*, for all other manuscripts very largely agree with C against it. Setting aside minor omissions and changes of word order, the only potentially significant variants where F agrees with other manuscripts against C are in its reading of 'transactis' for 'exactis',[186] agreeing with the thirteenth-century manuscript H and the fourteenth-century manuscripts L, T, and Y; and in its reading 'Mol' for 'mox'[187] in agreement with the late twelfth-century manuscript Ca. It may be that the working copy's text of O was imperfectly revised in converting it to version O_1, so that traces of these wordings remained, perhaps incompletely cancelled, to mislead a subsequent copyist. In the case of 'Mol' for 'mox', however, another explanation is possible. The word 'mox' follows the name of King Æthelwold who has earlier on in the passage been referred to as 'Aethelwoldum Mol', so it is easy to see how 'mox' could have been read 'Mol' independently on two different occasions.

Given the early date of C, the revision which produced O_1 is very likely to have been the work of Symeon and his collaborators. It is striking in addition that a number of the variants between F and C could be attributed to authorial intervention, as for example where F has 'obitum' for 'exitum',[188] 'incorruptionem' for 'pulchritudinem',[189] 'permodica' for 'non grandis',[190] and 'satiatus enim auro et argento aliisque rebus' for 'premissis enim auro et argento aliisque rebus'.[191]

A further version, Version O_2, was produced by a series of modifications to Version O_1. These may well have been made to

[185] See above, p. xxiii.   [186] See below, p. 30.

[187] See below, p. 84.   [188] See below, p. 74.

[189] See below, p. 118.   [190] See below, p. 148.

[191] See below, p. 170. In the case of one variant it is difficult to decide whether we are dealing with authorial revision, or careless copying from the working copy. This is where F adds a whole clause, 'hec enim duo sunt flumina quinque ferme ab inuicem milibus in mare decurrentia', where C records St Cuthbert's request that King Guthred should give him 'totam inter Weor et Tine terram'. F inserts its additional material after 'Tine' (below, p. 124). It is arguable that this clause was in the working copy of O_1 but was omitted by the scribe of C who had virtually reached the bottom of fo. 45^r in his copying and failed to include it through eye-skip (Doyle and Piper, *Catalogue*). This argument is weakened, however, because, although 'Tine' is on the last line of C's fo. 45^r, it is not the last word. It is more likely that the clause may have been dropped from O_1 as being superfluous in a book produced in a community which must have been familiar with the rivers of north-east England.

the working copy, but they were also made by erasure of text and substitution of new text in C itself. Some of them involved restoring by excision or replacement the text of O. They included the removal of the passages following the accounts of Carlisle and the expulsion of the canons, and the restoration of O's version of the story of the suicidal woman. Other modifications involved removing or replacing text found in O and O_1. In a reference to the monks brought from Jarrow to Durham, C has three erased words, which can more or less be read under ultra-violet light as 'numero uiginti tres', the words found at this point in F.[192] At the end of the account of Turgot, F has a sentence to the effect that he succeeded Aldwin as prior and held that office on the day of writing, where C has an erasure with enough surviving of the original writing to show that it originally had this statement, which is found in no other manuscript apart from F.[193] In the passage describing the gift of lands and privileges by King Guthred to the community of St Cuthbert, C has an erasure following the words 'terra quoque quam preceperat inter memorata duo flumina' where F reads 'a Deorestrete usque ad mare orientale'.[194] Although no trace of these words remains in C, there is just space for them. In the account of how Bishop Æthelric was accused of taking treasures from the church of Durham, C has an erasure of three words before its reference to his imprisonment and death in London. At this point F has 'reddere noluit, unde'.[195] As in the previous case, the space created by the erasure in C is sufficient to accommodate these words but no traces of writing remain.

In addition to these erasures where no new text was supplied, there were erasures to make space for revised wording. The new version of the story of the suicidal woman was erased and O's version was restored in its place. In this case, the new text was inserted in the hand of the scribe of the text as a whole, but in the other cases the hand concerned was that identified as Symeon's. In the account of the gift of Tynemouth to the monks of Jarrow (who later became the monks of Durham), F reads: 'ecclesiam sane sancti Oswini in Tinemuthe iamdudum donante Walchero episcopo cum comitatum regeret', but in C there has been an erasure of the final letter of 'donante' and the words 'Walchero . . . regeret' (the 'g' of the last

---

[192] Fo. 79; see below, p. 230.
[193] See below, pp. 206–7 and n. 85.
[194] Fo. 45ᵛ; see below, p. 126.
[195] Fo. 60ᵛ; see below, pp. 172–3 and n. 46.

word is partially visible under ultra-violet light), and Symeon has revised the sentence to read 'donantibus Northymbrie comitibus'.[196] There seems no doubt that F has preserved the original form, for not only is its version most likely to be historically correct, but there is space in C for the words found in F, whereas the present version leaves blank space. In the account of Copsig's tenure of the earldom of Northumbria, C states that 'iubente Willelmo rege procurator factus est', but this is over the erasure of a shorter phrase which seems to appear in F as 'comes factus est'.[197] Finally, in the account of the return of the canons of Durham from their temporary exile on Lindisfarne, C has 'reconciliata solenniter ecclesia octauum Kalendas Aprilis', but again this is over an erasure of a longer text, which could be the words found in F: 'ipsa die depositionis eius que est tredecim Kalendas Aprilis cum laudibus intrantes ecclesia'.[198]

Alterations to the prefatory material were probably also part of the production of version O_2 as found in C. The first fifteen and a half lines of the preface were erased, and Symeon wrote a new, shorter version over the erasure. A word was deleted after 'illum' in the sentence introducing the bishop-list with 'usque illum qui in presenti est'.[199] There is no trace of the original but presumably it was the name 'Ranulfus' for Bishop Ranulf Flambard (1099–1128) and the erasure was made when the extension of the bishop-list to later bishops made its inclusion misleading.

Finally, a number of minor additions and alterations were made to Version O_1 and are found in C, where they were executed by Symeon himself. Thus 'domini' was modified to 'dominice' in the clause 'cum Iuda traditore dominice dampnationis sententia feriantur'. F has 'domini', which is in this case arguably more correct.[200] The words 'prouincie' and 'plagam' were added above the line—they seem in fact required to complete the statement that Copsig was placed over the 'prouincie Northanhymbrorum, scilicet illorum qui ad septentrionalem plagam fluminis Tini habitant'.[201] Neither word is found in F. Symeon altered 'studii' to 'studium' in the clause 'hic nos id studii'; 'studii' is found in F and Ca, the latter presumably accidentally retaining it from the imperfectly revised working copy.[202] He

[196] Fo. 81ʳ; see below, pp. 234–5 and n. 26.
[197] Fo. 63ᵛ; see below, pp. 180–1 and n. 56.
[198] Fo. 65ᵛ; see below, pp. 186–7 and n. 62.
[199] Fo. 6ʳ; below, p. 2.   [200] See below, p. 136.
[201] See below, p. 180.   [202] See below, p. 18.

added above the line 'ad' in 'ad insulam nauigauit' from Bede's prose *Vita S. Cuthberti*, where this was omitted by F, and also by Ca and the early thirteenth-century D.[203] Symeon also added above the line the pronoun 'hic' to the sentence 'Hic habuerat unum de capillis sanctissimi Cuthberti'. It is omitted not only by F, but also by D and the fourteenth-century manuscripts, H, T, and V.[204] He added the epithet 'filius Westou' to the name of Elfred, which is found in Ca, Fx, L, and Y, although not in D, H, V, or T.[205] Lastly, he corrected 'decimo Kalendarum Iuniarum' for the date of King Ecgfrith's death to 'terciodecimo Kalendarum Iuniarum', which is factually correct.[206]

Version O_2 became the normative version for all subsequent manuscripts, apart from Ca, the version in which was nevertheless a modification of it (O_3). There are indications that C itself was regarded as the authoritative manuscript, kept in the monastic chancery (fo. 11^r) and used as an exemplar for later copies.[207] The working copy may also have survived, however, perhaps corrected and cancelled in a way which left earlier versions still legible, so that it may have been the source of those places in the text noted above where later manuscripts seem to have been influenced by earlier versions.

Version O_2 may have developed over a period of years. The replacement of the text about the suicidal woman was done by the main text scribe, and so was presumably made very early on. Those alterations in Symeon's hand must have been made before his death *c.*1129, and on grounds of the development of his hand as observed in other writings, before *c.*1120.[208] There is no way of dating the removal of the passages about Carlisle and the canons, but these were both sensitive issues in the first quarter of the twelfth century,[209] and it seems unlikely that the removals were made later than that. They were certainly made before *c.*1188, when Ca was made as a copy of the later version O_3.[210]

After Symeon's death, still further changes were made to version O_2 as represented by C. The summary beginning 'Regnante apud' was added as a separate quire to the front of C in the mid-twelfth century;[211] and the continuation beginning 'Tribus dehinc annis' was

[203] See below, p. 44.
[204] See below, p. 162.
[205] See below, p. 160.
[206] See below, p. 46.
[207] See below, p. lxiv.
[208] Gullick, 'Hand', pp. 21–2, 27.
[209] See below, pp. lxxxviii–lxxxix.
[210] See above, p. lvii.
[211] Gullick, 'Hand', p. 116.

added in the third quarter of that century.[212] The list of monks was continued up until the 1160s.[213] Apart from the list of monks, these became elements in version O₂ as found in other manuscripts.

Version O₂ was further modified to produce a fourth version, O₃, from which the text was copied into Ca, c.1188. For, although Ca agrees generally with C against F, there are nevertheless many differences. We cannot be sure whether a further working copy was made, or whether the modifications were introduced as Ca was being copied. Given Ca's *de luxe* character, the former is the most probable. The major differences between Version O₂ (as represented by C) and Version O₃ (as represented by Ca) are the following. In Ca, the ordering of the prefatory material has been changed: the preface beginning 'Exordium huius' precedes the summary beginning 'Regnante apud', and is followed by part of the introductory paragraph to the list of monks beginning 'Hic scripta'.[214] Moreover, a final sentence has been added to this paragraph and the list of monks, and the list of bishops in the preface have been omitted. The list of Bede's works has been truncated, and the *Libellus de exordio*'s version of Cuthbert's letter on the death of Bede, with the sentence which introduces it, has been omitted.[215] The list of estates alienated by the earls of Northumbria has also been omitted.[216]

Ca has in addition a considerable number of minor variants from C, as for example 'sedes episcopatus' for 'sedes episcopalis',[217] 'uocatus' for 'reuocatus',[218] 'paulum' for 'paululum',[219] and the omission of 'enim' and 'audieram'.[220] In the case of all these variants, Ca does not agree with any other manuscript, and the same is true of its system of chapter divisions. These admittedly correspond to those defined by the use of initials in C and F, but Ca has a list of chapter-headings and a system of chapter and book numbering which are found in no other manuscript.[221] In addition, it has a series of rubrics to the summary beginning 'Regnante apud' and the main text of the *Libellus de exordio* as well as to the preface beginning 'Exordium huius', which attribute the *Libellus de exordio* to Symeon. Of the other manuscripts, only H has a rubric attributing the work to Symeon, and this does not resemble in any other way the wording of the rubrics in

---

[212] Ibid., p. 117.
[214] See below, pp. 2–7.
[216] See below, p. 154.
[218] See below, p. 86.
[220] See below, pp. 190, 192.

[213] Piper, 'Lists', p. 185.
[215] See below, pp. 66–70.
[217] See below, p. 32.
[219] See below, p. 104.
[221] See below, Appendix C, pp. 328–33.

Ca.[222] Finally, the continuation begins like that in C but its wording soon becomes quite distinct.[223]

Version O₃ (as represented by Ca) was rejected as a normative text just as O and O₁ had been; and just as F was given away to Fountains, so Ca was given to Sawley, although it may have reached that house via Fountains.[224] It had no subsequent influence, either on the *Libellus de exordio* or its continuation.

(b) The text in D and H

D offers an early-thirteenth-century text of the *Libellus de exordio* which is almost certainly a direct copy of C. The relationship is obscured by D's numerous scribal errors, which include such blunders as 'ministri' for 'sinistri',[225] 'humilitatis' for 'humanitatis',[226] and 'mirabilis' for 'miserabilis',[227] but these have generally been corrected by a contemporary hand, either in the text itself or in pencil in the margin to yield a text which differs very little from C's. (It does have a few significant variants which it shares, as we shall see, with other manuscripts.) In addition, D agrees with C's chapter-divisions which, like C, it distinguishes by minor initials but (as it was originally written) without chapter numbers or rubrics. It lacks the list of monks and its introductory paragraph beginning 'Hic scripta', but in all other respects its prefatory material resembles C's; and it has the first and second continuations as in C, although continued further by the addition of an incomplete text of Geoffrey of Coldingham's *Liber de statu*.

H offers a text of the *Libellus de exordio* approximately a century younger than D's, prefaced by the same material as D (apart from the summary beginning 'Regnante apud'), and followed by the first and second continuations and by a now truncated text of Coldingham's *Liber de statu*. Its unique features include its rubric and its chapter-divisions, which represent a development of C's but are more numerous and furnished with numbers and rubrics quite different from those found in Ca. They embrace not only the *Libellus de exordio* but also its two continuations and Geoffrey of Coldingham's *Liber de statu*. They are closer to the chapter-system of the other fourteenth-century manuscripts, but they differ significantly from it and set H apart from all other copies of the *Libellus de exordio*.

[222] See above, p. xxx.
[224] See above, p. xxvii.
[226] See below, p. 216.
[223] See below, Appendix B, pp. 311–23.
[225] See below, p. 136.
[227] Ibid.

H is also notable for its very large number of unique variants. Many of these are relatively minor, but more significant are the omission of the whole of the Old English version of Bede's 'death-song' (in place of which H has five blank lines), and of such substantial phrases as 'sed de loco ad locum huc atque illuc',[228] 'exequentes imperii fines latius quam ullus progenitorum suorum extendendo',[229] and 'monachicum ab eis habitum susceperunt, et sub discipline regularis institutione'.[230] The names of four of the estates alienated by the earls of Northumbria are also omitted.[231] These omissions make it impossible to regard H as the source for later copies of the *Libellus de exordio*.

H does, however, share with D the addition of the words 'suis gloriosissimis'[232] and the substitution of 'Ianuarii' for 'Iuniarum'.[233] It is unlikely that H is a copy of D, since it has a text of Coldingham's *Liber de statu* which is fuller than D's and was probably complete as originally copied; but there is presumably some connection between them. Moreover, both D and H share with Fx, L, and Y the omission of the words 'quante erga fidei religionem deuotionis' from the *Libellus de exordio*'s account of Aidan,[234] and the addition of the words 'monachorum uel' to its quotation from Bede's description of Cedd's disciples.[235] Further, the addition of the words 'de Barthenay' to the reference to the monastery to which Oswald's body was translated links H to Fx, L, and Y,[236] as does the addition of a sentence from Bede's prose *Vita S. Cuthberti*,[237] and some thirty minor agreements.

(c) The text in Y, Fx, and L

The fourteenth-century manuscripts Y, Fx, and L are closely linked by their system of chapter-divisions, chapter-numbers, and (in the case of Y and Fx) rubrics which, as we shall see, they share with T and, as far as can be discerned, with V. They are unique, however, in that the text of the *Libellus de exordio* found in them has had five chapters interpolated into it from the compilation of St Cuthbert's miracles known as the *De miraculis*. These interpolations, which concern the appearance of St Cuthbert to King Alfred, the

---

[228] See below, pp. 72, 104.
[230] See below, p. 202.
[232] See below, p. 38.
[234] See below, p. 18.
[236] See below, p. 24.

[229] See below, p. 112.
[231] See below, p. 154.
[233] See below, p. 46.
[235] See below, p. 30.
[237] See below, p. 52.

swallowing of a Scottish army by the earth, the miraculous punishment of one of Earl Tostig's men for trying to violate the sanctuary of St Cuthbert, the miraculous death of a Norman soldier who stole from the priory, and the miraculous experience of Abbot Paul of St Alban's, have entailed the removal of the sentences from the original text of the *Libellus de exordio* which alluded to the incidents which they describe more fully.[238] They are also unique in that where the passage concerning the fate of the canons of Durham after 1083 had been erased in C they have a sentence describing how those canons were ensconced in Darlington, Norton, Auckland, and Easington.[239]

The three manuscripts share in addition over one hundred variants. Some of these are minor but cumulatively impressive. Some are variants of name forms, such as 'Balthredus' for 'Baltherus',[240] but some are much more substantial. Aside from the insertion of the chapters from the *De miraculis* and the statement about the canons, we should note in particular some substantial omissions which the three manuscripts have in common in their text of the *Libellus de exordio*. All omit the words 'monasterio quod uocatur';[241] 'omnibus diebus uite mee. Ecce iam beatus cum beatis habitas in domo Domini' (an omission clearly caused by a scribe skipping to the 'Domini' ending these words from the one preceding it);[242] and (by the same type of process) the very substantial passage: 'Aldwino quem pro insita illi prudentia et magne discretionis moderamine ac morum honestate ualde strenuum nouerat, intus et foris totius monasterii curam et dispensationem delegauit, et ut sine illius consilio uel prouidentia nil ageretur statuit. Denique'.[243]

The evidence of their scripts and of the last name in their bishop-lists suggests, as we have seen, that L is the youngest, Fx the next, and Y the oldest. What then is the relationship between them? Fx and Y have approximately fifty variant readings in common, including the omission of the words 'ut superius dictum est medias',[244] the reading 'intercedere deberent' for 'intercederent',[245] and the addition of the words 'episcopus Walcherus'.[246] Fx cannot, however, be a straight copy of Y since Y lacks the summary beginning 'Regnante apud' which is found in Fx. A study of the corrections made to Y is

---

[238] See below, pp. 110 n. 63, 127 n. 85, 177 n. 52, 220 n. 105, 236 n. 29.
[239] See below, p. 230 n. 20.   [240] See below, p. 80.
[241] See below, p. 32.   [242] See below, p. 38.
[243] See below, p. 232.   [244] See below, p. 118.
[245] See below, p. 198.   [246] See below, p. 202.

illuminating, for frequently a variant reading in Y is reproduced in Fx but corrected. For example, Y omits the word 'discipuli' which is found in Fx added above the line;[247] and where Y has 'paucis' for 'paucissimis', Fx has 'paucis' but altered to the superlative form.[248] In almost every place where Y has a variant peculiar to itself, Fx has been corrected to bring its text into line with that of C. The most likely explanation is that Fx is a copy of Y, which was subsequently corrected by reference to another copy. The likelihood is that this copy was that in C itself which may also have been the source for Fx's copy of the summary beginning 'Regnante apud'.

As we have seen, L agrees frequently with Fx and Y, but where Fx has been altered to bring its text into line with C's rather than Y's, L invariably follows the corrected text of Fx. This suggests that L is based on Fx, and there are indeed a large number of variant readings peculiar to Fx and L, some minor but some relatively substantial, such as the addition of the words 'et Ebraice',[249] the reading 'ecclesia' for 'insula',[250] and the erroneous reading 'emisit' for 'eum misit'.[251] Moreover, the way in which the list of Copsig's gifts to Durham has been transposed by Y and Fx, and then further transposed by L, confirms that L is based on Fx which is in turn based on Y.[252]

L cannot, however, be simply a copy of Fx. It has a number of variant readings which it shares with Y alone, notably the erroneous 'etatis' for 'quietis',[253] 'instructum' for 'institutum',[254] and 'minister-ium' for 'mysterium'.[255] Moreover, in its original form it lacked the summary beginning 'Regnante apud' which is found in Fx but not in L. The implication is that, although L may be a copy of Fx, it would seem to have been done with reference to Y. Where Fx has omitted 'contritos corde et alligauit', for example, L has supplied it, presumably from Y.[256] Such cross-influence is not surprising in view of the fact that Fx and Y were certainly Durham books and so too in all likelihood was L.

In two respects, however, L represents a further development in the text of the *Libellus de exordio*. First, the text has been equipped with an elaborate index section found in no other manuscript. Secondly, the final section concerning the death of William of

---

[247] See below, p. 164.
[248] See below, p. 216.
[249] See below, p. 42.
[250] See below, p. 52.
[251] See below, p. 226.
[252] See below, p. 180.
[253] See below, p. 84.
[254] See below, p. 160.
[255] See below, p. 172.
[256] See below, p. 54.

Saint-Calais has been augmented by the insertion in the original hand of the *De iniusta uexacione Willelmi primi*,[257] a tract defending William's actions at his trial for treason and his expulsion from England. Now, the earliest manuscript of this work is Fx, but in Fx it occurs before the *Libellus de exordio*, although in the same hand. The implication must be that L was based on Fx, but was conceived as an expanded work with the *De iniusta uexacione* absorbed into an appropriate part of the narrative of the *Libellus de exordio*.

This evidently struck the sixteenth-century owner of Fx, William Claxton, as a good idea, since he carefully marked in Fx's text of the *Libellus de exordio* the place where the *De iniusta uexacione* had been inserted in L, and he (or a contemporary) went to the lengths of inserting a text of it in his own hand into C.[258] Another piece of early modern interference in Fx and L concerns the Old English copy of Bede's 'death-song' at the appropriate point in the text of the *Libellus de exordio*. In both manuscripts this resembles that in C both in its text and in being written in a conscious imitation of Anglo-Saxon minuscule script, which some scholars have considered to be contemporary with the main text.[259] In Y, however, the song is written in a standard fourteenth-century script like that of the Latin text, and not in an imitation of Anglo-Saxon minuscule, so that suspicion is cast on the antiquity of the imitation of Anglo-Saxon minuscule in Fx and L. Moreover, A. I. Doyle has drawn attention to the slope of the letters in that imitation, which is not characteristic of medieval writing. It therefore seems likely that neither manuscript originally had a copy of the song but instead left a blank space such as is still to be seen in H. This was then filled by Claxton or some other early modern antiquary by copying from C and imitating its script.[260] It is in this connection significant that in Fx there was too small a space left for the song which therefore spills into the margin; and in L the song is written in brown ink quite different from that of the main text. T was similarly treated. It too had a blank space where the song is found in C, D, and Y, and into this the song was subsequently written, in this case in the hand of Archbishop Parker's secretary Jocelyn.[261]

---

[257] See above, p. xl.   [258] Doyle, 'Claxton', p. 344.

[259] *Old English Verse Texts from Many Sources: A Comprehensive Collection*, ed. F. C. Robinson and E. G. Stanley (EEMF xxiii; Copenhagen, 1991), p. 20.

[260] Doyle, 'Claxton', p. 344.

[261] David Yerkes, 'Joscelyn's text of Bede's death song', *Notes and Queries*, ccxxix (1984), 14–16.

(d) The text in T and V

As noted above, T appears to have been written in or soon after Anthony Bek's pontificate, and V, while difficult to date owing to the fragmentary condition of the text, may be nearly contemporary. T contains around 150 unique variant readings, most minor, but some major such as the omission of 'sed quantum scelus admiserint, mox pena uindice senserunt',[262] 'ad sui habitus reuerentiam, et ad ordinis obseruantiam precipue illos hortabatur',[263] and 'pontificatum officium se gerere monstrabat' for 'pontificem se monstrabat'.[264] Since T shares hardly any variant readings with other manuscripts and contains the same texts as those in C, it would appear to be derived independently from C, or possibly from D which is itself very close to C. It appears to have been influenced by Y, Fx, or L. Where they insert the account of the miracle of Barcwith from the *De miraculis*, the text in T has omitted the sentence alluding to the miracle which is also omitted in Y, Fx, and L: 'Quo tempore et illud (quod alibi plenius legitur) super Barcwid miraculum contigit, qui dum pacem sancti perfringere uellet, repente uindicta percussus interiit'.[265] But in T the appropriate chapter from the *De miraculis* does not in fact follow. It may be then that T was being written at the same time as Y and some discussion was taking place as to the desirability of incorporating the chapters from the *De miraculis*. Indeed the chapters are listed in the chapter-list even though they are not in the text. This discrepancy was evidently noted, for a hand of the late fourteenth or early fifteenth century copied the four chapters after the chronicle of Greystanes (fos. 127^r–132^r) and added marginal notes to the main text of the *Libellus de exordio* drawing attention to their correct position.

Like T, V has virtually no variant readings in common with other manuscripts, but unlike T it has very few variant readings of its own. It is not possible to comment on its original prefatory material and continuations because of its fragmentary condition, but like T it could be derived directly from C or possibly D.

(e) Conclusion

It is certain that C, D, Y, and Fx were in Durham during the Middle Ages, and L may well have been. The handling of the *De miraculis* in

[262] See below, p. 108.   [263] See below, p. 238.
[264] See below, p. 188.   [265] See below, p. 176.

T suggests strongly that it too was in Durham. Only in the case of F and probably Ca can we be reasonably certain that the books left Durham.[266] It is therefore not surprising that the evidence suggests cross-influence between the texts of the *Libellus de exordio* in various manuscripts, and this makes the construction of a stemma an unprofitable exercise, especially for the later medieval manuscripts. The following points can, however, be established with reasonable confidence on the basis of the variant readings and make-up of the texts of the *Libellus de exordio*.

As argued above, F can be seen as a copy of the working copy containing the original version, O. This was then revised to produce O_1 from which C was copied. C, and probably the working copy, were then revised to produce Version O_2. C, and possibly the working copy, were further corrected, C by Symeon, and, presumably after his death, C and possibly the working copy had added to them the summary beginning 'Regnante apud' and the continuation beginning 'Tribus dehinc annis'.

Version O_2 was modified to produce Version O_3, either in the working copy from which Ca was copied, or directly in the creation of Ca; but it was Version O_2 in its final form which was the normative version throughout the Middle Ages. D is a close copy of it, perhaps of C itself, but carelessly done and then corrected. H, T, and V could be copies of C, or possibly of D (certainty as to D's role is not possible until Geoffrey of Coldingham's *Liber de statu*, of which it contains the earliest copy, has been properly edited). L seems to be a copy of Fx, which is in turn a copy of Y, but as we have seen there has been considerable correction of Fx before L was copied from it. Like the other manuscripts, this group too may depend directly on C, despite their numerous variant readings. First, Y alone agrees with C in the erroneous reading 'humitate' for 'humilitate'.[267] This is one of the very few scribal slips in C and its appearance in Y must be significant. Presumably the scribe of Fx corrected it for himself. In the case of another slip, C reads 'aquiloni',[268] where D has presumably miscopied this as 'aquilone' and all other manuscripts except Fx, L, and Y read

---

[266] It may be significant that the only entry in any surviving Benedictine library catalogue, other than those of Durham which may conceivably relate to *LDE*, is an entry in a catalogue from Whitby (*De situ Dunelmensis ecclesie*, s. xii^ex); see *English Benedictine Libraries: The Shorter Catalogues*, ed. R. Sharpe *et al.* (London, 1996), p. 636 (B.109 no. 32).

[267] See below, p. 124.

[268] See below, p. 88.

'aquilonali' (C itself has been corrected to this in a later hand). The epithet 'filius Westou' applied to Elfred[269] is added to the text of C (by Symeon) and found only in Ca (which has presumably added it independently) and in Fx, L, and Y. Again, there seems to be a direct relationship between these three manuscripts and C. Striking too is the fact that Fx, L, and Y supply the sentence about the fate of the canons where C has a long erasure. Although it is tempting to regard this sentence as deriving from an earlier version of the *Libellus de exordio*, it seems more likely that it was introduced into the text by the scribe of Y.[270] The addition of the sentence therefore militates in favour of the scribe of Y having C before him, and the gap in the latter manuscript prompting him to fill it with the sentence in question.

Any conclusion has to be made with reference to the cross-influences between manuscripts. As noted above, even the relationship between Fx, L, and Y is not one of simple dependence, and the significant number of variant readings in common between D, H, Fx, L, and Y, and between Fx, H, L, and Y, indicate that D and H influenced the others. The position of D remains problematic, partly because we have no modern edition of Geoffrey of Coldingham to enable us to locate D's version in its textual history, partly because of the high level of scribal error in D.

The relations of the manuscripts show very clearly that as far as Durham was concerned the normative text was that offered by C in the form in which it had developed by the end of the twelfth century, omitting the list of monks and its introductory paragraph beginning 'Hic scripta', but including the summary beginning 'Regnante apud', the preface beginning 'Exordium huius', the erased and corrected passages, and the continuation beginning 'Tribus dehinc annis'. Setting aside the development represented by Ca, from then on the history of the text is one of additions: at the end, Geoffrey of Coldingham's *Liber de statu*, Robert Greystanes's *Historia de statu*, the lives of Richard of Bury, and the 'History of William Chambre'; at the beginning, the chapter-lists and corresponding rubrics in the text, and finally the elaborate index in L; to the text itself the incorporation of the four chapters from the *De miraculis* and finally in L the incorporation of the *De iniusta uexacione*, added in the sixteenth century to C.

---

[269] See below, p. 160.
[270] Rollason, 'Erasures', pp. 152–3.

5. Additions to the *Libellvs de exordio*

(a) The summary beginning 'Regnante apud Northanhymbros'

This text covers much the same ground as the *Libellus de exordio* itself but much more briefly. It has no material not contained in the latter, and it does not extend as far chronologically, drawing to a close with the establishment of monks at Durham in 1083. It is therefore possible that it was composed before the *Libellus de exordio*, possibly in the last years of the eleventh century, and that it was one of that text's sources.[271] Against this, however, the text reveals an attitude of hostility to the canons who were the Durham monks' predecessors which is out of tune with Symeon's relatively sympathetic view of them at the beginning of the twelfth century, but is in accord with the hostility displayed by a diploma of Pope Calixtus II, issued in May 1123, which referred to the clerks' 'depraved and incorrigible way of life', wording which was probably inspired by the Durham monks' representative at Rome.[272] This would suggest that the text was composed subsequently to the *Libellus de exordio*, summarizing it but modifying its approach to suit later circumstances, and this seems the likeliest explanation of its genesis. It is also in line with the evidence of the earliest copy which is that in C, written in or shortly after the first quarter of the twelfth century, as preliminary material before the preface beginning 'Exordium huius'.[273] Although it is possible that it was an earlier text added to C at that time, it seems a more economical hypothesis that it was composed at around the time that it was copied in C. In view of these arguments, the text is referred to in this edition as a summary of the *Libellus de exordio*.[274]

Although not found in F, H, V, or Y, in other manuscripts the summary is found as part of the textual tradition of the *Libellus de*

---

[271] B. Meehan, 'Notes on the preliminary texts and continuations to Symeon of Durham's *Libellus de exordio*', Rollason, *Symeon*, pp. 128–39, at 130–2.

[272] M. Foster, 'Custodians of St Cuthbert: the Durham monks' views of their predecessors 1083–*c*.1200', Rollason, *Anglo-Norman Durham*, pp. 53–65, at pp. 61–2, citing *Papsturkunden in England*, ed. W. Holtzmann (3 vols.; Berlin, 1930–52), ii. 138–40.

[273] See above, pp. xx–xxi; for the text, see Appendix A, pp. 258–65.

[274] Ca's rubric describing it as Symeon's preface to the *Libellus de exordio* (above, p. xxiv) may nevertheless have some basis in fact, since Symeon would still have been alive at the time of composition and may even have been its author.

exordio. It occurs before the preface, as in C, in D, Fx, and L, but after the preface in Ca and T.

(b) The continuation to the *Libellus de exordio*

Apart from F and the fragmentary V, all manuscripts of the *Libellus de exordio* contain a continuation beginning 'Tribus dehinc annis' and dealing with Bishop Ranulf Flambard (1099–28), more briefly with his successor Geoffrey Rufus (1133–41), and the usurpation of the bishopric by William Cumin (1141–4) before the installation of the rightful bishop, William of Sainte-Barbe (1143–52).[275] Ca's version has a variant account of the usurpation of Cumin, and ends with accounts of the episcopates of Sainte-Barbe and Hugh of le Puiset (1153–95) which are not found in any other manuscript.[276]

The date of composition of this continuation is uncertain. In C, the earliest manuscript of the *Libellus de exordio*, it has been copied in two stages: c. 1 and most of c. 2 (down to the word *restituta*) were written in the second half of the twelfth century by a scribe who also added to the list of monks, including entries for the 1160s. This section comprises an account of the career of Bishop Ranulf Flambard, down to his death-bed restitution of lands taken from Durham Cathedral Priory, and including narrative of colourful incidents in his early career, presumably derived from anecdotes told by himself. The same scribe, writing somewhat later, then wrote the remaining chapters, which form short notes on the vacancy following Flambard's death in 1128 and (c. 3) the episcopate of his successor Geoffrey Rufus and the account (cc. 4–10) of Cumin's usurpation, down to the installation of Sainte-Barbe.[277] Offler regarded the two sections as having been composed shortly after the last events described, but this view was based on too early a dating of the hand involved.[278] Viewed as a whole, the continuation must of course have been written after 1144, the date of Sainte-Barbe's installation described in it, and the date of the hand concerned, that is, some time in the second half of the twelfth century, perhaps the 1160s.

Down to the word *restituta*, Ca's version, which was copied probably *c.*1188,[279] is very close to C's. Admittedly it has a somewhat

---

[275] Appendix B, pp. 266–310.
[276] See below, pp. 310–23. Arnold printed this and some of the preceding section from Ca as 'continuatio altera' (Arnold, *Sym. Op.* i. 161–9).
[277] See above, p. xxi.
[278] See above, p.xxi n. 21.
[279] See above, p. xxvii.

different account of the vacancy after Flambard's death; but the collation shows that Ca was in other respects copying this section from C. As noted above, Ca's account of Cumin's usurpation is different from C's, and as in C it is the work of another scribe. The relationship between the two versions is not easy to discern. It has been suggested that Ca's version is a condensation of C's, but this disregards the fact that Ca's version, while unquestionably briefer than C's, contains additional material. It is possible therefore that the versions in C and Ca were composed contemporaneously. It is just possible that the compiler of Ca found in C only the section down to *restituta* because that was all which had at that time been written, and that Ca's version of Cumin's usurpation was then written as the first account, with C's being composed subsequently as an amplification of it. As with the text of the *Libellus de exordio*, however, C's version became the normative one, and all other manuscripts which contain the continuation follow C.[280]

6. Sources of the *Libellvs de exordio*

(a) Bede, *Historia ecclesiastica gentis Anglorum*[281]

Symeon drew extensively on this text, which was completed in 731, often extracting whole passages verbatim, and sometimes acknowledging it by name. Symeon was probably using the copy which Bishop William of Saint-Calais (1080–96) presented to Durham Cathedral Priory, and which is preserved in DCL B.II.35. As will appear from the apparatus, some distinctive readings are common to this copy and to the *Libellus de exordio*, but some are not, so that either Symeon had access to another copy also, or he knew the text well enough from memory to cite it without reference to any copy, introducing variants of his own in the process.

(b) Bede, prose *Vita S. Cuthberti*[282]

Symeon drew extensively on this text, which was written before 721,[283] extracting substantial passages verbatim. Palaeographical evi-

---

[280] For more detailed discussion of the above with references, see Meehan, in Rollason, *Symeon*, pp. 132–4; and cf. Meehan, in Rollason, *Anglo-Norman Durham*, p. 443 n. 31.

[281] Bede, *HE*.   [282] Bede, *V. Cuth.*

[283] Colgrave, *Two Lives*, pp. 46–9.

dence shows that he had himself made the copies contained in Bod. Lib., Digby 175, and Bodley 596. Nevertheless, collation of Symeon's text does not allow us to identify the particular copy which he had before him, and we can say no more than that he used a version or versions of the Durham recension, of which the earliest representative may be that in Digby 175, and which also include Cambridge, Trinity College O.3.55, Bod. Lib., Laud misc. 491, and Fx.

(c) Cuthbert, *Epistola de obitu Bede*

This letter, which is generally accepted to have been written shortly after the death of Bede,[284] is inserted more or less in its entirety into the *Libellus de exordio*, including the Old English poem, known as Bede's 'death-song' because, according to the letter, Bede recited it before his death.[285] There exist two distinct recensions: a 'continental version', represented by twelve surviving manuscripts, of which the oldest is St Gallen, Stiftsbibliothek 254 (St Gallen, s. ix); and a so-called 'Insular version', represented by thirty-three manuscripts of the twelfth century and later. These latter manuscripts can be divided into three groups: the 'Digby group', so-called because the best text is preserved in Bod. Lib., Digby 211 (Waltham, s. xii), a 'Symeon group', which comprises manuscripts C, F, D, and H of the *Libellus de exordio*;[286] and a 'Burney group', best represented by Cambridge, Trinity College R.5.27 (s. xii). According to Dobbie, the 'Digby group' preserves the earliest text of the 'Insular version', which must have broken away from the 'continental version' before the copying of St Gallen 254. The 'continental version' differs from the 'Insular version' in, for example, omitting the salutation, giving the date 'VII idus maias' for Bede's death, naming the scribe who took down Bede's dictation as Wilberht, the inclusion of the 'death song' in Northumbrian rather than West Saxon dialect, and adding material, notably a whole sentence at the end and phrases preceding the 'death song'.[287]

---

[284] Doubts on its authenticity suggested by W. F. Bolton, 'Epistola Cuthberti de obitu Bedae: a caveat', *Medievalia et Humanistica*, n.s. i (1970), 127–39, have not been found convincing.

[285] See below, pp. 72–3.

[286] For facsimiles of the text in C, F, and Y, see Robinson and Stanley, *Old English Verse Texts*, p. 20 and pl. 3. The inclusion in this work of Fx, L, and T was an error, since the poem has been added to them only in the 16th cent.; and it failed to include the text in D (A. I. Doyle, 'Bede's death song in Durham Cathedral, MS A.IV.36', Rollason, *Symeon*, pp. 157–60). H contains the letter but not the 'death-song'.

[287] Dobbie, *Cædmon's Hymn*, pp. 49–105. New studies and the discovery of new

It seems that Symeon drew on a copy of the 'Insular version' which was already very much altered from its original form and similar to the one accessible to the compiler of the *Annales S. Neoti* in Cambridge, Trinity College R.7.28 (s. xii). Comparison of this manuscript with the text of the letter preserved in the manuscripts of the *Libellus de exordio* suggests that Symeon edited the text he received in various ways, notably introducing *inquit* at the beginning to smooth the insertion of the letter into his history, noting that the language of the 'death song' was English ('hoc anglico carmine componens'), and adding a translation of that poem into Latin.[288] It is arguable that his alterations display a lack of understanding of the stylistic structure of the original letter, so that he produced an 'unhappy vulgar mess'.[289] In the present edition, the text of the letter in the *Libellus de exordio* has here been collated with that in Digby 211 in order to show its other variations from the earlier 'Insular version'. Italicized text represents text in common with that version.[290]

---

manuscripts, notably The Hague, Royal Library, 70.H.7, suggest that it is necessary to revise Dobbie's interpretation of the genesis of the groups he defined, since 'it is clear from a detailed investigation of his apparatus that the "Insular" texts . . . are derivatives of an earlier version which stood much closer to the Continental tradition' (*The Annals of St Neots with the Vita Prima Sancti Neoti*, ed. D. N. Dumville and M. Lapidge (The Anglo-Saxon Chronicle: A Collaborative Edition, xvii; Cambridge, 1985), pp. l–lii). For the manuscripts, see N. R. Ker, 'The Hague manuscript of the *Epistola Cuthberti de obitu Bedae* with Bede's song', *Medium Ævum*, viii (1939), 40–4, and K. W. Humphreys and A. S. C. Ross, 'Further manuscripts of Bede's "Historia Ecclesiastica", of the "Epistola Cuthberti de obitu Bedae", and further Anglo-Saxon texts of "Caedmon's Hymn" and "Bede's Death Song"', *Notes & Queries*, ccxx new ser. xxii (1975), 50–5.

[288] Dobbie, *Cædmon's Hymn*, pp. 96–7.

[289] D. R. Howlett, 'Symeon's structural style: experiments in deconstruction', Rollason, *Symeon*, pp. 254–81.

[290] See below, pp. 70–7. The best edition for the present purpose (without the Death Song) is that of Dobbie, *Cædmon's Hymn*, pp. 117–27, where the 'Insular version' represented by Digby 211 is critically edited facing the 'continental version' represented by Bamberg, Staatliche Bibliothek A.I.47 (?Eichstätt, s. xi). The 'death song' is edited and discussed in *The Anglo-Saxon Minor Poems*, ed. E. van Kirk Dobbie (The Anglo-Saxon Poetic Records, vi; London and New York, 1942), pp. c–cvii, 107–8 (where critical texts are given both of the Northumbrian dialect, based on St Gallen 254, and of the West Saxon dialect, based on Digby 211), and p. 199. See also Plummer, *Bede*, i. clx–clxiv, and Bede, *HE*, pp. 579–87, where the text of The Hague, Royal Library 70.H.7, is given without critical apparatus; and, for a reconstruction of the original text based on nearly eighty manuscripts, see Howlett, in Rollason, *Symeon*, pp. 255–67. See also D. R. Howlett, *British Books in Biblical Style* (Dublin, 1997), pp. 302–3.

(d) The Northern Annals and related sources

As we have seen, the early sections of the *Historia regum* embody various components, originally assembled by Byrhtferth of Ramsey (*c*.970–*c*.1020), before they were transmitted to the compiler of the *Historia regum*, who was probably Symeon himself.[291] The most important of these was a series of annals relating to Northumbrian history from the death of Bede to the beginning of the ninth century, which appear to have been derived from a set of annals drawn up in York around 800 but now lost in their original form. There is considerable uncertainty as to the nature of these Northern Annals, but what is clear is that there existed a common stock of annalistic material, which may perhaps be identified with them, and on this stock drew the compilers of the *Historia regum* as well as of the northern recensions (D and E) of the *Anglo-Saxon Chronicle*, which are preserved in manuscripts of the end of the eleventh century, the *De primo Saxonum aduentu*, and the continuation of Bede's *Historia ecclesiastica* (preserved in twelfth-century and later manuscripts).

Symeon, assuming him to have been the compiler of the *Historia regum*, apparently at the end of his life, obviously knew these annals as they were transmitted to him in Byrhtferth's compilation.[292] He used them also in compiling the *Annales Lindisfarnenses et Dunelmenses* and the *Libellus de exordio*.[293] But the discrepancies between these sources and the *Historia regum* leave open the question as to whether he knew Byrhtferth's compilation when he was working on them, or whether he had access instead to a unique recension of the lost Northern Annals which provided those pieces of information which find no parallel in other sources.[294] The matter cannot be resolved until more wide-ranging studies of Durham historiographical activity in the twelfth century have been made than are possible here, and this makes it particularly difficult to distinguish Symeon's sources in the *Libellus de exordio* from those texts which might be derived from it.

[291] See above, pp. xlix–l.

[292] See above, pxlix.

[293] *Chronica Rogeri de Houedene*, ed. W. Stubbs (4 vols.; RS li; London, 1868–71), pp. xxviii–xxix; *Two of the Saxon Chronicles Parallel with Supplementary Extracts from the Others*, ed. C. Plummer (2 vols.; Oxford, 1892–9), ii. lxviii–lxx; Blair, *Celt and Saxon*, ed. Chadwick, pp. 98–9; A. Gransden, *Historical Writing in England c.550 to c.1307* (London, 1974), pp. 31–2; and J. E. Story, 'Charlemagne and Northumbria: The Influence of Francia on Northumbrian Politics in the Later Eighth and Early Ninth Centuries', Ph.D. thesis (Durham, 1995), c. 3.

[294] See above, p. xlix and n. 161.

(e) *Historia de sancto Cuthberto*

This text includes a description of St Cuthbert's life culled in large measure from Bede's prose *Vita S. Cuthberti*; accounts of the endowments of Lindisfarne; an account of the wanderings of the Lindisfarne community in the face of Viking attack; an account of the endowment of the see by King Guthred and its establishment at Chester-le-Street; and records of the gifts made to the see when at Durham by King Cnut and certain eleventh-century nobles.[295]

Craster argued, first, that the text originally terminated with a description of the visit of King Edmund to the shrine of St Cuthbert at Chester-le-Street and that it was therefore written by the community there in the mid-tenth century, certainly before its move to Durham in 995, which is not mentioned; and, secondly, that the records of the gifts made to Durham in the eleventh century were added in a later recension to produce the text as we have it now. He recognized an objection to this argument in the fact that the text's account of how St Cuthbert appeared to King Alfred and promised him victory names the battle in which he won this as Ashingdon (*Assandun*), an error for *Ellandun*. Since the battle of Ashingdon was fought in 1016, this would suggest that the author of the *Historia de sancto Cuthberto* was familiar with it and was writing after it had taken place. Craster met this argument by proposing that this account of Alfred was stylistically distinct from the main body of the text and was also an addition of the eleventh century.[296]

Craster's arguments have recently come under attack from two directions. First, L. Simpson has demonstrated that the story about Alfred, despite its distinctive style, is an integral part of the main body of the text and that cross-references are made to it from the surrounding passages.[297] Secondly, T. Johnson-South has shown that Craster's use of the surviving manuscripts to support his hypothesis of an earlier and a later recension cannot be sustained. Detailed collation of the manuscripts offers no support for this idea and suggests either that the manuscripts were copied from each other, or that they were copying a single archetype.[298] The implication of

---

[295] Arnold, *Sym. Op.* i. 196–214.

[296] Craster, 'Patrimony', pp. 177–8.

[297] L. Simpson, 'The King Alfred/St Cuthbert episode in the *Historia de Sancto Cuthberto*: its significance for mid-tenth-century English history', Bonner, *Cuthbert*, pp. 397–411.

[298] T. Johnson-South, 'The *Historia de Sancto Cuthberto*: A New Edition and Trans-

this is that the text must be dated in or after the time of Cnut, and is presumably a work of the clerks of Durham, perhaps in the middle years of the eleventh century. As such, it should be noted that it is by no means an unsophisticated work, blending as it does records, hagiography, and history in a way reminiscent of such works as the *Liber Eliensis*.[299]

(f) William of Saint-Calais's letter to the monks of Durham

There is no reason to suppose that this letter, a general exhortation to the monks of Durham, which Symeon inserted verbatim into the *Libellus de exordio*, is not authentic. Although the original has not survived, there is a copy in DCL, B.IV.24, which is textually identical to that in the *Libellus de exordio*, and was written by the main scribe of C.[300] If we accept that DCL, B.IV.24 was the Durham cantor's book,[301] it seems likely that the copy in it was made for reading to the monks, as the letter itself instructs, and that it was transcribed thence into the *Libellus de exordio*.

(g) Profession-slips of the monks of Durham

Fo. 42[r-v] of the Durham *Liber Vitae* (BL, Cotton Domitian VII) contains a list of the bishops of Durham from Walcher to Ranulf Flambard and then a list of monks similar, but not identical, to that which forms in C part of the *Libellus de exordio*.[302] The first part of this list was compiled in the early twelfth century, probably before the first part of the list in C. From the name 'Brianus' onwards other near-contemporary hands have added names, notably those from 'Thomas' to 'Alanus' which were written by Symeon himself. The lists have been compared and collated by Piper, who shows that they are independent of each other, and were probably based on a collection of monastic profession-slips (that is, small pieces of parchment which were completed when a monk was professed) from which the names were drawn. Variations in order between the

lation, with Discussions of the Surviving Manuscripts, the Text, and Northumbrian Estate Structure', Ph.D. thesis (Cornell, 1990), *passim*.

[299] *Liber Eliensis*, ed. E. O. Blake (Camden Third Series, xvii; London, 1962).

[300] Gullick, in Rollason, *Symeon*, p. 108 n. 7.

[301] See above, p. xliii.

[302] Piper, 'Lists'; below, pp. 6–15.

two lists are therefore explicable because the slips became disordered. Piper's researches show further that the lists correspond broadly to the sequence in which monks joined the priory, and this has been indicated in the footnotes of the present edition.[303]

(h) *Cronica monasterii Dunelmensis*

This text is not extant in its putative original form, but a reconstruction of it was made by Craster on the basis of various late medieval sources, including the fifteenth-century *Libellus de exordio et statu ecclesie cathedralis Dunelmensis* of Prior Wessington and some historical notes in the margin of the Durham manuscript BL, Cotton Julius D.XII (s. xiii[2]). Craster adduced evidence to suggest that these were in fact drawing on a chronicle, which he called *Cronica monasterii Dunelmensis*, entered into the great gospel book kept until the sixteenth century on the high altar in Durham Cathedral.[304] As he reconstructed it, this chronicle covered some of the same ground as the *Historia de sancto Cuthberto*. Beginning with the endowment of Lindisfarne, it detailed the grants made to that church by King Ceolwulf; the ravaging by the Viking leader Halfdan; the grants to Chester-le-Street made by Kings Alfred and Guthred; gifts by kings of England in the tenth and early eleventh centuries; and finally the visit of William the Conqueror to St Cuthbert's shrine in 1072. Craster argued that the chronicle's failure to mention the introduction of monks and the foundation of Durham Cathedral Priory in 1083 meant that the chronicle was written between 1072 and 1083, and that it was therefore to be regarded as a composition of the clerks of Durham, probably under the reforming regime of Bishop Walcher (1071–80).[305]

---

[303] Piper, 'Lists'; for an example of a profession-slip (DCDCM, Misc. Ch. 6067a), see pl. 31).

[304] Craster, 'Red book'.

[305] Material shared with *CMD* and presumed to be derived from it has been italicized and noted in this edition, but it should be emphasized that the lateness of the sources from which the *CMD* has been reconstructed leaves considerable room for doubt. This is unlikely to be removed until late medieval Durham historical writings are much better known and edited. The work of Prior Wessington, for example, is not even in print, although the survival of what appears to be his autograph manuscript (Bod. Lib., Laud misc. 748) offers rich opportunities for research; see Craster, 'Red book', pp. 507–16; B. Dobson, 'Contrasting chronicles: historical writing at York and Durham in the later Middle Ages', *Church and Chronicle in the Middle Ages: Essays Presented to John Taylor*, ed. I. N. Wood and G. A. Loud (London and Rio Grande, 1991), pp. 201–18, at 205–7; and

(i) *De miraculis et translationibus sancti Cuthberti*

This is a collection of twenty-one stories concerning the miracles of St Cuthbert, which are often found appended to Bede's prose *Vita S. Cuthberti*, and which appear to have been written in three groups.[306] The first seven seem to have been written between 1083 and 1104, and comprise:

1. The story of St Cuthbert appearing to King Alfred and promising him victory.
2. The story of how three waves of blood prevented Bishop Eardwulf and Abbot Eadred from taking St Cuthbert's body to Ireland.
3. The story of the miraculous punishment of the pagan Onlafball.
4. The story of how a Scottish army attacking King Guthred was swallowed by the earth.
5. The punishment of one of Earl Tostig's men, Barcwith, for seeking to breach the sanctuary of St Cuthbert.
6. The miracle of how on the occasion of Bishop Æthelwine's flight from Durham to Lindisfarne the waters parted to allow him and the community to cross dry-shod to the island.
7. The story of the punishment of a Norman soldier who stole from Durham Cathedral Priory.

Of these, nos. 1–4 draw on the *Historia de sancto Cuthberto* and were themselves used by Symeon in the *Libellus de exordio*. Nos. 5 and 6 too were probably used by Symeon. Nos. 1, 4, 5, and 7 were amongst the five interpolated into the text of the *Libellus de exordio* in Y, Fx, and L.[307] A second group of eleven stories was written probably in the period 1100–15, and these include the story of the miraculous punishments of Earl Robert de Mowbray and Abbot Paul of St Albans for depriving the monks of Durham of the church of Tynemouth, which story was the fifth of those interpolated into the text of the the *Libellus de exordio* in Y, Fx, and L, and appears to have been used by Symeon himself.[308] A final group of three stories, including the account of the translation of St Cuthbert in 1104, was

---

A. J. Piper, 'The historical interests of the Durham monks', in Rollason, *Symeon*, pp. 301–32, at 324–6.

[306] *De miraculis*; B. Colgrave, 'The Post-Bedan miracles and translations of St Cuthbert', *The Early Cultures of North-West Europe (H. M. Chadwick Memorial Studies)*, ed. C. Fox and B. Dickins (Cambridge, 1950), pp. 305–32.

[307] See below, pp. 110, 127, 177, 220.

[308] See below, p. 236 n. 29.

composed around 1124, and these were not used in, or later interpolated into, the *Libellus de exordio*.

Although these stories are primarily hagiographical in character, they nevertheless have strong historiographical elements and must be considered in relation to the development of historical writing at Durham. Nothing is known of their authorship, apart from what can be derived from their subject matter, which indicates clearly that their authors were monks of Durham.[309]

(j) Oral tradition

Symeon evidently drew widely on oral tradition at least in an ecclesiastical context, for he lists amongst his sources the 'truthful accounts of our elders, who had seen the events themselves or had heard them related by their own elders who were religious and trustworthy men and who had been present at them', and in a specific instance the people who had witnessed the miracle of Oswulf and the snake.[310] He was on several occasions specific about his informants, as in the case of the monk Swartbrand who had seen the arm of St Oswald,[311] the descendants of the clerks of Durham who told him about the singing of the monastic office there,[312] the grandson of the deacon who heard Edmund miraculously named as bishop,[313] the old priests who had given him information about Elfred Westou, especially Gamel, later a monk of the monastery of Durham,[314] and Feoccher's son and two chaplains of the bishop.[315]

7. THE *LIBELLVS DE EXORDIO* AND JOHN OF WORCESTER

The relationship between the chronicle of John of Worcester and the *Libellus de exordio* was complex. At various points, John had information identical with that to be found in the *Libellus de exordio*. Since John is known to have drawn extensively on a now lost northern

---

[309] See also, W. M. Aird, 'The making of a medieval miracle collection: the *Liber de translationibus et miraculis sancti Cuthberti*', *Northern History*, xxviii (1992), 1–24.

[310] See below, pp. 20–1, 188–9, 176–7.

[311] See below, pp. 22–3.

[312] See below, pp. 104–5.

[313] See below, pp. 160–1.

[314] See below, pp. 162–3.

[315] See below, pp. 174–5; see also pp. 142–3.

version of the Anglo-Saxon Chronicle related to the extant D-version, it might be supposed that this or a related text was the source for both works.[316] There was, however, considerable interchange between Durham and Worcester. The two churches were bound by an early agreement (*conuentio*); an early version of John's chronicle was incorporated *in extenso* into the *Historia regum* for the years 848 to 1119 and to some extent for 1120 and 1121 as well; and John seems to have derived information from Durham sources, notably his detailed account of the murder of Bishop Walcher.[317] Study of the earliest manuscript of John's chronicle, CCCO 157, shows how extensive was the use made of the *Libellus de exordio* by the earliest scribes, who at one point, for example, entered into the margin its account of the election of Bishop Edmund.[318] Clearly, John had a copy of the *Libellus de exordio*, from which he extracted information. In such cases then, we must regard the *Libellus de exordio* as his direct source, rather than envisaging that he and Symeon drew independently on earlier sources.

8. THE HISTORIOGRAPHICAL BACKGROUND OF THE *LIBELLVS DE EXORDIO*

The *Libellus de exordio* was only one of a series of historical writings from Durham in the early twelfth century. For Offler, that period was 'the best period of historical activity in Durham'.[319] For D. N. Dumville, Durham was then 'a hot-bed of historiographic activity'.[320] A range of types of texts, some of them precocious in form, was produced. As we have seen, Symeon himself was concerned with a number of historical writings, including the *Historia regum*, which is closely related to, and was probably the source of, the *Historia post*

---

[316] R. R. Darlington and P. McGurk, 'The *Chronicon ex Chronicis* of Florence of Worcester and its use of sources for English history before 1066', *Anglo-Norman Studies*, v (1982), 185–96.

[317] M. Brett, 'John of Worcester and his contemporaries', *The Writing of History in the Middle Ages: Essays Presented to Richard William Southern*, ed. R. H. C. Davis and J. M. Wallace-Hadrill (Oxford, 1981), pp. 101–26.

[318] *JW* ii. 506.

[319] Offler, *Medieval Historians*, p. 6.

[320] D. N. Dumville, 'Textual archaeology and Northumbrian history subsequent to Bede', *Coinage in Ninth-Century Northumbria: The Tenth Oxford Symposium on Coinage and Monetary History*, ed. D. M. Metcalf (British Archaeological Reports, British Series, clxxx; Oxford, 1987), pp. 43–55, at 45 (repr. D. N. Dumville, *Britons and Anglo-Saxons in the Early Middle Ages* (Aldershot, 1993), no. x).

Bedam, a compilation extending to 1148, made probably at Durham, and itself used extensively by Roger of Howden.[321]

Other Durham writings included the *De iniusta uexacione Willelmi episcopi primi*, which begins with a short historical summary and proceeds to an eye-witness account of the trial for treason in 1088 of Bishop William of Saint-Calais, which ended in his condemnation and exile to Normandy.[322] Offler argued that it was not a genuine eye-witness account, given the errors in it and the (in his view) anachronistic use of canon law, and he proposed that it was composed in the second quarter of the twelfth century in Durham, as a response to Eadmer who had attacked William of Saint-Calais's reputation in his *Historia nouorum*.[323] Most scholars, however, have considered it to have been composed immediately after the trial, and this view is now supported by Philpott's research on canon law, showing that not only was canon law known in Durham in 1088 in the Durham manuscript, Cambridge, Peterhouse 74, but that the very canons used by William of Saint-Calais in his defence are marked in that manuscript in a manner consistent with these marks having been made by the bishop himself.[324] Whether composed in the late 1080s or in the second quarter of the twelfth century, however, the text is another piece of historical writing emanating from Durham in or around Symeon's time, and its introduction is related in some way to the *Libellus de exordio*.[325]

A quite different type of historical text, which contains extensive genealogical material, perhaps orally transmitted, is the *De obsessione Dunelmi et de probitate Vhtredi comitis, et de comitibus qui ei successerunt*, which begins with an account of a siege of Durham by the Scots, dated in the text to 969 but usually assumed to refer in fact to a siege in 1006.[326] The defence of Durham was then in the hands of Uhtred of the house of Bamburgh, whose success in this led to his being appointed earl of Northumbria. The text, however, is primarily

[321] *HpB;* and Gransden, *Historical Writing*, pp. 225–6.

[322] Offler, *DIV*.

[323] H. S. Offler, 'The tractate *De iniusta uexacione Willelmi episcopi primi*', *English Historical Review*, lxvi (1951), 321–41, with arguments restated in Offler, *DIV*, pp. 60–5.

[324] M. Philpott, 'The *De iniusta uexacione Willelmi episcopi primi* and canon law in Anglo-Norman Durham', Rollason, *Anglo-Norman Durham*, pp. 125–37.

[325] Gullick, 'Hand', p. 30.

[326] Arnold, *Sym. Op.* i. 215–20; for comment, B. Meehan, 'The siege of Durham, the battle of Carham and the cession of Lothian', *Scottish Historical Review*, lv (1976), 1–19; and C. J. Morris, *Marriage and Murder in Eleventh-Century Northumbria: A Study of 'De Obsessione Dunelmi'* (Borthwick Paper lxxxii; York, 1992).

concerned with his marriage to the daughter of Bishop Ealdhun of Durham, Ecgfrida, and the fate of her dowry following the break-up of her marriage to Uhtred and both partners' subsequent remarriages. The latest events described in it belong to the years 1073–4, but it is significant that certain of the estates which constituted Ecgfrida's dowry were being actively reclaimed by Durham Cathedral Priory from their lay owners in the early twelfth century. On these grounds, Morris has argued that the text may have been written then, rather than in the third quarter of the eleventh century as was previously supposed. There can be no doubt that it was written at Durham, for it was the Durham monks who were laying claim to the estates in question. If these arguments are accepted, it too must be viewed as a product of Durham Cathedral Priory in Symeon's time. Indeed, Morris has argued that its style and approach, albeit quite different from those of the *Libellus de exordio*, are most closely paralleled in Symeon's letter to Dean Hugh about the archbishops of York, raising the possibility that Symeon himself might have been involved with its composition.[327]

Yet another type of text is the *De primo Saxonum aduentu*, which comprises a series of histories of the kingdoms of Anglo-Saxon England, beginning with an account of the coming of the Saxons and proceeding to accounts of the kings of Kent, the kings of the East Saxons, the kings of the Northumbrians down to Eric Bloodaxe (948, 952–4), the archbishops of Canterbury and York, the bishops of Durham, and the earls of Northumbria.[328] The prominence given to the bishops of Durham and the manuscript tradition both suggest that this is a Durham compilation.[329] The text exists in different recensions, having evidently been updated, but the earliest version extant ends its list of Durham bishops with Ranulf Flambard (d. 1128), and was thus written in Symeon's time.[330] It was one of the earliest attempts to impose a clear framework on Anglo-Saxon history, a sort of *Handbook of British Chronology*, as Offler called it.[331] It is probably related to the text known as the *Series regum Northymbrensium*, a list of the kings of the Northumbrians and the lengths of their reigns from Ida to Henry I. This is found only in Ca,

[327] Morris, *Marriage and Murder*, pp. 9–10.
[328] Arnold, *Sym. Op.* ii. 365–84.
[329] Meehan, 'Symeon', pp. 157–60; Offler, *Medieval Historians*, pp. 11–12.
[330] Arnold, *Sym. Op.* ii. 381.
[331] Offler, *Medieval Historians*, p. 11.

where it is inserted, apparently as a space-filler, between the chapter headings and the *Libellus de exordio*.

Early twelfth-century Durham historical writing was unquestionably vigorous; and the *Libellus de exordio* itself stands as a very early post-Conquest history of a particular church, earlier for example than William of Malmesbury's account of Glastonbury,[332] or Hugh Candidus's of Peterborough.[333] It is tempting to attribute this vigour to Symeon himself. We have noted the range of his activity as a scribe;[334] Gullick has drawn attention to his activity as a supervisor of other scribes' work;[335] and we have seen his reputation, which led to Orm's vision being reported to him, and to Dean Hugh of York approaching him for an account of the prelates of his own church.[336] Even if we do not accept that all the texts attributed to him are really his, his role in stimulating historical writing may have been considerable. It is certainly true that after his death the scale of activity declined: brief and partisan accounts of the time of Flambard, Geoffrey Rufus, William Cumin, and William of Sainte-Barbe are all Durham Cathedral Priory could produce, aside possibly from the *Historia post Bedam*, itself derived from the *Historia regum*. Even the brilliant period of Bishop Hugh of le Puiset elicited only a thin and quite inadequate account.[337] The only historical writing of note was undertaken by the monk Geoffrey, and he was at Durham's cell of Coldingham,[338] although hagiographical writing was well represented in the work of Reginald of Durham and poetry by that of Lawrence of Durham.[339]

Important as Symeon's role no doubt was, however, it is not an adequate explanation of Durham's historiographical activity in his time. The impetus to historical writing began before him, with the *Historia de sancto Cuthberto* and possibly the *Cronica monasterii Dunelmi*, which share many of his preoccupations. In addition, the preface to the *Libellus de exordio* shows that Symeon wrote by the command of his superiors, who presumably included Prior Turgot

---

[332] J. Scott, *The Early History of Glastonbury Abbey: An Edition, Translation and Study of William of Malmesbury's De Antiquitate Glastonie Ecclesie* (Woodbridge, 1981).

[333] *The Chronicle of Hugh Candidus*, ed. W. T. Mellows (London, 1949).

[334] See above, pp. xlv–xlvii.

[335] Gullick, 'Hand', p. 20.

[336] See above, pp. xliii, xlvii.

[337] Appendix B, pp. 320–3.

[338] Raine, *Scriptores tres*, pp. 3–31.

[339] Raine, *Cuth. virt.*; *Dialogi Laurentii Dunelmensis monachi ac prioris*, ed. J. Raine (SS lxx; Durham, 1870).

and perhaps the sub-prior Algar.[340] Historical writing then was a wider concern of the Durham community, and it is to the reasons for this in the context of Durham's history in the eleventh and twelfth centuries that we must now turn.

Several issues which appear to have prompted historical writing and the composition of the *Libellus de exordio* in particular stand out both in the historical writings themselves and in the documents, particularly the forged documents, of Durham Cathedral Priory.[341] The first was the need for legitimacy following the events of 1083. As we have seen, it was in that year, according to Symeon, that Bishop William of Saint-Calais (1080–96) expelled the community of clerks who had served the cathedral until that time, and replaced them with Benedictine monks who had been established at Jarrow and Monkwearmouth under the leadership of Aldwin.[342]

Now, W. M. Aird has argued that Symeon overstated the events of 1083, which were in his view part of a much more gradual transition in the character and composition of the religious community of Durham.[343] The arguments adduced for this view are: the absence of authentic documents supporting Symeon's account when such might be expected to have been preserved;[344] the inconsistency of Symeon's handling of the pre-1083 monastic community; the failure of other writers, notably John of Worcester, to record what should have been a major upheaval at Durham; the parallels between Symeon's account of the reform of the Durham community and that of Eadmer with regard to Christ Church Canterbury, where charter evidence shows that the reform was in fact more gradual; occasions where named monks of Durham after 1083 may have been identical with or had links with members of the pre-1083 community;[345] and Symeon's deferential attitude to members of the pre-1083 community, with some of whom he clearly had contact.[346] These arguments deserve close consideration, but they are not conclusive, and it is not easy to accept that they provide grounds for rejecting Symeon's testimony, given the early date at which he was writing.

[340] See above, p. xliv.
[341] Offler, *Episcopal Charters*, nos. *3, *3a, *3b, *4, *4a, *4b, *7, and *passim*. See below, p. 242 n. 9.
[342] See above, p. xvi, below, pp. 228–31.
[343] Aird, 'The political context of the *Libellus de exordio*', in Rollason, *Symeon*, pp. 32–45, at 34–8, and Aird, *Cuthbert*, pp. 126–31, 137–8.
[344] See below, p. 230 n. 20.
[345] See below, p. 7 n. 19, and pp. 162–3 n. 28.
[346] See below, pp. lxxxii–lxxxiii.

An alternative interpretation remains possible. The *Libellus de exordio* certainly presents the reform of 1083 as having taken place peacefully and by agreement,[347] but if, contrary to Aird's view, the upheaval was a real one, this is unlikely to have been the case. The clerks of Durham were well connected with prominent local families and, to judge from their previous relations with Earl Uhtred, and the house of the native Northumbrian earls, it is unlikely that they gave up what they must have regarded as their hereditary church without a struggle. Moreover, their removal occurred in the aftermath of the military repression inflicted on the North as a reprisal for the murder of Bishop Walcher in 1080, with which the clerks may well have been implicated, even if unjustly.[348]

In short, the removal of the clerks in 1083 is likely to have been a source of dispute and mutual recrimination, and it is utterly improbable that the Benedictine monks' possession of Durham Cathedral was universally accepted or even universally supported. It is instructive that one of the major erasures in C, the earliest copy of the *Libellus de exordio*, is precisely its account of the fate of the displaced clerks.[349] It is reasonable to conjecture that this erasure was due to the sensitivity of the subject in the opening years of the twelfth century. If we can accept the information first supplied at this point by the fourteenth-century manuscript Y that the clerks were recompensed with the important county Durham churches of Darlington, Norton, Easington, and Auckland,[350] this suggests that their status was such that they could not simply be turned out in the way suggested by the *Libellus de exordio*.

It is significant in this context, however, that Symeon eschews any virulent attacks on them. True, he says that William of Saint-Calais removed them because their way of life was unsuitable, meaning presumably that they were married. But he makes no explicit attack on their conjugal status, which must have been from his Benedictine viewpoint one of the chief objections to them,[351] and he gives favourable portraits of them as individuals: those who were known

---

[347] See below, pp. 230–1.

[348] D. Rollason, 'Symeon of Durham and the community of Durham in the eleventh century', *England in the Eleventh Century: Proceedings of the 1990 Harlaxton Symposium*, ed. C. Hicks (Stamford, 1992), pp. 183–98. See also Foster, in Rollason, *Anglo-Norman Durham*, pp. 53–65.

[349] See below, p. 230 n. 20.

[350] Ibid.

[351] The most open attack is to be found in the *Visio Bosonis* (below, pp. 250–1).

as the bearers of St Cuthbert's coffin, for example, and particularly
the sacrist Elfred Westou, who was responsible for bringing the relics
of Bede and other saints to Durham.[352] Clerks of Symeon's own day,
presumably in some cases connected with the pre-1083 community,
appear in his pages as pious men, relaying stories of miracles and
events long past, worthy (as Symeon emphasizes) of credence and
respect.[353] Either Symeon felt unable to attack the clerks directly
because of their status, or he was writing in a spirit of reconciliation,
as we shall suggest below.[354]

Symeon's approach to the clerks was subtle. As Piper has shown,
he crafted the *Libellus de exordio* to underline the legitimacy of
Benedictine monks serving the shrine of St Cuthbert. After emphasizing the monastic character of the church of Lindisfarne and
Cuthbert in particular,[355] he put on the account of its flight in 875,
derived in essence from the *Historia de sancto Cuthberto*, a gloss to the
effect that the monks of Lindisfarne dispersed, leaving only the boys
they had been training to attend the body of their saint. These for
Symeon were the predecessors of the clerks who were expelled in
1083: merely interim guardians of the shrine of St Cuthbert, until
more appropriate guardians could be found, as in his view they were
in 1083.[356] No less telling is Symeon's emphasis on stories of the
misogyny of St Cuthbert, which the *Libellus de exordio* is the first to
tell. Although different interpretations are possible, it seems likely
that the point of these was to emphasize the unsuitability of the clerks
who were married and therefore must by inference have been
unacceptable to a saint who denied women admission even to the
churchyard of Durham Cathedral.[357]

Symeon's view of the monasticism of the pre-Viking period was of
course conditioned by his own training as a Benedictine monk,
influenced by the reforms of the eleventh century, and following
the monastic constitutions laid down by Archbishop Lanfranc (1070–
89).[358] He no doubt regarded the monks of Lindisfarne and other

[352] See below, pp. 110–11, 146–9, 160–7.

[353] See below, pp. 148–9, for example.

[354] Early 12th-cent. Durham monks were not as sympathetic: see above, p. lxvi.

[355] See below, pp. 26–7.

[356] A. J. Piper, 'The first generations of Durham monks and the cult of St Cuthbert',
Bonner, *Cuthbert*, pp. 437–46; and below, pp. 116–17.

[357] V. Tudor, 'The misogyny of St Cuthbert', *Archaeologia Aeliana*, 5th ser. xii (1984),
157–67; cf. Foster, in Rollason, *Anglo-Norman Durham*, pp. 57–8; and below, pp. 104–11.

[358] D. Knowles, *The Monastic Order in England: A History of its Development from the
Times of St Dunstan to the Fourth Lateran Council, 940–1216* (2nd edn.; Cambridge, 1963),

monasteries of the seventh, eighth, and earlier ninth centuries as living essentially the same lives as he and his colleagues did, and where he quotes Bede referring to the Rule there can be no doubt that he understood by this the Rule of St Benedict.[359] He was therefore able to draw a sharp distinction between the early monks and the clerks who were, according to him, expelled in 1083. Whether those early monks were in fact following the Rule of St Benedict is open to question, and there is no doubt that composite rules, such as the one devised by Benedict Biscop for Wearmouth and Jarrow, were in use, although the Rule of St Benedict may nevertheless have had a very considerable influence on them.[360] It has been argued also that early monasteries in England, and elsewhere in Europe, were of radically different character from those of Symeon's time, being much more committed to pastoral care and evangelization, to the extent that there was no distinction between 'monastic' and 'secular' religious communities and both should more properly be called by the Old English term 'minster' rather than 'monastery', which has connotations of the monasteries of Symeon's own time.[361] This argument, however, remains (in the present writer's view) open to question, both in terms of the evidence adduced to support it (which is of a topographical character as well as a documentary character and involves wide-ranging inferences as to the dates and origins of the ecclesiastical arrangements revealed by it), and in terms of evidence which can be adduced to suggest that monastic communities, with primarily devotional functions, were in fact distinct in the pre-Viking period from secular communities with primarily pastoral and evangelizing functions.[362] For the present purpose, however, the essential point is

cc. 5–7. Lanfranc's constitutions (*Monastic Constitutions*, ed. Knowles) were known, and almost certainly followed, at Durham from the late 11th-cent. DCL B.IV.24 (Piper, in Rollason, *Anglo-Norman Durham*, pp. 79–80).

[359] See below, pp. 24–5, 26–7, 34–5.

[360] C. P. Wormald, 'Bede and Benedict Biscop', *Famulus Christi*, ed. G. Bonner (London, 1976), pp. 141–69.

[361] See e.g. J. Blair, *Early Medieval Surrey: Landholding, Church and Settlement before 1300* (Stroud, 1991); *Minsters and Parish Churches: The Local Church in Transition 950–1200*, ed. J. Blair (Oxford, 1988); and *Pastoral Care before the Parish*, ed. J. Blair and R. Sharpe (Leicester, 1992), esp. papers by J. Blair, A. T. Thacker, and S. Foot.

[362] See D. Rollason and E. Cambridge, 'The pastoral organization of the Anglo-Saxon church: a review of the "minster hypothesis"', *Early Medieval Europe*, iv (1995), 87–104 (reply by J. Blair, 'Ecclesiastical organization and pastoral care in Anglo-Saxon England', *Early Medieval Europe*, iv (1995), 193–212). See also E. Cambridge, 'The early church in county Durham: a reassessment', *Journal of the British Archaeological Association*, cxxxvii (1984), 65–85; C. Cubitt, 'Pastoral care and conciliar canons: the provisions of the 747

Symeon's perception that his own community resembled that of Lindisfarne in Cuthbert's time, and differed sharply from that of the married clerks of pre-1083 Durham.

The legitimacy of the changes of 1083 at Durham Cathedral must have been tied up with the question of the continuity of its estates. As represented in the *Historia de sancto Cuthberto*, these were very widespread, embracing not only the area of County Durham, but also the areas of Islandshire and Norhamshire known as North Durham, Bedlingtonshire, and various lands in Yorkshire, including Crayke where the body of St Cuthbert was said to have rested on its seven-year wanderings.[363] As Craster has shown, these estates were indeed those held or claimed by Durham Cathedral in the early twelfth century, together with others given to it by the first Norman kings.[364] Yet the very turbulence of the church's history, and the changes of location from Lindisfarne, to Norham, then to Chester-le-Street, and finally to Durham, as well as the expulsion of the clerks in 1083, must have made title to these estates difficult to establish.[365] On the whole, the church of Durham relied on historical writing to justify its claims, rather than on forging charters purporting to relate to the pre-Conquest period. Of these latter, the only example is a charter of King Ecgfrith granting Crayke and Carlisle to St Cuthbert which is preserved in Ca.[366] From the eleventh century onwards, however, Durham historical texts display a preoccupation with estates claimed by the church: the *Historia de sancto Cuthberto* and the *Cronica monasterii Dunelmi* give many details of them, even purported summaries of charters, and the *De obsessione Dunelmi* is primarily concerned with those estates alienated from the church as a result of the marriage of Bishop Ealdhun's daughter.[367] Even the *Historia*

Council of Clofesho', *Pastoral Care*, ed. Blair and Sharpe, pp. 193–211; and, for distinctions between secular and monastic communities, D. A. Bullough, 'What has Ingeld to do with Lindisfarne?', *Anglo-Saxon England*, xxii (1993), 93–125. Although attention is drawn in the notes to evidence bearing on the arguments of Blair and others referred to on p. lxxxiv n. 361 in the case of individual churches, the term 'minster' has not been used in the translation or generally in the notes. *Monasterium* is consistently translated as 'monastery', which is unquestionably what Symeon meant, even if readers need to be aware of the possibility that his perception was unhistorical.

[363] *HSC*; D. Rollason, 'The wanderings of St Cuthbert', *Cuthbert: Saint and Patron*, ed. D. Rollason (Durham, 1987), pp. 45–61; and C. D. Morris, 'Northumbria and the Viking settlement: the evidence for landholding', *Archaeologia Aeliana*, 5th ser. v (1977), 81–104.

[364] Craster, 'Patrimony'.

[365] D. Rollason, *Saints and Relics in Anglo-Saxon England* (Oxford, 1989), pp. 211–12.

[366] See above, p. xxv.

[367] *HSC*, *CMD*, and Arnold, *Sym. Op.* i. 215–20.

regum devotes space to the question, notably an account of the possessions of Lindisfarne, different from a similar account in the *Historia de sancto Cuthberto*, which is inserted under the year 854.[368]

In the *Libellus de exordio*, however, Symeon is less preoccupied with details of estates. Although he does devote some space to them, notably the gifts of King Cnut and Earl Copsig,[369] he is sometimes content to refer readers to the *cartule* or *cartula* of the church, a word possibly referring to the *Historia de sancto Cuthberto*.[370] It may be that Symeon perceived a more pressing problem relating to his church's estates: the division of them between the monks and the bishop. Although it is likely that a division between the clerks and the bishop existed before 1083 by analogy with other churches, the situation in Symeon's time was apparently confused. He states that William of Saint-Calais and William I intended to provide properly for the monks but never in fact did so, and it is certain that the matter remained in dispute throughout the twelfth century.[371] The *Libellus de exordio* played an important part in the development of this dispute, not so much because it went into detail about the estates in question, although it did specify some; but more because its account of William of Saint-Calais's actions and intentions in establishing Durham Cathedral Priory formed the basis of the forged charters of William of Saint-Calais which the monks used subsequently to justify their claims to particular estates.[372]

These disputes between the monks and the bishop, which were only resolved in the early thirteenth century by the document known as *Le Conuenit*, embraced also disputes as to the status and functions of the prior of Durham. They were worsened by the fact that the bishops after William of Saint-Calais were secular clergy, who probably had little sympathy with the Benedictine community they found in possession of their cathedral. At issue in particular were questions of whether the prior should be elected by the monks, whether he should have the office of archdeacon over the churches held by the monks, and what seat he should occupy in the choir.[373]

---

[368] Arnold, *Sym. Op.* ii. 101–2.

[369] See below, pp. 166–7, 180–1.

[370] See below, pp. 46–7, 130–1, 137–8.

[371] See below, pp. 232–5. For an extended and lucid account of the dispute between the bishop and the monks, see E. U. Crosby, *Bishop and Chapter in Twelfth-Century England: A Study of the* Mensa Episcopalis (Cambridge, 1994), pp. 132–51.

[372] See below, p. 224 n. 9.

[373] F. Barlow, *Durham Jurisdictional Peculiars* (Oxford, 1950), pp. 1–40.

Symeon's contribution to the development of these issues was important. Whereas his account of the appointment by the bishop of the first two priors, Aldwin and Turgot, can have provided little support for those who believed the prior should be elected by the monks,[374] his picture of Turgot preaching and acting as archdeacon just as St Cuthbert was believed to have done must greatly have encouraged those who wished to see the prior fulfilling archidiaconal functions.[375] In fact, Symeon's picture was probably too extreme to be plausible, for in the course of the twelfth century the monks claimed only that the prior should be archdeacon for their own churches rather than for the diocese as a whole.[376] On the other hand, Symeon's picture of Prior Turgot as second in command to the bishop, assuming the latter's responsibilities during William's exile, must have been welcome indeed to those seeking to enhance the status of the prior in the course of the twelfth century.[377]

Tensions were especially acute between Durham Cathedral Priory and Bishop Ranulf Flambard, whose alienation of properties and dues from the monks was only made good in the death-bed restitutions which Symeon himself was responsible for copying. It has been argued that the monks' suspicions of Flambard's intentions towards them were the principal reason for the composition of the *Libellus de exordio*; and such an hypothesis would certainly account for the fact that the work finishes with William of Saint-Calais's death and, if it mentions Flambard at all, does so only to represent him earlier in his career as a tax-gatherer expelled from the diocese by St Cuthbert's miraculous intervention.[378] The *Libellus de exordio* continued to play a role in relations between the monks and the bishop, and Norton has argued that in the time of Bishop Hugh of le Puiset (1153–95) the copy of it in Ca was made as part of a complex iconographical and textual assemblage to press the monks' case on the bishop.[379]

The monks, however, were not always at odds with the bishop, for they were united with him in seeking the restitution of certain properties and parts of the diocese actually or allegedly alienated in the late eleventh or early twelfth century. The first of these was the

---

[374] See below, pp. 232–3, 240–1.

[375] See below, pp. 244–7.

[376] See below, p. 246 n. 46.

[377] See below, pp. 242–3.

[378] Piper, in Bonner, *Cuthbert*, pp. 437–46, at 442–3; Aird, in Rollason, *Symeon*, pp. 32–45; cf. Offler, *Medieval Historians*, p. 7. See below, pp. 196–9. Cf. below, pp. 48–9.

[379] Norton, in Rollason, *Symeon*, pp. 71–89. For Ca, see above, pp. xxiv–xxvii.

church of Tynemouth, which was, according to the *Libellus de exordio*, given to the monks of Jarrow prior to their removal to Durham.[380] It was, however, taken from them by Robert Mowbray, earl of Northumbria (1080/1–95), and given to the abbey of St Albans, and Durham never succeeded in recovering it. The sensitivity of this is shown by one of the early alterations in the two earliest manuscripts of the *Libellus de exordio*. According to F, Tynemouth was given to the monks of Jarrow by Bishop Walcher, presumably in his capacity as earl of Northumbria (he held this office in tandem with the bishopric of Durham). C appears to have read the same, but the passage has been altered, in Symeon's hand, to indicate that Tynemouth was granted to the monks of Jarrow by the earls of Northumbria.[381] Offler argued convincingly that F's version was correct, and that C was altered to strengthen Durham's title to Tynemouth, given that Walcher's tenure of both earldom and bishopric was unprecedented and probably regarded as irregular.[382] At all events, the *Libellus de exordio*'s preoccupation with Tynemouth stands at the beginning of a long and unsuccessful Durham campaign to recover it, a campaign which included the forging of charters, a court case at York in 1121 (recorded in the *Historia regum*), the composition of a miracle story describing the divine punishment inflicted both on Robert Mowbray and on Abbot Paul of St Albans who received the gift, and a settlement in 1174 by which Durham finally gave up its claims.[383]

A similar issue was Durham's claim to ecclesiastical jurisdiction over Carlisle and Teviotdale, areas which, according to the continuation beginning 'Tribus dehinc annis ecclesia uacante pastore', had been lost during Ranulf Flambard's exile from England.[384] Symeon in the *Libellus de exordio* emphasized Cuthbert's connections with Carlisle as originally indicated by Bede, and it is significant that another of the major erasures in C was of a substantial passage which followed a mention of Carlisle and presumably elaborated on Durham's claims to it.[385] Here too was evidently an issue of some

---

[380] For the history of Tynemouth, see H. H. E. Craster, *A History of Northumberland*, viii. *The Parish of Tynemouth* (Newcastle upon Tyne, 1907).

[381] See below, pp. 234–5 and n. 26.

[382] Offler, *Episcopal Charters*, pp. 4–6.

[383] Offler, *Episcopal Charters*, pp. 21–2, 39–46; Arnold, *Sym. Op.* ii. 260–2; and *De miraculis*, c. 13.

[384] See below, Appendix B, pp. 274–5.

[385] See below, pp. 94–5 and n. 38.

sensitivity. It is possible that Symeon drew up as a separate pamphlet the account of the see of Lindisfarne in Y (item 7), which stresses that church's relationship with Carlisle.[386]

Also lost permanently to Durham at this time was Hexham. It appears that from at least the early eleventh century this church was held on an hereditary basis by a family of provosts, the ancestors in fact of Ailred, abbot of Rievaulx. These provosts were also clerks of Durham, and one of them was none other than Elfred Westou, the sacrist of Durham. In 1083, the church of Hexham was in the hands of one of his descendants Eilaf, who declined to become a member of the new monastic community at Durham and retained possession of Hexham. Relations between the two churches must have been complex, for we find some years later his son Eilaf retiring to Durham as a monk and giving Hexham and its lands to Thomas, archbishop of York, who proceeded to found there the community of Augustinian canons which continued to hold Hexham until the Dissolution.[387] The loss of Hexham must have been a sore blow to Durham, not only because of its wide estates, but also because of its associations. Indeed Hexham emerges as the major cult centre rivalling Durham in the north-east, ably assisted in this by Ailred of Rievaulx himself, who wrote a sermon on the saints of Hexham.[388] The matter may already have been a sensitive one in the first years of the twelfth century, for the *Libellus de exordio* is suspiciously silent about Hexham, not even Elfred Westou's connection with that church being mentioned.

Symeon's perspectives, however, were not limited to the status and possessions of his church, but extended to the wider course of English history. In the pages of the *Libellus de exordio* we see something of the grimness of the post-Conquest decades in the North-East: the savage murder of the first Norman earl of Northumbria, Robert Cumin, and his followers,[389] and the ensuing harrying of the area; and the equally

---

[386] For text and comments, see Sharpe, in Rollason, *Symeon*, pp. 214–29. On Carlisle, see H. Summerson, *Medieval Carlisle: the City and the Borders from the Late Eleventh to the Mid-Sixteenth Century* (2 vols.; Cumberland and Westmorland Antiquarian and Archaeological Society, extra series, 25; Kendal, 1993), i. 31, 34; on Teviotdale, see below, p. 274 n. 15.

[387] *Priory of Hexham*, ed. Raine, i. lv–lxvi; and Offler, *Episcopal Charters*, pp. 22–3; see also W. Longstaffe, 'The hereditary sacerdotage of Hexham', *Archaeologia Aeliana*, new ser., iv (1860), 11–28; and D. J. Hall, 'The Community of St Cuthbert: Its Properties and Claims from the Ninth Century to the Twelfth', Ph.D. thesis (Oxford, 1984), pp. 109–14.

[388] *Priory of Hexham*, ed. Raine i. 173–203.

[389] See below, pp. 182–9.

savage murder of Bishop Walcher and his entourage, with its bloody aftermath.[390] Symeon describes these, but the *Libellus de exordio* seems never to adopt a hostile stance to the kings of England. William the Conqueror is made the subject of an unflattering miracle story, but the reason seems to be a local one: his disrespect for St Cuthbert.[391] William Rufus on the other hand is commended for his dealings with Prior Turgot and his restraint in not taking from the church of Durham.[392] Never once does Symeon show sympathy for the kings of Scots who were in his time serious contenders for power in the north. In what was presumably a diplomatic omission, Symeon fails to mention in the *Libellus de exordio* that King Malcolm III was present at the laying of the foundation stones of Durham Cathedral, even though his presence is attested in the *Historia regum*, and almost certainly corroborated by the *conuentio* drawn up by Symeon in the Durham *Liber Vitae*.[393] The author of the continuation beginning 'Tribus dehinc annis ecclesia uacante pastore' shows the same attitude; he never evinces any support for the king of Scots' candidate for the bishopric, William Cumin, although admittedly the priory had strong reasons of its own which led it to oppose his appointment.[394]

In a wider sense, the *Libellus de exordio* breathes the spirit of reconciliation between the native English and the continental in-comers, especially appropriate as Symeon was himself from France or Normandy. If we compare the account of Walcher's murder in the *Libellus de exordio* with that in John of Worcester's chronicle, we can see how much Symeon has played down the political ramifications, so that the killing is detached in his presentation from the intimate association with the affairs of the Northumbrian aristocracy which it has in John's.[395] As noted above, Symeon is also not unsympathetic to the clerks and priests of pre-1083 Durham.[396]

Such a spirit of reconciliation with the English past was no doubt apposite in Symeon's Durham. Aside from the wish of Durham Cathedral Priory to lay claim to the saintly traditions of Cuthbert, Oswald, Aidan, and Bede, the lists of monks in C and in the Durham

---

[390] See below, pp. 216–20.

[391] See below, pp. 196–7.

[392] See below, pp. 242–5.

[393] See below, pp. 244–5; Arnold, *Sym. Op.* ii. 220; see V. Wall, 'Malcolm III and the foundation of Durham Cathedral', Rollason, *Anglo-Norman Durham*, pp. 325–37, and *Liber Vitae*, fo. 52ᵛ. See also Aird, *Cuthbert*, pp. 238–40.

[394] Appendix B, pp. 282–311.

[395] See below, pp. 216–20; cf. JW iii. 32–7.

[396] See above, pp. lxxxii–lxxxiii.

Liber Vitae reveal the extent to which monks of the priory were English, or at least bore English names.[397] The origins of the reformed communities of Jarrow and Monkwearmouth had after all been traced by Symeon to an English monk who had read Bede's *Historia ecclesiastica* and to his two companions, one English, one Norman.[398] The treatment of Bede's 'death-song' in the *Libellus de exordio* is particularly instructive: Symeon adds the observation that it is in English, presumably for those who would not have recognized that language; he supplies a Latin translation; and in the earliest manuscripts of his work the scribes employ a careful imitation of semi-Insular minuscule script.[399] Nothing could be more appropriate for a monastic community established by a continental bishop, which had a copy of the Rule of St Benedict in Old English,[400] and identified so closely with the English past that even the reigns of its most obscure kings were an eagerly pursued subject of study.

Much of the this background is not peculiar to Durham. Rather it places the *Libellus de exordio* in line with the work of William of Malmesbury, Eadmer of Canterbury, John of Worcester, and other writers of the post-Conquest period.[401] Some of the features of it, however, are peculiar, at least in their emphasis, and highlight the precocity of such developments in this war-torn frontier church.

9. PREVIOUS EDITIONS AND PLAN OF THE PRESENT EDITION

The *Libellus de exordio* has been edited three times previously:

Historiae Anglicanae Scriptores Decem, ed. R. Twysden (2 vols., London, 1652), i. 1–58. This edition is based on Ca.
Symeonis monachi Dunhelmensis, *Libellus de exordio atque procursu*

---

[397] Piper, 'Lists', and W. M. Aird, 'The Origins and Development of the Church of St Cuthbert 635–1153, with Special Reference to Durham in the Period c.1071–1153', Ph.D. thesis (Edinburgh, 1991), pp. 157, 172, 391–4.

[398] See below, pp. 200–1. For comment, see A. Dawtry, 'The Benedictine revival in the North: the last bulwark of Anglo-Saxon monasticism?', *Studies in Church History*, xix (1982), 87–98, and R. H. C. Davis, 'Bede after Bede', *Studies in Medieval History Presented to R. Allen Brown*, ed. C. Harper-Bill, C. Holdsworth, and J. L. Nelson (Woodbridge, 1989), pp. 103–16.

[399] See below, pp. 72–3 and above, p. lxii n. 259.

[400] DCL B.IV.24, fos. 98ᵛ–123ᵛ.

[401] R. W. Southern, 'Aspects of the European tradition of historical writing: 4. The sense of the past', *Transactions of the Royal Historical Society*, 5th ser. xxiii (1973), 243–63; and Gransden, *Historical Writing*, cc. 8–9.

Dunhelmensis ecclesie, ed. Thomas Bedford (London, 1732). This edition is a fastidious representation of C, with variant readings from F and Ca (as edited by Twysden), and chapter headings and book and chapter numbers taken from Ca.

Symeonis monachi Opera omnia, ed. Thomas Arnold (RS lxxv; 2 vols., 1882–5), i. 3–135. This edition, which notes very few variant readings, is based on all the manuscripts discussed here except D, H, and V.

In view of the position of C established above, the aim of this edition, like that of Bedford's, is to represent the *Libellus de exordio* as it originally appeared in C, except where a strong case can be made that another manuscript preserves the original wording, as in the case of F's account of the gift of Tynemouth.[402] The text and translation therefore start with the preface beginning 'Exordium huius',[403] the bishop-list as originally written in C,[404] and the list of monks introduced by the paragraph beginning 'Hic scripta'.[405] There then follows the main body of the text from 'Gloriosi quondam' to the death of William of Saint-Calais, ending 'congregati fuerant monachi annus agebatur'.[406] As argued above, these items are the original components of the *Libellus de exordio*. As we have seen, however, two items were added in the course of the twelfth century and are found in C as later additions: the summary beginning 'Regnante apud' and the continuation beginning 'Tribus dehinc annis ecclesia uacante pastore', and because of their position in C and their interest for the early development of the *Libellus de exordio* they are edited and translated in Appendix A and Appendix B respectively, where the variant version of the continuation in Ca will also be found.[407] Previous editions of the *Libellus de exordio* have treated the summary as another preface as it is presented in Ca and other manuscripts, but as we have seen there is no authority for this in C and it is evidently a subsequent development. The five chapters from the *De miraculis* are not included, as they never formed part of C and they were not added to the *Libellus de exordio* until the fourteenth century, a little earlier than was the *De iniusta uexacione*. The latter's appearance in a definitive edition has in any case rendered its publication here unnecessary.[408]

---

[402] See below, p. 234 n. 26.
[404] See below, pp. 4–5.
[406] See below, pp. 16–256.
[408] Offler, *DIV*.

[403] See below, pp. 2–3.
[405] See below, pp. 4–15.
[407] See below, pp. 258–65 and 266–323.

C and F do not contain chapter headings or numbers, but do subdivide the text by minor and major initials. The development of chapter headings and numbers, and in the case of Ca the division of the work into four books, does, however, cast light on the means by which the text was integrated with those which continued its narrative, and also perhaps on the emphasis which was placed on it in the course of the Middle Ages. Moreover, scholars have often referred to the text by means of chapter and book numbering, sometimes using the subdivision into chapters found in varying forms in D, H, T, V, Y, Fx, and L, but more often using the system of four books divided into sixty-nine chapters found in Ca and in all previous editions. For this reason and for ease of reference, the present edition has retained Ca's book division and chapter-numbers (given as Arabic numerals) as its principal system of reference, which also corresponds to the use of minor and major initials in C and F. In order to show the other system of chapter division in the manuscripts and to permit reference to the other manuscripts, its chapter-numbers have been given in Roman numbers in square brackets in the margins. Where H diverges from the other manuscripts which use this system, this has been noted by a letter H against the number of the chapter in that manuscript. Where Fx, L, and Y diverge because of the insertion into them of additional material and the use of shorter chapter divisions, their chapter-numbers have been shown in round brackets. Where rubrics occur in manuscripts, they are noted in the apparatus, and the lists of chapter-headings as they occur before the text in the manuscripts are edited in Appendix C.[409]

The title by which this text has long been known, *Historia Dunelmensis ecclesie*, has no authority in the manuscripts, and seems to have been invented by Twysden. Although it was adopted as a running title by Bedford, he did not use it as the title of the text itself, but in Arnold's edition it appeared under the main rubric: *Symeonis monachi Historia Dunelmensis ecclesiæ*. It is not surprising therefore that scholars have used it widely, and it is with some trepidation that it is abandoned in the present edition. That the original title was *Libellus de exordio et procursu istius, hoc est Dunelmensis, ecclesie*, is clearly attested by C and F and there can be no justification for continuing to use a title fabricated in the seventeenth century, however convenient. Especially when the original title is more

---

[409] See below, pp. 324–33.

nearly descriptive of the nature of the text; for the parenthesis, *hoc est Dunelmensis*, hints at one of the central themes of the work: that the history of Durham was to be seen as a continuity with that of Chester-le-Street and Lindisfarne.

The original title changed in the course of the Middle Ages, partly in response to the work's changing character as additions were made to it. It has been suggested that an entry in the early twelfth-century catalogue of Durham Cathedral Priory's library for a *Liber de statu Dunelmensis ecclesie* refers to a manuscript of it, perhaps C itself, and thus shows that very soon after its composition the title by which it was known had changed. The catalogue reference is reflected in H's rubric, *Liber de statu Lindisfarnensis et Dunelmensis ecclesie*, and in the somewhat more elaborate versions in Y, T, and probably Fx, which are variations on *De statu Lindisfarnensis, id est Dunhelmensis ecclesie secundum uenerabilem Bedam presbiterum et postmodum de gestis episcoporum Dunelmie*. As we have seen, a reference in the 1392 Durham library catalogue suggests that, together with the texts added to it, it was known appropriately enough as *Gesta episcoporum*, and it was already as *Gesta episcoporum Dunelmensium* that Richard of Hexham knew it in the twelfth century. In the list of contents in Fx, it was known as *Gesta episcoporum Lyndisfarnensis et Dunelmensis ecclesie*. In the 1421 Durham Cathedral Priory library catalogue, it has become *Cronica de exordio et progressu ecclesie Dunelmensis*.[410] As with other aspects of Ca, its florid title, *Historia de exordio Christianitatis et religionis tocius Northumbrie de fide et origine sancti Oswaldi regis et martiris et de predicatione sancti Aidani episcopi*, is not reflected in any other manuscript. Variation and flexibility thus mark the development of the *Libellus de exordio*'s title, but there can be no doubt of its original appellation and it is that which is used in this edition.

Where text is shared with another source, with the exception of the Bible, it has been placed in italics in the Latin text and references given in the footnotes in both Latin text and English translation. Verbal echoes and dependencies are likewise indicated in the footnotes. Single quotation marks have been used for quotations from the Bible, quotations from other sources acknowledged by the author, and direct speech. Punctuation has been modernized, although it nevertheless reflects C as far as possible. Variations in the spelling of proper names have only been recorded for C and F.

---

[410] Botfield, *Catalogi veteres*, p. 124.

Otherwise minor scribal and orthographical variant readings have been ignored.

Where Symeon has extracted wholesale from his sources, for example Bede's *Historia ecclesiastica*, no attempt has been made to supply a full commentary, which is more properly to be found in editions of the texts in question; but some guidance as regards the content has been given.

Dates of kings and royal and ecclesiastical officers given in the notes are taken, unless otherwise stated, from E. B. Fryde, D. E. Greenway, S. Porter, *et al.*, *Handbook of British Chronology* (3rd edn.; Royal Historical Society Guides and Handbooks, 2; London, 1986), supplemented by Rollason, *Sources*.

SIGLA

Symeon of Durham

C	Durham University Library, Cosin V.II.6
Ca	CUL, Ff.1.27
D	DCL, A.IV.36
F	BL, Cotton Faustina A.V
Fx	Bod. Lib., Fairfax 6
H	Bod. Lib., Holkham misc. 25
L	Bod. Lib., Laud misc. 700
T	BL, Cotton Titus A.II
V	BL, Cotton Vespasian A.VI
Y	York, Minster Library, XV.I.12

Sources and related texts

ALf	*Annales Lindisfarnses et Dunelmenses*
ASC	Anglo-Saxon Chronicle
CMD	*Chronica monasterii Dunelmensis*
Dig.	*Bod. Lib., Digby 211*
HSC	*Historia de sancto Cuthberto*
JW	the Chronicle of John of Worcester

Symeon of Durham

LIBELLVS DE EXORDIO ATQVE PROCVRSV ISTIVS, HOC EST DVNHELMENSIS, ECCLESIE

Tract on the Origins and Progress of this the Church of Durham

Exordium *huius hoc est* Dunelmensis ecclesie describere maiorum auctoritate iussus, ingenii tardioris et imperitie michi conscius, non obedire prius cogitaueram.[1] Sed rursus obedientie hoc precipientium plus quam meis uiribus confidens, iuxta sensus mei qualitatem studium adhibui. Ea scilicet que sparsim in scedulis inuenire potui, ordinatim collecta digessi, ut eo facilius peritiores si mea non placent, unde *sue peritie* opus conueniens conficiant, in promptu inueniant.[2]

*Itaque congruum uidetur, ut omnium ipsius ecclesie episcoporum ab illo qui eius fundator primus extiterat, usque illum qui in presenti est,[3] hic ex ordine nomina ponantur, quibus et eos qui illis successuri fuerint episcopos, diligens futurorum cura scriptorum apponere non negligat.[4]

a–a om. Ca   *b–b* peritie sue T   *c–c (p. 4)* om. Ca

[1] The MSS have different headings here. Ca has in a contemporary (s. xii²) hand, 'Incipit apologia Symeonis', and concludes this section with the rubric, 'Explicit apologia Symeonis monachi'. H has, also in a contemporary hand (s. xiii), 'Incipit liber Symonis <sic> monachi Dunelmensis de statu Lindisfarnensis et Dunelmensis ecclesie usque ad electionem Hugonem de Puteaco'. In contemporary (s. xiv) hands, T has, 'Incipit de statu Lindisfarnensis ecclesie, id est Dunelmensis ecclesie, secundum uenerabilem Bedam presbiterum et primorum de gestis episcoporum Dunelmie'; and Y has 'Incipit (?) libellus (*seven words erased*) de statu Lindisfarnensis, id est Dunhelmensis ecclesie secundum uenerabilem Bedam presbiterum et postmodum de gestis episcoporum Dunhelmie.' There are no contemporary headings at this point in C, Fx, and L but early modern hands have written, 'Incipit libellus de statu Lindisfarnensis idem ⟨sic⟩ Dunelmensis ecclesie secundum uenerabilem Bedam presbiterum. Et postmodum de gestis episcoporum Dunelmensium'. In Fx the occurrence of a catchword 'Incipit libellus' at the foot of the previous folio (fo. 12ᵛ) and the survival in small 14th-cent. script above the preface beginning 'Exordium huius' of the partially legible words 'Bedam presbi...et postmo.. de gestis episcoporum' suggest that the early modern heading may have had some authority. C has in the top right-hand corner of the folio the 15th-cent. press-mark R apparently altered from Q.

[2] From the second word of the passage (*huius*) to this point C is written by a near-contemporary hand over an erasure. The original text was evidently longer, since half a line followed by a whole line and then a further half line have been left blank before *Itaque*. Under ultra-violet light traces of letters, possibly reading *um*, are visible at the end of this blank space.

[3] A word has been erased in C, and an early modern hand has added in the margin: 'erasa uidetur uox Rannulfum', that is Ranulf Flambard, bishop of Durham (1099–1128).

When I was commanded by the authority of my elders to describe the origins of this the church of Durham, I was conscious of my sluggish intellect and lack of skill, and I first of all considered disobeying.[1] But on reflection I placed my trust in the need for obedience to those who were ordering me to undertake this task rather than in my own strength, and I became eagerly absorbed in carrying out the work as well as the quality of my understanding would allow. I have gathered together and set out in order those things which I have been able to find scattered through the documents, in such a way that those more skilled than I may, if what I have done does not please them, find in my work the materials with which to create a work more suitable to their expertise.[2] Therefore it seems proper that I should note down here in order the names of all the bishops of this same church from him who was the first founder down to the one who is bishop at present,[3] and may the diligent attention of future scribes not neglect to add to these the names of those bishops who will have succeeded them.[4]

Although nothing is now legible, it seems very likely that this is what was originally written.

[4] It is possible, perhaps likely, that the author of *LDE* constructed this list of bishops on the basis of his own knowledge rather than drawing on a pre-existing list, for his list differs substantially from and runs on longer than any earlier lists. That in BL, Cotton Vespasian B.VI (s. ix^{in}), omits Tuda and runs only to Higbald, with later additions of Egbert and Edmund; those in CCCC 183 (s. x^1) and BL, Cotton Tiberius B.V (s. x^{ex}) run only to Egbert. All omit Tuda. For discussion and edition of these lists, see R. I. Page, 'Anglo-Saxon episcopal lists', *Nottingham Mediaeval Studies*, ix (1965), 71–95 [parts I, II], and x (1966), 2–24 [part III]. The closest parallel to *LDE*'s list is that in CCCO 157, p. 43, which is the partially autograph manuscript of John of Worcester's *Chronicle* and was probably completed by 1143, although the main body of the text was written by 1131 and the episcopal lists were drafted in or shortly after 1114. See JW, ii. xxi–xxxv, esp. xxxiv–xxxv; for the text of these lists and accompanying materials, which were evidently assembled from earlier sources, see *Florentii Wigorniensis monachi Chronicon ex chronicis*, ed. B. Thorpe (2 vols.; Publications of the English Historical Society ; London, 1848–9), i. 246, and JW, i (forthcoming). John's list of bishops of Lindisfarne runs to Ranulf Flambard and includes Tuda, but it omits Ecgred, and also Heathured and Eanberht who appear in his list of the bishops of Hexham, as they do in the lists of Hexham bishops in the other manuscripts cited above. In view of this, it is not impossible that Symeon's inclusion of them was intended to imply that Hexham had already been in some way amalgamated with Lindisfarne in the time of Heathured.

Aidanus[5]	Cutheardus
Finanus	Tilredus
Colmanus	Wigredus
Tuda	Vhtredus
Eata	Sexhelmus
Cuthbertus	Aldredus
Eadbertus	Elfsig
Eadfridus	Aldhunus
Ethelwoldus	Eadmundus
Kynewulfus	Eadredus
Higbaldus	Egelricus
Ecgbertus	Egelwinus
Heathuredus	Walcherus
Ecgredus	Willelmus
Eanbertus	Rannulfus[6]
Eardulfus	

Hic scripta continentur nomina monachorum in hac ecclesia ad incorrupti corporis sanctissimi Cuthberti presentiam iam professorum, quorum nominibus prescriptis etiam illorum nomina qui futuris temporibus annuente Christo ibidem professionem facturi fuerint, ut scribendo adiungat, posterorum quesumus sollertia semper meminisse studeat.[c7] Preterea lectorem petimus, ut tam pro illo qui hoc opus fieri iusserat, quam pro illis qui obediendo iussis id studio et labore perfecerunt,[a] Domino Iesu Christo preces fundere dignetur. Sed et pro omnibus quorum hic nomina uiderit, diuine pietatis abundantiam inuocare meminerit, uiuis quidem postulans sancte professionis augmentum et bone perseuerantie in futuro premium,

---

[a] perfecerint Ca

[5] Fx, L (fos. 10^v–12^v), H, T, and Y give lengths of reigns in the original hand after the names. Lengths of reigns have been added to C, mostly in the early modern period.

[6] In C the list is continued in a 13th-cent. hand to Hugh of le Puiset (1153–95), then in a gothic hand down to Walter Skirlaw (1388–1406), and then in various hands down to William Talbot (1721–30). In D the original hand continues to Philip of Poitiers (1195 × 9–1208). In T and Y the original hand continues to Anthony Bek (1283–1311). In Y there is then an erasure of approximately five lines which has impinged on the penflourishing of the 'G' of 'Gloriosi' (below, p. 16). In Fx the list is carried in a contemporary hand down to Richard of Bury (1333–45), then in a later hand down to Cuthbert Tunstall (1530–59), and in a still later hand to Tobias Matthew (1595–1606). In L the list on fo. 14^r is carried in the hand of the main scribe to John Fordham (1381–8), the length of whose reign seems to have been written over an erasure. The list on fos. 10^v–

Aidan[5]	Cutheard
Finan	Tilred
Colman	Wigred
Tuda	Uhtred
Eata	Sexhelm
Cuthbert	Aldred
Eadberht	Ælfsige
Eadfrith	Ealdhun
Æthelwald	Edmund
Cynewulf	Eadred
Higbald	Æthelric
Ecgberht	Æthelwine
Heathured	Walcher
Ecgred	William
Eanberht	Rannulf[6]
Eardwulf	

There now follows a list of the names of the monks who presently make profession in this church in the presence of the undecayed body of St Cuthbert, and we urge that those who come after us may have the conscientiousness to remember to add to this list the names of those who, Christ willing, will have made profession in the same place in the future.[7] Moreover, we beg the reader that he should deign to offer prayers to Our Lord Jesus Christ both for him who ordered this work to be composed and for those who in obedience to him laboured and studied to bring it to completion. May he also remember to invoke the abundance of God's mercy for all those whose names he will see here, asking for the living that they may adhere more fully to their holy profession and may in the future receive the reward of their virtuous perseverance, and for the dead that they may receive

12[v] is carried down to Hugh of le Puiset (1153–95) in the original hand, and is then extended to Cuthbert Tunstall. In H the list is carried down to Antony Bek in the original hand.

[7] This sentence and the following passage are found only in C and Ca, and the lists of monks are found only in C. Fx has a chapter-list after the bishop-list. C has a large initial H with a white lion inside it, and the first two words are in coloured capitals. The wording indicates that the list of monks which follows was of those who had become monks of Durham, whereas a similar list in the *Liber Vitae* included others, notably Reinfrid the refounder of Whitby (Piper, 'Lists', pp. 162–3). For a detailed comparison and collation of the lists, and a comparison of their contents with early 12th-cent. Durham obits, see Piper, 'Lists', where the relevant texts are edited. The dating of the hands followed here is that of Piper, 'Lists'; cf. Gullick, 'Scribes', p. 109 n. 61, and Meehan, 'Symeon', pp. 36–40.

et defunctis, ut percepta uenia peccatorum mereantur 'uidere bona Domini in terra uiuentium'.[8]

[1] ^aAldwinus[9]	[16] Godwinus[21]
[2] Elfwius[10]	[17] Wikingus[22]
[3] Willelmus[11]	[18] Godwinus[23]
[4] Leofwinus[12]	[19] Egelricus
[5] Wulmarus[13]	[20] Seulfus
[6] TVRGOTVS[14]	[21] Gregorius
[7] Edwinus[15]	[22] Edmundus
[8] Turkillus[16]	[23] Rotbertus
[9] Columbanus[17]	[24] Osbernus[24]
[10] Elfwinus	[25] Dunningus
[11] Godwinus[18]	[26] Ernanus[25]
[12] Elmarus	[27] Edmundus
[13] Helias	[28] Kytellus
[14] Suartebrandus[19]	[29] Romanus
[15] Gamelo[20]	[30] Godricus

^{a–a (p. 14)} Verumtamen quibus non uacat uel legere plurima non ualent, hoc si uoluerint legant, opus compendiosa breuitate poterunt scire *Ca*

---

[8] Ps. 26: 13 (27: 16). The phrasing here suggests that C was in part fulfilling the same function as the *Liber Vitae*, that is, as a memorial book. Figures representing the number of monks in the list have been added in a modern hand.

[9] Aldwin (OE Ealdwine), leader of the monks who refounded Jarrow and first prior of Durham (d. 1087; see below). Capitalization of names in the list seems to have been used to distinguish priors (see below, nos. 6, 93, 98, but cf. 47, 49, 67, 81, 180, 191). Aldwin's name was not entered in capitals, presumably because he was dead when the list was written in C.

[10] Elfwy (OE Ælfwig) was a monk of Evesham who accompanied Aldwin to Jarrow and was prior there for a short time *c*.1075 while Aldwin was at Melrose (see below, p. 208–9).

[11] This (or no. 35 or no. 52) could be the archdeacon William Havegrim who was present at the opening of St Cuthbert's tomb in 1104 (Raine, *Cuth. virt.* c. 40). On his position as a monk-archdeacon subordinate to Turgot as prior-archdeacon, see Offler, 'Early archdeacons', pp. 194–5. On monastic archdeacons at Durham and elsewhere, see below, p. 246 n. 46 and refs. therein.

[12] This is presumably the Leofwine who was prominent in the opening of St Cuthbert's tomb in 1104 and is mentioned both in *De miraculis* c. 7, and in Reginald's account of the opening (Raine, *Cuth. virt.* c. 40).

[13] This person is named in the 1121 plea of the Durham monks relating to their claim to Tynemouth, preserved in *HReg*, s.a.1121 (Arnold, *Sym. Op.* ii. 260–1; Piper, 'Lists', p. 163 n. 6). He is there said to have gone regularly to Tynemouth from Jarrow together with two other Jarrow monks Edmund and Eadred and a canon of Durham, Elfwald (OE Ælfwald), to perform services at Tynemouth. Neither Eadred nor Elfwald appear in this list or in the list in the *Liber Vitae*, but Edmund is presumably no. 22 On the implications of the naming of Edmund and Eadred for the veracity of the Durham monks' 1121 claim, see A. J. Piper, *The Durham Monks at Jarrow* (Jarrow Lecture; Jarrow, 1986), p. 4 (repr. *Bede and*

forgiveness for their sins and be found worthy 'to see the good things
of the Lord in the land of the living'.[8]

[1] Aldwin[9]	[16] Godwin[21]
[2] Elfwy[10]	[17] Wiking[22]
[3] William[11]	[18] Godwin[23]
[4] Leofwin[12]	[19] Ailric
[5] Wulmar[13]	[20] Seulf
[6] TURGOT[14]	[21] Gregory
[7] Edwin[15]	[22] Edmund
[8] Turkill[16]	[23] Robert
[9] Columbanus[17]	[24] Osbern[24]
[10] Elfwin	[25] Dunning
[11] Godwin[18]	[26] Ernan[25]
[12] Elmar	[27] Edmund
[13] Elias	[28] Kytel
[14] Swartbrand[19]	[29] Romanus
[15] Gamel[20]	[30] Godric

his World: The Jarrow Lectures 1958–93, ed. M. Lapidge (2 vols.; Aldershot, 1994), ii. 689–728); but cf. Offler, *Episcopal Charters*, pp. 44–5.

[14] Prior of Durham (1087–1109, or possibly 1115). The capitalization of his name, which seems to indicate that he was prior at the time of writing, is consistent with the passage referring to his current tenure of that office preserved by F but erased from C (see below, p. 207 n. 85).

[15] This is presumably the monk of that name who was present at the opening of St Cuthbert's tomb in 1104 (Raine, *Cuth. virt.* c. 40).

[16] This is presumably the monk allegedly sent from the refounded monastery of Jarrow to take charge of Tynemouth prior to Robert Mowbray's expropriation of it in 1090; see *HReg*, *s.a.* 1121 (Arnold, *Sym. Op.* ii. 261), and below p. 236 n. 29.

[17] This is presumably the Columbanus the anchorite, whose obit is recorded in DCL, B.IV.24, under 18 Sept. (Piper, 'Lists', p. 198).

[18] This (or nos. 16, 18, or 45) must be the sacrist of that name present at the opening of St Cuthbert's coffin in 1104 (Raine, *Cuth. virt.* c. 40).

[19] This is presumably the 'venerable, white-haired old man' of the name said below, (pp. 22–3) to have died 'recently in Bishop William's time', i.e. before 1096. It is possible that he was a member of the pre-1083 community, since his name occurs with the epithet 'priest' in what is probably an authentic witness list attached to a forged charter of 1074–5 (Offler, *Episcopal Charters*, p. 46). The list includes Leobwine *decanus*, evidently the dean killed with Bishop Walcher in 1080 (below, p. 215 n. 100).

[20] See below, p. 163 n. 28.

[21] See n. to no. 11.

[22] Presumably one of the monks who inspected Cuthbert's body in 1104 (Raine, *Cuth. virt.* c. 40).

[23] Ibid.

[24] This is presumably the sacrist present at the opening of St Cuthbert's tomb in 1104 (Raine, *Cuth. virt.* c. 40).

[25] See below, p. 191 n. 65.

[31]	Nicholaus	[56]	Leodgarus
[32]	Heinricus	[57]	Farmannus
[33]	Gregorius	[58]	Egelredus[34]
[34]	Alanus	[59]	Rotbertus[35]
[35]	Willelmus	[60]	Viuianus
[36]	Godselinus[26]	[61]	Eluricus
[37]	Eluredus	[62]	Radulfus
[38]	Symeon[27]	[63]	Elfwinus
[39]	Edwardus[28]	[64]	Clibernus[36]
[40]	Gamelo[29]	[65]	Brianus
[41]	Anskitillus	[66]	Bernardus
[42]	Walterus	[67]	Rogerius[37]
[43]	Martinus	[68]	Rotbertus
[44]	Osmundus	[69]	Baldwinus
[45]	Godwinus[30]	[70]	Siwardus
[46]	Edmundus	[71]	Paulinus
[47]	Rogerius[31]	[72]	Siwardus
[48]	Aldwinus[32]	[73]	Edmundus[38]
[49]	Algarus[33]	[74]	Ælfredus
[50]	Samuel	[75]	Normannus
[51]	Odo	[76]	Thurstanus[39]
[52]	Willelmus	[77]	Aidanus
[53]	Ricardus	[78]	Benedictus
[54]	Iohannes	[79]	Martinus
[55]	Normannus	[80]	Ioseph

[26] *Liber Vitae*, fo. 45, has 'Goscelinus', which seems preferable.

[27] This is presumably the author of the present work.

[28] This may be the monk of Durham sent to supervise the priory of Lindisfarne in *c*.1122. He appears in two notifications of Ranulf Flambard, dated respectively *c*.1122 and *c*.1124–8 (in the second of these he is said 'hitherto' to have held *Hewic* in Norhamshire and Islandshire). He may be identical with the Edward mentioned as a monk of Coldingham in two mandates of King David I of Scotland (1124–53). See Offler, *Episcopal Charters*, nos.19 and 21 and p. 63.

[29] See n. to no. 20.

[30] See n. to no. 11.

[31] Either this or no. 67 may be the future prior of Durham (?1138–49). Note that his name is not capitalized.

[32] This is presumably Aldwin, the sub-prior who was present at the opening of St Cuthbert's tomb in 1104 (Raine, *Cuth. virt.* c. 40).

[33] Future prior of Durham (1109–?38), he was present at the opening of St Cuthbert's tomb in 1104 (Raine, *Cuth. virt.* c. 40). Note that his name is not capitalized, presumably because he had not become prior when the list was compiled.

[34] In a charter of *c*.1122–8, Bishop Ranulf Flambard notifies 'Ægelr' monacho' of grants

[31]	Nicholas	[56]	Leodgar
[32]	Heinrich	[57]	Farmann
[33]	Gregory	[58]	Ailred[34]
[34]	Alan	[59]	Robert[35]
[35]	William	[60]	Vivian
[36]	Goscelin[26]	[61]	Elfric
[37]	Elfred	[62]	Ralph
[38]	Symeon[27]	[63]	Elfwin
[39]	Edward[28]	[64]	Clibern[36]
[40]	Gamel[29]	[65]	Brian
[41]	Ansketil	[66]	Bernard
[42]	Walter	[67]	Roger[37]
[43]	Martin	[68]	Robert
[44]	Osmund	[69]	Baldwin
[45]	Godwin[30]	[70]	Siward
[46]	Edmund	[71]	Paulinus
[47]	Roger[31]	[72]	Siward
[48]	Aldwin[32]	[73]	Edmund[38]
[49]	Algar[33]	[74]	Elfred
[50]	Samuel	[75]	Norman
[51]	Odo	[76]	Thurstan[39]
[52]	William	[77]	Aidan
[53]	Richard	[78]	Benedict
[54]	John	[79]	Martin
[55]	Norman	[80]	Joseph

he has made to St Cuthbert and his monks in Howden (Yorks.) (Offler, *Episcopal Charters*, p. 85).

[35] Robert the monk witnesses a notification of Ranulf Flambard *c.*1122–8, and Offler (*Episcopal Charters*, pp. 87–8) suggested that he might have been the Robert responsible for obtaining for the priory the confirmation by Pope Calixtus II of William of Saint-Calais's foundation.

[36] Members of a family with the names *Clibernus* and *Clibertus* appear as landholders in Durham charters of the period 1128–41, but there is no evidence that any of them ever became monks. See Offler, *Episcopal Charters*, pp. 109, 122–3, 125–6. The corresponding name in *Liber Vitae*, fo. 45[v], is Clement, which may have been a name in religion.

[37] See n. to no. 47.

[38] Names 1–73 were entered by the scribe of the rest of the text, probably during Turgot's period as prior (see n. to no. 6). A second scribe entered names 74–5.

[39] This is the first name written by a third scribe, who continued the list down to no. 88 inclusive. Since Thurstan's name occurs in the lists in both *LDE* and the *Liber Vitae* after the work of the first scribes had finished, it seems unlikely that he can have been the archdeacon Thurstan who is mentioned as a participant in a confraternity agreement made in 1081 × 5 between Bishop William of Saint-Calais and Abbot Vitalis of Westminster (*Lib. Vit.*, fo. 48[r]). Cf. Aird, *Cuthbert*, pp. 150–1.

[81] PAPA[40]
[82] Petrus
[83] Thomas
[84] Eduuinus
[85] Lambertus
[86] Thomas
[87] Fulco
[88] Leuiatus
[89] Turoldus[41]
[90] Ricardus
[91] Ainulfus[a]
[92] Aldredus[b][42]
[93] LAVRENTIVS[43]
[94] G[blank]s
[95] Y[blank]s
[96] D[blank]s
[97] M[blank]s[44]
[98] ABSALON[45]
[99] Willelmus
[100] Ysaac
[101] David
[102] Mauricius
[103] Henricus
[104] Daniel
[105] Laurentius
[106] Odo
[107] Alanus[c]
[108] Gregorius
[109] Radulfus
[110] Walterius
[111] Geruasius

[112] Antonius
[113] Suanus
[114] Moyses
[115] Adam
[116] Siluester
[117] Eilricus
[118] Albinus
[119] Simundus
[120] Vitalis
[121] Rogerius
[122] Iacob
[123] Daniel
[124] Rodbertus
[125] Rodbertus
[126] Petrus
[127] Samuel
[128] Iohannes
[129] Ernanus
[130] Lifricus
[131] Theodricus
[132] Radulfus
[133] Helyas
[134] Radulfus
[135] Æilricus
[136] Willelmus
[137] Ricardus
[128] Durandus
[139] Ælfredus
[140] Serlo
[141] Willelmus
[142] Ricardus

[a] *altered from* Arnulfus C   [b] Ald[blank]s C   [c] *on same line as Odo C*

---

[40] A monk of this name attests a charter of Ranulf Flambard of ?1127 and may have been a member of the bishop's clan, possibly a nephew; see Offler, *Episcopal Charters*, no. 23 and p. 105, and Offler, 'Early archdeacons', p. 201. Distinguishing his name by capitalization might suggest that Flambard (d. 1128) was still alive when this part of the list was written (Piper, 'Lists', p. 174).

[41] A fourth scribe continued the list down to and including no. 97, probably working in the time of Prior Lawrence (1149–54); see n. to no. 93.

[42] Possibly the monk to whom the vision of Orm was reported; see H. Farmer, 'The vision of Orm', *Analecta Bollandiana*, lxxv (1957), 72–82.

[81]	PAPA[40]	[112]	Antony
[82]	Peter	[113]	Swein
[83]	Thomas	[114]	Moses
[84]	Edwin	[115]	Adam
[85]	Lambert	[116]	Silvester
[86]	Thomas	[117]	Ailric
[87]	Fulk	[118]	Albinus
[88]	Leviat	[119]	Simund
[89]	Turold[41]	[120]	Vitalis
[90]	Richard	[121]	Roger
[91]	Ainulf	[122]	Jacob
[92]	Aldred[42]	[123]	Daniel
[93]	LAWRENCE[43]	[124]	Robert
[94]	G[*blank*]s	[125]	Robert
[95]	Y[*blank*]s	[126]	Peter
[96]	D[*blank*]s	[127]	Samuel
[97]	M[*blank*]s[44]	[128]	John
[98]	ABSALOM[45]	[129]	Ernan
[99]	William	[130]	Leofric
[100]	Isaac	[131]	Theodric
[101]	Dauid	[132]	Ralph
[102]	Maurice	[133]	Elias
[103]	Henry	[134]	Ralph
[104]	Daniel	[135]	Ailric
[105]	Lawrence	[136]	William
[106]	Odo	[137]	Richard
[107]	Alan	[128]	Durand
[108]	Gregory	[139]	Elfred
[109]	Ralph	[140]	Serlo
[110]	Walter	[141]	William
[111]	Gervase	[142]	Richard

[43] Prior of Durham (1149–54). The entering of his name in capitals suggests that he was currently prior when this part of the list was being written.

[44] For the possibility that nos. 94–7 were erased apart from their first and last letters because they had been accidentally duplicated by nos. 99–102 (*Willelmus* in no. 99 as a variant of a putative *Guillelmus* in no. 94), see Piper, 'Lists', p. 162.

[45] Nos. 98–230 were written in C in the second half of the 12th cent. by the scribe of the continuation beginning 'Tribus dehinc annis' (Appendix B, pp. 266–311), although name 98 may possibly have been written by a different scribe. A more exact dating can be derived from the fact that the name Absalom (98) was entered in capitals, probably indicating that he was currently prior (1154–58/9). Nos. 173 and 200 must have been entered after 1148 × 1155, and no. 177 after 1150 (see nn. ad locc.) and name 180 is probably that of the Prior Germanus (1163–89), presumably before he took office since his name is not capitalized.

[143]	Augustinus	[174]	Alanus
[144]	Asketinus[46]	[175]	Asketinus
[145]	Lambertus	[176]	Iohannes
[146]	Turoldus	[177]	Bartholomeus[50]
[147]	Leofwinus	[178]	Samson
[148]	Rodbertus	[179]	Helyas
[149]	Hugo	[180]	Germanus[51]
[150]	Iacobus	[181]	Walterius
[151]	Alanus	[182]	Ricardus
[152]	Waltheus[47]	[183]	Rodbertus
[153]	Ioseph	[184]	Henricus
[154]	Rogerius	[185]	Iohannes
[155]	Iacob[a]	[186]	Steinketel[52]
[156]	Moyses	[187]	Ricarius
[157]	Alexander	[188]	Ambrosius
[158]	Willelmus	[189]	Leofwinus
[159]	Albanus	[190]	Huctredus
[160]	Henricus	[191]	Thomas[53]
[161]	Siluester	[192]	Alanus
[162]	Rodbertus	[193]	Arkillus
[163]	Iuo	[194]	Wigotus
[164]	Benedictus	[195]	Gaufridus
[165]	Reginaldus	[196]	Elfredus
[166]	Aculfus	[197]	Iohannes[54]
[167]	Reginaldus	[198]	Siluanus
[168]	Ysaac	[199]	Bainardus
[169]	Walterius	[200]	Iohel[55]
[170]	Turoldus	[201]	Walterius
[171]	Reginaldus	[202]	Rannulfus
[172]	Iurdanus[48]	[203]	Asketinus
[173]	Rodbertus[49]	[204]	Willelmus

[a] *interlin. C (below line, s. xii[1])*

[46] A sacristan of this name occurs in Raine, *Cuth. virt.* c. 104 (cf. no. 175).

[47] This name has been added by the original hand over erasure. The *Liber Vitae* has *Waldeuus*, which suggests the appropriate English version of the name.

[48] The corresponding name in *Liber Vitae* is 'Iohannes archidiaconus'; but this was probably based on a misreading (Piper, 'Lists', p. 165).

[49] This entry probably refers to Robert of St Martin who, on becoming a monk, issued a charter assigned to 1148 (Piper, 'Lists', p. 172).

[50] This is almost certainly the famous hermit of Farne who professed with Prior Germanus (no. 180) and within a year went to establish a hermitage on Farne. Since this

[143] Augustine		[174] Alan
[144] Asketin[46]		[175] Asketin
[145] Lambert		[176] John
[146] Turold		[177] Bartholomew[50]
[147] Leofwin		[178] Samson
[148] Robert		[179] Elias
[149] Hugh		[180] Germanus[51]
[150] Jacob		[181] Walter
[151] Alan		[182] Richard
[152] Waldeve[47]		[183] Robert
[153] Joseph		[184] Henry
[154] Roger		[185] John
[155] Jacob		[186] Steinketel[52]
[156] Moses		[187] Richer
[157] Alexander		[188] Ambrose
[158] William		[189] Leofwin
[159] Alban		[190] Uthred
[160] Henry		[191] Thomas[53]
[161] Silvester		[192] Alan
[162] Robert		[193] Arkil
[163] Ivo		[194] Wigot
[164] Benedict		[195] Geoffrey
[165] Reginald		[196] Elfred
[166] Aculf		[197] John[54]
[167] Reginald		[198] Silvanus
[168] Isaac		[199] Baynard
[169] Walter		[200] Joel[55]
[170] Turold		[201] Walter
[171] Reginald		[202] Ranulf
[172] Jordan[48]		[203] Asketin
[173] Robert[49]		[204] William

event can be calculated as Dec. 1150, this provides a *terminus post quem* for the writing of this part of the list.

[51] See n. to no. 98.

[52] The corresponding name in the *Liber Vitae* is Stephen, possibly a name in religion (Piper, 'Lists', p. 165).

[53] This may be the prior of Durham (?1161/2–3).

[54] This may be John, archdeacon from *c*.1155–74 (A. I. Doyle, pers. comm. regarding the opinion of H. S. Offler). A green suprascript cross above his name in the manuscript may be a sign of status (Piper, 'Lists', p. 165).

[55] A monk of this name is mentioned in a document assigned to 1155 (Piper, 'Lists', p. 172).

[205]	Elfredus	[218]	Walterius
[206]	Odo	[219]	Willelmus
[207]	Rodbertus	[220]	Ricardus
[208]	Clibertus	[221]	Osmundus[56]
[209]	Alcwinus	[222]	Gilebertus
[210]	Fabianus	[223]	Rodbertus
[211]	Herebertus	[224]	Gregorius
[212]	Hugo	[225]	Petrus
[213]	Gaufridus	[226]	Absalon
[214]	Olaf	[227]	Patricius
[215]	Elwinus	[228]	Suanus
[216]	Constantinus	[229]	Theodbaldus
[217]	Willelmus	[230]	Girardus[a][57]

[56] Nos. 221, 222, 224, 225, and 226 have above them respectively the letters 'd', 'e', 'a', 'b', and 'f'. These were presumably to show that the names had been entered in the wrong order and should be read in the alphabetical order of the small letters (Piper, 'Lists', p. 162).

[205]	Elfred	[218]	Walter
[206]	Odo	[219]	William
[207]	Robert	[220]	Richard
[208]	Clibert	[221]	Osmund[56]
[209]	Alcuin	[222]	Gilbert
[210]	Fabian	[223]	Robert
[211]	Herbert	[224]	Gregory
[212]	Hugh	[225]	Peter
[213]	Geoffrey	[226]	Absalom
[214]	Olaf	[227]	Patrick
[215]	Elfwin	[228]	Swein
[216]	Constantine	[229]	Theobald
[217]	William	[230]	Gerard[57]

[57] The third column begins with a red initial 'V' possibly followed by an erasure; the remainder of the column and the next two leaves are ruled but blank.

^aINCIPIT LIBELLVS DE EXORDIO ATQVE PROCVRSV ISTIVS HOC EST DVNHELMENSIS ECCLESIE.^{a 1}

⟨Liber primus⟩

1. Gloriosi^b quondam regis Northanhymbrorum et preciosi martyris Oswaldi feruentissima in Christo fide, hec sancta ecclesia, uidelicet que in Dei laudem et perpetuam sui tutelam^c ipsas sacre uenerationis reliquias, incorruptum scilicet sanctissimi patris Cuthberti corpus, et eiusdem regis ac martyris caput uenerandum, intra unius loculi conseruat hospitium,² ^dsui status^d ac religionis sacre sumpsit exordium. Licet enim causis existentibus alibi quam ab ipso sit locata, nichilominus tamen stabilitate fidei, dignitate quoque et auctoritate cathedre pontificalis, statu etiam monachice habitationis que ab ipso rege et Aidano pontifice ibidem instituta est, ipsa eadem ecclesia Deo auctore fundata^e permanet.³ Quoniam igitur ^fde ipsa^f quedam ueritate subnixa scribere decreuimus, congruum uidetur ut de ^gfundatoris ipsius^g prefati scilicet regis ingenita secundum carnem nobilitate pauca premittamus.

Siquidem claris admodum natalibus est ortus, non solum patre sed etiam auis dignitate regia precellentibus, fratribus quoque uno ante

---

^a *This heading only in C F; no contemporary heading here in D Fx H L T and Y; Ca in a contemporary hand:* Incipit historia sancte et suauis memorie Simeonis monachi sancti Cuthberti Dunelmi de exordio Christianitatis et religionis tocius Northumbrie et de exortu et processu Lindisfarnensis siue Dunelmensis ecclesie. *Fx L have in early modern archaicizing hands:* Cronica de exordio et progressu ecclesie Dunelmensis. *C has above the contemporary heading in a 15th-cent. hand first the press-mark O and then the heading:* Cronica de exordio et progressu ecclesie Dunelmensis. De registro siue officio cancellariatus ecclesie Dunelmensis.   ^b *With a large decorated initial C F*   ^c inter *add. Fx L Y after* tutelam   ^{d–d} status sui *D Fx H L Y*   ^e est et *add. T*   ^{f–f} *om. H*   ^{g–g} ipsius fundatoris *L*

---

¹ The word *libellus* may carry the implication that the text is intended to prove a case of some sort, hence the translation 'tract', which follows Gransden, *Historical Writing c.550 to c.1307*, p. 115. The word is also used in the title of Reginald of Durham, *Libellus de admirandis beati Cuthberti uirtutibus quae nouellis patratae sunt temporibus* (Raine, *Cuth. virt.*), where, given the length of the work (almost three hundred printed pages), the meaning cannot be 'little book' any more than in the case of *LDE*. 'Tract' would certainly be an appropriate translation in the case of another late 11th- or 12th-cent. Durham text, *Libellus de iniusta uexacione Willelmi episcopi primi* (Offler, *DIV*), which was written to defend the reputation of William of Saint-Calais, bishop of Durham (1080–96). The title in Ca, p. 131, may be translated: 'Here begins the history of the holy Symeon of good memory, monk of St Cuthbert's church in Durham, concerning the origin of the Christian

HERE BEGINS THE TRACT ON THE ORIGINS AND
PROGRESS OF THIS THE CHURCH OF DURHAM.[1]

⟨Book i⟩

1. This venerable church derived its status and its divine religion
from the fervent faith in Christ of the former glorious king of the
Northumbrians and estimable martyr Oswald. In praise of God and
under his perpetual guardianship it preserves those relics of devout
veneration, the undecayed body of the most saintly father Cuthbert
and the venerable head of that same king and martyr Oswald, both
lodged in a single shrine.[2] Although for various reasons this church
no longer stands in the place where Oswald founded it, nevertheless
by virtue of the constancy of its faith, the dignity and authority of its
episcopal throne, and the status of the dwelling-place of monks
established there by the king himself and by Bishop Aidan, it is
still the very same church founded by God's command.[3] Therefore,
because we have resolved to write about this church on the basis of
truth, it seems proper to include by way of introduction a few words
about the nobility of the flesh inherited by its founder King Oswald.

He was indeed of distinguished birth, for not only his father but
also his forefathers were pre-eminent in royal majesty—and his
brothers also, one before him and the other after him—were

religion in the whole of Northumbria and concerning the origin and progress of the church
of Lindisfarne or in other words Durham.'

[2] Oswald was king of the Northumbrians (634–42); on the problems of dating his reign
and those of other early Northumbrian kings, see D. P. Kirby, *The Earliest English Kings*
(London, 1991), pp. 77–112. On Oswald's career and the history of his relics, see *Oswald:
Northumbrian King and European Saint*, ed. C. Stancliffe and E. Cambridge (Stamford,
1995), and below, pp. 18–25. Cuthbert was bishop of Lindisfarne (685–7) and a hermit on
the Inner Farne island. On his career and relics, see Bonner, *Cuthbert*, and Battiscombe,
Relics. When St Cuthbert's shrine was opened in 1104, the head of St Oswald and
numerous relics of other saints were found with Cuthbert's undecayed body, and it was the
only relic to be allowed to remain with that body. See *De miraculis* c. 7 (*Sym. Op.* i. 252,
255); see also R. N. Bailey, 'St Oswald's heads', in *Oswald: Northumbrian King*, pp. 164–
77, and below, pp. 102–3.

[3] A central theme of *LDE* is the transference of the church of Lindisfarne, first to
Chester-le-Street (Co. Durham) in 883 and then in 995 to Durham itself. The monastic
community to which the author of *LDE* belonged had in fact only been established in
1083, although he here implies that it could trace its history back to the time of King
Oswald. Aidan was an Irishman from Iona who came in 635 at King Oswald's request to
evangelize Northumbria, and established the church of Lindisfarne. He died on 31 Aug.
651. See below, pp. 24–5, and, for Aidan's career, Bede, *HE* iii. 3, 5, 14–17, 26.

altero uero post illum regni apice pollentibus. Erat nanque filius potentissimi regis Ethelfridi, cuius pater Ethelricus rex, cuius pater Ida rex, *a quo* (ut[a] Beda refert) *regalis Northanhymbrorum prosapia* cepit[b] originem.[4] Nec ʿtantum paterna,ʿ sed et materna quoque origine clarissimam duxit genealogiam, ex sorore uidelicet[d] Edwini regis procreatus.[5] Sed progenitoribus fidei Christiane prorsus[e] ignaris, ille ut rosa de spinis effloruit, salutari utique fonte Christo[f] regeneratus, atque ipsa sacrosancta regeneratione dignissime uiuens.[6] Regno enim potitus, gentem sibi subditam secum mox Christo subdidit, utpote in uerbo fidei pontifici Aidano socius et cooperator existens egregius. Predicante nanque in sua (id est Scottorum) lingua episcopo, ille qui hanc eque ut suam perfecte nouerat rex utique regis eterni minister deuotus assistere, et fidus interpres fidei ducibus suis ac ministris ministrare solebat[g] uerba salutis.[7] Verum qualis quantusque fuerit, [h]quante erga fidei religionem deuotionis,[h] quanteque in pauperes misericordie ac benignitatis, et quam maxime inter curas regni deditus orationi, que et quanta post mortem illius ad indicium eius iam cum Christo uiuentis claruerint miracula, *Ecclesiastica Gentis Anglorum* Beda describente declarat *Hystoria*.[8]

[i]Porro hic nos id studium[i] occupat ut [j]ex huius sancte hoc est[j] [k]ecclesie Dunhelmensis[k] exordio, procursu, queque in prefata historia aliis quoque opusculis inueniri poterant, ad memoriam posterorum in unum ex ordine compacta, quoddam libelli corpusculum perficiant.

---

    [a] *om. H*   [b] sumpsit *H L Y*   [c-c] paterna tantum *Fx L Y*   [d] *om. Fx*
L Y   [e] penitus *Ca*   [f] *om. Fx L Y*   [g] *om. T*   [h-h] *om. D Fx H L Y*
[i-i] hic nos id studii *Ca D H C* (*corr. to* studium *C*); id nos hic studii *F*   [j-j] ex hoc
huius sancte *H*   [k-k] Dunelmensis ecclesie *F*

    [4] The statement about Ida's rule is from Bede, *HE* v. 24. Oswald's father was
Æthelfrith, king of the Bernicians (592–604) and king of the Northumbrians (604–16);
the forefathers (whose dates are very uncertain) were Æthelric, king of the Bernicians
(568–72); and Ida (547–59). The brothers were Eanfrith, king of the Bernicians (633–4),
and Oswiu, king of the Bernicians (642–55) and of the Northumbrians (655–70). Eanfrith
was in fact an apostate, killed by King Cædwalla of Gwynedd (Bede, *HE* iii. 1). Bede does
not mention Æthelric nor the family relationships set out here. They could have been
derived directly or indirectly from 9th-cent. Old English genealogies (D. Dumville, 'The
Anglian collection of royal genealogies and regnal lists', *Anglo-Saxon England*, v (1976),
23–50), and they are actually to be found in the list of kings of the Northumbrians and
England inserted after the table of chapter headings for *LDE* in Ca, pp. 129–30 (Arnold,
Sym. Op. ii. 389–92).
    [5] Bede, *HE* iii. 6, states that Oswald was the nephew of Edwin, king of the North-
umbrians (616–33), through his sister Acha. For a discussion of the chronological
difficulties surrounding his death and the possibility that his reign really extended from
617–34, see Kirby, *Earliest English Kings*, p. 67, and Rollason, *Sources*, pp. 46–7.

mighty in the kingdom's highest office. For Oswald was the son of the most powerful King Æthelfrith, whose father was King Æthelric, son of King Ida, from whom (as Bede relates) the royal family of the Northumbrians was descended.[4] Moreover, Oswald's outstandingly distinguished lineage derived not only from his father's side but also from his mother's, for she was the sister of King Edwin.[5] But on the stock of his ancestors who were utterly ignorant of the Christian faith, he bloomed like a rose amongst thorns, for he had been reborn in Christ in the font of salvation, and he lived as one most worthy of that sacred rebirth.[6] Once he had gained possession of his kingdom, he soon caused his people to become subjects of Christ like himself, since in the word of faith he was the distinguished colleague and collaborator of Bishop Aidan. When the bishop was preaching in his own language (that is Irish), the king, who knew it as perfectly as his own, was accustomed to stand beside him as the devoted servant of the eternal king, and to act as a faithful interpreter, administering the words of salvation to his counts and thegns.[7] How great and what manner of man he was is set out in Bede's *Ecclesiastical History of the English People*: how deep his devotion was to the Christian faith, how much mercy and kindliness he showed to the poor, how earnestly he devoted himself to prayer even in the midst of the cares of his kingdom, and after his death how many and what kind of miracles were worked as a sign that he was already dwelling with Christ.[8]

Our present purpose is that everything concerning the origin and progress of this church of Durham which could be found in Bede's *History* and in other little works should, in order to preserve its memory for posterity, be assembled and arranged to form the substance of this tract. We also believe it proper to add to the

---

[6] Bede, *HE* iii. 3, states simply that Oswald had been baptized a Christian while Edwin was king and he was in exile amongst the Scots. According to the *Vita Oswaldi* attributed to Reginald of Durham, Oswald derived his Christian doctrine from Acha, with whom he is said to have fled on Edwin's accession (Arnold, *Sym. Op.* i. 341; cf. 344, 385). It seems likely, however, that this text, written in 1165 (Arnold, *Sym. Op.* i. 382), was merely embroidering the account in *LDE* in a plausible way. Note e.g. the similarity of its phraseology 'de spineto pagane gentis uelut florens rosa' (p. 344) and *LDE*'s 'ut rosa de spinis effloruit'.

[7] Bede, *HE* iii. 3.

[8] Bede, *HE* iii. 1–2, 9–13; iv. 14. For the miracles, see further Rollason, *Saints and Relics*, pp. 26–7, 101–2, 102–3, 104, 110–11, C. Stancliffe, 'Where was Oswald killed?', in *Oswald: Northumbrian King*, pp. 84–96, at 90–6, and A. T. Thacker, '*Membra disjecta*: The division of the body and the diffusion of the cult', ibid., pp. 97–127, at 101, 104, 107, 108, 114.

Nonnulla etiam, que defectu scriptorum litteris non fuerant tradita, seniorum autem ueracium relatione qui ea uel uiderant, uel a patribus suis uiris religiosis fideque dignissimis qui interfuere sepius audierant, ad nostram notitiam peruenerunt, uel que et nos ipsi uidimus, his que ex aliorum scriptis collecta sunt adiungenda credimus.[9]

[i] **2.** Anno[a] igitur Dominice Incarnationis sexcentesimo tricesimo quinto, qui est annus[b] [c]aduentus Anglorum[c] in Brittanniam centesimus octogesimus octauus, aduentus uero sancti Augustini tricesimus nonus, piissimus rex Osuualdus secundo imperii sui anno *uenienti ad se* Aidano sedem episcopalem *in insula Lindisfarnensi* constituit,[10] ubi et ipse antistes iubente,[d] suffragante et cooperante rege, monachorum qui secum uenerant habitationem instituit, hoc illis [e]rege scilicet[e] et episcopo procurantibus, ut et[f] pontificali auctoritate fides roboraretur nouella, et monachica institutione semper in posterum caperet [i (H)] augmentum religionis obseruantia. Vnde[g] sicut[h] legimus et seniorum traditione percepimus, ad ipsius ecclesie presulatum monachi solebant eligi, exemplo nimirum primi antistitis Aidani qui et monachus erat, et monachicam [i]uitam cum suis omnibus[i] agere solebat.[11] Quod ab anno Incarnationis Dominice sexcentesimo tricesimo quinto obseruatum est usque[j] annum Incarnationis eiusdem millesimum septuagesimum secundum, quando de clericali ordine in episcopatum [k]est consecratus[k] uir religiosus de Hlothariorum gente Gualcherus. Nam inter episcopos nec commemorandum arbitror illum, qui multo

---

[a] Omnes (Quod *T*) episcopi a sancto Aydano usque ad Walcherum preter unum symoniacum monachi fuerunt *rubric Fx T Y*; De sancto Aidano primo episcopo Lindisfarnense *rubric in marg. H*   [b] *om. Y*   [c‑c] Anglorum aduentus *H*   [d] et *add. Fx L Y*   [e‑e] scilicet rege *Fx L Y*   [f] *om. Fx H L Y*   [g] Omnes episcopi a sancto Aydano usque ad Walcherum preter unum simoniacum monachi *rubric H*   [h] *om. H*   [i‑i] cum suis omnibus uitam *Fx L Y*   [j] ad *add. Fx L*   [k‑k] consecratus est *Ca*

---

[9] For *LDE's* sources, see above, pp. xlviii–lxxxvi.

[10] The establishment of the see of Lindisfarne is described by Bede, *HE* iii. 3, from which the words italicized here are taken, but he gave no date, writing only 'soon after he [Oswald] acceded to the kingdom'. In *HE* v. 24, he gave the date of St Augustine's arrival as 597, which conforms with *LDE's* statement here, but that for the coming of the English as 449, which does not. *LDE's* statement agrees rather with Bede's dating in *HE* ii. 14, where he gives 627 as 'about 180 years after the coming of the English to Britain'. The date 635 is given in ASC, *s.a.*, in *ALf*, *s.a.*, and JW ii. 90–1, where a marginal note, probably by John of Worcester and possibly derived from *LDE*, says of Aidan: 'per quem et per ipsum clarissimum et sanctissimum Oswaldum in prouincia Berniciorum primum funditur ecclesia Christi et instituitur'. Bede notes Aidan's death in 651 (*HE* v. 24) and that this

information collected from the writings of others a number of facts
which have not been handed down in written form because of a lack
of writers to record them, but which have either come to our notice
through the truthful accounts of our elders, who had seen the events
themselves or had often heard them related by their own elders who
were religious and most trustworthy men and who had been present
at them, or which we have witnessed ourselves.[9]

2. In the year of Our Lord's Incarnation 635, which is the one [i]
hundredth and eighty-eighth year from the coming of the English
into Britain and the thirty-ninth from the arrival of St Augustine, the
most pious king Oswald, who was then in the second year of his reign,
received Aidan and established for him an episcopal see on the island
of Lindisfarne.[10] There that bishop, by the order of the king and with
his support and co-operation, established a dwelling-place for the
monks who had accompanied him. The king and the bishop saw to
this so that the new faith should be strengthened by pontifical
authority, and so that religious observance should always afterwards
gain increase through the monastic institution. For this reason, as we [i (H)]
read and also learn from the traditions of our elders, it was customary
for monks to be elected as bishops of this church, following doubtless
the example of the first bishop Aidan who was a monk and
accustomed to lead the monastic life together with all his companions.[11] This practice was observed from the year of the Incarnation
of Our Lord 635 until the year of the Incarnation 1072, when
Walcher, a religious man of the Lotharingian race, was chosen
from the order of clerks to be consecrated bishop. For I do not
judge it proper to commemorate amongst the bishops the one who as

was when he had been bishop for seventeen years (*HE* iii. 26, 17 (16)) which is consistent
with the date 635. On the use of 'multiple datings' of the type given here, see K.-U.
Jäschke, 'Remarks on datings in the *Libellus de exordio atque procursu istius hoc est
Dunhelmensis ecclesie*', in Rollason, *Symeon*, pp. 46–60. For references to the foundation
of Lindisfarne in Irish annals, Anderson, *Early Sources*, i. 148. For the history and
character of Lindisfarne in the Anglo-Saxon period, see D. O'Sullivan and R. Young,
English Heritage Book of Lindisfarne (London, 1994), cc. 4–5.

[11] See below, pp. 160–1. On the constitution of Lindisfarne, see Bede, *V. Cuth.* c. 16;
and Bede, *HE* iv. 27 (25); and for the influence on arrangements at Lindisfarne of Irish
monastic *paruchiae*, see K. Hughes, *The Church in Early Irish Society* (London, 1966),
pp. 82–3, although reference should also be made to R. Sharpe, 'Some problems
concerning the organization of the church in early medieval Ireland', *Peritia* iii (1984),
230–70, where Hughes's views on the monastic character of the early Irish church are
questioned.

ante de clero per symoniacam heresim ordinatus,[a] sed morte preuentus nullum episcopale officium est facere permissus.[12]

At ut ad propositum redeatur, Aidanus ipsius ecclesie primus et[b]
presul et monachus omnibus sibi successuris et episcopis et monachis
in uia Domini qua precesserat se sequendum premonstrauit.
Cuius uitam cum multa laude uenerabilis Beda prosecutus esset, '*Vt multa*',
inquit, '*breuiter comprehendam, quantum ab eis qui illum nouere
didicimus, nichil ex omnibus que in euangelicis siue apostolicis siue[c]
propheticis litteris facienda cognouerat, pretermittere, sed cuncta pro suis
uiribus [d]operibus[e] explere[d] curabat.*'[13]

Huius presulatus anno octauo, regni autem sui nono, sanctissimus
ac piissimus rex Oswaldus, primus in tota Berniciorum gente
signifer fidei Christiane, et fundator ecclesie Lindisfarnensis, ex
qua omnium eiusdem prouincie ecclesiarum manarunt primordia, a
paganis in bello prostratus occubuit.[14] Cuius *caput in cimiterio ecclesie
prefate, manus* uero *cum brachiis* quas rex interfector a corpore
precidi iusserat, in urbe regia [f]condite sunt,[f][15] dextera cum brachio
uotum benedictionis [g]Aidani episcopi[g] per incorruptionem prefer-
ente, que etiam ad nostram usque etatem utriusque meritum [h]regis
scilicet[h] et pontificis gratia sue incorruptionis ostendit, sicut nostre
(hoc est Dunhelmensis) ecclesie monachus uenerande caniciei et
multe simplicitatis uocabulo Swartebrandus[i] qui nuper [j]Willelmo
episcopatum[j] administrante defunctus est [k]sepius se uidisse attes-
tatus[l] est.[k] Nam ut Beda narrat, die sancto pasche sedente ad
mensam rege, cum [m]discus illi *argenteus*[m] esset *appositus epulis
regalibus refertus, subito* nuntiatur multitudinem pauperum in
platea sedere, et elemosine [n]aliquid a rege[n] expectare. Nec mora
dapes sibimet appositas pauperibus deferri, et eundem discum inter
eos precepit *minutatim diuidi*. Quo facto pietatis pontifex[o] qui
assidebat delectatus, apprehendens dexteram eius, ait, '*Nunquam*

[a] ordinatus est *Fx L*   [b] *om. T*   [c] uel (*Bede, p. 266*); siue *over erasure*
BL, *Cotton Tiberius C.ii and A.xiv* (*Plummer, Bede, i. 161 n. 4*); siue *DCL, B.II.35,*
fo. 134[r]   [d-d] explere operibus *Fx L Y*   [e] *om. H*   [f-f] sunt condite *H*
[g-g] episcopi Aidani *Fx L Y*   [h-h] scilicet regis *Fx L Y*   [i] Svartebrandus *F*
[j-j] episcopatum Willelmo *Ca*   [k-k] *om. H*   [l] testatus *L*   [m-m] illi
discus argenteus *H*; discus argenteus illi *Fx L*   [n-n] a rege aliquid *D H L Y*
[o] episcopus *T*

[12] This was Eadred (c.1040; below, pp. 168–9, 194–5), erroneously identified as
Sexhelm (bishop of Chester-le-Street for six months at some time between 942 and
946) by B. Meehan, 'Notes on the preliminary texts and continuations to Symeon of
Durham's *Libellus de exordio*', in Rollason, *Symeon*, pp. 128–39, at 129.

a clerk was ordained bishop long ago through the heresy of simony, but was prevented by death from fulfilling the episcopal office.[12]

To return to our theme, Aidan, the first bishop and monk of this church, showed to all those bishops and monks who will come after him that they should follow in the way of the Lord as he had done before them. The venerable Bede described the course of his life with much praise: 'To summarize many things briefly, so far as we can learn from those who knew him, he strove to neglect nothing which he had learned from the writings of the evangelists, the apostles, and the prophets should be done, but he did everything in his power to put these things into practice in his deeds.'[13]

In the eighth year of Aidan's episcopate and the ninth year of Oswald's reign, that most saintly and pious king, the first standard-bearer of the Christian faith in the whole of the people of the Bernicians, and the founder of the church of Lindisfarne, from which all the churches of the Bernician kingdom originated, was overthrown and killed in battle by the heathens.[14] His head was buried in the cemetery of the church of Lindisfarne; his hands and arms, which the king who had killed him had ordered to be cut off, were preserved in the royal city.[15] The right hand with the arm bears witness in its preservation from decay to Bishop Aidan's blessing on it, and right down to our own age it demonstrates by virtue of its undecayed state the merits of both the king and the bishop. Swartebrand, a monk of our church of Durham, a venerable white-haired man of great honesty who died recently during the time that William was governing the bishopric, attested that he had often seen it. For as Bede narrates, when the king was sitting at table on the holy day of Easter and a silver dish loaded with a royal feast had been set before him, it was suddenly announced to him that a multitude of poor people were sitting in the courtyard and expecting something in the way of alms from the king. At once he ordered the feast set for him to be carried to the poor, and the dish itself to be divided up in pieces among them. The bishop who was sitting by was delighted by this act of piety and, seizing the king's

[13] Bede's words are from *HE* iii. 17.
[14] Oswald was killed in battle against Penda, the pagan king of the Mercians (d. 654), at the battle of *Maserfelth* in 642 (Bede, *HE* iii. 9, v. 24). Aird, *Cuthbert*, p. 15, interprets the account of Lindisfarne in this sentence to mean that it was regarded as 'the mother-church of Bernicia'; but, although possible, this does not seem to be required by the Latin.
[15] The italicized words concerning the arm and head of Oswald are from Bede, *HE* iii. 12. From *HE* iii.6 it is clear that the 'royal city' was Bamburgh (Northumberland).

inueterascat hec manus.[^a][16] Porro ossa illius in monasterium[^b] quod in prouincia Lindissi[^c] [^d]situm est,[^d] translata sunt.[17]

3. Peractis[^e] in episcopatu decem et septem annis presul Aidanus uiam patrum est ingressus, cui mors temporalis letum uite alterius pandebat introitum.[^f][18] Cuius [^g]sullimium in Christo[^g] meritorum gloriam, etiam miraculorum quibus et ante et post mortem sullimiter effulserat, tercio superius memorate hystorie declarante libro testantur indicia.[19] Huius ad celos felicem triumphum celestium agminum choris eximia cum claritate deducentibus, 'ille Israhelita in quo dolus non erat,'[20] in carne non secundum carnem uiuens,[21] ille[^h] cuius a puero [^i]tota conuersatio erat[^i] in celis,[^j][22] ille inquam conuersationis angelice iuuenis egregius, sanctissimus uidelicet[^k] Cuthbertus uidere promeruit. Nam cum pastor futurus animarum, agens in montibus custodiam pecorum iuxta fluuium Leder solus secretis pernoctaret in orationibus,[^l] iamque studio et amore totus in celum raperetur, tante glorie ac beatitudinis contemplatione dignus habebatur. Qua uisione dilectus Deo adolescens incitatus ad subeundum artioris propositi gradum, ad promerendam inter magnificos uiros altioris premii gloriam, mane facto statim *commendans suis pecora que pascebat dominis*, perfectioris uite gratia *monasterium petere decreuit*.[23]

[ii]   Anno[^m] enim Dominice Incarnationis sexcentesimo quinquagesimo primo, ab aduentu uero sancti Augustini in Brittaniam quinquagesimo quinto, ex quo autem[^n] prouincia Berniciorum industria[^o] regis

---

[^a]: inueterascat, *Bede, HE*; inueterascat *BL, Cotton Tiberius A.xiv (s. viii^{med}), C.ii (s. viii²)* and *DCL, B.II.35 (s. xi^{ex}), fo. 126′*,   [^b]: de Barthenay *add. Fx L H Y*   [^c]: Lindisfarnensi *D*   [^d–d]: est situm *Fx L Y*   [^e]: Moritur sanctus Aidanus (episcopus et monachus *add. T) rubric Fx T*   [^f]: *om. H*   [^g–g]: in Christo sublimium *Ca*   [^h]: *om. D Fx H L Y*   [^i–i]: erat tota conuersatio *D*; erat conuersatio *Fx H Y*; conuersatio erat *L*   [^j]: celo *H*   [^k]: *om. T*   [^l]: montibus *H*   [^m]: Sanctus Cuthbertus factus est monachus *rubric Fx H T Y*   [^n]: enim *Fx L Y*   [^o]: per industriam *T*

---

[16] The story of Aidan's blessing is from Bede, *HE* iii. 6, somewhat reordered, with the italicized words verbatim. For Swartebrand, see above, pp. 6–7, n. 19. It is not clear where Swartebrand had seen the arm. There is no trace of it in the Durham relic-lists (I. G. Thomas, 'The cult of saints' relics in medieval England', Ph.D. thesis (London, 1974), *s.u.*). Possibly there was still an arm-relic at Bamburgh at the beginning of the 12th cent.; possibly Swartebrand had seen it at Peterborough where the arm of St Oswald was a highly prized relic (see *The Chronicle of Hugh Candidus*, ed. W. T. Mellows (Oxford, 1949), p. 52, and Reginald of Durham, *Vita Oswaldi*, c. 48 (Arnold, *Sym. Op.* i. 374–5)). See also Rollason, *Saints and Relics*, pp. 26, 27–8.

[17] For the translation of Oswald's body to Bardney (Lincs.) by his niece Osthryth, see Bede, *HE* iii. 11, and A. T. Thacker, '*Membra disjecta*: the division of the body and the

right hand, he said: 'May this hand never decay.'[16] The king's
bones, however, were translated to a monastery situated in the
kingdom of Lindsey.[17]

3. After seventeen years as bishop, Aidan went the way of his fathers,
and temporal death opened for him a joyous entrance to another life.[18]
As the third book of Bede's *History* describes, signs bore witness to
the glory of his sublime merits in Christ and also of the miracles with
which he was blazoned forth before and after his death.[19] The one
who was worthy to witness him being led up to heaven with
extraordinary radiance and in happy triumph by the heavenly hosts
was 'that Israelite in whom there was no guile',[20] living in the flesh
but not in the way of the flesh,[21] he whose whole life had from his
boyhood been directed towards heaven,[22] that distinguished youth, I
say, who lived like the angels, the most holy Cuthbert himself. For
when the future shepherd of souls was keeping watch over his flocks
in the mountains near the river Leader and was passing the night
alone in secret prayers, he was bodily carried up into heaven through
his striving and love, and was held worthy to contemplate such great
glory and blessedness. Exultant from this vision, the youth beloved of
God was inspired to submit to the rule of a stricter way of life in order
that he might merit, along with distinguished men, the glory of a
higher prize. In the morning he at once handed over the flocks he was
caring for to their masters and decided to seek a monastery in order to
follow a more perfect way of life.[23]

In the year of the Incarnation of Our Lord 651, the fifty-fifth from [ii]
the arrival of St Augustine in Britain, but the seventeenth from the
year in which the kingdom of the Bernicians received the faith of
Christ through the diligence of King Oswald, the year in which

diffusion of the cult', in *Oswald: Northumbrian King*, ed. Stancliffe and Cambridge, pp. 97–
127, at 104–5. Oswald's body was subsequently translated from Bardney to Gloucester in
909; see ASC, *s.a.* 909, and *Willelmi Malmesbiriensis monachi, De gestis pontificum Anglorum
libri quinque*, ed. N. E. S. A. Hamilton (RS lii; London, 1870), p. 293; see also D. Rollason,
'St Oswald in post-Conquest England', *Oswald: Northumbrian King*, ed. Stancliffe and
Cambridge, pp. 164–77, at 168.

[18] Bede, *HE* iii. 14, 17, gives Aidan's death as 31 August after completing seventeen
years as bishop, which is consistent with the date of 651 given by JW ii. 100–1.

[19] Bede, *HE* iii. 6, 14, 15, 17.

[20] John 1: 47; quoted in Bede, *V. Cuth.* c. 6.

[21] Cf. Rom. 8: 13, 8: 4; Cor. 10: 3.   [22] Phil. 3: 20.

[23] The italicized words concerning Cuthbert's decision are from Bede, *V. Cuth.* c. 4.
The river is the Leader Water, which flows south from the Lammermuir Hills to the river
Tweed at Melrose.

Oswaldi fidem Christi perceperat[a] anno septimo decimo, quo pontifex Aidanus ad celestia transiit, qui est annus imperii regis Oswiu nonus, iuuenis ille sanctissimus Christo soli famulaturus monasterium Mailrosense intrauit,[24] susceptus a reuerentissimo abbate Eata, suggerente ei de Cuthberto Boisilo eximie sanctitatis et prophetici spiritus uiro, qui ipsum monasterium secundus ab abbate prepositi iure gubernabat. Iunctus fratrum consortio, qualis quantusque fuerit, quam maioris super ceteros uirtutis per obseruantiam[b] discipline regularis, per instantiam legendi, operandi, uigilandi, *ab omni quod inebriare potest* abstinendi, et per exercitia cuiusque pii laboris, in libro uite ipsius[c] luculento sermone Beda prosequitur.[25]

Et ut nos plurima paucis comprehendamus, factus est monachus. [d]Plane monachus![d] Monachus inquam uenerabilis ac per cuncta digne[e] laudabilis, corpore, mente, habitu castris [f]associatus dominicis.[f][26] Hunc beatus Boisilus pro insita illi[g] puritate ac pia intentione pre ceteris dilexit, et scripturarum scientia erudiuit, sicut in hac ecclesia seruatus codex, in quo eo docente ipse didicerat, per tanta annorum curricula prisca nouitate ac decore mirabilis hodieque demonstrat.[27]

---

   [a] conceperat *T*   [b] obedientiam *Fx L Y*   [c] illius *H L*   [d-d] *om. Fx L Y*   [e] *om. Fx L*   [f-f] dominicis associatus *F H*   [g] sibi *Ca*

[24] The story of Cuthbert's vision makes it clear that his entry into Melrose was in the same year as Aidan's death, i.e. 651. This is consistent with the ninth year of the reign of Oswiu, king of the Northumbrians (642–70). JW ii. 100 records the event in a contemporary marginal note against the year 651. Melrose figured prominently in Bede's writings as Boisil's monastery where Cuthbert first became a monk. See, for example, Bede, *HE* iv. 27 (25), and Bede, *V. Cuth.* c. 6. The site of Melrose is presumed to be that of Old Melrose, a promontory in the river Tweed, approximately two miles downstream of Melrose, where there is a later chapel and an earthen bank cutting off the neck of the promontory (NT 587 340). See C. Thomas, *The Early Christian Archaeology of North Britain* (Oxford, 1971), pp. 35–6, fig. 11, and M. R. Wakeford, 'The British church and Anglo-Saxon expansion: the evidence of saints' cults', Ph.D. thesis (Durham, 1998), pp. 21–3. For the possibility that some but not all members of the monastery exercised pastoral functions, see C. Cubitt, in Blair and Sharpe, *Pastoral Care*, pp. 203–4; cf. Thacker, ibid., p. 166, and S. Foot, '"By water in the spirit": the administration of baptism in early Anglo-Saxon England', ibid., pp. 171–92, at 175, 186.

[25] Bede, *V. Cuth.* c. 6, citing Judg. 13 and Num. 6: 3. Cf. Bede, *HE* iv. 27 (25). The gloss on the role of the provost is not found in that text. Eata, who was a pupil of Bishop Aidan, was abbot of Melrose, then abbot of Lindisfarne, and subsequently bishop of Hexham (678–81, 685–6) and Lindisfarne (681–5); Boisil was prior of Melrose, dying of plague in *c.*660 or 661; see *The Blackwell Encyclopaedia of Anglo-Saxon England*, ed. M. Lapidge, J. Blair, S. Keynes, and D. Scragg (Oxford, 1998), *s.u.*, and, further on Eata, below, pp. 32–3. On the possible significance of *LDE*'s allusion to the Rule, see above, pp. lxxxiii–lxxxv.

[26] According to *LDE* (below, pp. 228–31), almost all the secular clerks of Durham Cathedral were expelled in 1083 to make way for Benedictine monks from Monkwearmouth and Jarrow who formed Durham Cathedral Priory as it subsisted throughout the Middle Ages. Symeon's repeated emphasis on Cuthbert's status as a monk here may have

Bishop Aidan went to heaven, being the ninth year of the reign of King Oswiu, that most holy young man Cuthbert entered the monastery of Melrose to serve Christ only.[24] There he was received by the most reverend abbot Eata, to whom he was introduced by Boisil, a man of outstanding sanctity and prophetic spirit who was provost and therefore ruled the monastery in second place after the abbot. In the book about his life, Bede describes in lucid terms what Cuthbert was like and how great he was when he had been enrolled in the company of the brothers, how his virtue excelled that of the others in his observance of the discipline of the Rule, in his attention to reading, good works, vigils, abstention from any intoxicating liquor, and in the exercise of every pious labour.[25]

To express many things in few words, he became a monk. Wholly a monk! A monk, I say, venerable and in all respects worthy of praise, and one who was in body, mind, and way of life a dweller in the camps of the Lord.[26] The blessed Boisil loved him more than all the others for the purity which was rooted in his soul and for his striving after piety, and he grounded him in knowledge of the scriptures, as is shown in our day by a book which is preserved in this church and which was one from which Cuthbert learned under Boisil's instruction—it is a wonderful thing that after so many years it retains its original newness and elegance.[27] When Boisil had been taken up to

been intended to underpin the claim that the church of St Cuthbert, first at Lindisfarne, then at Chester-le-Street, and finally at Durham, had always been a church of monks, and so therefore the introduction of monks in 1083 was justified (see above, Introduction, pp. lxxxii–lxxxiii, and references therein). It is also consistent with Symeon's claim that the bishop of that church had, with only insignificant exceptions, always been a monk - a veiled criticism perhaps of Ranulf Flambard, bishop of Durham (1099–1128), who was not a monk (see below, pp. 197–9). See further Piper, in Bonner, *Cuthbert*, pp. 439–41; and, on Symeon's attitude to Ranulf Flambard, Aird, in Rollason, *Symeon*, pp. 42–5

[27] Bede, *V. Cuth.* c. 8, describes how on his death-bed Boisil, who knew he had only seven days to live, said to Cuthbert, 'I have a book [of the evangelist John] consisting of seven gatherings of which we can get through one every day, with the Lord's help, reading it and discussing it between ourselves so far as is necessary.' That a book thought to have been this one was preserved at Durham is shown by the entry in the 14th-cent. relic-list of the church of *Liber sancti Boisili magistri sancti Cuthberti*. This book may in fact have been the early 8th-cent. copy of the gospel of St John (the Stonyhurst Gospel, now on loan to the British Library (Loan 74)) , which has a 12th-cent. inscription stating that it was found with Cuthbert's body at his translation in 1104, and this may in turn have been the 'beati Cuthberti libellus precipui honoris' which, according to Reginald of Durham, Hugh of le Puiset showed to William, archbishop of York. See R. A. B. Mynors, 'The Stonyhurst Gospel, (a) Textual description and history', Battiscombe, *Relics*, pp. 358–60, *The Stonyhurst Gospel of St John*, ed. T. J. Brown (Roxburghe Club; Oxford, 1969), and *Codices latini antiquiores*, ed. E. A. Lowe (11 vols. and supplement, Oxford, 1934–71; 2nd edn. of vol. ii, 1972), ii. 260.

Translato*a* ad celestia Boisilo, uir Domini Cuthbertus in prepositi officium magistro successit, et cotidiano uirtutum profectu equiperare uel etiam supergredi contendit.[28] Qui quam studiose uerbo et exemplo uniuersos ad celestia uocauerit, quam sullimiter miraculorum gloria choruscauerit, quanta gratie prophetalis luce*b* prefulserit, qui nosse desiderat, prefatum uite ipsius*c* librum legat.

4. Successit*d* autem Aidano in episcopatum Finan, ab eadem gente et monasterio unde et predecessor eius fuerat missus. *Qui in insula Lindisfarnensi fecit ecclesiam sedi episcopali congruam, quam tempore sequente reuerentissimus archiepiscopus Theodorus in honore beati Petri apostoli dedicauit, sed episcopus loci ipsius*e* Eadbertus,* de quo in sequentibus dicemus, *ablata arundine plumbi laminis eam totam (hoc est et*f* tectum et ipsos quoque parietes eius*g*) cooperire curauit.*[29]

Ab *h*hoc episcopo*h* (scilicet*i* Finano) princeps Mediterraneorum Anglorum Peada in prouincia Northanhymbrorum baptizatus est *et acceptis quattuor presbiteris, qui ad docendam baptizandamque gentem illius eruditione et uita uidebantur idonei, multo cum gaudio reuersus est.*[30] Nec multo post rex Orientalium Saxonum Sigbertus ab eodem episcopo lauacrum salutis accepit. Siquidem prouincia illa fidem quam olim expulso Mellito antistite abiecerat, industria regis Oswiu*j* conuerso ad fidem Christi rege prefato recepit, predicante ibi uerbum Christi de natione Anglorum presbitero et Lindisfarnensis ecclesie monacho Cedd a rege Oswiu*k* illuc in hoc ipsum misso, qui prius etiam apud Mediterraneos Anglos uerbo predicationis multum fructificauerat. Cum ergo in prouincia Orientalium Saxonum *multam Domino ecclesiam congregasset, contigit quodam tempore ut ad Lindisfarnensem ecclesiam propter colloquium Finani episcopi* rediret. *Qui ubi prosperatum*l* ei opus euuangelii comperit, fecit eum episcopum in gente*

---

a Translatoque *Fx L Y*   *b* uite *L*   *c* illius *D H Y*   *d* Successit Aydano Fynan, qui construxit Lindisfarnensem ecclesiam et dedicari fecit *rubric Fx*; Aydano succedit Finanus *rubric T*; De episcopo Finano *rubric H*   *e* illius *Fx L*   *f* om. *Fx L*   *g* om. *Fx L Y*   *h–h* episcopo hoc *H*   *i* om. *Fx L Y*   *j* Oswyni *Fx L*   *k* Oswyno *Fx L*; Owyn *with a final letter erased Y*   *l* prosperum *Fx L*

---

[28] Bede, *V. Cuth.* c. 9, and *HE* iv. 27.

[29] This chapter is drawn largely verbatim from Bede, *HE* iii. 25. Finan, who came from Iona, was bishop of Lindisfarne from 651 to 661, Eadberht from 688 to 698 (on him, see below, pp. 54–5); on Theodore, who was archbishop of Canterbury from 668–90, see M. Lapidge, 'The career of Archbishop Theodore', *Archbishop Theodore: Commemorative Studies in his Life and Influence*, ed. M. Lapidge (Cambridge Studies in Anglo-Saxon England, xi; Cambridge, 1995), pp. 1–29. No remains of the church referred to here have survived (see below, p. 54 n. 68).

heaven, Cuthbert, the man of God, succeeded his master in the office of provost, and daily he strove to equal or to surpass him by the increase of his virtue.[28] Anyone who desires to know how strenuously he summoned everyone to heaven by word and by example, how sublimely he radiated the glory of miracles, what light of prophetic grace shone in him, should read the book of his life mentioned above.

4. Aidan was succeeded as bishop by Finan, who came from the same people and monastery as those whence his predecessor had been sent. He built a church on the island of Lindisfarne suitable for a bishop's see, which later on the most reverend Archbishop Theodore dedicated in honour of the blessed apostle Peter; but Eadberht, bishop of Lindisfarne, of whom we shall speak subsequently, removed the reed thatch and had the whole church, that is the roof and also the walls themselves, covered with sheets of lead.[29]

It was by Bishop Finan that Peada, prince of the Middle Angles, was baptized in the kingdom of the Northumbrians and then returned home with great joy, taking with him four priests who were seen to be well-qualified in learning and manner of life for the task of teaching and baptizing Peada's people.[30] Not long afterwards Sigeberht, king of the East Saxons, also received from Bishop Finan the baptism of salvation. For indeed that kingdom, which had formerly cast off the faith after expelling its bishop Mellitus, received it again once King Sigeberht had been converted to the faith of Christ through the efforts of King Oswiu. The word of Christ was preached there by Cedd, a priest of the English nation and monk of the church of Lindisfarne who had been sent to the East Saxons for that purpose by King Oswiu but who had previously achieved great success in preaching the word among the Middle Angles. When he had assembled a large church for the Lord in the kingdom of the East Saxons, it happened at a certain time that he returned to the church of Lindisfarne in order to consult with Bishop Finan who, when he learned how his work of evangelization had prospered, made him bishop of the people of the East Saxons. After accepting the rank of

[30] Bede, *HE* iii. 21, with the italicized words verbatim. Peada was the son of King Penda of Mercia (d. 654), who had made him king of the Middle Angles and, although a pagan, permitted him to be baptized, which was a condition of his marriage to Alhflæd, daughter of King Oswiu of Northumbria. The baptism took place between 653 and 655, as Bede indicates (loc. cit.). The four priests were Cedd (see below, n. 31), Adda, Betti, and Diuma. See also, Bede, *HE* iii. 24.

Orientalium Saxonum. Qui accepto gradu episcopatus rediit ad prouinciam, et in ciuitate que Ythancester appellatur sed et in illa que Tilaburg cognominatur, quarum prior est in ripa Pente amnis, secunda in ripa Tamensis, collecto examine[a] famulorum Christi disciplinam uite regularis custodire[b] docuit.[31]

Tercium quoque monasterium in prouincia Northanhymbrorum in Lestingaheu construxit, *et religiosis moribus iuxta ritus Lindisfarnensium ubi educatus erat instituit.* In quo ipse moriens, dedit illud regendum Ceadda[c] fratri suo, qui et ipse monachus erat ecclesie Lindisfarnensis, unus uidelicet de discipulis Aidani, qui postea iubente rege Oswiu[d] Eboracensis ecclesie ordinatus est episcopus; nec multo post Theodoro archiepiscopo precipiente prouincie Merciorum prelatus, in loco qui Licetfeld nuncupatur sedem habuit pontificalem.[e][32]

5. Defuncto[f] autem Finano decimo sui episcopatus anno, Colmannus et ipse a Scotia missus, ad ecclesie regimen successit. Qui tribus annis in episcopatu exactis,[g] orta dissensione de obseruatione pasche, malens ipse morem sue gentis sequi, relicto episcopatu patriam [h]reuersus est,[h] anno scilicet pontificatus Scottorum *quem gesserunt in prouincia Anglorum tricesimo. Quante autem parsimonie, cuius continentie fuerint, testabatur[i] etiam locus ille quem regebant, ubi abeuntibus eis excepta ecclesia paucissime domus reperte sunt. Nil pecuniarum absque pecoribus habebant. Siquid enim pecunie a diuitibus accipiebant, mox pauperibus dabant. Nam neque ad susceptionem potentium seculi uel[j] pecunias colligi, uel domos preuideri necesse fuit, qui nunquam ad ecclesiam*

---

[a] monachorum uel *add. D Fx H L Y*   [b] custodiri *Bede, HE*; custodire, *DCL, B.II.35, fo. 138r*   [c] Cedda *F; om. Fx L Y but add. above line by later hand*   [d] Oswyn *Fx L*   [e] episcopalem *Fx L Y*   [f] Succedit Finano Colemannus *rubric Fx T*; De Colmanno episcopo *rubric H. V starts here with heading in early modern archaicizing hand:* Cronicon de statu Lindisfarnensis et Dunelmensis ecclesie ab anno 635 ad annum 1151 Turgoto Dunelmensi auctore. Desunt tria capitula que inuenienda in alio. Defuncto. . . tribus *also in modern hand*   [g] transactis *F Fx H L T Y*   [h–h] est reuersus *H*   [i] testatur *Fx L Y*   [j] *om. Fx L Y*

---

[31] This account of the East Saxons is drawn from Bede, *HE* iii. 22, the last two sentences largely verbatim. Sigberht II ('sanctus') was king of the East Saxons from *c.*653 to an unknown date before 664. Mellitus was bishop of London (i.e. of the East Saxons) from 604 until his expulsion in *c.*617, and archbishop of Canterbury from 619 to 624 (Bede, *HE* ii. 3–7). Cedd was a disciple of St Aidan and one of the four priests sent to evangelize the Middle Angles (see above, n. 30). The date of his appointment as bishop of the East Saxons is uncertain but may have been *c.*653, and he may have died in *c.*664. *Ythancester* is identified with Bradwell-on-Sea (Essex), where a small, early Anglo-Saxon

bishop, he returned to that kingdom and both in the city called
Ythancester and in that called Tilbury (the former being on the banks
of the river Blackwater, the latter on the banks of the river Thames)
he gathered a multitude of servants of Christ and taught them to keep
the discipline of the regular life.[31]

He constructed a third monastery at Lastingham in the kingdom of
the Northumbrians and established there religious customs according
to the rites of Lindisfarne where he himself had been educated. As he
was dying there, he handed the monastery over to be governed by his
brother Chad, who was also a monk of the church of Lindisfarne and
was indeed one of the disciples of Aidan. Afterwards Chad was
ordained bishop of the church of York by order of King Oswiu, and
not long after that he was by command of Archbishop Theodore
made bishop of the kingdom of the Mercians and had his episcopal
see in the place called Lichfield.[32]

5. After the death of Finan in the tenth year of his episcopate,
Colman, who was himself sent from Ireland, succeeded to the
government of the church. When he had been bishop for three
years, there arose a dissension concerning the observance of Easter.
Preferring to follow the custom of his own people, Colman left his
bishopric and returned to his own country—it was then the thirtieth
year of the episcopate which the Irish had exercised in the kingdom of
the English. How frugal and abstemious they were was shown by the
place over which they ruled, where very few buildings apart from the
church were to be found when they had left. They had no property
apart from cattle. If they accepted any money from the rich, they at
once gave it to the poor. For it was not necessary for them to amass
money or to provide buildings for receiving the powerful of this
world, who used to come to church only to pray or to hear the word of

church occupies the west gate of the Roman fort of *Othona*; see H. M. Taylor and
J. Taylor, *Anglo-Saxon Architecture* (3 vols.; Cambridge, 1965–78), i. 91–2, iii. 1079, and
J. Blair, 'Anglo-Saxon minsters: a topographical review', in *Pastoral Care before the Parish*,
ed. J. Blair and R. Sharpe (Leicester, 1992), pp. 227–66, at 239, 244.

[32] This paragraph is derived from Bede, *HE* iii. 23, 28, iv. 3, with the italicized words
verbatim from iii. 23. Lastingham, which was founded on land granted by King Æthelwald
of Deira, is located in the southern fringes of the North Yorkshire Moors (SE 728 905).
Chad was made bishop of York in 664 while Wilfrid, who had been granted the see
formerly, was abroad; he was removed in 669 to allow Wilfrid to be reinstated (a fact not
mentioned by Symeon), and was then bishop of Lichfield until his death in 672 (*HE* iii. 28,
iv. 3; cf. *The Life of Bishop Wilfrid by Eddius Stephanus*, ed. and trans. B. Colgrave
(Cambridge, 1927), cc. 14–15).

nisi orationis tantum et audiendi uerbi Dei causa ueniebant. Rex ipse cum oportunitas exegisset, cum quinque tantum aut sex ministris ueniebat, et ^a *expleta oratione discedebat. Quod si forte eos ibi refici contingeret, simplici tantum et cotidiano fratrum cibo contenti nichil ultra* ^b *querebant. Tota enim* ^c*fuit sollicitudo tunc* ^c *doctoribus illis* ^d*Deo seruiendi* ^d *non seculo, tota* ^e *cura cordis excolendi non uentris, qui in tantum erant ab omni auaritie peste castigati, ut nemo territoria ac possessiones ad construenda monasteria nisi a potestatibus seculi coactus acciperet. Que consuetudo per omnia aliquanto post hec tempore in ecclesiis Northanhymbrorum seruata est.*

Abiens autem domum Colmanus assumpsit secum partem ossium reuerentissimi patris Aidani, partem uero in ecclesia cui preerat reliquit, et in secretario ^f *eius condi precepit.* Quo^g *patriam reuerso, suscepit pro illo pontificatum Northanhymbrorum famulus Christi Tuda, qui apud Scottos Austrinos eruditus erat atque ordinatus episcopus, uir quidem bonus ac religiosus,* sed eodem anno superueniente pestilentia ac prouinciam Northanhymbrorum depopulante *raptus est de mundo. Porro fratribus qui in Lindisfarnensi ecclesia Scottis abeuntibus remanere maluerunt, prepositus est abbatis iure uir reuerentissimus ac mansuetissimus Eata, qui erat abbas in* ^h*monasterio quod uocatur* ^h *Mailros; quod* ⁱ *aiunt Colmanum abiturum petisse, et impetrasse a rege Oswio,* ^j eo quod esset idem Eata unus de duodecim pueris Aidani, *quos primo episcopatus sui tempore de natione Anglorum erudiendos in Christo accep*erat. *Multum nanque eundem episcopum Colmanum rex pro insita illi prudentia diligebat.*³³

[iii] 6. Anno^k ab Incarnatione Domini sexcentesimo sexagesimo quarto, ex quo autem^l sedes^m episcopalisⁿ in insula Lindisfarnensi et monachorum habitatio a studiosissimis^o Christi cultoribus rege Oswaldo et pontifice Aidano institute sunt anno tricesimo, quo Scotti domum redeuntes ipsam ecclesiam reliquerant, abbas Eata (ut dictum est) cura ipsius ecclesie siue monasterii suscepta, beatum Cuthbertum,

^a *om.* H   ^b amplius *Fx H L Y*   ^{c–c} tunc fuit sollicitudo *Fx L* ^{d–d} seruiendi Deo (Deo *above line*) *F*   ^e totaque *Fx L*   ^f secreta *H* ^g De Tuda episcopo *rubric H*   ^{h–h} *om. Fx L Y; Bede, HE,* dicitur, *but* uocatur, *DCL, B.II.35, fo. 145r*   ⁱ autem *add. H*   ^j Oswyno *V L*   ^k Episcopi et abbates simul in una eademque ecclesia Lindesfarnensi fuerunt *rubric Fx Y;* De abbate Eacta *rubric H;* Cuthbertus translatus (Translatus Cuthbertus *T*) est de Mailros ad Lindisfarnensem insulam, prepositus efficitur idem et qualiter idem (ibidem *V*) docuit (docuerit *V*) *rubric T V*   ^l *om. H*   ^m *om. F*   ⁿ *om. T;* episcopatus *Ca* ^o studiosis *F*

God. When the occasion required it, the king himself would come with only five or six thegns and would leave after finishing his prayers. If it happened by chance that they took refreshment there, they were content with only the simple daily food of the brethren and they sought nothing more. So great then was the solicitude of those teachers to serve God and not the world, to attend wholly to the needs of the heart and not the belly, so completely were they purged of the pestilence of avarice, that none of them would accept lands or possessions for the construction of monasteries unless forced to do so by worldly rulers. This practice was observed universally in the Northumbrian churches for some time afterwards.

When he returned home, Colman took with him part of the bones of the most reverend father Aidan, but he left the rest in the church which he had ruled, and ordered them to be buried in the sanctuary. After Colman had gone back to his homeland, the bishopric of the Northumbrians was received in his place by the servant of Christ, Tuda, who had been educated and ordained bishop among the southern Irish. He was indeed a good and religious man, but he was snatched from the world in that same year by a pestilence which came and devastated the kingdom of the Northumbrians. Now the brothers who preferred to stay in the church of Lindisfarne after the Irish had left received as their abbot a very reverend and gentle man called Eata, who was abbot of the monastery called Melrose. It is said that when he was departing, Colman asked and obtained this of King Oswiu, because Eata was one of the twelve English boys, whom Aidan had chosen when he first became bishop to educate in Christ. For the king greatly loved Bishop Colman for the wisdom that was ingrained in him.[33]

6. In the year of the Incarnation of Our Lord 664, the thirtieth year [iii] from when the episcopal see and the dwelling of monks on the island of Lindisfarne was established by those most attentive worshippers of Christ, King Oswald and Bishop Aidan, the year in which the Irish had returned home and left the church of Lindisfarne, Abbot Eata (as has been said) took on the care of that church and monastery; and he transferred the blessed Cuthbert, who was then in the fourteenth year

---

[33] This chapter is derived, in large part verbatim, from Bede, *HE* iii. 25–6. The bishops referred to here were Finan (651–61); Colman (661–4); Tuda (664); and Eata (before 681–685). The dissension referred to was that leading to the Synod of Whitby in 664 (Bede, *HE* iii. 25; see e.g. R. Abels, 'The council of Whitby: a study in early Anglo-Saxon politics', *Journal of British Studies*, xxiii (1983), 1–25).

cum in Mailrosensi monasterio in monachice uite perfectione iam quartum decimum ageret annum, illo transtulit, ut ibi quoque fratribus custodiam discipline regularis et auctoritate prepositi intimaret, et exemplo uirtutis premonstraret.[34]

[iii (H)] Cur[a] autem idem locus et supra sub[b] episcoporum et nunc sub abbatis regimine fuerit, uel cur ad ipsius ecclesie curam de monachica (ut supradictum est) magis[c] quam de[d] clericali professione consuetudo fuerit episcopos eligendi, in prefato[e] libro quem[f] de uita et uirtutibus ipsius[g] patris Cuthberti componit uenerabilis presbiter et monachus Beda commemorat. His enim uerbis inter alia loquitur:

'*Neque aliquis*', [h]inquit, '*miretur*,[h] quod in eadem insula Lindisfarnea cum permodica sit, *et supra episcopi et nunc abbatis et monachorum esse locum dixerimus.*[i] [j]*Re uera enim ita est.*[j] *Nanque*[k] *una eademque seruorum Dei habitatio utrosque simul tenet, immo omnes monachos tenet. Aidanus quippe, qui primus eiusdem loci* [l]*episcopus fuit,*[l] monachus erat,[m] *et monachicam* [n]*cum suis omnibus uitam*[n] [o]*semper agere solebat.*[o] *Vnde ab illo omnes*[p] [q]*loci ipsius*[q] *antistites usque hodie sic episcopale exercent officium,*[r] *ut regente monasterium abbate, quem ipsi cum consilio fratrum elegerint, omnes presbiteri, diacones, cantores, lectores, ceterique gradus ecclesiastici monachicam per omni* [s]*cum ipso episcopo*[s] *regulam seruent.*'

Sed de hoc satis dictum.[t] *Vir* autem *Domini Cuthbertus ad Lindisfarnensem ecclesiam siue monasterium adueniens, mox instituta monachica fratribus uiuendo pariter et docendo tradebat, sed et*[u] *morantem circumquaque uulgi multitudinem more suo crebra uisitatione ad celestia querenda ac promerenda succendebat. Nec non etiam signis clarior effectus, plurimos* '*uariis languoribus et tormentis comprehensos*'[35] *orationum instantia prisce*[v] *sanitati restituit; nonnullos ab immundorum spirituum uexatione non solum presens orando, tangendo, imperando, exorcizando, sed et absens uel tantum orando, uel certe eorum sanationem*[w] *predicendo curauit.*

[a] Cur episcopi et abbates simul in una eadem ecclesia Lindisfarnensi fuerunt *rubric* H   [b] *om.* T   [c] *om.* T   [d] *om.* Fx T   [e] autem *add.* Y   [f] *om.* Fx L Y   [g] eius H   [h–h] miretur inquit H   [i] diximus H   [j–j] *om.* H   [k] enim *add.* Fx Y   [l–l] fuit episcopus D Fx H L Y   [m] fuit T   [n–n] uitam cum suis omnibus F   [o–o] agere solebat F H; agere solebat semper Fx L Y   [p] *om.* L   [q–q] ipsius loci H; loci illius V   [r] studium T   [s–s] *om.* Ca, *but* cum *in marg. with omission sign and other words presumably cut off by binder*   [t] est *add.* Fx H L Y   [u] *om.* L   [v] pristine Fx L Y   [w] sanitatem Fx H L Y

[34] The information about Eata is from Bede, *HE* iii. 26. The chronological relationships given here are consistent with dates of 635 for the establishment of Lindisfarne (above,

of his life of monastic perfection in the monastery of Melrose, to Lindisfarne so that he could there direct and guide the brothers in keeping the discipline of the Rule both by his authority as provost and by the example of his own virtue.[34]

In the book which he wrote about the life and miracles of father [iii (H)] Cuthbert and which we have mentioned before, the venerable priest and monk Bede recounts why this same place was formerly under the rule of bishops and then under that of an abbot, and why it was the custom (as was said above) to elect bishops from the monastic rather than the clerical profession. Amongst other things, Bede wrote:

> Let no one be surprised that in this same island of Lindisfarne, which is quite small, we have spoken previously of there being the place of a bishop and now the place of an abbot and monks. This is indeed truly the case. For one and the same habitation of the servants of God holds simultaneously both, or rather it holds all monks. For Aidan, who was the first bishop of this place, was a monk and was always accustomed to lead the monastic life with all his companions. So in succession to him all the bishops of this same place down to the present day exercise the episcopal office in such a way that, whilst the monastery is ruled by an abbot whom they elect with the counsel of the brothers, all the priests, deacons, cantors, lectors and other ecclesiastical grades keep in all things the monastic Rule along with the bishop.

But enough has been said about this. When Cuthbert, that man of the Lord, came to the church—that is monastery—of Lindisfarne, not only did he soon educate the brothers in the monastic institutions by his way of life as well as by his teaching, but also according to his custom he made frequent visits to the multitude of common people living thereabouts and inspired them to seek heaven and to make themselves worthy of it. He became still more famous for his miracles, and by the force of his prayers he restored to their former health many 'who were in the grip of various illnesses and torments';[35] and several others he cured of the vexation of unclean spirits not only by praying, touching, commanding, and exorcizing when he was actually present, but also by prayer alone when he was absent, or indeed simply by predicting their return to health.

p. 20) and 651 for Cuthbert's entry as a monk into Melrose (above, p. 26). On the possible significance to Symeon of this reference to the Rule, see above, pp. lxxxiii–lxxxiv.

[35] Matt. 4: 24.

Erant autem[a] [b]quidam in monasterio[b] fratres qui prisce [c]sue consuetudini[c] quam regulari mallent obtemperare custodie. Quos tamen ille modesta patientie sue uirtute superabat, et cotidiano exercitio paulatim ad melioris propositi statum conuertebat. Erat nanque patientie uirtute precipuus, atque ad perferenda [d]fortiter omnia[d] que uel animo uel corpori aduersa ingerebantur inuictissimus; nec minus inter tristia que contigissent faciem pretendens hilarem,[36] ut palam daretur intelligi, quia interna Spiritus Sancti consolatione pressuras contempneret extrinsecas. His et huiusmodi spiritualibus exercitiis uir uenerabilis et bonorum quorumque[e] ad se imitandum prouocabat affectum, et improbos quosque ac rebelles uite regulari[f] a pertinatia sui reuocabat erroris.[37]

Legant[g] qui scire uolunt ipsius uitam, et in uno sancti spiritus uasculo omnium uirtutum considerent exuberare gratiam. Discant tanti uiri auctoritate et subiecti et prelati ordinis obseruantiam, iustitie ac pietatis excellentiam, mansuetudinis atque seueritatis temperantiam. Discant, inquam, eius exemplo, discant qui [h]ei nunc[h] deseruiunt monachi, sibi prepositis humilitatem exhibere, obedientiam, dilectionem, reuerentiam, et omnem ex cordis puritate subiectionem. Discant[i] eius magisterio, qui illius in prioratu successores sunt, contradicentium iniurias modesta uirtute patientie superare; discant et iustitie zelo feruere ad arguendum peccantes, et spiritu mansuetudinis modestos esse ad ignoscendum penitentibus.[38] Ipse enim nonnunquam confitentibus sibi peccata sua his qui deliquerant, prior miserans infirmos lacrimas fudit, et[j] quid peccatori esset agendum ipse iustus suo premonstrauit exemplo. *Nullus ab eo sine gaudio consolationis abibat, nullum[k] dolor animi quem ad illum attulerat redeuntem comitatus est.*[39]

---

[a] *om.* F   [b–b] in monasterio quidam *D Fx H L Y*   [c–c] consuetudini sue *H*
[d–d] omnia fortiter *Ca*   [e] quorumcumque *V*   [f] regularis *Bede, V. Cuth.; but* regulari *in Cambridge, Trinity College, O.3.55 (s. xii^med, Durham), Bod. Lib., Laud. misc. 491 (s. xii², Durham), Paris, Bibliothèque Nationale, lat. 5362 (s. xii) (Colgrave, Two Lives, pp. 212, 21–2, 26, 35)*   [g] De moribus beati Cutberti *rubric H*
[h–h] nunc ei *Fx L Y*   [i] Discant etiam *D Fx L Y*   [j] *om.* D Fx H L Y
[k] etiam *add.* H L

---

[36] Cf. Eccl. 7: 26.

[37] From 'Let no one' to this point, *LDE* extracts verbatim from Bede, *V. Cuth.* c. 16, with the sentence 'But enough has been said about this' covering an omission. On Lindisfarne, see above, pp. 20–1.

[38] It is tempting to connect *LDE's* comments here, which must be directed at Turgot

Now there were in the monastery certain brothers who preferred to conform to their own former customs than to place themselves in the custody of the Rule, but these Cuthbert overcame with his forbearance and patience, and little by little through daily exercise he converted them to acceptance of the better way of life. For he was outstanding for his patience, and he was invincible in enduring bravely all the adversities which were inflicted on his spirit or his body; and when things turned out sadly, he nevertheless showed a happy face,[36] so that it might openly be given to understand that through the inner consolation of the Holy Spirit he held pressures from outside in contempt. By these and other spiritual exercises the venerable man stimulated the desire of every good man to imitate him, and he called back from the pertinacity of their error all those who were reprobate and rebellious towards the way of life of the Rule.[37]

Those who wish to know should read his Life and should consider how this one vessel of the Holy Spirit overflowed with the grace of all virtues. They should learn from the authority of such a man how to observe the duties of subjects and rulers, the excellence of justice and piety, and the moderation of gentleness and severity. Those who now serve him as monks should learn, I say, should learn by his example to show to those placed over them humility, obedience, affection, reverence, and all that subjection which derives from purity of heart. Those who are his successors in the office of prior should learn by his teaching to overcome the injuries of those who speak against them with the mild power of patience; and they should learn to burn with zeal for justice to reprove sinners, and to be mild with the spirit of gentleness to forgive the penitent.[38] For often when those who had erred confessed their sins to him, he first took pity on these weak ones and wept. Then, righteous as he was, he showed by his example what the sinner should do. No one left his presence without the joy of consolation; no one who had brought spiritual pain to him departed uncomforted.[39]

---

who was prior at the time of its composition (above, p. xx), with William of Malmesbury's comment that Turgot's use of his privileges so angered Bishop Ranulf Flambard that he had the prior appointed bishop of St Andrews in order to be rid of him (*De gestis pontificum*, ed. Hamilton, pp. 273–4).

[39] This sentence is taken verbatim from Bede, *V. Cuth.* c. 22.

7. Anno[a] Incarnationis Dominice sexcentesimo septuagesimo sexto[b] qui est annus imperii regis[c] Ecgfridi sextus, cum uir Domini Cuthbertus in[d] Lindisfarnensis monasterii prioratu duodecimum et eo amplius annum transegisset, tandem comitante prefati abbatis sui simul et fratrum gratia, *anachoretice quoque contemplationis secreta silentia* petiit, ibi sicut ubique contendens ut ex bono melior, ex meliore fieret optimus.[40] *Ibi quanto ab strepitu mundane sollicitudinis liberior, tanto Deo uicinior,* o [e]pater dulcissime, sanctissime,[e] reuerentissime; *sedebas cum Maria 'secus pedes Domini, optimam partem eligens que a te non auferetur in eternum'.*[41] Ibi sitiens anima tua[42] ad Deum fontem uiuum concupiuit et defecit in atria Domini; ibi cor tuum et caro tua exultauerunt in Deum uiuum;[43] ibi gustasti et uidisti quam suauis est Dominus; beatus es quoniam sperasti in eo.[44] Qua ibi meditatione, quo amoris suspirio, quanto studio, quanta compunctione, quantis lacrimarum effusionibus, cogitasti, optasti, requisisti, petisti et cum propheta conclamasti: 'Domine, dilexi decorem domus tue, et locum habitationis glorie tue.'[45] Postpositis nanque aliis omnibus, tota uita tua hoc solum clamabat: 'Vnam petii a Domino, hanc requiram, ut inhabitem in domo Domini [f]omnibus diebus uite mee.' Ecce iam beatus cum beatis habitas in domo Domini,[f] in secula seculorum laudabis illum.[46]

Vbi uero talia uir Domini promeruerat est insula Farne, *que hinc altissimo, inde infinito clauditur oceano,* tunc *aque prorsus inops, frugis quoque et arboris, malignorum* etiam *spirituum frequentia humane habitationi minus accommoda.*[47] Verum illo quoque uirum Dei comitante miraculorum gloria, de rupe saxosa[g] precibus fontem elicuit,[h] de tellure durissima segetem produxit, hoste antiquo cum satellitum

---

[a] Sanctus Cuthbertus factus est anachorita in insula de Farne *rubric Fx T V*; Sanctus Chuthbertus petiit desertum gratia tamen fratrum *rubric H*   [b] *om.* L   [c] *om.* T   [d] *om.* Ca   [e-e] sanctissime pater dulcissime *D H*   [f-f] *om.* Fx L Y   [g] suis gloriosissimis *add. D H before* precibus   [h] elicuit et *D H*

---

[40] The italicized words are from Bede, *HE* iv. 26 (28). Ecgfrith was king of the Northumbrians from 670 to 685. The date 676 is not found in eighth-century sources, but it occurs in *ALf*, and, given that Cuthbert became bishop in 685, it could be deduced from the statement in *HSC* c. 3 (Arnold, *Sym. Op.* i. 197), that Cuthbert spent nine years on the Inner Farne. See further C. Stancliffe, 'Cuthbert and the polarity between pastor and solitary', Bonner, *Cuthbert*, pp. 21–44, at 33.
[41] Luke 10: 39, 42.
[42] Cf. Ps. 146: 6.
[43] Cf. Ps. 83 (84): 3.
[44] Ps. 33 (34): 9.
[45] Ps. 25 (26): 8.

7. In the year of Our Lord's Incarnation 676, which was the sixth year of the reign of King Ecgfrith, when Cuthbert, the man of the Lord, had passed twelve and more years as prior of the monastery of Lindisfarne, at length with the full permission of his aforementioned abbot and also of the brothers, he sought also the secluded tranquillity of eremitic contemplation, striving in that as in all things to raise himself from being good to being better, and from being better to being best of all.[40] O dearest, most holy, most reverend father, as much freer as you were there from the din of worldly cares, so much closer were you to God; you sat with Mary 'at the feet of the Lord, choosing the better part which may not be taken from you in all eternity'.[41] There your soul, longing for God, thirsted[42] for the living fountain and withdrew into the courts of the Lord; there your heart and your flesh exulted in the living God;[43] there you tasted and saw how dear is the Lord; and you are blessed because you placed your hope in him.[44] With what meditation, with what sighs of love, with how much striving, with how much remorse, with how many outbursts of tears, you there pondered, longed for, sought, beseeched and with the prophet cried out: 'Lord, I have loved the beauty of your house and the place where your glory dwells.'[45] For having set aside everything else your whole life cried out this alone: 'I have asked one thing of the Lord, I shall seek this, that I may live all the days of my life in the house of the Lord.' See as one blessed you dwell now with the blessed in the house of the Lord, and you will praise him for ever and ever.[46]

The place where the man of the Lord merited such things is the island of Farne, which is surrounded on one side by a deep channel and on the other by the boundless ocean. It was then a place entirely unsuitable for human habitation, for it was absolutely wanting in water, produce and trees, and also frequented by evil spirits.[47] But the glory of miracles accompanied the man of God there and he elicited through prayers a spring from a rock, he produced corn from the hardest of ground and, after putting to flight the ancient enemy with

[46] Ps. 26 (27): 4 and cf. Ps. 83 (84): 5. *Domus Domini* ('house of the Lord') was 'an established synonym for a church or monastery' (A. J. Piper, 'The first generations of Durham monks and the cult of St Cuthbert', in Bonner, *Cuthbert*, pp. 437–46, at 439, citing R. E. Latham and D. R. Howlett, *Dictionary of Medieval Latin from British Sources* (Oxford, 1975–), p. 720 *domus* defs. 6–7).

[47] The latter part of this sentence is taken verbatim from Bede, *V. Cuth.* c. 17, and *HE* iv. 28 (26). The island is the Inner Farne, approximately two miles off the coast of Northumberland, opposite Bamburgh.

turba fugato locum ipsum*ᵃ* habitabilem fecit.⁴⁸ Postquam enim inhabitator sancti spiritus suam ibidem habitationem*ᵇ* instituit, in tantum spiritus nequam deinceps ipsam*ᶜ* insulam exhorruit, ut qui eam Christo famulaturus ingreditur, nullas ex phantasiis demonum inquietudines sustinere dicatur.⁴⁹

[iv] 8. Huius*ᵈ* sanctissimi patris *ᵉ*solitarie uite anno secundo,*ᵉ* qui est Incarnationis sexcentesimus septuagesimus septimus, imperii uero regis Ecgfridi septimus, ex quo autem Theodorus archiepiscopus Brittanniam uenerat nonus, Beda *natus est* in prouincia Northanhymbrorum, *in territorio* monasterii apostolorum *ᶠ*Petri et Pauli,*ᶠ* quod est ad Wiramutha et in Gyruum. In quod monasterium *cura propinquorum cum esset septem annorum datus est educandus reuerentissimo abbati Benedicto ac deinde Ceolfrido*, anno scilicet decimo postquam idem monasterium sancti Petri apostoli fundatum est, ex quo autem [v] sancti Pauli monasterium fuerat inceptum anno tercio.⁵⁰ Que*ᵍ* utraque monasteria, tanta pace et concordia et eadem familiaritate et *fraterna societate ᵸfuerant coniunctaᵸ* ut, sicut ipse Beda postea describit,*ⁱ* pro uno in duobus locis posito haberentur monasterio.⁵¹ Vnde ipse in *Historia Anglorum* unius mentionem faciens, '*Monasterium*,' inquit, '*Petri ʲet Pauliʲ quod est ad hostium Wiri amnis, et iuxta amnem Tinaᵏ in loco qui uocatur in Gyruum.*'⁵²

Hic itaque infantulus bone spei et diuina et seculari litteratura diligenter imbuitur, quandoque sancti spiritus organum futurus quo eius precordia irradiante in sancte uniuersalis ecclesie munimentum, plurimos in noui et ueteris testamenti expositionem libros erat

---

ᵃ illum *Fx L*   *ᵇ* inhabitationem *Ca*   *ᶜ om. H*   *ᵈ* Sanctus Beda doctor (*om. H*) natus est in territorio Girwensi *rubric Fx H T V Y*   *ᵉ⁻ᵉ* anno secundo solitarie uite *F*   *ᶠ⁻ᶠ om. T*   *ᵍ* Vnum monasterium in Weremutha et Gerue erat (erat *om. H*) *rubric Fx H Y*   *ᵸ⁻ᵸ* coniuncta fuerant *Fx L Y* *ⁱ* descripsit *H*   *ʲ⁻ʲ om. V*   *ᵏ* Tinam *Bede, HE, but* Tina *in DCL, B.II. 35, fo. 203v*

---

⁴⁸ Bede, *V. Cuth.* c. 17.
⁴⁹ The use of the present tense suggests that hermits were resident on Farne at the time of *LDE*'s composition. A certain Ailric is known to have been a hermit there in the 12th cent., probably in the early 12th cent. since he was the uncle of Bernard, probably the sacrist who occurs in the Durham records in *c.*1114 (Raine, *Cuth. virt.*, pp. 61, 151–3; Alan Piper, pers. comm.; cf. Victoria Tudor, 'Durham Priory and its hermits in the twelfth cent.', in Rollason, *Anglo-Norman Durham*, pp. 67–78, at 67). After that a series of hermits is known to have occupied the island (Tudor, ibid.).
⁵⁰ The italicized words are from Bede, *HE* v. 24. On Bede's career, see e.g. B. Ward, *The Venerable Bede* (Harrisburg, 1990), pp. 2–6, and G. H. Brown, *Bede the Venerable*

his crowd of henchmen, he made the place itself habitable.[48] For after this man in whom dwelled the Holy Spirit had established his dwelling there, the vile spirit henceforth held the island itself in such horror that it is said that no one who goes on to the island to serve Christ suffers any anxieties from the fantasies of demons.[49]

8. In the second year of this most holy father's life as a hermit, that is [iv] the year of the Incarnation 677, the seventh year of the reign of King Ecgfrith, and the ninth since Archbishop Theodore came to Britain, Bede was born in the kingdom of the Northumbrians, in the territory of the monastery of the apostles Peter and Paul which is at Wearmouth and Jarrow. When he was seven years old, he was given by his relatives to that monastery to be educated first by the most reverend abbot Benedict and then by Ceolfrith, that was in the tenth year after the foundation of the monastery of St Peter the Apostle, the third year after the establishment of the monastery of St Paul.[50] These two [v] monasteries were joined in such peace, concord, familiarity, and brotherly fellowship that, as Bede himself afterwards describes, it was as if they were a single monastery located in two places.[51] Hence when he mentions one of them in his *History of the English* he refers to 'the monastery of Peter and Paul which is at the mouth of the river Wear, and by the river Tyne at the place called Jarrow.'[52]

Here then this most promising infant was diligently imbued with divine and secular literature, for he was to be the organ of the Holy Spirit, and with this lighting up his heart he was to compose for the defence of the holy and universal church many books of exposition of the Old and New Testaments. When he had become erudite in the

(Boston, 1987), c. 1. Symeon confusedly took Bede's statement that he was in his 59th year when he completed *HE*, i.e. in 731, as information about his age at his death in 735 (below, pp. 64–5), and so arrived at 677 for his birth, which was in fact around 673. The error is shared by *ALf* and JW ii. 134–5, which may have derived it from *LDE*. It is consistent with a date of 676 for Cuthbert becoming a hermit (above, pp. 38–9), 670 for the arrival of Theodore, and 671 for the accession of Ecgfrith. A date of 684 × 5 for Bede's entry into Jarrow is also consistent with dates of 674 for the foundation of St Peter's, Monkwearmouth, and 681 × 2 for the foundation of St Paul's, Jarrow; see e.g. P. H. Blair, *The World of Bede* (2nd edn.; Cambridge, 1990), pp. 165–83.

[51] Bede, *Historia abbatum*, c. 7 (Plummer, *Bede*, i. 370).

[52] Bede, *HE* v. 21. For the sites of the monasteries, see e.g. R. J. Cramp, 'Excavations at the Saxon monastic sites of Wearmouth and Jarrow, co. Durham: an interim report', *Medieval Archaeology* xiii (1969), 21–66; id., 'Monkwearmouth and Jarrow: the archaeological evidence', in *Famulus Christi*, ed. Bonner, pp. 5–18; and, for more recent discussion including the argument that these monasteries had pastoral responsibilities in the surrounding countryside, *Pastoral Care*, ed. Blair and Sharpe, pp. 140–1, 260–2.

compositurus. Et cum in*a* Latina erudiretur lingua, Grece quoque*b*
[vi] peritiam non mediocriter percepit.[53] Quippe*c* per id temporis in
monasterio prefato deditus erat studio, quando Theodorus archiepiscopus et Adrianus abbas qui *litteris sacris simul et secularibus*
abundanter ambo erant instructi, peragrata tota Brittannia congregantes
discipulorum cateruam scientie salutaris cotidie flumina irrigandis eorum
cordibus emanabant, ita ut etiam metrice artis, astronomie, et arithmetice
ecclesiastice disciplinam inter sacrorum apicum uolumina suis auditoribus
[vi (H)] *contraderent*. Sic*d* enim de his ipse Beda loquitur. Deinde*e* et istud*f*
subiungit: '*Indicio est*',*g* inquit, '*quod usque hodie supersunt de eorum*
discipulis qui Latinam Grecamque linguam eque ut propriam in qua nati
sunt norunt.'[54]

Transeunte autem ad celestia patre Cuthberto, ille uite ipsius
egregius quandoque scriptor futurus Beda, etatis iam tunc undecim,
studii uero in monasterio quattuor habebat annos. Verum de illo
latius in sequentibus dicemus, nunc ad ea unde digressi sumus
narrando redeamus.[55]

[vii] **9.** *Anno*^h *Dominice Incarnationis sexcentesimo septuagesimo octauo, qui*
est annus imperii regis Ecgfridi octauus, Wilfridus, qui totius Northanhymbrorum prouincie pontificatum non paruo tempore adminis-
trauerat, *orta inter ipsum* et predictum*i regem dissensione* ab episcopatu
pulsus^j *est, et duo in locum eius episcopi* ordinati sunt Eboraci ab
archiepiscopo Theodoro qui Northanhymbrorum genti preessent,
Bosa uidelicet qui Deirorum, et *^k sepe memoratus*^k abbas *Eata qui*
Berniciorum prouinciam gubernaret, hic in ciuitate Eboraci, ille in
Hagustaldensi et *Lindisfarnensi ecclesia cathedram habens episcopalem*,
ambo de monachorum collegio in episcopatus gradum asciti. Igitur Eata
cum quattuordecim annis ecclesie Lindisfarnensi abbatis iure pre-

---

a om. H   *b* et Ebraice *Fx L*   *c* A quibus doctoribus eruditus erat Beda
rubric *Fx Y*   *d* A quibus doctoribus eruditus erat Beda *rubric H*   *e* Dein *Ca*
f illud *H*   *g* enim *D*   *h* Vuilfridus ab episcopatu tocius Northanhimbrie
(tocius Northanhimbrie om. *H*) expulsus est *rubric Fx H T V Y*   *i* prefatum *Ca*
j depositus *T*; expulsus *L*   *k–k* om. *Ca but* et sepe m *add. in marg.; remainder*
truncated by binder

---

[53] Bede himself stated only that he had revised a bad translation from the Greek of a
Vita Anastasii (*HE* v. 24, quoted below, pp. 68–9). Anastasius was a Persian monk,
martyred in 628 under Chosroes II. For the possibility that his work has in fact survived in
the form of *Bibliotheca Hagiographica Latina Antique et Mediae Aetatis*, ed. Society of
Bollandists (2 vols.; Brussels, 1898–1901), no. 408, see P. Meyvaert and C. Vircillo
Franklin, 'Has Bede's Version of the "Passio Anastasii" Come Down to us in "BHL"

Latin language, he also obtained a by no means mediocre skill in
Greek.[53] For indeed he was given over to study in the aforementioned [vi]
monastery at the time when Archbishop Theodore and Abbot
Hadrian, who were both equally well instructed in sacred and secular
writings, travelled through Britain and, collecting together a crowd of
disciples, they poured forth every day rivers of salvation-giving
knowledge to irrigate their hearts, in such a way that they passed
on to their pupils the discipline of the art of metre, astronomy, and
ecclesiastical compute, as well as the books of sacred scripture. It is [vi (H)]
thus that Bede tells of these things and then adds: 'The proof of this is
that even today some of their disciples are still living who know Latin
and Greek as well as they do their native language.'[54]

When father Cuthbert went to heaven, Bede, who was to be the
distinguished author of his life, was eleven years old, having studied
at the monastery for four years. Since we shall have more to say about
him in what follows, let us now return to narrating those matters from
which we digressed.[55]

9. In the year of our Lord's Incarnation 678, which was the eighth [vii]
year of the reign of King Ecgfrith, Wilfrid, who had for some
considerable time been administering the bishopric of the whole
kingdom of the Northumbrians, was expelled from his see after a
dissension had arisen between him and King Ecgfrith, and at York
Archbishop Theodore ordained two bishops in his place to rule over
the Northumbrian people. These were Bosa who was to govern the
kingdom of the Deirans, and Abbot Eata, whom we have often
mentioned, who was to govern the kingdom of the Bernicians, the
former with his episcopal throne in the city of York, the latter with
his in the churches of Hexham and Lindisfarne; both were received
into the episcopate from the fellowship of monks. So Eata, when he
had been abbot of the church of Lindisfarne for fourteen years, took

408?', *Analecta Bollandiana*, c (1982), 373–400. On Bede's own knowledge of Greek, see
A. C. Dionisotti, 'On Bede, grammars, and Greek', *Revue bénédictine*, xcii (1982), 111–41,
and *Bedae Venerabilis Expositio Actuum apostolorum et retractatio*, ed. M. L. W. Laistner
(Cambridge, Mass., 1939), pp. xxxviii–xli.

[54] This and the previous sentence are largely taken verbatim from Bede, *HE* iv. 2. For
evidence of Greek and Latin scholarship under Theodore, archbishop of Canterbury (668–
90), and Hadrian, abbot of St Augustine's Abbey, Canterbury, see *Biblical Commentaries
from the Canterbury School of Theodore and Hadrian*, ed. M. Lapidge and B. Bischoff
(Cambridge Studies in Anglo-Saxon England, x; Cambridge, 1994).

[55] Since Cuthbert died in 687, the chronological indications given here are consistent
with *LDE*'s erroneous date of 677 for Bede's birth (see above, p. 41 n. 50).

fuisset, duarum ecclesiarum suscepit presulatum, tercio anno ex quo pater Cuthbertus anachoretice sedis adierat solitudinem. *Post tres autem annos abscessionis Wilfridi*, Theodorus ordinauit Tunbertum *ad Hagustaldensem ecclesiam*, Eata ad Lindisfarnensis ecclesie presula- [viii] tum per quattuor annos remanente.[56] Quadriennio*[a]* uero exacto,*[b]* contigit *ut congregata synodo non parua sub presentia* piissimi ac Deo dilecti *regis Ecgfridi iuxta fluuium Alne in loco qui dicitur* Æt Twiforda, *quod significat 'ad duplex uadum'*, *cui beate memorie Theodorus archiepiscopus presidebat, unanimo omnium consensu ad episcopatum ecclesie*[c] *Lindisfarnensis beatus pater Cuthbertus eligeretur.*[d] Qui cum multis legatariis ac litteris ad se premissis nequaquam suo loco *posset erui, tandem rex ipse prefatus una cum sanctissimo antistite Trumwino, necnon et aliis religiosis ac potentibus uiris* ad[e] *insulam* [viii (H)] *nauigauit. Conueniunt*[f] *et de ipsa insula Lindisfarnensi in hoc ipsum*[g] *multi de fratribus, genu flectunt omnes, adiurant per Dominum, lacrimas fundunt, obsecrant, donec ipsum* [h]*quoque lacrimis*[h] *plenum dulcibus extrahunt latebris, atque ad synodum pertrahunt. Quo dum perueniret, quamuis multum renitens unanima cunctorum uoluntate superatur, atque ad suscipiendum episcopatus officium collum summittere compellitur, eo maxime uictus sermone, quod famulus*[i] *Domini Boisilus cum ei mente prophetica cuncta que eum essent superuentura pate*fecit, *antistitem quoque eum futurum predixerat. Nec statim ordinatio*[j] *decreta, sed peracta hieme que imminebat*[k] *completa est.* Cum ergo per nouem annos in solitaria uita soli Deo uacasset, in pontificatus honorem auctore Deo leuatur, consecratus *Eboraci* septimas Kalendas Aprilis in ipso die sancto[l] Pasche *sub presentia regis Ecgfridi, conuenientibus ad consecrationem eius septem episcopis, in quibus* [m]*beate memorie Theodorus*[m] ordinator eius *primatum tenebat*, anno Dominice Incarnationis sexcentesimo octogesimo quinto, regni autem Ecgfridi duodecimo.

[ix]   *Electus*[n] *est autem*[o] *primo in episcopatum Hagustaldensis ecclesie pro Tunberto qui ab episcopatu fuerat depositus, sed quoniam plus Lindisfarnensi ecclesie in qua conuersatus fuerat dilexit prefici, placuit ut Eata*

[a] Sanctus Cuthbertus ad episcopatum electus est Hagustaldensem *rubric Fx Y*; Cuthbertus consecratus est in episcopatum Lyndisfarnensem septem Kalendas Aprilis die paschale *rubric T*   [b] elapso *T*   [c] *om. Y; add. over line Fx*   [d] eligitur *Fx L Y*   [e] *above line by Symeon C; om. Ca D F Y*   [f] Corruerunt *H*; Sanctus Cuthbertus ad episcopatum electus Hagustaldensis ecclesie *rubric H*   [g] ipsum negotium *Fx L Y*   [h–h] lacrimis quoque *F*   [i] seruus *T*   [j] ordinatio eius *Ca*   [k] eminebat *Fx L Y*   [l] *om. Fx L*   [m–m] beatus Theodorus *H*   [n] Commutauerunt sedes episcopales Eata et Cuthbertus sanctus (sanctus *om. H*) *rubric Fx H Y*   [o] *om. H*

charge of the two churches in the third year after father Cuthbert had retired to the solitude of his hermitage. Three years after the departure of Wilfrid, however, Theodore ordained Tunberht to the church of Hexham, whilst Eata remained bishop of Lindisfarne for four years.[56] After four years had passed, it came about that a large [viii] synod was held in the presence of the most pious King Ecgfrith, beloved of God, by the River Alne at a place called Twyford, which means 'At the Two Fords'. There Archbishop Theodore of blessed memory presided and, by the unanimous consent of all, the blessed father Cuthbert was elected bishop of the church of Lindisfarne. When despite the many messengers and letters sent to him he could in no way be torn away from the place where he was, at length King Ecgfrith himself together with the most holy bishop Trumwine and many other religious and powerful men sailed to the island. Assembled there also were many of the brothers from the island of [viii (H)] Lindisfarne. Everyone knelt down, entreated him in the name of the Lord, shed tears, and beseeched him, until finally they dragged him, weeping bitterly, from his beloved refuges and led him to the synod. When he arrived there, although he resisted stoutly, he was overcome by the unanimous will of all and compelled to bow his neck to receive the episcopal office. In this matter his resistance was chiefly overcome by the words of the servant of the Lord, Boisil, when he had revealed to Cuthbert with prophetic spirit all that was to befall him, and had also predicted that he would become a bishop. The ordination was not resolved upon at once, but was carried out after the winter which was then approaching. So when he had devoted himself to God in the life of a solitary for nine years, he was raised to the honour of the pontificate by the will of God, and consecrated at York on 26 March on the holy day of Easter itself, in the presence of King Ecgfrith. Seven bishops were assembled for his consecration, amongst whom Theodore of blessed memory held the chief place and ordained him, this being in the year of Our Lord's Incarnation 685, the twelfth of Ecgfrith's reign.

Now, he was elected first to the bishopric of the church of Hexham [ix] in place of Tunberht, who had been deposed from the episcopate. Because he preferred to be set over the church of Lindisfarne in

---

[56] This paragraph is derived from Bede, *HE* iv. 12. For Eata, see above, p. 26 n. 25. Bosa was bishop of York from 678/9 to 706, Tunberht was bishop of Hexham from 681 until his deposition in 684 (Bede, *HE* iv. 28 (26)). On the departure (or expulsion, as his biographer Stephen saw it) of Wilfrid, see *Life of Wilfrid*, ed. Colgrave, c. 24.

reuerso ad sedem ecclesie[a] Hagustaldensis, cui regende primo fuerat ordinatus, Cuthbertus ecclesie Lindisfarnensis gubernacula susciperet.[57] Cui [b]rex prefatus[b] et Theodorus in ciuitate Eboraca *dederunt totam terram a muro ecclesie sancti Petri usque[c] magnam portam uersus occidentem, et a muro* ipsius *ecclesie usque[d] murum ciuitatis uersus austrum. Villam* quoque[e] Crecam et tria in circuitu ipsius uille miliaria ei dederunt, ut haberet Eboracum iens uel inde rediens *mansionem* ubi requiescere posset. Vbi monachorum habitationem instituit, et quia illa terra minus sufficiens erat, Lugubaliam que Luel uocatur *in circuitu quindecim miliaria* habentem in augmentum suscepit. Vbi [f]etiam *sanctimonialium[f] congregatione* stabilita, reginam dato habitu religionis consecrauit, et in profectu diuine seruitutis *scolas* instituit. Alie quoque terrarum possessiones ei donate sunt, quas hic longum est et non necessarium ponere. Scripte sunt enim in cartulis ecclesie.[58]

At rex Ecgfridus, anno quo fecerat hunc uenerabilem patrem ordinari episcopum, *cum maxima parte copiarum* quas ad deuastandam[g] terram Pictorum secum duxerat, secundum [h]prophetiam eiusdem patris Cuthberti[h] [i]extinctus est[i] apud Nechtanesmere (quod est stagnum Nechtani) die terciodecimo[j] Kalendarum Iuniarum,[k] anno regni sui quintodecimo, cuius corpus in Hii, insula Columbe, sepultum est.[59]

---

[a] *om.* T   [b-b] prefatus rex F   [c] usque ad *Fx H L Y HSC*   [d] usque ad *Fx H L HSC*   [e] autem D   [f-f] etiam *in marg.* Y; sanctimonialium etiam *Fx L*   [g] deuastandum T   [h-h] eiusdem patris Cuthberti prophetiam *L Y*   [i-i] *om.* T; extinctus *add. in marg. in rough hand* C; tercio F   [j] tercio *with* decimo *above line in contemporary hand* C; tercio F   [k] Ianuarii D H

---

[57] This and the preceding paragraph to this point are derived from Bede, *HE* iv. 28 (26); cf. Bede, *V. Cuth.* c. 24. On the business and location (*Adtuifyrdi*, possibly Whittingham (Northumberland)) of the synod at which these matters were decided, see C. Cubitt, *Anglo-Saxon Church Councils c.650–c.850* (Leicester, 1995), pp. 258–9, 302–3. The date was the beginning of winter, 684. Trumwine was bishop of the Picts until his expulsion from his see of Abercorn (Midlothian) after the defeat of King Ecgfrith by the Picts in 685 (Bede, *HE* iv. 13, 26).

[58] This account of gifts to Cuthbert is derived from *HSC* c. 5 (Arnold, *Sym. Op.* i. 199), but the reference to the queen is peculiar to *LDE*. The 'charters' (*cartule*) of the church may be a reference to *HSC* which describes other gifts supposed to have been made to Cuthbert, notably that of land around the Bowmont Water (Northumberland); see *HSC* c. 3 (Arnold, *Sym. Op.* i. 197). It is possible, however, that Symeon knew free-standing documents, such as the forged charter of King Ecgfrith purporting to record the grant of land at Crayke and Carlisle to Cuthbert and preserved in Ca, p. 186, as well as in the later MSS (P. H. Sawyer, *Anglo-Saxon Charters: An Annotated List and Bibliography* (London, 1968), no. 66). For discussion of the possible locations of the land in York, see Rollason, *Sources*, pp. 140–1. On

which he had lived, however, it was arranged that, once Eata had returned to the see of the church of Hexham which he had originally been ordained to rule, Cuthbert should assume the government of the church of Lindisfarne.[57] King Ecgfrith and Archbishop Theodore gave to him in the city of York all the land from the wall of the church of St Peter as far as the great gate on the west side, and from the wall of the church of St Peter as far as the wall of the city on the south. They also gave him the vill of Crayke with a circuit of three miles around it, so that on his journeys to and from York he might have a staging-post where he might rest. There he established a house of monks and, because that land was by no means sufficient, he received as an addition to it Carlisle, which is called Luel, with a circuit of fifteen miles around it. There he established a congregation of nuns, and consecrated the queen, to whom he had given the habit of a nun; and for the advancement of divine service he established schools. Other landed possessions were also given to him which it would be lengthy and unnecessary to set out here. They are recorded in writing in the charters of the church.[58]

In the very year that he had had Cuthbert ordained bishop and in fulfilment of this venerable father's prophecy, King Ecgfrith was killed with most of the forces he was leading to lay waste the land of the Picts at a place called *Nechtansmere* (that is Nechtan's water) on 20 May in the fifteenth year of his reign, and his body was buried on Iona, the island of Columba.[59]

Crayke, see below, p. 91 n. 29, and E. Cambridge, 'Why did the community of St Cuthbert settle at Chester-le-Street?', in Bonner, *Cuthbert*, pp. 367–86, at 380–5.

[59] For Cuthbert's prophecy, which he made to Abbess Ælfflæd on Coquet Island (Northumbria), see Bede, *V. Cuth.* c. 24. The battle (Bede, *HE* iv. 26 (24)) took place in 685. The name is not found in any English source prior to *LDE*. The only one to give any indication of its site is ASC E, *s.a.* 685, according to which Ecgfrith was defeated 'be norðan sae', presumably a reference to a location north of the Firth of Forth. It appears as the battle of *Duin Nechtain*, however, in *The Annals of Ulster (to A.D. 1131): Part I: Text and Translation*, ed. S. Mac Airt and G. Mac Niocaill (Dublin, 1983), *s.a.* 685, and in *The Annals of Tigernach*, ed. W. Stokes (2 vols.; Felinfach, 1993), *s.a.* 685. This would seem to be connected with Dunnichen, three miles south-east of Forfar; the name means 'fortress of Nechtan' and there was formerly a lake in the vicinity which could have been the 'mere' of Symeon's name and that of Nennius. See F. T. Wainwright, 'Nechtansmere', *Antiquity*, xxii (1948), 82–97. The battle may even be represented on the carved stone at nearby Aberlemno (J. Romilly Allen and J. Anderson, *The Early Christian Monuments of Scotland*, introduction by I. Henderson (2 vols.; Balgavies, 1993, repr. from edn. of 1903), ii. 209–14, and, for the interpretation, A. Ritchie, *Picts: An Introduction to the Life of the Picts and the Carved Stones in the Care of Historic Scotland* (Edinburgh, 1989), pp. 22–7, and S. Foster, *Picts, Gaels and Scots* (London, 1996), p. 103. The reference to the burial of Ecgfrith's body is peculiar to *LDE*.

[x] **10.** Venerabilis*a* autem Cuthbertus *susceptum episcopatus gradum, ad imitationem beatorum apostolorum uirtutum ornabat operibus, commissam nanque sibi plebem et orationibus *b*protegebat assiduis,*b* et admonitionibus saluberrimis ad celestia uocabat, et—quod maxime doctores iuuat—ea que agenda docebat, ipse prius agendo premonstraret.*c* 60* Vt enim patri spirituali quondam subiectus exemplum subiectis dederat humilitatis et obedientie, prepositus quoque monasteriorum prepositis formam in se magisterii expresserat, sic episcopus etiam episcopis imitandam uite pontificalis normam reliquit. Quapropter qui ei in culmen honoris succedit, uitam quoque imitari studeat, ut dignus successor tanti predecessoris placita Deo conuersatione uices digne peragat. Sollicitus hinc illius uitam consideret, illinc suam. Consideret, inquam, ne peccatis oneratus occupet cathedram, quam ille uniuersarum effulgens decore uirtutum effecerat gloriosam.61 Namque ut in illius laudem *d*gratias Deo*d* agens ecclesia canit, castitate angelica, dignitate prophetica, uirtute apostolica, omniumque iustorum sanctitate insignis enituit. *Erat quippe*e* ante omnia diuine caritatis igne feruidus, patientie uirtute modestus, orationum deuotioni sollertissime intentus, affabilis omnibus qui ad se consolationis gratia ueniebant, hoc ipsum quoque *f*orationis loco*f* ducens, si infirmis fratribus opem sue exhortationis tribueret, sciens quia qui dixit 'Diliges Dominum Deum tuum', dixit et 'Diliges proximum tuum.'*g*62 Erat abstinentie castigatione insignis, erat gratia conpunctionis semper ad celestia suspensus. Denique cum sacrificium Deo uictime salutaris*h* offerret, non elata*i* in altum uoce sed profusis ex imo pectore lacrimis Domino sua uota commendabat.63*

*Duobus autem annis in episcopatu peractis, repetiit insulam ac monasterium*j* suum;*k* 64* mox *l*peracto die sollenni*l* natiuitatis Dominice,

a Quale exemplum uenerabilis Cuthbertus prebuit suis successoribus *rubric Fx T V Y*; Egfridus rex eodem anno quo sanctus Cuthbertus consecratus fuit occisus est *rubric H* *b–b* assiduis protegebat *Ca* *c* premonstrauit *F* *d–d* Deo gratias *Ca* *e* nanque *F* *f–f* loco orationis *H*; loco *expunctuated with* lucrum *in marg.* *Y*; lucrum *with* uel loco *in marg.* *Fx*; lucrum *L* *g* tuum *add. by BL, Cotton Tiberius C.II, DCL, B.II.35* *h* salutis *F* *i* elata *for* eleuata *poss. derived from* eleuatum, *DCL, B.II.35* *j* mansionem *H* *k* om. *Fx L* *l–l* peractis diebus solempnibus *T*

60 This sentence is taken verbatim from *HE* iv. 28 (26); cf. Bede, *V. Cuth.* cc. 26, 16–22.
61 *LDE* later explicitly relates Cuthbert's position as provost to that of the prior of Durham in the author's time (below, pp. 246–7). The reference to bishops here is likely to be directed at Bishop Ranulf Flambard (above, p. lxxxvii).
62 Luke 10: 27.
63 The italicized section is verbatim from Bede, *HE* iv. 28 (26), citing Deut. 6: 5, Lev. 19: 19, Matt. 19: 19 and 22: 37 and 39, and Mark 12: 30–1. The addition of *tuum* after

10. Now the venerable Cuthbert adorned the episcopal office which [x]
he had received with virtuous works in imitation of the blessed
apostles; he protected the people committed to him with assiduous
prayers; with admonitions for their salvation he called them to
heaven; and—that which is the greatest assistance to teachers—
everything he taught should be done he himself first of all demonstrated by his own actions.[60] For just as formerly he had as a subject
of the spiritual father given the example of humility and obedience to
those subjected to him, and also as provost he had expressed through
himself the manner of rule to be followed by provosts of other
monasteries, so as a bishop he also left a model of the episcopal life to
be imitated by other bishops. Therefore whoever would succeed him
in this highest office should strive also to imitate his life, and as a
worthy successor of such a man should worthily pass through all
vicissitudes with a manner of life pleasing to God. He should
carefully consider on the one hand his own life, on the other
Cuthbert's. He should consider, I say, lest he should be burdened
with sins when he occupies the episcopal throne, a throne which
Cuthbert himself, radiant with the splendour of all virtues, had made
glorious.[61] For, as the church sings in praise of him when giving
thanks to God, he excelled in the chastity of the angels, the dignity of
the prophets, the virtue of the apostles, and the holiness of all just
men. Above all he burned with the fire of divine love, he was gentle
with the virtue of patience, he was most earnest and gifted in his
devotion to prayer, and he was affable to all who came to him seeking
the grace of his consolation—for he considered it equivalent to prayer
itself for him to give the succour of his exhortation to his weaker
brothers, knowing that he who said, 'You should love the Lord your
God', said also, 'You should love your neighbour'.[62] He was
distinguished by the abstinence with which he castigated himself,
he was always straining towards heaven according to the dictates of
his conscience. So when he offered to God the sacrifice of the mass,
he commended his vows to Him not with raised voice but with tears
which came from his heart.[63]

After he had spent two years as bishop, he returned to his island
and his monastery.[64] Shortly after the feast of the nativity of Our

---

proximum is found in BL, Cotton Tiberius C.II and DCL, B.II.35, and the form *elata* for
eleuata may be based on the erroneous *eleuatum* in DCL, B.II.35.

[64] This sentence is from Bede, *HE* iv. 29 (27). This was after Christmas 686 (Bede, *V.
Cuth.* c. 34; Stancliffe, in Bonner, *Cuthbert*, p. 36).

diuino admonitus oraculo quia dies sibi mortis uel uite magis illius que sola uita dicenda est iam appropiaret introitus.[65] *Qui cum duos ferme menses in magna repetite sue quietis exultatione transigeret, correptus infirmitate subita temporalis igne doloris ad perpetue cepit beatitudinis gaudia preparari.* Tribus *enim ebdomadibus continuis infirmitate decoctus, sic ad extrema peruenit. Siquidem* ᵃquarta feriaᵃ *cepit egrotare, et rursus quarta feria finita egritudine migrauit ad Dominum.*

Qui infirmatus, hec per *Herefrid*um *deuote religionis presbiter*um *qui tunc Lindisfarnensi monasterio* ᵇ*abbatis iure*ᵇ *prefuit,* demandauit dicens: '*Cum* Dominusᶜ *susceperit animam meam, sepelite me in hac mansione iuxta oratorium meum ad meridiem contra orientalem plagam sancte crucis quam ibidem erexi. Est autem ad aquilonem*ᵈ *eiusdem oratorii partem sarcofagum terre cespite abditum, quod olim michi Cudda uenerabilis abbas donauit. In hoc corpus meum reponite, inuoluentes in sindone quam inuenietis istic. Nolui quidem ea uiuens indui,*ᵉ *sed pro amore dilecte Deo femine que hanc michi misit, Verce uidelicet abbatisse, ad obuoluendum corpus meum reseruare curaui.*'

At fratribus eum rogantibus ut eius corpus in Lindisfarnensium ecclesia tumulandum transferre ac secum habere sibi liceret, respondens ille: '*Et mee*', inquit, '*uoluntatis erat hic requiescere corpore, ubi quantulumcunque pro Domino certamen certaui, ubi cursum consummare desidero, unde ad coronam iusticie sulleuandum me a pio iudice spero. Sed et uobis quoque*ᶠ *commodius esse arbitror ut hic requiescam propter incursionem profugorum uel noxiorum quorumlibet. Qui cum ad corpus meum forte confugerint, quia qualiscunque sum, fama tamen exiuit*ᵍ ʰ*de me*ʰ *quia famulus Christi*ⁱ *sim,*ʲ *necesse habetis* ᵏ*sepius pro talibus*ᵏ *apud potentes seculi intercedere, atque ideo*ˡ *de presentia corporis mei multum tolerare laborem.*' At fratribus *multum diu precantibus laboremque huiusmodi gratum sibi ac leuem fore asseuerantibus, tandem cum consilio locutus uir Domini: 'Si meam' inquit 'dispositionem superare, et meum corpus illo reducere*ᵐ *uultis,* ⁿ*uidetur michi optimum*ⁿ *ut in interioribus basilice uestre*ᵒ *illud tumuletis, quatinus et ipsi cum uultis meum*

ᵃ⁻ᵃ quarta *Ca;* feria quarta *H*   ᵇ⁻ᵇ *om. F*   ᶜ Deus *T L Y*
ᵈ aquilonalem *F Ca*   ᵉ uti *F*   ᶠ *om. T*   ᵍ exiuit *for* exiit *found in Cambridge, Trinity College, O.3.55, Bod. Lib., Laud misc. 491, Fx (Colgrave, Two Lives, pp. 280-2)*   ʰ⁻ʰ *om. L*   ⁱ Dei *F*   ʲ sum *T V*   ᵏ⁻ᵏ pro talibus sepius *T*   ˡ *om. T*   ᵐ ducere *H*   ⁿ⁻ⁿ michi optimum uidetur *H*
ᵒ nostre *T*

Lord, he was forewarned by a vision that the day of his death—or rather of his entry into that life which alone should be called life—was approaching.[65] When he had passed almost two months in the exultation of his regained quietitude, he was suddenly stricken with illness and the fire of worldly pain began to prepare him for the joys of perpetual blessedness. Wasted by the illness for three weeks on end, he came at length to his last moments. He was indeed taken ill on a Wednesday, and also on a Wednesday his illness came to an end and he passed on to the Lord.

During his illness he made this request through Herefrith, a devout and religious priest who was then ruling the monastery of Lindisfarne as abbot: 'When the Lord has received my soul, bury me in this dwelling to the south of my oratory, on the east side of the holy cross which I have erected there. Now, on the north side of that oratory there is hidden under sods of earth a sarcophagus which was once given to me by the venerable abbot Cudda. Place my body in this, wrapping it in the cloth which you will find there. For indeed I did not wish to wear it during my lifetime but, for love of the abbess Verca, a woman loved of God, who gave it to me, I have taken care to keep it so that my body might be wrapped in it.'

When the brothers asked him to allow them to take his body for burial to the church of Lindisfarne and so to keep it with them, he replied: 'It was my wish that my body should rest here, where I have for a little while fought the fight for the Lord, where I desire to run the race to the end, and whence I hope that the righteous judge will raise me up to receive the crown of justice. Furthermore, I believe that it would be more convenient for you if I were to rest here, on account of the incursion of fugitives and criminals of all sorts who will perhaps flee for sanctuary to my body—because whatever my real nature may be, the report has nevertheless gone out that I am a servant of Christ—it will very often be necessary for you to intercede with the powerful of this world on behalf of such men, and so indeed you will have to suffer much labour on account of the presence of my body.' But when the brothers beseeched him long and hard, asserting that such labour would be light and pleasant for them, the man of God at length gave them this counsel: 'If you wish to overturn my decision and to take my body back with you, it seems best to me that you should bury it in the interior of your church, so that you

[65] This is presumably a reference to the vision of his approaching end which Cuthbert communicated to Hereberht, the hermit of Derwentwater (Bede, *V. Cuth.* c. 28, and Bede, *HE* iv. 29 (27)), although it is not clear whence *LDE* derives its chronology.

sepulchrum uisitare possitis, et in potestate sit uestra an aliqui illo de aduenientibus accedant.' Gratias egerunt fratres *permissioni et consilio illius*[a] *flexis* [b]*in terram genibus.*[b] [66]

Cui permissioni et consilio nos quoque gratias agamus non solum flexis genibus, sed et totis corporibus pariter et cordibus ei suppliciter[c] prostratis. Nos, inquam, [d]gratias illi[d] referamus, quibus incorruptum [e]corpus eius[e] quadringentesimo et octauo decimo dormitionis eiuṣ anno quamuis indignis diuina gratia uidere et manibus quoque contrectare donauit. Agamus, inquam, gratias, laboremque defendendi confugientes ad illius sepulchrum, dulcedine amoris eius gratum ac leuem ducamus, et omne quicquid nutante[f] seculi statu aduersum ingruerit despectui habeamus, dummodo talem ac tantum sacri corporis thesaurum in medio nostri nos habere gaudeamus.[67]

[xi] Cum[g] uero increscente languore uideret tempus [h]sue resolutionis[h] instare, hunc[i] hereditarium sermonem, hoc ultimum uale fratribus reliquit, disserens pauca sed fortia de pace et humilitate, cauendisque eis qui his obluctari quam oblectari mallent: *'Pacem' inquit 'inter uos semper et caritatem custodite diuinam et, cum de uestro statu consilium uos agere necessitas poposcerit, uidete attentius ut unanimes existatis in*
[xi (H)] *consiliis.'* Et cetera que in uita illius leguntur ad fidei [j]caritatisque custodiam,[j] ad uite regularis obseruantiam salubria monita.[k] *At ubi consuetum nocturne orationis tempus aderat, acceptis sacramentis salutaribus exitum suum*[l] *muniuit, atque eleuatis ad celum oculis, extensisque in altum manibus, intentam supernis laudibus animam ad gaudia regni celestis emisit,* biennio in episcopatu suo exacto, anno [m]sexcentesimo octogesimo septimo Dominice incarnationis,[m] ex quo autem rex Oswaldus et Aidanus pontificalem sedem et monachorum habitationem in sepe dicta insula[n] instituerant quinquagesimo tertio, [o]ex eo uero quo[o]

---

[a] eius *H*   [b-b] genibus in terram *L*; terram *for* terra *found in Cambridge, Trinity College, O.3.55, Bod. Lib., Laud misc. 491, Fx (Colgrave, Two Lives, pp. 280-2)*   [c] om. *T*   [d-d] illi gratias *Ca*   [e-e] eius corpus *F*   [f] in tanto *H*; mutante *L*   [g] Obitus sancti Cuthberti *rubric Fx V Y*   [h-h] resolutionis sue *D*   [i] corr. over erasure *C F*   [j-j] et caritatis custodiam *L*; caritatis custodiam et *H*   [k] Obitus sancti Cuthberti *rubric H*   [l] quem iam uenisse cognouit Dominici corporis et sanguinis communione *add. Fx H L Y (Bede, V. Cuth. c. 39)*   [m-m] Dominice incarnationis sexcentesimo octogesimo septimo *H Fx L Y*   [n] ecclesia *Fx L*   [o-o] ex eo uero *T;* uero ex quo *L Y*

---

[66] The whole of this account of Cuthbert's last illness is taken, largely verbatim, from Bede, *V. Cuth.* c. 37. Nothing is known of Cudda, Verca, or Herefrith, other than the information contained in this passage.

[67] The reference is to the translation of Cuthbert's undecayed body into the new

yourselves may visit my tomb when you wish, but so that it may be in your power whether any visitors should have access to it.' The brothers knelt down and gave thanks for his permission and for his advice.[66]

For this permission and counsel we too give thanks, not only upon bended knees but also with our whole bodies and our hearts prostrate before him in supplication. We give thanks to him, I say, we to whom it was given by divine grace, unworthy as we are, to see and even to touch his undecayed body in the four hundredth and eighteenth year after his death. Let us give thanks, I say, and delighted by his love let us hold as light and pleasant the labour of defending those who flee to his tomb; and let us hold in contempt whatever adversity may assail us in the changeable state of this world, so long as we may rejoice in having so great a treasure as his holy body in our midst.[67] When with [xi] his illness worsening he saw that the time of his release was approaching he left to the brothers this sermon to be handed down, this final farewell, discoursing briefly but powerfully on peace and humility and on the need to avoid those who contended against these virtues rather than taking pleasure in them: 'Always keep the peace and love of God among yourselves and, when necessity demands that you hold discussions concerning your situation, see to it attentively that you are unanimous in your counsels.' And he gave other wholesome advice, which can be read in his life, for the keeping of faith and love and for the observation of the life of the Rule. So when [xi (H)] the time of his accustomed nightly prayers came, he fortified his departure by receiving the redeeming sacraments and, with his eyes raised to heaven and his hands stretched out on high, he sent forth his soul which was bent on celestial praises to the joys of the heavenly kingdom. He had been bishop for two years, the year being the six hundredth and eighty-seventh of the Incarnation of Our Lord, the fifty-third since King Oswald and Aidan had established an episcopal see and a dwelling of monks on the island we have often mentioned,

Norman cathedral on 29 Aug. 1104, described and dated in *De miraculis* c. 7, and in Raine, *Cuth. virt.* c. 40. See Battiscombe, *Relics*, pp. 55–9, and, for the dating, Jäschke, in Rollason, *Symeon*, pp. 48–50. For the importance of the reference in *LDE* for dating and attributing *LDE*, see above, p. xlii. It also provides evidence for the existence of sanctuary rights at Cuthbert's tomb in the early 12th-cent.; cf. the account of an attempted breach of sanctuary there in the time of Earl Tostig (1055–65) in *De miraculis* c. 5 (Arnold, *Sym. Op.* i. 243–5). See also D. Hall, 'The sanctuary of St Cuthbert', in Bonner, *Cuthbert*, pp. 425–36, esp. 425, and, for evidence of sanctuary rights in the eighth cent., below, pp. 78–81.

monachicum in Mailros habitum sumpserat tricesimo septimo anno, quamuis ab ipso puericie sue tempore monachus mente semper et actu uixerit. *Impositum autem naui uenerabile corpus patris, ad insulam Lindisfarnensium* fratres retulerunt. *Quod magno occurrentium agmine chorisque canentium susceptum est, atque in ecclesia beati Petri apostoli[a] ad dexteram altaris petrino in sarcophago repositum.*[68]

Sepulto autem *uiro Dei tanta ecclesiam illam temptationis aura concussit, ut plures e fratribus loco magis cedere, quam talibus uellent interesse periculis, episcopatum [b]ecclesie illius[b] anno ipso serua*nte *uenerabili antistite Wilfrid*o, *donec eligeretur qui pro Cuthberto antistes ordinari deberet.* Ordinatus est autem[c] post annum Eadbertus in episcopatum, *uir scientia scripturarum diuinarum simul et preceptorum celestium obseruantia, ac maxime elemosinarum operatione insignis, ita ut iuxta legem omnibus annis decimam[d] non solum quadrupedum, uerum etiam frugum omnium atque pomorum necnon et[e] uestimentorum partem pauperibus daret.* Eo itaque in pontificatum sullimato, prefate temptationis tempestate sedata, ut scriptura loquitur, '*edificauit Ierusalem*' *(id est uisionem pacis)* '*Dominus et dispersiones Israel congregauit. Sanauit [f]contritos corde et alligauit[f] contritiones eorum.*'[69]

[xii] **11.** *Transactis[g]* autem *sepulture ipsius annis undecim, aperientes sepulchrum eius fratres inuenerunt corpus totum quasi adhuc uiueret integrum, et flexibilibus artuum compagibus multo dormienti quam mortuo similius. Sed et uestimenta omnia quibus indutum erat non solum intemerata, uerum etiam prisca nouitate et* claritate *miranda parebant. Quod ubi uiderunt[h] fratres, nimio mox timore et tremore sunt perculsi, adeo ut uix aliquid*

---

[a] *om.* Y; *add. over line* Fx   [b-b] illius ecclesie H   [c] *om.* H   [d] *om.* T
[e] *om.* H   [f-f] *om.* Fx   [g] Post undecim annos (annos undecim T) corpus sancti Cuthberti incorruptum inuentum est *rubric* Fx H T Y   [h] uidebant H

---

[68] Much of this paragraph is derived from Bede, *V. Cuth.* cc. 39, 40. The chronology, which is added by *LDE*, is consistent with dates of 635 for the foundation of Lindisfarne and 651 for Cuthbert's entry into Melrose. Nothing is known from archaeological excavation about the location of the tomb or indeed of the location and layout of St Peter's Church; see D. O'Sullivan, 'The plan of the early Christian monastery on Lindisfarne: a fresh look at the evidence', in Bonner, *Cuthbert*, pp. 125–42, and for a speculative approach based on the alignment of the priory church with the present parish church, J. Blair, 'The early churches at Lindisfarne', *Archaeologia Aeliana*, 5th ser. xix (1991), 47–53. Inscribed gravestones and sculpture of pre-Viking date were recovered from the general area of the medieval priory church, but without precise records being kept (C. R. Peers, 'The inscribed and sculptured stones of Lindisfarne', *Archaeologia*, lxxiv (1925, for 1924), 255–70, and Cramp, *Corpus*, pp. 194–208). In 698, Cuthbert's undecayed body was raised from the sarcophagus referred to in this passage and placed in a light wooden chest (*theca*) on the floor of the church (Bede, *V. Cuth.* c. 42; and, on the

the thirty-seventh indeed since Cuthbert had assumed the monastic habit at Melrose, although from the time of his boyhood he had lived always as a monk in thought and deed. The brothers placed the venerable body of the father in a ship and took it back to the island of Lindisfarne. There it was received by a great crowd who came to meet it and by choirs of singers, and it was placed in a stone sarcophagus to the right of the altar in the church of the St Peter the Apostle.[68]

When the man of God had been buried, such a wind of trial shook that church that many of the brothers preferred to leave rather than to face such perils there. For in that particular year the position of bishop in Cuthbert's church was held by the venerable bishop Wilfrid, until he who was to be bishop in Cuthbert's place was elected. After a year, however, Eadberht was ordained to the episcopate. He was a man distinguished for his knowledge of the sacred scriptures, for his observance of heavenly precepts, and above all for his giving of alms, so that according to the law he gave every year to the poor a tenth part not only of the livestock but also of all the crops and the fruit and of the clothing. After he had been raised to the bishopric and the aforementioned storm of trial had died down, 'the Lord built Jerusalem', as scripture says, that is the vision of peace; 'he brought together the dispersal of Israel; he cured the contrite in heart and he bound up their griefs'.[69]

11. When eleven years had passed since Cuthbert's burial, the brothers opened his grave and found his body wholly undecayed as if it were still living and the joints still flexible, more as if it were asleep than dead. Moreover all the garments in which it was clad not only appeared undecayed but had even miraculously preserved their newness and brightness. When the brothers saw this, they were struck with great fear and trembling, so that they could hardly speak, [xii]

preservation at Durham of a chest identified with the *theca*, see Battiscombe, *Relics*, pp. 202–307, C. V. Horie and J. M. Cronyn, *St Cuthbert's Coffin: The History, Technology and Conservation* (Durham, 1985), and Bonner, *Cuthbert*, pp. 231–85).

[69] Most of this paragraph is taken verbatim from Bede, *HE* iv. 29 (27), and Bede, *V. Cuth.* c. 40, quoting Ps. 146: 2, 3. The etymology of Jerusalem was presumably derived from Ezechiel 13: 6 ('Prophete Israel, qui prophetant ad Ierusalem, et uident ei uisionem pacis, et non est pax'). Wilfrid (d. 709), the founder of Ripon and Hexham, and bishop of York (*Blackwell Encyclopaedia*, ed. Lapidge *et al.*, *s.u.*) administered the see of Lindisfarne from 687 to 688. Reference to his having administered the see of Lindisfarne from 687–8 is found only in Bede, *HE* v. 29 (27), and Bede, *V. Cuth.* c. 40 alludes to the period in question as a very troubled one. See also, below, p. 58–9 and, for Eadberht's dates, p.58 n. 74.

loqui, uix intueri auderent[a] *miraculum quod parebat, uix ipsi quid agerent nossent.* Extremam *autem indumentorum eius partem pro ostendendo incorruptionis*[b] *signo tollentes, nam que carni illius proxima aderant prorsus tangere timebant, festinarunt referre antistiti quod inuenerant. Que cum ille et munera gratanter acciperet, et miracula libenter audiret, nam et ipsa indumenta quasi patris adhuc corpori circumdata miro deosculabatur affectu, 'Noua', inquit, 'indumenta corpori pro his que tulistis circumdate, et sic reponite in theca*[c] *quam parastis. Scio autem certissime quia non diu uacuus remanebit locus, qui tanta celestis miraculi uirtute consecratus est, et quam beatus est cui in*[d] *eo* facultatem *quiescendi* Dominus totius *beatitudinis auctor atque largitor* prestare dignabitur.'

Hec et huiusmodi plura ubi multis cum lacrimis et magna compunctione antistes, lingua etiam[e] *tremente compleuit, fecerunt fratres ut iusserat, et inuolutum nouo amictu corpus,* nouaque *in theca reconditum supra pauimentum sanctuarii* digne uenerationis gratia *posuerunt.* Tulerunt autem fratres *partem*[f] *de capillis*[f] *eius, quam more reliquiarum rogantibus amicis dare uel ostendere in signum miraculi possent.*[70]

Nec mora Deo dilectus antistes Eadbertus morbo correptus[g] *est acerbo, ac per dies crescente ardore languoris, non multo post (id est pridie Nonas Maias) etiam ipse*[h] *migrauit ad Dominum, impetrato ab eo munere quod diligentissime petierat, uidelicet ut non repentina morte sed longa excoctus egritudine migraret*[i] *e corpore. Cuius corpus in sepulchro beati patris Cuthberti ponentes, apposuerunt desuper arcam in qua incorrupta eiusdem patris membra locauerant.*[71]

Huius uero scilicet beati Cuthberti gloriosissime conuersationis exordium, progressum, terminum, sicut ab his qui cum eo conuersati fuerant fratribus, indubiis testibus didicerat, puro ac simplici sermone Beda explicat, gratia Dei hoc prouidente ut[j] angelicam uitam quam in extremis mundi partibus uir tantus duxerat, uir tante in ecclesia quaque diffusa[k] auctoritatis scribendo[l] propalaret. Vnde conuenienter ordinante Deo actum est, ut ossa ipsius defuncti cum corpore eiusdem[m] patris quandoque[n] requiescerent, cuius corporis pios pro

---

[a] *om.* H   [b] eius *add.* T   [c] thecam F   [d] *om.* H   [e] et L
[f-f] capillorum F   [g] arreptus D   [h] *om.* T   [i] migrauit H   [j] ac T V
[k] diffuse Ca   [l] *om.* H   [m] ipsius H   [n] *om.* T

---

[70] This paragraph is taken, almost wholly verbatim, from Bede, *HE* iv. 30, and, to a greater extent, Bede, *V. Cuth.* c. 42; the last sentence from Bede, *HE* iv. 32. As this passage shows, the elevation of the body took place in 698. On the context, see Rollason, *Saints and Relics*, pp. 35–7.

[71] This paragraph is verbatim from Bede, *HE* iv. 30, and Bede, *V. Cuth.* c. 43. Eadberht's relics were taken from Lindisfarne with those of Cuthbert (below, pp. 102–

they hardly dared look at the miracle which had appeared, they hardly knew what they should do. They removed a part of his clothing furthest from the body in order to use it as a witness to his undecayed state, for they were very much afraid to touch that which had been closest to his flesh, and they hastened to tell the bishop what they had found. When he had gratefully accepted the gifts and willingly listened to their account of the miracles, he kissed the garments themselves with wonderful affection as if they were still clothing the father's body, and he said: 'Put new clothes around the body in place of these which you have taken, and so place it in the casket which you have prepared. For I know for certain that the place consecrated by virtue of such a heavenly miracle will not long remain empty, and how blessed is he to whom the Lord, the maker and giver of all holiness, will deign to grant permission to rest there.' When the bishop had said these and many other such things with many tears, great compunction and a trembling tongue, the brothers did as he had ordered, and so that it might be venerated worthily they placed the body, wrapped in a new covering and placed in the new casket, on the floor of the sanctuary. The brothers took some of his hairs so that, in the manner of relics, they could be given or shown to friends who asked as a sign of the miracle.[70]

Without delay Eadberht, the bishop beloved of God, was seized by a cruel illness and, as the severity of the disease increased day by day, he shortly afterwards went to the Lord (that is on 6 May) having obtained from him the gift that he had most diligently requested, that is that he should be taken from the body not by a sudden death but wasted by a long illness. They laid his body in the grave of the blessed father Cuthbert, and above they erected a shrine in which they had placed that same father's undecayed remains.[71]

Bede, who had learned about the beginning, course, and end of the most glorious life of the blessed Cuthbert from witnesses who were above doubt, as from those brothers who had lived with him, expounded it in pure and simple words, the grace of God thus providing that the angelic life which such a man had led in the farthest corners of the world should be made known by the writing of a man of such authority wherever the church is to be found. Thus by the ordinance of God it happened fittingly that after his death Bede's bones came at length to rest with the body of that same father, whose

3), and were found in Cuthbert's shrine in 1104 (*De miraculis* c. 7, Arnold, *Sym. Op.* i. 252).

Christo labores et incorruptionem post undecim sepulture annos secuturis temporibus manifestando descripserat.[72]

Post obitum uero patris Cuthberti Wilfridus (ut supradictum est) *uno anno* ecclesie illius episcopatum tenuit. Iam enim Aldfrido *rege inuitante qui post* fratrem *Ecgfridum regnauit, sedem et episcopatum* receperat.[73] Deinde Eadbertus per decem annos, post quem *Eadfridus per uiginti quattuor* sancti ac Deo digni presules ecclesie* prefuerunt.[74] Cuius Eadfridi tempore Beda tricesimo etatis sue anno, gradu presbiteratus accepto, libros suos incepit facere, in quibus faciendis per uiginti nouem annos (id est ad* finem uite) in lege Domini meditans die ac nocte indesinenter laborauit.[75] Fecit inter alia et sepe dictum librum uite patris Cuthberti ad prefatum episcopum ita scribens: '*Domino sancto ac beatissimo patri* Eadfrido episcopo, sed et omni congregationi fratrum qui in Lindisfarnensi insula Christo derseruiunt, Beda fidelis uester conseruus salutem. Quia iussistis, dilectissimi, ut libro, quem de uita beate memorie patris nostri Cuthberti uestro rogatu composui, prefationem aliquam iuxta morem prefigerem*', et cetera que in proemio eiusdem opusculi ipse prosequitur.[76] Eius uero ostensa in alios beneficia predicaturus, ipse primum in se *per curationem lingue* dum eius miracula caneret, est expertus, sicut in prefatione libelli quem de uita ipsius metro composuit ad Iohannem presbiterum ipsemet affirmat.[77]

Predictus itaque reuerentissimus pontifex Eadfridus[78] multum feruens amore sui predecessoris, beati Cuthberti oratorium in sue anachoretice conuersationis insula, longa iam *uetustate dissolutum, a fundamentis* restaurauit, Felgildo tunc ibidem in uita solitaria post

---

a–a om. F *b–b* per uiginti quattuor Eadfridus *T* *c om. T* *d* usque ad Fx *L* *e om. V* *f–f* Reuerentissimus itaque predictus *H*

---

[72] Reference is presumably to Bede, *V. Cuth.*, rather than to his linguistically difficult metrical *uita* (see below, n. 77). On the subsequent transfer of the relics of Bede to Durham in the early eleventh cent., see below, pp. 164–7.

[73] On Wilfrid's administration of Lindisfarne, see above, p. 55 n. 69. Aldfrith was king of the Northumbrians from 686–705 (for discussion of the complications surrounding these dates, see Rollason, *Sources*, p. 49). The statement that he gave Wilfrid responsibility for Lindisfarne is peculiar to *LDE*.

[74] Eadberht was evidently bishop of Lindisfarne from 688–98, Eadfrith from 698–721. Bede, *HE* iv. 30 (28), implies that Eadberht died in the same year as the first translation of St Cuthbert, i.e. 698, which would give him a pontificate of ten years, following the year in which Wilfrid administered the see. Eadfrith's succession to Eadberht is dated 698 in JW ii. 158–61, but in a contemporary addition to the original annal. As for Eadfrith's death, *ALf* gives 722; and JW (ii. 176–7) gives 721, but this information is also added to the original annal. 721 is consistent with *LDE's* twenty-four-year pontificate for Eadfrith.

[75] Bede, *HE* v. 24, states that he became a priest in his thirtieth year and from then

pious labours for Christ and the undecayed state of whose body after eleven years he had described so that it might be made known to later times.[72]

After the death of father Cuthbert, Wilfrid (as we said before) held the episcopal see of that church for a year. For he had received the see and the episcopal office at the invitation of King Aldfrith who ruled after his brother Ecgfrith.[73] After that the church was ruled by two holy bishops worthy of God, Eadberht for ten years and after him Eadfrith for twenty-four.[74] It was in the time of Eadfrith that Bede, in his thirtieth year and having accepted the rank of priest, began to write his books, on which for twenty-nine years (that is to the end of his life) he laboured without ceasing, meditating day and night on the law of the Lord.[75] Among others he wrote the book of the life of father Cuthbert which we have often mentioned, and he dedicated it thus to the aforementioned bishop: 'To my lord the holy and most blessed father Bishop Eadfrith and to the whole congregation of brothers who serve Christ on the island of Lindisfarne, Bede your faithful fellow servant sends greeting. Because, dearly beloved, you have ordered that I should place at the beginning of the book about the life of our father Cuthbert of blessed memory, which I have composed at your request, some preface as is the custom,' and so on as he himself continues in the preface to that same work.[76] This same man, who was to make known the saint's miracles shown to others, first of all experienced in himself a cure of his tongue, which happened while he was singing of the saint's miracles, as he affirms to the priest John in the preface to the little book which he composed in metre concerning Cuthbert's life.[77]

The aforementioned[78] most reverend bishop Eadfrith, burning with a great love for his predecessor, restored from its foundations the blessed Cuthbert's oratory, which was then ruined because of its great age, on the island where he had lived the life of an anchorite; and Felgild was then living the solitary life there in succession to

until his 59th year, presumably 731, he had been writing works. Symeon has taken Bede's reference to his 59th year as being to the year of his death rather than to that of the composition of the *HE* and has thus calculated erroneously that Bede was engaged in writing for 29 years. Bede in fact died in 735. See also above, p. 40 n. 50.

[76] The quotation is from Bede, *V. Cuth.* preface.

[77] *Bedas metrische Vita sancti Cuthberti*, ed. W. Jaager (Palaestra, cxcviii; Leipzig, 1935), preface (p. 57). On this text, see M. Lapidge, 'Bede's metrical *Vita sancti Cuthberti*', in Bonner, *Cuthbert*, pp. 77–93.

[78] V breaks off here at the foot of fo. 66ᵛ and the end of a gathering. The word *itaque*, possibly a catchword, has been written below.

Ethelwoldum conuersante. Qui uidelicet Aethelwoldus cum *iam multis annis in monasterio quod dicitur in Hripum acceptum presbiteratus officium condignis gradu* condecorasset *actibus*, successit uiro Domini[a] Cuthberto in exercenda uita solitaria *in insula Farne*, mansitque ibidem *duodecim*[b] *annis*, ubi et *defunctus* est, *sed in insula*[c] *Lindisfarnensium iuxta prefatorum episcoporum corpora in ecclesia beati Petri apostoli sepultus.*[d][79]

[xiii] **12.** Defuncto[e] Eadfrido episcopo, religiose ac modeste uite abbas et presbiter monasterii Mailrosensis Ethelwoldus successit in episcopatum, predecessorum suorum cathedram per sedecim annos et ipse condignis[f] honore actibus seruans. Hic plane antequam monasterium prefatum iure abbatis regeret, beati patris Cuthberti (ut in eius uita legitur) dignus minister extiterat.[80] Fecerat iste[g] de lapide crucem artifici opere expoliri, et in sui memoriam suum in eo nomen exarari. Cuius summitatem multo post tempore dum ipsam ecclesiam Lindisfarnensem pagani deuastarent, fregerunt, sed post artificis ingenio relique parti infuso plumbo ipsa fractura est adiuncta; semperque[h] deinceps cum corpore sancti Cuthberti crux ipsa cirumferri solebat, et a populo Northanhymbrorum propter utrumque sanctum in honore haberi, que etiam usque hodie in huius (id est Dunelmensis) ecclesie[i] cimiterio stans sullimis utrorumque pontificum intuentibus exhibet monimentum.[81]

[xiv] **13.** Anno[j] [k]Dominice incarnationis[k] septingentesimo uicesimo nono,[l] pontificatus uero Ethelwoldi quinto, *Osricus rex Northanhymbrorum filius Aldfridi regis uita decessit,*[m] cum ipse regni quod undecim annis gubernabat successorem pro se *Ceolwulfum decreuisset, fratrem illius*

---

[a] Dei *H*   [b] uiginti *H*   [c] *om. L*   [d] est sepultus *H*
[e] Etheluualdus episcopus fecit crucem lapideam que adhuc cernitur in cimiterio Dunelmi *rubric Fx H T Y*   [f] *om. F*   [g] ipse *Fx H L Y*   [h] semper *H*   [i] *om. H*   [j] De genealogia Ceowlphi regis et omnium regum Northanimbrorum (Northumbrie *H*) *rubric Fx H T Y*   [k-k] ab incarnationis Dominice *Fx L Y*   [l] *Numerals; above in words in contemp. hand C*   [m] discessit *Fx H L Y*

---

[79] This paragraph is taken, largely verbatim, from Bede, *HE* v. 1; cf. *V. Cuth.* c. 46. The name occurs as *Oidiluald* in *HE* and also, amongst those of hermits and anchorites, in *Liber Vitae*, fo. 15. Ripon (Yorks.), which was originally founded by Abbot Eata but then refounded by Wilfrid, was evidently a major monastery, and the present church preserves the 7th-cent. crypt (*Blackwell Encyclopaedia*, ed. Lapidge *et al.*, *s.u.*, and H. M. and J. Taylor, *Anglo-Saxon Architecture*, iii. 1014–17).

[80] Bede, *V. Cuth.* c. 30. Æthelwald was bishop of Lindisfarne from before 731 to 737/40, possibly 724–40. The date of his death is given as 740 in *HReg*, *s.a.* (Arnold, *Sym. Op.*

Æthelwald. Now when Æthelwald had for many years in the monastery called Ripon been adorning the office of priest, which he had accepted, with actions worthy of that rank, he succeeded the man of God Cuthbert in leading the life of a solitary on the island of Farne. He stayed there for twelve years and died there, but he was buried on the island of Lindisfarne near the bodies of the aforementioned bishops in the church of the blessed Peter the Apostle.[79]

12. After the death of Bishop Eadfrith, Æthelwald, a man of religious [xiii] and gentle life and abbot and priest of the monastery of Melrose, succeeded to the bishopric, and occupied the throne of his predecessors for sixteen years, himself performing acts worthy of the honour conferred on him. Before he ruled the aforesaid monastery as abbot, he had been a worthy servant of the blessed father Cuthbert (as can be read in his Life).[80] He had had embellished by the work of craftsmen a stone cross, and in memory of the saint he had his name inscribed on it. Much later the heathens broke the top of this cross when they sacked the church of Lindisfarne, but afterwards with the ingenuity of a craftsman the broken part was joined again to the remainder by means of pouring in lead. Always afterwards it was the custom to carry this cross round with the body of St Cuthbert, and for it to be held in honour by the people of Northumbria on account of both saints. Down to the present day it stands loftily in the cemetery of this church (that is the church of Durham), and it exhibits to onlookers a monument to both bishops.[81]

13. In the year of Our Lord's Incarnation 729, the fifth of the [xiv] episcopate of Æthelwald, King Osric of the Northumbrians, son of King Aldfrith, departed this life, after he himself had decreed that his successor in the kingdom which he had ruled for eleven years should

ii. 32) and the *HECont*, *s.a.*, but as 737 by ASC DEF and 738 by JW ii. 186–7. Æthelwald's accession had occurred by 731, when he was mentioned as the current bishop of Lindisfarne by Bede (*HE* v. 12, 23), but the only source to give an exact date (722) is *ALf*. Since *LDE* regarded 729 as the fifth year of Æthelwald's episcopate (below), and made the unique statement that he was bishop for sixteen years, Symeon presumably believed that he became bishop in 724 and died in 740. This is not inconsistent with other sources. Bishop Eadberht died in 698 (see above, p. 58 n. 74), and the dates of his successor Eadferth are entirely unknown. On Melrose, see above, p. 26 n. 24.

[81] This cross is not thought to have survived, but it has been suggested that its influence on sculpture produced in later centuries by the community of St Cuthbert can be discerned, especially in the cross shaft from St Oswald's, Durham; see Rosemary Cramp, 'The artistic influence of Lindisfarne within Northumbria', in Bonner, *Cuthbert*, pp. 213–28, at 223–5, 228; and Cramp, *Corpus*, p. 67.

qui ante se regnauerat Coenredi regis.[82] Qui uidelicet Ceolwlfus de
stirpe quidem Ide primi regis Northanhymbrorum fuerat, sed non de
filio eius Ethelrico rege, de quo gloriosissimi reges Oswaldus et Oswiu
descenderant, genealogiam duxit sed de fratre ipsius[a] Ethelrici
nomine Ocga[b] originem traxisse inuenitur. Fuerat quippe Ceolwlfus
filius Cuthe, cuius pater Cuthwine, cuius pater Liodwald, [c]cuius pater
Ecgwald,[c] cuius pater Aldhelm, cuius pater Ocga, cuius pater Ida rex.
Duodecim nanque filios habuit Ida, ex quibus reges Northanhymbrorum exorti sunt: Addas, Ethelricum, Theodericum, Edricum,
Theudheri, Osmer, Alricum, Eccam, Osbaldum, Scor, Sceotheri,
Ocga ex cuius progenie fratres ambo reges Coenred scilicet et Ceolwlf
processerant.[83] Cuius Ceolwlfi regni *principia et processus* multis
redundauere rerum aduersantium motibus, sed post *arridente pace ac
serenitate temporum plures in gente Northanhymbrorum tam nobiles quam
priuati se suosque liberos depositis armis sategerunt magis accepta tonsura
monasterialibus ascribere uotis, quam bellicis exerceri[d] studiis,* quod etiam
ipse rex (ut post dicemus) facere curauit.[84] Qui quoniam studiis
liberalibus erat imbutus, eius diligentiam legendi et audiendi scrip-
turas sacras et gesta priorum Beda laudibus commendans, *Historiam
Gentis[e] Anglorum* quam fecerat ei dicauit, ad illum[f] ita scribens:
'*Gloriosissimo regi Ceolwlfo, Beda famulus Christi et presbiter, Hystoriam
Gentis Anglorum Ecclesiasticam quam nuper edideram, libentissime tibi
desideranti, rex, et prius ad legendum ac probandum transmisi; et nunc ad
transcribendum ac plenius ex tempore meditandum[g] retransmitto; satisque
tue studium sinceritatis amplector, quo non solum audiendis scripture
sacre[h] uerbis aurem sedulus accommodas, uerum etiam noscendis priorum*

---

[a] eius *H*   [b] om. *H*   [c-c] om. *Fx L*   [d] exercere *DCL, B.II.35*
[e] om. *H*   [f] eum *Ca*   [g] meditaturus *HReg (Arnold, Sym. Op. ii. 42)*
[h] om. *L*

---

[82] The italicized words are verbatim from *HE* v. 23. Osric was king of the Northumbrians from 718 to 729, Coenred from 716 to 718, and Ceolwulf from 729 until his
resignation to become a monk of Lindisfarne in 737 (*HECont, s.a.* 737 and *HReg, s.a.* 737
(Arnold, *Sym. Op.* ii. 32), and below, pp. 78–9). The reference to the fifth year of the
episcopate of Æthelwald being 729 is peculiar to *LDE* (see above, p. 60 n. 80).
[83] This genealogy is closest to that in the *DPSA*: 'Erat iste Ceolwulfus filius Cuthe, qui
Cuthwini, qui Leodwaldi, qui Ecgwaldi, qui Aldelmi, qui Ocgge, qui fuit filius Ide, primi
regis Nothanhymbrorum.' The same text gives an identical list of Ida's sons, but
distinguishes between legitimate and illegitimate. The same list is found in the notes on
Northumbrian kings interpolated after the chapter list of *LDE* in Ca, but there the
genealogy of Ceolwulf which follows omits Cutha, so that Ceolwulf's father is named as
Cuthwine (Arnold, *Sym. Op.* ii. 390). This is in line with the 9th-cent. Anglian

be Ceolwulf, brother of that Coenred who had reigned as king before him.[82] Now Ceolwulf was certainly of the stock of Ida, the first king of the Northumbrians, but he did not derive his line from Ida's son Æthelric, from whom the most glorious kings Oswald and Oswiu were descended, but he is found to have derived his origin from Æthelric's brother, who was called Ocga. For Ceolwulf was the son of Cutha, whose father was Cuthwine, whose father was Leodwald, whose father was Ecgwald, whose father was Aldhelm, whose father was Ocga, whose father was King Ida. Ida had twelve sons, from whom arose the kings of the Northumbrians: Adda, Æthelric, Theodoric, Edric, Theudhere, Osmer, Alric, Ecca, Osbald, Scor, Sceotheri, and Ocga, from whose progeny were descended the two kings and brothers, Coenred and Ceolwulf.[83] The beginnings and the course of Ceolwulf's reign were filled to overflowing with the tumults of adverse events; but later on, when peace and serene times smiled on them, many of the people of the Northumbrians, both nobles and commons, laid down their arms, took the tonsure, and strove to bind themselves and their children to monastic vows rather than to exercise themselves in the arts of war—and the king himself undertook to do just this, as we shall explain later.[84] Because he was grounded in liberal studies, Bede dedicated to him the *History of the English People* which he had written, praising his diligence in reading and listening to the holy scriptures and the deeds of his predecessors, and writing to him thus: 'To the most glorious King Ceolwulf. I Bede, servant of Christ and priest, sent to you most willingly at your wish, O king, the *Ecclesiastical History of the English People*, which I had recently written, first so that you might read and correct it; now I send it again so that you may have it transcribed and ponder it more fully at your leisure. Warmly do I embrace the zeal and sincerity with which you not only lend your ear sedulously to hearing the words of sacred scripture, but you also devote your energy to learning attentively of

geneaologies which give, as in that in BL, Cotton Vespasian B.VI (Mercia, s. ix^in): 'Ceolulf Cuðuining, Cuðuine Liodualding, Lioduald Ecgualding, Ecguald Edelming, Edhelm Ocgting, Ocg Iding'; see Dumville, 'Genealogies', pp. 30, 32, 35. The genealogy in CCCO 157, p. 274, gives the same names as *LDE* but omits Leodwald. The dates of the kings mentioned here in *LDE* are very uncertain. According to Bede, Ida began to reign in 547 (Bede, *HE* v. 24), but the dates of the kings of the Bernician line are uncertain until the accession of Æthelfrith in 592/3.

[84] This sentence is taken, largely verbatim, from Bede, *HE* v. 23. The adverse events of Ceolwulf's reign presumably included his being 'captured and tonsured and then restored to his kingdom' in 731 (*HECont, s.a.*).

gestis siue dictis et maxime nostre gentis uirorum illustrium curam uigilanter impendis', et cetera.[85]

[xv] **14.** Anno[a] autem Dominice incarnationis septingentesimo tricesimo quinto,[b] imperii autem Ceolwlfi [c]septimo, episcopatus uero Aethel-woldi[c] anno undecimo,[d] illa ecclesie catholice lucerna ad eam[e] que se illuminauerat lucem, illa uena aque salientis in uitam eternam ad fontem uiuum Deum peruenit, sacrorum scilicet librorum compositor uenerabilis presbiter et monachus Beda defunctus anno etatis sue quinquagesimo nono, ex quo autem rex Oswaldus et antistes Aidanus pontificalem cathedram et monachorum habitationem in Lindisfar-nensi insula instituerant anno centesimo primo, a constructione uero monasterii Petri apostoli in Wiramuthe sexagesimo secundo,[f] porro a patris Cuthberti transitu quadragesimo nono anno.[g][86] Qui uidelicet Beda *in extremo* quidem *mundi angulo* uiuens latuit, sed post mortem per uniuersas mundi partes omnibus in libris suis uiuens innotuit.[87] In quibus terrarum regionumque diuersarum situs, naturas, qualitates subtiliter ac si cuncta ipse peragrasset plerumque describit, cum ab infantia in monasterio nutritus, totam ibidem usque[h] euocationis sue diem uitam transegerit.[i]

[xvi] Ne[j] uero quisquam aliud quam est de illo nos dicere suspicetur, ipsius de semetipso[k] dicta congruum subiungere uidetur:

'Ego', inquit, *'Beda famulus Christi et presbiter monasterii beator-um[l] apostolorum Petri et Pauli quod est ad Wiramutha [m]et in Gyruum,[m] natus in territorio eiusdem monasterii, cum essem annorum septem cura propinquorum datus sum educandus reuerentissimo abbati Benedicto ac deinde Ceolfrido, cunctumque ex eo tempus uite in eiusdem monasterii habitatione peragens; omnem meditandis scripturis operam dedi, atque inter obseruantiam discipline regularis et cotidianam [n]cantandi in ecclesia[n] curam semper aut discere aut docere aut scribere dulce habui. Nono decimo autem uite mee anno diaconatum, tricesimo*

---

[a] Obiit Beda doctor *rubric Fx H T Y*; Capitulum xv *rubric L*   [b] *Numerals; above in words in contemp. hand C*   [c–c] *om. T*   [d] *Numerals; above in words in contemp. hand C*   [e] illam *T*   [f] *Numerals; above in words in contemp. hand C*   [g] *Numerals; above in words in contemp. hand C*   [h] usque ad *Ca*   [i] et cetera add. *L*   [j] De libris quos fecit Beda doctor *rubric Fx H Y*; Quo tempore Beda incepit componere libros et quot *rubric T*; Capitulum sextum decimum *rubric L*   [k] seipso *Fx L Y*   [l] *om. H*   [m–m] *om. F*   [n–n] in ecclesia cantandi *Fx H L Y*

---

85 The quotation is from Bede, *HE* preface.

86 See above, pp. 20–1, 40–1, 52–3. The totals of years given here are consistent with

the deeds or words of your predecessors, and above all of the illustrious men of our race', and so on.[85]

14. In the year of Our Lord's Incarnation 735, the seventh year of [xv] Ceolwulf's reign and the eleventh of the pontificate of Æthelwald, that lamp of the catholic church went to the light which had illuminated it, that vein of water leaping toward eternal life reached the living spring which is God, the writer of holy books, the venerable priest and monk Bede, died in the fifty-ninth year of his age, the hundred and first year since King Oswald and Bishop Aidan had established a pontifical see and a dwelling-place of monks on the island of Lindisfarne, the sixty-second year from the construction of the monastery of Peter at Wearmouth, and the forty-ninth year from the passing of father Cuthbert.[86] Now Bede lived hidden away in the extreme corner of the world, but after his death he lived on in his books and became known to everyone all over the world.[87] In these books he frequently and subtly describes the sites, natures and characters of diverse lands and regions as if he himself had travelled through all of them, when he had been brought up from childhood in the monastery and there had passed his whole life to the day of his calling away.

Lest anyone suspect us of saying anything which is not derived [xvi] from Bede himself, it seems appropriate to give here what he said about himself:

'I Bede, servant of Christ and priest of the monastery of the blessed apostles Peter and Paul, which is situated at Wearmouth and Jarrow, was born in the territory of that same monastery. When I was seven years old I was given by my relatives to the most reverend Abbot Benedict to be educated, and later to Ceolfrith, and from that time I lived all my life in that monastery. I devoted all my efforts to meditating on the scriptures and, between observance of the discipline of the Rule and the daily labour of singing in the church, I held always as sweet the task of learning and teaching and writing. In the nineteenth year of my life I received the rank of

---

dates given above, i.e. 635 for the foundation of Lindisfarne, 674 for the foundation of Wearmouth, and 687 for the death of Cuthbert.

[87] The comment on Bede's remoteness is from Bede, *HE* v. 15. The vast circulation of Bede's writings is evident from M. L. W. Laistner and H. H. King, *A Hand-list of Bede Manuscripts* (Ithaca, NY, 1943), and see also D. Whitelock, *After Bede* (Jarrow, 1960), repr. Lapidge, *Bede and his World*, ii. 35–50.

gradum presbiteratus, utrunque per ministerium reuerentissimi[a] episcopi Iohannis, iubente Ceolfrido abbate suscepi. Ex quo tempore accepti *presbiteratus usque ad[b] annum etatis mee quinquagesimum[c] nonum, hec in scripturam sanctam mee meorumque necessitati ex opusculis uenerabilium patrum breuiter annotare, siue etiam ad formam sensus et interpretationis eorum superadicere curaui:*

In principium Genesis usque ad natiuitatem Ysaac et eiectionem Ismaelis, libros tres.[d]

De tabernaculo et uasis eius ac uestibus sacerdotum, libros tres.

In primam partem Samuelis (id est usque ad mortem Saulis), libros quattuor.[e]

De edificatione templi allegorice expositionis sicut et cetera, libros duos.

Item in [f]Regum librum,[f] triginta questionum.

In Prouerbia Salomonis, libros tres.

[g]In Cantica Canticorum, libros sex.[h]

In Ezram et Neemiam, libros tres.

In Canticum Abbacuc, librum unum.

In librum beati patris[i] Tobie, explanationis allegorice de Christo et ecclesia, librum unum.

Item capitula lectionum in Pentatheuchum Moysi, Iosue, Iudicum; in libros Regum et uerba dierum; in libros[j] beati patris Iob; in Parabolas, Ecclesiasten, et Cantica Canticorum; in Ysaiam prophetam, Ezram quoque[k] et Neemiam.

In Euangelium Marci, libros quattuor.

In Euangelium[l] Luce, sex.[m]

Omeliarum Euangelii,[n] libros duos.

In Apostolum quecunque in opusculis sancti Augustini exposita inueni, cuncta per ordinem transcribere curaui.

In Actus Apostolorum, libros duos.

In epistolas [o]septem canonicas,[o] libros singulos.

In Apocalipsi[p] sancti Iohannis, libros tres.

Item capitula lectionum in totum Nouum Testamentum excepto euangelio.

Item librum epistolarum ad diuersos, quarum de sex etatibus seculi

---

[a] sanctissimi *T*   [b] om. *T*   [c] nonagesimum *H*   [d] quattuor *Bede, HE;* tres *DCL, B.II.35*   [e] tres *Bede, HE;* quattuor *DCL, B.II.35*   [f-f] librum Regum *F T*   [g-g] (p. 68) et alios tractatus qui in Historia Anglorum attitulati sunt *Ca*   [h] septem *Bede, HE;* sex *DCL, B.II.35*   [i] om. *H*   [j] libro *Bede, HE (all MSS)*

deacon, in the thirtieth that of priest, both through the ministry of the most reverend Bishop John and at the command of Abbot Ceolfrith. From the time that I accepted the priesthood until the fifty-ninth year of my age, I have striven to meet the needs of myself and my brothers by commenting briefly in the following books on holy scripture by drawing on the works of the venerable fathers, and even by amplifying the manner of their understanding and interpretation:

On the beginning of Genesis up to the birth of Isaac and the casting out of Ishmael, three books.

Concerning the Tabernacle, its vessels, and the priestly vestments, three books.

On the first book of Samuel (that is, to the death of Saul), four books.

On the building of the temple, an allegorical interpretation like the others, two books.

On the book of Kings, thirty questions.

On the Proverbs of Solomon, three books.

On the Song of Songs, six books.

On Ezra and Nehemiah, three books.

On the Song of Habbakuk, one book.

On the book of the blessed father Tobias, an allegorical interpretation concerning Christ and the church, one book.

Chapters of readings on the Pentateuch of Moses, Joshua, and Judges; on the books of Kings and Chronicles; on the books of the blessed father Job; on Proverbs, Ecclesiastes, and the Song of Songs; on the prophets Isaiah, Ezra, and Nehemiah.

On the Gospel of Mark, four books.

On the Gospel of Luke, six books.

Homilies on the Gospel, two books.

On the Apostle, I have taken care to transcribe in order whatever I found expounded in the works of St Augustine.

On the Acts of the Apostles, two books.

On the seven canonical epistles, one book each.

On the Apocalypse of St John, three books.

Chapters of the readings on the whole of the New Testament except the Gospels.

A book of letters to various people, one on the six ages of the

k om. *Fx L*   *l* om. *F*   *m* sex libros *H*   *n* om. *H*   *o–o* canonicas septem *T*   *p* Apocalipsin *Bede, HE (all MSS)*

una est; de mansionibus filiorum Israel una; una de eo quod ait Ysaias, 'Et claudentur ibi in carcerem et post dies multos uisitabuntur'; de ratione bissexti una; de equinoctio iuxta Anatolium una.

Item de hystoriis sanctorum, librum uite et passionis sancti Felicis confessoris de metrico Paulini opere in prosam transtuli; librum uite et passionis sancti^a Anastasii, male de Greco translatum et peius a quodam imperito emendatum, prout potui ad sensum correxi; uitam sancti patris monachi simul et antistitis Cuthberti et prius heroico metro, et postmodum plano sermone descripsi.

Hystoriam abbatum monasterii huius, in quo superne pietati deseruire gaudeo, Benedicti, Ceolfridi, et Huetberti in libellis duobus.

Hystoriam Ecclesiasticam nostre insule ac gentis in libris quinque.

Martyrologium de nataliciis sanctorum martyrum diebus, in quo omnes quos inuenire potui non solum qua die, uerum etiam quo genere certaminis, uel sub quo iudice mundum uicerint, diligenter annotare studui.

Librum hymnorum de diuerso metro siue rithmo.

Librum epigrammatum heroico metro siue eliaco.

De natura rerum^b et de temporibus, libros singulos.

Item de temporibus, librum unum maiorem.

Librum de orthographia alphabeti ordine distinctum.

Item librum de metrica arte, et huic adiectum alium de scematibus siue tropis^c libellum, hoc est de figuris modisque locutionum quibus scriptura sancta contexta est.'^{g 88}

Cum ^dergo hos^d libros peruigili studio edidisset, obiit septimas^e Kalendas Iunii in Gyruue, ibique sepultus est; sed post multa annorum curricula ossa illius inde translata, et cum incorrupto sanctissimi patris Cuthberti corpore ^fsunt collocata.^f In cuius (uidelicet Bede) honorem porticus ad aquilonalem plagam ecclesie sancti Pauli in Gyrwe consecrata, uenerandam fidelibus nominis eius ibidem prestat memoriam. Ostenditur etiam ^ghodie locus^g ubi de lapide mansiunculam habens, ab omni inquietudine liber sedere, meditari,

---

^a om. T   ^b rei T   ^c de tropis H   ^{d–d} ergo L; hos ergo Fx Y
^e septimo Ca   ^{f–f} collocata sunt Y   ^{g–g} locus hodie Ca

---

⁸⁸ This long quotation is taken verbatim from Bede, *HE* v. 24, with the epithet 'servant of Christ' drawn from the preface. The list of works shares the omission of the item 'In Isaiam, Danihelem, XII prophetas, et partem Hieremie' with DCL, B.II.35, fo. 213^v, but also (according to Plummer, *Bede*, i. 358–9) with BL, Cotton Tiberius C.II, Winchester, Cathedral Library 3, Oxford, Bodleian Library, Digby 101, Bodley 163, Laud misc. 243, and Douce 368, and the OE version of Bede's *HE* (*The Old English Version of Bede's*

world; one on the houses of the sons of Israel; one on the words of Isaiah, 'And they shall be shut up in the prison and after many days shall be visited'; one on the reason for the intercalary day; and one on the equinox, following Anatolius.

Of the histories of the saints, I translated into prose from the metrical work of Paulinus a book of the life and passion of St Felix; as well as I was able I corrected, to restore the sense of it, a book of the life and passion of St Anastasius, badly translated from the Greek and emended in an even worse manner by some unskilled person; and I described the life of the holy father Cuthbert, monk and bishop, first in heroic metre and afterwards in prose.

The history of the abbots of this monastery, in which I rejoice in serving the sublime piety, Benedict, Ceolfrith and Hwaetberht, in two little books.

The ecclesiastical history of our island and people in five books.

A martyrology of the 'birthdays' of the holy martyrs, in which I have striven to note down diligently everything I could find about them, not only on what day, but also by what manner of struggle, and under what judge, they overcame the world.

A book of hymns in various metres and rhythms.

A book of epigrams in heroic and elegiac metre.

Two books, one on the nature of things and one on time; also a larger book on time.

A book about orthography, arranged in order of the alphabet.

A book on the art of metre, and to this is added another small book on the rhetorical figures or tropes, that is the figures and modes of speech with which the holy scriptures are composed.'[88]

When he had completed these books with ever-watchful zeal, he died on 26 May at Jarrow and was buried there; but after many years had passed his bones were translated thence, and were placed with the undecayed body of the most holy father Cuthbert. A chapel was dedicated in his (that is Bede's) honour on the north side of the church of St Paul at Jarrow, and there this provides the faithful with a memorial to his name which they should revere. Even today the place is shown where he had a little cell made of stone, in which he was

Ecclesiastical History of the English People, ed. T. Miller (2 vols. in 4; Early English Text Society, 1891–8). For the works listed here, see R. Sharpe, *A Handlist of Latin Writers of Great Britain and Ireland before 1540* (Publications of the Journal of Medieval Latin, i; Turnhout, 1997), pp. 70–6, and M. Gorman, Wigbod and the *lectiones* on the Hexateuch attributed to Bede in Paris lat. 2342', *Revue bénédictine*, cv (1995), 310–47, at 343–7.

legere, dictare consueuerat, et scribere.[89] Transiit autem ipsa die solenni ascensionis Dominice. *[a]Cuius nos transitum melius uerbis ipsius[b] scribendum putamus, qui eius discipulus uocabulo Cuthbertus presens affuit, ad condiscipulum taliter scribens:[a]*

15. *'Dilectissimo',[c]* inquit, *'in Christo* collectori[d] Cuthwino,[e] *Cuthbertus condiscipulus in Deo[f] eternam salutem.*[90]

Munusculum quod misisti multum libenter accepi, multumque gratanter litteras tue[g] deuote eruditionis legi. In quibus quod maxime desiderabam, missas uidelicet et orationes sacrosanctas pro Deo dilecto patre ac nostro magistro Beda, a uobis diligenter celebrari repperi. Vnde delectat magis pro eius caritate, quantum fruor ingenio, paucis sermonibus dicere, quo ordine migraret e[h] seculo, cum etiam hoc te desiderasse et poscere[i] intellexi.

Grauatus quidem est infirmitate maxima creberrimi anhelitus, sine dolore tamen, ante diem resurrectionis Dominice (id est fere duabus ebdomadibus), et sic postea letus et gaudens gratiasque agens omnipotenti Deo omni die et nocte, immo horis omnibus, usque ad diem ascensionis Dominice (id est septimas Kalendas Iunii)[91] uitam ducebat; et nobis suis discipulis cotidie lectiones dabat, et quicquid reliquum erat diei, in psalmorum decantatione[j] occupabat, [k]totam quoque[k] noctem in letitia et gratiarum actione peruigil ducebat, nisi tantum modicus somnus impediret. Euigilans autem statim consueta repetiuit, et expansis manibus Deo gratias agere non desinit.[l] O uere beatus uir! Canebat sententiam beati Pauli apostoli: 'Horrendum est, incidere in manus[m] Dei uiuentis',[92] *et multa alia de sancta scriptura et in nostra [n]quoque lingua[n]* (hoc est Anglica), *ut erat doctus in nostris*

[a-a] *om.* Ca *(i. 15 also om.* Ca)   [b] illius *T*   [c] Epistola uenerabilis Bede *rubric* Y.   [d] lectori *Dig*   [e] Cuthberto *Y*   [f] Domino *H*   [g] tuas *H* [h] a *T*   [i] poposcisse *Dig*; poposcere *altered to* poscere *C*; poposcere *F*   [j] cantu *Dig*   [k-k] totam *F;* totamque *H*; totam uero *Dig*   [l] desiuit *Dig* [m] manibus *T*   [n-n] lingua quoque *Fx* L

---

[89] *LDE's* words seem to suggest that St Paul's, Jarrow, was a pilgrimage site connected with Bede in the early twelfth cent.. No surviving feature of the site of Jarrow can be convincingly associated with this structure (for references, see above, p. 41 n. 52).

[90] Symeon's text of this letter, which is probably the work of a contemporary (above, p. lxix n. 284), is derived from the so-called 'Insular version' rather than the 'Continental version', as is shown *inter alia* by the fact that it gives Bede's 'death-song' in West Saxon rather than Northumbrian dialect (both versions are edited in *Anglo-Saxon Minor Poems*, ed. Dobbie, vi. 107–8). Symeon edited the text he received in various ways, notably

accustomed to sit, free from all disquietude, and to meditate, read, dictate, and write.[89] He died on the solemn day of the Ascension of Our Lord itself. We have thought it better to describe his passing in the words of his pupil called Cuthbert, who was present and who wrote thus to a fellow pupil:

15. 'To his most beloved fellow reader in Christ Cuthwin, Cuthbert his fellow pupil in God sends eternal greetings.[90]

The little gift which you sent I have most willingly accepted, and I have most gratefully read the letter composed by your devoted erudition. In this I discovered what I most desired, that masses and holy prayers are being diligently celebrated by you for the beloved father and our teacher Bede. Whence it delights me, more from love of him, to set down in a few words, insofar as I have the ability, the manner in which he left the world, especially since I understand that you had desired and have requested this.

He was weighed down with a very great infirmity of frequent breathlessness, although without pain, before the day of Our Lord's Resurrection (that is for about two weeks). After that he lived his life happily until the day of Our Lord's Ascension (that is 26 May),[91] rejoicing and giving thanks to almighty God day and night, indeed at every hour. To us, his disciples, he gave lessons every day and whatever was left of the day he devoted to singing psalms, and he kept vigil all night in happiness and thanksgiving excepting only when a short sleep prevented this. As soon as he woke, however, he would repeat the accustomed things and spreading out his hands he would not cease giving thanks to God. O truly blessed man! He would sing the sentence of St Paul the Apostle, 'Dreadful it is to fall into the hands of the living God.'[92] Many other things from holy scripture he would recite, and also several in our language, that is English, for he was learned

---

introducing *inquit* at the beginning, noting that the language was English, and adding a translation of the poem into Latin. For further details and references, see above, pp. lxxix–lxx. Cuthbert was abbot of Wearmouth-Jarrow by *c.*764 when he corresponded with Archbishop Lul of Mainz (*Die Briefe des heiligen Bonifatius und Lullus*, ed. M. Tangl (*MGH Epp. selectae*, i; Berlin, 1916), nos. 116, 126–7). Cuthwin is otherwise unknown, although an abbot of that name appears in *Liber Vitae*, fo. 6ʳ (J. Gerchow, *Die Gedenküberlieferung der Angelsachsen mit einem Katalog der Libri Vitae und Necrologien* (Munich, 1987), p. 306).

[91] Bede actually died on the eve of Ascension Day, 25 May 735.

[92] Heb. 10: 31.

carminibus, nonnulla dixit. Nam et tunc[a] [b]hoc Anglico[b] carmine componens, multum compunctus aiebat:

[c]*For þam neodfere*[d] [e]*nenig wyrþeð*[e]
þances[f] *snottra,*[g] *þonne him þearf sy,*
to gehiggenne[h] *ær his heonengange,*
hwæt[i] *his gaste godes oððe*[j] *yfeles,*[k]
æfter[l] *deaðe*[m] *heonen*[n] *demed wurðe.*[oc]

Quod ita latine sonat:
Ante necessarium exitum[93] prudentior quam opus fuerit nemo existit, ad cogitandum uidelicet antequam hinc[p] proficiscatur anima quid boni uel mali egerit, qualiter post exitum iudicanda fuerit.

Cantabat etiam antiphonas secundum [q]*nostram* consuetudinem[q] *et sui, quarum una est: 'O rex glorie, domine uirtutum, qui triumphator hodie super omnes celos ascendisti, ne derelinquas nos*[r] *orphanos, sed mitte promissum patris in nos, spiritum ueritatis. Alleluia.'*[94] *Et cum uenisset ad illud uerbum, 'ne derelinquas nos orphanos', prorupit in lacrimas et multum fleuit, et post horam cepit repetere que inchoauerat. Et nos hec*[s] *audientes, luximus cum illo. Altera uice legimus, altera plorauimus, immo semper cum fletu legimus.*

In tali letitia quinquagesimales dies usque ad[t] *diem prefatum deduximus,*[u][95] *et ille multum gaudebat, Deo*que[v] *gratias agebat quia sic meruisset infirmari. Referebat et sepe dicebat, 'Flagellat Deus omnem filium quem recipit',*[96] *et multa alia de sancta scriptura,* [w]*sententiam* quoque[w] *sancti Ambrosii: 'Non sic uixi ut me pudeat inter uos uiuere, sed nec mori timeo, quia bonum Deum habemus.'*[97] *In istis autem diebus duo opuscula multum memoria digna, exceptis lectionibus quas accepimus ab eo, et cantu psalmorum, facere studebat: Euangelium* scilicet[x] *sancti*[y] *Iohannis in nostram linguam ad*

[a] nunc *T* [b–b] Anglico hoc *Fx L Y* [c–c] *om. Fx H L T* [d] neofere *Y*; nedfere *Dig* [e–e] næni wyrþeþ *Dig* [f] þancer *D* [g] snotera *Dig* [h] gehiggene *F*; gehisgenne *Y;* gehicgenne *Dig* [i] hwet *F* [j] oþþe *Dig* [k] yueles *F* [l] æften *L* [m] ð *on erasure C;* deaþe *F;* daðe *Fx* [n] heonon *Dig* [o] weorþe *Dig* [p] *om. Fx* [q–q] ob nostram consolationem *Dig* [r] *om. H* [s] hoc *H* [t] *om. T* [u] duximus *Fx L Y* [v] et Deo *Dig* [w–w] et sententiam *Dig* [x] uero *Dig* [y] *om. Fx L*

[93] On the dialect, see above, p. lxix. The Old English word *neodfere* here causes difficulties of interpretation, but in view of the appearance in the earliest manuscripts of the 'Continental version' of Bede's letter of the words 'dicens de terribili exitu animarum e

in our poetry. For then indeed he composed this in English verse
and would recite it with much compunction:

> For þam neodfere   nenig wyrþeð
> þances snottra,   þonne him þearf sy,
> to gehiggenne   ær his heonengange,
> hwæt his gaste   godes oððe yfeles,
> æfter deaðe heonen   demed wurðe.

In Latin this means:

Before his inevitable departure,[93] there is no one who is more
attentive than is needful in considering in his soul before his
departure what he has done of good or of evil and how these things
are to be judged after his death.

He would also sing antiphons according to our custom and his,
of which one was: 'O king of glory, lord of power, who have
ascended today in triumph over all the heavens, do not leave us as
orphans, but send to us the spirit of truth promised by the father.
Alleluia.'[94] And when he came to the words, 'Do not leave us as
orphans,' he burst into tears and wept bitterly, and after an hour he
resumed reciting what he had begun. We who were listening
lamented with him. Alternately we read and wept, or rather we
read always with weeping.

In such happiness we spent the quinquagesimal days[95] until the
aforesaid day, and he rejoiced greatly, giving thanks to God that he
had merited to sicken in this way. He often called to mind and
recited, 'God flogs every son he receives.'[96] Many other things he
recited from holy scripture and also the sentence of St Ambrose: 'I
have not lived so that I am ashamed to live among you, but I am not
afraid to die, because the God we have is good.'[97] In those days he
strove to fulfil two very memorable tasks, aside from the lessons
which we received and the singing of the psalms: translating the
Gospel of St John into our language for the use of the church, and

corpore' to introduce the Death Song, it is possible that Symeon correctly translated
neodfere as *necessarium exitum;* see Dobbie, *Manuscripts of Caedmon's Hymn*, p. 53. It is
conceivable that the Old English poem did not appear in the Continental version and was
not by Bede, but, since it is found in the earliest manuscripts (s. ix) and seems to fit well in
the text, this is unlikely (cf. op. cit., p. 120 and p. 121).

[94] This appears as the antiphon of the *Magnificat* of Ascension Day in later texts.

[95] The period of fifty days between Easter and Pentecost.

[96] Heb. 12: 6.

[97] Attributed to Ambrose in *Vita Ambrosii* (*PL*, ed. Migne, xiv. 43).

utilitatem ecclesie conuertit, et de libris rotarum Ysidori episcopi excerptiones quasdam, dicens, 'Nolo ut discipuli[a] mei [b]mendacium legant,[b] et in hoc post obitum meum sine fructu laborent.[98] Cum [c]uenisset autem[c] tercia feria ante ascensionem Domini, cepit uehementius egrotare in anhelitu, et modicus tumor in pedibus apparuit. Totum [d]autem illum[d] diem ducebat[e] et hilariter dictabat, et nonnunquam inter alia dixit: 'Discite cum festinatione, nescio quamdiu subsistam, et si post modicum tollat me factor meus.[99] Nobis autem uidebatur quod suum exitum[f] bene sciret, et sic noctem in gratiarum actione peruigil duxit. Et mane illucescente[g] (id est quarta feria) precepit diligenter scribi que ceperamus. Et hoc facto usque ad terciam horam[h] ambulauimus deinde cum reliquiis sanctorum, ut consuetudo illius diei poscebat.[i][100] Vnus[j] uero [k]erat ex nobis cum illo,[k] qui dixit illi,[l] 'Adhuc, magister dilectissime, capitulum unum deest, uideturne[m] tibi "difficile plus te interrogari?"[n] At ille, [o]'Facile est', inquit.[o] 'Accipe tuum calamum et tempera, et festinanter scribe.' [p]Quod ille fecit.[p] [q]Nona autem hora[q] dixit michi, 'Quedam[r] preciosa in mea capsella habeo, id est piperem,[s] oraria, et incensa. Sed curre uelociter, et presbiteros nostri[t] monasterii adduc ad me, ut et ego munuscula qualia Deus[u] donauit illis distribuam. Diuites autem in hoc seculo aurum,[v] argentum, et alia queque preciosa dare student; ego autem cum multa caritate et gaudio fratribus meis dabo quod Deus[w] dederat.'[x] Et allocutus est unumquemque, monens et obsecrans pro eo missas et orationes diligenter facere, quod[y] illi libenter spoponderunt. Lugebant autem et flebant omnes, maxime [z]quod dixerat quia[z] amplius faciem eius[aa] in hoc seculo non essent uisuri.[101] Gaudebant autem quia dixit, 'Tempus est ut reuertar ad eum qui me fecit, qui me[bb] creauit, qui me ex nichilo formauit. Multum tempus uixi, bene michi pius iudex uitam meam preuidit, tempus[cc] resolutionis mee instat,[102] quia cupio

---

[a] pueri Dig   [b–b] legant mendacium L   [c–c] autem uenisset H
[d–d] illum autem T   [e] docebat Dig   [f] obitum F   [g] illuscescente Dig
[h] A tercia autem hora add. Dig   [i] postulat F   [j] Et unus Dig   [k–k] ex nobis cum illo erat Fx L Y   [l] om. T   [m] uidetur Dig   [n–n] difficile esse plus te interrogare Dig   [o–o] inquit, 'Facile est' Dig   [p–p] Et ille hoc fecit Dig
[q–q] Ad nonam autem horam Dig   [r] Quedam autem Dig   [s] piperum Dig
[t] mei Fx L   [u] Deus michi Fx L   [v] aurum et Dig   [w] Deus michi Fx L
[x] Et hoc cum tremore fecit add. Dig   [y] et Dig   [z–z] quia dixerat quod Dig
[aa] suam F   [bb] om. Dig   [cc] iam tempus Dig

---

[98] According to the Continental version, the section of John's gospel was from the beginning to 6: 9. The term *libri rotarum* (Books of Wheels) was frequently applied in manuscripts to Isidore of Seville (d. 636), *De natura rerum*, probably because of the circular figures found in that text (Dobbie, *Manuscripts of Caedmon's Hymn*, pp. 101–2). That Bede

making certain excerpts from the Books of Wheels of Bishop
Isidore, saying, 'I do not wish that my disciples should read
untruths, or should labour fruitlessly on this after my death.'[98]

When the Tuesday before the Ascension of Our Lord came,
however, he began to be more critically ill in his breathing and a
small swelling appeared in his feet. He passed all that day and
happily dictated, and among other things he several times said to
us: 'Learn in haste, for "I do not know how long I shall be here,
and whether in a little while my maker will take me".'[99] It was
clear to us that he knew well when his end would come, and thus
he passed the night in vigil and thanksgiving. When day dawned,
it being Wednesday, he ordered us to write diligently what we
had begun. When we had done this, we then processed at the
third hour with the relics of the saints, as the custom of that day
required.[100] One of us, who was with him, said to him: 'Dearest
master, there is still one chapter lacking, but does it not seem
hard to ask more of you?' But he replied, 'It is easy. Take up
your pen and your ink and write in haste.' This he did. At the
ninth hour he said to me, 'I have a few precious things in my
box—pepper, napkins, and incense. Run quickly and bring the
priests of our monastery to me, so that I may distribute among
them such little gifts as God has given. Just as the rich in this
world strive to give gold, silver, and other such precious things,
so with much love and rejoicing will I give to my brothers what
God has given me.' He spoke to each in turn, advising and
beseeching that masses and prayers should be said diligently for
him, which they willingly promised to do. Everyone grieved and
wept, above all because he had said that his face would no more
be seen in this world.[101] Everyone rejoiced, however, because he
said, 'It is time for me to return to him who made me, who
created me, who formed me from nothing. I have lived for a long
time, the just judge has provided well for me during my life, and
now the time of my release is at hand,[102] for I wish to be released

---

was merely excerpting from it in the original Latin, not also translating the excerpts into
Old English, seems clear from Cuthbert's words (see P. Meyvaert, 'Bede the Scholar',
Famulus Christi, ed. Bonner, pp. 40–69, at 59).

[99] Words in double quotation marks from Job 32: 22.

[100] A reference to the Rogation Processions used in the Gallican liturgy; see M. Förster,
Geschichte der Reliquienkultus in Altengland (Munich, 1943), pp. 4–5.

[101] Cf. Acts 20: 38.

[102] 2 Tim. 4: 6.

dissolui et esse cum Christo.' Sic et alia multa locutus, in leticia diem usque ad^a uesperum duxit. Et prefatus puer dixit: 'Adhuc una sententia, magister dilecte, non est descripta.' ^b*At* ille, *'Scribe,' inquit, 'cito'.*^b *Post modicum dixit puer, 'Modo sententia descripta est.'* ^c*At ille, 'Bene,' inquit,^c 'ueritatem dixisti, consummatum est.*¹⁰³*Accipe* ^d*meum caput*^d ^e*in manus tuas,^e quia multum me delectat sedere ex aduerso loco sancto meo in quo orare solebam,* ^f*ut* et *ego*^f sedens ^g*patrem meum inuocare possim.'*^g *Et sic in pauimento sue casule decantans 'Gloria patri et filio et spiritui sancto', cum*^h *spiritum sanctum* ⁱnominasset, spiritumⁱ *e corpore exalauit ultimum, ac sic regna migrauit ad celestia. Omnes autem qui^j uidere beati patris obitum, nunquam se uidisse ullum alium in tam*^k *magna deuotione atque tranquillitate uitam^l finisse dicebant. Quia, sicut audisti, quousque anima in corpore fuit, 'Gloria patri' et alia* ^m*quedam spiritalia,*^m *expansis manibus Deo uiuo et uero gratias agere non cessabat.*

Scito autem, frater karissime, quod multa narrare possemⁿ *de eo, sed breuitatem sermonis^o ineruditio lingue facit.'*

---

^a *om. H*   ^{b–b} At inquit, 'Scribe cito' *Dig*   ^{c–c} At ille inquit, 'Bene' *Dig*
^{d–d} caput meum *Dig*   ^{e–e} *om. F*   ^{f–f} ut ego *H;* et ut ego *T;* ut ibi *Dig*
^{g–g} possim inuocare patrem meum *F*   ^h et cum *Dig*   ^{i–i} uocauit suum *Dig*
^j qui audiere uel *Dig*   ^k tanta *H*   ^l uitam sic *Dig*   ^{m–m} quedam cecinit
spiritalia et *Dig;* spiritualia quedam *F*   ⁿ possum narrare *Dig*   ^o *om. H*

and to be with Christ.' This and many other things he said, and thus in happiness he passed the day until evening. Then the boy who was mentioned above said, 'Still there is one sentence not written, beloved master.' He replied, 'Write quickly.' After a little while, the boy said, 'Now the sentence is written.' He replied, 'You have said well; it is completed.[103] Take my head in your hands, for it would delight me much to sit opposite my holy place, in which I was accustomed to pray, so that sitting I may call upon my father.' Thus on the floor of his cell he sang 'Glory to the father and to the son and to the holy spirit', and as he named the holy spirit, he breathed out his spirit at last from his body and thus migrated to the heavenly realms. Everyone who saw the blessed father's death said that they had never seen anyone finish their life in such great devotion and tranquillity. For, as you have heard, he did not cease while his soul was still in his body to sing to the living God, with his hands outspread, 'Glory to the father' and other such spiritual things, and to give thanks.

Know, dearest brother, that I could tell many things of him, but my lack of erudition forces me to be brief.'

---

[103] John 19: 30.

[xvii] 1. Post*a* dormitionem eius in Christo anno tercio, rex Ceolwulfus relicto regno et curis mundialibus, uoluntaria paupertate secutus est pauperem Christum, ut cum illo quandoque ditaretur in gloria, Eadberto filio patrui eius in regnum Northanhymbrorum ei succedente. Intrauit autem Lindisfarnense monasterium, sancto*b* Cuthberto secum conferens *thesauros regios et terras, id est Bregesne et Werceworde cum suis appendiciis* simul *et ecclesiam quam* ibidem *ipse edificauerat*, alias *quoque quattuor uillas: Wudecestre, Hwitingham, Eadulfingham, et Ecgwlfingham. Accepta* itaque *tonsura in* prefato *monasterio* monachicam cum monachis uitam ducere, et post imperium regni terrestris, celesti regno gaudebat militare.[1] Vbi gloriose conuersationis consummans terminum sepultus est, sed succedente tempore ab Ecgfrido eiusdem loci antistite (ut post dicemus) ad Northam translatus.[2] Decursis post hec multorum *c*curriculis annorum,*c* caput illius Dunhelmum translatum, una cum aliis sanctorum reliquiis in ecclesia sancti Cuthberti, quem semper amauerat, uenerabiliter est locatum.[3]

[xviii] 2. Regnante*d* post Ceolwulfum quem prediximus Eadberto, Cynewlf episcopatum ecclesie Lindisfarnensis suscepit, quem non paruo quidem tempore sed multis rerum aduersantium molestiis uexatus tenuit.[4] Denique Offa*e* de genere regio persequentibus inimicis ad

---

a Ceouulfus rex (*om. T Fx*) factus est monachus Lindisfarnensis *rubric Fx H T Y*   *b om. L*   *c–c* annorum curriculis *Ca*   *d* Obiit Baltherus anachorita de Tynhyngham *rubric Fx Y*   *e om. L*

---

[1] ASC DE, *s.a.* 737, describes how Ceolwulf 'received St Peter's tonsure' and gave his kingdom to Eadberht, son of his paternal uncle, and the account in *HECont, s.a.* 737, is similar. JW ii. 186–7, however, places the event under 738: 'Ceoluulfus, rex Northymbrorum, regni gubernaculo relicto, et Eadbrihto patrueli suo, Eate scilicet filio, tradito, monachus efficitur.' Eadberht reigned from 737/8 to 758. Symeon's emphasis on Ceolwulf's monastic poverty is presumably his own and may be reflected in *ALf, s.a.* 738: 'Ceoluulf dimisso regno fit monachus in Lindisfarne, cui filius patrui sui Æatbertus successit XXI'. This is very similar to *HReg, s.a.* 737 (Arnold, *Sym. Op.* ii. 32). The gifts of lands are described in identical words (italicized in the Latin here) in *CMD* (Craster, 'Red book', p. 523), which may be the source, drawing in turn on *HSC* c. 8 (which gives the bounds of Warkworth; NU 248 062) and a chronologically garbled account in c. 11. The estates are all in Northumberland, although Woodchester is an unknown location unless it is to be identified with Woodhorn (Hart, *Early Charters*, p. 135; NZ 301 889). On Whittingham (NU 066 120) as a possible site of a council, see above, p. 46 n. 57. Edlingham (NU 119 091) and Eglingham (NU 106 195) lie to the west of Alnwick.

Book ii

1. In the third year after Bede had fallen asleep in Christ, King [xvii]
Ceolwulf gave up his kingdom and his worldly cares, and in voluntary
poverty followed Christ the pauper, so that in the end he might with
him be enriched with glory; and Eadberht, the son of his uncle,
succeeded him to the kingdom of the Northumbrians. He himself
entered the monastery of Lindisfarne, bringing with him to confer
upon St Cuthbert royal treasures and lands, namely Brainshaugh and
Warkworth with its appurtenances, together with the church which
he himself had built there, and four other vills: Woodchester,
Whittingham, Edlingham, and Eglingham. After he had received
the tonsure in the aforesaid monastery, he rejoiced in leading the
monastic life with the monks and, after having ruled an earthly
kingdom, in fighting for the kingdom of heaven.[1] When he reached
the end of his glorious life, he was buried there, but in later times he
was translated to Norham (as we shall explain later) by Ecgred,
bishop of that church.[2] When many years had run their course after
these events, his head was translated to Durham, together with many
other relics of the saints, and was reverently placed in the church of
St Cuthbert, whom he had always loved.[3]

2. While Eadberht (whom we mentioned above) was reigning in [xviii]
succession to Ceolwulf, Cynewulf received the bishopric of the
church of Lindisfarne, and held it for a not inconsiderable time,
although much vexed and troubled by the adversity of his circumstances.[4] For Offa, who was of the royal race, took sanctuary from the

---

[2] Ceolwulf's death is given *s.a.* 760 in ASC DE, and by JW ii. 202–3; but in *HReg* it is
given *s.a.* 764 (Arnold, *Sym. Op.* ii. 42). The translation of Ceolwulf's relics to Norham is
described in *HSC* c. 9; see also, below, pp. 92–3. *Ecgfrido* here is presumably a variant
spelling of *Ecgredo*, i.e. Ecgred, bishop of Lindisfarne from 830 to 845 (for the correct
spelling, which is also found in other texts, see below, p. 82). On Norham, see below, p. 92
n. 33.

[3] An early or mid-12th-cent. Durham relic-list records 'caput Ceolwulfi regis et postea
monachi in lindispharnensi ecclesia', and the item is also found in later Durham relic-lists
(Battiscombe, *Relics*, pp. 112–13).

[4] Cf. *ALf, s.a.* 740: 'Cyneuulf suscepit episcopatum Lindisfarnensem et rexit XL annis.'
HReg (Arnold, *Sym. Op.* ii. 32) and *HECont* record Cynewulf's appointment *s.a.* 740. In the
earliest manuscript of John of Worcester (CCCO 157), Cynewulf's accession is noted in the
margin alongside the annal for 738; but the note straddles the annals for 739 and 740 (JW ii.
186), so that it is uncertain to which year it relates. ASC E gives the date of his consecration
as 737, and his death as 779. *HReg* gives the latter *s.a.* 780. See also below, p. 85 n. 18.

corpus sancti Cuthberti confugerat, indeque post ui abstractus, nefanda *est nece* peremptus. Vnde offensus rex Eadbertus, episcopum cepit, captum in Bebbanburch teneri precepit, Friothuberto Hagustaldensi episcopo Lindisfarnensem episcopatum administrante, donec placato rege de captione relaxatus Cynewulf ad suam rediret ecclesiam.[5]

[xviii (H)]   Huius*b* pontificatus anno septimodecimo, regni uero Eadberti uicesimo, uir Domini et presbiter Baltherus,*c* qui uitam anachoreticam in Tiningaham duxerat, uiam sanctorum patrum ingressus est, migrando ad eum*d* qui se reformauit*e* ad imaginem filii sui pridie nonas Martias.*f*[6]

[xix]   3. Verum*g* intermissa paululum de episcopis narratione, de ipso rege Eadberto breuiter aliquid dicendum uidetur congruum. Patrui (ut dictum est) Ceolwlfi regis uocabulo Eata filius erat,[7] qui suscepto regno efficacem se ualde ac strenuum ad tenendum regendumque imperium exhibebat. Omnibus denique*h* aduersariis uel sibi subiectis uel bello prostratis, reges circunquaque morantes Anglorum, Pictorum, Britonum, Scottorum non solum cum eo pacem seruabant, sed et honorem illi deferre gaudebant.[8] Cuius excellentie fama ac operum uirtutis longe lateque diffusa, etiam ad regem Francorum

---

a-a nece est *H L Y*   *b* Obiit Bartholomeus anachorita de Tinhingham *rubric H*
c Balthredus *Fx L Y*   *d* Deum *T*   *e* formauit *H*   *f* Martii *H*; et cetera *add. L*   *g* Eadbertus rex dimisso regno clericatum suscepit *rubric Fx Y*; Obiit Baltherus anacorita de Tinigham *rubric T*   *h* itaque *Ca*

[5] Frithuberht was bishop of Hexham (734–66); Eadberht was king of the Northumbrians (737–58). According to *HReg*, *s.a.* 750 (Arnold, *Sym. Op.* ii. 39–40), Offa was the son of Aldfrith, presumably the king of the Northumbrians of that name (686–705). *HReg*'s account of the affair differs significantly from that in *LDE* in that Cynewulf's arrest is made to precede Offa's flight to sanctuary whereas in *LDE* it follows it. Nor does *HReg* make any mention either of the killing of Offa or of the role of Frithuberht. *LDE's* wording is confused as to the reasons for Eadberht's displeasure, although from the sense it is clear that it was caused by the granting of sanctuary to Offa. On sanctuary at St Cuthbert's tomb, see above, p. 52 n. 67; on the general political context, see D. Rollason, 'Hagiography and politics in eighth-century Northumbria', *Holy Men and Holy Women: Old English Prose Saints' Lives and their Contexts*, ed. P. Szarmach (SUNY Series in Medieval Studies; New York, 1996), pp. 95–114, at 97.

[6] The date of Balthere's death would therefore have been 756, under which year *ALf* records: 'Balthere obiit in Tiningham anachorita.' *HReg's* entry for the same year shares with *LDE* the words 'uiam sanctorum patrum est secutus, migrando ad eum qui se reformauit ad imaginem filii sui' (Arnold, *Sym. Op.* ii. 41). The place of Balthere's death was Tyningham (East Lothian), where a church of St Balthere was burned in 941 (ibid. ii. 94). Nothing now remains of early medieval date, but the Bass Rock, a prominent offshore island, was identified as the site of Balthere's hermitage (mentioned in *Alcuin, The Bishops*,

pursuit of his enemies at the body of St Cuthbert, and afterwards he was taken away by force, and wickedly put to death. Eadberht was offended on account of this, and he seized the bishop, and ordered him to be held prisoner at Bamburgh. Frithuberht, bishop of Hexham, administered the see of Lindisfarne until the king was placated and Cynewulf, who was then released from his captivity, returned to his own church.[5]

In the seventeenth year of his pontificate, the twentieth of the reign [xviii (H)] of Eadberht, the man of the Lord and priest Balthere, who had been leading the life of an anchorite at Tyningham, went the way of the holy fathers on 6 March, migrating to him who had formed him in the image of his son.[6]

3. Now that we have inserted this short account of the bishops, it [xix] seems appropriate to say something briefly about King Eadberht himself. As we said, he was the son of Ceolwulf's uncle Eata,[7] and after becoming king he really showed himself to be effective and strenuous in holding and governing the kingdom. When he had either made his enemies subject to him or had destroyed them in war, the neighbouring kings of the English, Picts, Britons, and Scots not only kept the peace with him, but rejoiced to do him honour.[8] Report of his superiority and of the valour of his deeds spread far and wide, and

Kings, and Saints of York, ed. P. Godman (OMT, 1982), lines 1325 ff.) in the Breviary of Aberdeen, which also referred to a rock which he caused to sail out of the way of navigation and is now identified with that called St Baldred's Boat (Anderson, *Early Sources*, i. 242 n. 3). Tyningham formed one of the later rural deaneries of Lothian (M. Ash, 'The diocese of St Andrews under its "Norman" bishops', *Scottish Historical Review*, lv (1976), 105–26, at pp. 125–6), and had been the centre of a shire (G. W. S. Barrow, *The Kingdom of the Scots* (London, 1973), p. 35, and Aird, *Cuthbert*, p. 245). On the claims of Lindisfarne and, later, Durham to the lands of Tyningham which are embodied in *HSC* c. 4, see H. E. Craster, 'The patrimony of St Cuthbert', *English Historical Review*, lxix (1954), 177–99, at p. 179. Balthere's miracles are described only in *Bishops, Kings, and Saints*, ed. Godman, lines 1319–87. For the translation of his relics to Durham in the early eleventh century, see below, pp. 162–3. There is no evidence that the feast was observed at Durham, and there is no trace of it in the Durham calendars edited in *English Benedictine Kalendars after A.D. 1100*, ed. F. Wormald (Henry Bradshaw Society, lxxvii; 1938), pp. 166–79.

[7] ASC and JW, *s.a.* 738, name Eadberht's father as Eata (JW ii. 186–7).

[8] Eadberht's victories over the Britons and the Picts are recorded in *HReg*, *s.a.* 756 (Arnold, *Sym. Op.* ii. 40–1), and in *HECont*, *s.a.* 750. The general tenor of the *LDE's* comments, however, seems peculiar to it, as does the claim that Eadberht defeated the Scots and the English (*HECont*, *s.a.* 740, describes how King Æthelbald of the Mercians devastated his kingdom). A favourable account of his reign, including a reference to his 'extending the bounds of his own kingdom, subduing the enemy's forces in many a terrible defeat', is given by Alcuin (*Bishops, Saints, and Kings*, ed. Godman, lines 1248–72).

Pipinum peruenit, propter quod ei amicitia iunctus^a multa ei ac diuersa dona regalia transmisit.[9]

[xix (H)] Anno^b autem imperii sui uicesimo primo, cum undique pace ac dignitate cum omnium amore et gratia floreret, filio nomine Osulfo regnum contradedit, seque in clericatu omnipotentis Dei seruitio mancipauit, rogatus multum antea ne id faceret^c a regibus Anglorum et partem regni sui eius regno adicere uolentibus, dummodo retinens honorem suo in regno resideret.[10] At ille omnibus diuitiis et regnis seruitutem Dei pretulit, in qua per decem annos usque ad finem uite permansit,^d sepultusque^e est Eboraci in eadem porticu qua et frater eius Ecgbertus, qui tribus annis ante illum obierat.[11]

Iste siquidem Ecgbertus in infantia a patre Eata in monasterium traditus fuerat, qui prouectiori etate cum fratre Ecgredo Romam profectus, diaconatus gradum suscepit, mortuoque ibi fratre patriam reuersus.[12] Regnante Ceolwlfo atque iubente, primus post Paulinum accepto ab apostolica sede pallio, genti Northanhymbrorum in archiepiscopatum confirmatus est, et per triginta duos annos tenuit.[13]

[xx] 4. Anno^f ab Incarnatione Domini septingentesimo sexagesimo, presulatus uero Cynewlfi uicesimo primo, Osulf cum post patrem uno anno regnasset, impia nece a sua familia peremptus,^g Aethelwoldum

---

^a coniunctus H   ^b Eadbertus rex dimisso regno clericatum suscepit rubric H
^c faciat T   ^d mansit H   ^e sepultus H   ^f Higbaldus factus est episcopus Lindisfarnensis rubric Fx H Y   ^g est add. H

---

[9] Pippin III, father of Charlemagne, was mayor of the palace of Neustria, Burgundy, and Provence from 741 to 747, then mayor of the palace for all Frankia from 747 to 751, when he was anointed king of the Franks, an office he held until his death in 768. This reference to friendship with Eadberht is peculiar to *LDE*, and no other source refers to contacts between the two kings. J. E. Story, however, argues that Symeon may have had access to otherwise unpreserved Frankish annals; and that *LDE*'s account here is made plausible by what is known of Pippin's relations with the Northumbrian missionary Willibrord (Bede, *HE* v. 10), and by parallelism between Eadberht's coinage reform and that of Pippin, suggesting the possibility that the two kings may have been in contact with each other (J. E. Story, 'Charlemagne and Northumbria: The Influence of Francia on Northumbrian Politics in the Later Eighth and Early Ninth Centuries', Ph.D. thesis (Durham, 1995), pp. 72–3, 75–8; see also J. Booth, 'Sceattas in Northumbria', *Sceattas in England and on the Continent*, ed. D. Hill and D. M. Metcalf (British Archaeological Reports, British Series, cxxviii, 1984), pp. 71–112).

[10] Eadberht's assigning his kingdom to Oswulf is recorded *s.a.* 758 in *HReg* (Arnold, *Sym. Op.* ii. 41) and *HECont*, of which the latter refers to him taking 'St Peter's

even reached the king of the Franks Pippin, who became his friend because of this and sent him many and varied royal gifts.[9]

In the twenty-first year of his reign, when peace and dignity were flourishing on all sides with the love and good will of all, he handed over his kingdom to his son called Oswulf, and devoted himself as a priest to the service of almighty God, although he had long before been asked not to do this by the kings of the English who were willing to add part of their own kingdoms to his, so long as he retained the honour of king and remained in his kingdom.[10] But above all riches and kingdoms he preferred the service of God, in which he spent the last ten years of his life; and he was buried at York in the same chapel as his brother Ecgberht, who had died three years before him.[11] [xix (H)]

Now this Ecgberht, who had been placed in a monastery in infancy by his father Eata, went to Rome in later life with his brother Ecgred, received the rank of deacon and, after his brother had died there, returned to his own country.[12] In the reign of Ceolwulf and by his command, he became the first since Paulinus to accept the pallium from the apostolic see, and he was confirmed as archbishop of the Northumbrians, which position he held for thirty-two years.[13]

4. In the year of Our Lord's Incarnation 760, the twenty-first of the pontificate of Cynewulf, when Oswulf had reigned for one year after his father, he was wickedly put to death by his household and was [xx]

---

tonsure'. An account of his resignation and tonsuring is given in ASC DE, *s.a.* 757, *ALf*, *s.a.* 757, and JW, *s.a.* 757 (ii. 184–5). Only *LDE* relates the protests of the other kings.

[11] The death of Eadberht is recorded *s.a.* 768 in *HReg* (Arnold, *Sym. Op.* ii. 44) and *HECont*, and it is assigned to the 21st year of his reign in *DPSA*.

[12] This information about Ecgberht is unique to *LDE*, there being no hint of it in other sources, including the extended account of Ecgberht given by Alcuin (*Bishops, Saints, and Kings*, ed. Godman, lines 1248–72).

[13] Ecgberht became bishop of York in 732/3 and archbishop in 735, dying in 766. The information and wording of this sentence are close to *ALf* and *HECont.*, *s.a.* 735, and are echoed in *HReg*, *s.a.* 735 (Arnold, *Sym. Op.* ii, 31); all of these share the words 'primus post Paulinum'. The date 735 for Ecgberht's receipt of the pallium is also given in ASC, *s.a.* His death is recorded *s.a.* 766 *in ASC DE and HReg* (Arnold, *Sym. Op.* ii. 43). Counting his first year, *LDE's* figure of 32 years for his pontificate is consistent with this. The details of the burial of Ecgberht and Eadberht are found in ASC, *s.a.* 738, closely followed by *The Chronicle of Æthelweard*, ed. A. Campbell (NMT, 1962), p. 22.

Mol successorem habuit.[14] Qui ubi sex annis regnauerat, Alchred de stirpe Ethrici filii Ide regis in imperium successit.[15] Nono autem anno regni fraude suorum primatum exilio imperium mutauit, pro quo[a] Aethelred filius Aethelwoldi mox[b] in regnum substitutus est.[16] Quo imperii quarto anno in exilium fugato, Aelfwold[c] filius Osulfi regnum adeptus Northanhymbrorum decem annis tenuit.[17] Huius regni tercio anno qui est ab Incarnatione Domini septingentesimo octogesimo, Cynewulf (de quo supra diximus) quadragesimo primo sui episcopatus anno senio ac labore confectus, cum consensu totius congregationis uices suas in ecclesie regimine Higbaldo uiro strenuo delegauit; ipse uero liber ab huiusmodi[d] curis tribus post hec annis quieti et orationi operam dabat.[e] Quarto autem sue quietis[f] anno eo migrante ad Dominum, Higbald cathedram ascendens pontificalem per uiginti annos gubernauit.[18]

Anno presulatus eius sexto, prefatus rex Ælfwoldus[g] a duce suo

---

[a] om. H   [b] Mol Ca F   [c] Ethelwold T   [d] huius L   [e] dedit Ca; marginal correction probably destroyed in binding   [f] etatis L Y   [g] Ethelwoldus F L

---

[14] Æthelwald Moll was king of the Northumbrians from 759 until his expulsion in 765. He was seemingly of aristocratic stock, and he is probably to be identified with the *patricius* Moll referred to in a letter of Pope Paul I of 757/8 (*Councils and Ecclesiastical Documents Relating to Great Britain and Ireland*, ed. A. W. Haddan and W. Stubbs (3 vols.; Oxford, 1869–71), iii. 395). Placing the 21st year of Cynewulf's episcopate in 760 is consistent with a date for his accession in 740, but the end of Oswulf's one-year reign is placed in 759 by *HReg* (Arnold, *Sym. Op.* ii. 41) and *HECont*, although it is placed *s.a.* 757 by JW ii. 200–1. The chronology of *ALf* appears confused, since it gives Oswulf's accession *s.a.* 757 but then notes *s.a.* 759 that 'Oswulfus regnauit anno I super Northanhymbros.' *HReg* shares with *LDE* the information that he was killed 'a sua familia', but it adds the place of the killing, 'iuxta Mechil Wongtune'. According to *HECont*, Oswulf was killed 'a suis ministris facinore'. All these sources note the accession of Æthelwald Moll, in 759 according to *HReg*, *HECont*, and ASC DE; in 760 according to *ALf*.

[15] The length of Æthelwald Moll's reign, six years, agrees with *ALf*, *s.a.* 760, and with *HReg* (Arnold, *Sym. Op.* ii. 43), ASC DE, JW (ii. 204–5), and *HECont*, all of which place Alhred's accession in 765. He was expelled in 774 (see below, n. 16). Although *HReg* and *DPSA* describe him as 'ex prosapia Ide', only JW (ii. 204) gives genealogical information comparable to that in *LDE*: 'Alhredus filius Eanuuini successit, qui fuit Byrnhom, qui fuit Bofa, qui fuit Beacmon, qui fuit Earic, qui fuit Ide'. *LDE*'s Ethricus is found as a son of Ida in *DPSA* (Arnold, *Sym. Op.* ii. 374).

[16] *LDE*'s 'ninth year of his reign' is consistent with a date of 774, in which year Alhred's expulsion and replacement by Æthelred is recorded by *HReg* (Arnold, *Sym. Op.* ii. 45), ASC DE, and JW ii. 210–11. ASC adds that the expulsion took place at Easter and was from York. The length of his reign is given as nine years by ASC D, s.a. 765 (E has 'eight years'), and also by *DPSA* (Arnold, *Sym. Op.* ii. 376). There is one verbal echo

succeeded by Æthelwald Moll.[14] When he had reigned for six years, Alhred, who was of the line of King Ida's son Æthric, succeeded to the kingdom.[15] In the ninth year of his reign he was forced through the deceitfulness of his leading men to exchange the kingdom for exile, and Æthelwald's son Æthelred was soon substituted for him.[16] After he in his turn had fled into exile in the fourth year of his reign, Ælfwald, son of Oswulf, assumed the rule of the Northumbrians and held it for ten years.[17] In the third year of his reign, that was the seven hundredth and eightieth from Our Lord's Incarnation, Cynewulf (of whom we spoke above), in the forty-first year of his pontificate, worn out with age and labour, with the consent of the whole congregation delegated his post in the government of the church to that strenuous man Higbald; and he himself, free from such cares, devoted himself for three years after this to quietness and prayer. When he passed on to the Lord in the fourth year of his retirement, Higbald ascended the episcopal throne and governed the see for twenty years.[18]

In the sixth year of his pontificate, the aforementioned King

---

between *LDE* on the one side and *HReg*, which has the expression, 'exilio imperii mutauit maiestatem'.

[17] V begins again here at fo. 67ʳ. *HReg* places the expulsion of Æthelred in 779 (Arnold, *Sym. Op.* ii. 46), which would be the fifth year of his reign. *ALf* and ASC DE give 778, as does JW ii. 212–13, although this text gives him what appears to be his alternative name of Æthelberht (cf. JW ii. 210 n. 3). Ælfwald I reigned from 779 to 788.

[18] Cynewulf was bishop of Lindisfarne from 737/740 to 779/780 (see above, p. 79 n. 4), Higbald from 780 × 782–803. *LDE*'s account of his period of retirement is unique. It may have been based on a genuine tradition, or it may have derived from a misunderstanding of the wording of some account of Cynewulf's death such as that found in *HReg*, *s.a.* 780 (Arnold, *Sym. Op.* ii. 47) : 'Cyniwulf quoque episcopus . . . relictis secularibus curis, Higbaldo gubernacula ecclesie cum electione totius familie commisit.' Notice the similarity betwen *LDE*'s 'cum consensu totius congregationis' and *HReg*'s 'cum electione totius familie'. That the *HReg* is here referring to Cynewulf's death rather than his retirement is clear from the mention in ASC DE for the same year of Higbald's consecration at Sockburn (Co. Durham; NZ 349 069). *ALf*, *s.a.* 780, has 'Cineuulf Lindisfarnensis episcopus commisit episcopatum Higbaldo .xxii. annis', and the length of his pontificate is consistent with its reference to his death *s.a.* 803. *LDE*'s statement that he ruled for 20 ('XX' in the manuscripts) years is presumably an error, since it states later that Higbald died after having been bishop for 22 years (below, pp. 90–1). ASC DE mention Higbald's death *s.a.* 803, and an annal to this effect has been added *s.a.* 803 to *HReg* (Arnold, *Sym. Op.* ii. 68). This last source, however, has in addition a reference to the consecration of Higbald *s.a.* 781, which has been added by a hand other than that of the main scribe at the foot of a column (Arnold, *Sym. Op.* ii. 47). JW (ii. 230–1) has a marginal note relating Higbald's death and Ecgberht's election; in CCCO 157, this note, which is by the second scribe of the manuscript, is opposite the annals for 802–3. *LDE* presumably regarded Higbald's consecration as having occurred in 782, since it later refers to 793 as the eleventh year of his pontificate (below, pp. 86–7).

Sicga[a] miseranda morte peremptus in loco qui dicitur Scytlescester[b][19] iuxta murum, sepultus est in Hagustaldensi ecclesia. Fuerat quippe pietatis eximie ac iustitie, unde in loco occisionis eius lux celitus emissa sepe a plurimis uisa est.[20] Cui suus nepos Osred Alchredi quondam regis filius successit, sed post annum pulsus regno, in Eufoniam insulam (que Man uocatur) aufugit, et Aethelred de exilio reuocatus[c] regnum quod dudum amiserat recepit.[d][21]

[xxi] 5. Anno[e] ab Incarnatione Domini septingentesimo nonagesimo tertio, a transitu uero patris Cuthberti centesimo septimo, pontificatus autem Higbaldi undecimo, qui est annus imperii impiissimi regis Aethelredi quintus, uastatio miserrima Lindisfarnensem ecclesiam sanguine et rapina replens, pene usque ad interneciem[f] deleuit.[22] Sed antequam de ipsa[g] uastatione dicamus, de ipso loco antiquorum dicta paucis ponenda putamus. Sic enim scriptum[h] inuenimus:[23]

---

[a] Sioga *H*   [b] Scydescester *Ca H*   [c] uocatus *Ca*   [d] accepit *T*
[e] Descripcio Lindisfarnensis insule *rubric Fx H T V Y*   [f] internitionem *Ca*
[g] ista *Fx L Y*   [h] scripta *Ca*

---

[19] This place is popularly identified with Haltonchesters (Northumberland) on Hadrian's Wall.

[20] This account of Ælfwald's death is closely related to those in *HReg*, *s.a.* 788 (Arnold, *Sym. Op.* ii. 52), *DPSA*, ASC DE, *s.a.* 789; JW, *s.a.* 789 (ii. 222–3). In view of *LDE*'s interest in SS Cuthbert and Oswald, it may be significant that it does not make any mention of the church dedicated to these saints which was, according to *HReg*, built at the site of Ælfwald's death. *LDE* presumably dated the killing to 788 since it considered 793 to be the fifth year of Æthelred's second reign (below). On the cult of Ælfwald, see D. Rollason, 'The cults of murdered royal saints in Anglo-Saxon England', *Anglo-Saxon England*, xi (1983), 1–22, at 3–5.

[21] The one-year reign of Osred and his parentage is recorded *s.a.* 788 in *HReg* (Arnold, *Sym. Op.* ii. 52) and *ALf*; *s.a.* 789 in ASC DE; and *s.a.* 789 in JW ii. 222–3. *ALf* also mentions under that year the beginning of the reign of Æthelred, which it gives as seven years; but *HReg* (Arnold, *Sym. Op.* ii. 52) and ASC DE place it *s.a.* 790. They, however, reverse the sequence of events relative to *LDE*, thus making Æthelred's recall precede Osred's expulsion. *LDE*'s version is paralleled in this respect by that in *DPSA*, but there Osred is said to have been killed prior to Æthelred's return, rather than exiled. This is clearly erroneous in view of the 792 annal in *HReg* (Arnold, *Sym. Op.* ii. 54) and ASC DE relating to Osred's return to be captured and killed. This annal in *HReg* refers to Osred returning from Eufonia and thus corroborates *LDE*'s statement that Osred was exiled there. *LDE*'s identification of Eufonia with the Isle of Man is important, because it corroborates the identification of e.g. *Eufania* in the *Annals of Ulster*, *s.a.* 576 (Anderson, *Early Sources*, i. 88–9; *Annals of Ulster*, ed. Mac Airt and Mac Niocaill, *s.a.*).

[22] This is a reference to the Viking attack on Lindisfarne in 793, which Symeon describes below (pp. 88–9). It evidently caused considerable consternation, not least with Alcuin from whom it elicited a series of letters (*Epistolae Karolini Aevi, Tomus II*, ed.

Ælfwald was put to a grievous death by his duke Sicga in a place by the Wall called *Scytlescester*,[19] and he was buried in the church of Hexham. He had been of such outstanding piety and justice, that at the place where he was killed a light sent down from heaven was often seen by many.[20] His nephew Osred, son of the former King Alhred, succeeded him, but he was driven from his kingdom after a year, and he fled to the Euphonian island (which is called Man), and Æthelred was recalled from exile to receive again the kingdom which he had lost long before.[21]

5. In the seven hundredth and ninety-third year from Our Lord's [xxi] Incarnation, the hundred and seventh from the passing of father Cuthbert, the eleventh of the pontificate of Higbald, and the fifth of the reign of the most impious King Æthelred, the church of Lindisfarne was destroyed almost to the point of extermination by a most lamentable devastation, abounding in blood and rapine.[22] But before we describe this devastation, we think we should set down in a few words what our forefathers said about this place. For we have found the following written:[23]

E. Dümmler (*MGH, Epp.* iv, *Karolini Aevi ii* ; Berlin, 1895), nos. 19–22. On the context of the attack, see e.g. P. H. Sawyer, *Kings and Vikings: Scandinavia and Europe AD 700–1100* (London and New York, 1982), pp. 78–9, 81, 94–5. It is recorded *s.a.* 793 in *HReg* (Arnold, *Sym. Op.* ii. 55), ASC DE, and *ALf. LDE*'s placing of this event on the seventh of the Ides of June (7 June; below, p. 88) is close to the reference in *ALf*, which has the sixth, and is more plausible than the date of the sixth of the Ides of January (8 January) given in ASC DE. The latter's version, however, may have influenced the scribe of H to substitute *Ianuarium* for *Iuniarum*.

[23] This description of Lindisfarne, without the explanation of the name which is unique to *LDE*, is found in only one other text, *HReg*, *s.a.* 793, where it occurs in the following expanded form (words in common italicized): '*Lindisfarnensis insula* magna est *per ambitum*, uerbi gratia *octo* uel amplius *miliariis se extend*ens. *In qua est nobile monasterium quo eximius Cuthbertus antistes* positus erat *cum aliis presulibus qui eius successores dignissimi exititerant. De quibus dici* congruenter *potest quod canitur*, 'Corpora Sanctorum in pace sepulta sunt'. Lindis* dicitur flumen quod *excurr*it *in mare, duorum pedum latitudinem habens*, quando ledon fuerit, id est, minor estus, et *uideri potest:* quando uero malina fuerit, id est, major estus maris, tunc nequit Lindis uideri.' In *HReg* it is followed by an excursus on tides derived from Bede's *De natura rerum* and illustrated by one of Aldhelm's *Enigmata* (Arnold, *Sym. Op.* ii. 54–5). It has been convincingly argued that these items were amongst those added by Byrhtferth of Ramsey (*c*.970–*c*.1020), when he made the compilation of the 'Northern Annals' (above, p. lxxi) and other material which formed the core of *HReg* down to the death of Alfred (Arnold, *Sym. Op.* ii. 92; see Lapidge, *Anglo-Saxon England*, x (1982), 97–122). It is not certain whether this account of Lindisfarne formed part of Byrhtferth's compilation and was taken from there by Symeon, or was added by Symeon himself, first to *LDE* and then to *HReg* when Symeon expanded it (see above, p. xlix).

Lindisfarnensis insula octo miliariis se extendit per ambitum, in qua est nobile monasterium quo eximius antistes Cuthbertus, cum aliis presulibus qui eius successores dignissimi extiterant, corpore requieuit, de quibus apte dici potest quod canitur: 'Corpora eorum in pace sepulta sunt, et uiuent nomina eorum in eternum.'[24] Vocatur autem Lindisfarne a fluuiolo scilicet Lindis excurrente in mare, qui duorum pedum [a]habens latitudinem[a] non nisi cum recesserit mare uideri potest.

Hec de ipsa insula. Cuius cladem et aliorum quoque[b] sanctorum necem futuram presignantia, horrenda fulmina[c] et dracones igneis iactibus per era uibrantes et uolitantes uidebantur.[25]

[xxii]　Mox[d] eodem anno pagani ab aquilonali[e] climate nauali exercitu Brittanniam uenientes, hac illacque discurrentes, predantes interficiunt non solum iumenta, uerum etiam sacerdotes leuitasque[f] chorosque monachorum atque[g] sanctimonialium. Veniunt septimum Iduum Iuniarum[h] ad Lindisfarnensem ecclesiam, miserabili predatione cuncta uastant, sancta pollutis uestigiis calcant, altaria suffodiunt, omnia thesauraria ecclesie rapiunt. Quosdam e fratribus interficiunt, nonnullos secum uinctos assumunt, plurimos opprobriis uexatos nudos proiciunt, aliquos in mare demergunt.[26] Verum non impune ista fecerunt, Deo iniurias quas sancto Cuthberto irrogauerant maturius iudicante.[i] Denique anno sequente dum portum Ecgfridi regis (hoc est Gyruum) uastantes, monasterium quoque ad hostium Doni amnis depredarentur, dux eorum ibidem crudeli nece interiit; nec multo post ui tempestatis eorum collise contriteque naues perierunt. Illorum uero quidam fluctibus absorti, alii qui ad terram uiui quoquomodo[j] fuerant eiecti, mox indigenarum gladio sunt

---

[a-a] habens *om.* F; latitudinem habens *Fx L Y*　　[b] *om.* H　　[c] flumina *Fx L V Y*　　[d] Prima uastacio Lindisfarnensis insule a paganis *rubric Fx T V Y*; Vastacio Lindisfarnensis insule prima a paganis *rubric H*　　[e] *corr. from* aquiloni *in a later hand* C; aquilone *D*; aquiloni *Fx L Y*　　[f] et leuitas *H*; leuitas *T*　　[g] *at* T　　[h] Ianuarium *H*　　[i] uindicante *Ca H*　　[j] quomodo *D H V*

---

[24] Eccles. 44: 14.
[25] This sentence is closely related to *HReg*, *s.a.* 793 (words in common italicized): 'Siquidem *fulmina* abominanda, et *dracones* per aera, igneique ictus sepe uibrare et uolitare uidebantur; que scilicet signa famem magnam, et multorum hominum stragem pessimam atque inedicibilem, que subsecuta est, demonstrauere' (Arnold, *Sym. Op.* ii. 54–5). The substance of this is also to be found in ASC DE, *s.a.* 793. The word *inedicibilem* was one favoured by Byrhtferth of Ramsey who made the compilation on which the early sections of *HReg* are based (above, p. xlix).

The island of Lindisfarne is eight miles round, and on it is a noble monastery where there rest the bodies of the distinguished bishop Cuthbert and other bishops who were his most worthy successors, and of whom can justly be said the words which are sung: 'Their bodies are buried in peace, and their names will live for ever.'[24] Lindisfarne is called after the little stream *Lindis* which flows into the sea and, being only two feet in width, cannot be seen unless the tide is out.

So much for the island itself. Horrendous thunderbolts and dragons hurling fiery missiles and flying through the air were seen, presaging the destruction of the island and the approaching deaths of many holy men.[25]

Soon afterwards, in that very same year, heathen men from [xxii] northern climes came with a naval force to Britain and traversed the country in all directions, looting and killing not only beasts of burden but also priests, deacons, and congregations of monks and nuns. They came to the church of Lindisfarne on 7 June, devastated everything with pitiless looting, trampled the holy things under their sacrilegious feet, dug up the altars, and pillaged all the treasures of the church. Some of the brothers they killed, several they bound and took with them, many they tormented with opprobrium and threw out naked, and others they drowned in the sea.[26] But they did not do these things with impunity, for God very soon gave judgment on the injuries which they had inflicted on St Cuthbert. In fact in the following year, as they were ravaging the port of King Ecgfrith (that is Jarrow), and pillaging also the monastery at the mouth of the river Don, their leader died a cruel death; and not long afterwards their ships were destroyed, being driven into collision by the force of a storm and broken up. Some of the heathens were swallowed by the waves and others, who were somehow thrown up on to the land alive,

---

[26] This account of the Viking attack on Lindisfarne is almost identical to *HReg*, *s.a.* 793 (Arnold, *Sym. Op.* ii. 55; words in common are italicized in the Latin text): '*Eodem* sane *anno pagani ab aquilonali climate nauali exercitu* ut aculeati crabones *Brittanniam uenientes, hac illacque* ut dirissimi lupi *discurrentes, predantes,* mordentes, *interfici*entes *non solum iumenta,* oues et boues, *uerum etiam sacerdotes leuitasque chorosque monachorum atque sanctimonialium, ueniunt,* ut prefati sumus, *ad Lindisfarnensem ecclesiam, miserabili predatione cuncta uastant, sancta pollutis uestigiis, altaria suffodiunt, omnia thesauraria* sancte *ecclesie rapiunt. Quosdam e fratribus interficiunt, nonnullos secum uinctos assumunt,* per*plurimos opprobriis uexatos nudos proiciunt, aliquos in mare demergunt.*'

interfecti.[27] Taliter ecclesia Lindisfarnensi uastata et suis ornamentis spoliata, nichilominus tamen in ea sedes episcopalis et qui barbarorum manus effugere poterant monachi apud sacrum corpus beati Cuthberti multo post tempore permanserunt.

A cuius ecclesie depopulatione undecimo[a] anno, Higbald [b]completis in episcopatu[b] uiginti duobus annis defunctus est[c] octauas Kalendas Iunii,[28] et Ecgbertus in locum eius electus et consecratus, Eanbaldo archiepiscopo, et Eanberto et Badulfo aliis quoque episcopis in locum qui dicitur Biguell tertias Idus Iunii ad eius ordinationem conuenientibus,[29] septimum tunc annum imperii agente filio Earulfi[d] Eardulfo, qui occiso regi Aethelredo successerat.[30] Sed eo decimo regni sui anno de prouincia fugato, Aelfwold[e] per biennium illud tenuit, deinde Eanred filius Eardulfi regis[f] triginta tribus annis imperauit.[31] At Ecgberto peractis in episcopatu decem et octo annis

---

[a] nono *Ca*   [b-b] in episcopatu completis *H*   [c] *om. L*   [d] Eardulfi *F*
[e] Ethelwold *Fx L T;* Aelfwado *H;* Ethelwald, *V*   [f] *om. H*

---

[27] These two sentences are closely related to the more elaborate account in *HReg, s.a.* 794 (Arnold, *Sym. Op.* ii. 56), with which they share some phrases (italicized here): 'Predicti pagani *portum Ecgfridi regis uastantes, monasterium ad ostium Doni amnis* predarunt. Sed Sanctus Cuthbertus non sine punitione eos sinebat abire. Princeps quoque eorum ibidem *crudeli nece* occisus est ab Anglis, et, post exigui temporis spatium, *uis tempestatis eorum naues* quassauit, perdidit, contriuit; et perplurimos mare operuit. Nonnulli itaque ad littus sunt *eiecti*, et mox interfecti absque misericordia. Et recte illius hec contigerunt, quoniam se non ledentes grauiter leserunt.' These details are also found in ASC DE, *s.a.* 794, where the place in question is referred to as 'Ecgferþæs mynster æt Done muþan'. *LDE* is unique, however, in making an identification with Jarrow. In a letter to King Eadbert, Pope Paul I referred to a monastery called *Donæmuthe* which he linked with Stonegrave and Coxwold (both in the North Riding of Yorkshire) as having been subject to the same abbess (Haddan and Stubbs, *Councils and Ecclesiastical Documents*, iii. 394–6). For the possibility that the monastery attacked in 794 was in fact on the river Don in the West Riding, see W. Richardson, 'The Venerable Bede and a lost Saxon monastery in Yorkshire', *Yorkshire Archaeological Journal*, lvii (1985), 15–22.

[28] The eleventh year after the pillaging of Lindisfarne in 793 would be 803–4, and this accords with ASC DE, *s.a.* 803, recording the death of Bishop Higbald of Lindisfarne (780 × 782–803) and the consecration of Bishop Ecgberht (803–21); see above, p. 85 n. 17.

[29] The consecrating bishops were Eanbald II, archbishop of York (796–808 × ?), Eanberht, bishop of Hexham (800–13), and Beadwulf, bishop of Whithorn (791–803 × ?). Bywell is on the river Tyne, four miles downstream from Corbridge. It has two churches very close together. St Peter's has Anglo-Saxon fabric of the second half of the 7th cent. St Andrew's, although its earliest fabric is no earlier than the mid-10th cent., has preserved a sculptured stone dated to the late 7th or early 8th cent. (H. M. and J. Taylor, *Anglo-Saxon Architecture*, i. 121–6, and Cramp, *Corpus*, p. 168). In view of this, it seems very likely that Bywell was the site of an early ecclesiastical centre of some importance, and it has been suggested that it was the monastery described in Ædiluulf's poem *De abbatibus* (D. R. Howlett, 'The provenance, date and structure of the *De Abbatibus*', *Archaeologia Aeliana*, 5th ser., iii (1973), 121–30; Blair, in Blair and Sharpe, *Pastoral Care*, pp. 227–8, 250; but cf. K. Ward, 'The monastery of the *De abbatibus:* a

were soon killed by the swords of the inhabitants.[27] So the church of Lindisfarne was ravaged and despoiled of its ornaments, but nevertheless for a long time afterwards an episcopal see remained there with the holy body of the blessed Cuthbert and those monks who had been able to escape from the hand of the barbarians.

In the eleventh year after the pillaging of that church, Higbald, who had completed twenty-two years as bishop, died on 25 May;[28] and Ecgberht was elected and consecrated in his stead on 11 June, at a place called Bywell, by Archbishop Eanbald and other bishops, including Eanberht and Beadwulf, who had assembled for his ordination.[29] This was in the seventh year of the reign of Earulf's son Eardwulf, who had succeeded King Æthelred when the latter had been killed.[30] But in the tenth year of his reign he was driven from the kingdom which was then held by Ælfwald for two years, after which King Eardwulf's son Eanred ruled it for thirty-three years.[31] When

reconsideration of its location', *Durham Archaeological Journal*, vii (1991), 123–7, and M. Lapidge, 'Aediluulf and the School of York', in his *Anglo-Latin Literature 600–899* (London and Rio Grande, 1996), pp. 382–98, at 394–8 (repr. from *Lateinische Kultur im VIII. Jahrhundert*, ed. A. Lehner and W. Berschin (St Ottilien, 1990), pp. 161–78), who argues in favour of identifying the monastery with Crayke, which lies approximately twelve miles north of York (see below, pp. 98–9, 122–3).

[30] Eardwulf reigned from 796 until his expulsion in 806, and was then restored in 808 and reigned until an indeterminate date, possibly as late as *c.*830 (see below, n. 31). Cf. this passage with *HReg*, *s.a.* 796 (Arnold, *Sym. Op.* ii. 57–8): 'Eardulf enim, de quo supradiximus, filius Eardulfi, de exilio uocatus, regni infulis est sublimatus.' This is consistent with the date of 803 for Bishop Ecgberht's consecration (above, p. 85 n. 17). *LDE* differs from *HReg* with regard to the circumstances of Eardwulf's accession. According to *HReg* Æthelred was indeed murdered but was succeeded for a period of 27 days by the *patricius* Osbald, whose expulsion opened the way for Eardwulf's recall from exile.

[31] *HReg* has no annals between 803 and 830, but ASC DE notes the expulsion of Eardwulf *s.a.* 806, and *DPSA* assigns reigns of ten and two years to Eardwulf and Ælfwald respectively. Roger of Wendover, however, dates the expulsion to 808 (Coxe, *Flores* i. 270), Henry of Huntingdon seemingly to 807 (*Henry, Archdeacon of Huntingdon, Historia Anglorum, The History of the English People*, ed. and trans. D. E. Greenway (OMT, 1996), pp. 260–1). According to contemporary Frankish and papal sources, Eardulf was restored in 808 by envoys of Charlemagne and Pope Leo III, but there is no record of this in Northumbrian sources. See *Annales Regni Francorum*, ed. F. Kurze (*MGH, Scriptores Rerum Germanicarum in usum scholarum*, vi; Hanover, 1895), pp. 126–7, Haddan and Stubbs, *Councils and Ecclesiastical Documents*, iii. 566, and, for comment, Kirby, *Earliest English Kings*, pp. 157 and 196. Eanred's 33-year reign would presumably have ended in 841, but although the span given here conforms with the king-list prefixed to *LDE* in Ca, it differs from the *DPSA* which gives a reign of 32 years. Moreover, the dates of all 9th-cent. Northumbrian kings are open to question as a result of numismatic studies, the evidence of which suggests that Eardwulf's second reign may have lasted until *c.*831, with Eanred ruling until as late as *c.*854; see H. E. Pagan, 'Northumbrian numismatic chronology in the ninth century', *British Numismatic Journal*, xxxviii (1969), 1–15, and P. Grierson and M. Blackburn, *Medieval European Coinage with a Catalogue of the Coins in the Fitzwilliam Museum, Cambridge, i, The Early Middle Ages (5th–10th Centuries)* (Cambridge, 1986), pp. 301–2.

defuncto, Heathured successit et in officio regiminis nouem annos transegit. Post quem Ecgredus *ᵃuicesimo secundo anno imperii Eanrediᵃ* regis in presulatum est sullimatus,³² uir natu nobilis et operum efficatia strenuus, qui patris *ᵇCuthberti ecclesiamᵇ* amplius predecessoribus suis*ᶜ* rerum et*ᵈ* terrarum largitionibus locupletare studuerat et honorare.

[xxiii]   Edificata*ᵉ* nanque in Northam ecclesia, eaque in honore sanctorum Petri apostoli et*ᶠ* Cuthberti pontificis necnon et Ceolwlfi regis et post monachi dedicata, transtulit illo*ᵍ* corpus eiusdem Deo dilecti Ceolwlfi;³³ ipsamque uillam cum duabus aliis, quas ipse condiderat, eodem nomine nuncupatis—Geddeworde—cum suis appendiciis,³⁴ ecclesiam quoque et uillam quam edificauerat in loco qui Geinforde appellatur*ʰ* et quicquid ad eam pertinet a flumine Teisa usque Weor, sancto confessori Cuthberto contulit.³⁵ Duas quoque*ⁱ* uillas Ileclif et Wigeclif,*ʲ* sed et Billingham in Heorternesse quarum ipse conditor fuerat, locis superioribus que predicto confessori donauerat, perpetuo

---

ᵃ⁻ᵃ om. L   *ᵇ⁻ᵇ* ecclesiam Cuthberti *Fx L Y*   *ᶜ om. H*   *ᵈ* ac *D F H T V*   *ᵉ* Ecclesia in Northam sancti Cuthberti (sancti Cuthberti in Norham *H*) edificata est *rubric Fx H V Y*   *ᶠ* sancti *add. L*   *ᵍ* illuc *H*   *ʰ* dicitur *F* *ⁱ om. T*   *ʲ* Wileclif *F*

---

³² Ecgberht, who was consecrated in 803 (above, p. 90 n. 28), would have completed eighteen years as bishop in 821, but the only other source to notice his death is JW ii. 240–1, which has *s.a.* 819 (an alteration over some erasure by the second scribe of CCCO 157): 'Defuncto Ecgberto Lindisfarnensi episcopo, Heathoredus successit.' The length of Heathured's pontificate given in *LDE* and its date for the accession of Ecgred agree with *HReg*, which has an isolated annal for 830 recording the latter (Arnold, *Sym. Op.* ii. 68). Heathured's dates are therefore probably 821–30. Ecgred was bishop of Lindisfarne (830–46 × 7; see below, p. 94 n. 37).

³³ Norham stands on the south bank of the river Tweed approximately ten miles upstream from Berwick. The present church, which is dedicated to St Cuthbert, is late medieval, but it contains a large collection of sculptured fragments, some of which are 9th-cent. in date (Cramp, *Corpus*, pp. 208–14). An abbot of Norham is mentioned at the beginning of the 10th-cent. in *HSC* c. 21. This latter text has an account of Ecgred's activities at Norham which differs from that of *LDE*: 'Successit Egred episcopus, qui transportauit quandam ecclesiam olim factam a beato Aidano, tempore Oswaldi regis, de Lindisfarnensi insula ad Northham, ibique eam reedificauit, et illuc corpus sancti Cuthberti et Ceoluulfi regis transtulit, ipsamque uillam sancto confessori dedit.' The use of the singular *transtulit* raises the possibility that the reference to Ceolwulf has been interpolated into this text (see Thomas, 'Cult of Saints' Relics', p. 74). *LDE* alludes to the resting-place of Ceolwulf at Norham (above, pp. 78–9). The purported diploma of Bishop William of Saint-Calais relating to the foundation of Durham Cathedral Priory, which drew heavily on *LDE* iv. 2 and was entered into the *Liber Vitae* soon after the

Ecgberht died after being bishop for eighteen years, Heathured succeeded and held that office for nine years. After him Ecgred was raised to the episcopate in the twenty-second year of the reign of King Eanred.[32] He was a man of noble birth and strenuous and effective in his actions, and more than his predecessors he strove to adorn and enrich the church of father Cuthbert with donations of land and property.

For, when he had built a church in Norham and dedicated it in [xxiii] honour of saints Peter the apostle, Cuthbert the bishop, and Ceolwulf king and later monk, he translated to it the body of that same Ceolwulf beloved of God;[33] and he gave to the holy confessor Cuthbert the vill itself with two other vills which he had founded and which were called by the same name, Jedburgh, with all their appurtenances,[34] and also the church and vill which he had built in a place called Gainford and whatever pertained to it between the river Tees and the river Wear.[35] To these places which he had given to the aforesaid confessor, he added to be held in perpetuity the two vills of Cliffe and Wycliffe and also Billingham in Hartness, of all of which he

completion of that work, does show knowledge of the tradition that Cuthbert's body was at Norham: 'Norham quam ipse ibi corpore quiescendo illustrauerat' (Offler, *Episcopal Charters*, pp. 8, 12). According to *HReg*, *s.a.* 854, Ceolwulf's body was taken to Norham and there, 'ut fertur ab habitatoribus ipisus loci, claruit miraculis' (Arnold, *Sym. Op.* ii. 102). An account of the possessions of Lindisfarne at the beginning of the same annal includes Norham which it states was formerly known as *Ubbanford* (Arnold, *Sym. Op.* ii. 101–2). In fact the list of saints' resting places, *Secgan be þæm Godes sanctum*, has in what is probably a 9th-cent. series of entries a reference to St Cuthbert's body resting at *Ubbanford* on the river Tweed (F. Liebermann, *Die Heiligen Englands* (Hanover, 1889), p. 9, and for comment D. W. Rollason, 'Lists of saints' resting-places in Anglo-Saxon England, *Anglo-Saxon England*, vii (1978), 61–93, at p. 68). Norham was an important possession of the bishops of Durham in later times and Ranulf Flambard built a castle there (Appendix B, below, pp. 276–7).

[34] *HSC* c. 9 (Arnold, *Sym. Op.* i. 201) mentions this gift and defines the territories belonging to the two Jedburghs as 'a Duna usque ad Tefegedmuthe, et inde ad Wiltuna, et inde ultra montem uersus austrum', interpreted by Hinde as describing from the hill called Dunion near Jedburgh, down the river Teviot to Jedmouth, 'and so up that river to Wilton, immediately opposite to the town of Hawick' (*Symeonis Opera*, ed. Hinde, p. 140).

[35] Gainford (Co. Durham) is on the river Tees downstream of Barnard Castle. *HSC* c. 9 mentions this grant and adds further that its appurtenances were defined as 'a flumine Tese usque ad Weor, et a uia que uocatur Deorstrete usque ad montem uersus occidentem'. Gainford church has no pre-Conquest fabric, but thirty-one items of pre-Conquest sculpture, mostly dated to the 10th cent. and later but one possibly of the mid-9th, have been found there (Cramp, *Corpus*, pp. 80–90). Gainford cannot have been a new foundation in Ecgred's time, however, since *HReg*, *s.a.* 801 (Arnold, *Sym. Op.* ii. 65), refers to the burial there of a certain abbot called Edwin.

possidenda adiecit.[36] Sexto decimo autem episcopatus sui anno, qui
est quintus annus regni Aethelredi qui patri Eanredo successerat,
defunctus est, pro quo Eanbertus electus octo annis ecclesiam[a]
gubernauit.

[xxiv] Post[b] quem anno ab Incarnatione Domini octingentesimo quinquagesimo quarto, imperii autem Osberti qui occiso Aethelredo in
regnum successerat anno quinto, Eardulfus uir magni meriti cathedre
pontificalis gubernacula suscepit;[37] nec minorem quam proximis
Lindisfarnensium quibusque longe positis episcopatus sui locis
pastoralis cure sollicitudinem impendebat. Quorum Luel (quod
nunc Carleol appellatur) non solum proprii iuris sancti Cuthberti
fuerat, sed etiam ad sui episcopatus regimen ab Ecgfridi regis
temporibus semper adiacebat.[38] Nemo sane predecessorum eius[c] uel
successorum usque in presens[d] tantum sacratissimi corporis Cuthberti presentia laborauit, qui cum illo de loco ad locum per septem
annos fugitando, inter gladios ubique seuientes, inter barbarorum
impetus feroces, inter monasteriorum concremationes, inter rapinas
et hominum strages eius obsequio amore semper[e] inseparabili adhesit
sicut in consequentibus dicetur.[39]

[xxv] 6. His[f] temporibus coadunati undecumque infinita multitudine
populi Danorum scilicet et Fresonum aliarumque gentium paga-
narum multa classe aduecti,[g] [h]hisque regibus ac ducibus[h] Halfdene,
Inguar, Hubba, Beicgsecg, Guthrum, Oscytello, Amundo, Sidroc

---

  a om. L   *b* Carlel episcopatui Lindisfarnensis ecclesie subiacebat *rubric Fx H*
T Y   *c* suorum Ca   *d* in *adds Ca*.   *e* om. Ca   *f* Secunda et
extrema (ultima T) Lindisfarnensis insule deuastacio ab (sub *H*) Inguar et Hubba *rubric*
H T V Y   *g* adducti Fx *(corr. in marg.)* L Y   *h–h* hisque regibus ducibus Ca
with regibus *add. above line;* hiisque quoque regibus et ducibus H

---

[36] Although the tower of St Cuthbert's Church, Billingham is post-Conquest
(E. Cambridge, 'Early Romanesque architecture in north-east England: a style and its
patrons', Rollason, *Anglo-Norman Durham*, pp. 141–60, at 141–5), the nave is early and a
number of items of pre-Conquest sculpture have been found there, including a grave-
marker possibly to be dated to the second half of the 9th cent. and one dated to the first
half of the 8th (Cramp, *Corpus*, pp. 48–53). This last find suggests that Ecgred was not in
fact the founder of Billingham. *Cliue* and *Witcliue* appear in *Domesday Book*, fol. 309a, as
sokes of Gilling (Yorks.) (*Yorkshire*, ed. and trans. M. L. Faull and M. Stinson (2 vols.;
Domesday Book, xxx; Chichester, 1986), i. 6N1). They can be identified as Cliffe Hall (NZ
207152) and Wycliffe (NZ 115 143), both on the Tees upstream from Darlington (Faull
and Stinson, *Yorkshire*, map II).

[37] The dates of the bishops of Lindisfarne mentioned here are: Ecgred (830–846 × 7),
Eanberht (846 × 7–854), Eardulf (854–880 × 5), then bishop of Chester-le-Street until
899. Eanred's accession is dated to 841 (above, p. 91 n. 30), hence Ecgred's death is
dated 846 × 7. In JW (ii.260–1), it is given *s.a.* 845; but in CCCO 157 this is an addition

himself was the founder.[36] In the sixteenth year of his pontificate, however, which was the fifth year of the reign of Æthelred who had succeeded his father Eanred, Ecgred died and Eanberht was elected in his place and governed the church for eight years.

After him, in the year 854 of the Incarnation of Our Lord, the fifth [xxiv] of the reign of Osberht who had succeeded Æthelred when the latter had been killed, Eardwulf, a man of great merit, accepted the governance of the pontifical throne.[37] He devoted no less effort to the pastoral care of the distant places in his diocese than he did to those nearest to Lindisfarne. Of the former, Luel (which is now called Carlisle) had not only been under the personal jurisdiction of St Cuthbert, but also from the time of King Ecgfrith it was always placed under the governance of his bishopric.[38] It is certain that none of his predecessors or successors down to the present day laboured so much in the presence of Cuthbert's most sacred body, for, fleeing with it from place to place for seven years, beset by swords wreaking violence everywhere, ferocious attacks of barbarians, burning-down of monasteries, rapine and massacre, he always held fast with unremitting love to his obedience to the saint, as we shall subsequently recount.[39]

6. At this time an infinite multitude of people drawn together from [xxv] all parts—from the Danes, the Frisians, and other heathen peoples— came in a great fleet; and led by their kings and dukes, Halfdan, Inguar, Hubba, Beicsecg, Guthrum, Osketel, Amund, Sidroc, and

by the second scribe. Another note by the same scribe agrees with *LDE*, however, in giving the date of Eanberht's death *s.a.* 854 (JW ii. 268–9), which accords with *LDE*'s eight-year pontificate.

[38] An extremely thorough erasure of seventeen lines now follows in C. Under ultraviolet light the only marks visible are the remains of a *ur* abbreviation in the middle of the first line. For the alleged grant of Carlisle to St Cuthbert and his foundation of a monastery and schools there, see above, pp. 46–7. The early lives of St Cuthbert associate the saint with Carlisle but do not suggest that he had any jurisdiction there (Anon., *V. Cuth.* cc. 5 and 8–9, and Bede, *V. Cuth.* c. 27). *LDE*'s wording here must relate to Durham's late 11th-cent. claim to exercise authority over Carlisle, which was disputed by both Glasgow and York. The erasure of seventeen lines at this point in C has presumably removed text which elaborated on that. See Rollason, 'Erasures', pp. 148–50, and Sharpe, in Rollason, *Symeon*, pp. 214–29; for the claim to authority over Carlisle, see Offler, *Episcopal Charters*, p. 22, Sharpe, op. cit., pp. 216–17. Summerson's assumption that the claim was undisputed is misleading (Summerson, *Medieval Carlisle*, i. 31, 34).

[39] The period of seven years is specified in *HSC* c. 20 (Arnold, *Sym. Op.* i. 207), in *HReg*'s second annal for 875 (Arnold, *Sym.Op.* ii. 110), and also in *DPSA* ('nomina episcoporum Dunelmensium'). *HReg*'s first annal, however, gives a period of nine years (Arnold, *Sym.Op.* ii. 82). For details of the places visited, see below, pp. 112–27.

cum alio eiusdem nominis duce,[a] Osberno quoque et Frana necnon Haroldo adducti, Angliam occupant, cunctamque peruagantes, incendio, rapinis et strage deuastant. Subactis ac[b] perditis australium Anglorum pene omnibus prouinciis, Northanhimbrorum quoque regionem expugnare aggrediuntur.[40]

Anno enim[c] ab Incarnatione Domini octingentesimo sexagesimo septimo, presulatus uero Eardulfi anno quarto decimo, qui est [d]quintus annus[d] imperii [e]Aelle regis[e] Northanhymbrorum, quem expulso Osberto in regnum substituerant, predictus paganorum exercitus Kalendas Nouembris capta Eboraca, hac illacque discurrit, cruore atque luctu omnia repleuit; ecclesias longe lateque et monasteria ferro atque igne deleuit, nil preter solos sine tecto parietes abiens reliquit, in tantum ut illa que in presenti est aetas ipsorum locorum uix aliquod—interdum nullum—antique nobilitatis possit reuisere signum. Et[f] hac quidem uice ultra Tini fluminis ostium non processerant barbari, sed inde Eboracum sunt[g] reuersi. At[h] Northanhymbrorum populi, in tanta necessitate placatis alterutrum [i]suis regibus[i] (scilicet Osberto et Ella), congregatoque exercitu non paruo, hostium uires quoquomodo debilitare conabantur.

[xxvi]   Igitur[j] duobus regibus et octo comitibus perducti, Eboracum duodecimas Kalendas Aprilis irrumpunt, quorum quidam intus, alii uero extrinsecus satis pertinaciter agunt. Quorum repentino aduentu hostibus aliquantulum perterritis sed post acriter resistentibus, ex utraque parte atrociter pugnatur.[41] Tandem cum maxima parte

---

[a] duce et H   [b] et H   [c] om. H   [d-d] annus quintus T   [e-e] regis Aelle Ca   [f] In Ca   [g] om. L   [h] om. Y; ins. over line Fx   [i-i] regibus suis Ca   [j] De Osberto et Ella regibus qui Cretham abstulerunt et Bilingham de Sancto Cuthberto rubric Fx T V Y

---

[40] The Viking 'Great Army' (micel here) landed in East Anglia in 865, captured York in 866–7, and conquered East Anglia in 869 and Mercia in 873 (see F. M. Stenton, Anglo-Saxon England (3rd edn., Oxford, 1971), pp. 245–76). The source for LDE's account of its activities is probably Asser, although this is not certain. For its reference to Frisians, LDE is probably using HSC c. 10 (Arnold, Sym. Op. i. 202), or De miraculis c. 1 (Arnold, Sym. Op. i. 229–34), both of which describe Ubba as 'duke of the Frisians'. Asser, c. 69, mentions Frisians only as enemies of the Danes on the continent. The names of the leaders given here are at no point found together in Asser's text and the spellings are notably different from LDE's. Asser refers to the arrival in England of Inwar and Healfdene in 878 (further on Halfdan, see below, pp. 100–1, 104–5); and their alleged brother Hubba is mentioned in an interpolation in the same section (c. 54). Bæcscecg, Sidroc, Osbern, Fræna, and Hareld appear as the defeated leaders at the Battle of Ashdown in 871 (c. 39). Gothrum, Osscytil, and Anuind first appear as wintering at Cambridge in 875 (c. 47); see Stenton, Anglo-Saxon England, p. 246 n. 2.

[41] The date 867 given by ASC is by our reckoning 866, since in this part of ASC the

another duke of the same name, and also Osbern and Frana, together with Harold, they occupied England, roaming everywhere and devastating everything with fire, rapine, and carnage. After subjugating or destroying almost all the kingdoms of the southern English, they assaulted the region of the Northumbrians to conquer it as well.[40]

In the year of Our Lord's Incarnation 867, the fourteenth year of the pontificate of Eardwulf, that is the fifth year of the reign of King Ælle of the Northumbrians, whom they had installed in the place of the expelled Osberht, the aforementioned heathen army captured York on 1 November and ranged hither and thither, filling everywhere with blood and lamentation. They destroyed monasteries and churches far and wide with sword and fire, and when they departed they left nothing except roofless walls, to such an extent that the present generation can recognize hardly any sign—sometimes none at all—of the ancient nobility of these places. At this time, however, the barbarians did not advance beyond the mouth of the river Tyne, but returned to York. Driven by necessity, the kings of the Northumbrians (that is, Osberht and Ælle) were reconciled to each other, and the Northumbrian peoples gathered together a not inconsiderable army and strove in every way possible to cripple the enemy's power.

So, led by two kings and eight counts, they burst into York on 21 [xxvi] March, and fought stubbornly, some on the inside, some on the outside. At first the enemy was terrified by the sudden arrival of the attackers, but then they resisted fiercely, and on both sides there was savage fighting.[41] At length both the aforementioned kings fell with

year began on 24 Sept. and this incident is here placed on 1 Nov. *LDE*'s statement that Ælle was in the fifth year of his reign in 867 (866) can be made to conform with other sources, although *ALf*, *s.a.* 863, assigns to him only a four-year reign. The chronology of all the 12th-cent. writers may be defective, however; see above, p. 91 n. 31. *LDE*'s account of the Viking capture of York and the failed Northumbrian counter-attack is the most detailed extant, and is unique in describing the first capture of York. It is described by Asser, c. 27, who gives a broadly similar account of how the kings Ælle and Osberht joined forces to counter-attack but were defeated after they had successfully broken through the Vikings to enter York. ASC, *s.a.* 867, gives a compatible but more general account, and both it and Asser refer to the expulsion of Ælle in favour of Osberht. *HReg*'s first entry for 867 is based on Asser (Arnold, *Sym. Op.* ii. 74–5), and its second for 867 (ibid., ii. 105–6) resembles Asser, who was followed verbatim by JW ii. 280–3. In its second entry *HReg* adds a phrase giving the same date as *LDE* for the Northumbrian counter-attack. Roger of Wendover (Coxe, *Flores* i. 298) also gives a date for this, but according to him it was Palm Sunday (23 March in 867). *LDE*'s statement that the Vikings did not on this occasion cross the Tyne is presumably related to the information that *HReg* adds to its sources in its second entry for 867, namely that the Vikings 'omniaque uastauerunt usque Tinemuthan'. The reference to eight counts is otherwise found only in Roger of Wendover (Coxe, *Flores*

[*See p. 98 for n. 41 cont.*]

suorum ambo prefati reges occubuerunt, et iniurias quas ecclesie sancti Cuthberti aliquando irrogauerant, uita priuati et regno per-
[xxvi (H)] soluerunt. Denique[a] Osbertus Wercewrde et Tillemuthe, Aella uero Billingham, Ileclif, et Wigeclif, Crecam quoque, sacrilego ausu ipsius ecclesie abripuerant.[42] Quibus (ut dictum est) interfectis, regem Northumbris qui supererant Ecgbertum Dani constituerunt, qui eis tantum qui ad septentrionalem plagam [b]fluminis Tini[b] habitabant sub eorum dominio imperaret.[43] His ita gestis, ab Eboraco ad regnum Merciorum exercitus proficiscitur, sed post annum reuersus Eboracum solita crudelitate grassatur.[44]

[xxvii]   Inde[c] altero anno diuertens duce omnium crudelissimo Inguar Orientales Anglos inuadit, sanctissimumque regem Eadmundum diuersis penis laceratum cum suo pontifice Hunberto peremit.[45] Inter hec Northumbrani regem suum Ecgbertum et archiepiscopum Wlfhere[d] de prouincia expellunt, et quendam uocabulo Ricsig in regnum[e] sibi constituunt.[46] Nec multo post Halfdene rex Danorum

---

[a] Osbertus et Ella reges qui Crecam et Billingham sancto Cuthberto abstulerunt *rubric* H   [b-b] Tini fluminis H   [c] Martirizatus sanctus rex Edmundus *rubric* H; Occiditur sanctus Eadmundus *rubric Fx* Y; Sanctus Edmundus occiditur *rubric T* [d] Wilfred H   [e] regem H

---

i. 298). *LDE*'s interest in the archaeology of York should be noted, although the destruction noted by Symeon is more likely to have resulted from the burning of York by the Normans in Sept. 1069 (*HReg, s.a.* , *Hugh the Chanter: The History of the Church of York 1066–1127*, ed. and trans. C. Johnson, rev. M. Brett, C. N. L. Brooke, and M. Winterbottom (2nd edn.; OMT, 1990), pp. 2–3; for comment, Rollason, *Sources*, pp. 184–5, 193–5). Nevertheless, Symeon's account of the destruction arising from the attack agrees with that of William of Malmesbury (*Gesta Regum Anglorum: The History of the English Kings*, ed. and trans. R. A. B. Mynors, completed R. M. Thomson and M. Winterbottom (2 vols., OMT, 1998–9), i. 180–1, and with the *Annales Cambriae, s.a.* 866 (*Nennius: British History and the Welsh Annals*, ed. J. Morris (History from the Sources; London and Chichester, 1980), pp. 48, 89.

[42] The source here is clearly *HSC* c. 10 (Arnold, *Sym. Op.* i. 201–2). According to that text, Tillmouth (Northumberland) had been part of the early lands of Lindisfarne (c. 4); Warkworth (Northumberland), the bounds of which it gives, had been a gift of King Ceolwulf when he retired as a monk to Lindisfarne in 737 (c. 8 and above, p. 78–9); Billingham, Cliffe, and Wycliffe had been established by Bishop Ecgred of Lindisfarne (830–45); and Crayke had been given by King Ecgfrith to Cuthbert, who founded a monastery there and whose body was later to rest there for a short time (cc. 5, 20; see also above, pp. 46–7). Billingham (Co. Durham) possesses a pre-Conquest church, into the tower of which early sculpture is embedded (H. M. and J. Taylor, *Anglo-Saxon Architecture*, i. 66–70; Cramp, *Corpus*, pp. 48–53; but cf. E. Cambridge, 'Early Romanesque architecture in North-East England: a style and its patrons', in Rollason, *Anglo-Norman Durham*, pp. 141–60, at 141–4). For Cliffe and Wycliffe, see above, p. 94 n. 36. For the context of these places in the land-claims of the church of Durham, see Craster, *English Historical Review*, lxix (1954), 179, 182, 185, 186. It may be significant that the lands alienated by Osberht were in Bernicia, those by Ælle were in Deira.

most of their men, and deprived of life and kingdom they paid for the injuries which they had formerly inflicted on the church of St [xxxvi (H)] Cuthbert. For Osberht had with sacrilegious daring seized from Cuthbert's church Warkworth and Tillmouth, and Ælle had done the same with Billingham, Cliffe, and Wycliffe, and also Crayke.[42] When these two kings had been killed (as has been described), the Danes set up Ecgberht as a king over the surviving Northumbrians, but he ruled only over those who lived to the north of the river Tyne, and that under the authority of the Danes.[43] When all this had been done, the army marched from York to the kingdom of the Mercians, but after a year it returned to York and ravaged with its customary cruelty.[44]

It left in the following year and, under its most cruel of all leaders [xxvii] Inguar, it invaded the East Angles, and killed the most holy King Edmund, on whom had been inflicted various tortures, and with him his bishop Hunberht.[45] Meanwhile the Northumbrians expelled their king Ecgberht and their archbishop Wulfhere from the kingdom, and set up as their king a certain man called Ricsige.[46] Not long afterwards

[43] The appointment of Ecgberht is known only to northern sources. In his letter to Dean Hugh, Symeon of Durham assigns to him a reign of seven years (Arnold, *Sym. Op.* i. 225), but in the lists of kings prefixed to *LDE* in Ca he is assigned a reign of six years (Arnold, *Sym. Op.* ii. 391) and this agrees with *HReg* (below). *DPSA* assigns him five (Arnold, *Sym. Op.* ii. 377). *LDE*'s statement here is related to *HReg*'s second annal for 867, in which text taken from JW and Asser has had added to it the words, 'Quibus peractis, predicti pagani sub suo dominio regem Ecgberhtum prefecerunt. Ecgberhtus uero regnauit post hec super Northumbros ultra Tine .vi. annis' (Arnold, *Sym. Op.* ii. 106).

[44] This expedition into Mercia, during which the Vikings were besieged in Nottingham by a combined force of Mercians and West Saxons, is described by ASC, Asser, cc. 30–1, and JW ii. 282–5, following Asser, *s.a.* 868, with the return to York being placed in 869. *HReg*'s two entries for 868–9 are related to this (Arnold, *Sym. Op.* ii. 75–6, 106–7) but the first of these adds words which reflect *LDE*'s observation that the Vikings were engaged in ravaging on their return to York: 'rursum ad gentem Northanhymbrorum profectus est . . . debacchans et insaniens, occidens et perdens perplurimos uiros et mulieres.'

[45] According to the *Annals of St Neots*, *s.a.* 856, Hunberht, bishop of the East Anglians, anointed Edmund as king (*The Annals of St Neots with the Vita Prima Sancti Neoti*, ed. D. N. Dumville and M. Lapidge (The Anglo-Saxon Chronicle: A Collaborative Edition, xvii; Cambridge, 1985), p. 51), and a Hunberht is named by William of Malmesbury as bishop of the East Angles, but in the first half of the 9th cent. (*De gestis pontificum*, ed. Hamilton, p. 148). He does not, however, occur in Abbo's *Passio S. Eadmundi* (*Three Lives of English Saints*, ed. M. Winterbottom (Toronto, 1972), pp. 67–87), and *LDE* is unique in describing him as having been martyred with Edmund.

[46] The expulsion of Ecgberht and Wulfhere and the installation of Ricsige is mentioned by Symeon in his letter to Dean Hugh (Arnold, *Sym. Op.* i. 255), but is otherwise noted only in *HReg*'s second annals for 872–3, which differ from *LDE* in that the annal for 872 mentions only the expulsions, while that for 873 states: 'Ecgberhtus rex Northanhymbrorum moriens successorem habuit Ricsig, qui regnauit tribus annis; et Wlfere in suum archiepiscopatum receptus est' (Arnold, *Sym. Op.* ii. 81, 110).

assumpta de Rheoppandune, ubi tunc sederat, plurima parte predicti exercitus, *multa cum classe Tinam ingrediens, circa Tomemuthe*[a] hiematurus *applicuit*, totam ad aquilonalem plagam[b] predicti fluminis prouinciam, que pacem eatenus habuerat, peracta hieme depopulaturus.[47]

[xxviii] Cuius[c] aduentu audito memoratus antistes Eardulfus, futuram cladem ecclesie Lindisfarnensis et totius episcopatus ultimam depopulationem preuidens, fugam [d]cum suis[d] arripere meditabatur, sed[e] quid de sacratissimo [f]patris Cuthberti corpore[f] fieret[g] sollicitabatur. Sine illo enim[h] thesauro nusquam esse uolebat, siue in sua [xxviii (H)] ecclesia residens, siue inde[i] discedens. Ascito[j] ergo probande[k] sanctitatis uiro Eadredo, qui, ab eo quod in Luel, in monasterio dudum ab ipso Cuthberto instituto educatus,[l] officium abbatis gesserit, Lulisc[m] cognominabatur; dum quid potissimum agerent inuicem tractarent, dictorum ipsius[n] patris Cuthberti, *que ultima ab hac uita migraturus suis contradiderat*, recordantes, *loco magis* eligunt *cedere quam* barbaris collum[o] summittere. *Sic enim inter* alia suis paterna sollicitudine *consuluit dicens: 'Si uos unum e*[p] duobus aduersis[q] eligere necessitas coegerit,[r]* multo plus diligo ut eruentes[s] de tumulo tollentesque uobiscum *'mea ossa*[t] recedatis ab his locis, et ubicunque Deus prouiderit incole maneatis, quam ut ulla ratione consentientes iniquitati, scismaticorum iugo colla subdatis.' Hec illi relegentes, patrem Cuthbertum cum ista[u] diceret, futurum sui temporis periculum prophetie spiritu preuidisse, sibique[v] reputabant[w] talia mandasse.[48] Tollentes ergo sacrum illud et incorruptum patris corpus, et

---

[a] Tynemuthe *Fx H L T Y*   [b] partem *H*   [c] De fuga Ardulfi episcopi cum corpore sancti Cuthberti de insula Lindisfarnensi *rubric Fx T V Y*   [d-d] *om. T*
[e] et si *L*   [f-f] corpore patris Cuthberti *H and Y but with* corpore *add. in marg. in Y*; corpore beati Cuthberti patris *Fx L*   [g] *om. T*   [h] *om. H*   [i] *om. V*
[j] De fuga Ardulfi episcopi cum corpore sancti Cuthberti de insula Lindisfarnensi *rubric H*
[k] *om. T V*   [l] inducatus *Fx Y*   [m] Luliso *Fx L T Y*   [n] illius *H*
[o] *om. L*   [p] de *H*   [q] *om. L*   [r] poposcerit *F*   [s] irruentes *L*
[t-t] ossa mea *F*   [u] ita *T*   [v] ubique *L*   [w] putabant *H*

---

[47] Repton was a Mercian royal monastery (M. Biddle, 'Archaeology, architecture, and the cult of saints in Anglo-Saxon England', *The Anglo-Saxon Church: Papers on History, Architecture and Archaeology in Honour of Dr H. M. Taylor*, ed. L. A. S. Butler and R. Morris, CBA Research Report 60 (London, 1986), pp. 1–31, at 14–22; and *Blackwell Encyclopaedia*, ed. Lapidge, *s.u.*); on Tynemouth, see below, p. 234 n. 26. This passage is close to the first annal for 875 in *HReg*: 'Exercitus Repadun deseruit, seseque in duas partes diuisit. Vna pars cum Haldene ad regionem Northanhymbrorum secessit, et eum uastauit, et hiemauit iuxta flumen quod dicitur Tyne et totam gentem suo dominatui subdidit' (Arnold, *Sym. Op.* ii. 82), itself nearly identical to ASC, *s.a.* 875, Asser, c. 47, and JW ii. 304–5 *(s.a.* 875), which is drawn from Asser. The words 'multa cum classe Tinam

Halfdan, king of the Danes, took the chief part of the aforesaid army from Repton where he had been based, entered the mouth of the river Tyne with a great fleet, and landed in the vicinity of Tynemouth with the intention of wintering there and, after the winter was over, of devastating the whole region north of that river, which had hitherto enjoyed peace.[47]

When Bishop Eardwulf heard of his arrival, he foresaw that the church of Lindisfarne would be finally destroyed and the whole bishopric laid waste, and he considered taking to flight with his people, but he was uneasy as to what would become of the most holy body of father Cuthbert. Wherever he might go, whether he stayed in his church or departed from it, he wished never to be parted from that treasure. He summoned to him a man of proven holiness, Eadred, who was surnamed Lulisc because he had been educated and had held the office of abbot in Carlisle (*Luel*), in the monastery founded long ago by Cuthbert himself. While they were discussing between themselves what they should do for the best, they recalled the instructions that the same father Cuthbert had given to his monks when he was about to pass on from this life, that they should choose rather to leave the place than to bow their necks to the barbarians. Thus amongst other things he advised this with paternal solicitude: 'If necessity forces you to choose one of two evils, I should much prefer it that you should raise up my bones from the grave, take them away with you, and dwell as inhabitants of whatever place God may provide for you, than that you should for any reason condone iniquity, and bow your necks to the yoke of the schismatics.' Reading these words again, they concluded that when he had said these things father Cuthbert had in his own time foreseen with the spirit of prophecy the future peril of his church, and they considered that these instructions were binding on them.[48] So they took up the holy

[xxviii]

[xxviii (H)]

---

ingrediens, circa Tynemuth applicuit' occur in this context in *CMD* (Craster, 'Red book', p. 525).

[48] Nothing else is known of Eadred. Eardwulf was bishop of Lindisfarne (854–880 × 5), and subsequently bishop of Chester-le-Street until 899. The ultimate source of Cuthbert's words and the phrases introducing them (italicized in the Latin here) is *Bede, V. Cuth.* c. 39, but they are quoted in *De miraculis* c. 2 (Arnold, *Sym. Op.* i. 234–5), which is closely related to *LDE* and may have been its source, although it does not mention Eadred's participation in the decision. Bede is not explicit as to the identity of the schismatics Cuthbert was supposed to have had in mind, but presumably they were those who had not adopted the 'Roman' method for the keeping of Easter. In *HSC* c. 13 (Arnold, *Sym. Op.* i. 203), the departure of Eardwulf and Eadred with the body of St Cuthbert is said to have been occasioned by a vision experienced by Eadred.

una cum eo in eiusdem thece loculo (ut in ueteribus libris inuenitur) collocatas sanctorum reliquias, uidelicet caput Deo dilecti regis ac martyris Oswaldi antea in eiusdem ecclesie cimiterio sepultum, partem quoque ossium sancti Aidani (nam ut supradictum est ᵃalteram partemᵃ Colmanus ad Scotiam rediens secum tulerat), preterea etiam successorum eiusdem patris Cuthberti uenerabilium sacerdotum ossa ueneranda, scilicet Eadberti , Eadfridi,ᵇ Aethelwoldi, quorum supra mentionem fecimus.⁴⁹ Hecᶜ ergo tollentes, illam nobilem et primam in gente Berniciorum ecclesiam⁵⁰ in qua plurimorum ᵈfuerat conuersatio sanctorum,ᵈ illam, inquam, barbaros fugiendo relinquunt,ᵉ anno scilicetᶠ ab Incarnatione Domini octingentesimo septuagesimo quinto, ex quo autem rex Oswaldus et pontifex Aidanus ipsam ecclesiam ᵍfundantes sedemᵍ in ea pontificalem cum monachorum congregatione locauerant ducentesimo quadragesimo primo, a transitu uero patris Cuthberti centesimo octagesimo nono,ʰ episcopatus ueroⁱ Eardulfi anno uicesimo secundo.⁵¹ Hic est octogesimus ʲtercius annusʲ ex quo a piratis ecclesia illa (ut supradictum est) sub Higbaldo episcopo deuastata, omnesque monachi uaria sunt morte necati, preter paucissimos qui quoquomodo euaserant.⁵²

Qui etiam, hac clade de qua nunc agimus superueniente, omnes defecerunt, sed qui inter eos ab etate infantili in habitu clericali fuerant nutriti atque eruditi, quocunque sancti patris corpus ferebatur secuti sunt, moremque sibi a monachis doctoribus traditum in officiisᵏ—dumtaxat diurne uel nocturne laudis—semper seruarunt.⁵³

ᵃ⁻ᵃ om. F   ᵇ Ealfridi Fx L Y   ᶜ Vltima uastacio Lindisfarnensis ecclesie rubric Y   ᵈ⁻ᵈ sanctorum fuerat conuersatio T   ᵉ reliquerunt H ᶠ om. F   ᵍ⁻ᵍ consederant sedemque F   ʰ octauo Fx L   ⁱ om. Fx L ʲ⁻ʲ annus tercius T   ᵏ officio Fx L Y

⁴⁹ The word used for chest (theca) is the one used in Bede, V. Cuth. c. 42, to describe the receptacle into which Cuthbert's body was placed after its elevation in 698. It is usually identified with the coffin-reliquary now preserved in the Treasury of Durham Cathedral (E. Kitzinger, 'The coffin-reliquary', in Battiscombe, Relics, pp. 202–304, at 202). In retelling the story of its being drawn on a cart (below), Reginald of Durham calls it a 'theca lignea' (Raine, Cuth. virt., p. 17). The present account should be compared with De miraculis c. 7 (Arnold, Sym. Op. i. 252), which reads: 'Quas profecto reliquias, ut in ueteribus libris legitur, constat esse caput gloriosi regis et martyris Oswaldi, ossa quoque uenerabilium confessorum Christi ac sacerdotum, Aidani uidelicet, et successorum ipsius uenerandi patris Cuthberti, scilicet Eadberti, Eadfridi, et Ethelwoldi.' The saints in question were: Oswald, king and martyr (d. 642; on the burial of his head at Lindisfarne, see Bede, HE iii. 12), Aidan, bishop of Lindisfarne (d. 642; on the removal of his relics by Colman, see LDE i. 5), Eadberht, bishop of Lindisfarne (688–98), Eadfrith, bishop of Lindisfarne (dates uncertain but some time between 698 and 731), and Æthelwald, bishop

and undecayed body of the father, and placed together with it in the same coffin (as is to be found in old books) relics of other saints, namely the head of Oswald, king and martyr beloved of God, which had formerly been buried in the cemetery of this same church, also part of the bones of St Aidan (for as mentioned earlier Colman had taken part of them with him when he went back to Ireland), and in addition the bones of the venerable priests who were the successors of father Cuthbert and whom we mentioned earlier, that is Eadberht, Eadfrith, and Æthelwald.[49] Taking up all these, they left that noble church, the first in the nation of the Bernicians[50] and in which so many saints had lived their lives. They left it, I say, to flee from the barbarians, it being the year of the Incarnation of Our Lord 875, the two-hundredth and forty-first since King Oswald and Bishop Aidan had founded that same church and placed in it an episcopal see with a congregation of monks, the one hundredth and eighty-ninth from the passing of father Cuthbert, the twenty-second of the episcopate of Eardwulf.[51] That is the eighty-third year since that church (as was said above) was sacked in the time of Bishop Higbald, and almost all the monks, apart from a very few who somehow escaped, perished by various deaths.[52]

With the coming of this new devastation of which we are now speaking, these survivors also dispersed, but those who had been brought up and educated among the monks from childhood, albeit in the habit of clerks, followed the body of the holy father wherever it was carried, and they always preserved the custom—which had been handed down to them by their teachers the monks—of singing the day and night offices.[53] As a result all their descendants who

of Lindisfarne (? × 731–737/40). On Eadberht's burial in Cuthbert's former grave, see above, pp. 56–7. On the finding of his relics and those of the other two bishops of Lindisfarne in Cuthbert's shrine in 1104, see *De miraculis* c. 7 (Arnold, *Sym. Op.* i. 252). The identity of the 'old books' is unclear, unless *HSC* is meant.

[50] This is presumably based on Bede's statement that at the time of Oswald's victory at Heavenfield, just before the foundation of Lindisfarne, 'nullum altare in tota Berniciorum gente erectum est' (Bede, *HE* iii. 2); but cf. *LDE*'s description of Lindisfarne as 'ex qua omnium eiusdem prouincie ecclesiarum manarunt primordia' (above, pp. 22–3).

[51] Both annals for 875 in *HReg* (Arnold, *Sym. Op.* ii. 82, 110) mention the departure in that year of Eardwulf and Eadred with the body of St Cuthbert. Lindisfarne was founded in 635 and Cuthbert died in 687, so *LDE*'s computations of the time elapsed since those events are correct. *LDE* evidently regarded Eardwulf's episcopate as beginning in 854, and this is in harmony with *HReg*'s first annal for that year which mentions Eardwulf's accession (Arnold, *Sym. Op.* ii. 71).   [52] See below, pp. 116–17.

[53] On the place of this account in Symeon's treatment of the continuity of monastic life in some form around the body of St Cuthbert, see Piper, in Bonner, *Cuthbert*, p. 440, and above, pp. xliv–xlv.

Vnde tota nepotum suorum successio magis secundum instituta monachorum quam clericorum consuetudinem canendi horas usque[a] tempus Walcheri episcopi paterna traditione obseruauit, sicut eos [b]sepe canentes[b] audiuimus, et usque hodie nonnullos de illa progenie narrantes audire solemus.[54] Nec tamen corpori eiusdem patris Cuthberti pontificis simul et monachi, monachorum unquam usque ad predicti Walcheri tempora sedulitas defuit uel obsequium. Eardulfus denique pontifex et sicut predecessores eius monachus, Eadredus quoque monachus et abbas, quoad uixerant, indiuiduo comitatu ei semper adherebant, post quos episcopi sequentes usque ad sepe dictum Walcherum monachi, sine duobus uel tribus monachis nunquam fuisse noscuntur.[55]

Cum ergo episcopus una cum uenerandis reliquiis fugiens insulam[c] prefatam et ecclesiam deseruisset, mox et ipsius loci et totius Northanhymbrorum prouincie seua depopulatio est secuta, exercitu Danorum ductu Halfdene regis [d]crudeliter ubique[d] debachante, qui etiam monasteria passim et ecclesias ignibus contradidit, seruos ancillasque[e] Dei ludibriis affectos interfecit et, ut breuiter dicam, ab orientali mari usque ad occidentale cedem et incendium continuauit. Vnde antistes et qui cum illo[f] sancti patris corpus comitabantur nusquam locum requiescendi habere poterant, [g]sed de loco ad locum, huc atque illuc[g] euntes et redeuntes, ante crudelium barbarorum faciem discurrebant.

[xxix] 7. In[h] nullam autem[i] pene ecclesiarum, quas confessor beatus siue ante siue nunc, in tempore fuge uel post, sui sacri corporis presentia illustrauit, ulla usque hodie feminis esse constat[j] [k]intrandi licentia.[k] Cuius rei consuetudo ut [l]qua de[l] causa oriri ceperit indicemus, intermisso paululum[m] narrandi ordine breuiter superiora replicemus.[56]

---

  [a] usque ad T   [b-b] canentes sepe Ca   [c] in insulam T   [d-d] ubique crudeliter Fx L Y   [e] et ancillas H   [f] eo H   [g-g] om. H   [h] Quare mulieres non intrant ecclesiam (ecclesias H) sancti Cuthberti rubric Fx H T V Y   [i] nanque T   [j] om. Ca   [k-k] licentia intrandi F   [l-l] de qua H   [m] paulum Ca

---

[54] For the possible implications of this statement for Symeon's own career, see above, pp. xliv–xlv.

[55] On Walcher, bishop of Durham (1071–80), see below, pp. 194–7 and nn. For LDE's claim that all the bishops before Walcher were monks and attended by monks, see Piper, in Bonner, Cuthbert, pp. 440–1.

[56] On the implications of the misogyny attributed to St Cuthbert by LDE but of which

succeeded them down to the time of Bishop Walcher followed the tradition of their fathers in the custom of singing the hours according to the regimen of the monks rather than that of the clerks. Indeed we ourselves have often heard them singing in this manner, and even today we are accustomed to hear several of their descendants describe it so.[54] So the body of that same father Cuthbert, who was at the same time both bishop and monk, never lacked the zeal and obedience of monks down to the time of the aforementioned Walcher. For Eardwulf, who was bishop and like his predecessors a monk, and also Eadred, monk and abbot, always kept close to Cuthbert in undivided companionship as long as they lived, and the bishops who came after them, down to the time of Walcher whom we have often mentioned, are known to have been monks and never to have failed to have two or three monks with them.[55]

Now when the bishop had taken with him the venerable relics, and had fled from the aforesaid island and deserted the church, there soon followed a dreadful destruction of that place and of the whole kingdom of the Northumbrians, the army of the Danes led by King Halfdan ravaging cruelly everywhere. Putting monasteries and churches to the flames wherever they passed, they killed servants and handmaids of God whom they had first subjected to mockery, and, to put it briefly, spread fire and slaughter from the eastern sea to the western. So the bishop and those who with him were accompanying the body of the holy father could have nowhere to rest but wandered from place to place, moving hither and thither, backwards and forwards, fleeing in the face of the cruel barbarians.

7. It remains the case even today that women are not given [xxix] permission to enter virtually any of the churches which the blessed confessor has sanctified with the presence of his sacred body either now or formerly, in the time of his flight or afterwards. So as to indicate why it was that the custom with regard to this matter originated, we will briefly interrupt the order of the narrative and then return to what we were saying above.[56]

there is no trace in the 8th-cent. lives of the saint or in the miracle described below, pp. 150–1, see V. Tudor, 'The misogyny of St Cuthbert', *Archaeologia Aeliana*, 5th ser., xii (1984), 157–67; and Piper, in Bonner, *Cuthbert*, p. 443. See also Aird, *Cuthbert*, pp. 125–6, who points out that there was apparently no prohibition on women being buried in the cemetery when Bishop Ealdhun's daughter Ecgfrida was interred there (p. 122 n. 95, citing *De obsessione Dunelmi*, Arnold, *Sym. Op.* i. 217).

Ante paucos sane sui episcopatus annos monasterium in Coldingham *per culpam incurie flammis absumptum est. Quod tamen a malitia inhabitantium in eo contigisse, omnes qui nouere facillime potuerunt aduertere.* Erant siquidem in eodem loco diuersis tamen[a] separate mansionibus monachorum sanctimonialiumque congregationes, qui paulatim a regularis discipline statu defluentes, inhonesta inuicem familiaritate decipiendi occasionem inimico prebuerant. *Nam et domunculas que ad orandum uel legendum facte fuerant,* [b]in commessationum, potationum, confabulationum,[c] et ceterarum cubilia[d] illecebrarum conuertebant.[b] *Virgines quoque Deo dicate contempta reuerentia sue professionis, texendis subtilioribus indumentis operam dabant, quibus aut seipsas ad uicem[e] sponsarum in periculum sui status adornarent, aut externorum sibi uirorum amicitiam* compararent. *Vnde merito loco illi et habitatoribus eius grauis de celo uindicta flammis seuientibus* facta fuerat. Sed non defuit puniendis admonitio premissa diuine pietatis, qua aliquantulum correcti paucis post diebus timere, et seipsos intermissis facinoribus ceperunt castigare. *Verum post obitum religiose abbatisse Ebbe redierunt ad pristinas sordes, immo sceleratiora fecerunt, et cum dicerent 'Pax et securitas', diuine ultionis pena[f] sunt multati.*[57]

Nec multo post uir Domini Cuthbertus episcopali sullimatus cathedra, ne sui[58] uel presentes uel futuri quandoque tali exemplo Dei super se iram prouocarent, omne ab eis feminarum separauit consortium, ne indiscreta illarum societas seruis Dei aliquod sui propositi periculum, et ex eorum ruina inimico generaret gaudium. Omnibus ergo et uiris et feminis consentientibus, omne suis et in presenti et post futuris temporibus muliebre interdixit consortium, earumque ab ecclesie sue ingressu penitus[g] amouit introitum. Vnde in insula sedis episcopalis eius facta ecclesia que lingua indigenarum Grene Cyrice (id est 'uiridis ecclesia') appellatur, eo quod in campi uirentis planitie sita sit, iussit ut illo missas et uerbum Dei auditure mulieres conuenirent, ne propius ecclesie in qua ipse cum monachis

---

[a] *om.* H   [b-b] conuertebant in commessacionum . . . illecebrarum T
[c] fabulationum *Fx L Y*   [d] cubicula *F*   [e] inuicem *Fx (corr. to* uicem) *H Y*
[f] *ins. over line Fx Y*   [g] *om.* T

---

[57] This paragraph is derived, much of it verbatim, from Bede, *HE* iv. 25. For identification of the site of Coldingham with Kirk Hill, near St Abb's Head (Berwicks.; NT 917 687), see L. Alcock *et al.*, 'Reconnaissance excavations on early historic fortifications and other royal sites in Scotland, 1974–84: 1, Excavations near St Abb's Head, Berwicks', *Proceedings of the Society of Antiquaries of Scotland*, cxvi (1986), 255–79; and on the site and its possible lay-out, see Blair, in Blair and Sharpe, *Pastoral Care*, pp. 227–8, 233, 259–61.

Now, a few years earlier in his pontificate the monastery at Coldingham was consumed by fire caused by culpable negligence. Everyone who was in a position to know, however, was aware that this had really happened because of the evil ways of the inhabitants. In that same place indeed there were congregations of monks and nuns, albeit living separately in different dwellings, who had gradually fallen away from the discipline of the Rule and had by their improper familiarity with each other given the Enemy the opportunity of ensnaring them. For the cells which had been made for the purpose of prayer and reading they converted into dens of feasting, drinking, story-telling, and other enticements. The virgins dedicated to God held the reverence due to their vows in contempt, and devoted their efforts to weaving fine clothes, with which they would either adorn themselves like brides, imperilling their status as nuns, or use them to procure for themselves the friendship of men from outside the abbey. Hence the raging flames of heaven's stern vengeance were justly inflicted on this place and its inhabitants. But those who were to be punished were not deprived of an admonition from the divine piety, after which they were fearful for a few days, and refraining from their misdeeds they began to chastise themselves. After the death of the religious abbess Æbbe, however, they returned to their former unclean ways, or rather they did still more wicked things, and just as they were saying 'Peace and security' they were punished with the torment of divine vengeance.[57]

Not long after this the man of the Lord, Cuthbert, now raised to the episcopal throne, severed his monks[58] from all female company, so that neither they nor their successors should ever at any time provoke the wrath of God against themselves by setting such an example, and so that the indiscreet association of women with God's servants the monks should not endanger their resolve and so ruin them, thereby giving joy to the Enemy. With the consent of all, both men and women, he forebade to his monks then and in the future all female company, and he completely removed from women the right of entry into his church. For this reason he built on the island of his episcopal see a church, which is called in the language of the inhabitants Grene Cyrice (that is 'green church') because it is sited on the verdant greenness of the plain, and he ordered that women should gather there to hear masses and the word of God, so that they should never come any nearer to the church in which he

[58] Note that *sui*, here translated as 'his monks', qualifies no substantive.

conuersabatur, unquam accederent. Que consuetudo usque hodie diligenter obseruatur, in tantum ut nisi metus hostilis uel concrematio loci compellat, nec in cimiteria quidem^a ipsarum ecclesiarum ubi ad tempus corpus eius requieuerat, mulieribus introire liceat.[59]

8. Fuerant^b autem^c nonnulle^d que ausu temerario hec instituta infringere temptauerunt, ^esed quantum scelus admiserint, mox pena uindice senserunt.^e Harum quedam uocabulo Sungeoua, filii Beuonis qui Gamelo uocabatur uxor, que nocte quadam cum de conuiuio domum redire uellet, querebatur marito quod uiam propter lutosas platearum uoragines nusquam mundam habere potuisset. Ad ultimum utrisque placuit, ut per cimiterium huius (hoc est Dunhelmensis) ecclesie transitum facerent, atque postea hoc peccatum elemosinis expiarent. Cum ergo simul irent, repente cepit ipsa nescio quid exhorrere,^f et se iamiamque extra sensum fore clamare. Increpata a marito ut tacens absque ullo timore pergeret, cum^g iam extra sepem que cimiterium ecclesie ambierat, pedem poneret, ilico repente cecidit, domumque portata ipsam noctem huius uite terminum habuit.

9. Sequitur^h et aliud non dissimiliter factum. Erat nanqueⁱ uxor cuiusdam diuitis, qui postea nobiscum in hac ecclesia in monachico habitu conuersatus est, que audiens narrari a pluribus uariam ecclesie ornamentorum pulchritudinem, feminea auiditate uidendi noua succenditur. Nec ualens impetum animi refrenare, que se pre ceteris mariti potentia extulerat, arripuit uiam^j per ecclesie cimiterium. Sed non impune. Postea enim sensum perdidit, suam morsibus linguam precidit, nec prius^k insaniam quam propria manu inciso sibi^l gutture uitam amisit. Nam in domo non facile retineri ualens, dum incertis sedibus uagaretur, die quadam inuenta est sub arbore cruentato gutture mortua iacere, et cultellum quo semetipsam extinxerat in manu retinere.

Plura quidem contra similem aliarum feminarum audaciam diuinitus ostensa adhuc narrari poterant, sed quoniam ad alia

---

^a om. H   ^b Alia causa *rubric Fx*; Capitulum *rubric V*   ^c om. H   ^d om. Ca   ^{e–e} om. T   ^f exorare H   ^g ut D H   ^h Tertia causa *rubric Fx*; Capitulum *rubric* V   ⁱ autem L Y   ^j iter Ca   ^k plus L   ^l om. T

[59] *LDE* is the first source to record this arrangement either at Lindisfarne or at Durham. Nothing is known of the later history of the Green Church.

and his monks were. This custom is still meticulously observed today, to such an extent that women are not even given permission to enter the cemeteries of those churches where his body rested for a time, unless they are forced to seek refuge there, either from fear of enemy attack,or because the place where they are living has been burned down.[59]

8. There have been several women who tried with rash daring to infringe these decrees, but through the avenging punishment inflicted on them they soon learned how great a crime they had committed. One of these was a certain woman called Sungeova, the wife of Bevo's son Gamel. One night when she wanted to go home from a feast, she complained to her husband that she could nowhere find a clean way on account of the muddy potholes in the streets. At last they both agreed that they should make their way across the cemetery of this church of Durham and that they should afterwards expiate this sin by alms-giving. So they went together, but suddenly the woman began to be terrified of I know not what and to cry out that she was already losing her senses. Her husband told her angrily to be quiet and to go on without fear, but as soon as she placed a foot outside the fence which surrounded the cemetery of the church she suddenly fell down on the spot. She was carried home and her life came to an end that very night.

9. A similar sort of thing happened later on to the wife of a certain rich man, who afterwards took the monastic habit and lived his life with us in this church. She had heard many people tell of the varied beauty of the ornaments of the church and was fired with womanly eagerness to see new things. She was unable to restrain her heart's desire, for the powerful position of her husband had set her above others, so she took the path through the cemetery of the church. But not with impunity! For after this she went out of her mind and bit out her own tongue; and the madness did not leave her before she had lost her life by cutting her own throat. For, as it was not easy to keep her in the house, she wandered about without a fixed home, and one day she was found dead under a tree, her throat bleeding and the knife with which she had ended her own life in her hand.

Many other divine signs against similar audacity in other women could be related here but, because we must pass on to other things,

nobis transeundum est, hec breuitatis causa de his dicta sufficiant.[60]

[xxx] 10. His[a] interpositis, ad ea que inceperamus ordine narrationis redeamus. [b]Discurrentibus undique[b] paganis et per multos annos Northanhymbrorum prouinciam inhabitantibus, Christianus indigenarum populus cum liberis et coniugibus sacrum [c]beati confessoris[c] corpus comitabatur, omnia que amiserat—patriam, domos, suppellectilem—in uno ipsius corpore se reputans conseruasse, dummodo secum illud habere mereretur. Itaque omnes Northanhymbrorum partes incertis semper sedibus percurrebant, et tanquam oues ora luporum fugientes, solo sui pastoris ductu et patrocinio confidebant.[61] Nec tamen sacri corporis loculum, nec in quo ferebatur uehiculum passim cuilibet attingere licitum fuerat, sed obseruata tante sanctitati[d] reuerentia,[e] ex omnibus specialiter septem ad hoc ipsum[f] constituti fuerant, ut si quid in his cura[g] uel emendatione indigeret, preter ipsos nemo [h]manum apponere auderet.[h] Vnde singuli eorum ex officiis quibus deputati fuerant, positis sibi agnominibus [i]uocari solebant.[i][62]

[j]Inter hec rex occidentalium Saxonum Aelfredus, immanes hostium uires ferre non ualens, tribus annis in *Glestingiensibus latitauit*[k] *paludibus.* Sed qualiter ibi manifesta uisione sanctus ei Cuthbertus apparuerit, et eius suffragante auxilio subactis hostibus regnum receperit, quoniam alibi plene per ordinem scriptum habetur,[63] hic non esse repetendum uidetur. Breuiter tamen hic memoretur, quod inter admonitiones ceteras et promissa, regnum Brittannie ei suisque filiis pollicetur. '*Misericordiam,*' inquit, '*et iusticiam precipue diligas moneo, eademque filios tuos seruare pre omnibus semper doceto, quoniam*

---

[a] De septem uiris qui portabant feretrum sancti Cuthberti et de Elfredo rege cui sanctus Cuthbertus apparuit (et de. . . apparuit *om. H*) *rubric* Fx H T V Y   [b-b] Vndique discurrentibus T   [c-c] confessoris beati H   [d] sanctitatis Ca   [e] obseruantia H   [f] *om.* H   [g] *om.* T   [h-h] auderet manum apponere Ca   [i-i] uocabatur T   [j-jj (p. 112)] *om.* Fx L Y   [k] latitabat F

---

[60] In C, 'Nam in domo . . . sufficiant' has been written over an erasure of 13½ lines in the main hand but in a different ink and with the words more widely spaced. Two lines have been left blank after *sufficiant*. Nothing of the erased text is now visible. On the possible significance of this alteration, see Rollason, 'Erasures', pp. 147–8.

[61] For the possibility that this picture of wandering as refugees did not reflect historical reality but was itself derived from a hagiographical topos, see Rollason, in his *Cuthert: Saint and Patron*, pp. 45–59.

[62] See below, pp. 116–17, 146–9 and n. 7.

[63] From the beginning of this sentence to the end of the chapter, Fx, L, and Y insert *De miraculis* c. 1 (Arnold, *Sym. Op.* i. 229–34), which covers the same ground as the present

these few words about such matters must suffice in the interests of brevity.[60]

10. After this digression, let us return to those matters with which we [xxx] had in the course of the narrative begun to deal. While the heathens roamed everywhere and settled for many years in the kingdom of the Northumbrians, the indigenous Christian people with their children and their wives accompanied the holy body of the blessed confessor, regarding everything they had lost—country, homes, possessions—as preserved in the one and only body of the saint, so long as they were worthy to have it with them. So they travelled through all parts of Northumbria always without any fixed home, and like sheep fleeing from the jaws of wolves they placed their faith entirely in the leadership and protection of their shepherd.[61] No one was allowed heedlessly to touch the coffin of the holy body or the vehicle on which it was carried, but the reverence due to such holiness was observed, and from among all of them seven men were specially designated for this purpose that, if the coffin or the vehicle needed any attention or repair, none but these should dare to lay a hand on them. For this reason individuals amongst them were accustomed to be called by names given to them as a result of the offices to which they had been assigned.[62]

Meanwhile Alfred, king of the West Saxons, being unable to withstand the massive power of his enemies, spent three years hiding in the marshes of Glastonbury. Since these events are fully described in their proper order in other writings, [63] it does not seem necessary to repeat here how St Cuthbert appeared to Alfred there in a vision, and lent him assistance to overcome his enemies and gain his kingdom. Here, however, we may briefly recall that amongst other admonitions and pledges he promised the kingdom of Britain to him and his sons. 'I advise you,' he said, 'that you should above all love mercy and justice, and that you should always teach your sons to uphold these principles above all, because by my intercession and by

chapter but in more detail. Down to the end of Cuthbert's speech to Alfred, *LDE* is similar (the italicized sections in the Latin text verbally identical) to this, but the details of the number of men who came to Alfred and of how Edward took gifts to Cuthbert, however, seem to be derived from *HSC* cc. 18–19 (Arnold, *Sym. Op.* i. 206–7). Fx, L, and Y number as the inserted matter a separate chapter (xxxi), so that their next chapter is numbered xxxii, and not xxxi as for the other MSS which use this system of subdivision. From here on, the chapter divisions of Fx, L, and Y, which diverge in other ways from the other MSS, will be indicated by Roman numerals in round brackets.

me impetrante Deoque donante totius Brittannie imperium uobis concedetur disponendum. Si autem Deo michique fideles[a] extiteritis, me posthac ad conterendum robur omne inimicorum inexpugnabile defensionis scutum[64] habebitis.' Igitur in crastino iuxta promissum sancti de melioribus amicis quingenti circa horam nonam bene armati ad eum uenerunt, et post septem dies apud Assandune Anglorum exercitus concurrit.[b] Vbi de hostibus uictoria Aelfredus potitus, per filium suum Edwardum regalia dona transmisit sancto Cuthberto. Cuius monita ipse Elfredus postque ipsum filii eius Deo et ipsi[c] sancto confessori fideles existendo [d]exequentes, imperii fines latius quam ullus progenitorum suorum extendendo,[d] promissorum eius effectibus potiti sunt. Que tamen in nepote [e]ipsius Aelfredi[e] Aethelstano maxime sunt completa, qui primus regum Anglorum subactis ubique hostibus, totius Brittannie dominium obtinuit. Cuius quanta erga sanctum Cuthbertum, quantaue [f]illius erga[f] ecclesiam eius munificentia[g] extiterit, suo loco in sequentibus dicemus.[ij][65]

[xxxi (xxxii)] **11.** Verum[h] ut ad superiora redeamus, episcopus Eardulfus et abbas Eadredus tota pene prouincia cum thesauro corporis sacri peruagata, *propter diuturnum[i] laborem nimio tandem confecti tedio, ut suis[j] finem laboribus et sancto corpori sedem in Hibernia quererent, mutuo inter se [k]diu consilio[k] uentilabant, presertim quia nullam in [l]tota hac[l] terra remanendi spem habebant. Proinde adhibitis ad hoc quoque de omnibus qui sapientiores erant et etate prouectiores, sui secreta consilii eis pandebant. Placuit itaque illis[m] hoc consilium, et 'Euidenter,' inquiunt, 'in Terra Peregrina requiescendi locum querere monemur, quia nisi hoc Dei fuisset uoluntas ipsiusque sancti, procul dubio iampridem et sue sanctitati locus ad requiescendum condignus, et nobis ad manendum oportunus fuisset prouisus.'*

Ergo ad hostium fluminis quod *Dyrwenta* uocatur,[n] *omnes simul*

---

[a] filios fideles *T*   [b] cucurrit *F*   [c] om. *F*   [d-d] om. *H*   [e-e] eius *H* [f-f] erga illius *T*   [g] magnificentia *V*   [h] De fuga Ardulfi episcopi cum corpore sancti Cuthberti uersus Hiberniam et de amissione texti euuangeliorum (et de. . . euuangeliorum *om. H) rubric Fx H T V Y*   [i] diurnum *H*   [j] om. *L* [k-k] consilio diu *F*   [l-l] hac tota *L*   [m] eis *H*   [n] om. *T*

---

[64] Cf. Wisd. 5: 20.
[65] Alfred was king of Wessex (871–99); on Æthelstan's dates, see below, p. 132, n. 96. The references here are to King Alfred's withdrawal west of Selwood after the Danish attack on Chippenham in 878, and in the same year the victory of the Battle of Edington (not Ashingdon) foretold to him by St Cuthbert (ASC, *s.a.* 878, and Asser, cc. 55–6). In

God's gift the kingdom of all Britain will be granted to you and placed under your dominion. If you and your sons are faithful to me and to God, you will thereafter have in me an invincible shield[64] to crush all the strength of your enemies.' So on the following day, according to the promise of the saint, five hundred of the best of his friends came to him well armed around the ninth hour, and seven days later the army of the English gave battle at Ashingdon. There Alfred was victorious over his enemies, and by his son Edward he sent royal gifts to St Cuthbert. Alfred and his sons after him followed the saint's advice by remaining faithful to him and to God, and his promises were fulfilled in their interests when they extended the boundaries of their kingdom more widely than any of their predecessors. These promises attained their greatest fulfilment in Alfred's nephew Æthel-stan, who subjugated his enemies everywhere and became the first of the kings of the English to obtain dominion over the whole of Britain. We shall subsequently describe in its proper place the scale of his munificence towards St Cuthbert and his church.[65]

11. To return to what we were describing earlier, Bishop Eardwulf [xxxi and Abbot Eadred, having wandered through almost the whole (xxxii)] kingdom with the treasure of the holy body, were worn down at length with the fatigue of their daily labours; and they discussed between themselves for a long time a plan to seek an end of their labours and a resting place for the holy body in Ireland, particularly because they had no hope of finding in all this land a place where they could stay. Accordingly they called together those from amongst them who were wiser and more advanced in age, and told them secretly of their plan. They approved the plan, saying: 'Our clear advice is that a resting place should be sought in the Land of Pilgrims, because if this had not been the will of God and of the saint himself, there is no doubt that a resting place worthy of his holiness would long since have been provided for the saint, and for us a suitable place to settle.'

So everyone—the bishop, the abbot, and the people—gathered at

these sources, however, no mention is made of the period of three years, and the refuge is given as Athelney (Somerset), not Glastonbury (Somerset); on the possible significance of the reference to Glastonbury in *HSC* for positing a mid-10th-cent. context for this tradition in that text, see Simpson, in Bonner, *Cuthbert*, p. 406. Other accounts of Cuthbert miraculously assisting Alfred are given by William of Malmesbury (*De gestis pontificum*, ed. Hamilton, pp. 199, 269, and of St Neot assisting Alfred in the *Vita S. Neoti*, c. 16 (*Annals of St Neots*, ed. Dumville and Lapidge, pp. 130–2).

episcopus et abbas et populus conueniunt.[66] *Ibi nauis ad transponendum paratur,*[a] *uenerabile patris corpus imponitur, cum episcopo et abbate pauci quibus* [b]*hoc innotuerat*[b] *consilium ingrediuntur, ceteris omnibus quid agere uellent ignorantibus.* Quid plura? *Sociis a litore se spectantibus ualedicunt, secundis uela flatibus expediunt, recto*[c] *uersus Hiberniam ductu proram dirigunt. Quis tunc planctus residentium?* 'Heu,' *inquiunt,* 'miseri, nos in hec misera cur nati sumus tempora? Tu pater et patrone noster, en tanquam captiuus in exilium duceris, nos tanquam oues luporum dentibus, ita miseri et captiui aduersariis exponimur seuientibus.' Nec illi plura. Continuo uenti mutantur, fluctus intumescentes eleuantur, et quod nunc erat tranquillum, mare fit tempestuosum, nauisque iam non ualens gubernari, huc et*[d] *illuc inter fluctiuagas iactabatur undas. Qui enim intus erant, uelut mortui obriguerant. Interea tres mire magnitudinis unde*[e] *horrifico cum murmure superuenientes, nauim medias pene usque tabulas impleuerunt, atque terribili miraculo postque Egypti plagas inaudito protinus in sanguinem conuertebantur.*[67] *Qua tempestate dum nauis uerteretur in latera, cadens ex ea textus euangeliorum auro gemmisque perornatus, in maris ferebatur profunda.*[68] *Ergo postquam sensu*[f] *aliquantulum recepto semetipsos qui uel ubi essent recordantur,* genua flectunt, *ueniamque stulti ausus toto corpore ad pedes sancti corporis prostrati petunt. Arrepto itaque gubernaculo, nauim ad litus et ad socios retorquent, et continuo flantibus a tergo uentis, illuc sine aliqua*[g] *difficultate perueniunt. Tunc qui prius fleuerant dolendo, uersa uice plus iam flebant gaudendo. Episcopus uero cum sociis suis*[h] *pudore simul et dolore* [i]*non minus*[i] *lacrimans, toto corpore in terram prosternitur, sibique indulgeri obnoxius precatur.*[69]

---

[a] *om.* H   [b-b] innotuerat hoc *Fx L Y*; innotuerat *om.* T   [c] retro H
[d] *om. Fx L*   [e] *om.* H   [f] *om.* H   [g] *om.* T   [h] *om.* H
[i-i] *om.* H

---

[66] This is presumably the river Derwent which flows into the Irish Sea at Workington (Cumberland). The *Terra peregrinorum* was Ireland, as emerges in what follows. On Eadred, abbot of Carlisle, and Eardwulf, bishop of Lindisfarne (854–83), see above, pp. 100–1 and n. 48. The use of *populus* here and below (index, *s.n.*, also *populus sancti*) must refer to the 'people of the saint' or in the vernacular *haliwerfolc*, a designation applied in documents of the 12th and 13th cents. to the tenants of the church of Durham, and so to the lands which they occupied. In this latter sense it came to be a name cognate with Norfolk and Suffolk and meaning in effect County Durham. See G. T. Lapsley, *The County Palatine of Durham: A Study in Constitutional History* (London, 1900), pp. 22–4, 109–10, and Hall, 'Community of St Cuthbert', c. 1. See also Aird, *Cuthbert*, pp. 5–8 and *passim*.

the mouth of the river which is called Derwent.[66] There a ship was prepared for the crossing, the venerable body of the father was placed on it, and the bishop and the abbot and the few to whom this plan had been made known went aboard, all the rest being still ignorant of what they intended to do. What more is there to relate? They said goodbye to their fellows who were watching them from the shore, they unfurled the sails to a following wind, and they steered the ship on a true course towards Ireland. Who can describe the lamentation of those left behind? 'Alas,' they cried, 'we unhappy ones, why were we born in these miserable times? Our father and our protector, you are being led away into exile like a captive, while we unhappy captives are exposed to the ravages of adversity like sheep to the fangs of wolves.' They said no more. Straightaway the winds changed, towering waves rose up, and the sea which had been calm became stormy, so that the ship could not be steered, but was buffeted hither and thither among the driving waves. Those who were on board became rigid as if they were dead. Meanwhile three waves of marvellous size broke over the ship with a horrifying roar. They filled it almost to the middle planks and by an awesome miracle unheard of since the plagues of Egypt, they were at once changed into blood.[67] In the course of this storm the ship turned on its side, and a gospel book ornamented with gold and gems fell from it and was carried down to the depths of the sea.[68] After they had recovered their senses a little and had remembered who they were and where they were, they knelt down, and throwing themselves down full length at the feet of the holy body, they asked forgiveness for their stupid rashness. One seized the tiller and steered the ship back towards the shore and their comrades, and at once the winds blew from behind them and they arrived there without difficulty. Then those who had previously wept in sorrow, now instead wept rather for joy. But the bishop with his companions wept no less than the others, but in his case from shame and distress, and threw himself full length on the ground, praying that guilty as he was he might be forgiven.[69]

[67] Cf. Exod. 4: 9, 7: 17.

[68] For this book, which must be the Lindisfarne Gospels, see below, pp. 118–21 and n. 75, where the story of its miraculous recovery is related.

[69] This chapter is based, largely verbatim (as italicized in the Latin text), on *De miraculis* c. 2 (Arnold, *Sym. Op.* i. 234–7), which now proceeds directly to a brief account of the sojourn of St Cuthbert's body at Crayke, which is incorporated into *LDE* (below, pp. 122–3).

[xxxii   12. Interea*^a* populus*^b* longo per annorum spatia labore, famis neces-
(xxxiii)]   sitate, cunctarumque rerum egestate compulsus, a comitatu sancti
corporis dilabitur, et per loca inhabitata ut qualitercunque uitam
sustentarent, dispergitur.*^c* Exceptis enim episcopo et abbate cum suis
admodum paucis omnes discesserunt, preter illos septem qui eius
obsequio corporis familiarius (ut dictum est) *^d*semper adherere*^d*
consueuerunt.*^e* Hi nimirum fuerunt illi qui deficientibus monachis
nutriti ab eis et educati (ut superius diximus) de insula Lindisfarnensi
uenerandum sancti confessoris corpus sunt secuti, nunquam illud
quousque uiuerent relicturi.[70] Quorum quattuor qui tribus aliis
maiores esse memorantur,*^f* hec fuerunt nomina: Hunred, Stitheard,
Edmund, Franco, de quorum stirpe multi*^g* in Northanhymbrorum
prouincia tam clerici quam laici se descendisse tanto magis gloriantur,
quanto progenitores sui sancto Cuthberto fidelius deseruisse narrantur.[71]

Cum ergo cunctis discedentibus*^h* soli cum tanto thesauro relicti
essent, aduersis undique*ⁱ* rebus maximas sustinuerunt angustias, nec
tamen quo consilio euaderent, quoue*^j* solacio respirarent, excogitare
potuerunt. 'Quid,' inquiunt, 'facturi sumus? Quo patris reliquias
ferentes ibimus? Barbaros fugientes per septem annos totam prouinciam lustrauimus, iamque nullus in patria fuge superest locus. Ne
uero peregrinantes alicubi requiem queramus, manifesta flagelli
castigatione prohibiti sumus. Super hec omnia fames dira incumbens,
quacunque solacium uite querere compellit, sed gladius Danorum
ubique seuiens nobis cum hoc*^k* thesauro transitum non permittit.
Porro si illo relicto nobis ipsis prouiderimus, inquirenti postmodum
eius*^l* populo ubinam sit pastor et patronus eorum, quid respondebi-
mus?[72] Furto an*^m* uiolentia nobis ablatum dicemus? In exilium
transportatum,*ⁿ* an solum in desertis nunciabimus*^o* relictum? Profecto
manu illorum iusta confestim morte interibimus, omnibusque post
futuris seculis infamiam *^p*nostri relinquemus,*^p* cunctorum maledicta
lucrabimur.' Tanta rerum angustia gementibus, tandem consuetum
piissimi patroni affuit auxilium, quo et animos eorum merore, et

---

^a Nomina quattuor uirorum principalium (*om. H*) qui sanctum secuti sunt
Cuthbertum *rubric Fx H T V Y*   ^b *om. T*   ^c dilabitur *F*
^{d–d} adherere semper *Ca*   ^e consueuerant *H*   ^f uidebantur *Ca*   ^g *om. H*
^h descendentibus *T*   ⁱ *om. T*   ^j quo *H*   ^k *om. H*   ^l *om. H*
^m aut *Fx L Y*   ⁿ *om. T*   ^o *om. L*   ^{p–p} relinquemus nostri *F*

---

[70] *LDE*'s cross-references are to pp. 110–11. For the significance of the word *populus*
('people') here, see above, p. 114 n. 66.

12. Meanwhile the people were compelled by long labour over many years, by the exigency of hunger and want, for they had nothing, to give up accompanying the body of the saint, and they dispersed to uninhabited places to sustain themselves by whatever means they could. Apart from the bishop and the abbot with a very few followers everyone left, except those seven who (as has been said) were accustomed always to hold themselves in close association with and obedience to his body. It was these who (as we said above) had been supported and educated by the monks, and when the monks left, they had followed the venerable body of the holy confessor from the island of Lindisfarne, vowing never to part company with it as long as they lived.[70] Four of these, who are remembered as being more important than the other three, had these names: Hunred, Stitheard, Edmund, and Franco. Many of their descendants in the kingdom of the Northumbrians—clergy and laity—take pride that their ancestors are said to have served St Cuthbert so faithfully.[71]

[xxxii (xxxiii)]

Now when all the rest had gone and they were left alone with so great a treasure, they suffered the greatest distress with everything against them wherever they turned, and they could not devise any plan by which they might escape, nor could they imagine by what comfort they might be relieved. 'What are we to do?' they said. 'Whither shall we carry the relics of the father? Fleeing from the barbarians we have travelled across the whole kingdom for seven years, and now in the whole country there is no place of refuge left. We have been prohibited by the manifest punishment of the scourge which befell us from seeking a haven as strangers in another country. On top of all this the burden of dire hunger presses upon us, and compels us to seek solace for our lives anywhere we can, but the swords of the Danes ravage everywhere and prevent us from travelling with this treasure. But if we abandon it and look to ourselves, what shall we say to the saint's people when they afterwards ask where is their pastor and patron? Shall we say it was taken from us by theft or violence?[72] Shall we announce that it was transported into exile, or left alone in desert places? We shall certainly and justly perish at once at their hands, we shall leave an infamous reputation to future ages, and we shall earn the curses of all. While they were bewailing their indigence, the accustomed aid of the most pious patron came to them at last, through which he relieved their

---

[71] On the bearers, see below, pp. 146–9 and n. 7; on Hunred, see also below, pp. 118–19. [72] On *eius populo* ('the saint's people'), see above, p. 114 n. 66.

corpora releuauit labore, quia 'factus est Dominus refugium pauperum, adiutor in opportunitatibus in tribulatione'.[a73]

[xxxiii (xxxiv)] Cuidam[b] nanque illorum uidelicet[c] Hunredo per uisum assistens, iussit[d] [e]ut estu maris recedente codicem, qui de naui (ut superius dictum est) medias[e] ceciderat in undas, quererent, fortassis enim contra hoc quod ipsi sperare possent, Deo miserante inuenirent.[f] Nam et de illius libri[g] amissione, maxima illorum mentes perturbauerat mestitia. Quibus uerbis hec quoque adiungens, 'Tu,' inquit, 'citius[h] surgens frenum, quod [i]in arbore uidebis[i] pendere, equo quem non longe hinc inuenies ostendere,[j] moxque ad te sponte accurrentem curabis frenare, quem deinceps carrum in quo meum corpus circumfertur trahentem, uos leuigato labore sequi ualebitis.' His perceptis, confestim somno expergefactus, uisionem se uidisse narrauit, moxque [k]aliquos e sociis[k] ad mare quod erat uicinum, librum quem amiserant quesituros misit. Per id quippe temporis in locum qui Candida Casa (uulgo autem Huuiterna) uocatur, deuenerant.[74]

[xxxiv (xxxv)] Itaque[l] pergentes ad mare, multo quam consueuerat longius recessisse conspiciunt, et tribus uel[m] eo amplius miliariis gradientes, ipsum sanctum euangeliorum codicem reperiunt, qui sicut[n] forinsecus gemmis et auro sui decorem, ita[o] intrinsecus litteris et foliis priorem preferebat pulchritudinem,[p] ac si ab aqua minime tactus fuisset. Que res animos eorum anxios non parum [q]gaudio releuauit,[q] uirumque memoratum de ceteris que audierat, minime dubitare permisit. Pergens ergo frenum sicut per somnium didicerat in arbore suspensum inuenit, deinde hac illacque circumspiciens, paulo remotius caballum rufi coloris aspexit, qui unde uel quomodo in illum solitudinis locum peruenerit, sciri nullatenus potuit. Cui sicut iussus fuerat, dum manu elata frenum ostenderet, concite adueniens manibus illius sese frenandum obtulit. Quo ad socios

---

[a] et ceteris *add.* L   [b] Visio Hundredi *rubric* Fx H T V Y   [c] scilicet H
[d] Cuthbertus iussit Fx L Y.   [e-e] *om.* Fx Y   [f] inquirerent H   [g] *om.* T
[h] *om.* H   [i-i] uidebis in arbore L   [j] ostende H L Y   [k-k] aliquos de sociis Fx L Y; socios T   [l] De inuentione texti euuangelii (ewangeliorum H) *rubric* Fx H T V Y   [m] et H   [n] ita F Ca Fx H L T V Y   [o] *om.* Ca *but with a signe de renvoi*   [p] incorruptionem F   [q-q] letificabat F

---

[73] Ps.(A) 9: 10
[74] The name *Ad Candidam Casam* applied to Whithorn (Wigtownshire; NX 445 403) is found in Bede, *HE* iii. 4, where a British bishop called Ninian is said to have had his see at a church dedicated to St Martin there. Whithorn later became an Anglian see and bishops are recorded from 681 to the early 9th cent., when the episcopal succession came to an end. Archaeological excavations suggest that the place had developed by the 10th cent. as a

souls of sadness and their bodies of labour, because 'the Lord is made
a refuge of the poor and a timely helper of those in distress'.[73]

He appeared in a vision to the one called Hunred, and ordered that [xxxiii
when the tide went out they should look for the book which (as was (xxxiv)]
said above) had fallen out of the ship into the midst of the waves, and
perhaps contrary to anything they themselves might hope, they would
by God's mercy find it. For their minds were troubled with the
greatest sadness on account of the loss of this book. To these words he
added the following: 'Rise up quickly and show the bridle, which you
will see hanging from a tree, to the horse, which you will find not far
away. It will come to you at once of its own accord and you should
take care to bridle it. After that it will pull the cart on which my body
is carried, and you will be able to follow it with lightened labour.'
When Hunred had understood these things he awoke suddenly from
sleep, and told of how he had seen the vision. Soon he sent several of
his comrades to the sea which was nearby, to look for the book which
they had lost. Now at this time they had come to a place called the
White House or by the common people Whithorn.[74]

So they came to the sea and saw that it had receded much farther [xxxiv
than normal. When they had walked three miles or more they found (xxxv)]
that same holy book of the gospels, which retained its enrichment of
gems and gold on the outside, as on the inside it showed the former
beauty of its letters and pages, as if it had not been touched by the
water at all. This event filled their minds with no small measure of
joy, and it was now impossible to doubt the aforementioned man as to
the other things which he had heard. He went on and found the bridle
hanging, as he had learned in his dream, from a tree; and then he
looked around and a little way off he saw a horse of reddish colour—
where it had come from and how it came to be in that lonely place he
could by no means discover. As he had been instructed he raised his
hand and showed it the bridle, and it came swiftly to him and
presented itself to be bridled at his hands. When he had led it to his
companions, they rejoiced to labour afterwards all the more willingly

Viking trading centre; see P. Hill, *Whithorn and St Ninian: The Excavation of a Monastic
Town 1984–91* (Stroud, 1997), cc. 3–5. Aside from this story in *LDE*, there is no evidence
of any connection between Whithorn and the Community of St Cuthbert. In the 8th cent.,
a metrical account of the miracles of St Ninian was composed at York (*Poetae Latini aeui
Carolini*, ed. E. Dümmler and K. Strecker (4 vols., *MGH*; 1881–1923), iv. 943–62; see
W. Levison, 'An eighth-century poem on St Ninian', *Antiquity*, xiv (1940), 280–91), and
ASC, *s.a.* 762 (*recte* 763), records the consecration of Pehtwine as bishop of Whithorn 'æt
Ælfet ee', usually identified with Elvet on the east bank of the river Wear at Durham.

perducto, pro*a* patris Cuthberti corporis*b* presentia tanto libentius postmodum laborare gaudebant, quanto eius suffragia nunquam in necessitate sibi defutura pro certo sciebant. Adiungentes itaque caballum uehiculo quod illum celestem thesaurum theca inclusum ferebat, eo securius per quelibet loca ipsum sequebantur, quo a Deo sibi prouiso equo ductore utebantur.

Porro liber memoratus in hac ecclesia, que corpus ipsius sancti patris habere meruit, usque hodie seruatur, in quo nullum omnino (ut diximus) per aquam lesionis signum monstratur. Quod plane et ipsius sancti Cuthberti et ipsorum quoque meritis qui ipsius libri auctores extiterant gestum creditur: Eadfridi uidelicet uenerande memorie episcopi, qui hunc in honorem beati Cuthberti manu propria scripserat; successoris quoque eiusdem uenerabilis Aethelwoldi, qui auro gemmisque perornari iusserat; sancti etiam Bilfridi anachorite, qui uota iubentis manu artifici*c* prosecutus, egregium opus composuerat. Erat enim aurificii*d* arte precipuus. Hi pariter amore dilecti Deo confessoris et pontificis feruentes, suam erga ipsum deuotionem posteris omnibus innotescendam hoc opere reliquerunt.*e* 75

13. Cum*f* ergo et corpori suo sedem prouidere, et seruientes sibi*g* a longo per septem annos labore uellet respirare, rex impius*h* Halfdene crudelitatis sue, quam in ecclesiam ipsius sancti cetera quoque*i* sanctorum loca exercuerat, uindictam Deo iudice persoluit. *Nam cum insania mentis grauissimus* *j*corpus eius*j* *inuasit cruciatus, unde etiam*k* *fetor exhalans intolerabilis,* toto *eum* exercitui *reddidit exosum.*

a om. H   *b om. V*   *c* aritificis *Ca*   *d* artificii *D*; aurifici *H*   *e* et cetera *add. L*   *f* De morte Alfdene *rubric Fx H T V Y*   *g ins. over line Fx; om. Y*   *h om. Fx L Y*   *i* que *Ca*   *j-j* eius corpus *Fx L Y*   *k om. F*

75 The book referred to must be the Lindisfarne Gospels (BL, Cotton Nero D.IV), the Old English colophon of which (fo. 259) may be translated: 'Eadfrith, bishop of the Lindisfarne Church, originally wrote this book, for God and for St Cuthbert and—jointly—for all the saints whose relics are in the Island. And Æthelwald, bishop of the Lindisfarne islanders, impressed it on the outside and covered it—as he well knew how to do. And Billfrith, the anchorite, forged the ornaments which are on it on the outside and adorned it with gold and with gems and also with gilded-over silver—pure metal. And Aldred, unworthy and most miserable priest, glossed it in English between the lines with the help of God and St Cuthbert.' The bishops mentioned are bishops of Lindisfarne ?698–? × 731, and respectively from ? × 731–737 or 740. The glossator, Aldred, was active in the Community of St Cuthbert at Chester-le-Street from c.960 to c.970 (G. Bonner, 'St Cuthbert at Chester-le-Street', in Bonner, *Cuthbert*, pp. 387–95, at 392–5), and he was responsible for the colophon. The authority of the colophon is

to protect the body of father Cuthbert, now that they knew for certain that his help would never fail them in their need. Harnessing the horse to the vehicle on which they were carrying that heavenly treasure encased in its chest, they followed it wherever it went, all the more safely because they were using as a guide the horse provided for them by God.

Now the aforementioned book is today preserved in this church which has merited to have the body of that same holy father, and in it (as we have said) there is no sign that it has been harmed by the water. This circumstance is believed certainly to be due to the merits of St Cuthbert himself and also of those who had been the makers of the book, that is: Bishop Eadfrith of venerable memory, who wrote it with his own hand in honour of St Cuthbert; his own successor, the venerable Æthelwald, who ordered it to be adorned with gold and gems; and also St Billfrith the Anchorite, who executed Æthelwald's wishes and commands with a craftsman's hand, producing an out-standing piece of work. For he was distinguished in the goldsmith's art. These men, who were all fervent in their love of the confessor and bishop beloved of God, left in this work something through which all those who come after them may appreciate their devotion towards the saint.[75]

13. Since therefore Cuthbert wished to provide a resting place for his body, and to give a breathing space from their long seven years' labour to those who served him, the impious king Halfdan paid by the judgment of God the penalty of the cruelty which he had inflicted on the saint's own church and on other places of the saints. For as insanity afflicted his mind so the direst torment afflicted his body, from which there rose such an intolerable stench that he was rendered

[xxxv (xxxvi)]

debated, particularly as regards whether Eadfrith personally wrote the book. *LDE*'s assertion that he did so 'with his own hand' may be an independent tradition, or it may simply represent an elaboration of the colophon. The latter seems the more likely, since its statement that Æthelwald ordered the book to be adorned appears to be a misreading of the Old English statement in the colophon that Æthelwald actually bound the book himself. The author of *LDE* would seem to have confused the rare words *geðryde* and *gebelde* with *gebeodan*, which means 'to command'. *LDE*'s account is none the less important as showing that the book was at Durham at the beginning of the 12th cent. and apparently had its binding, which has since been lost. *LDE*'s observation that there was no sign that it had been harmed by water has been confirmed by modern research. See *Euangeliorum quattuor Codex Lindisfarnensis*, with commentary by T. D. Kendrick, T. J. Brown, R. L. S. Bruce-Mitford (2 vols., Lausanne, 1960), ii. 5–11, 21–3; vol. i contains a full facsimile.

Contemptus ergo[a] ab omnibus et proiectus, cum tribus tantum nauibus de Tina profugit, nec multo post cum suis omnibus periit.[76]

His[b] ita[c] gestis, ad monasterium quod in sua quondam uilla *uocabulo Creca fuit, illud uenerabile corpus deferunt, ibique ab abbate cui nomen erat Geue benignissime suscepti, uelut in proprio quattuor mensibus residebant.*[77] Interea cum exercitus et qui supererant de indigenis sine rege nutarent, sepe nominato abbati Eadredo religiose conuersationis uiro, ipse beatus Cuthbertus per somnium astitit, iamque suorum quieti prouidens, ei hec facienda iniunxit: 'Pergens', inquit, 'ad exercitum Danorum, mea te ad illos missum legatione dices, ut scilicet puerum, quem uidue illi uendiderant, uocabulo Guthredum filium Hardacnut, ubinam sit tibi ostendant. Quo inuento et precio libertatis eius uidue persoluto, ante totius exercitus frequentiam producatur,[d] atque ab omnibus me uolente ac iubente, in Oswiesdune (hoc est monte Oswiu) electus, posita in brachio eius dextro armilla in regnum constituatur.' Euigilans ergo abbas, rem sociis retulit, moxque profectus iussa per ordinem compleuit.

Productoque[e] in medium iuuene, tam barbari quam indigene reuerenter iussa sancti Cuthberti suscipiunt, atque unanimi fauore puerum ex seruitute in regnum constituunt. Quo cum gratia cunctorum et amore regni sede potito, cum [f]sopitis iam[f] perturbationum procellis tranquillitas redderetur, *sedes episcopalis quam in Lindisfarnensi insula superius diximus, in Cuncacestre restauratur.*[78] Translato

---

[a] om. *Fx L Y*   [b] De uisione Eadredi de Guthredo faciendo regem (regem faciendo *Fx V Y*) *rubric Fx H T V Y*   [c] itaque *L*   [d] perducatur *L*   [e] Sedes episcopalis in Conkescestre restauratur *rubric Fx H T V Y*   [f-f] iam sopitis *H*

---

[76] The Viking leader Halfdan came to Northumbria in 875 and in 876 he shared out the land, although in fact his dominance was probably limited to the area south of the Tees (ASC, *s.a.*, Arnold, *Sym. Op.* ii. 82, 111, Coxe, *Flores* i. 326–7; see also Rollason, *Sources*, pp. 63–4). The source for the present account may be *CMD* (Craster, 'Red book', p. 524), with which it shares the words italicized in the Latin text, but the ultimate source is probably *HSC* c. 12: 'Sed mox ira Dei et sancti confessoris super eum uenit. Nam adeo cepit insanire ac fetere, quod totus eum exercitus suus a se expulit, et longe in mare fugauit, nec postea comparuit' (Arnold, *Sym. Op.* i. 203). The reference to Halfdan's departure with three ships is peculiar to *LDE*. A. P. Smyth, *Scandinavian Kings in the British Isles 850–880* (Oxford, 1977), pp. 263–4, has identified him with the *Albann* killed in Ireland in 877 (*Annals of Ulster*, ed. Mac Airt and Mac Niocaill, pp. 332–3), thus dating his departure to 877 or perhaps 876.

[77] Most of this sentence is derived verbatim from *De miraculis* c. 2 (Arnold, *Sym. Op.* i. 237); the details are also to be found in *HSC* c. 20 (op. cit. i. 209). On Crayke, see above, pp. 46–7, 91 n. 29, 98–9, 115 n. 69. Nothing more is known of Abbot Geve.

[78] For Abbot Eadred, see above, pp. 100–1. *Oswiesdune* has not been identified, but

odious to his whole army. So, held in contempt and driven out by all, he fled with only three ships from the Tyne, and soon afterwards perished with all his men.[76]

When these things had happened, they carried that venerable body to the monastery which was in his former vill called Crayke, where they were received in kindly fashion by the abbot whose name was Geve, and remained for four months as if in their own home.[77] Meanwhile since the army and those of the native inhabitants who had survived were in a state of uncertainty without a king, St Cuthbert himself appeared in a dream to Abbot Eadred, that man of religious life whom we have frequently mentioned, and so as to provide for the peace of his people he enjoined him to act thus: 'You shall go', he said, 'to the army of the Danes, and shall say that you have been sent to them as my representative, that they may show you the whereabouts of a boy called Guthred, son of Harthacnut, whom they have sold to a widow. When he has been found and the price of his freedom paid to the widow, he should be led before the assembled army; by my wish and command he should be elected by all at *Oswiesdune* (that is Oswiu's Mount), an armlet should be placed on his right arm, and he should be made king.' When the abbot woke up, he told all this to his companions, and he soon set out and carried out the saint's commands in due order.

When the young man had been led into the midst of them, barbarians as well as native inhabitants reverently received the commands of St Cuthbert, and by the favour of all they raised the boy from slavery to kingship. When by the grace and love of all he had been placed on the throne of the kingdom, and when the storms of disorder had been calmed and tranquillity had returned, the episcopal see, which we spoke of above as being on the island of Lindisfarne, was restored at Chester-le-Street.[78] When after four

[right margin: [xxxvi (xxxvii)]]

[right margin: [xxxvii (xxxviii)]]

Guthred is probably identical with the king Guthfrith, buried at York Minster in 895 (see below, p. 127 n. 86, and, for references to numismatic evidence, Rollason, *Sources*, p. 64). Chester-le-Street lies approximately six miles north of Durham on the river Wear; on the site and remains of early medieval date there, see E. Cambridge, 'Why did the Community of St Cuthbert settle at Chester-le-Street?', Bonner, *Cuthbert*, pp. 367–86, and, for discussion of comparanda, Blair, in Blair and Sharpe, *Pastoral Care*, pp. 236–8. The establishment of the Community of St Cuthbert there, and thus also the inception of Guthred's reign, can be dated to 883, 885, or 880. *LDE* dates the community's departure from Lindisfarne to 875 and gives its period of wandering as seven years (above, pp. 102–3 and 94–5), which would suggest 883 for its arrival at Chester-le-Street. This agrees with *HReg* (Arnold, *Sym. Op.* ii. 86). Another entry in *HReg*, however, gives nine years as the period of wandering (ibid., ii. 92), which would suggest 885. Finally, *LDE* states that

[*See p. 124 for n. 78 cont.*]

igitur illuc post quattuor menses de Creca beatissimi patris incorrupto corpore, *simul et qui Deo seruirent ibidem* institutis, eximius antistes Eardulfus, uir ubique in prosperis et aduersis sancto Cuthberto adherens, primus ibi cathedram pontificalem conscendit.[79]

[xxxviii (xxxix)] Nec[b] parum[c] honoris et donorum illi ecclesie rex Guthredus contulit, eique qui ex seruo se in regem promouerat, deuota deinceps humilitate[d] subditus, fideliter seruiuit. Vnde cuncta que pro priuilegiis ecclesie sue ac libertate atque pro sibi ministrantium sustentatione mandauerat, ille ut promptus minister mox adimplere festinauit. Denique memorato abbati per uisum astans ipse[e] sanctus: 'Dicito,' inquit, 'regi, ut totam inter Weor et Tine[f] terram michi et in mea ecclesia ministrantibus[g] perpetue possessionis iure largiatur, ex qua illis ne inopia laborent, uite subsidia procurentur.[80] Precipe illi preterea ut ecclesiam meam tutum profugis locum refugii constituat, ut quicunque qualibet de causa ad meum corpus confugerit, pacem per triginta et septem dies nulla unquam occasione infringendam habeat.'[81] Hec per fidelem internuntium abbatem audita, tam ipse rex Guthredus[h] quam etiam rex[i] potentissimus (cuius superius mentio facta est) Aelfredus declaranda populis propalarunt, eaque toto non solum Anglorum sed etiam Danorum consentiente atque collaudante exercitu in perpetuum seruanda constituerunt. Eos autem qui institutam ab ipso sancto pacem quoquomodo irritare presumpserint, dampno pecunie multandos censuerunt, ut scilicet quantum regi

---

a–a et simul qui ibidem Deo seruierunt *H*   *b* De libertatibus et pace ecclesie sancti Cuthberti a regibus anglie Elfredo et Guthredo statutis *rubric Fx T V Y*; De libertatibus et pace ecclesie sancti Cuthberti datis *rubric H*   *c* quidem *add. Fx and Y expunctuated in Fx*; nisi *add. L.*   *d* humitate *C Y*   *e* iste *Fx L*   *f* hec enim duo sunt flumina quinque ferme ab inuicem milibus in mare decurrentia *add. F*   *g* seruientibus *Ca*   *h* Cuthred *F*   *i* om. *Ca*

Bishop Eardwulf died in the same year as King Alfred (899), nineteen years after the establishment at Chester-le-Street (below, pp. 128–9), which would suggest 880. *DPSA* assigns Guthred a fourteen-year reign (Arnold, *Sym. Op.* ii. 377), which agrees with that, since his death is probably to be assigned to 895 (see above). As regards *LDE*'s sources, the words italicized in the Latin text here are from *De miraculis* c. 2 (Arnold, *Sym. Op.* i. 237). The source for the story of Cuthbert's appearance to Abbot Eadred and the establishment of Guthred as king seems to be *CMD* (Craster, 'Red book', p. 524), with which there are some verbal echoes; but some details are drawn from *HSC* c. 13 (Arnold, *Sym. Op.* i. 203), although the wording there is different. The linkage made in *LDE* between the installation of Guthred and the establishment of the see at Chester-le-Street is not made by *HSC* or *De miraculis*. *HReg*'s first entry for 883 (Arnold, *Sym. Op.* ii. 86) has an interlineated sentence: 'Guthred ex seruo factus est rex, et sedes episcopalis in Cunkecestra restauratur.' *HReg*'s second entry for 883 (Arnold, *Sym. Op.* i. 114) has a more elaborate description, which is not identical to *LDE* and contains information not found in *LDE*: 'Tunc sanctus

months the undecayed body of the most blessed father had been translated there from Crayke, and at the same time those who were to serve God in that place had been established, the distinguished Bishop Eardwulf, a man who always stood by St Cuthbert everywhere in prosperity as well as in adversity, was the first to ascend the pontifical throne there.[79]

King Guthred gave to that church no small quantity of honour and [xxxviii gifts, and from then on he subjected himself in devout humility and (xxxix)] faithful service to the saint who had raised him from a slave to a king. So whatever the saint had commanded for the privileges and liberty of his church and for the sustenance of those who ministered to him, the king as a willing servant hastened at once to grant. Now the saint appeared in a vision to the aforesaid abbot and said: 'Tell the king that he should give rights of perpetual possession to me and to those who minister in my church all the land between the Wear and the Tyne, so that they may not struggle in want, but may be able to procure from these lands a living for themselves.[80] Order him further that he should constitute my church as a safe place of refuge for fugitives, so that whoever flees to my body for whatever cause may have for thirty-seven days peace which may not on any pretext ever be broken.'[81] When they had heard these things through the abbot as faithful intermediary, not only King Guthred himself but also the most powerful King Alfred (whom we mentioned earlier) made them known by declaration to the people and, with the consent and approval not only of the army of the English but also of that of the Danes, they established them to be observed in perpetuity. They laid down that those who presumed to violate in any way the sanctuary which the saint had instituted should be punished with a fine so that,

Cuthbertus abbati Eadredo (qui pro eo quod in Luel habitauit Lulisc cognominabatur) assistens per uisionem precepit, ut episcopo et omni exercitui Anglorum et Danorum diceret, quatinus Guthredum filium Hardecnut, quem Dani uendiderant in seruum cuidam uidue apud Hwitingaham, dato pretio, redimerent, et redemptum sibi in regem leuarent; regnauitque super Eboracum; Egbert uero super Northimbros.'

[79] Eardwulf, bishop of Chester-le-Street (880 × 5–99), formerly bishop of Lindisfarne (854–83).

[80] The words 'pro sibi ministrantium sustentatione' and 'in mea ecclesia ministrantibus' may be significant in the context of the dispute between the bishop and the priory over the division of the church's lands. *LDE* may here be emphasizing the claim of the priory to the estates of Jarrow and Monkwearmouth which lay between the rivers Tyne and Wear. See *Feodarium Prioratus Dunelmensis*, ed. W. Greenwell (SS lviii; Durham, 1871), p. xvii.

[81] This speech represents in different words the second half of the speech attributed to Cuthbert in *HSC* c. 13 (Arnold, *Sym. Op.* i. 203), in the first part of which he instructs Abbot Eadred to make Guthred king.

Anglorum pace ipsius fracta debeant,[a] tantundem ipsi sancto uiolata eius pace persoluant, uidelicet ad minus octoginta et sedecim[b] libras.[82] Terra quoque quam[c] preceperat inter memorata duo flumina[d] mox [e]ei donata,[e 83] communi regum supradictorum et totius populi sententia decretum est, ut quicunque sancto Cuthberto terram donauerit, uel pecunia ipsius empta fuerit, nemo deinceps ex ea cuiuslibet seruitii aut[f] consuetudinis sibi ius aliquod usurpare audeat, sed sola ecclesia inconcussa quiete ac libertate, cum omnibus consuetudinibus et (ut uulgo dicitur) cum saca et socne et infangentheof perpetualiter possideat. Has leges et hec statuta quicunque quolibet nisu infringere presumpserint, eos in perpetuum, nisi emendauerint, gehenne ignibus puniendos anathematizando sententia omnium contradedit.[84]

[xxxix] Interiecto[g] tempore aliquanto gens Scottorum innumerabili exer-citu coadunato, inter cetera sue crudelitatis facinora Lindisfarnense monasterium seuiens et rapiens inuasit. Contra quos dum rex Guthredus per sanctum Cuthbertum confortatus pugnaturus staret, subito terra dehiscens hostes uiuos omnes absorbuit, renouato ibi miraculo antiquo, quando 'aperta est terra et degluttiuit Dathan, [h]et operuit super congregationem Abiron'.[h] Qualiter autem[i] gestum sit, alibi constat esse scriptum.[g 85]

[(xli)] **14.** Anno[j] ab Incarnatione Domini octingentesimo nonagesimo quarto rex Guthredus cum non paucis annis prospere regnasset moriens,[86] priuilegia ecclesie[k] patris Cuthberti de quiete, de[l] libertate ipsius, de pace confugientium ad sepulchrum eius a nullo unquam

---

[a] debebant *Ca*   [b] xvii *H*   [c] quoquomodo *H*   [d] a Deorestrete usque mare orientale *add. F*   [e–e] donata ei *Fx L*   [f] *om. Fx L*   [g–g] *om. Fx L Y*; Scotti absorpti sunt uiui apud Mundigene *rubric H*   [h–h] et cetera *H*   [i] *om. H* [j] De priuilegiis Guthredi regis sancto Cuthberto concessis *rubric Fx T V Y*   [k] *om. L* [l] *om. V*

---

[82] On sanctuary, see above, pp. 50–3 and n. 67. *LDE*'s figure for the fine differs from that of 1,200 *ore* given in *CMD* (Craster, 'Red book', p. 524), although in practice the amounts would have been similar since 1,200 *ore* was probably equivalent to £80–£100. On the plausibility and significance of these amounts, see Hall, in Bonner, *Cuthbert*, pp. 425–36, esp. 426–30, who argues that Alfred's role, which is first referred to in *CMD* and *LDE*, was plausible in view of the fact that Alfred's law code was the first to deal with sanctuary at length, and referred specifically to a period of 37 days allowed to a fugitive.

[83] C has here an erasure of approximately five words in the space of which has been added later in pencil and in a 17th- or 18th-cent. hand, 'Weor et Tine'; F has 'from Dere Street as far as the North Sea'; see also Rollason, 'Erasures', p. 155. On the term *totius populi* ('of all the people'), see above, p. 114 n. 66.

[84] This is related to but not verbally identical to *CMD* (Craster, 'Red book', p. 524). If it is ultimately based on a charter, no such document has survived.

however much they would owe to the king of England for breach of the royal peace, they should pay the same amount to the saint for the violation of his peace, that is at least ninety-six pounds.[82] When soon afterwards the land between the two aforementioned rivers had been given to the saint as he had commanded,[83] it was decreed by the common resolve of the aforesaid kings and of the whole people that if anyone should give land to St Cuthbert, or if land should be bought with the saint's own money, no one thenceforth should dare to arrogate to themselves from it any right of service or custom, but that the church alone should possess it perpetually in undisturbed liberty and freedom from claims, with all its customary rights and with (as it is called in the vernacular) sake and soke and infangentheof. Anyone who by whatever effort presumed to infringe these laws and statutes was condemned by the judgment of all, unless he mended his ways, to anathema and perpetual punishment in the fires of hell.[84]

Some time later the people of the Scots gathered together an [xxxix] innumerable army, and among other cruel crimes they attacked the monastery of Lindisfarne with ravaging and rapine. While King Guthred, strengthened by St Cuthbert, had taken up his position to fight against them, the earth suddenly opened and swallowed all the enemy alive, there having been repeated there a former miracle in which 'the ground opened and swallowed Dathan and covered the congregation of Abiron'. How this came about has been described in writing elsewhere.[85]

14. In the year of Our Lord's Incarnation 894, King Guthred died [(xli)] after he had reigned for many years,[86] and he left in perpetuity to all the kings, bishops, and peoples who came after him the privileges of the church of father Cuthbert establishing its freedom from claims, its liberties, the sanctuary rights of those fleeing to the saint's tomb

[85] Ps. 105:17 (106: 18); cf. Eccles. 45: 22. This account of Guthred's resistance to the Scots seems to be based on *De miraculis* c. 4, with which it is replaced in Fx, L, and Y as their c. xl. T has a note at the foot of the page (s. xiv^ex^/s. xv^in^) regarding the lack of this insertion. For the story, cf. *HSC* c. 33 (Arnold, *Sym. Op.* i. 240–2), where the site of the miracle is named as *Mundingedene*, evidently the place named in the rubric here in H. In another version of the story by Reginald of Durham, the place is called *Munegedene* and identified as a hill in the vicinity of Norham (Northumberland) (*Cuth. virt.*, ed. Raine, p. 149 (c. 73)).

[86] *Chronicle of Æthelweard*, ed. Campbell, p. 51, records *s.a.* 895 the death of a king of the Northumbrians called Guthfrid who was buried in York minster, and is presumably to be identified with the Guthred of *LDE* (on Guthred, see above, p. 122 n. 78).

irritanda, alia quoque in ecclesie ipsius munimentum statuta, omnibus post se regibus, episcopis et populis in eternum conseruanda reliquit, que etiam usque hodie*[a]* seruantur.[87] Denique nemo ea unquam impune conabatur infringere. Quorum Scotti (ut prefati sumus), cum pacem eius uiolassent, subito terre hiatu absorti in momento disparuerunt. Alios quoque in simili presumptionis scelere, quam terribilis uindicta percusserit, in sequentibus dicetur.

Mortuo Guthredo, rex Aelfredus Northanhumbrorum regnum suscepit disponendum. Postquam enim*[b]* sanctus Cuthbertus ei apparuerat, paterno regno (id est*[c]* Occidentalium Saxonum), et prouinciam Orientalium Anglorum et Northanhymbrorum post Guthredum adiecit.[88]

[(xlii)] **15.** Anno*[d]* ab Incarnatione Domini*[e]* octingentesimo nonagesimo nono,*[f]* idem piissimus rex Anglorum Elfredus, peractis in regno uiginti octo annis et dimidio, defunctus est, Edwardo filio in regnum patri succedente. Qui ab ipso diligentissime admonitus fuerat, ut sanctum Cuthbertum eiusque ecclesiam quam maxime diligendo semper honori haberet, recolendo ex quantis angustiis et calamitatibus*[g]* patrem eripiens regno restituerit, et plus quam antecessores eius habuerant, ei subactis hostibus augmentauerit.

16. Eodem*[h]* anno quo rex Elfredus mortuus est, ille*[i]* sepe memoratus antistes Eardulfus*[j]* in senectute bona, suorum premia laborum recepturus, ab hac uita migrauit, anno scilicet nono decimo ex quo sacrum beati patris Cuthberti corpus in Cunecacestre*[k]* translatum fuerat, sui uero episcopatus anno quadragesimo sexto.[89] In cuius loco Cutheardus et ipse coram Deo et hominibus uita probabili commendatus, omnium electione cathedram episcopalem suscepit regendam. Qui*[l]* magna sollicitudine, rerum sufficientiam Deo coram*[m]* incorrupti corporis presentia seruituris prouidens, quas et quot *[n]*uillas ipsius sancti*[n]* pecunia comparatas prioribus regum

---

[a] *om.* L   *[b]* *om.* T   *[c]* est regno *Ca*   *[d]* De morte Egfridi (Elfredi *Fx*) *rubric Fx T V Y*   *[e]* *om.* H   *[f]* viii *Fx H L*   *[g]* calamitate *F* *[h]* Capitulum *rubric Fx T V Y*   *[i]* ipse *F*   *[j]* *om.* L   *[k]* Cuncacestre *F* *[l]* Qui in *Fx L Y*   *[m]* *add. over line in later hand Fx; om.* Y   *[n-n]* ipsius sancti uillas *T*

---

[87] No trace of any such documents has survived.

[88] There is no factual basis to the claim that Alfred took possession of Northumbria. L. Simpson has noted that 'the author . . . was anticipating tenth-century events here, as if

which should never be violated by anyone, and other statutes for the defence of the church itself—and all these are still preserved today.[87] And no one has ever striven with impunity to infringe them. Amongst those who did so were the Scots who (as we related above), when they violated the saint's peace, were suddenly swallowed by an opening of the earth and disappeared in a moment. We shall describe subsequently with what terrible a vengeance the saint struck others also who committed a similar crime of presumption.

After Guthred's death, King Alfred received under his rule the kingdom of the Northumbrians. For after St Cuthbert had appeared to him, he added to his father's kingdom (that is the kingdom of the West Saxons) both the kingdom of the East Angles and after Guthred's death the kingdom of the Northumbrians.[88]

15. In the year of Our Lord's Incarnation 899, that same most pious [(xlii)] king Alfred died after reigning for twenty-eight and a half years, and his son Edward succeeded his father in the kingdom. He had been most diligently exhorted by his father that he should always hold St Cuthbert and his church in the greatest possible love and honour, recalling from what dire straits and calamities the saint had rescued his father and restored him to his kingdom, and how having subjugated his enemies, he had augmented that kingdom beyond that which his predecessors had ruled.

16. In the same year in which Alfred died, Bishop Eardwulf, to whom we have often referred, migrated from this life in ripe old age to receive the rewards of his labours, that was in the nineteenth year after that in which the holy body of the blessed father Cuthbert had been translated to Chester-le-Street, being the forty-sixth of Eardwulf's episcopate.[89] In his place Cutheard, a man commendable in the sight of God and of men for the worthiness of his life, received the rule of the episcopal throne by unanimous election. He made provision with great solicitude for the sustenance of those who were to serve God in the presence of the undecayed body. The cartulary of the church, which records the former munificence of

he wanted to minimize discontinuities in Anglo-Saxon rulership over these territories' (Simpson, in Bonner, *Cuthbert*, pp. 397–411, esp. 408).

[89] The year meant is 899, in which year Alfred died and Eardwulf was in the 46th year of an episcopate which had begun on Lindisfarne in 854. On the significance of the statement that this was the nineteenth year after the translation of Cuthbert's body to Chester-le-Street, see above, p. 124 n. 78.

donariis adiecerit, ecclesie cartula, que antiquam regum et quor-
umque^a religiosorum munificentiam erga ipsum sanctum continet,
^{b}manifeste declarat.$^{b\,90}$

[xl (xliii)]   Itaque^c Edwardo non solum Occidentalium Saxonum, uerum etiam
Orientalium Anglorum Northanhymbrorum quoque regna dispo-
nente, et Cutheardo Berniciorum administrante presulatum, *rex
quidam paganus* uocabulo *Reingwald multa ^{d}cum classe^d Northanhymbrorum partibus applicuit*; nec mora irrupta^e Eboraca, indigenas
quosque meliores uel occidit, *uel extra patriam fugauit.*^{91} *Occupauit
quoque totam mox terram ^{f}sancti Cuthberti,^{f} uillasque ipsius duobus suis
militibus quorum unus Scula, alter uero Onlafbal   appellabatur.*$^{g\,92}$
Horum Scula, a uilla que ^{h}uocatur Iodene^h usque Billingham sortitus
dominium,^{93} miseros indigenas grauibus tributis et intolerabilibus
afflixit. Vnde usque hodie Eboracenses quotiens tributum regale
soluere coguntur, ei parti terre sancti Cuthberti quam Scula posse-
derat, in leuamentum sui multam pecunie imponere nituntur. Scilicet
legem deputant, quod paganus per tirannidem fecerat, qui non
legitimo regi Anglorum, sed barbaro et alienigene et regis Anglorum
hosti militabat. Nec tamen quamuis ^{i}multum in hoc^i laborauerint,
prauam consuetudinem huc usque sancto Cuthberto resistente intro-
ducere potuerunt.^{94}

[xli (xliv)]   Aliam^j uero partem^k uillarum Onlafbal occupauit, qui multo quam
socius eius *immaniorem et crudeliorem ^{l}se in sui^l perniciem omnibus
exhibebat.* Denique cum *multis sepe iniuriis episcopum, congregationem*

---

^{a} quorumcumque *L V* $^{b-b}$ om. *L* ^{c} Raynwaldus quidam rex paganus
Northumbriam uastauit *rubric H Fx T Y* $^{d-d}$ om. *T* ^{e} om. *T*
$^{f-f}$ Cuthberti sancti *D* ^{g} distribuit *add. Ca* $^{h-h}$ Iodene uocatur *T*
$^{i-i}$ in hoc multum *H* ^{j} De crudeli morte (morte crudeli *H*) Onlafbal *Fx H V Y*
^{k} tempore *H* $^{l-l}$ sui se in *T*

---

^{90} The cartulary *(cartula)* referred to is presumably what purports to be a summary of a
charter in *HSC* c. 21 (Arnold, *Sym. Op.* i. 208), which lists the purchases Cuthheard made
with St Cuthbert's 'own money' as Sedgefield (Co. Durham) and Bedlington (Northumberland) with its appendages Netherton, ?Gubeon *(Grubba)*, Twizell, Choppington,
Sleekburn, and ?Cambois *(Commer)*. See Hart, *Early Charters*, nos. 159, 160 (p. 140).

^{91} Edward the Elder was king of the Anglo-Saxons (899–924); Rægnald was king of
York from some date between 914 (or earlier) and 919 and his death in 920/1. His capture
of York is recorded in *HReg, s.a.* 919 (Arnold, *Sym. Op.* ii. 93), which is a more likely date
than that of 923 given by ASC DE, *s.a.* It is possible that Rægnald had in fact made
himself ruler of York after, or even before, his first victory at Corbridge in 914 *(HSC* c. 22
(Arnold, *Sym. Op.* i. 209): see F. T. Wainwright, 'The battles at Corbridge', *Scandinavian
England: Collected Papers by F. T. Wainwright*, ed. H. P. R. Finberg (Chichester, 1975),
pp. 163–79); and *LDE* implies that his conquests in Bernicia, which presumably flowed
from that victory, were the result of, rather than the prelude to, his taking of York. Thus

kings and other religious men towards the saint, clearly shows which vills and how many he bought with the saint's own money and added to the gifts of former kings.[90]

While Edward was ruling the kingdoms not only of the West [xl (xliii)] Saxons but also of the East Angles and the Northumbrians, and Cutheard was administering the see of the Bernicians, a certain heathen king called Rægnald came with a large fleet and landed in Northumbria. Without delay he attacked York and either killed or drove out of their homeland all the better sort of inhabitants.[91] He soon occupied the whole of the land of St Cuthbert and distributed the vills to two of his armed followers, one of whom was called Scula, the other Onlafball.[92] Of these the lordship of the lands from the vill called Eden as far as Billingham fell to Scula,[93] and he inflicted heavy and intolerable tributes on the unfortunate inhabitants. For this reason even today, the people of York attempt to impose a mulct of money on that part of the land of St Cuthbert which Scula possessed equivalent to whatever sum in royal tax they are compelled to pay. Thus they deem to be law what was done tyrannically by a heathen who was fighting not for the legitimate king of the English but for one who was a barbarian, a foreigner, and the enemy of the king of the English. With St Cuthbert resisting them, however, they have not hitherto been able to introduce this bad custom, although they have worked hard to do so.[94]

Now the other group of vills was occupied by Onlafball, the [xli (xliv)] manner of whose destruction showed to all how much more savage and cruel he was than his colleague. At length, when he was molesting

HReg's account of how he 'broke into York' in 919 must refer to a later retaking of that city (Rollason, *Sources*, p. 66, citing A. P. Smyth, *Scandinavian York and Dublin: The History and Archaeology of Two Related Kingdoms* (2 vols., Dublin, 1975–9), i. 102–3).

[92] From the beginning of this sentence, the story of Onlafball is taken almost verbatim from *De miraculis* c. 3 (Arnold, *Sym. Op.* i. 238–40), with the exception of the account of the lands of Scula and the contemporary claims of the people of York, which is unique to *LDE*. The definition of the land, 'a uilla que uocatur Iodene, usque ad Billingham', is found, however, in *HSC* c. 23 (Arnold, *Sym. Op.* i. 209), where the story of Onlafball is told in different words and with a description of Onlafball's lands as extending from Eden to the river Wear. This version also has a more precise ending: 'Sanctus uero Cuthbertus, sicut iustum erat, terram suam recepit.' Onlafball also names the gods he invokes as Thor and Odin.

[93] Castle Eden (Co. Durham) is presumably meant; see Hart, *Early Charters*, no. 164 (p. 141). On Billingham, see above, p. 94 and n. 36. School Aycliffe (Co. Durham; NZ 257 235), south of Darlington, is supposed to preserve Scula's name (E. Ekwall, *The Concise Oxford Dictionary of English Place-Names* (4th edn.; Oxford, 1960), p. 20).

[94] The account of the contemporary claims of the people of York is peculiar to *LDE* and nothing further is known of it.

atque populum sancti Cuthberti[95] *molestaret, prediaque ad* episcopium *iure attinentia*[a] sibi *pertinaciter usurparet, episcopus uolens eum*[b] *Deo lucrari, 'Queso,'* inquit, *'pertinacis animi rigorem deponas, et ab illicita rerum peruasione ecclesiasticarum iam te cohibeas.* Nam si hec monita spreueris, ipsum *confessorem suas suorumque iniurias per te irrogatas, grauiter uindicaturum esse non dubites.'* At ille contra hec[c] diabolico spiritu inflatus, *'Quid,'* inquit, *'huius* [d]*hominis mortui*[d] *minas cotidie michi obicitis? Quid contra me uobis ualebit ipsius in quo speratis auxilium? Deorum meorum* [e]potentiam *contestor,*[e] *quod tam ipsi mortuo quam uobis omnibus deinceps inimicissimus ero.'* At episcopus omnesque *fratres in terram prostrati, a Deo* [f]*et sancto confessore*[f] *superbas illius minas annullari flagitabant. Iam miser ille ad hostium uenerat, iam alterum intra limen alterum extra pedem posuerat, et ibi tanquam clauis per utrumque pedem confixus* [g]*nec egredi nec regredi*[g] *ualebat, sed immobilis ibi prorsus* manebat. Vbi diutius tortus, *beatissimi confessoris sanctitatem palam confitebatur, sicque impiam animam eodem in loco* [h]*reddere compellebatur.*[h] Quo *exemplo* [i]*alii omnes*[i] *conterriti, neque terras neque aliud quid quod ecclesie iure competebat, quoquomodo ulterius peruadere presumebant.*[j]

17. Defuncto[k] autem Cutheardo cum iam quintum decimum [l]suo in episcopatu ageret annum,[l] substitutus est ad ecclesie regimen bone actionis uir Tilredus. Cuius pontificatus [m]septimo anno[m] Edwardo rege defuncto, filius eius Aethelstanus suscepta regni gubernacula gloriosissime rexit,[96] primusque regum totius Brittannie quaquauersum adeptus est imperium,[97] adiuuante atque impetrante hoc apud Deum beato Cuthberto, qui auo illius Elfredo quondam apparens

---

[a] pertinentia *Ca*   [b] *om. Ca*   [c] *om.* L   [d-d] mortui hominis *F*
[e-e] contestor potentiam *H*   [f-f] ac sancto Cuthberto *H*   [g-g] nec regredi nec
egredi *T*   [h-h] compellebatur reddere *H*   [i-i] omnes alii *H*
[j] presumpserunt *Ca*   [k] De Athelstano rege *rubric T*   [l-l] annum suo in
episcopatu ageret *T*   [m-m] anno septimo *H*

---

[95] On this term, see above, p. 114 n. 66.

[96] *LDE*'s chronology is confused. According to it Cuthheard would have become bishop in 899 so his fifteenth year would have been 913–14, which agrees with the date of 913 given for Tilred's accession in *ALf* s.a., but its reference to Edward the Elder's death in the seventh year of Bishop Tilred is problematic, since it would date the king's death (*recte* 924) to 920–1. Later, *LDE* implies that Tilred's accession occurred in 911/12 (below, pp. 135, 101); and that Edward died in 919 (below, pp. 134–5), which is not even consistent with *ALf*, which gives 920 (*s.a.*). Æthelstan was king of Wessex (924/5–7) and of England (927–39).

the bishop, community, and people of St Cuthbert[95] with many injuries, and was persistently expropriating estates belonging by right to the bishopric, the bishop, who wished to win him for God, said: 'I beseech you to moderate the hardness of your stubborn mind, and to refrain from the illicit annexation of church property. For if you spurn this advice, you should have no doubt that the confessor himself will wreak a severe vengeance for the injuries which you have inflicted on him and his people.' But inflated with arrogance against this by the spirit of the devil, Onlafball replied: 'Why do you burden me every day with the threats of this dead man? What force can the help of him in whom you place your hope have against me? I call to witness the power of my gods, that henceforth I shall be the bitterest of enemies to that dead man and to you all.' Then the bishop and all the brothers threw themselves on the ground, and beseeched God and St Cuthbert to nullify his proud threats. As soon as that unhappy man had come to the door, and had placed one foot outside the threshold and the other inside, he was fixed as if by a nail through each foot and, unable to go out or to come back in, he remained there immobile. After he had for a long time been thus tormented, he acknowledged publicly the sanctity of the most blessed confessor, and thus he was compelled to give up his most impious soul in that same place. All the others were terrified by this example, and presumed no more to misappropriate in any way lands or anything else which belonged by right to the church.

17. When Cutheard died, while he was in the fifteenth year of his episcopate, his place at the head of the church was taken by a man called Tilred, who was noted for good works. In the seventh year of his pontificate King Edward died, and his son Æthelstan received the government of the kingdom and ruled most gloriously.[96] He was the first of the kings to accede to the rule of the whole length and breadth of Britain,[97] in which the blessed Cuthbert assisted him and interceded with God on his behalf, as he had previously promised when he had appeared to Æthelstan's grandfather Alfred with the

---

[97] Cf. *ALf*, *s.a.* 920: 'Hic primus obtinuit totius Anglie monarchiam.' Asser had referred to King Alfred in similar terms ('omnium Brittanie insule Christianorum rectori'; Asser, c. 1), but the use of such styles really began with Æthelstan (Simpson, in Bonner, *Cuthbert*, p. 401). These were not only on charters (e.g. 'rex Anglorum . . . totius Bryttannie regni solio sublimatus' in Sawyer, *Charters*, no. 405), but also on coins (e.g. 'rex totius Britannie' on a coin of *c.*930; J. J. North, *English Hammered Coinage, i, Early Anglo-Saxon to Henry III, c.600–1272* (3rd edn.; London, 1994), pp. 134–6.)

promiserat, '*Totius,*' inquiens, '*Brittannie* regnum filiis tuis me impetrante *concedetur disponendum.*'[98] Denique huic Ethelstano pater moriturus uniuersa replicare cepit, que et quanta suo patri pietatis beneficia beatus Cuthbertus impenderit, qualiter ex latibulis ad que metu hostium confugerat, ad bellandum contra hostem prodire iusserit, moxque ad illum totius Anglie exercitum congregauerit, nec difficulter hoste prostrato, patrio illius regno plurimam Brittannie partem adiecerit, semperque deinceps promptus illi adiutor extiterit. 'Iccirco,' inquit, 'fili, tanto patrono tamque benigno liberatori nostro deuotum te semper et fidelem exhibe, memor quid filiis Aelfredi si pietatem et iustitiam fecerint, si ei fideles extiterint, ipse promiserit.'[99] Hec pii patris monita Aethelstanus libenter suscipiens, libentius regno potitus est executus. Denique ante illum nullus regum ecclesiam sancti Cuthberti tantum dilexit, tam diuersis tamque multiplicibus regiis muneribus decorauit. Vnde hostibus passim emergentibus ubique preualens, omnibus illis uel occisis uel seruitio sibi*[a]* subactis uel extra terminos Brittannie fugatis, maiori quam ullus regum Anglorum ante illum gloria regnabat.

[xlii (xlv)]   Huius*[b]* *[c]*primo imperii*[c]* anno, qui est annus Dominice Incarnationis nongentesimus nonus decimus, natus est sanctus Dunstanus, qui septuagesimo etatis sue anno, regnante Aethelredo rege transiit ad Dominum.[100]

[(xlvi)]   18. Anno*[d]* Incarnationis Dominice nongentesimo uicesimo quinto, Tilredus, cum in episcopatu iam tredecim annos et quattuor menses egisset, defunctus est et in eius locum Wigredus eligitur episcopus et consecratur.[101] Cuius pontificatus anno decimo Aethelstanus rex dum

---

[a] om. F   *[b]* Natus est sanctus Dunstanus *rubric H*; sanctus Dunstanus natus est *rubric Fx V Y*   *[c–c]* imperii primo *Ca*   *[d]* Tilredus episcopus moritur Vigredus consecratur *rubric H*; Ethelstanus rex leges et libertates sancto Cuthberto confirmauit *rubric Fx T V Y*

---

[98] This sentence is found in *De miraculis* c. 1 (Arnold, *Sym. Op.* i. 232), but the story is also told in *HSC* c. 16 (Arnold, *Sym. Op.* i. 204–5).

[99] This account of Edward's death-bed admonitions seems to be a re-writing and amplification of *HSC* c. 25, with reference to cc. 15–16 (Arnold, *Sym. Op.* i. 210–11, 204–5).

[100] Dunstan was archbishop of Canterbury (959–88). The date of his birth is problematical. According to his earliest biographer, he was born in the reign of Æthelstan (*Memorials of Saint Dunstan, Archbishop of Canterbury*, ed. W. Stubbs (RS lxiii; London, 1874), p. 6), and the date 919 will not fit with this since Æthelstan became king in 924.

words: 'By my intercession the kingdom of all Britain will be conceded to your sons and placed at their disposal.'[98] Then when he was about to die Æthelstan's father had related everything to him, the number and scale of the benefits of piety which the blessed Cuthbert bestowed upon his own father, how the saint ordered him to leave the hiding-places to which he had fled for fear of the enemy and to make war on that enemy, how shortly afterwards Cuthbert brought together under him the army of all England, how after laying low his enemies without difficulty he added the greater part of Britain to his father's kingdom, and how thereafter he was always prompt to be his helper. 'Therefore, my son', he said, 'show yourself always devoted and faithful to such a patron and our so benign liberator, mindful of what he promised to the sons of Alfred if they upheld piety and justice and if they were faithful to him.'[99] Æthelstan received willingly his pious father's advice, and followed it still more willingly when he had come to the throne. No king before him held the church of St Cuthbert in so much affection, nor adorned it with such diverse and numerous royal gifts. For that reason he prevailed everywhere over enemies who from time to time rose up against him; once he had killed them all, or made them all his slaves, or driven them all beyond the bounds of Britain, he reigned with greater glory than any of the the kings of the English before him.

In the first year of Æthelstan's reign, which was the year of Our [xlii (xlv)] Lord's Incarnation 919, St Dunstan was born. He passed away to the Lord in the seventieth year of his life, in the reign of King Æthelred.[100]

18. In the year of Our Lord's Incarnation 925, Tilred died after he [(xlvi)] had been bishop for thirteen years and four months, and Wigred was elected and consecrated in his place.[101] In the tenth year of Wigred's pontificate, King Æthelstan, while he was on his way to

---

ASC F gives 925; and JW (ii. 384–5) notes the birth in the annal for 924, but observes that it occurred in the time of Archbishop Æthelhelm (923 × 5–926). Some modern scholars have argued for *c.*909–10, but there is no firm foundation for such an early dating; see N. Brooks, 'The career of St Dunstan', in *St Dunstan: His Life, Times and Cult*, ed. N. Ramsay, M. Sparks, and T. Tatton-Brown (Woodbridge, 1992), pp. 1–23, at 3–5. Dunstan's death in 988 in the reign of King Æthelred (978/9–1016) is well attested (e.g. *Alf s.a.* , ASC *s.a.* , and JW ii. 436–7).

[101] This implies that Tilred had become bishop in 912 or even 911 (cf. above, pp. 132–3). Wigred may have been bishop of Chester-le-Street from 925 until around 942, but the dates are uncertain.

Scotiam tenderet, cum totius Brittannie exercitu sancti Cuthberti patro-
cinia querens eius sepulchrum expetiit;[102] *suffragia* postulauit; eique
diuersis speciebus in ecclesie ornamentum multa que regem deceret
donaria contulit, que in hac Dunelmensi ecclesia usque hodie seruata,
piam ipsius regis erga ecclesiam sancti patris Cuthberti deuotionem,
et eternam representant memoriam. Que autem et quanta sint,
descripta per ordinem cartula comprehendit. His ornamentorum
donariis, uillarum quoque non minus quam duodecim possessiones
ad sufficientiam inibi seruientium superadiecit,[a] quorum nomina
quoniam alibi scripta tenentur, hic ea ponere necessarium non
habetur. Leges quoque et consuetudines ipsius sancti[b] quas auus
eius rex Elfredus et Guthredus rex instituerant, ipse approbauit, et[c]
inuiolabili firmitate in perpetuum seruandas censuit.

[xliii] Oblatione[d] autem facta, eos[e] si qui aliquid ex his auferre uel
quoquo modo minuere presumpsissent, grauissime maledictionis
anathemate percussit, ut scilicet *in die iudicii cum Iuda traditore*
dominice[f] dampnationis sententia feriantur. Exercitus quoque iussu
regis sepulchrum sancti confessoris nonaginta sex et eo amplius
libris argenti honorauit. Ita se suisque sancti confessoris patrocinio
commendatis, disposito itinere profectus est, fratrem Eadmundum
multum obtestatus, *ut si quid sinistri[g] [h]in hac* sibi[h] *expeditione*
eueniret, corpus suum ad[i] ecclesiam sancti Cuthberti sepeliendum
referret.[103] Fugato deinde Owino[j] rege Cumbrorum et Constantino

---

[a] adiecit *H*   [b] ecclesie *F*   [c] *om.* L   [d] Ethelstanus rex leges et
libertates sancto Cuthberto confirmauit *rubric H*   [e] omnes *F*   [f] domini *corr.*
in contemp. hand to dominice *C;* domini *F;* diuine *Fx L Y*   [g] ministri *corr. to*
sinistri *D*   [h–h] sibi in *H*   [i] in *Ca*   [j] Oswyno *L*

---

[102] This expedition to Scotland is given *s.a.* 934 in ASC (933, presumably in error, in
ASC A) and twice under the same date in *HReg* (Arnold, *Sym. Op.* ii. 92, 134). *CMD*
(Craster, 'Red book', p. 525), however, with which this sentence shares the italicized
words, gives 935.

[103] This account of Æthelstan's gifts is derived from *HSC* cc. 26–7 (Arnold, *Sym. Op.* i.
211–12). It seems likely that the cartulary (*cartula*) referred to is in fact that text. The
detail about the laws, however, is found in *CMD* (Craster, 'Red book', p. 525), which
echoes *HSC* in specifying South (Bishop's) Wearmouth (Co. Durham) as the vill given by
Æthelstan on this occasion and listing its dependencies as Westoe, Offerton, Silksworth,
the two Ryhopes, Burdon, Seaham, Seaton, Dalton-le-Dale, Dawdon, and Cold Heseldon
(see Hart, *Early Charters*, no. 120 (p. 118), for the identifications). It should be noted that
LDE's figure of twelve vills can only have been arrived at by adding South Wearmouth to
its eleven dependencies. The money gift attributed to Æthelstan is given as 'twelve
hundred' in *HSC* c. 27, on the significance of which for sanctuary rights, see Hall, in
Bonner, *Cuthbert*, p. 430. The only purported gifts of Æthelstan known to have been

Scotland, came to the tomb of St Cuthbert with the army of the whole of Britain to seek the patronage of the saint.[102] He requested Cuthbert's intercession, and he gave him for the adornment of his church many different kinds of gifts worthy of a king, which are still preserved today in this church of Durham and serve as a monument to the king's pious devotion to the church of the holy father Cuthbert and to his undying memory. The cartulary contains an inventory of them and how great they were. To these gifts of ornaments he added for the sustenance of those serving there property amounting to not less than twelve vills, the names of which it is not necessary to insert here because they are to be found in writing elsewhere. He approved and ordered to be observed inviolably and in perpetuity the laws and customs of the saint which his grandfather King Alfred and King Guthred had instituted.

After making this offering, he imposed on those who presumed to [xliii] take anything from them or in any way to diminish them the anathema of the gravest of curses, that is, that on the Day of Judgment they should be smitten with the sentence of the Lord's damnation along with Judas the traitor. By order of the king the army also honoured the tomb of the holy confessor with more than ninety-six pounds of silver. Having thus commended himself and his men to the protection of the holy confessor, he arranged his march and set out, urgently entreating his brother Edmund that, if anything untoward should happen to him on this expedition, his body should be brought back for burial to the church of St Cuthbert.[103] After this he put to flight Owain, king of the Cumbrians, and Constantine, king of the Scots; and he conquered

preserved at Durham in the Middle Ages were a copy of Bede's prose and metrical lives of St Cuthbert now preserved as CCCC 183, which is probably that mentioned in *HSC* c. 26; and the gospel book preserved in a burned state as BL, Cotton Otho B. IX. On these see S. Keynes, 'King Athelstan's books', in *Learning and Literature in Anglo-Saxon England*, ed. M. Lapidge and H. Gneuss (Cambridge, 1985), pp. 143–201, at 170–85, and cf. D. Rollason, 'St Cuthbert and Wessex: the evidence of Cambridge, Corpus Christi College, MS 183', in Bonner, *Cuthbert*, pp. 413–24. *HSC* c. 26 mentions also a stole and maniple, which are probably those preserved in Durham Cathedral Treasury, and which were produced in Winchester in the early 10th cent. (Battiscombe, *Relics*, pp. 33, 375–432); and seven *pallia* (cloths) which may have included the Nature Goddess silk preserved in Durham Cathedral Treasury (ibid., pp. 470–83, and now C. Higgins, 'Some new thoughts on the Nature Goddess silk', Bonner, *Cuthbert*, pp. 329–37, and H. Granger-Taylor, 'The inscription on the Nature Goddess silk', ibid., pp. 339–41). The same source (c. 28; Arnold, *Sym. Op.* i. 212) describes King Edmund as having presented *duo pallia Greca*, however, and the silk may equally well have been one of these (see Higgins, op. cit., p. 333, below, pp. 138–9)

rege Scottorum, terrestri et nauali exercitu Scotiam sibi subiugando perdomuit.[104]

Quarto post hec anno (hoc est nongentesimo tricesimo septimo Dominice Natiuitatis anno) apud Weondune,[a] quod alio nomine Aet Brunnanwerc uel Brunnanbyrig appellatur, pugnauit contra Onlaf Guthredi quondam regis filium, qui sexcenti et quindecim nauibus aduenerat, secum habens [b]contra Aethelstanum[b] auxilia regum prefatorum, [c]scilicet Scottorum[c] et Cumbrorum. At ille sancti Cuthberti patrocinio confisus, prostrata multitudine infinita reges illos de regno suo propulit, [d]suisque gloriosum[d] reportans triumphum;[105] hostibus circumquaque tremendus, suis erat pacificus, et in pace postmodum uitam terminauit,[e] fratri Edmundo imperii monarchiam relinquens.[106]

Huius [f]regni anno[f] tercio Wigredus cum decem et septem annos in episcopatu habuisset defunctus, Vhtredum habuit successorem.[107] Interim[g] rex Edmundus et ipse in Scotiam [h]cum exercitu tendens,[h] sancti Cuthberti suffragia postulaturus ad eius sepulchrum diuertit, et ut frater eius quondam Ethelstanus regalibus donis illud honorauit,

---

[a] Wendune F   [b-b] om. F   [c-c] Scottorum scilicet F   [d-d] et gloriosus inde F   [e] finiuit H   [f-f] anni regno H   [g] Post hec F   [h-h] tendens cum exercitu L

---

[104] Owain was king of Strathclyde (i.e. the Cumbrians) c.925–37; Constantine II was king of Scots 900–43. ASC, s.a. , and HReg (Arnold, Sym. Op. ii.124) state that Æthelstan made a combined military and naval expedition to Scotland in 934; and HReg adds the information that he ravaged as far as Dunnottar (presumably Dunnottar Castle just south of Stonehaven) and the unidentified Wertermorum, and that his fleet ravaged as far as Caithness. HReg, which is similar to The Chronicle of Melrose, ed. A. O. Anderson, M. O. Anderson, and W. C. Dickinson (London, 1936), p. 12, and JW, s.a. 934 (ii. 388–91), states that Æthelstan intervened in Scotland because King Constantine had broken his pledges, and that the latter was forced to give gifts and his son as a hostage. The pledges in question were presumably those made to Æthelstan by Constantine and King Owain of Strathclyde in 927; on this see A. P. Smyth, Warlords and Holy Men: Scotland AD 80–1000 (London, 1984), pp. 200–4. LDE is unique, however, in connecting Owain explicitly with the 934 campaign and in stating that both he and Constantine were put to flight.

[105] LDE's account of the Battle of Brunanburh is closest to the first annal for 937 in HReg (Arnold, Sym. Op. ii. 93): 'Ethelstanus rex apud Wendune pugnauit, regemque Onlafum cum DC. et XV. nauibus Constantinum quoque regem Scottorum, et regem Cumbrorum, cum omni eorum multitudine in fugam uertit.' The date 937 is correct, and Æthelstan's principal opponent was indeed Olaf, son of King Guthfrith of Dublin, who succeeded his father at Dublin in 934 and also became king of York in 939. See e.g.

Scotland with a land army and a naval force in order to make it subject to him.[104]

In the fourth year after this (that is the year 937 of Our Lord's Nativity), at *Weondune* which is called by another name *Æt Brunnanwerc* or *Brunnanbyrig*, he fought against Olaf, son of the former king Guthred, who had come against Æthelstan with 615 ships and had with him the help of the aforesaid kings, that is of the Scots and the Cumbrians. But Æthelstan trusted in the protection of St Cuthbert, and laid low an infinite multitude, driving those kings from his kingdom and bringing back to his people a glorious triumph.[105] To his enemies everywhere he was fearsome, but he was peaceful towards his own people, and he afterwards ended his life in peace, leaving the rule of his empire to his brother Edmund.[106]

In the third year of his reign Wigred died after being bishop for seventeen years, and Uhtred was his successor.[107] Meanwhile King Edmund also marched on Scotland with an army, and he turned aside to the tomb of St Cuthbert to ask for the saint's intercession. As his brother Æthelstan had done before him he honoured it with royal gifts, namely with gold and palls, and he also confirmed the laws of

Stenton, *Anglo-Saxon England*, pp. 342–3; Smyth, *Scandinavian York and Dublin*, ii. 31–88. The site of the battle is unidentified. For a survey of the forms of the name preserved (that in *LDE* is unique to it) and possible identifications, see *The Battle of Brunanburh*, ed. A. Campbell (London, 1938), pp. 43–80, who concludes that the site cannot be identified. See also J. McN. Dodgson, 'The background of Brunanburh', *Saga Book of the Viking Society*, xiv (1953–7), 303–16, who favours Bromborough in the Wirral; Smyth, op. cit., ii. 41–55, who favours Bromwich between Bedford and Huntingdon; M. Wood, 'Brunanburh Revisited', *Saga Book of the Viking Society*, xx (1978–81), 200–17, who favours a location on Northumbria's southern frontier, possibly Brinsworth on the outskirts of Rotherham. The name *Weondune* is peculiar to *LDE* and *HReg*, and it may conceivably reflect the name *Vinheiðr* which is given to the battle in *Egil's Saga*, although that account is a very garbled one (*Brunanburh*, ed. Campbell, pp. 68–80, A. Campbell, *Skaldic Verse and Anglo-Saxon History* (London, 1971), pp. 5–7, and see Smyth, op. cit., ii. 49; for the text, *Egils Saga Skalla-Grímssonar*, ed. S. Nordal (Islenzk Fornrit 2; Reykjavík, 1933), i. 132; translation in *Egils Saga*, trans. C. Fell (London, 1975), p. 76).

[106] Æthelstan died on 27 Oct. 939 and his brother Edmund reigned from then until his murder on 26 May 946.

[107] This would be 941–2, which agrees with *LDE*'s earlier statement that Wigred became bishop in 925. *HReg* places the death of Wigred and the accession of Uhtred (whose name it spells *Getredus)* in its second annal for 941 (Arnold, *Sym. Op.* ii. 125). The length of Uhtred's episcopate is unknown, but Ealdred had succeeded him at some date before 948 (below, p. 141 n. 110).

auro scilicet et palliis, *a*leges quoque illius*b* sicut unquam meliores fuerant firmauit.*a* [108]

[xliv
(xlvii)]

19. Defuncto*c* autem Vhtredo episcopo, Sexhelm loco eius *d*est ordinatus,*d* sed uix *e*aliquot mensibus*e* in ecclesia residens, sancto Cuthberto illum expellente aufugit. Cum enim a uia predecessorum suorum aberrans, populum ipsius sancti[109] et eos qui in ecclesia eius seruiebant, auaritia succensus affligeret, exterritus a sancto per somnium iussus est quantotius abscedere.*f* Dum ille differret, secunda nocte uehementius eum increpans festinanter abire iussit, penam ei intentans si tardaret. Nec sic quidem ille obedire uoluit, cum ecce tertio multo quam ante seuerior illum aggreditur, et quam citius eum aufugere precepit, nec quicquam de rebus ecclesie secum asportare presumeret. Si aliquandiu tardaret, mortem*g* illi citius affuturam minabatur. Expergefactus de somno, cepit infirmari, et ne mortem mox incurreret, abire quamuis egrotans festinauit. Dum autem fugiens circa Eboracum uenisset, sanitatem recepit, pro quo Aldredus cathedram episcopalem conscendit.[110]

[(xlviii)]

20. Anno*h* ab Incarnatione Domini nongentesimo quadragesimo octauo Edmundo rege mortuo, frater eius Eadredus solium regni conscendit,[111] uir pietatis cultor et iustitie, qui etiam sicut et*i* fratres eius ecclesiam sancti Cuthberti regalibus donariis uisitauit. Mortuo autem Aldredo episcopo, Aelfsig pro eo ipsius ecclesie gubernacula in Cunecacestre*j* suscepit, ordinatus Eboraci ab Oscekillo archiepiscopo,

---

a–a leges illius ipse quoque uiolatores earum eterno dampnans anathemate firmauit *F*
b illi *Fx L Y*   *c* Sexhelm episcopus per sanctum Cuthbertum fugatus est *rubric Fx*
H T V Y   *d–d* ordinatus est *H*   *e–e* mensibus aliquot *T*   *f* discedere *Ca*
g om. T   *h* De consecratione Alduni primi episcopi Dunelmi (*om. Fx*) *rubric Fx T*
V Y   *i om. H*   *j* Cuncacestre *F*

---

[108] The information that Edmund led an expedition against Scotland is unique to *LDE*, but *ASC, s.a.*, *HReg* (Arnold, *Sym. Op.* ii. 126), and *Chronicle of Melrose*, ed. Anderson, p. 13, mention that he ravaged Strathclyde in 945 and gave it to King Constantine as a fief. This operation is mentioned briefly in Welsh sources (Anderson, *Early Sources*, ii. 449). *LDE*'s source for Edmund's visit is clearly *HSC* c. 28 (Arnold, *Sym. Op.* i. 212), which reads: 'Eo [Æthelstano] defuncto Eadmundus frater eius in regnum successit, magnum rursus exercitum congregauit, et in Scottiam properauit. In eundo tamen ad oratorium sancti Cuthberti diuertit, ante sepulchrum eius genua flexit, preces fudit, se et suos Deo et sancto confessori commendauit. Exercitus sexaginta libras obtulit; ipse uero manu propria duas armillas aureas et duo pallia Graeca, supra sanctum corpus posuit; pacem uero et legem quam unquam habuit meliorem, omni terre sancti Cuthberti dedit, datam

the saint so that they had greater force than they had ever had before.[108]

19. After the death of Bishop Uhtred, Sexhelm was ordained in his place, but he had hardly been resident in the church for a few months when St Cuthbert expelled him and he fled. When, turning aside from the ways of his predecessors and consumed with avarice, he had brought ruin to the people of the saint[109] and those who served in his church, he was terrified by the saint in a dream and ordered to depart summarily. Since he put off leaving, the saint rebuked him more vehemently on the second night and ordered him to go away in haste, threatening him with punishment if he delayed. As indeed he was not willing to obey, the saint set about him on the third night much more severely than before, and instructed him to flee immediately and not to presume to take with him any of the possessions of the church. If he delayed any longer, he threatened that death would soon come to him. Awoken from sleep he began to grow ill, and so that he should not shortly suffer death, he hastened to leave, ill as he was. When in the course of his flight he arrived at York, he recovered his health. Aldred ascended the episcopal throne in his place.[110]

20. In the year of Our Lord's Incarnation 948, after King Edmund's death his brother Eadred ascended the throne of the kingdom.[111] He was a man of piety and a lover of justice, and like his brothers visited the church of St Cuthbert bringing royal gifts. After Bishop Aldred's death, Ælfsige took over the government of the church in Chester-le-Street in his place, being ordained at York by Archbishop

confirmauit.' Note that F's wording is farther removed from this. On the possibility of identifying one of Edmund's gifts, see above, p. 137 n. 103.

[109] On the significance of this term, see above, p. 114 n. 66.

[110] Neither the date of Uhtred's death nor those of Sexhelm's pontificate are known. Sexhelm should not be confused with the simoniac Eadred (above, p. 22 n. 12). Note the similarity of the miracle described here to that described in connection with the expulsion from Durham of the tax-gatherer Ranulf (below, pp. 196–9). The date of Ealdred's accession is not known, but Symeon presumably believed it to have occurred before 948, since he assigns the death of King Edmund to that year in the immediately following passage.

[111] The death of Edmund is recorded *s.a.* 948 in ASC E and in the first entry for that year in *HReg* (Arnold, *Sym. Op.* ii. 94), but other versions of ASC, JW (ii. 398–9), and the second series of annals for the 10th cent. in *HReg* (Arnold, *Sym. Op.* ii. 126) assign it to 946, which appears to be correct. On this chronology, Eadred reigned 946–55. He led an expedition to Northumbria in 948 (ASC D) or in 950 (*HReg* (Arnold, *Sym. Op.* ii. 94, 126–7)), but no other source mentions a visit to Chester-le-Street.

tempore Eadgari regis qui *fratri Eadwio* in regnum successerat.
Transactis autem in episcopatu suo uiginti duobus annis Aelfsig
defunctus est, pro quo electus est et consecratus episcopus uir
eximie religionis Aldhunus, anno ab Incarnatione Domini nongentesimo nonagesimo,*b* qui est *duodecimus annus* imperii *Aethelredi
regis,* qui post mortem fratris Edwardi fraude nouerce sue
miseranda nece perempti, sceptrum regnandi obtinuit.[112] Erat
autem idem antistes prosapia nobilis, sed placita Deo conuersatione
multo nobilior, habitu sicut omnes predecessores eius *et actu*
probabilis monachus. Cuius probitatis laudem a maioribus sibi
traditam indigene pene omnes ac si eum hodie uiderent, predicare
solent.[113]

---

a–a fratri Eadwino *T V;* Eadwio fratri *Ca*   *b* om. *Y (ins. over line Fx)*
c–c annus duodecimus *H*   *d–d* regis Ethelredi *Ca*   *e–e* om. *Y (ins. over line Fx)*

---

[112] Osketel, archbishop of York (956–71); Edgar, king of England (957–75), Æthelred,
king of England (978–1016). The information given here suggests that Ælfsige became
bishop in 968. The accession of Bishop Ealdhun in 990 is found also in *HReg, s.a.* (Arnold,

Osketel, in the time of King Edgar who had succeeded his brother
Eadwig to the kingdom. After he had spent twenty-two years as
bishop, Ælfsige died and in his place was elected and consecrated as
bishop Ealdhun, a man distinguished by his religion. This was in the
year of Our Lord's Incarnation 990, which was the twelfth year of the
reign of King Æthelred, who obtained the sceptre of the kingdom
after the death of his brother Edward who was put to death miserably
by the treachery of his stepmother.[112] This bishop was of noble stock,
but he was even nobler in the life he led which was pleasing to God,
and he was a worthy monk by his habit (as were all his predecessors)
and by his actions. Almost all the native inhabitants are accustomed to
praise his uprightness, of which they have learned from the traditions
of their ancestors, as if he were still among them today.[113]

Sym. Op. ii. 134); but, for the possibility that there has been chronological confusion, see
below, p. 144 n. 1.

[113] For the significance for Symeon's own day of *LDE*'s claim that Ealdhun and all his
predecessors were monks, and for that of his reliance on the oral traditions of his own time,
traditions which presumably derived ultimately from the pre-1083 clerks of Durham, see
above, pp. lxxxii–lxxxvi and lxxvi.

[xlv (xlix)] 1. Anno[a] autem ab Incarnatione Domini nongentesimo nonagesimo quinto, imperii uero [b]regis Ethelredi[b] septimo decimo, idem antistes incipiente iam accepti[c] presulatus sexto anno, celesti premonitus oraculo ut cum incorrupto sanctissimi patris corpore quantotius fugiens superuenturam [d]pyratarum rabiem[d] declinaret, tulit illud centesimo [e]tertio decimo[e] anno ex quo in Cunecacestre locatum fuerat, et inde cum omni qui eius dicitur populo in Hripum transportauit.[1] In qua fuga illud memorabile[f] fertur, quod in tanta multitudine nemo a minimo usque ad maximum ulla infirmitatis molestia affligebatur, sed sine ullo labore, sine ullo incommodo uiam gradiendo peragebant. Nec solum homines sed etiam[g] animalia tenera et nuper quoque nata (erat enim tempus ueris) sana et incolumia sine aliqua[h] difficultate et uexatione toto itinere gradiebantur.

Post tres autem uel quattuor menses pace reddita, cum uenerandum corpus ad priorem locum reportarent, iamque prope Dunhelmum ad orientalem plagam in locum qui Wrdelau dicitur aduenissent,[2] uehiculum quo sacri corporis theca ferebatur, ulterius promoueri non poterat.[i] Accedunt plures, sed nil quanuis multum laborantes proficiunt. Quibus adhuc multo plures coniunguntur, sed illud mouere nequaquam ualebant. Itaque incorrupti corporis theca, ueluti mons quidam mansit immota.[3] Quo facto omnibus aperte clarebat, quod ad eum ubi prius fuerat locum se transportari nollet;

---

[a] Aldunus episcopus cum corpore sancti Cuthberti fugam iniit *rubric Fx H T V Y*; Liber Tertius *Ca marg.*   [b-b] Ethelredi regis *Ca*   [c] *om. H*   [d-d] rabiem pyratarum *L*   [e-e] xiii *over erasure C*; quinto decimo *F*   [f] memoriale *L Y*   [g] *om. H*   [h] *om. Ca (signe de renvoi in marg.)*   [i] potuit *Ca*

---

[1] The chronological indications given here for the move of the Community of St Cuthbert to Durham are consistent with a date of 995, although it should be noted that C's '113th year' is written over erasure and F has '115th year'. For the dates of Ealdhun's accession and the establishment of the see at Chester-le-Street, see above, pp. 122–3 and n. 78). *HReg*, *s.a.* 995 (Arnold, *Sym. Op.* ii. 136), has simply: 'Aldunus episcopus transtulit de Cestre in Dunholm corpus Sancti Cuthberti'; and JW ii. 444–7 notes in the course of a marginal excursus on the history of Lindisfarne that the see was transferred to Durham in 995. No other source mentions a threatened Viking attack in that year. ASC, *s.a.*, 993 records a Viking sack of Bamburgh and ravaging of Lindsey and Northumbria. For the possibility that the date of the move was in fact 992 and that the chronology has been confused by a three-year vacancy prior to Ealdhun's accession, see J. Cooper, 'The dates of the bishops of Durham in the first half of the 11th cent.', *Durham University Journal*, lx (1968), 131–7, at pp. 133–4. In seeking to explain why the community moved to Ripon, Aird, *Cuthbert*, p. 45 n. 131, draws attention to Cuthbert's connection with the

1. Now, in the year of our Lord 995, that is in the seventeenth year of [xlv (xlix)]
the reign of King Æthelred, the said bishop, who was then entering
the sixth year of the episcopal office which he had accepted, was
forewarned by a heavenly premonition that he should flee as quickly
as possible with the incorrupt body of the most holy father Cuthbert,
to escape the fury of the Vikings whose arrival was imminent.
Accordingly he raised that body in the 113th year since it had been
brought to Chester-le-Street and, accompanied by all those people
who are called the 'people of the saint', he transported it to Ripon.[1] It
is related that one very memorable circumstance about the flight was
that in all that multitude no one from the lowest to the highest was
afflicted by any scourge of illness, but instead the whole party
completed their journey with neither suffering nor inconvenience.
It was not only men but also young and even new-born animals (for it
was springtime) who accomplished the whole journey safe and sound
and without any difficulty or hardship.

When three or four months later peace had returned, they were
taking the venerable body back to its former resting place, and they
had reached a place called *Wrdelau*, which is near Durham on the east
side,[2] the cart on which they were carrying the coffin containing the
holy body could be moved no further. Many came to help but,
although they laboured mightily, still the cart could not be moved.
Even when many others added their strength, they were unable to
budge it at all, and so the coffin of the incorrupt body remained as
immoveable as a mountain.[3] This occurrence clearly revealed to all
that the saint did not wish to be taken back to his former resting place;

place (Bede, *V.Cuth.* c. 7), and speculates that only the religious community made the
move. On the significance of the term *eius populo* ('the people of St Cuthbert'), see above,
p. 114 n. 66.

[2] A marginal note in F gives this place as Bearpark, but this is not a possible
identification since Bearpark lies west of Durham. The place-name *Wrdelau* has not
survived in an appropriate location, but the place is traditionally identified with Mountjoy,
just to the south-east of Durham city; see *VCH Durham*, ii. 8. It should be noted, however,
that this place is not 'in the middle of a plain' as *LDE* subsequently states (below, pp. 146–
7). J. Raine, *St Cuthbert, with an Account of the State in which his Remains were found upon
the Opening of his Tomb in Durham Cathedral, in the year 1827* (Durham, 1828), p. 55 n.,
suggested Wardley (parish of Jarrow); see Aird, *Cuthbert*, p. 45 n. 133.

[3] This story is a hagiographical topos. Cf. similar accounts of the Kentish saints
Æthelberht and Æthelred, and of St Alchmund of Hexham (Arnold, *Sym.Op.* ii. 9–10, 49).
The last of these may be in deliberate imitation of *LDE's* account of Cuthbert.

quo autem transferre deberent, ignorabant. Nam ubi tunc fuerant medio scilicet in campo, locus erat inhabitabilis. Alloquens ergo populum[4] episcopus, precepit ut omnes simul per triduum ieiunio*a* uigiliis ac*b* precibus celestis ostensionem indicii expeterent, quo cum sacro patris corpore diuertere deberent. Quo*c* facto,*d* cuidam religioso nomine Eadmero reuelatum est, ut in Dunhelmum illud transferre, ibidemque requiescendi sedem debuissent preparare.

[xlvi]   Qua*e* reuelatione omnibus patefacta, releuati gaudio gratias cuncti egerunt Christo, moxque accedentes paucissimi corporis *f*sancti loculum*f* leuarunt, quod tota prius multitudo nec mouere poterat. Itaque ad locum celitus ostensum (uidelicet Dunhelmum) cum letitia et laude corpus sanctum detulerunt, factaque citissime de uirgis ecclesiola, ibidem illud ad tempus locarunt.[5]

[xlvii (l)]   Ex*g* his autem*h* qui tunc *i*cum sancti confessoris*i* corpore in hunc locum conuenerant, erat quidam uocabulo Riggulfus, qui omne tempus uite sue ducentos et decem annos habuerat, quorum quadraginta in monachico habitu ante mortem duxerat. Erat autem nepos Franconis, qui (ut superius dictum est) unus erat de septem qui uenerandum patris corpus indiuiduo comitatu sunt secuti. Franco quippe pater*j* erat Reingualdi, a quo illa*k* quam condiderat uilla Reiningtun est appellata. Reingualdus uero pater extitit Riggulfi, cuius filius Ethric, ex cuius Ethrici filia progenitus est presbiter*l* Alchmundus, pater eius qui nunc usque superest Elfredi.[6] Huius Franconis socius erat (ut supra dictum est) Hunred, cuius filius*m* *n*Eadulf, cuius filius*n* Eadred fuerat, qui ut fertur sex annis ante finem uite extra ecclesiam nunquam *o*loqui poterat,*o* cum in ecclesia nemo ad cantandum uel psallendum expeditior et promptior esse potuisset. Fuerant nonnulli qui hoc ei propterea putauerant euenisse, ut nulla

---

a ieuniis *Fx L Y*   *b* et *H*   *c* Corpus sancti Cuthberti Dunhelmum delatum est *rubric Fx V Y*   *d* facto autem *Fx L Y*   *e* Corpus sancti Cuthberti Dunhelmum delatum est *rubric H*   *f-f* loculum sancti *T*   *g* Genealogia eorum qui corpus sancti Cuthberti Dunhelmum tulerunt *rubric Fx H T (s. xiv) V Y*   *h* om. *T*   *i-i* confessoris sancti cum *T*   *j* om. *F*   *k* om. *H*   *l* om. *F*   *m* om. *Y*; *ins. over line Fx*   *n-n* om. *H*   *o-o* poterat loqui *Fx L*

[4] On the significance of the term *populus* ('the people of St Cuthbert'), see above, p. 114 n. 66.

[5] Although there is no evidence for an earlier church on the peninsula at Durham, it is possible that St Oswald's in Elvet just across the river Wear was already in existence; and it is even possible that it was an episcopal residence associated with an admittedly undocumented pre-Viking royal site on the peninsula of Durham (see E. Cambridge, 'Archaeology and the cult of St Oswald in Pre-Conquest Northumbria', in *Oswald: Northumbrian King*, ed. Cambridge and Stancliffe, pp. 128–63, at 148–54).

but they did not know to what place he did wish to be taken. For the place where they were, which was in the middle of a plain, was uninhabitable. So the bishop spoke to the people[4] and ordered that everyone together should with three days of fasting, prayers, and vigils beseech the manifestation of a heavenly sign to indicate where they were to take the holy body of the father. When this had been done, it was revealed to a certain religious man called Eadmer that they should translate the body to Durham, and there prepare a resting place for it.

When this revelation had been made known to everyone, they were [xlvi] elated with joy and all gave thanks to Christ. At once they went to the coffin of the holy body and now just a very few of them were able to lift it, whereas before the whole assembly had been unable even to move it. So with rejoicing and praise they took the holy body to the place revealed to them by heaven, that is Durham, and there they quickly made a little church of branches, and in it they placed the body for the time being.[5]

Amongst those who came to Durham at that time with the body of [xlvii (l)] the holy confessor was a certain man called Riggulf, who lived for 210 years, the last forty of which he spent as a monk. Now, he was the grandson of Franco who (as noted above) was one of the seven who followed the father's venerable body in inseparable companionship. In point of fact, Franco was the father of Reinguald, after whom was named the vill of Rainton, which he had founded. It was Reinguald who was the father of Riggulf, whose son Ethric had a daughter who became the mother of the priest Alchmund, the father of that Elfred who is still alive.[6] As stated above, Franco was a companion of Hunred, whose son Eadwulf had a son called Eadred, of whom it is said that for the last six years of his life he was never able to speak outside the church, although inside the church no one could have been readier and prompter to sing or to recite psalms. Several people thought that this had happened to him so that his tongue, which he

---

[6] *LDE* is the only source of information about this family, apart from the reference in Reginald of Durham (below, p. 148 n. 7), and its appearance here implies that the author had good contacts with the families of the pre-1083 clerks of Durham (on which, see above, p. lxxxiii). The age of Riggulf must of course be apocryphal. The identification of *Reiningtun* with Rainton just to the east of Durham rather than with Rennington north of Alnwick in Northumberland seems more plausible on topographical grounds, although both are possible in terms of etymology; see E. Ekwall, *Concise Dictionary*, *s.u.*, and A. Mawer, *The Place-Names of Northumberland and Durham* (Cambridge, 1920), pp. xxvi, 162, 165, who favours Rennington.

inutili uel noxia locutione illius lingua macularetur, que tam*a* studiose in precibus et psalmodia exercebatur. Huius Eadredi filius erat Collanus, *b*cuius filius Eadred, cuius filius Collanus,*b* ex cuius sorore progeniti sunt Eilafus, et qui *c*usque hodie*c* supersunt Hemmingus et Wlfkillus presbiteri.[7] De his tantum dixisse sufficiat; nunc ad ea unde digressus est sermo redeat.

[(li)] **2.** Comitans*d* sanctissimum patris Cuthberti corpus uniuersus populus in Dunhelmum, locum quidem natura munitum sed non facile habitabilem inuenit, quoniam densissima undique silua totum occupauerat. Tantum in medio planicies erat *e*non grandis,*e* quam arando et seminando excolere consueuerant, ubi episcopus Aldhunus non paruam de lapide postea ecclesiam erexit, sicut in consequentibus apparebit.[8] Igitur prefatus antistes*f* totius populi auxilio, et comitis Northanhymbrorum Vhtredi adiutorio totam extirpans siluam*g* succidit, ipsumque locum in breui habitabilem fecit.[9] Denique a flumine Coqued usque*h* Tesam*i* uniuersa populorum multitudo tam ad hoc opus quam ad construendam postmodum ecclesiam prompto animo accessit, et donec perficeretur deuota insistere non cessauit.[10] Eradicata itaque silua, et unicuique mansionibus sorte distributis, presul antedictus, amore Christi et sancti Cuthberti feruens, ecclesiam honesto nec paruo opere inchoauit, et ad perficiendam omni studio

---

a om. H   *b-b* om. Y; add. over line Fx   *c-c* nunc usque Ca   *d* De constructione ecclesie Dunelmensis *rubric* Fx T V Y   *e-e* permodica F *f* om. H   *g* siluas T   *h* usque ad Ca T   *i* Teisam F

---

[7] The names of the bearers were known to Reginald of Durham, who was familiar with other traditions about them, notably concerning their various roles in the story of the finding of bridle, horse, and cart (see above, pp. 118–19) which led to Stitheard being surnamed *Rap* (rope), another bearer *Coite* (horse), and Hunred *Cretel* (which meant cart according to Reginald). In addition, Reginald told a story about Eilaf, who is supposed to have been a bearer and to have stolen some cheese, a crime revealed by the appearance of a vixen—hence Eilaf's surname *Tod* (fox). See Raine, *Cuth. virt.*, pp. 25–9. The development of these stories by Reginald's time in the 1160s seems to corroborate *LDE's* statement (above, pp. 116–17) that the families of the bearers took pride in their ancestors' roles. Their status is confirmed by Reginald's information that the descendants of one of the bearers held Bedlington in his time, as well as his information about the presence among them of Eilaf, and also by *LDE's* account of how a descendant of Franco founded the vill of Rainton (above). Hunred may have been the founder of the hereditary priests of Hexham, one of the family names of which was Eilaf (Hall, 'Community of St Cuthbert', pp. 109–12, and *Priory of Hexham*, ed. Raine, i. Appendix IV). The story of Eadred's dumbness is unique to *LDE*. Hemming and Wulfkill appear as priests respectively of Sedgefield and Brancepeth in the possibly authentic witness list of a purported confirmation of Bishop William of St Calais relating to 27 Apr. 1085 (Offler, *Episcopal Charters*, no. 5, pp. 41–5). See also Aird, *Cuthbert*, pp. 116–17, 119, 121.

used so assiduously for prayers and psalms, should not be defiled by pointless or harmful speech. The son of this Eadred was Collan, who had a son called Eadred, the father of another Collan, whose sister was the mother of Eilaf and of two priests who are still alive today, Hemming and Wulfkill.[7] Now, however, we have said enough about these things, so let us return to the narrative from which we digressed.

2. All of the people who accompanied the most holy body of father [(li)] Cuthbert to Durham found there a place which, although it possessed natural defences, was not easily habitable because it was completely covered on all sides by very dense forest. Only in the middle was there a piece of level ground and this was not large. At first they were accustomed to cultivate this by ploughing and sowing, but later Bishop Ealdhun built a stone church of some size on it, as will appear subsequently in our account.[8] So the aforesaid bishop, with the help of all the people and assistance of Uhtred, earl of the Northumbrians, cut down and uprooted the whole forest and soon made the place habitable.[9] Later, a multitude of people from the whole area between the river Coquet and the river Tees readily came to help not only with this task but also afterwards with the construction of the church, and they persevered devotedly until it was finished.[10] When the forest had been cleared and dwellings assigned to each by lot, Bishop Ealdhun, burning with love for Christ and St Cuthbert, began to build a church of noble workmanship and by no means small in

---

[8] The cross-reference is to pp. 148–51, below.

[9] The area referred to is presumably the peninsula in an incised meander of the river Wear on which Durham stands. It is not clear whether this passage means that the community itself was cultivating the central area of the peninsula (which is the meaning given to this translation) or whether it had been cultivated before their arrival as might be implied by the use of the pluperfect tense in the original Latin. See M. O. H. Carver, 'Early medieval Durham: the archaeological evidence,' *Medieval Art and Architecture at Durham Cathedral*, ed. N. Coldstream and P. Draper (British Archaeological Association Conference Transactions for 1977, 1980), pp. 11–12. The participation of Uhtred in the clearing of the site is made more comprehensible by reference to the late 11h- or early 12th-cent. text *De obsessione Dunelmi*, in which Uhtred, son of Earl Waltheof I of Bamburgh, is said to have been made earl as a result of his successful defence of Durham against the Scots and to have married the daughter of Bishop Ealdhun. For the text, see Arnold, *Sym.Op.* i. 215–20, and for a translation and commentary see Morris, *Marriage and Murder*. On the significance of the term *populus* ('the people of St Cuthbert'), see above, p. 114 n. 66.

[10] The significance of the river Coquet as a boundary in this connection is not clear, except that Warkworth and Bedlington, both ancient possessions of the church of St Cuthbert, lay south of it, Warkworth on the south bank itself (cf. above, pp. 78–9).

intendit. Interea sanctum corpus de illa (quam superius diximus) ecclesiola in aliam translatum que Alba Ecclesia uocabatur, tribus ibidem annis dum maior ecclesia construeretur requieuit.[11]

[xlviii (lii)]   3. Vbi[a] autem prius iacuerat, miracula coruscare, et infirmi sanitatem ceperunt recuperare. Transacto nanque tempore non paruo, quedam femina de natione Scottorum, toto corpore ab infantia debilis Dunhelmum fuerat perducta, cuius miserie nemo tam inhumanus qui non posset condolere. Pedes nanque et crura post tergum retorta post se trahebat, atque ita manibus reptando de loco ad locum se miseranda ferebat. Contigit autem ut ad prefatum locum ubi sanctissimum corpus paucis diebus requieuerat, miserabilis illa se trahendo perueniret. Vbi se in suum officium retorquentibus neruis, subito illa exilire cepit et rursus ad terram cadere, et clamore uniuersos perturbare, que post paululum erecta, pedibus suis sanissima constitit, et saluatori suo Christo per intercessionem beati[b] Cuthberti gratiarum actiones retulit. Hoc audito ciuitas tota festinat ad ecclesiam, signa pulsantur, clerus *Te Deum laudamus* personat, populus suis uocibus in laudem Dei concrepat, Cuthbertum uere magnum et Deo dilectum predicat. Illa uero que sanata fuerat, per multas regiones ac nationes discurrit et iter omne pedes incedendo peregit. Nam et Romam gratia orationis adiit, et inde reuertens in Hiberniam profecta est, omnibus perfactum in se miraculum Dei gloriam, et eius dilecti confessoris [c]sanctitatis ubique predicans excellentiam.[c] Hoc sane ita factum quemadmodum descripsimus, a quibusdam presbiteris qui uiderunt religiosis et etate prouectis et omnino simplicibus frequenter audiuimus.[12]

---

[a] De miraculis factis in parua ecclesia ubi sanctus Cuthbertus post (prius *Fx T V Y*) iacuit *rubric Fx H T V Y*   [b] sanctissimi *H*; sancti *Ca Fx L T Y*   [c-c] *om. L*

---

[11] *LDE* probably means that this White Church, which has not previously been mentioned, was built by Ealdhun after the construction of the wooden church. On the other hand, it could have been St Oswald's in Elvet (above, p. 146 n. 5) or some other pre-existing church on or near the peninsula of Durham. Reginald of Durham seems to have regarded the pre-Conquest cathedral itself as the White Church but this does not seem to be consistent with *LDE*, although of course the appellation may have been transferred to the pre-Conquest cathedral in the course of the 12th cent. (Raine, *Cuth. virt.*, c. 16 (p. 29)). The late 16th-cent. monk of Durham who wrote *The Rites of Durham* solved the problem by regarding the White 'Chapel' as part of the cathedral church which Ealdhun was building; see *The Rites of Durham*, ed. J. T. Fowler (SS cvii, Durham, 1903), pp. 71–2. Note the inference that the clerks had separate dwellings and did not live in common.

scale, and to the completion of this he devoted all his efforts. Meanwhile the holy body was translated from that little church (which we mentioned above) into another which was called the White Church, and there it remained for three years while the larger church was being built.[11]

3. At the place where it had formerly rested, however, miracles [xlviii (lii)] began to be manifested and the sick to be cured. Now after some considerable time had passed, there was brought to Durham a certain woman of the Scottish nation, who had been crippled in her whole body since childhood, and whose misery was such that no one could have been so inhuman as not to sympathize with it. For she dragged after herself her feet and legs which were twisted against her back, and so she moved pitifully from place to place by crawling on her hands. One day it happened that this miserable woman managed by dragging herself in this way to reach that place where the most holy body had remained for a few days. There her sinews twisted themselves back to their proper function, and suddenly she began to leap up, only to fall again to the ground, and to disturb everyone with her cries. After a short time, however, she stood erect on her feet, completely healed, and she gave thanks to her saviour Christ for the intercession of the blessed Cuthbert. As soon as they heard of this, everyone in the city hurried to the church, the bells were rung, the clergy chanted the *Te Deum laudamus*, the people let their voices resound in praise of God, and proclaimed Cuthbert to be truly great and beloved of God. The woman who had been cured travelled through many regions and nations and accomplished the whole journey on foot. In fact, she went to Rome in order to pray and she returned from there to Ireland, and everywhere the miracle which had been performed for her proclaimed to everyone the glory of God and the excellence of the sanctity of his beloved confessor. We have truly described how this miracle occurred just as we have often heard it from certain devout and entirely trustworthy priests who saw it and who are now advanced in age.[12]

[12] On the foundation of Lindisfarne, see above, pp. 20–1 and nn. The absence of any reference to monks in connection with this miracle shows that it pre-dates the establishment of the cathedral priory in 1083. It therefore provides further evidence of Symeon's contacts with the pre-1083 community. It must also have pre-dated the exclusion of women from places connected with the saint (above, pp. 104–7 and nn.).

[(liii)] **4.** Verum*ᵃ* ut ad superiora*ᵇ* sermo redeat, uenerandus antistes Aldhunus ecclesiam tercio ex quo eam fundauerat anno pridie Nonas Septembris solenniter dedicauit, cunctisque gaudentibus et Deum collaudantibus sanctissimi patris Cuthberti incorruptum corpus in locum quem parauerat*ᶜ* translatum *ᵈ*debito cum honore*ᵈ* locauit. Taliter usque in*ᵉ* presens cum sancto corpore sedes episcopalis hoc in loco permansit, que a rege quondam Oswaldo et pontifice Aidano primitus in insula Lindisfarnensi fuerat instituta. A quo anno scilicet quo Aidanus in ipsa insula cathedram conscenderat pontificalem usque annum quo Aldhunus eandem in Dunhelmo ascenderat, trecenti sexaginta unus, a transitu uero patris Cuthberti trecenti nouem, computantur anni.¹³ Igitur antistes uehementer cum uniuerso populo huius loci habitatione delectatus exultauit, ubi omnipotens Deus famuli sui corpus requiescere uoluit, atque uoluntatem suam (sicut supradictum est) signi *ᶠ*ostensione manifestauit*ᶠ* et reuelatione. Erat sane idem episcopus multe religionis et humilitatis, uerbo et actu bonis hominibus amabilis.

Fuerunt per id temporis plurimi qui diuersa dona in ornamentum ecclesie, et ad sufficientiam inibi sancto confessori ministrantium terras contulerunt, inter quos unus ex nobilibus uocabulo Styr filius Vlfi a rege Ethelredo impetrauit, ut Dearningtun*ᵍ* cum suis appendiciis sancto Cuthberto donaret, atque coram rege et presentibus archiepiscopo Eboracensi Wlstano et episcopo Dunhelmensi Aldhuno et *ʰ*aliis principalibus*ʰ* uiris qui cum rege Eboracum conuenerant ita hoc donum firmatum est, ut qui sancto Cuthberto auferret, eterno anathemate dampnaretur. Alias quoque terras supradictus uir adiecit, quas alibi descriptas pagina ostendit.¹⁴ *His donariis alias terras eterno*

ᵃ De dedicacione ecclesie Dunelmensis *rubric Fx V Y*; De dedica . . . *rubric T*
ᵇ ecclesie *add. L*   *ᶜ* preparauerat *F*   *ᵈ⁻ᵈ* cum honore debito *T*   *ᵉ om. T*
ᶠ⁻ᶠ manifestauit ostensione *T*   *ᵍ* Derlingtonam *Fx;* Derlyngton *L;* Dearlingtun *T*
ʰ⁻ʰ hiis *T*

---

¹³ The date 4 Sept. is assigned to the 'translation of St Cuthbert' in a number of pre-1100 calendars; see e.g. *English Kalendars before AD 1100*, ed. F. Wormald (Henry Bradshaw Society, lxxii; London, 1934, repr. Woodbridge, 1988), nos. 1, 6, 7–16, 18–20. Since the manuscript which preserves the first of these, Bod. Lib., Digby 63, dates to the late 9th cent., however, 4 Sept. originally represented an earlier translation of the saint's body, perhaps to Norham in the early 9th cent. or to Chester-le-Street in 883; see above p. 92 n. 33 and pp. 122–3, and Rollason, in Bonner, *Cuthbert*, pp. 416–17 and references therein.

¹⁴ Wulfstan II was archbishop of York (1002–23); Ealdhun was bishop of Durham (990 × 5–1018); Æthelred was king of the English (978–1016). Styr, son of Ulf, is described in the *De obsessione Dunelmi* as a rich citizen of York and to have married his daughter to Earl Uhtred after the latter's separation from Ecgfrida, daughter of Bishop

4. Returning now to what we were describing earlier, the venerable [(liii)] Bishop Ealdhun solemnly dedicated the church on 4 September in the third year after he had founded it. While everyone rejoiced and praised God, he translated the incorrupt body of the most holy Cuthbert into the place which he had prepared for it and enshrined it there with due honour. In this way the episcopal see, which had been founded originally on the island of Lindisfarne by the former King Oswald and Bishop Aidan, has remained in this place until the present day in the presence of the holy body. From the year in which Aidan ascended his episcopal throne on that island to the year in which Ealdhun ascended the same throne in Durham are reckoned 361 years, that is 309 years from the death of St Cuthbert.[13] So the bishop and all the people rejoiced greatly, delighted to be inhabitants of this place where Almighty God wished the body of his servant to rest and made manifest his will (as described above) by a miraculous sign and revelation. This same bishop was truly very devout and humble, worthy of the love of all good men by his words and actions.

At that time there were many who gave various gifts for the decoration of the church, and lands for the sustenance of those who served the holy confessor in it. One of the most noble amongst these was Styr, son of Ulf, who obtained from King Æthelred permission to give to St Cuthbert Darlington with all its appurtenances, and in the presence of the king, Archbishop Wulfstan of York, Bishop Ealdhun of Durham, and other principal men who had assembled in York with the king, this gift was confirmed so that any who should take it from St Cuthbert should be condemned to eternal anathema. This same man added other lands which are recorded in writing elsewhere.[14] To these gifts Snaculf, son of Cytel, added further

Ealdhun (Arnold, *Sym.Op.* i. 216). *LDE's* source here and the record of other lands given to which it refers is presumably *HSC* c. 29 (Arnold, *Sym. Op.* i. 212–13), which preserves the summarized text of a charter by which Styr grants to Durham not only Darlington but also lands in High Coniscliffe (NZ 226 152), Cokerton (on the western outskirts of Darlington), Haughton-le-Skerne (NZ 31 20) and Ketton on the north-east (NZ 318 164), Normanby near Middlesborough (NZ 56 18), and Lumley near Chester-le-Street (NZ 297 492). For the identifications, I am very grateful to V. Watts. Hart, *Early Charters*, no. 130 (pp. 126–7), dates the gift to 1003 × 16 (on Styr, see his p. 360); see also E. Craster, 'The patrimony of St Cuthbert', *English Historical Review*, lxix (1954), 177–99, at p. 193. These places are also listed as gifts of Styr in *CMD* (Craster, 'Red book', p. 526), but there the gift of 'Dearningtun cum omnibus suis appendiciis' is attributed to King Æthelred. Darlington, Cokerton, and Haughton-le-Skerne appear in the 1183 survey of the lands of the bishop of Durham known as *Boldon Book* (*Boldon Book: Northumberland and Durham*, ed and trans. D. Austin (Chichester, 1982), pp. 56–63, with reference for criticism of the edition to H. S. Offler, 'Rereading Boldon Book', Offler, *North of the Tees*, no. XII).

iure possidendas Snaculf Cykelli filius superaddidit, scilicet Brydbyrig,[a]
Mordun, Socceburg,[b] Grisebi cum saca et socne.[15]

[xlix (liv)] *Sunt autem[c] nonnulle terrarum possessiones quas Aldhunus episcopus sui*
temporis comitibus Northanhymbrorum dum necessitatem paterentur, ad
tempus quidem prestitit, sed uiolentia comitum qui eis successerunt pene
omnes eas a dominio ecclesie[d] alienauit. [c]Quarum quedam hic nominatim
ponuntur: Gegenforde[f] quam Ecgredum episcopum superius[g] condi-
disse, sanctoque Cuthberto donasse superius[h] dictum[i] est, *Cueorn-*
ingtun,[j] [k]Sliddeuesse, Bereford, Stredford,[k] Lyrtingtun,[l] Marawuda,
Stantun, Stretlea,[m] Cletlinga,[n] Langadun, Mortun, Persebrige, [o]Alclit
duo, Copland,[o] Weardsetle,[p] Bincestre, Cuthbertestun, Ticcelea, Ediscum,
Wudetun, [q]Hunewic, Neowatun,[q] Helme. Hec omnia fuerant ecclesie que,
dum prestans indigentibus prerogaret beneficium, suarum rerum passa est
dampnum.[e][16]

[l (lv)] **5.** Anno[r] Incarnationis Dominice mille duodeuicesimo, Cnut regnum
Anglorum disponente, Northanhymbrorum populis per triginta
noctes cometa apparuit, que terribili presagio futuram prouincie

---

[a] Bradeberie *H*; Bradbiri *Fx L T;* Bradbyri *(first four letters over erasure) Y*
[b] Sockeburne *L;* Socceburn *Y*   [c] Aldhunus episcopus quasdam terras et uillas
quibusdam accomodauit que numquam ad ecclesiam redierunt *rubric Fx Y*   [d] *om. D*
[e-e] *om. Ca*   [f] Gayndforde *H*   [g] *om. F*   [h] *om. F T*   [i] scriptum *T*
[j] Cuerningtun *F*   [k-k] *om. H*   [l] *Stratford T*   [m] Gretham *corr. to* Stretlea
Fx; Gretham *L*   [n] Clethama *corr. to* Cletlinga *Fx;* Cleteham *H;* Cletham *L;* Cletlain
(altered) Y   [o-o] Alkelande duo Coplande *H;* Aldit Aukland *corr. to* Alclit duo
Copland *Fx;* Aldit, Aukland *L;* Alclit duo Auckland *(last word over erasure) Y*
[p] Wersetle *F*   [q-q] *om. L*   [r] Populus Northanimbrorum apud Carrum
interfectus est a Scotis *rubric Fx H T V Y*

---

[15] These estates and their donor are listed in *HSC* c. 30, but the sentence here is
verbally identical to *CMD* (Craster, 'Red book', p. 526). Hart, *Early Charters*, no. 131
(p. 127) dates the grant to 1003 × 16. Bradbury (NZ 317 282, possibly the Isle of Bradbury
a little to the west is meant) and Mordon (NZ 265 330) are to the north-east of Bishop
Auckland (co. Durham); Girsby (NZ 356 083) and Sockburn (348 072) are on the river
Tees to the south-east of Darlington (for identifications, V. Watts, pers. comm., but see
also Ekwall, *Concise Dictionary*, and Mawer, *Place-Names*). Only the Isle of Bradbury
appears as a possession of the church of Durham in later documents; it figures in *Boldon
Book* (*Boldon Book*, ed. Austin, p. 47).

[16] This chapter is taken, in large part verbatim (italicized in the Latin text) from
CMD (Craster, 'Red book', pp. 526–7). Cf. *HSC* c. 31 (Arnold, *Sym. Op.* i. 213), where
the earls in question are named as Æthelred, Northman, and Uhtred. As Hart has noted
(*Early Charters*, p. 323), only the last of these is readily identifiable as the earl of the
Northumbrians mentioned above (pp. 148–9), so the others may have been subordinates.
Northman appears in *Liber Vitae*, fo. 33[v] as the grantor of Escomb to Durham; and an
ealdorman of this name attested a charter of King Æthelred in 994 (Sawyer, *Anglo-Saxon*

estates to be held in perpetuity, namely Bradbury, Mordon, Sock-burn, and Girsby, with sake and soke.[15]

There are, however, several landed possessions which Bishop [xlix (liv)] Ealdhun transferred on a strictly temporary basis to the contemporary earls of the Northumbrians when they were in need, but the violence of the earls who succeeded them resulted in virtually all of them being alienated from the dominion of the church. Certain of these will be named here: Gainford which (as we noted above) Bishop Ecgred built and gave to St Cuthbert, Whorlton, Sledwich, Barford, Startforth, Lartington, Marwood, Stainton, Streatlam, Cleatham, Langton, Morton Tinmouth, Piercebridge, Bishop and West Auckland, Copeland, *Weardsetle*, Binchester, *Cuthbertestun*, Thickley, Escomb, Witton-le-Wear, Hunwick, Newton Cap, and Helmington. All these had belonged to the church which suffered loss of her possessions through granting benefices to indigent men.[16]

5. In the year of our lord 1018, while Cnut was ruling the kingdom of [l (lv)] the English, there appeared to the Northumbrian peoples a comet, which persisted for thirty nights, presaging in a terrible way the

---

Charters, no. 881; and S. Keynes, *An Atlas of Attestations in Anglo-Saxon Charters, c.670–1066* (Cambridge, 1995), table lxii(1)). See also Craster, *English Historical Review*, lxix (1954), 194–5. The cross-reference to the activities of Bishop Ecgred is to pp. 92–3. For the identifications of the places mentioned, I rely on V. Watts, pers. comm., but see also Ekwall, *Concise Dictionary*, and Mawer, *Place-Names*. Some lie in the valley of the river Tees between Darlington and Barnard Castle, from west to east: Stainton (NZ 070 186), Streatlam (NZ 082 199), Sledwich (NZ 095 150), Barford (NZ 103 178), Whorlton (NZ 108 148), Cleatham (NZ 118 188), Langton (NZ 168 195), Gainford (NZ 169 167), Barforth (NZ 161 168), Morton Tinmouth (NZ 188 212), and Piercebridge (NZ 210 155). Marwood (NZ 062 219) lies to the north-east of Barnard Castle, Startforth (NZ 04 16) to the north-east, Lartington (NZ 015 178) to the west. Around Bishop Auckland (NZ 210 290) and the valley of the river Wear lie: to the west, Witton-le-Wear (NZ 148 312), Escomb (NZ 189 301), Copeland (NZ 167 261), and West Auckland (NZ 183 265); to the north, Helmington (NZ 179 346), Hunwick (NZ 180 325), Binchester (NZ 209 312), and Newton Cap (NZ 202 305); to the south, ?West Thickley (NZ 222 250). Bishop Auckland itself was presumably at this time centred on the ancient South Church (NZ 217 285). It was apparently restored to Durham by King Cnut (below, pp. 166–9). *Weardsetle* and *Cuthbertestun* have not been identified. On Gainford, see above, p. 93 n. 35. For the place of these vills in the development of Durham's estates, see Craster, loc. cit. Gainford and the lands belonging to it formed the Balliol barony after the Conquest; but most of the lands around Bishop Auckland are recorded in *Boldon Book* as possessions of the bishop of Durham in 1183 (*Boldon Book*, ed. Austin, pp. 37, 39, 69, 71).

cladem premonstrauit.[17] Siquidem paulo post (id est post triginta dies) uniuersus a flumine Tesa usque[a] Twedam populus, dum contra infinitam Scottorum multitudinem apud Carrum dimicaret, pene totus cum natu maioribus suis interiit.[18] Episcopus audita populi sancti Cuthberti[19] miseranda nece, alto cordis dolore attactus grauiter ingemuit, et 'O[b] me', inquit, 'miserum! ut quid in hec tempora seruatus sum? An ideo huc usque uixi, ut tantam uiderem cladem populi? Iam in pristinum [c]sui statum[c] amplius terra non reformabitur. 'O', inquit, 'sanctissime, o dilecte Deo confessor Cuthberte! si quid [d]tibi unquam[d] placitum feci, nunc queso michi uicem repende. Illam dico uicem, ut tuo populo mortuo, non sim[e] [f]diutius ego[f] superstes.' Nec multo post consecutus est quod desiderans orauerat. Post paucos etenim[g] dies morbo correptus obiit, peractis in episcopatu uiginti nouem annis, quorum quinque in Ceastre, uiginti quattuor autem[h] in Dunhelmo transegit;[20] qui de ecclesia quam inceperat solam turrim occidentalem imperfectam reliquit, cuius perfectionem et dedicationem eius successor adimpleuit.[21]

[(lvi)]   **6.** Defuncto[i] Aldhuno episcopo, tribus pene[j] annis ecclesia pastorali destituebatur solatio.[22] Cuius longam destitutionem hi [k]qui in ea[k] fuerant moleste ferentes, facto in unum conuentu tractabant, quem ex

---

[a] usque ad *L*   [b] *om. H*   [c–c] statum sui *H*   [d–d] unquam tibi *Ca*
[e] *om. D*   [f–f] ego diutius *Ca T*   [g] *om. L*   [h] *om. T*   [i] De electione
Edmundi episcopi *rubric Fx T V Y*   [j] *om. H*   [k–k] in ea qui *V*

---

[17] According to Japanese and Korean sources, a large comet appeared on 3 Aug. 1018 which became more intense, according to the Japanese, on 13 Aug.; see Ho Peng Yoke, *Vistas in Astronomy 5* (Oxford, 1962), p. 182. European chroniclers also note the comet as having been visible in 1018, with Thietmar of Merseburg assigning to it a duration of fourteen days in August; see M. Pingré, *Cométographie ou traité historique et théorique des comètes* (Paris, 1783), i. 366–7. I am very grateful to F. R. Stevenson for these references and for his advice and help.

[18] Carham is just south of the river Tweed, about three miles above Coldstream (NT 798 385). For this passage, cf. *HReg, s.a.* 1018 (Arnold, *Sym. Op.* ii. 155–6): 'Aldunus episcopus Dunholmensis obiit. Ingens bellum apud Carrum gestum est inter Scottos et Anglos, inter Huctredum filium Waldef comitem Northymbrorum, et Malcolmum filium Cyneth regem Scottorum. Cum quo fuit in bello Eugenius Caluus rex Clutinensium.' Note that Ealdhun's death is there placed before the battle rather than after it as in *LDE*. The occurrence of the battle at Carham and the participation in it of King Malcolm is confirmed by a Scottish chronicle written before 1214 (Anderson, *Early Sources*, i. xlv–xlvi, 544). On the difficulties raised by the battle and its date, see B. Meehan, 'The siege of Durham, the battle of Carham and the cession of Lothian', *Scottish Historical Review*, lv (1976), 1–19; A. A. M. Duncan, 'The battle of Carham, 1018', *Scottish Historical Review*, lv (1976), 20–8; and Smyth, *Warlords and Holy Men*, pp. 233–7.

future devastation of the province.[17] For soon afterwards (that is after thirty days) the whole people between the River Tees and the river Tweed fought a battle at Carham against a countless multitude of Scots and almost all perished, including even their old folk.[18] When the bishop heard of the miserable death of the people of St Cuthbert,[19] he was stricken with deep sorrow of heart, and sighed, saying: 'O why—wretched as I am—was I spared to see these times? Have I lived up till now only to see such a massacre of the people? Now the land will never again be restored to its pristine state. O most holy Cuthbert, o confessor beloved of God! if I have ever done anything that was pleasing to you, now I beg you to make recompense to me. That recompense, I say, should be that now that your people are dead, I should myself live no longer.' Not long afterwards he obtained what he had desired and prayed for. For a few days later he succumbed to an illness and died, having been bishop for twenty-nine years, five of them spent in Chester-le-Street and the other twenty-four in Durham.[20] Of the church which he had begun, he left only the western tower unfinished, and the church was brought to completion and dedicated by his successor.[21]

6. After the death of Ealdhun, the church was for three years [(lvi)] without the care of a pastor.[22] Those who were members of the church found this long period of deprivation vexatious, and so they came together in a council to discuss whom from amongst

---

[19] On the significance of the term *populus sancti Cuthberti* ('the people of St Cuthbert'), see above, p. 114 n. 66.

[20] This calculation would suggest that Ealdhun's death occurred in 1019, but *LDE* (above) dates the Battle of Carham to 1018 and states that Ealdhun died a few days later. See Stenton, *Anglo-Saxon England*, p. 418 n. 2, and Cooper, *Durham University Journal*, lx (1968), 133–4.

[21] This west tower is mentioned in *HReg*, s.a. 1069 (Arnold, *Sym.Op.* ii. 186–7), as having been saved from the fire started by the killers of Earl Robert Cumin. Two towers are mentioned by Reginald in his description of the cathedral, which he erroneously calls the White Church (Raine, *Cuth. virt.* c. 16 (p. 29)). On the basis of these accounts the church has been compared to surviving churches at Dover and Norton near Stockton and has been interpreted as a cruciform building, with one tower at the west end and another over the crossing. See W. St John Hope, 'Notes on recent excavations in the cloister of Durham Abbey', *Proceedings of the Society of Antiquaries*, xxii (1901), pp. 416–23, A. W. Clapham, *English Romanesque Architecture before the Conquest* (Oxford, 1930), p. 88, and, more speculatively, H. D. Briggs, R. N. Bailey, and E. Cambridge, 'A new approach to church archaeology: dowsing, excavation and documentary research at Woodhead, Ponteland and the pre-Norman cathedral of Durham', *Archaeologia Aeliana*, 5th ser. xi (1983), 79–100.

[22] This vacancy might have been connected with Cnut's wish to increase his control over the church of Durham.

sese[a] ad episcopatum eligere possent. Et dum illorum unicuique durum esset mundi gaudia deserere, blandimenta seculi relinquere, uoluptates[b] abicere, graue erat ad suscipiendum sanctitatis officium consentire. Nam secundum instituta canonum non nisi ex eadem ecclesia pontifices eligi consueuerant, et nisi honeste ac religiose conuersationis esset, sedem sancti Aidani et sancti Cuthberti aliorumque[c] sanctorum episcoporum, nemo facile ausus fuerat conscendere.[23]

De hoc itaque illis conferentibus, superuenit ex eorum numero quidam bone actionis presbiter uocabulo Eadmundus, et unde agerent uel cur tam tristes essent requisiuit. Et cum didicisset quod de episcopi electione tractarent, iocose alloquens, 'Cur me', inquit, 'episcopum non eligitis?' At illi scientes eum uirum religiosum ac strenuum, iocum illius non iocose accipiebant, sed in eius electione omnes concorditer intendebant. Ipse autem primo putauit illos secum iocari, sed ubi [d]eos serio[d] agnouit agere grauiter tulit, seque in nullo tanto gradu dignum reclamauit. Illis uero ut hoc susciperet insistentibus, 'Ego', ait, 'omnino me non esse idoneum agnosco, uerumtamen Deo nichil impossibile scio, ipsius et sancti Cuthberti uoluntas ut de me fiat exoro.' Igitur cum ad tumbam sancti confessoris triduo precibus et ieuniis, sicut ante semper consueuerant, intentius orarent, ut quem [e]ad episcopatum uellet eligi aperto declararet indicio, religiosus quidam presbiter cum missam propter hoc ipsum indictam ad caput ipsius sancti[e] celebraret, in medio canone quasi de ipso patris sepulchro uocem audiuit, que tribus uicibus Eadmundum episcopum nominauit.

[li] Mox[f] presbiter genua suppliciter ante altare flexit, deinde se erigens nichilominus eandem uocem sicut[g] prius Eadmundum ter episcopum [h]nominantem audiuit.[h] Missa[i] peracta, quesiuit a diacono qui ad altaris sacrificium ei astiterat, utrumne aliquid inter ipsa misse secreta audisset. Respondens ille, 'Ter', inquit, 'nominari Eadmundum episcopum audiui, sed a quo uox illa facta fuerit scire non potui.' Presbiter ergo mirantibus et percunctantibus uniuersis, cur in canone contra morem ecclesie genua flexisset, rem cum diacono sicut erat aperuit. Tunc omnes pariter Deum in

[a] se Y (corr. to sese Fx)   [b] uoluptatem Y   [c] aliorum Y (corr. to aliorumque Fx)   [d–d] serio L; serio eos Fx Y   [e–e] om. Ca. (ad capud in marg.)   [f] De electione Edmundi episcopi rubric H   [g] quam F; sicut et H   [h–h] audiuit nominantem F   [i] Missa uero Fx L Y

themselves they could elect as bishop. Since it was hard for any of them to give up the joys of the world, to relinquish the charms of life, to eschew pleasures, it was difficult to find anyone willing to consent to assume an office of such sanctity. For according to the canonical institutes they had been accustomed to elect bishops from amongst none but members of the same church, and no one had dared lightly to accept the see of St Aidan, St Cuthbert, and the other saintly bishops, unless they were of honest and religious life.[23]

As they were thus discussing this matter, there arrived one of their number who was a priest of good bearing called Edmund, and he asked them what they were doing and why they were so sad. When he had learned that they were discussing the election of a bishop, he asked jokingly, 'Why do you not elect me as bishop?' Since they knew that he was a strenuous and religious man, they received seriously the suggestion which he had made in jest, and all unanimously resolved on his election. For his part, he at first thought that they were joking with him in their turn, but when he realized that they were in earnest he demurred and declared himself to be in no way worthy of such a position. When they insisted that he should receive it, he said: 'I acknowledge that I am in no way suitable, but since I also know that nothing is impossible for God, I pray that the will of God and St Cuthbert be done in my case.' So when, as had always previously been their custom, they had spent three days in diligent prayer and fasting at the tomb of the holy confessor, so that he might declare by a clear sign whom he wished to be elected as bishop, a certain devout priest, who was celebrating a mass devoted to this purpose at the head of the saint, heard in the middle of the canon a voice which seemed to be coming from the tomb of that father and which three times named Edmund as bishop.

At once the priest knelt in supplication before the altar, then rising [li] he still heard the same voice as before three times naming Edmund as bishop. When the mass was finished, he asked the deacon who had been assisting him in the sacrament of the altar, whether he had heard anything during the secret of the mass. He replied: 'Three times I heard Edmund named as bishop, but I could not tell from whom the voice came.' So when everyone wondered and asked why in the canon of the mass the priest had knelt contrary to the custom of the church, he and the deacon made known what had happened. Then everyone

---

[23] On *LDE's* attitude to the clerks of Durham, see Piper, in Bonner, *Cuthbert*, pp. 437–47; and M. Foster, 'Custodians of St Cuthbert: the Durham monks' views of their predecessors, 1083–*c*.1200', Rollason, *Anglo-Norman Durham*, pp. 53–65.

sancto Cuthberto collaudantes et gratias agentes, Eadmundum *ᵃ*rapiunt, et*ᵃ* ecclesie *ᵇ*gubernacula suscipere*ᵇ* compellunt. Hec sane de illius electione quidam *ᶜ*prouecta etate*ᶜ* presbiter solet referre, quemadmodum ab auo suo ipso scilicet diacono qui tunc euangelium ad missam legerat atque ipsam uocem audierat, sepius se audisse testatur.²⁴

Igitur Eadmundus multo cum honore ad regem Cnut deducitur, cuius electioni et ipse congaudens, solenniter eum ordinari precepit. At ille cathedram predecessorum suorum qui monachi fuerant, nullo modo se posse ascendere fatebatur, nisi illos et ipse monachico habitu indutus imitaretur. Quapropter religioso habitu suscepto, honorifice a Wulstano Eboracensi archiepiscopo apud Wintoniam episcopus consecratur, multumque ab ipso rege diligitur*ᵈ*²⁵ et honoratur.*ᵉ* Rediens autem*ᶠ* domum ad monasterium Burch diuertit, indeque postulans ab abbate accepit quendam monachum in ecclesiasticis officiis simul et regularis discipline obseruantia excellenter institutum,*ᵍ* qui ei semper indiuiduo comitatu adhereret, et monachice uite disciplinam edoceret. Vocabatur autem Aegelricus, qui postea eiusdem (hoc est Dunhelmensis) ecclesie fuerat*ʰ* episcopus. Igitur Eadmundus nobili prosapia oriundus, persona simul et conuersatione honorabilis, nemini de sua uita ullam praue suspicionis occasionem dederat, et*ⁱ* in ecclesie regimine ualde strenuum se exhibuerat. Ecclesie nanque hostibus et prauis quibusque multum erat metuendus, *ʲ*bonis uero*ʲ* omnibus humilis et amandus. Nulli potentum timoris causa adulabatur, nullius uiolentia res ecclesiasticas pessundari patiebatur.

[lii (lvii)] **7.** Sub*ᵏ* hoc antistite in ipsa ecclesia claruit quidam presbiter, qui piis et religiosis operibus magne apud sanctum Cuthbertum familiaritatis extiterat, uocabulo Elfredus,*ˡ* qui usque tempus Egelwini episcopi permansit. Erat in omnibus sancto Cuthberto deuotus, uir multum

---

ᵃ⁻ᵃ om. *Ca*   *ᵇ⁻ᵇ* suscipere gubernacula *Ca*   *ᶜ⁻ᶜ* prouecte etatis *Ca*
ᵈ diligibatur *Fx L; altered to* diligibatur *Y*   *ᵉ* honorabatur *Fx L*   *ᶠ* om. *H*
ᵍ instructum *L Y*   *ʰ* fuit *H*   *ⁱ* om. *H*   *ʲ⁻ʲ* bonisque *T*   *ᵏ* De
Alfredo larue *rubric H T V Y*; De Alfredo de Jarowe *rubric Fx*   *ˡ* filius Westou *add.*
C Ca Fx L Y

---

²⁴ On the importance of this sentence for demonstrating Symeon's links with the pre-1083 community at Durham, see Aird, *Cuthbert*, p. 120, and above, pp. lxxxi–lxxxii.
²⁵ Wulfstan II was archbishop of York from 1002 to 1023, which is consistent with Edmund becoming bishop of Durham three years after Ealdhun's death, i.e. in 1021 or 1022. JW (ii. 508–9) gives 1025 as the date of Edmund's accession, in a note added to CCCO 157 by the second scribe. That it may have been misplaced is suggested by the fact that the original hand had entered in the margin opposite the annals for 1020–1 an account

together praised and gave thanks to God working through St Cuthbert, and they took Edmund and compelled him to accept the governance of the church. A certain priest who is very advanced in years is accustomed to relate these things about Edmund's election, just as, according to his testimony, he very often heard them from his grandfather, who was none other than that deacon who read the gospel at mass on that occasion.[24]

So Edmund was led with great honour to King Cnut, who also rejoiced in his election, and solemnly commanded that he should be ordained. But he confessed that he could in no way ascend the episcopal throne of his predecessors who had been monks, unless he were to emulate them and be vested in the monastic habit himself. After receiving for that reason the monastic habit, he was honourably consecrated bishop at Winchester by Archbishop Wulfstan of York, and he was much loved and honoured by the king himself.[25] On his way home he turned aside to the monastery of Peterborough, and received from the abbot at his own request a certain monk who was very well trained both in ecclesiastical offices and in the observance of the discipline of the monastic rule, and who was always to be a constant companion to him and to teach him the discipline of the monastic life. He was called Æthelric and later on he became bishop of this same church, that is the church of Durham. Now in his lifetime Edmund, who was both noble in his family descent and honourable in his person and his way of life, gave no one cause for suspicion of any depravity, and he showed himself very strenuous in governing the church. For he was very formidable to enemies of the church and evil people, but he was truly humble and amiable towards the good. He did not flatter any of the powerful out of fear of them, and he did not suffer the possessions of the church to be damaged by the violence of anyone.

7. In the time of this bishop there flourished in this church a certain [lii (lvii)] priest called Elfred, who lived until the time of Bishop Æthelwine and enjoyed through pious and religious works a relationship of great familiarity with St Cuthbert. He was in all things devoted to St Cuthbert; he was a man of great sobriety, ready in alms-giving,

of Edmund's election clearly derived from *LDE*, with which it shares some words (JW ii. 506–7). On the implication of this passage that at the time there was 'no one at Durham who was recognised as a monk or knowledgeable in monastic practices', see Aird, *Cuthbert*, p. 114.

sobrius, elemosinis deditus, in orationum studio assiduus, lasciuis et impudicis terribilis, honestis uero et Deum timentibus uenerabilis, custos ecclesie fidelissimus. Hunc etiam episcopi timuerunt offendere, quem sancto confessori tam familiarem nouerant esse. Nam cum Egelricus episcopus et qui ei successit frater Egelwinus, sed et illi qui cum eis erant monachi, cum rebus ecclesie quas rapuerant etiam sacras sanctorum^a reliquias uellent auferre, et ad sua monasteria transmittere, timor prefati sacerdotis eos ab hac iniuria noscitur refrenasse.[26] Singulis noctibus psalterium decantare, quo completo ad uigilias nocturnas solebat signum pulsare. Sed et in pueris in^b Dei seruitium educandis multum erat studiosus, quos cotidie cantu et lectione instituere,^{c} et ecclesiasticis officiis curabat informare. Habuerat^d unum de capillis sanctissimi^e patris Cuthberti, quem aduentantibus sepe amicis ostendere, et ex illo sanctitatem eius mirantibus plus admirationis consueuit adicere. Solebat nanque impleto prunis ardentibus turibulo super eas ipsum capillum ponere, ubi diutius iacens nequaquam consumi poterat, sed candescere ac uelut aurum in igne consuerat^f rutilare, indeque^g post longas moras sullatus, in propriam formam paulatim redire.[27] Hoc sane miraculum^h multi ^{i}discipulorum eius^i sed et^j quidam huius monasterii frater multe simplicitatis et humilitatis nomine Gamelo, qui nunc in Christo dormit, sepius se uidisse attestati sunt.[28]

[liii (lviii)]   Cum^k ergo presbiter prefatus honestam ac religiosam ageret uitam, iussus per uisionem per antiqua monasteriorum et ecclesiarum loca in prouincia Northanhymbrorum discurrit, ossa sanctorum que in illis sepulta^l nouerat, de terra eleuauit,^{m} ac declaranda populis et ueneranda supra humum locata reliquit, ossa ^{n}uidelicet Baltheri^n et Bilfridi anachoritarum,[29] Acce quoque et Alchmundi

---

^{a} om. H ^{b} om. D ^{c} instruere Fx H L; altered to instituere Y ^{d} Hic habuerat C (hic in contemp. hand over line C) Ca Fx L ^{e} om. H ^{f} consueuerat Ca D Fx L ^{g} inde Fx ^{h} miraculorum Fx L $^{i-i}$ om. F ^{j} om. T
^{k} De ossibus plurimorum sanctorum que Alfredus de terra leuauit rubric Fx H T V Y
^{l} ins. over line Fx; om. Y ^{m} leuauit Ca $^{n-n}$ Balteri uidelicet T

---

[26] See below, pp. 170–3. Æthelric and Æthelwine were bishops of Durham respectively from 1041 to 1056 and from 1056 to 1071. The Elfred referred to here was Elfred son of Westou (as is noted in some manuscripts of LDE, including C in which the information is an addition made by Symeon's hand). He was great-grandfather of Ailred, abbot of Rievaulx; and he held the church of Hexham from Bishop Edmund (Priory of Hexham, ed. Raine, Appendix IV).
[27] For a more elaborate version of this story, see Raine, Cuth. virt. c. 26 (pp. 57–8), trans. Raine, St Cuthbert, p. 59.

assiduous in the practice of prayer, severe to the lascivious and the
unchaste, respected by the honest and the god-fearing; and he was a
most faithful sacristan of the church. Even the bishops feared to
offend one who they knew to be such a familiar of the holy confessor.
For when Bishop Æthelric and his brother Æthelwine who succeeded
him, as well as the monks who were with them, wanted to take away
holy relics of the saints, together with the property of the church
which they had seized, and send them to their monasteries, it is
certain that fear of the priest Elfred deterred them from doing so.[26]
Every night he would chant the psalms, and then he would ring the
bell for mattins. He was also very assiduous in the education of the
boys who were being brought up to the service of God, and every day
he would attend to teaching them singing and reading and to
informing them about the offices of the church. He had in his
possession one of the hairs of the most holy father Cuthbert, which
he would often show to his friends when they came to visit. They
marvelled at Cuthbert's sanctity and the hair served to increase their
admiration. When he had filled a thurible with burning coals, he was
accustomed to place the hair on them, where it lay for a long time and
could in no way be burned, but rather it shone and glowed as if it
were gold in the fire. After a long while Elfred would take it up and
slowly it would return to its original form.[27] Now many of his
disciples have borne witness that they very often saw this miracle,
and especially one called Gamel, a brother of this monastery and a
man of great honesty and humility who now sleeps in Christ.[28]

As Elfred was living an honest and religious life, he set out at the   [liii (lviii)]
command of a vision and visited the former sites of monasteries and
churches in the kingdom of the Northumbrians. He raised from the
earth the bones of those saints whom he knew to be buried in these
places, and enshrined them above ground so that they might be better
known to the people and venerated by them. The bones in question
were those of the anchorites Balthere and Billfrith,[29] the bishops of

---

[28] Gamel's name is fifteenth in the list of monks at the beginning of *LDE* (above,
pp. 6–7). It is tempting to speculate that he may have been a descendant of Gamel Hamel
and Gamel the Younger who successively held the prebend of Hexham from Elfred son of
Westou (*Priory of Hexham*, ed. Raine, Appendix IV). Aird, *Cuthbert*, pp. 120–2, speculates
that he may have been a member of the pre-1083 community of St Cuthbert who
subsequently became a monk.

[29] Balthere was a hermit at Tyninghame in Lothian (see above, pp. 80–1 and n. 6.);
Billfrith was the binder of the Lindisfarne Gospels (see above, p. 120–1). Nothing is
known of the fate of either of these persons' remains before Elfred's time. Both appear in a
mid-12th-cent. Durham relic-list (Battiscombe, *Relics*, p. 113).

episcoporum Hagustaldensium,[30] et regis Oswini,[31] *necnon etiam*
abbatissarum uenerabilium Ebbe[32] et Aethelgithe.[b33] De quorum
omnium reliquiis aliquam secum partem in Dunhelmum asportauit,
et cum patris Cuthberti corpore locauit. Ad Mailrosense quoque
monasterium per reuelationem admonitus proficiscens, ossa sancti
Boisili qui beati Cuthberti *magister quondam* in eodem monasterio
extiterat, inde in ipsius *discipuli ecclesiam* transtulit, et iuxta illius
corpus in altero scrinio decenter sicut hactenus habentur condidit.[34]

[liv (lix)] Ad* monasterium quoque quod est in Gyruum ubi Bedam
doctorem conuersatum, defunctum et sepultum nouerat, singulis
annis adueniente anniuersaria dormitionis* eius die uenire, ibique
precibus et uigiliis solebat insistere.[35] Quodam tempore iuxta morem
illo pergens, cum aliquot ibidem dies solus in ecclesia orando et
uigilando transegisset, nescientibus sociis summo diluculo solus
(quod *ante nunquam* consueuerat) Dunhelmum rediit, sui uidelicet
secreti nullum uolens testem habere. Nam cum multis postea uixisset
annis, ad prefatum monasterium, tanquam iam* adeptus id quod
concupiuerat,* amplius uenire non curauit. Vnde sepius* a suis
familiariter requisitus, ubinam uenerabilis Bede ossa requiescerent,
certus de re inquisita sic erat solitus respondere: 'Hoc', inquit, 'nemo*
me certius nouit. Firmum, o dilectissimi! et procul omni dubio
certum habeatis, quod eadem theca que sacratissimum corpus patris*
Cuthberti seruat, etiam ossa uenerandi* doctoris et monachi Bede
contineat. Extra huius loculi hospicium nemo querat portionem eius
reliquiarum.' Hec dicens, familiares suos silentio precepit tegere, ne
scilicet extranei qui tunc in ecclesia ipsa conuersabantur, iniurias
aliquas machinarentur, quorum summum erat studium reliquias
sanctorum et maxime Bede si quas possent auferre. Vnde cum ipse

a–a struck through *Fx;* et *L;* necnon *Y*   *b* Etheldrithe *Fx L;* Ethelgithe *altered*
to Etheldrithe *Y*   *c–c* quondam magister *T*   *d–d* ecclesiam discipuli *L;*
ecclesiam *Y;* discipuli *add. over line Fx*   *e* De reliquiis Bede doctoris *rubric Fx*
H V Y   *f* depositionis *H*   *g–g* nunquam ante *H*   *h om. F H*
i cupiuerat *F*   *j om. H*   *k* nullus *Fx L;* nemo *altered to* nullus *Y*
l patris beati *H*   *m om. H*

[30] Respectively 709–31 and 767–80/1. For a fuller account of Elfred's treatment of their
remains in which it is claimed that he was prevented from removing any of their relics
from Hexham, see the Hexham material apparently interpolated into the *HReg*, *s.a.* 781
(Arnold, *Sym.Op.* ii. 48–50).
[31] King of the Deirans, murdered at the behest of King Oswiu of the Bernicians in 651
(Bede, *HE* iii. 14). This is the earliest reference to his relics which according to *Fl. Wig.* i.
222, were translated at Tynemouth by Bishop Æthelwine of Durham in 1065. This is

Hexham Acca and Alchmund,[30] and King Oswine,[31] together with those of the venerable abbesses Æbbe[32] and Æthelgitha.[33] He took a certain part of all these relics back to Durham with him, and enshrined them with the body of father Cuthbert. At the bidding of a revelation he went to the monastery of Melrose, and from there he translated the bones of St Boisil, who had once been the blessed Cuthbert's teacher in that same monastery, to the church of his former disciple, where he installed them fittingly in another shrine near to Cuthbert's body, just as they are preserved to this day.[34]

Every year on the anniversary of the death of Bede the teacher, [liv (lix)] Elfred was accustomed also to visit Jarrow, where he knew Bede to have lived, died, and been buried, and there he would stay saying prayers and keeping vigil.[35] On one occasion when he had gone there according to his custom, and had passed several days alone in the church engaged in praying and keeping vigil, he left at the crack of dawn without his companions knowing (which he had never been accustomed to do before) and returned to Durham, clearly not wishing to have any witness to his secret. For, although he afterwards lived for many years, he never again visited the aforesaid monastery, as if he had gained possession of what he had desired. So that when he was asked by those close to him, as he very often was, where the bones of the venerable Bede rested, he was accustomed to reply as if he were quite sure of the answer: 'No one knows this more certainly than I. O beloved friends! you may regard it as firm and certain and beyond any doubt, that the same coffin which contains the most sacred body of father Cuthbert also contains the bones of the venerable doctor and monk Bede. No one should look for any portion of his relics outside the shelter of this coffin.' Having said this, he instructed those close to him to keep silent about it, lest the outsiders who were at that time living in the church, should contrive some mischief, for their chief aim was to carry off relics of saints, and above all those of Bede, if they could. For this reason, when he

consistent with the *Vita Oswini*, which assigns the translation to the time of that bishop (1056–71) and Earl Tostig (1055–65); see *Miscellanea biographica*, ed. Raine, pp. 11–17.

[32] Seventh-cent. abbess of Coldingham (Bede, *HE* iv. 19).

[33] The context suggests that this otherwise unknown saint may also have been an early abbess of Coldingham.

[34] Boisil was prior of Melrose; see Bede, *V. Cuth.* c. 6; and above, pp. 26–7 and n. 25.

[35] The anniversary of Bede is 25 May in a Durham calendar edited in *English Benedictine Kalendars after A.D. 1100*, ed. F. Wormald (Henry Bradshaw Society, lxxvii, 1938), pp. 161–79. On the day of his death as given in Cuthbert's letter, see above, pp. 70–1 and n. 91.

sanctorum ossa cum sancti Cuthberti corpore (ut supradictum est) locaret, id omnino occulte facere studebat. Cuius de Beda sententie*ᵃ* concordat etiam*ᵇ* illud Anglico sermone compositum carmen, ubi cum de statu huius loci et de sanctorum reliquiis que in eo continentur agitur, etiam reliquiarum Bede una cum ceteris ibidem mentio habetur.³⁶ Cuius nimirum ea ossa fuisse noscuntur, que multis post annis cum incorrupto patris Cuthberti corpore a ceteris reliquiis segregata in lineo saccello inueniebantur*ᶜ* locata.³⁷

Alia quoque multa memorie digna de supradicto uiro narrantur, que specialiter illi sancto Cuthberto per manifestam uisionem precipiente faciebat uel etiam uentura prenuntiabat. Innocentia enim et pia illorum simplicitas qui per id temporis erant, plurimum apud ipsum sanctum confessorem*ᵈ* ualebat, unde *ᵉ*semper illos*ᵉ* ab hostibus defendere, et ab aduersariis illatas iniurias maturius solebat uindicare.*ᶠ*

[lv (lx)] 8. Huius*ᵍ* sancti presulis et Deo digni confessoris Cuthberti *ʰ*ecclesiam etiam*ʰ* pius et religiosus rex Anglorum Cnut multo*ⁱ* uenerabatur honore, in tantum ut ad ipsius sacratissimum corpus nudis pedibus a loco qui uia Garmundi dicitur (id est per quinque miliaria) incedens ueniret, et ei suisque seruitoribus mansionem Standrope cum omnibus suis appendiciis libere in perpetuum possidendam donaret, id est Cnapatun, Scottun, Rabi, Wacarfeld, Efenwuda,*ʲ* Alclit,*ᵏ* Luteringtun, Elledun, Ingeltun, Ticcelea, Middeltun. Hec *ˡ*itaque ea*ˡ* quidem ratione dedit, ut preter eos qui ipsi sancto in ecclesia derseruirent, nemo se intromitteret. Eum autem qui aliter faceret uel auferre uel *ᵐ*inde minuere presumeret,*ᵐ* rex ipse cum Eadmundo episcopo excommunicauit, et excommunicando discessuris in die

---

ᵃ sententia *Fx L;* sententie *altered to* sententia *Y*   *ᵇ om. F L*
ᶜ inueniebamus *F*   *ᵈ om. F*   *ᵉ⁻ᵉ* illos semper *Ca*   *ᶠ* et cetera *add. L*
ᵍ Donacio de Stayndrope *rubric H*; Knut rex (Anglie *added T V*) uenit ad sanctum Cuthbertum nudis pedibus *rubric Fx T V Y*   *ʰ⁻ʰ om. H*   *ⁱ om. V*
ʲ Euenwuda *F*   *ᵏ* Alclend *H*   *ˡ⁻ˡ* ea itaque *Fx L Y*   *ᵐ⁻ᵐ* minuere presumeret inde *F*; inde *om. H*

---

³⁶ This is evidently a reference to the poem entitled *De situ Dunelmi* in Ca (item 8, above, p. xxv), which also mentions the presence at Durham of the relics of Boisil. For the text, see *Anglo-Saxon Minor Poems*, ed. Dobbie, p. 27, and D. Howlett, 'The shape and meaning of the Old English poem "Durham"', Rollason, *Anglo-Norman Durham*, pp. 485–95, at 492, where favourable comments are also made on the poem's literary quality. The

enshrined the bones of these saints with the body of St Cuthbert (as
was described above), he took care to do this very secretly. His
account of Bede agrees also with that poem in the English language
which, when it speaks of the condition of this church and the relics
of saints which are contained in it, mentions the relics of Bede there
together with those of other saints.[36] It is known for certain that it
was his bones which were found many years later enshrined with
the incorrupt body of the father Cuthbert, where they had been
kept separate from the other relics by being contained in a linen
bag.[37]

Many other things worthy of note are told of Elfred, things which
he did when specially told to do so by St Cuthbert in a vision, and
things which he foretold would happen in the future. The innocence
and pious honesty of the men of that time achieved much with the
holy confessor, so that he always defended them from their enemies,
and was quick to avenge injuries done to them.

8. The pious and religious king of the English Cnut so venerated and   [lv (lx)]
honoured the church of that holy bishop and confessor worthy of
God, Cuthbert, that he walked barefoot to the saint's most sacred
body from the place called Garmondsway (that is a distance of five
miles). Moreover, he gave freely and in perpetual possession to the
saint and those who served him the vill of Staindrop with all its
appurtenances, that is *Cnapatun*, Shotton, Raby, Wackerfield, Evenwood, West Auckland, Lutterington Hall, Eldon, Ingelton, Thickley,
and *Middeltun*. The terms of this gift were that no one should
interfere with it, except those who served the saint himself in his
church. Anyone who should do otherwise, or should presume to take
anything away from these possessions, or to diminish them, the king
himself together with Bishop Edmund excommunicated, and by
excommunicating them they consigned them to the company of

mention of the poem in *LDE* indicates that it was composed before 1104 × 9; see H. S.
Offler, 'The date of Durham (*Carmen de situ Dunelmi*)', *Journal of English and Germanic
Philology*, lxi (1962), 591–4 (repr. Offler, *North of the Tees*, no. IV).

[37] This is presumably a reference to the translation of 1104, at which the author of *LDE*
seems to have been present (see above, pp. xlii, xliv). The early 12th-cent. account of that
(*De miraculis* c. 7 (Arnold, *Sym.Op.* i. 252–3)) mentions the presence in Cuthbert's coffin
when it was opened of many relics, including those of Bede, but it says nothing about any
linen bag, which is information unique to *LDE*.

iudicii in ignem eternum associauit. Simili ratione idem rex et uillam que Brontun appellatur sepedicto sancto donauit.[38]

[lvi (lxi)] 9. Anno ab[a] Incarnatione Domini millesimo tricesimo quinto defuncto Cnut, cum filius eius Haroldus iam quintum annum in regno, et Eadmundus uicesimum in pontificatu gereret, Dunecanus rex Scottorum cum immensis copiis[b] adueniens, Dunhelmum obsedit, et ad eam expugnandam[c] multum quidem sed frustra laborauit. Nam magna parte equitum suorum ab his qui obsidebantur interfecta confusus aufugit, fugiens pedites omnes interfectos amisit, quorum capita in forum collata,[d] in stipitibus sunt suspensa.[39] Nec multo post ipse rex cum iam in Scotiam redisset a suis occisus interiit.[40] Cum autem Eadmundus uicesimum tertium annum sui pontificatus ageret, defunctus est in Gloecestre cum apud regem ibidem moraretur, sed a suis corpus eius Dunhelmum perlatum honorifice sepulture est traditum.

[lvii (lxii)] Quo[e] facto Eadredus qui post episcopum secundus fuerat,[f] presulatum illius ecclesie primus ex ordine clericali festinabat obtinere. Siquidem sumpta ex thesauris ecclesie pecunia non modica, a rege scilicet[g] Hardecnut episcopatum emit, sed episcopale officium facere illum diuina ultio non permisit. Intraturus quippe ecclesiam subita infirmitate corripitur, decidensque[h] in lectum decimo mense moritur.[i]

[lviii Quo[j] anno, scilicet Incarnationis Dominice millesimo quadrage-
(lxiii)] simo secundo, et ipse rex mortuus est, succedente illi in imperium

---

[a] Duncanus rex Scottorum Dunhelmum obsedit sed nichil (nil *H*; nec *T*) proficiens postea de (a *H*) suis interfectus est *rubric Fx H T V Y*   [b] copiis hominum *L Y*
[c] expugnandum *Ca*   [d] collocata *Fx L*   [e] De Eadredo episcopo symoniaco episcopo *rubric H*; De Aldredo episcopo symoniaco de ordine clericali primo *rubric Fx V Y*
[f] erat *Ca F*   [g] om. *H*   [h] decidens *L Y*   [i] et cetera add. *L*   [j] De Egilrico episcopo expulso *rubric H*; De Egilrico episcopo expulso sed per uim reconciliato *rubric Fx Y*; De Aldredo episcopo symoniaco ordine clericorum primo *T in marg.*

---

[38] Staindrop lies north-east of Barnard Castle (NZ 131 126). The dependent vills which can be identified (V. Watts, pers. comm.; cf. Ekwall, *Concise Dictionary*, and Mawer, *Place-Names)* are Shotton (NZ 10 23 near Raby), Raby (NZ 128 220), Wackerfield (NZ 152 126), Evenwood (NZ 155 250), West Auckland (NZ 183 264, on which see above, pp. 154–5), Lutterington Hall (NZ 1824), Eldon (NZ 2427), Ingelton (NZ 175 205), and ?East Thickley (NZ 222 250). In view of the fact that Staindrop was a conventual manor alienated by Ranulf Flambard, the wording here may be significant: see Offler, *Episcopal Charters*, pp. 107–9. Staindropshire is represented as held of the prior and convent of Durham in 15th-cent. surveys of the priory's lands (*Feodarium*, ed. Greenwell, pp. 56, 156). *CMD* links the gift of other lands in Yorkshire with that of Brompton (two miles north-east of Northallerton, N. Yorks.; SE 374 964). All the lands mentioned in *LDE* are listed as gifts of Cnut, king of England (1016–35), to the church of Durham in *HSC* c. 32, where the spellings of the names are notably similar to those in *LDE*. The barefoot

those who on the Day of Judgment should go down into the eternal fire. On a similar basis, the same king gave to the saint the vill called Brompton.[38]

9. After the death of Cnut which occurred in the year of Our Lord's [lvi (lxi)] Incarnation 1035, when his son Harold was in the fifth year of his reign, and Edmund was in his twentieth year as bishop, King Duncan of the Scots came with immense forces, besieged Durham, and expended much labour to conquer it, but in vain. For when the greater part of his cavalry had been killed by those who were being besieged, he fled in confusion, and in this flight he lost all his foot soldiers who were killed and their heads taken to the market place and stuck up on stakes.[39] Not long afterwards the king himself, when he had returned to Scotland, was killed by his own men.[40] When Edmund was in the twenty-third year of his pontificate, he died in Gloucester when he was staying there with King Harold, but his people brought his body back to Durham to be honourably buried.

After this Eadred, who had been second in rank to the bishop, [lvii (lxii)] hastened to obtain the position of bishop of that church, the first from the order of clerks to do so. Since he had taken no small amount of money from the church's treasure, he purchased the bishopric from the king, who was Harthacnut, but divine vengeance did not allow him to assume episcopal office. As he was about to enter the church, he was seized with sudden infirmity, collapsed, and died in bed in his tenth month as bishop.

In the same year, that is the year 1042 of Our Lord's Incarnation, [lviii King Harthacnut himself died, and was succeeded on the throne by (lxiii)]

pilgrimage from Garmondsway (now a deserted village near Ferryhill, NZ 432 348), however, is otherwise mentioned only in *CMD* (Craster, 'Red book', pp. 526–7), where Cnut's gifts are also listed and there is reference to the anathema clause which, as in *LDE*, is said to have been enacted jointly by Cnut and Bishop Edmund. These lands are listed as possessions of the church of Durham in *Liber Vitae*, fo. 50[v].

[39] Duncan I was king of Scots (1034–40), Harold Harefoot was king of England (1035/6–40). This siege, here dated to 1040, is not mentioned in any other source. The detail of the impaling of the defeated Scots' heads around the market-place is reminiscent of the account in *De obsessione Dunelmi* (on which see above, pp. lxxviii–lxxix) of a siege which is alleged to have taken place in 969 (Arnold, *Sym. Op.* i. 215–16). On the possibility that the author of the latter text was confusing the two sieges, see Meehan, 'Siege of Durham', p. 16, and D. Whitelock, 'The dealings of the kings of England with Northumbria', *The Anglo-Saxons: Studies presented to Bruce Dickins*, ed. P. Clemoes (London, 1959), pp. 70–88, at 86 n. 1 See also below, p. 186 n. 60.

[40] The killing of Duncan by Macbeth in 1040 is mentioned in the chronicle of Marianus Scotus, the Annals of Tigernach, and the D version of the Chronicle of the Kings of Scotland (Anderson, *Early Sources*, i. 579–81).

piissimo Eadwardo*a* Aethelredi regis et Emme filio. Episcopatum uero Dunhelmensem ille (cuius superius mentio facta est) Egelricus*b* suscepit, Siwardo cum iam Eadulfum comitem interfecisset, totius prouincie Northanhymbrorum comitatum ab Humbra usque Twedam administrante.[41] Tertio autem anno *c*accepi episcopatus*c* Aegelricus a clericis, eo quod extraneus esset et contra uoluntatem illorum*d* electus, de ecclesia expulsus Siwardum comitem expetiit, et munere oblato eius gratiam et auxilium contra obstinatos obtinuit. Illius enim*e* timore ac potentia exterriti ac*f* deiecti,*g* siue uolentes siue nolentes compulsi sunt episcopo reconciliari, et in sedem sui pontificatus recipere. Habuerat autem *h*episcopus secum*h* fratrem suum monachum uocabulo Egelwinum, qui sub eo totius episcopatus curam gerebat, et cum eo alios quoque monachos, qui omnes una cum episcopo pecunias et ornamenta ecclesie minuere et inde studuerant abstrahere.*i* [42]

[lix (lxiv)]   Placuerat*j* eidem antistiti ecclesiam in Cunecaceastre*k* (que corrupte nunc Ceastre*l* uocatur) de ligno factam destruere, et pro eo quod aliquando beati *m*Cuthberti corpus*m* ibidem quieuerat, aliam de lapide fabricare.[43] Cum ergo altius terra foderetur, grandis ibidem thesaurus est inuentus, quem dudum propter auaritiam et tirannidem Sexhelmi (de quo supra dictum est)*n* secretarius et pauci cum eo ibidem dicuntur abscondisse.[44] Episcopus itaque tollens ipsam pecuniam ad monasterium*o* unde ipse fuerat misit, quam illuc sequi omnino*p* deliberauit. Premissis*q* enim auro et argento aliisque rebus quas de ecclesia tulerat, decreuit episcopatum dimittere et fratrem Egelwinum in locum suum substituere. Itaque piissimo rege Eadwardo quintodecimum annum in*r* imperio habente, auxilio et fauore comitis Tostii qui Siwardo successerat,

---

a confessore C *(over line)* D   *b* monachus C *(over line)*   *c-c* episcopatus accepti T   *d* eorum H   *e* enim a L   *f* et H   *g* eiecti T *h-h* secum episcopus L   *i* et cetera *add.* L   *j* De thesauro inuento apud Castere et ab Egelrico asportato *rubric Fx* H T *(in marg.)* Y   *k* Cuncacestre F *l* Cestre F   *m-m* corpus Cuthberti L Y   *n* om. C   *o* ecclesiam T *p* continuo H   *q* Satiatus F   *r* om. H

---

[41] *LDE*'s calculations are consistent with a 1042 date for Edmund's death, the brief episcopate of Bishop Eadred, and the accession of Bishop Æthelric. The king with whom Bishop Edmund was staying was thus Harthacnut (effective 1040–2), *LDE* having failed to note the death of Harold Harefoot in 1040. A note, presumably derived from *LDE*, has been added in a different hand in a note to the annal for 1042 at the foot of the page in the manuscript of *HReg*, CCCC 139: 'Cui Edredus per pecuniam in episcopatum successit, et decimo mense moritur' (Arnold, *Sym.Op.* ii. 162). The main text of *HReg*, however,

the most pious Edward, son of King Æthelred and Emma. Æthelric (whom we mentioned above) received the see of Durham, while Siward, after he had killed Earl Eardwulf, governed the earldom of the whole of Northumbria from the Humber to the Tweed.[41] In the third year after he had received the bishopric, Æthelric, who had been expelled from his church by the clerks because he was an outsider and had been elected against their wishes, appealed to Earl Siward and, after giving him a gift, he received his favour and help against the obstinate clerks. Terrified and overwhelmed by the fearful power of the earl, they were compelled willy nilly to be reconciled to the bishop, and to admit him into his episcopal see. Now this bishop had with him his brother, a monk called Æthelwine, who under him saw to the running of the whole bishopric, and with him there were also other monks, who all collaborated with the bishop to diminish the treasure of the church by removing money and ornaments.[42]

This same bishop decided to demolish the wooden church in [lix (lxiv)] *Cunecaceastre* (which is now corruptly called Chester-le-Street), and because the body of the blessed Cuthbert had once rested there, to build another of stone.[43] When a deep hole had therefore been dug in the ground there, a huge treasure was found, which is said to have been hidden long ago by the sacristan and a few others on account of the avarice and tyranny of Sexhelm, whom we mentioned above.[44] So the bishop took up the money and sent it to the monastery from which he himself had come, and he firmly resolved to follow it there himself. For after sending on ahead the gold and silver and other things which he had taken from the church, he decided to give up the bishopric, and put his brother Æthelwine in his place. So, while the most pious King Edward was in the fifteenth year of his reign, with the help and favour of Earl Tostig who had succeeded Siward,

---

simply records the death of Edmund and succession of Æthelric but *s.a.* 1043. Siward was earl of Northumbria (*c.*1041–55), who killed Eardwulf, earl of Northumbria (1038–*c.*1041).

[42] On the possible reasons for *LDE's* hostility to these bishops, who were after all monks and therefore might expect the author's approval, see B. Meehan, 'Outsiders, insiders, and property in Durham around 1100', *Studies in Church History*, xii (1975), 45–58.

[43] Since the church of St Cuthbert had been located at Chester-le-Street for over a century from 883 to 995, the continued existence of a church built only of wood is at first sight surprising. For the possibility that wood was the normal building material for even important non-monastic churches, see E. Cambridge, 'The early church in County Durham: a reassessment', *Journal of the British Archaeological Association*, cxxxvii (1984), 65–85, at 80–1. The rebuilding described here may have been an early example of a general trend discussed by Blair, *Minsters and Parish Churches*, p. 9.

[44] On Seaxhelm, see above, pp. 140–1.

Egelwinus in episcopatum sullimatur, et Egelricus, cum iam quindecim annos in pontificatu egisset, ad monasterium suum reuertitur, ibique in locis palustribus lapide et ligno uias construit, et ecclesias aliaque multa ex prefata pecunia fabricauit.[45] Regnante autem postmodum Willelmo, accusatus apud illum quod multas de ecclesia Dunhelmensi pecunias tulisset, reddere noluit, unde[46] Lundoniam perductus et custodie deputatus, in captione regis est defunctus.

[lx (lxv)] 10. Quo[a] adhuc pontificatum regente, res inusitate facta terribili exemplo ministris altaris proculdubio iram Dei ostendit imminere, si ad sacrosanctum mysterium[b] sine castitate presumant accedere. Quidam etenim[c] presbyter uocabulo Feoccher, non longe ab urbe habens ecclesiam habitabat, sed cum uxori copulatus esset, indignam sacerdotis officio uitam ducebat. Quadam die multi[d] tam nobiles quam priuati primo mane ad ipsum locum placitaturi conuenerunt, sed ante placitum ut presbyter eis missam celebraret rogauerunt. At ille qui ipsa nocte cum uxore dormierat, ad sacrum altaris officium accedere formidabat. [e]Itaque negauit[e] se id facturum. Illis autem semel, bis, terque rogantibus sibi missam celebrari, presbyter nimis ex utraque parte angustabatur, hinc uerecundia inde timore. Si enim eis non obediret, uerecundabatur illos causam suspicari; si obediret, iudicium[f] timebat iusti iudicis Dei. Vicit tamen humana uerecundia diuinum timorem. Itaque missam celebrauit. Hora uero qua sacrosancta mysteria sumere deberet, in calicem introspexit, et ecce particulam Dominici corporis que iuxta morem [g]missa fuerat in calicem,[g] ita cum sanguine in teterrimam speciem commutatam uidit, ut (sicut postea fatebatur) magis in calice picis colorem quam panis et uini conspiceret. Ilico reatum intelligens presbyter, pallere, et quasi iam tunc flammis ultricibus tradendus cepit nimium pauere.

[a] De Fochero presbitero cui in calice pro sanguine Christi nigra species (specie *Fx Y*) apparuit *rubric Fx H T V Y*   [b] ministerium *L Y*   [c] enim *H*   [d] *om. Ca* *(signe de renvoi poss. indicating lost marginal correction)*   [e-e] Ipse negauit itaque *H* [f] iusticiam *H*   [g-g] miscuerat in calice *H*

[45] Edward the Confessor was king of England 1042–66. Tostig, son of Earl Godwine of Wessex, was earl of Northumbria from 1055–65 when he was expelled by a Northumbrian revolt and subsequently killed at the Battle of Stamford Bridge in 1066; see e.g. Stenton, *Anglo-Saxon England*, pp. 547, 565, 570–2, 579, 586–7, 588, 590. The dating of Æthelwine's appointment given here agrees with *HReg*, *s.a.* 1056 (Arnold, *Sym.Op.* ii. 173), in a passage also found in JW for the same year (ii. 580–1), which states that Æthelric left his see and returned to Peterborough of his own free will. It says nothing, however, of the removal of any treasures from Durham.

Æthelwine was raised to the bishopric, and Æthelric who had then passed fifteen years in the episcopate, returned to his monastery, and there laid causeways of stone and wood across the marshy places, and constructed churches and many other things with the aforesaid money.[45] Afterwards in the reign of William, however, he was accused before the king of having taken much money from the church of Durham and he refused to return it. So he was escorted to London[46] and handed over into custody, where he died as a prisoner of the king.

10. While this man was still bishop, an unusual thing happened, [lx (lxv)] which by a terrible example showed the ministers of the altar that they are without doubt threatened with the wrath of God if they presume to approach the sacred mystery without chastity. For a certain priest called Feoccher lived not far from the city in a place where he had a church, but since he was united with a woman he led a life unworthy of the office of priest. One day many nobles and ordinary men met together in that place early in the morning to hear pleas, but before the court began they asked the priest to celebrate mass for them. He feared to undertake the office of the altar, however, having slept with the woman that very same night. So he replied that he would not do it. But they demanded once, twice, even three times that mass should be celebrated for them, so that the priest was hemmed in on both sides, on the one by shame, on the other by fear. For if he did not obey them, he was ashamed to give them cause for suspicion, and if he did obey them he feared the judgment of God the just judge. Human shame, however, overcame fear of God. So he celebrated mass. But at the moment when he should have received the sacred mysteries, he looked into the chalice and saw that the small portion of the Lord's body, which had been put in the chalice in the accustomed way, had been changed along with the blood into a most hideous form, so that (as he afterwards confessed) he saw it in the chalice the colour of pitch rather than of bread and wine. The priest immediately realized his guilt, turned pale, and began to tremble violently as if he were to be handed over straightaway to the avenging

[46] The words 'reddere noluit, unde' are visible in normal light only in F. C has here an erasure of three words above which the words found in F have been supplied in small letters by Thomas Rud. In fact the words *noluit* and *unde* are clearly visible under ultra-violet light and so are traces of a word preceding them although the *r* is hard to distinguish and it is not certain that it read *reddere*. The three words are found in no other manuscript.

Preterea multum anxius erat, quid de hoc quod in calice uiderat, facere deberet. Exhorrebat illud uelut suam mortem sumere. Volebat in terram effundere,ᵃ sed quoniam consecratum erat, id metuebat facere. Reputans ergo quoniam quicquid faceret, Omnipotentis iudicium effugere non ualeret, magno cum tremore ac formidine illud sumpsit, sed tante amaritudinis fuit, ut nil ad gustandum amarius esse potuisset.

Vix missa peracta, confestim equum ascendens ad episcopum festinauit, cuius pedibus prostratus rem ex ordine retulit. Cui indicta penitentia precepit, ut si Deum sibi propitium habere uellet, sinceram deinceps et castam ei uitam offerre studeret. Quod presbyter libenter promisit et promissum usque finem uite caste ac religiose uiuendo custodiuit. Hoc sane ita factum sicut retulimus, ab ipsius presbyteri filio presbitero et duobus capellanis episcopi qui postea nobiscum in hac ecclesia in monachili habitu conuersati sunt, sicut ab ipso ᵇin quo factum est presbyteroᵇ didicerant, frequenter referentibus audiuimus.⁴⁷

[lxi (lxvi)] **11.** Susceptoᶜ episcopatu Egelwinus, nichilominus ecclesie nichil inferre, immo multo magis quam frater eius ᵈante illumᵈ ornamenta resque alias satagebat auferre. Verum sicut exitus rerum edocuit,ᵉ nec ipse hoc impune fecit. Sed de hoc paulo post dicemus.⁴⁸ Illo pontificatum regente, supradictus comes Tosti cum Northanhymbrorum disponeret comitatum, in ueneratione semper ecclesiam sancti Cuthberti habuit, et donariis non paucis que inibi adhuc habentur ornauit. Ipsa quoque coniunx illiusᶠ Iudith filia comitis Flandrensium Blandwini, honesta ualde ac religiosa, multo plus sanctum Cuthbertum diligens, diuersa ᵍillius ecclesieᵍ ornamenta contulerat;⁴⁹ et adhuc plura cum multis

ᵃ fundere T   ᵇ⁻ᵇ presbytero in quo factum est H   ᶜ De Iudith comitissa (Northanymbrie *added* T V) et famula eius *rubric* Fx H T V Y   ᵈ⁻ᵈ *om.* T   ᵉ docuit F   ᶠ eius H   ᵍ⁻ᵍ ecclesie illius Ca Fx L Y

⁴⁷ Since it took place in the time of Bishop Æthelwine, this incident must be dated to the period 1056–71. It is of interest for the prevalence of married priests in the second half of the 11th cent. and for *LDE's* attitude to them; see e.g. C. Brooke, 'Gregorian reform in action: clerical marriage in England, 1050–1200', in his *Medieval Church and Society: Collected Essays* (London, 1971), pp. 69–99, esp. 82–3. The fact that the story is told at the expense of a parish priest rather than one of the (married) clerks of Durham may indicate that the author of *LDE* was unable or unwilling to attack their way of life in this respect; see Rollason, *England in the Eleventh Century*, ed. Hicks, pp. 189–90; and Foster, in Rollason, *Anglo-Norman Durham*, pp. 53–65. The fact that the informants of the author of *LDE* were Bishop Æthelwine's chaplains who had become monks of Durham may indicate

flames. Meanwhile he was very anxious as to what should be done with what he had seen in the chalice. He was horrified at the thought of receiving it as if it was his own death. He wanted to pour it out on the ground, but he was afraid to do that because it had been consecrated. Reflecting therefore that whatever he did, he could not escape the judgment of the Almighty, he received it with great trembling and fear, but it was of such bitterness, that nothing could have been more bitter to taste.

Hardly was mass over than he immediately mounted his horse and hastened to the bishop, throwing himself at his feet and relating the whole matter to him as it had happened. The bishop imposed penance on him and ordered that, if he wished God to be well-disposed towards him, he should strive from then on to offer him a sincere and chaste life. This the priest freely promised and he kept his promise till the end of his life, living chastely and piously. We have related how these things occurred as we have frequently heard them described by the priest's son (himself a priest) and two chaplains of the bishop, who afterwards lived with us in this church in the monastic habit, just as they had learned of them from the priest to whom this happened.[47]

11. Once he had received the episcopate, Æthelwine nevertheless [lxi (lxvi)] brought nothing to the church, but rather he was to a much greater extent than his brother before him intent on removing from it ornaments and other things. As the upshot showed, however, he did not do this with impunity. But we shall speak of this a little later.[48] While he was governing the bishopric, Earl Tostig, who was governing the earldom of Northumbria, held the church of St Cuthbert always in veneration, and he embellished it with several gifts, which it still has today. His wife Judith, daughter of Count Baldwin of Flanders, a very honest and religious woman who loved St Cuthbert even more than did her husband, also gave various ornaments to the saint's church;[49] and she promised to give more

that the discontinuity between the pre-1083 clerical community and the post-1083 cathedral priory was not as great as *LDE's* general remarks on this suggest (below, pp. 228–31, and above, pp. lxxxi–lxxxiii and refs.).   [48] See below, pp. 192–5.

[49] For Tostig, see above, p. 172 n. 45. JW (ii. 560–1) also names Judith as a daughter of Count Baldwin, but ASC D, *s.a.* 1052, refers to her merely as a kinswoman. She also patronized the cult of St Oswald (D. Ó Riain-Raedel, 'Edith, Judith, Matilda: the role of royal ladies in the propagation of the continental cult', *Oswald: Northumbrian King*, ed. Stancliffe and Cambridge, pp. 210–29, at 216–22) and that of Oswine (*Miscellanea Biographica*, ed. Raine, pp. 12, 14–16); see Aird, *Cuthbert*, pp. 55, 58 n. 180.

terrarum possessionibus se donaturam promiserat, si eius ecclesiam intrare, et ad ipsius sepulchrum sibi liceret adorare. Sed tantam*a* rem per se non ausa temptare, unam de pedissequis suis cogitauerat premittere, ut si hoc ipsa impune facere posset, domina post sequens securior ingredi auderet. Puella ergo, domine sue uoluntate agnita, hora secretiori ad hoc temptandum conata est aggredi. Iam pedem intra cimiterium erat positura, cum subito ueluti*b* uentorum uiolentia repelli cepit et uiribus deficere, et*c* grauiter infirmata uix ad hospitium ualuit redire, decidensque in lectum, graui torquebatur cruciatu, tandem dolore cum uita caruit. Hoc facto comitissa uehementer exterrita contremuit,[50] atque humiliter satisfaciendo, imaginem crucifixi (que—sicut in sequentibus dicetur—a raptoribus suo fuerat spoliata ornatu) imaginem quoque sancte Dei genitricis Marie et Iohannis Euangeliste ipsa et eius coniunx fieri iusserunt et auro argentoque*d* uestierunt, aliaque perplura ad decorem ecclesie obtulerunt.[51]

*e*Quo tempore et illud (quod alibi plenius legitur) super Barcwid miraculum contigit, qui dum pacem sancti perfringere uellet, repente uindicta percussus interiit.*e* [52]

12. Fuit*f* et alius praue actionis uir Osulfus uocabulo, in quo factum est hoc*g* quod narrabimus, *h*sicut a multis qui uiderant quam sepe audiuimus.*h* [53] Quadam nanque die ubi in campo obdormiens*i* expergefactus fuerat, serpentem sibi collum stringere sentiebat. Quem manu comprehendens in terram elidit,*j* sed mox iterum *k*eius collum*k*

---

a tanquam *V*   *b* uelut *F*   *c* om. *H*   *d* et argento *H*   *c–e* om. *Fx L T Y.*   *f* De serpente constringente collum cuiusdam *rubric Fx H T V Y*   *g* om. *Ca*   *h–h* add. above line *Fx;* om. *Y*   *i* dormiens *Fx H L Y*   *j* elisit *Ca*   *k–k* collum eius *Ca*

---

[50] On the significance of *LDE's* representation of the veneration of Cuthbert as excluding women, see above, pp. 104–11 and nn.

[51] That Judith was a notable patron of the arts is shown by the survival of a number of manuscripts owned by her (R. Gameson, *The Role of Art in the Late Anglo-Saxon Church* (Oxford, 1995), pp. 128–9, adding to the list of manuscripts given in E. Temple, *Anglo-Saxon Manuscripts 900–1066* (A Survey of Manuscripts Illuminated in the British Isles, ii; London, 1976), pp. 108–12)); that she was particularly devoted to the Crucifixion is suggested by the fact that in one of these (New York, Pierpont Morgan Library, 709, fo. 105ᵛ; Temple, op. cit., ill. 289) she is represented embracing the foot of the cross, while another manuscript which she owned (New York, Pierpont Morgan Library, 708; ibid., p. 109) has a Crucifixion on the binding. The crucifix described in the present text obviously comprised a group of figures, presumably made of stone or wood, with Mary and John the Evangelist at the foot of the cross. Patronage of such an object by a married couple is parallelled in the Waltham Cross, which was adorned by Tovi the Proud, a

still together with many landed possessions, if she were allowed to enter his church and to adore him at his tomb. Since she did not dare to attempt such a thing herself, she devised the plan of sending one of her servants ahead of her, so that if she were able to do this with impunity, the mistress would follow after her and would dare to enter the church with more confidence of her safety. So when the girl had learned her mistress's will, she undertook to approach the church at a very quiet time in order to attempt this. As she was about to place her foot inside the cemetery, she was suddenly repelled by a violent force as of the wind, her strength failed, and stricken with a grave infirmity, she was scarcely able to return to the hospice, where falling on to her bed, she was racked with terrible torment until at length she was deprived of both the pain and her life. The countess was absolutely terrified at what had happened and began to tremble all over.[50] Humbly and in order to make amends, she and her husband ordered to be made and clad in gold and silver an image of the crucified Christ (which as will be explained subsequently was despoiled of its enrichment by robbers) and also an image of St Mary, the mother of God, and John the Evangelist, and they also gave to the church many other things for its adornment.[51]

At this time that miracle (which is fully described elsewhere) was performed on Barcwith, who since he wished to infringe the peace of the saint, was struck down with sudden retribution and died.[52]

12. There was another man of evil character named Oswulf. We shall now narrate what happened to him, as we have very often heard about it from many people who saw it.[53] One day he was sleeping in a field, when he was awakened to feel a snake wound tightly round his neck. Seizing it with his hands he threw it to the ground, but it soon coiled

[lxii (lxviii)]

follower of King Cnut (1016–35) and his wife Gytha (C. R. Dodwell, *Anglo-Saxon Art: A New Perspective* (Manchester, 1982), p. 119). The despoliation of the Durham crucifix is described below, pp. 186–9.

[52] The miracle referred to is *De miraculis* c. 5, which in Fx, L, and Y is actually inserted into the text of *LDE* at this point with the heading 'Quomodo miles comitis Tosti Barwith dum ianuas monasterii eius infringere cupit subito percussus interierit (interiit *Fx*)', *L with rubric* 'Capitulum lxvii'. T omits the last sentence of the chapter but does not have the text of the miracle story; instead there is at the foot of the page a 14th-cent. note: 'Require capitulum lxvii quod hic deficit, 'Quomodo miles Tosti' et cetera.' The story concerns a robber called Aldan-hamal who is imprisoned at Durham by Tostig. He escapes after appealing to St Cuthbert and seeks sanctuary in the cathedral. One of Tostig's men, Barcwith, proposes breaking down the doors in order to take him by force, but he is miraculously stricken and dies in agony.

[53] Nothing is known of Oswulf. On *LDE*'s use of oral sources, see above, p. lxxvi.

complexus circundedit. Rursus eum ad terram proiecit, sed eodem mox momento ab eodem constringebatur.[a] Ita serpentem siue in ignem siue in aquam uel in terram semper proicere potuit, sed qualiter mox in eius collum redierit scire non ualuit. Aliquotiens etiam in particulas ferro consueuit diuidere, sed protinus idem ipse[b] serpens [c]collum eius uidebatur[c] constringere. Et in primis quidem admodum paruus erat, sed paulatim in maius et maius excreuerat, nec tamen ulla eum ueneni infusione ledebat. Quotiens autem ecclesiam, quam sanctissimi confessoris Cuthberti corporis[d] presentia illustrat, intrauit, mox in ipso introitu serpens illum dimittebat, nec quamdiu in ecclesia morabatur, ad eum accedere audebat. Cum uero exiret, protinus collum eius complectens[e] stringebat. Itaque dum per multum tempus [f]tale sustinuisset[f] incommodum, inuento tandem salubri consilio, tribus continue[g] diebus ac noctibus in ecclesia orans perstitit, et postmodum exiens a serpentis complexu deinceps liberatus, in peregrinationem profectus est, nec unquam postea uisus in patria.

13. Eodem[h] tempore quidam ad solenne sanctissimi confessoris festum cum domino suo uenerat, qui cum super sepulchrum oblatione aduenientium multitudinem denariorum conspiceret, furtum animo concepit. Itaque accessit, et astantes fallendo dum quasi sepulchrum oscularetur, quattuor uel quinque nummos ore attraxit. Nec mora os illius cepit intus uehementer ardere, [i]adeo ut (sicut[i] postea fatebatur) ferrum ex igne candens in ore portare sibi uideretur. Respuere nummos uolebat, sed nec aperire os poterat. Cum ita[j] intolerabili cruciatu torqueretur, huc atque[k] illuc per ecclesiam mutus discurrebat, atque omnes dum insanire putabatur, in pauorem conuertebat. Tandem per medium populi prorumpens de ecclesia, de loco ad locum se incessabiliter cursibus ferebat, et cum ore non posset, horrendis motibus et nutibus grauiter se cruciari cunctis ostendebat. Ad ultimum reuersus in se, ad sepulchrum concite recurrit, et prostrato corpore tota cordis intentione ueniam a sancto quesiuit, res quascunque habuerat obtulit. Cunque iam suam oblationem super sepulchrum ponens illud oscularetur, cum ipso osculo de illius ore nummi super sepulchrum ceciderunt. Taliter ab illo cruciatu liberatus, confestim equum ascendens quantotius abire

---

[a] constringitur F   [b] om. F   [c–c] uidebatur collum eius Fx L Y   [d] om. Ca   [e] amplectens T   [f–f] sustinuisset tale H   [g] commune F
[h] De denariis ardentibus in ore cuiusdam (om. H) latronis rubric Fx H T V Y
[i–i] adeo sicut ut Fx Y; adeo sicut L   [j] itaque Ca   [k] itaque Fx L Y

itself around his neck afresh. Again he threw it to the ground, but a moment later it was again entwined around him. However often he might throw the snake into the fire or the water or to the ground, he could not discover how it almost at once returned to his neck. Several times he would cut it into small pieces with a knife, but immediately the very same serpent was again seen to be wrapped around his neck. At first it was very small, but little by little it grew larger and larger, although it did no harm by any spitting out of venom. Every time he entered the church which was irradiated by the presence of the body of the most holy confessor Cuthbert, however, directly on his going in the snake left him, and did not dare to return to him as long as he stayed in the church. When he came out, it immediately wound itself around his neck. So when he had suffered this misfortune for a long time, he was given wholesome advice, and he remained continuously in the church for three days and nights praying. When he came out after this, he was thenceforth freed from the embrace of the snake and, setting off on a pilgrimage, he was never afterwards seen in his homeland.

13. At this same time a certain man, who had come with his master to the solemn feast of the most holy confessor, saw on the tomb a multitude of coins which were the oblations of visitors, and conceived in his mind a theft. So he drew near and in order to deceive those who were standing there he made as if to kiss the tomb, but in fact he took four or five coins into his mouth. At once his mouth began to burn violently inside just as if (as he afterwards confessed) he were carrying an iron glowing from the fire in his mouth. He wanted to spit the coins out, but he was unable to open his mouth. As he was being racked thus by intolerable torment, he ran mutely hither and thither in the church, inducing fear in everyone, for they thought he was mad. At length he burst out of the church through the midst of the people, and made incessant dashes from place to place, showing to all by horrendous gestures and nods (since he could not tell them with his mouth) that he was being severely tortured. At last he came to his senses, and rushed headlong to the tomb where, throwing himself on the ground, he begged forgiveness from the saint with all his heart, and offered everything which he had. When as he was placing his offering on the tomb he kissed it, with that kiss the coins fell out of his mouth on to the tomb. In this way he was freed from his torment, and mounting his horse at once, he hastened to leave as soon as

[lxiii (lxix)]

festinauit, nec unquam *postea Dunhelmum* rediit. Nam cum *sepius ei* *a domino suo multa* fuissent oblata ut secum illo* ueniret, non solum non uenire, sed nec tam prope ut ecclesiam uideret ausus fuerat accedere.

14. Nec* solum comes supradictus et illius uxor, sed etiam familiares illorum* erga sancti Cuthberti ecclesiam multum deuoti extiterant et munifici. Quorum quidam uocabulo Copsi, qui sub Tosti totius comitatus curas gerebat, ecclesiam sancti Germani in Merscum ab Aegelrico episcopo dedicatam et ipsam uillam aliasque infra subscriptas* terras sancto Cuthberto et ad sepulchrum eius seruituris in perpetuum donauit, atque illos qui eis aliquid ex his auferrent, cum episcopo et aliis qui affuerant cum diabolo dampnandos excommunicauit. In Merscum* decem carrucatas terre et dimidiam. *In Thorntun duo carrucatas terre. In Theostcota decem bouetas terre. In Readecliue dimidiam carrucatam terre. In Gisburham unam carrucatam terre.* [54] In cuius donationis signum etiam sciphum argenteum obtulit, qui in hac ecclesia* seruatus* eternam illius facti *retinet memoriam.* [55] Hic idem Copsi postea quanuis breui tempore prouincie* Northanhymbrorum, scilicet illorum qui ad septentrionalem plagam* fluminis Tini habitant, *iubente Willelmo rege procurator est factus.* [56]

---

a–a Dunhelmum postea *Fx H L Y*   *b–b* ei sepius *Fx L Y*   *c–c* multa a domino suo *H*; multa a domino *Fx L Y*   *d* illuc *Fx*   *e* Capitulum *rubric Fx T V Y*   *f* eorum *Fx H L Y*   *g* scriptas *Fx L Y*   *h* Mercum *F*   *i–i* In Redecliue dimidiam carrucatam terre. In Geseburn (Gosebini *Fx*) unam carrucatam terre. In Thornetun (Thorneton *Fx*) duo carrucatas terre. In Teostcota decem bouatas terre *Fx Y*; In Redecliue dimidiam carrucatam terre. In Theoscota decem bouetas terre. In Goseburn unam carrucatam terre. In Thorntun duo carrucatas terre *L;* Redecliue *for* Readecliue *F*   *j* om. *T*   *k* seruatur et *Fx H L Y*   *l–l* memoriam retinet *Ca*   *m* above line *C; om. F*   *n* above line *C; om. F*   *o–o* comes factus est *F;* iubente Willelmo rege procurator factus est *H*

---

[54] The church of St Germanus was at Marske-by-the-Sea (North Yorks.), where there is today a church so dedicated, but no fabric of medieval date survives (N. Pevsner, *Yorkshire: The North Riding* (The Buildings of England ; Harmondsworth, 1966), p. 239); the other lands, which were presumably intended for its support, are approximately five miles to the south-west, now represented by Thornton Fields (NZ 461 518), Tocketts Farm (NZ 461 517), and Rawcliff Banks (NZ 464 516), which lie close to Guisborough (*Yorkshire*, ed. Faull and Stinson, ii. map III). The gift in question must have been made before the Norman Conquest (when Copsig was made earl of Northumbria, below, p. 181 n. 56) but after the consecration of St Germanus's by Bishop Æthelric between 1042 and 1056. For the history of these estates in Domesday Book and their subsequent restoration to Bishop Ranulf Flambard, see *Early Yorkshire Charters*, ii, ed. W. Farrer (Edinburgh, 1915), pp. 261–2 (no. 925) and pp. 295–6 (no. 963). The attribution of the gift to Tostig in Prior Wessington's *Libellus de exordio et statu ecclesie cathedralis Dunelmensis* is unlikely to be correct (London, Lincoln's Inn, Hales 114, fo. 26, printed Raine, *Scriptores tres*, p. ccccxxiii; on Wessington, see Craster, 'Red book', pp. 507–19).

possible and never afterwards returned to Durham. For although he was frequently offered many things by his lord that he should accompany him, not only would he not come, but he did not even dare to come within sight of the church.

14. It was not only Earl Tostig and his wife but also the members of their household who were very devout and munificent towards the church of St Cuthbert. One of these called Copsig, who presided over the affairs of the whole earldom under Tostig, gave in perpetuity to St Cuthbert and to those who were to serve at his tomb the church of St Germanus in Marske, which had been dedicated by Bishop Æthelric, and the vill itself together with the other lands set out below; and together with the bishop and the others who were present, he excommunicated any who might take anything away from these gifts and consigned them to damnation with the devil. In Marske ten and a half carucates. In Thornton two carucates of land. In Tocketts ten bovates of land. In Rawcliff half a carucate of land. In Guisborough one carucate of land.[54] As a token of this gift, he also presented a silver cup, which is preserved in this church and serves as an eternal memorial to this deed.[55] Later on, although only for a short time, this same Copsig was by order of King William made procurator of the earldom of the Northumbrians, that is of those who dwell on the north side of the river Tyne.[56]

[55] For the use of objects, in this case knives, in the Durham archive as records of gifts, see M. Clanchy, *From Memory to Written Record: England 1066–1307* (2nd edn; Oxford, 1993), pp. 38–9, 258–9.

[56] Copsig's origins are unknown, but Aird, *Cuthbert*, p. 64 n. 19, suggests that he was a Yorkshire thegn. According to the account of the earls of Northumbria in *HReg, s.a.* 1072 (Arnold, *Sym. Op.* ii. 198–9), Copsig was given the *comitatus* north of the Tyne which was held by Morcar's deputy, Oswulf, whom Copsig expelled, only to be killed by him on 12 Mar. in the fifth week of his tenure of office. *DPSA* has a similar account (Arnold, *Sym. Op.* ii. 383–4). For other sources and for reasons for assigning Copsig's period of office to 1067, see Freeman, *Norman Conquest*, iv. 741–4; see also W. E. Kapelle, *The Norman Conquest of the North: The Region and its Transformation 1000–1135* (London, 1979), pp. 106–8. *LDE*'s account is somewhat confused, particularly its statement at the beginning of c. 4 that Copsig presided over the whole earldom. Moreover, in C the words *iubente Willelmo rege* ('by order of King William') have been written over an erasure, and the remainder of the sentence, including the word *procurator*, fitted in on a section of the leaf previously left blank; the original words may have been those found in F, *comes factus est* ('was made earl'). This alteration may have been a correction made after the information contained in *HReg* had become available to Symeon; but it may also have had some significance, which now eludes us, in the context of the relations between Durham Cathedral Priory and Bishop Ranulf Flambard who was referred to by contemporaries as *procurator* of England (Rollason, 'Erasures', p. 155).

15. Anno*a* Incarnationis Dominice*b* millesimo sexagesimo sexto, piissimus rex Edwardus uicesimo quarto regni sui anno Nonas Ianuarii defunctus est, pro quo Haroldus regni solium ascendit, sed paruo tempore gubernauit. Ingruentibus enim*c* undique aduersis, contra fortissimum regem Norewegensium, primo per duos comites sed mox terga uertentes, deinde per seipsum non longe ab Eboraco iniit bellum. Ibi quidem uictoria potitus, sed inde diuertens contra potentissimum Normannorum comitem, qui iam in Angliam cum multo exercitu aduenerat dimicauit, sed cum toto pene Anglorum exercitu occubuit.[57]

Willelmus autem regnum adeptus Anglorum, populos Northanhymbrorum diu rebelles sustinuit, quibus tertio regni sui anno quendam Rotbertum cognomine*d* Cumin comitem prefecit. Quem illi ubi aduenientem audierant, omnes relictis domibus fugere parabant. Sed subito niuis tanta nimietas, tantaque hiemis obuenit asperitas, ut omnem eis fugiendi possibilitatem adimeret. Quapropter omnibus idem fuit consilium, ut aut comitem extinguerent, aut simul ipsi caderent. Quod episcopus comiti occurrens nuntiauit, atque ut reuertetur*e* admonuit. At ille qui suos rapinis et cedibus seuire permiserat, iam *f*enim plures ecclesie*f* rusticos interfecerant, datum est illi*g* *h*ne tunc consilium salutis*h* audiret.

Intrauit ergo Dunhelmum cum septingentis hominibus ubique per domos hostiliter agentibus. Summo autem diluculo, Northanhymbrenses congregati per omnes portas irrumpunt, totaque urbe discursantes, socios comitis interficiunt. Tanta denique fuit *i*interfectorum multitudo,*i* ut omnes platee*j* cruore atque*k* cadaueribus replerentur. Supererant adhuc non pauci, qui hostium domus in qua comes erat defendentes, oppugnantium prohibebant accessum. *l*Illi ergo igne*l* iniecto, domum cum his qui intus erant conati sunt incendere. Itaque flammarum globis altius uolitantibus, turris*m* occidentalis que iuxta stabat, iamiamque ab igne cremanda uidebatur. Populis ergo*n* genua flectentibus et sanctum Cuthbertum, ut

a De morte regis sancti Edwardi et de rege Oraldo et Willelmo Conquestore et de occisione Roberti Cumin apud Dunelmum *rubric H*; De occisione Roberti Comin apud Dunhelmum *rubric Fx T V Y* *b* Dominice Incarnationis *Ca* *c* om. *Fx L Y* *d* ex nomine *Fx L Y* *e* reuerteretur *F* *f-f* ecclesie enim plures *F* *g* om. *H* *h-h* tunc illi consilium salutis ut *L* *i-i* multitudo interfectorum *Fx L Y* *j* om. *T* *k* ac *T* *l-l* Igne ergo illi *F* *m* turris ecclesie *Fx H L Y* *n* autem *Fx H L Y*

[57] For the battles mentioned in this passage, that is, the battle of Stamford Bridge on 25 Sept. and the battle of Hastings on 14 Oct., see Stenton, *Anglo-Saxon England*, pp. 588–96;

15. In the year of Our Lord's Incarnation 1066, the most pious King Edward died on 5 January in the twenty-fourth year of his reign, and Harold ascended the throne of the kingdom in his place, but he ruled it for only a short time. With adversities hemming him in on all sides, he first ordered two earls to confront the very powerful king of the Norwegians but they soon fled, and he himself engaged that king in battle not far from York. There indeed he won the victory, but he had to turn back to fight the very powerful duke of the Normans, who had then invaded England with a large army, and in that battle he fell with almost the whole English army.[57]

When William had obtained the kingdom of the English, however, he still had to suffer for a long while the rebelliousness of the Northumbrian people, over whom in the third year of his reign he set an earl called Robert Cumin. When they heard that he was coming, all the Northumbrians left their homes and prepared to flee. But suddenly there came such a heavy fall of snow and such harsh winter weather that all possibility of flight was denied them. Because of this, everyone was of the same opinion, that they should either kill the earl, or themselves perish together. The bishop rushed to the earl, informed him of this, and advised him to go back. But since he had allowed his men to ravage the countryside by pillaging and killing, and they had killed many of the church's peasants, the Lord granted that he should not accept this salutary advice.

He therefore entered Durham with seven hundred men, and they acted towards all the homes in a hostile manner. At first light, however, the Northumbrians who had assembled burst in together through all the gates, and rushed through the whole town killing the earl's companions. So great was the multitude of the slain, that all the streets were full of blood and corpses. Several remained alive, and these defended the house of the enemy in which the earl was, and denied access to the attackers. So the latter threw fire, and tried to burn down the house together with those who were inside. As balls of fire flew up high to a great height, it seemed that the west tower which stood nearby was bound to be burned. So the people knelt down and beseeched St Cuthbert that he should preserve his

for a more detailed discussion of Hastings, R. A. Brown, 'The battle of Hastings', *Anglo-Norman Studies*, iii (1980), 1–21, and for the wider issue of Anglo-Saxon military incompetence, M. Strickland, 'Military technology and conquest: the anomaly of Anglo-Saxon England', *Anglo-Norman Studies*, xix (1996), 353–82. The king of the Norwegians was Harold Hardrada and the two earls ordered to confront him were Edwin of Mercia and Morcar of Northumbria.

ecclesiam suam a flammis illesam seruaret rogantibus, continuo
surgens ab oriente uentus globos flammarum ab ecclesia reiecit,
atque longius omne*a* ab inde periculum reppulit. Attamen domo ut
ceperat ardente, qui intus erant quidam concremati, alii uero*b* dum
foras prorumperent protinus *c*sunt obtruncati.*c* Ita comite secundas*d*
Kalendas Februarii cum suis omnibus preter unum qui uulneratus
euaserat deleto,*e* 58 rex Willelmus grauiter offensus, ducem quendam
cum exercitu ut eius mortem ulcisceretur direxit.*f*

[lxv (lxxi)]　　Cum*g* autem ad Aluertonam uenissent, et iam mane facto
Dunhelmum profecturi essent, tanta nebularum densitas orta est,
ut uix astantes sese alterutrum uidere, uiam uero nullo modo
ualerent*h* inuenire. Stupentibus illis cur hoc esset, et conferentibus
inuicem quidnam facerent, affuit quidam*i* qui diceret homines illos
quendam in sua urbe sanctum habere, qui eis semper in aduersis
protector adesset, quos nemo impune illo uindicante ledere unquam
ualeret. Quibus auditis, mox ad propria sunt reuersi. Hi uero ad quos
interficiendos missi fuerant, nichil ex*j* hostibus antequam reuersi
fuissent agnouerunt, atque ita factum est Deo eos per sanctum
Cuthbertum miserante, ut prius inimicorum abscessum quam aduentum audirent.59

[(lxxii)]　　Attamen*k* eodem anno *l*rege Willelmo*l* cum exercitu Eboracum
ueniente et omnia circumcircaque*m* uastante, episcopus Egelwinus et
maiores natu habito inuicem consilio, incorruptum sanctissimi patris
Cuthberti*n* corpus septuagesimo quinto anno ex quo ab Aldhuno in
Dunhelmum perlatum est tollentes, ad ecclesiam Lindisfarnensem
*o*ceperunt fugere.*o*60

---

a om. Y　　　　　　*b* om. H　　　　　*c–c* obtruncati sunt Fx L Y　　　　*d* iii F
e deleto uitam finiuit Fx L Y　　　*f* et cetera add. L　　　　*g* De nebula apud
Aluertonam rubric Fx H T (truncated by binding) V (s.xv) Y　　　*h* ualebant Fx L Y
i om. T　　*j* de D Fx H L Y　　　*k* De fuga cum corpore sancti Cuthberti ad
insulam Lindisfarnensem et de recessu maris rubric Fx T V Y　　　*l–l* Willelmo H;
Willelmo rege Fx L　　　*m* circumquaque H T; circumcirca Fx L Y　　　*n* om. Y;
ins. over line Fx　　　*o–o* fugere ceperunt Ca

---

58 A passage in *HReg, s.a.* 1069 (Arnold, *Sym. Op.* ii. 186–7), gives a very similar
account of this affair, omitting some details and adding only that the house in which
Cumin was killed was that of the bishop. It does, however, state that he was being sent
north of the Tyne (p. 186), so that Durham would have been a staging post on his journey
(Aird, *Cuthbert*, p. 71). By contrast, Orderic Vitalis (*The Ecclesiastical History of Orderic
Vitalis*, ed. M. Chibnall (6 vols.; OMT, 1969–80), ii. 220) states that he was given the
county of Durham, and that he was killed by the *ciues* of Durham; but Orderic is unlikely
to have been well informed (see Aird, *Cuthbert*, pp. 70–1). For a general account, see
Kapelle, *Norman Conquest of the North*, p. 112. For the significance of *LDE*'s reference to
the west tower of the cathedral, see above, p. 157 and n. 21.

church unharmed from the flames, and at once a wind sprang up
from the east and blew the balls of flame away from the church, and
diverted all danger from it. But the house where the fire had started
blazed fiercely. Some of those who were inside were burned to
death, others rushed out through the doors and were at once cut
down. Thus the earl was killed on 31 January with all his men apart
from one who had escaped wounded.[58] King William reacted angrily
and sent a certain duke with an army in order to avenge the earl's
death.

However, when they had reached Allerton, with the intention of [lxv (lxxi)]
going on to Durham as soon as morning had broken, such a dense fog
covered everything that those who were there could hardly see one
another, and they were quite unable to find the way. While they were
wondering why this was and discussing amongst themselves what
they should do, someone came to them and told them that those men
had in their town a certain saint, who was always their protector in
adversity, and that with him as their avenger no one was ever able to
harm them with impunity. Once they had heard this, they soon
returned home. Indeed those whom they had been sent to kill knew
nothing of their enemies before they had gone away, and thus it
happened that, by God's mercy on them through St Cuthbert, they
heard of their foes' departure before they heard of their arrival.[59]

In that same year, however, when King William came with an army [(lxxii)]
to York and devastated everything round about, Bishop Æthelwine
and the elders of the community took counsel together, and decided
to take up the undecayed body of the most holy father Cuthbert and
to flee to the church of Lindisfarne, this being in the seventy-fifth
year since Ealdhun had brought it to Durham.[60]

---

[59] Allerton is the region of Northallerton (Yorks.; SE 366 942). This abortive expedition
is mentioned only in *LDE*, and may be an invention. *De miraculis* c. 6 (Arnold, *Sym. Op.* i.
245–6) states that Æthelwine and the community fled to Lindisfarne in fear of King
William's reprisals for Cumin's death, whereas in *LDE* their flight is linked rather to the
king's expedition to York. *HReg*, *s.a.* 1069 (Arnold, *Sym. Op.* ii. 189), also seems to link it
to William's expedition to York.

[60] This expedition, the so-called 'Harrying of the North', was precipitated by the
capture of York by a Danish army in Sept. 1069, and the king's campaign of ravaging
continued through to 1070. The dating given here is consistent with the establishment of
Durham being in 995 (above, p. 144 and n. 1). The most vivid account of the 'Harrying' is
that of Orderic Vitalis (*Ecclesiastical History*, ed. Chibnall, ii. 230–3), but see also William
of Malmesbury (*Gesta regum*, ed. Mynors *et al.*, i. 462–3). For other sources and comment,
see Rollason, *Sources*, pp 188–90. For discussion, see Kapelle, *Norman Conquest of the
North*, pp. 120–33, Freeman, *Norman Conquest*, iv. 294–308, and, on the impact of the
'Harrying', D. M. Palliser, 'Domesday Book and the "Harrying of the North"', *Northern*

[*See p. 186 for n. 60 cont.*]

[lxvi]　Et*a* prima quidem nocte in ecclesia sancti Pauli in Gyruum, secunda in Betlingtun,*b* tercia in loco qui Tughala dicitur mansit, quarto die ad ipsius insule aditum comitante omni eius populo peruenit. Sed quoniam*c* illo uenerant*d* *circa uesperam, qua uidelicet hora secundum* tempus suum *circumquaque plenum erat mare,* episcopus et quique maiores *sexui infirmiori et etati teneriori,* ne frigore hiemis que solito asperior ingruerat omnes nocte periclitarentur, erat enim paulo ante Natale Dominicum, condolentes et condolendo gementes, '*Quid*', inquiuunt, '*faciemus?* Ne modo insulam *intremus, fluctuum altitudine prohibemur, nec quo tantam frigoris asperitatem declinemus, manendi locum habemus.*' Illis ita gementibus *subito* mare *siccum*e eis *intreundi aditum illo tantum loco* recedens permisit, cum *circunquaque plenissimum fluctuaret. Mox omnes ingressi,* Deo *laudes* et *beatissimo confessori decantantes, siccis pedibus* cum sacro sui*f* patroni corpore *insule litus attingebant.* Hoc quoque in illo facto ualde fuit mirabile, quod*g* (sicut illi qui *htunc feretrumh* portabant attestari solent) *se precedentes* continuo *fluctus marini sequerentur,i ita ut nec paulatim euntibus precurrerent, nec concite pergentibus diutius remanerent.*[61]

Instante autem Quadragesima tranquillitate reddita sacrum corpus Dunhelmum reportauerunt, atque *j*reconciliata solenniter ecclesia octauum*j* Kalendas Aprilis cum laudibus intrantes ecclesiam, suo in loco illud reposuerunt.[62] Inuenerunt autem imaginem crucifixi in solum deiectam, et a suo ornatu quo a comite supradicto uidelicet Tosti et eius coniuge fuerat uestita, omnino spoliatam.[63] Hanc enim

---

　a De fuga cum corpore sancti Cuthberti ad insulam *rubric H;* Et *om. H*　　*b* Bethlingtun F　　*c* quia L　　*d* peruenerant H　　*e* om. Y; ins. over line Fx　　*f* sancti T　　*g* quia Fx L Y　　*h–h* feretrum tunc Ca　　*i* sequentur H　　*j–j* ipsa die depositionis eius que est tertium decimum F

History, xxix (1993), 1–23. As regards the defensibility of Durham, the only reference to the city's fortifications is that in the late 11th- or early 12th-cent. text *De obsessione Dunelmi* (on which, see above, pp. lxxviii–lxxix), which describes the repulse of a Scottish siege, possibly in 1006, and how the heads of the besiegers were impaled 'per circuitum murorum in stipitibus' (Arnold, *Sym. Op.* i. 216). This text, which probably dates from the period when Durham was acquiring, or had acquired, the walls which it was to preserve through the Middle Ages, does not inspire confidence as regards the fortifications of Durham (cf. M. Bonney, *Lordship and the Urban Community: Durham and its Overlords 1250–1540* (Cambridge, 1990), p. 18, who is incautious in her interpretation of it and speculative in assigning it to Symeon). Note further that *LDE* itself gives an account of the impaling of the heads of dead Scots around the market-place after a siege in 1040, but without reference to walls (above, pp. 168–9). For the possibility that the *De obsessione Dunelmi* may have confused this with the siege it purported to describe, see above, p. 169 n. 39.

[61] This paragraph is an abbreviated version of *De miraculis* c. 6, but the account of the itinerary followed to Lindisfarne is original to *LDE*. Even today, Lindisfarne is cut off

On the first night the body rested in the church of St Paul at [lxvi]
Jarrow, on the second at Bedlington, on the third in the place called
Tughall, and on the fourth day in company with all the saint's people
it reached the approach route to the island itself. But because they
had arrived there sometime in the evening, when on that date it was
high tide around the island, the bishop and certain of the elders were
distressed on account of those of the weaker sex and of tender age, lest
they should all be put in danger during the night by the cold of
winter, which was more severe than usual (for it was shortly before
Christmas), and they groaned: 'What shall we do? We are prevented
from reaching the island by the height of the tide, nor is there any
place where we can stay which is protected from the harshness of the
cold.' As they were thus bewailing their plight, the sea suddenly drew
back from just that one place and allowed them dry passage across,
while in other places the tide remained at its highest. Soon everyone
crossed, singing praises to God and to the most blessed confessor, and
with the holy body of their patron they reached the shore of the island
dry-shod. What was truly miraculous in this was the fact that (as
those who were carrying the shrine at that time are accustomed to
bear witness) the sea-tide followed hard on their heels as they made
their way, so that it neither drew ahead of them while they were
making slow progress, nor did it remain long behind them while they
were advancing rapidly.[61]

When peace returned just before Lent, they carried the holy body
back to Durham, and after reinstating the church they entered it with
praises on 25 March and laid the body back in its place.[62] They found
the crucifix thrown down on to the ground, and completely despoiled
of the decoration with which it had been adorned (as was mentioned
earlier) by Earl Tostig and his wife.[63] This was the only one of the

from the mainland at high tide. The same information about the itinerary is given in *HReg*,
s.a. 1069 (Arnold, *Sym. Op.* ii. 189), which adds the detail that the date of departure was
11 Dec. St Paul's Jarrow was Bede's former church, which had probably been given to the
church of Chester-le-Street by King Guthred (above, p. 125 n. 80). Bedlington (NZ 261
818) and Tughall (NU 215 265) are both in Northumberland; Bedlington with its shire was
in the bishop's hands in 1183 (*Boldon Book*, ed. Austin, pp. 28–9, 32–3).

[62] F gives the date as 20 March, 'the feast-day of St Cuthbert'; but C has been altered
over erasure to give 25 March. This was probably considered to be a correction (or at least
it became the authoritative version), since *HReg*, *s.a.* 1069 (Arnold, *Sym. Op.* ii. 188–9)
also has 25 March as the date on which the community returned to Durham, and this
account is later than that of *LDE*. For discussion of the possible circumstances of the
correction, see Jäschke, in Rollason, *Symeon*, pp. 51–3; and also Rollason, 'Erasures',
p. 153.

[63] On the crucifix, see above, pp. 176–7.

solam ex ornamentis post se in ecclesia reliquerant, ob hoc uidelicet quod ^adifficile in fuga^a portari poterat, simul sperantes quod propter illam maiorem loco reuerentiam hostes exhibere uellent. Verum quidam illorum superuenientes, quicquid in ea auri et argenti uel gemmarum inuenerant, penitus abstrahentes abierunt.

Quo facto rex grauiter indignatus, iussit eos perquisitos comprehendi, et comprehensos ad episcopum et presbyteros eorum iudicio puniendos perduci. At illi nichil ^beis triste^b facientes, permiserunt illesos^c abire.

Nec multo post episcopatum regente Walchero rex predictus magnam auri argentique^d quantitatem, gemmas quoque ^epreciosas perplures^e ad ipsius imaginis ornatum transmisit, quibus episcopus partim ipsam sicut hodie cernitur ^fuestiri fecit,^f partem pro rerum penuria in suos usus expendit.[64]

[lxvii
(lxxiii)] **16.** Sed^g ut parumper ad superiora redeatur, in fuga memorata qua cum sancti patris corpore ad predictam insulam fugerant, quidam ultra amnem Tinam prepotens Gillo Michael per contrarium (id est puer Michaelis) appellatus, nam rectius puer diaboli nuncuparetur, multas fugientibus iniurias irrogauit, iter illorum^h impediendo, ipsosⁱ affligendo, predas ex eis agendo, et quodcunque mali poterat faciendo. Sed non impune. Locato enim in insula sancto corpore, quidam ex clero prouecte etatis ab episcopo domum remittebatur, ut uidelicet qualiter se res circa Dunhelmum et illam ecclesiam haberet, diligenter exploraret. Vbi aliquantulum^j uie peregerat, incumbente iam nocte paululum^k medio in campo requiescens obdormiuit, ubi manifestam de interitu prefati uiri uisionem uidit, quam sicut ipsius uerbis frequenter audiuimus, ita ^lex ordine hic^l scribendam esse iudicauimus:

'Ductus', inquit, 'Dunhelmum, in ecclesia ut michi uidebatur astabam, ubi duos ^msumme auctoritatis^m uiros ante altare uersis ad orientem uultibus assistere uidi.ⁿ Alter etatis medie uir,^o episcopalibus ^psolenniter uestimentis^p indutus, habitu uenerando et uultu honorabili^q magne reuerentie ^rpontificem se monstrabat.^r Alter a dextris eius assistens, rubicundi coloris pallio circumamictus, facie

^{a–a} in fuga difficile *Fx L T Y*   ^{b–b} triste eis *Ca*   ^c illos *T*   ^d et argenti *H*   ^{e–e} perplures preciosas *Ca*; plures preciosas *H*   ^{f–f} fecit uestiri *F* ^g De morte Gillo Michaelis (et eius dampnacione *added H*) *rubric Fx H T V Y* ^h eorum *Ca*   ⁱ illos *T*   ^j cum aliquantum *Fx Y*   ^k paululum iam *H* ^{l–l} hic ex ordine *H Y*; ex ordine *Fx*; hoc ex ordine *L*   ^{m–m} auctoritatis summe *T* ⁿ aspexi *Fx Y*   ^o om. *T*   ^{p–p} uestimentis solempniter *T*   ^q uenerabili *Ca V*   ^{r–r} pontificatum officium se gerere monstrabat *T*

ornaments which they had left behind them in the church, because it would have been difficult to carry with them in their flight, and they also hoped that because of it the enemy would show greater reverence towards the place. But in truth some of them had come and had taken away absolutely everything they could find in the way of gold, silver, and gems. The king was very angry about this and ordered the men in question to be sought out and captured, and to be delivered bound to the bishop and his priests to be punished according to their judgment. They did no harm to them, however, and allowed them to go away unscathed.

Not long afterwards while Bishop Walcher was ruling the see, the aforesaid king sent a great quantity of gold and silver and also many precious stones to ornament this image, and these the bishop used in part to adorn it as it is to be seen today, and in part appropriated on account of his penury.[64]

16. Let us now speedily return, however, to what we were discussing above. In the flight which we have described to the aforesaid island with the body of the holy father, a certain powerful man beyond the river Tyne called Gillo Michael (a perverse naming since it means the servant of Michael whereas he should more properly have been called the servant of the Devil) did much harm to the fugitives, obstructing their way, afflicting them with hardship, robbing them, and doing whatever mischief to them he could. But not with impunity! For when the holy body had been established on the island, a certain member of the clergy of advanced age was sent home by the bishop, so that he might diligently enquire how things stood with Durham and with the church. When he had travelled some distance along the way, night fell and he lay down to rest for a while in the middle of a field where he fell asleep and saw a clear vision of the death of the aforesaid man. We have judged it appropriate to write this down here in his own words as we have frequently heard it:

'I was taken to Durham', he said, 'and there it seemed to me that I was standing in the church, when I saw two men of the highest authority who stood before the altar and looked towards the east. One of them was a middle-aged man, whose solemn episcopal vestments, venerable appearance, and dignified features showed him to be a very reverend bishop. The other, who stood on his right and was clad in a robe of reddish colour, had a long face, a very wispy beard, a noble

[lxvii (lxxiii)]

---

[64] Walcher was bishop of Durham (1071–80); the king was William I (1066–87).

paululum producta, barba admodum tenui, statura procera, pulcherrimi iuuenis formam gerebat. Post aliquod temporis interuallum, reflectentes ab altari oculos per ecclesiam uertunt, cuius desertionem quasi grauiter ferens episcopus ait, "Ve tibi Cospatrice,[a] [b]ue tibi Cospatrice![b] ecclesiam meam suis rebus euacuasti, et in desertum conuertisti." Hic enim Cospatricus hoc maxime [c]consilium dederat,[c] ut fugientes ecclesiam relinquerent, et ipse maximam [d]ornamentorum eius partem[d] secum abduxerat.

Interea dum cupiens ad illos accedere nequaquam tamen auderem, iuuenis ille digito innuens, moderata uoce me nomine meo aduocauit, et an nossem que esset illa pontificalis persona, interrogauit. Cui dum me nescire responderem,[e] "Iste," [f]ait, "est[f] tuus dominus, sanctus uidelicet antistes Cuthbertus." Confestim ad [g]pedes eius[g] procidi, obsecrans ut sue ecclesie atque[h] suis miseriis[i] subueniret. Aliquanto post inclinatis reuerenter ad altare capitibus, [j]lento inde maturoque[j] incessu simul procedebant; atque ubi ad hostium peruenerant, iuuenis ille prior egrediens paulum[k] processit, sed episcopus in ipso hostio substitit. Qui respiciens, meque qui a longe sequebar aduocans, "Dic," inquit, "Earnane,[65] [l]an nosti[l] quis sit iuuenis ille?" [m]Cui ego, "Domine," inquam,[m] "non noui." Et ille, "Hic," inquit, "est sanctus Oswaldus."

Inde simul ad australem plagam urbis paulo longius progredientes[n] subsistunt. Quo et ego uocatus ab episcopo ueni, iussusque[o] deorsum respicere, uallem [p]infinite profunditatis[p] plenam animabus hominum uidi. Vbi et memoratus Gillo Michael penis atrocibus torquebatur, in locis enim[q] teterrimis[r] [s]prostratus iacebat,[s] et fenaria falce preacuta ultra citraque transfossus, intolerabiles patiebatur cruciatus. Clamabat miser et diros ululatus ac flebiles miserabiliter uoces sine intermissione emittebat. Nulla [t]erat misero temporis[t] intercapedo, qua uel ad horam a pena respirare potuisset.[u] Similes cruciatus et [v]ceteri omnes[v] patiebantur. Inquisitus a sancto Cuthberto an aliquem ibi agnoscerem, respondi [w]me ibidem agnouisse[w] Gillonem. Et ille, "Vere," ait, "hic est ipse. Mortuus nanque his

---

[a] Gospatric- *throughout* F   [b-b] *om.* H   [c-c] dederat consilium *Ca*
[d-d] partem ornamentorum eius *Fx Y (partem ins. above line)*   [e] respondissem *F*
[f-f] est ait *F Fx H Y*   [g-g] eius pedes *Fx Y*   [h] et *Fx (corr. to atque in marg.)*
H Y   [i] ministris *L*   [j-j] lentoque inde maturo *T*   [k] paululum *Ca D Fx*
H L V Y   [l-l] agnosti *L V*   [m-m] Cui inquam domine *H Y*
[n] procedentes *Fx H Y*   [o] iussus *Fx (with que ins. over line) Y*
[p-p] profunditatis infinite *Fx;* infinite profunditatis infinite *Y*   [q] *om. Ca*
[r] tenebrosis *H*   [s-s] iacebat prostratus *Fx Y*   [t-t] erat temporis *H;* erat

stature, and the appearance of a very handsome young man. After some time had passed, they turned their eyes away from the altar towards the church, and the bishop, who seemed to take it very hard that the church was deserted, said: "Woe to you Cospatrick, woe to you Cospatrick! You have emptied my church of its possessions, and turned it into a desert." Now it was this Cospatrick who had chiefly given the advice, that they should flee and leave the church, and he himself had taken away with him the largest part of the ornaments.

While I was yearning to approach them but in no way dared to do so, the young man pointed to me and in a quiet voice called me by name, asking me whether I knew the identity of that episcopal personage. When I replied that I did not know, he said: "He is your lord, that is the holy bishop Cuthbert." At once I threw myself at his feet, begging him to come to the aid of his church in its adversity. Shortly afterwards they both bowed their heads to the altar, and then together they set off first at a slow pace and then more quickly. When they had reached the door, the young man went out first a little way ahead of the bishop, who stood on the doorstep. Looking round Cuthbert called to me as I was following at a distance. "Tell me, Ernan,"[65] he said, "do you know who that young man is?" "I do not know, my lord," I replied. "This," he said, "is St Oswald."

Then they went on together a short distance on the southern side of the city and there they stopped. The bishop called me to come and, when I looked down as I was ordered to, I saw a valley of infinite depth full of the souls of men. There Gillo Michael was being tormented with appalling sufferings, for he lay stretched out in the foulest places and, run through from one side of his body to the other with a sharp hay scythe, he suffered intolerable tortures. The miserable man cried out wretchedly and incessantly with dire wails and doleful howls. No respite was given to the wretch, in which he might for a time have been relieved of his suffering. All the others there were suffering similar torments. St Cuthbert asked me if I knew anyone there, and I replied that I recognized Gillo. "That is indeed he," the saint said. "For he has died and been consigned to these

temporis misero *Fx (corr. in marg.) Y*; enim misero erat temporis *T*   " posset *F* ⱽ⁻ᵛ omnes ceteri *Fx Y*   ʷ⁻ʷ me agnoscere ibi *Fx;* ibidem me agnouisse *H*; me agnouisse ibi *Y*

---

[65] Monks of Durham of this name appear 26th and 129th in the list at the beginning of *LDE* (pp. 6–7, 10–11). The name is an unusual one, and a family connection with the clerk named here is not impossible.

miseriis et doloribus *^a*est deputatus."*^a* At ego, "Domine," inquam, "non est mortuus. Sero nanque sanus et incolumis in domo sua epulatus est, grandeque conuiuium nunc illis *^b*et illis*^b* locis preparatum, eum expectat." At ille, *^c*"Et ego,"*^c* inquit, "dico, uere nunc mortuus est. Ipse enim*^d* et alii quos cum eo uidisti, quoniam pacem meam fregerunt, et michi in*^e* meis iniurias fecerunt, hos cruciatus et hec tormenta compelluntur sustinere."

His dictis euigilaui, statimque ascendens equum, hortatus sum socios ut mecum festinarent. Mirantibus illis causam tam subite festinationis prefatum hominem mortuum, et a quo illius mortem audierim indicaui. Quod*^f* illi credere noluerunt, et me quia credidi deriserunt. Itaque tota nocte pergentes, mane*^g* facto diuertimus parumper de uia ad proximam ecclesiam audituri missam. Interrogatus ut solet a popularibus quos rumores afferrem, predicti hominis mortem nuntiaui. Illi uero quoniam pridie sanum nouerant, falsum me dicere respondebant.*^h* Sed mox quidam ex illius familia aduenientes, dominum suum ipsa nocte mortuum nuntiabant. Ego diligenter coram omnibus horam mortis eius inquirens, eadem noctis hora eum mortuum agnoui, qua illum horrendis cruciatibus traditum *ⁱ*sancto michi*ⁱ* ostendente Cuthberto conspexi.

Cuius tormenta intolerabilia comiti Cospatrico,*^j* sed et ea que de illo a predicto sancto audieram,*^k* dum referrem, *^l*pauens ille*^l* intremuit, moxque nudis pedibus ad insulam ubi sanctum corpus fuerat incedens, ueniam eorum que in eum deliquerat, precibus et muneribus petiuit. Veruntamen postea nunquam *^m*ei fuerat idem*^m* qui prius status honoris, expulsus enim*ⁿ* de comitatu multas quamdiu uixit, aduersantium rerum importunitates et afflictiones pertulit."⁶⁶

[lxviii (lxxiv)] **17.** Reportato*^o* in Dunhelmum (sicut iam dictum est) beatissimi confessoris corpore, Egelwinus quinto decimo *^p*sui episcopatus*^p*

---

^{a–a} deputatus est *T*   *^{b–b}* om. *L T V*   *^{c–c}* om. *T*   *^d* ins. over line *Fx*; om. *Y*   *^e* et *Fx Y*   *^f* Quo *C*   *^g* mane autem *Fx*   *^h* responderunt *Ca*   *^{i–i}* michi sancto *Fx (corr. in marg.) Y*   *^j* sic *F*   *^k* om. *Ca*   *^{l–l}* ille pauens *H*   *^{m–m}* fuerat ei eidem *Fx Y*   *ⁿ* namque *Fx*   *^o* Deportato *F H Y*; Egelwynus episcopus cum thesauris ecclesie fugit *rubric Fx H T V Y*   *^{p–p}* episcopatus sui *T*

---

⁶⁶ *HReg*, *s.a.* 1072 (Arnold, *Sym. Op.* ii. 196), records that in that year William the Conqueror deprived Cospatrick of his office. The account of the earls of Northumbria which is inserted into the text immediately afterwards (p. 199) states that he was the son of Maldred, son of Crinan, and Algitha, daughter of Earl Uhtred of Bamburgh, and that he bought the earldom. After his deprivation he fled to Malcolm, king of Scots, and was

miseries and sufferings." "But, lord," I said, "he is not dead. This evening he dined safe and sound in his home, and he is expected at a great feast prepared for him in such and such a place." "And I say," said he, "that he is indeed now dead. For he and the others whom you see with him are compelled to suffer these agonies and torments because they have infringed my peace and have done harm to me through my people."

When he had said this, I woke up and mounting my horse at once I called to my companions that they should hasten to come with me. When they wondered as to the reason for this sudden haste, I told them that the aforesaid man was dead, and I explained to them from whom I had heard of his death. They refused to believe this, and laughed at me because I believed it. So we travelled all night and in the morning we turned aside for a little while to a nearby church to hear mass. When as is the custom the people asked me what news I was bringing, I informed them of the death of the aforementioned man. Because they knew that he had been well the day before, however, they replied that I was speaking a falsehood. But soon certain members of his household arrived and announced that their lord had died that very night. In the presence of all I enquired diligently as to the hour of his death, and I learned that he had died at the very time when St Cuthbert had shown me him handed over to horrendous torments.

When I told Earl Cospatrick of Gillo Michael's intolerable torments and also of what I had heard from the aforesaid saint about Cospatrick himself, he was stricken with fear, and he soon came barefoot to the island where the holy body was, and asked forgiveness with presents and gifts for those things which he had done to offend the saint. Notwithstanding, he never afterwards regained his former position of honour, for he was expelled from his earldom and as long as he lived he was beset by many misfortunes and afflictions.'[66]

17. When the body of the most blessed confessor had been brought back to Durham as we have described, Æthelwine, in the fifteenth year of his episcopate, took part of the treasures of [lxviii (lxxiv)]

granted Dunbar. Nothing is known of Gillo Michael, although the name occurs in *Liber Vitae*, fo. 16, and in documents from Northumberland and Durham, *c.*1200 (G. W. S. Barrow, 'Northern English society in the early Middle Ages', *Northern History*, iv (1969), 1–28, at p. 9, and Aird, *Cuthbert*, pp. 78–9, arguing further that the episode which follows may be symptomatic of the hostility of the Northumbrians north of the Tyne to the community of St Cuthbert.

anno, partem thesaurorum ecclesie asportans, Angliam relicturus nauem ascendit. Sed cum iam cupito itinere uersus Coloniam nauigaret, uento repulsus in Scotiam ibidem hiemauit. Inde proficiscens, apud Elig ab hominibus regis capitur, et usque Abendunam perductus, ex precepto regis diligenti custodia tenetur.[67] Admonitus frequenter reddere ea que de ecclesia tulerat, nichil se inde accepisse[a] iuramento affirmabat. Sed dum[b] quadam die manducaturus manus lauaret, ex illius brachiis armilla usque[c] manum cunctis intuentibus delabens, manifesto periurio episcopum notabat. Itaque iubente rege in carcerem detruditur, ubi dum ex nimia cordis anxietate comedere nollet, fame ac dolore moritur.[68]

[lxix]   18. Cum[d] uero post illius discessum ecclesia per annum pontificali[e]
(lxxv)]   ministerio uacasset, anno ab Incarnatione Domini millesimo septuagesimo secundo, qui est annus regni Willelmi septimus, Walcherus de gente Hlothariorum natu nobilis, diuina et seculari scientia[f] non mediocriter institutus, ab ipso rege eligitur, et ad pontificatum ecclesie sancti Cuthberti consecratur, uir uenerande canitiei, sobrietate morum[g] et honestate uite tali dignus honore. Ipse quidem excepto illo de quo supradictum est simoniaco et post aliquot menses mortuo, primus post Aidanum ex clericali ordine ipsius ecclesie suscepit presulatum, sed uite laudabilis conuersatione religiosum preferebat monachum.[69]

Qui cum clericos ibidem inueniret, clericorum morem in diurnis et nocturnis officiis eos[h] seruare docuit, nam antea magis consuetudines monachorum in his imitati fuerant, sicut a progenitoribus

---

 a cepisse *Fx Y*   *b* cum *Fx Y*   *c* usque ad *Fx H Y*   *d* Walcherus factus est Dunelmensis ecclesie (*om. Fx T*) episcopus *rubric Fx H T V Y*   *e om. Y* (*ins. over line Fx*)   *f* sentencia *L*   *g om. T*   *h om. T*

---

[67] According to ASC D Æthelwine, bishop of Durham (1056–71), was outlawed at Easter 1070 (which was the fifteenth year of his episcopate), apparently at a council at Westminster, and this is presumably the reason for his flight from Durham. See Freeman, *Norman Conquest*, iv. 335–8, 812–13, who proposes the unnecessarily strained argument that the king's displeasure resulted from Æthelwine's failure to discipline those who had desecrated the crucifix at Durham during the bishop's flight to Lindisfarne. According to ASC DE, Æthelwine joined Hereward the Wake and the rebels at Ely and was captured and sent to Abingdon, as *LDE* describes, in 1071 where he died during the winter of that year (ASC D wrongly places this under 1072). Æthelwine's original intention of sailing to Cologne is itself noteworthy as a possible indication of links between northern England and the Rhineland; on links between Cologne and England generally, see e.g. V. Ortenberg, *The English Church and the Continent in the Tenth and Eleventh Centuries: Cultural, Spiritual, and Artistic Exchanges* (Oxford, 1992), pp. 75–6. See also the reference in the laws of Æthelred (IV.8) to 'the subjects of the emperor [of Germany] who came in their

the church and boarded a ship to leave England. But when he had set
sail with the intention of travelling to Cologne, he was blown by the
wind to Scotland and there he spent the winter. Setting out again
from there, he was captured by the king's men at Ely, and taken to
Abingdon where he was held in close custody by the king's orders.[67]
He was frequently admonished to give back what he had taken from
the church, but he always affirmed on oath that he had taken nothing
from it. But as one day he was washing his hands before eating, a
bracelet slipped down from his arm on to his hand with everyone
watching, and thus the bishop was shown to be guilty of clear
perjury. So on the king's orders he was thrown into jail, where he
refused to eat because of the great anguish he felt in his heart, and he
died of hunger and sorrow.[68]

18. After his departure the church was for a year lacking anyone to [lxix
fulfil the episcopal office, but then in the year of Our Lord's (lxxv)]
Incarnation 1072, which was the seventh year of the reign of William,
Walcher, a noble-born man of Lotharingian race, exceedingly well
instructed in divine and secular knowledge, was elected by the king
himself, and consecrated to the bishopric of the church of St
Cuthbert. He was a venerable white-haired man, worthy of such an
honour by the sobriety of his ways and the integrity of his life.
Although, apart from that simoniac whom we described above and
who was dead after a few months, he was the first from the order of
clerks to become bishop of this church since the time of Aidan, he
showed himself by the manner of his praiseworthy life to be at heart a
pious monk.[69]

Finding his church served by clerks, he instructed them to observe
the day-time and night-time offices according to the customs of
clerks, for previously they had rather imitated the customs of monks

ships [to or through] London' (*The Laws of the Kings of England from Edmund to Henry I*,
ed. and trans. A. J. Robertson (Cambridge, 1925), pp. 72–3).

[68] This account of Æthelwine's end is peculiar to *LDE* and seems very partial.

[69] The simoniac was Eadred (see above, pp. 20–3, 168–9). Regarding Walcher, *HReg*,
s.a. 1072 (Arnold, *Sym. Op.* ii. 195) adds that he was of the clergy of Liège, as does the
summary beginning *Regnante apud* (below, pp. 260–1), and that after his election he was
escorted to York by a housecarl called Eilaf, and thence by the king's order Earl Cospatrick
escorted him to Durham, where he was installed in the middle of Lent (3 Apr. 1072). On
Walcher's appearance and character, cf. William of Malmesbury's account of him as 'uir
neque immodestus neque illiteratus', and also his story of how Edward the Confessor's
widow Edith was so struck at his consecration by him 'cesarie lacteolum, uultu roseum,
statura pregrandem' that she predicted that he would be a martyr (*De gestis pontificum*, ed.
Hamilton, p. 272).

suis (ut supradictum est) qui inter monachos nutriti et educati extiterant, hereditaria semper traditione didicerant.[70]

[lxx 19. Exacto[a] tempore aliquanto rex supradictus de Scotia [b]quo cum[b]
(lxxvi)] exercitu uenerat,[c] rediens Dunhelmum intrauit,[71] et diligenter inter-
rogans an corpus beati Cuthberti ibidem requiesceret, cunctis[d]
uociferantibus et iurantibus illud ibi haberi, credere noluit. Decreuit
ergo rem [e]uisu explorare,[e] habens secum episcopos et abbates qui eo
iubente id deberent perficere. Iam enim disposuerat, ut si sanctum ibi
corpus inuentum non esset, nobiliores et natu maiores uniuersos
obtruncari preciperet. Omnibus itaque pauentibus et Dei[f] misericordiam per sancti Cuthberti merita implorantibus, in ipsa Omnium
Sanctorum festiuitate predicto episcopo missam celebrante, rex cum
id quod animo conceperat, iamiamque perficere uellet, repente nimio
calore cepit estuare et estuando fatigari, ut uix [g]tolerare tantum
calorem[g] potuisset. Festinans ergo de ecclesia exire, relictoque
quod[h] ingenti copia preparatum fuerat conuiuio, equum confestim
ascendit, et quousque ad Tesam ueniret, in cursum urgere non
cessauit. Quo indicio magnum Dei confessorem Cuthbertum ibi
requiescere fatebatur, et populum Deo prohibente ledere non per-
mittebatur.[72]

[lxxi 20. Post[i] tempus aliquot quendam uocabulo Rannulfum illo miserat,
(lxxvii)] qui ipsius sancti populum regi tributum soluere compelleret. Quod
illi grauiter ferentes (scilicet quod nouas consuetudines cogerentur
subire), consuetum in aduersis sancti Cuthberti auxilium studebant

  [a] Willelmus rex de Dunelmo fugit incredulus incorrupti corporis Cuthberti *rubric H*;
De Dunelmo fugit Willelmus incredulus de incorruptione corporis sancti Cuthberti
rubric Fx T V Y [b-b] cum quo *Fx Y* [c] ierat *Fx Y* [d] cunctisque *Fx
H Y* [e-e] explorare uisu *V* [f] *om. H* [g-g] tantum calorem tolerare *Fx
H Y* [h] *add. above line C*; quia *D* [i] De fugacione cuiusdam Ranulfi *rubric
Fx H T V Y*

  [70] The cross-reference is to pp. 102–3, 116–17, above. For the present passage, cf.
Malmesbury's words: 'canonicos monachili seruitio assuetos, quod semper monachum
habuisset episcopum, ad usum clericorum redegit' (loc. cit.). See J. Barrow, 'English
cathedral communities and reform in the late tenth and eleventh centuries', Rollason,
Anglo-Norman Durham, pp. 25–39, at 33–4. The possibility that Walcher may have found
the constitution of the community of St Cuthbert difficult to understand is suggested by a
letter of Lanfranc to him, indicating that he had asked advice regarding 'a priest brought
up in a monastery without being professed as a monk' (*The Letters of Lanfranc, Archbishop
of Canterbury*, ed. H. Clover and M. Gibson (OMT, 1979)), no. 45 (pp. 140–3), on which
see Aird, *Cuthbert*, p. 112.

in these offices, as they had always learned them from the traditions of their forefathers (as mentioned earlier) who had been cared for and educated among monks.[70]

19. Some time later King William entered Durham on his way back from Scotland where he had been with his army.[71] He diligently enquired whether the body of St Cuthbert rested there, but although everyone cried aloud and swore on oath that it was there, he refused to believe it. So he decided to investigate the matter by a visual inspection, having with him bishops and abbots who were to perform this task on his orders. For he had resolved that if the holy body were not found there, he would give orders for all the most noble and most senior to be executed. While everyone was in great fear and was imploring the mercy of God through the merits of St Cuthbert, and the bishop was celebrating mass, it being the feast of All Saints, the king wanted to put into effect the idea which he had conceived, when suddenly he began to burn with a terrible heat and to be so wearied by it, that he could hardly bear such a high temperature. Hastening to leave the church, he left behind a great feast which had been lavishly prepared for him, and he at once mounted his horse, ceaselessly urging it to a gallop until he reached the river Tees. By this sign he acknowledged that the great confessor of God Cuthbert rests there, and he was not permitted to harm the people because God prohibited him from doing so.[72]

    [lxx (lxxvi)]

20. Some time later the king sent there a certain man called Ranulf, who was to compel the people of St Cuthbert to pay tribute to the king. They took this badly, because it meant that they were being subjected to new customs, and they devoted their efforts to seeking the aid which St Cuthbert usually gave them in adversity. So during

    [lxxi (lxxvii)]

[71] The campaign in question began with William the Conqueror's invasion of Scotland on 15 Aug. 1072 to subjugate King Malcolm, on which see Freeman, *Norman Conquest*, iv. 514–18, and D. C. Douglas, *William the Conqueror: The Norman Impact on England* (London, 1964), pp. 226–8.

[72] All Saints day is 1 Nov. The story of William the Conqueror's doubts about St Cuthbert's body is told in different words by Roger of Howden, who describes those who were to investigate the body simply as chaplains, and also links William's confirmation of Durham's privileges and his grant of Hemingbrough directly to this incident; see *Cronica Rogeri de Houedene*, ed. Stubbs, i. 126–7. In *CMD* (Craster, 'Red book', p. 528), however, William's visit is described much more favourably. According to this the king gladly learned about St Cuthbert's life, and was so impressed that he granted money, confirmation of privileges, and also Waltham with all its appurtenances.

inquirere. Nocte igitur*a* qua finita tributum populo erat impositurus, beatus Cuthbertus ei per somnium assistens, baculo pastorali quem manu gestabat illum*b* impulit, et auctoritate pontificali et uultu minaci increpauit, quod illuc ad populum suum affligendum*c* ausus fuerit uenire, dicens quod non impune hoc presumpserit, et nisi cito*d* recederet peiora passurus esset. Itaque de somno euigilans, tanta detinebatur infirmitate ut nullo modo de stratu ualeret resurgere. Mox coram omnibus que uiderat et audierat narrauit, et ut pro se apud sanctum confessorem intercederent*e* humiliter rogauit, deinceps nil tale in eius *f*populum presumpturus,*f* si modo euaderet uiuus. Mittens ergo ad eius sepulchrum pallium (quod huc usque in hac ecclesia in huius facti memoriam seruatur), se illi et suis omnibus fidelem *g*ac deuotum seruum*g* fore promisit, si nunc*h* culpam et culpe penam sibi dimittere dignaretur. Verum inualescente infirmitate, per diuersa episcopatus loca in feretro se circumferri fecit, *i*reatumque suum et*i* uindictam ubique *j*omnibus ostendit.*j* Qui quamdiu in locis ad episcopatum pertinentibus morabatur, graui iugiter egritudine laborauit, cum uero ea derelinquens ad propria remeare cepisset, confestim ab infirmitate conualuit.[73]

His et aliis uirtutum miraculis per sanctum Cuthbertum declaratis, rex ipse*k* Willelmus sanctum confessorem et illius ecclesiam in magna semper ueneratione habuit, et regiis muneribus honorauit, terrarum quoque*l* illius possessiones augmentauit. Nam et Billingham quam olim ab Ecgredo episcopo conditam sancto Cuthberto diximus, quam uiolentia malignorum abstulerat, ipse rex ecclesie*m* restituit, et pro sua suorumque filiorum salute ad uictum in ipsa ecclesia *n*sancto Cuthberto*n* ministrantium, quietam et ab omni aliorum consuetudine liberam in perpetuum possidendam donauit. Leges quoque et consuetudines ipsius sancti sicut antiqua regum auctoritas stabilierat, ipse

---

a uero F   *b* ipsum Fx Y   *c* confligendum F   *d* citius T
e intercedere deberent Fx Y   *f-f* populo (populum Fx) presumpturus iureiurando promisit Fx Y   *g-g* seruum ac deuotum F   *h* om. Fx L   *i-i* reatum et suam L   *j-j* ostendit omnibus Ca   *k* ille Y   *l* que Y   *m* om. H
n-n om. F

---

73 The tax-gatherer may have been Ranulf Flambard, bishop of Durham (1099–1128), that is, while *LDE* was being composed, although this would imply considerable hostility towards that prelate on the part of *LDE*; see Freeman, *Norman Conquest*, iv. 521–2, and, for the implications of the possible identification, Aird, in Rollason, *Symeon*, p. 44, and

the night before the day on which the tribute was to be imposed on the people, St Cuthbert appeared to Ranulf in a dream, struck him with the pastoral staff which he held in his hand, rebuked him with episcopal authority and with a threatening countenance that he should have dared to have come there to afflict his people, and told him that he had not presumed to do this with impunity, and that he would suffer still worse if he did not go away quickly. When he woke from sleep, he found himself stricken with such infirmity that he could not rise from his bed at all. He soon related in the presence of everyone what he had seen and heard, and he humbly asked that they should intercede for him with the holy confessor, declaring that he would henceforth not presume to do anything of this sort to the saint's people if only he might escape alive. So he sent a precious cloth to his tomb (which is still preserved in this church as a memorial to this event), and promised that he would be a faithful and devoted servant to the saint and all his people, if the saint would deign now to remit his guilt and the punishment attached to it. His illness only got worse, however, and he had himself carried around the various parts of the bishopric on a litter to show to everyone his guilt and the vengeance which had been wreaked on him. As long as he remained in places belonging to the bishopric he suffered continuously from this grave illness, but when he left them and began his return journey to where he came from, he at once recovered from his infirmity.[73]

When these and other miracles of St Cuthbert had been made known, King William himself held the holy confessor and his church always in great veneration, honoured it with royal gifts, and also increased its landed possessions. For he restored to the church Billingham, which had formerly been founded for St Cuthbert by Bishop Ecgred (as we said) but which had been taken away by the violence of evil men; and for the salvation of himself and his sons the king gave it for the sustenance of those serving St Cuthbert in this church, quit and free of all customs and to be held in perpetuity. He also confirmed by his authority and consent the laws and customs of the saint, as they had been established by the

---

above, p. 141 n. 110. For the potential significance of the taxation itself, see Kapelle, *Norman Conquest of the North*, pp. 134–5, who dates the taxation to 1073 or 1074 on the grounds that in *LDE*'s narrative it comes between King William's Scottish expedition of 1072 and Aldwin's arrival in the north in 1073 or 1074 (pp. 269–70 n. 56; above, pp. 196–7, below, pp. 200–3).

quoque suo consensu et auctoritate confirmauit, et illibatas ab omnibus seruari imperauit.[a][74]

[lxxii 21. His[b] temporibus quidam in prouincia Merciorum presbiter ac
(lxxviii)] prior in monasterio quod in Wincelcumbe situm est, habitu et actione monachus uocabulo Aldwinus habitabat, qui uoluntariam paupertatem et mundi contemptum cunctis seculi honoribus ac diuitiis pretulerat. Didicerat[c] ex Historia Anglorum quod prouincia Northanhymbrorum crebris quondam [d]choris monachorum,[d] ac multis constipata fuerit agminibus sanctorum, qui in carne non secundum carnem uiuentes celestem in terris conuersationem ducere gaudebant. Quorum loca (uidelicet monasteria) licet iam in solitudinem sciret redacta, desiderauit inuisere, ibique ad imitationem illorum pauperem uitam ducere. Perueniens ergo ad Eoueshamense monasterium, desiderium suum quibusdam ex fratribus patefecit, e quibus duos mox in sui propositi societatem sibi[e] adiunxit, quorum alter diaconus postea presbiter Elfwius,[f] alter ignarus litterarum uocabatur Reinfridus. Quibus abbas ipsorum non aliter [g]abeundi licentiam[g] dare uoluit, nisi prius Aldwinum eis preponeret, et curam animarum illorum ipsi[h] commendaret.[75]

Perrexerunt itaque simul[i] pedibus incedentes tres monachi, unum tantummodo secum[j] ducentes asellum, quo libri necessarii et uestimenta sacerdotalia ad diuinum celebrandum mysterium[k] ferebantur.[76] Et primo quidem super [l]ripam Tini[l] fluminis ad plagam septentrionalem in loco qui dicitur[m] Munecaceastre[n] quod 'Monachorum Ciuitas' appellatur, habitare ceperunt, qui locus [o]licet ad episcopatum Dunhelmensem[o] pertineat,[p] iuris tamen[q] Northanhymbrorum comitis

---

[a] precepit *Ca*   [b] De aduentu Aldwini monachi sociorumque eius in Northumbriam *rubric Fx H T V Y*   [c] Hic didicerat *Ca*   [d-d] monachorum choris *Fx Y*   [e] *om. H*   [f] Elwius *F*   [g-g] licentiam abeundi *Fx Y*   [h] illi *Fx Y*   [i] *om. H*   [j] *om. H*   [k] ministerium *L*   [l-l] Tinam *T*   [m] *om. H Y; ins. above line Fx*   [n] Muncacestre *F*   [o-o] licet *ins. above line Fx;* ad episcopatum Dunhelmensem licet *Y*   [p] *om. T*   [q] *Ins. above line Fx; om. Y*

---

[74] The cross-reference concerning Billingham is to pp. 92–3, above. The laws and customs referred to were presumably those granted by the kings Guthred and Alfred (above, pp. 124–7). Cf. the account of Roger of Howden (*Cronica Rogeri de Houedene*, ed. Stubbs, i. 127): 'legesque ecclesie ipsius, et consuetudines, quam meliores retro actis temporibus habuerat, in perpetuum firmauit seruandas.'

[75] The *Historia Anglorum* mentioned here was certainly Bede's *Ecclesiastical History of*

authority of former kings, and ordered that they should be kept by all without infringement.[74]

21. At this time there lived a certain man called Aldwin in the [lxxii province of the Mercians, a priest and prior in the monastery at (lxxviii)] Winchcombe, a man who was a monk by his habit and by his actions, and who had preferred voluntary poverty and contempt of the world to all worldly honours and riches. He had learned from the *History of the English* that the kingdom of the Northumbrians had once been full of numerous choirs of monks and many hosts of saints, who rejoiced to lead a heavenly life on earth, living in the flesh but not according to the flesh. He desired to visit the places of these people, in other words their monasteries, although he knew that they had been deserted; and there to lead a life of poverty in imitation of them. So he went to the monastery of Evesham and revealed his desire to certain of the brothers, two of whom soon joined him in his plan. One of these was a deacon and later a priest, Elfwy, the other was a man called Reinfred who was ignorant of letters. Their abbot was unwilling to give them permission to go, unless he might first of all appoint Aldwin over them and commend to him the cure of their souls.[75]

So the three monks set out together on foot, leading with them only one donkey on which were borne books and priestly vestments necessary for the celebration of the divine mystery.[76] They first of all began to live on the bank of the river Tyne on the northern side at a place called Monkchester, which means 'City of the Monks', a place which although it belongs to the bishopric of Durham is under the

---

the *English People*; on its significance for monastic reformers of the late 11th and 12th cents., see Davis, *Studies in Medieval History*, ed. Harper-Bill, pp. 103–16. *LDE* later (below, pp. 210–11) states that Aldwin arrived in the third year of Bishop Walcher, which, since he was consecrated in March 1071, would place Aldwin's arrival between March 1073 and March 1074. For an account of the three monks' mission and its date, see Knowles, *Monastic Order*, pp. 165–71. For a re-appraisal of the possible significance of Evesham and Winchcombe in this connection, see Dawtry, *Studies in Church History*, xviii (1982), 87–98.

[76] It is not possible to identify any of these books amongst surviving manuscripts of Durham Cathedral priory, which was the house most likely to have inherited them. Two of the scribes of the late 11th- or early 12th-cent. Durham copy of Flavius Josephus's works (DCL, B.II.1) had west country connections, however, probably with either Winchcombe or Evesham (see M. Gullick, D. Marner, and A. J. Piper, *Anglo-Norman Durham 1093–1193: A Catalogue for an Exhibition of Manuscripts in the Treasury, Durham Cathedral, September 1993*, ed. D. Rollason (Durham, 1993), p. 7). But it seems unlikely that this was one of the books concerned.

habetur.[77] Quapropter uenerandus pontifex Walcherus ad illos mittens rogauit ut ad se uenirent, et sub iure potius ecclesie quam sub potestate secularium manendi locum acciperent. Quos aduenientes, multo cum honore et gaudio suscepit, magnasque Deo gratiarum actiones retulit, quod in hac prouincia monachice professionis uiros ad habitandum suscipere, et sub suo regimine meruisset habere.

[lxxiii
(lxxix)] Dedit^a ergo^b ^{c}eis monasterium^c beati Pauli apostoli^d a Benedicto quondam abbate constructum in Gyruum, quod stantibus adhuc solis sine culmine parietibus, uix aliquod ^{e}antique nobilitatis seruauerat signum.^{e}[78] Quibus culmen de lignis informibus et feno superponentes, diuine seruitutis officia ibidem celebrare ceperunt, factaque sub ipsis parietibus casula ubi dormirent et manducarent, religiosorum elemosinis pauperem uitam sustentarunt. Ibi pariter in frigore ac^f fame et rerum omnium penuria pro Christo residentes degebant, qui in monasteriis que reliquerant, omnem rerum affluentiam habere poterant.[79]

Interea multi exemplo illorum^g prouocati, seculo abrenuntiantes ^{h}monachicum ab eis habitum susceperunt, et sub discipline regularis institutione^h Christo militare didicerunt. Quorum pauci de ipsa Northanhymbrorum prouincia, plures uero de australibus Anglorum partibus fuerant,[80] qui exemplo Abrahe 'de terra sua et de

---

^{a} Habitacio monachorum restauratur in Garue rubric Fx H T V Y ^{b} ergo episcopus Walcherus Fx; ergo et episcopus Walcherus Y $^{c-c}$ eis ergo monasterium H; ergo monasterium eis T ^{d} om. F $^{e-e}$ signum antique nobilitatis seruauerat Fx Y ^{f} et Fx ^{g} eorum Fx H $^{h-h}$ om. H

[77] The identification of Monkchester with Newcastle is made in HReg, s.a. 1074 (Arnold, Sym. Op. ii. 201): 'usque locum qui Munekeceastre, id est monachorum ciuitas, appellatur, qui nunc Nouumcastellum nominatur'. It is found also in Vita Oswini in the account of a miracle worked there when William the Conqueror was returning from his 1072 expedition to Scotland: 'circa locum qui nunc Nouum Castellum dicitur, quondam uero Moneccestre dicebatur' (Miscellanea Biographica, ed. Raine, p. 21). The name is not otherwise recorded. Newcastle seems to have been so-called after the construction of the castle there in 1080 by Robert Curthose (HReg., s.a., Arnold, Sym. Op. ii. 211). That there was a pre-existing settlement there is indicated by the presence within the Roman fort of a cemetery, the graves of which were cut into by the construction of the castle, but there is no further evidence for that settlement and even coin evidence for the pre-Conquest period from Newcastle is very limited. Antiquarian traditions that Newcastle was the royal centre known to Bede as Ad Murum are speculative (for this and for the details of the excavations, see C. P. Graves, The Archaeology of Newcastle upon Tyne (English Heritage Monograph; London, forthcoming)). Note LDE's implication that the bishop of Durham's powers ended and the earl of Northumbria's began at the river Tyne, on which see Lapsley, County Palatine of Durham, pp. 15, 128, 149, 156.

[78] For the original construction of Jarrow, see Historia abbatum c. 12 in the anonymous version, c. 7 in that by Bede (Plummer, Bede i. 370, 392); for the site, see above, p. 41 n. 52.

jurisdiction of the earl of Northumbria.[77] For this reason the venerable Bishop Walcher sent to them and asked them to come to him, and to accept a place to live which was rather under the jurisdiction of the church than under that of secular power. When they came he received them with much honour and joy, and gave hearty thanks to God that he had been worthy to receive in that province and under his episcopal rule men of monastic profession who came to dwell there.

He therefore gave them the monastery of the blessed Paul the Apostle, which had been built at Jarrow by the former abbot Benedict. Its walls alone were standing roofless, and it had preserved hardly any sign of its former nobility.[78] After building a roof of rough timber and straw, the monks began to celebrate the divine office there. They made a hut for themselves under the walls, where they might sleep and eat, and they sustained their life of poverty by the alms of the faithful. There they lived and endured for Christ in cold and hunger and penury, although in the monasteries which they had left they could have had abundance.[79]

Meanwhile many were inspired by their example to renounce the world and to receive from them the monastic habit, learning to fight for Christ under the instruction of the Rule's discipline. A few of these men were from the province of the Northumbrians itself, but more were from the southern parts of England.[80] Following the

The ruin of Jarrow presumably dated from William the Conqueror's harrying of the North in 1069–70, when according to *HReg*, *s.a.* 1069 (Arnold, *Sym. Op.* i. 189), St Paul's Church at Jarrow was burned during Æthelwine's self-imposed exile to Lindisfarne (above, pp. 184–7). *LDE's* account of Elfred son of Westou's theft of Bede's relics from Jarrow suggests that the church was functioning in his time (above, pp. 162–7). That the central tower of St Paul's was constructed in the period just before the Norman Conquest (H. M. and J. Taylor, *Anglo-Saxon Architecture*, i. 344–5) is now disputed; and it seems more likely to belong to work carried out at Jarrow after the establishment of Aldwin's community there. See Cambridge, in Rollason, *Anglo-Norman Durham*, p. 149 n. 29; and M. Thurlby, 'The roles of the patron and the master mason in the first design of the Romanesque cathedral of Durham', Rollason, *Anglo-Norman Durham*, pp. 161–84, at 177.

[79] *LDE's* account seems to imply that Aldwin's community was in origin eremitical in inspiration; see H. Leyser, *Hermits and the New Monasticism: A Study of Religious Communities in Western Europe, 1000–1150* (London, 1984), p. 36.

[80] It is not possible to verify this statement. Setting aside names of Biblical derivation, the names of the first monks of Durham, who must have included those who had joined Aldwin and survived until the move to Durham in 1083 (above, p. xlv), show a mixture of English and continental, although the latter could of course have been settled in England. The only recruit to Aldwin's community whose origin is known is Turgot who came from Lincolnshire (below, n. 85). *HReg*, *s.a.* 1074 (Arnold, *Sym. Op.* ii. 202) states in general that the recruits came 'de remotis Anglie partibus'.

cognatione sua et de*a* domo patrum suorum egredientes', terram repromissionis[81] (id est supernam patriam) ingredi desiderabant, religiose conuersationis magistrum habentes Aldwinum. Erat nanque mundi contemptor egregius, habitu et mente humillimus, patiens in aduersis, modestus in prosperis, ingenio acutus, consilio prouidus, sermone grauis et actione, humilibus socius, contra contumaces iustitie zelo feruidus, semper celestia desiderans, et secum quoscunque poterat illuc prouocans.

Igitur episcopus uidens numerum *b*Deo ibidem*b* seruientium cotidie augeri, et iam per multa annorum uolumina*c* in illis partibus extinctam monachice conuersationis reuiuiscere *d*suo tempore*d* lucernam, gratias agens Deo uehementer exultauit, et pastoralem illis*e* sollicitudinem*f* et paternam cum omni affectu impendebat benignitatem. Cum enim *g*eos ecclesiam*g* ipsam reedificare, et destructa monachorum habitacula uideret uelle restaurare, dedit eis ipsam uillam Gyruum cum suis appenditiis, scilicet Preostun, Munecatun, Heathewurthe,*h* Heabyrm, Wiuestou, Heortedun, ut et opera perficere et sine indigentia ipsi*i* possent uiuere.[82] Taliter illi ex diuersis locis Christo pastore congregante in unum ouile adducti, didicerunt quam bonum sit et quam iocundum habitare fratres in unum.

[(lxxx)] 22. Cum*j* autem famulus Christi Aldwinus ibidem (sicut iam dictum est) aliquatenus fructificasset, ad alia quoque loca cogitauit transire, et simile opus Domino adiuuante perficere. Igitur constituto fratribus quem communiter ipsi*k* elegerant priore, proficiscens inde reliquit ibidem socium sue peregrinationis de quo supradictum est Elfwium, uirum simplicitatis et innocentie merito predicandum, orationibus et lacrimis iugiter intentum. Tercius *l*uero illorum*l* socius, uidelicet Reinfridus ad Streoneshalch (quod

---

a om. H   *b–b* ibidem Deo Fx Y   *c* curricula Ca; curricula uolumina Fx (with curricula struck out) H Y   *d–d* tempore suo Y   *e* om. Fx Y *f* solicitudinem illis H   *g–g* ecclesiam eos H   *h* Heawurthe F   *i* ibi F; om. Y (inserted over line Fx)   *j* Qualiter Aldunus monachus cum Turgoto discipulo suo Giruensem ecclesiam dereliquerunt rubric Fx T V Y   *k* om. Fx Y *l–l* eorum Fx Y

---

[81] Gen. 12: 1 (cf. Act. 7: 3); and cf. Heb. 11: 9.

example of Abraham 'they left their land and their kindred and the home of their fathers,' and desired to enter the promised land[81] (that is the heavenly kingdom). As the master of their religious life they had Aldwin. For he was distinguished in his contempt for the world, very humble in character and in mind, patient in adversity, modest in prosperity, sharp of mind, wise in counsel, grave in word and deed, a companion to the humble, burning with zeal for justice against those who were contumacious, desiring always heavenly things, and inspiring everyone he could to go along with him.

When the bishop saw that the number of those serving God there was growing daily, and the light of monastic life which had been extinct for so many years was being rekindled in his time, he gave fervent thanks to God and rejoiced greatly, and with all his heart lavished on them his care as a pastor and his blessing as a father. When he saw that they wished to rebuild the church itself and to restore the ruined dwelling of the monks, he gave them the vill of Jarrow with its appurtenances, that is Preston, Monkton, Heworth, Hebburn, Westoe, and Harton, so that they might complete the work and live without poverty.[82] In this way they were gathered together from various places as one flock, and with Christ as their shepherd, they learned how fitting and pleasant it is for brothers to live in unity.

22. When Aldwin the servant of Christ had (as we have said) been [(lxxx)] labouring fruitfully there for some time, he decided to go also to other places, and with God's help to carry out similar work there. So having set over the brothers a prior whom they themselves had elected in common, he set out leaving there the companion of his pilgrimage Elfwy, whom we mentioned earlier, a man of outstanding simplicity and innocence, constantly devoted to prayers and tears. The third companion, Reinfred, went to *Streoneshalch* (which is called

---

[82] Neither an original charter nor a copy survives relating to this gift. For the identification of the places named, which are all in the parish of Jarrow, see Offler, *Episcopal Charters*, p. 3. They are located as follows: Preston (NZ 34 69), Monkton (NZ 33 63), Heworth (NZ 29 61), Hebburn (NZ 32 64), Westoe (NZ 38 66), and Harton (NZ 38 64).

Hwitebi appellatur) secessit,[83] ubi aduenientes suscipiens monachorum habitationem instituere[a] cepit, qui post eius obitum
migrantes Eboracum, monasterium in honorem sancte[b] Marie
semper uirginis quod nunc abbas [c]Stephanus strenue[c] regit, con-
struxerunt.[84] At Aldwinus de Gyrwensi monasterio[d] egrediens,
comitem itineris et propositi in clericali adhuc habitu Turgotum
habuit, amore tamen et actu uitam monachorum imitantem.
Veniens enim Dunhelmum, benigne ab episcopo susceptus, et
cum eius intentionem agnouisset, ad prefatum monasterium [e]ab
eo[e] missus est, ibique sub magisterio Aldwini clericus inter
monachos degebat. Non enim habitum monachicum prius suscipere
audebat, quam maiori et[f] diuturniori sese districtione probasset.
[g]Ipse est qui in locum magistri uidelicet Aldwini succedens, hodie
in hac id est Dunelmensi ecclesia dudum sibi traditum a Willelmo
episcopo prioratum tenet.[g][85]

---

[a] instruere *Fx*　　　[b] beate *Fx Y*　　　[c-c] strenue Stephanus *L*　　　[d] ecclesia
Fx Y　　　[e-e] om. *Fx H Y*　　　[f] ac *F L T V*　　　[g-g] only in *F*

---

[83] Elfwy appears in the list of monks (above, pp. 6–7 no. 2, and n.). The date of the
departure of Aldwin and Reinfrid is not specified in either *LDE* or *HReg*, *s.a.* 1074
(Arnold, *Sym. Op.* ii. 201), but Burton suggests 1077 for Reinfrid's arrival at Whitby
(below, n. 84). As regards Whitby, the name is first attested in *Domesday Book* (fo. 305a).
LDE is the earliest source to identify it with the place which Bede names *Streaneshalch* and
knew as the site of a monastery founded in the mid-7th cent. by Abbess Hild (Bede, *HE* iv.
23). The discovery of early Anglo-Saxon remains interpreted as those of Hild's monastery
on the site of the medieval abbey has made *LDE*'s identification plausible (see R. J. Cramp,
'Monastic sites', *The Archaeology of Anglo-Saxon England*, ed. D. M. Wilson (Cambridge,
1976), pp. 223–9, id., 'A reconsideration of the monastic site at Whitby', *The Age of
Migrating Ideas: Early Medieval Art in Northern Britain and Ireland*, ed. R. M. Spearman
and J. Higgitt (Edinburgh and Stroud, 1993), pp. 64–73; J. Higgitt, 'Monasteries and
inscriptions in early medieval Northumbria: the evidence of Whitby', *From the Isles of the
North: Early Medieval Art in Ireland and Britain: Proceedings of the Third International
Conference on Insular Art held in the Ulster Museum, Belfast, 7–11 April 1994*, ed. C. Bourke
(Belfast, 1994), pp. 229–36; P. Rahtz, 'Anglo-Saxon and later Whitby', *Yorkshire
Monasticism: Archaeology, Art and Architecture, from the Seventh to the Sixteenth Centuries*,
ed. L. R. Hoey (Leeds, 1995), pp. 1–11). No church has been discovered on the site,
however, so the remains may not be monastic at all; and Bede's place-name may in fact
survive as Strensall just to the north of York (Ekwall, *Concise Dictionary, s.u.* Strensall, and
R. Coates, 'The slighting of Strensall', *Journal of the English Place-Name Society*, xiii
(1980–1), 50–3). The view that Bede's interpretation of *Streaneshalch* as *sinus fari* means
'Bay of the Lighthouse' and refers to a place by the sea is undermined in view of P. H.
Blair's argument that Bede intended it to be understood figuratively, the light in question
being Hild herself ('Whitby as a centre of learning in the seventh century', *Learning and
Literature in Anglo-Saxon England*, ed. H. Gneuss and M. Lapidge (Cambridge, 1985),
pp. 3–32, at 10–12). Cf. T. W. Bell, 'A Roman signal station at Whitby', *Archaeological
Journal*, clv (1998), 303–22. A. Thacker's suggestion that there were at pre-Viking Whitby

Whitby).[83] There he received people coming to him and he began to establish a dwelling of monks. After his death these monks moved to York and constructed a monastery in honour of St Mary the Virgin, which Abbot Stephen now rules vigorously.[84] Aldwin left the monastery of Jarrow, taking with him as travelling companion and partner in his plans Turgot, a man still in clerical habit but who was emulating the life of the monks by his love and his deeds. When he came to Durham, he was received kindly by the bishop who, when he had learned of his intent, sent him to the monastery of Jarrow to live as a clerk among monks under the rule of Aldwin. For he had not been bold enough to receive the monastic habit earlier, until he had undergone a longer and more rigorous probation. He it is who, having succeeded his master Aldwin, still to this day holds in the church of Durham the office of prior, which was some time ago entrusted to him by Bishop William.[85]

'an abbatial church for the nuns and a parochial or cemeterial church for the priests' is based on 11th-cent. and later evidence and is speculative ('Monks, preaching and pastoral care in early Anglo-Saxon England', in Blair and Sharpe, *Pastoral Care*, pp. 138–70, at 143–4).

[84] Sources deriving both from Whitby and from St Mary's Abbey, York, corroborate *LDE's* statement that the latter was founded from the former, but they indicate that the sequence of events was more complex than it is presented as being here. According to J. Burton, 'The monastic revival in Yorkshire: Whitby and St Mary's Abbey, York', Rollason, *Anglo-Norman Durham*, pp. 41–51, Reinfred settled as a hermit at Whitby around 1077 and attracted followers to him. Within a year or so authority over them was in the hands of a recruit called Stephen who eventually moved part of the community to Lastingham (Yorks.). This was in fact before Reinfred's death, for the remainder of the community stayed with him, removing for a time to Hackness (Yorks.), where Reinfred was killed. By 1086, Stephen and his followers had moved to St Olave's, York, and St Mary's in that city is said to have been founded for them in 1088; but cf. *HReg*, *s.a.* 1078 (Arnold, *Sym. Op.* ii. 208): 'fundata est abbatia sancte Marie Eboraci.' Stephen is recorded as alive in 1108 and may have died in 1112 (*Heads of Religious Houses*, p. 84). The sources mentioned above are printed in *Cartularium Abbathiae de Whiteby*, ed. J. C. Atkinson (SS lxix, lxxii; Durham, 1879–81), i. 1–10 and xxxviii–xxxix, and W. Dugdale, *Monasticon Anglicanum*, rev. J. Caley, H. Ellis, and B. Bandinel (London, 1817–30), iii. 544–6.

[85] The sentence 'Ipse est . . . prioratum tenet' is visible in normal light only in F. C has an erasure of over three and a half lines above which the hand of Thomas Rud has supplied the sentence from F. Under ultra-violet light the words 'Ipse . . . locum mag. . . . . . . Willelmo episcopo prioratum tenet' are still visible in C. *HReg*, *s.a.* 1074 (Arnold, *Sym. Op.* ii. 202–5), gives a detailed account of Turgot's career: how he was taken hostage by the Normans at Lincoln and escaped to Norway to be kindly received by King Olaf; and how while returning he was shipwrecked and lost all his possessions, apparently deciding to become a monk as a result. *HReg* then gives the same information as *LDE* with regard to how Aldwin made Turgot a monk (below, pp. 208–9) and how Turgot succeeded him as prior (below, pp. 240–1). It adds, however, an account of Turgot's appointment to the see of St Andrews, his difficulties there, and his return to die in Durham in 1115. The bishop who sent him to Jarrow must have been Walcher, bishop of Durham (1072–80).

[lxxiv]   Hic[a]86 magistrum de monasterio ut dictum est[b] proficiscentem secutus, indiuiduo illi[c] comitatu semper adherebat. Igitur ad Mailrosense quondam monasterium tunc autem solitudinem peruenientes, secreta [d]illius loci[d] habitatione delectati,[e] Christo ibidem seruientes ceperunt conuersari. Sed cum regi Scottorum Malcolmo, ad quem locus[f] ipse[g] pertinebat, eorum ibi conuersatio innotuisset, graues [h]ab illo[h] iniurias et persecutiones pertulerunt, pro eo quod euangelicum preceptum seruantes iurare illi fidelitatem noluerunt.87 Inter hec uenerabilis episcopus Walcherus frequentibus eos litteris et mandatis rogauit, monuit, adiurauit, ad ultimum cum clero et[i] omni populo coram sacratissimo sancti Cuthberti corpore sese illos excommunicaturum minatur, nisi ad se sub sancto Cuthberto mansuri reuerterentur. Illi ergo excommunicationem magis quam [j]iram regis[j] que mortem eis minabatur formidantes (nam mori tunc omnino[k] statuerant), locum illum relinquunt, et[l] ad episcopum perueniunt.

[lxxv (lxxxi)]   Quibus[m] statim monasterium beati Petri apostoli in Wiramuthe donauit, olim (sicut habitator eius ab infantia Beda describit) egregium satis ac nobile, tunc autem quid antiquitus fuerit uix per ruinam edificiorum uideri poterat.88 Vbi de uirgis facientes habitacula, quoscunque poterant 'artam et angustam uiam que ducit ad uitam' secum ingredi docere[n] studebant. Ibi Aldwinus Turgoto monachicum habitum tradidit, et ut carissimum in Christo fratrem diligens, uerbo et exemplo iugum Christi suaue illum portare docuit.89 Quos episcopus familiari caritate amplectens, sepius ad colloquium suum euocauit,[o] et interdum suis adhibens consiliis, libentissime illorum dictis dignatus est obedire.

Donauerat autem illis ipsam uillam Wiramutham, cui postea successor eius Willelmus aliam proximam uidelicet Suthewic[p] adiecit, ut cum his qui secum erant fratribus sine magna difficultate ibidem[q]

---

[a] Hic itaque F; Alduuinus et Turgotus apud Mailros habitare ceperunt *rubric* H   [b] *om.* D   [c] *om.* H   [d-d] loci illius *Fx Y*   [e] dilecti *L*   [f] locus etiam *Fx Y (over erasure)*   [g] ille *Fx H*   [h-h] *om.* L   [i] et cum *D H*   [j-j] regis iram *Fx Y*; iram *ins. over line* L   [k] *om.* H   [l] *om.* L   [m] Habitacio monachorum apud Weremuthe *rubric* H; Turgotus factus est monacus Gyrwyensis *rubric Fx T V Y*   [n] *om.* H   [o] uocauit *H*   [p] Suthwic *F*   [q] *om.* H

---

86 C now has an erasure of one word after the first word of this sentence ('Hic') which must have contained approximately four or five letters.

Turgot[86] followed his master (as we said) when he left the [lxxiv] monastery, and always stayed with him in undivided companionship. So they came to Melrose, formerly a monastery but then deserted, and delighted by the seclusion of that place, they began to live there in the service of Christ. But when King Malcolm of the Scots, to whom the place itself belonged, learned of their living there, they suffered grave injuries and persecutions at his hands, because they refused to swear fealty to him, adhering as they did to the precepts of the Gospels.[87] Meanwhile the venerable Bishop Walcher was asking, advising, and adjuring them with frequent letters and commands, and at length threatening to excommunicate them with the clergy and all the people in the presence of the most holy body of St Cuthbert, unless they should return to him and remain under St Cuthbert's protection. They feared the excommunication more than the anger of the king who was threatening them with death (for they were entirely resolved to die then), and so they left the place and came to the bishop.

He at once gave them the monastery of the blessed Peter the [lxxv] Apostle in Wearmouth, formerly (as Bede who had dwelled there (lxxxi)] since childhood described it) very distinguished and noble; but at that time it was hardly possible to see what it had formerly been because of the ruin of the buildings.[88] There they made dwellings out of twigs, and strove to teach anyone they could to enter with them on the 'straight and narrow way which leads to life'. There Aldwin gave Turgot the monastic habit, and with affection as his dearest brother in Christ, taught him by word and example how sweet it is to carry the yoke of Christ.[89] The bishop embraced them with familiar love and often called them to confer with him; and sometimes he received their advice and most willingly condescended to obey their instructions.

Now he had given them the vill of Wearmouth itself, to which his successor William later added the neighbouring vill of Southwick, so that with those brothers who were with them they could continue in

---

[87] On Melrose, see above, p. 26, n. 24. The king was King Malcolm III Canmore (1058–93). On the significance of this passage of *LDE* for disproving the view expressed in the continuation of *LDE* (below, pp. 274–5) that Teviotdale, with which the upper Tweed was linked, was ecclesiastically subject to Durham rather than being part of Cumbria, see Kapelle, *Norman Conquest of the North*, pp. 266–7.

[88] Bede's description of Wearmouth is in his *Historia abbatum* (Plummer, *Bede* i. 364–404). According to *HReg*, *s.a.* 1070 (Arnold, *Sym. Op.* ii. 190–1), St Peter's church there was burned in that year by King Malcolm III of Scots.

[89] Matt. 7: 14 and cf. Matt. 11: 30.

in Christi famulatu possent*a* perseuerare.[90] Nam etiam de remotis Anglorum partibus illuc aliqui aduenientes,[91] monachicam cum eis uitam agere, et*b* uno corde ac*c* una anima Christo didicerunt seruire. Tunc ecclesiam sancti Petri cuius adhuc *d*soli parietes*d* semiruti steterant, succisis arboribus, eradicatis uepribus et spinis que totam occupauerant, curarunt expurgare; et culmine imposito, quale hodie cernitur, ad agenda diuine laudis officia sategerant restaurare. Plane a tempore quo a paganis ecclesie in prouincia Northanhymbrorum euerse, et monasteria sunt*e* destructa atque incensa, usque*f* tercium annum presulatus*g* Walcheri, quando per Aldwinum in ipsam prouinciam uenientem monachorum *h*in illa cepit*h* habitatio reuiuiscere, ducenti et octo *i*computantur anni.*i*[92]

Igitur episcopo protegente placidam et quietam uitam monachi duxerunt, quos ille ut*j* pater benignissimus toto affectu fouere, et sepius per semetipsum dignatus est inuisere, et ea quibus indigebant largius prebere. Hic quoque si diuturniora sibi huius uite tempora extitissent, monachus fieri et monachorum habitationem ad sacrum corpus beati Cuthberti stabilire decreuerat. Vnde positis fundamentis monachorum habitacula ubi nunc habentur Dunhelmi construere cepit. Sed heu proh dolor! morte preuentus quod disposuerat perficere nequiuit, quod tamen eius successor sicut in sequentibus demonstrandum est perfecit.[93]

[(lxxxii)] **23.** Huius*k* strenuitas pontificis uidelicet*l* Walcheri non solum nullum rerum ecclesiasticarum passa est detrimentum, uerum etiam in earum augmentum dante sibi rege locum egregium, scilicet Waltham cum ipsius nobili ecclesia que canonicorum congregatione

---

a om. T   *b* ac L   *c* et H L   *d–d* parietes soli Fx Y   *e* om. L *f* usque ad Fx Y; om. L   *g* om. F   *h–h* cepit in illa Ca   *i–i* anni computantur Fx H Y   *j* sicut Fx H Y   *k* De moribus Walcheri Dunelmensis episcopi (episcopi Dunelmensis Fx) et de uisione cuiusdam morientis *rubric* Fx T V Y   *l* scilicet H

---

[90] Southwick lies approximately one mile upstream (NZ 381 585). Neither an original charter nor a copy survives relating to this gift (Offler, *Episcopal Charters*, pp. 63). It is found among the lands of Durham Cathedral Priory in a late 12th-cent. forgery of a purported notification of Bishop William of Saint-Calais of the liberties and possessions granted to the prior and monks of Durham (ibid., no. *7, p. 57), in an inventory of 1464 (*Feodarium*, ed. Greenwell, p. 119), and in other late medieval documents (op. cit., pp. 15, 79, 81, 85, 94, 208, 309, 311, 329; and Raine, *Scriptores tres*, pp. xxvi, cxli, ccxcii).

the service of Christ there without undue difficulty.[90] For men came from the remotest parts of England[91] to live the monastic life with them, and to learn to serve Christ with heart and soul. Then they worked to clear out the church of St Peter, of which only the walls were still standing in a semi-ruinous state, and they cut down the trees and cleared the creepers and thorn-bushes which had completely taken it over. Then they roofed it, as it can be seen today, and they strove to restore it so that services of divine praise could be held in it. In plain terms, two hundred and eight years had elapsed from the time when the churches of the kingdom of the Northumbrians were overthrown by the pagans, and the monasteries destroyed and burned, up to the third year of the pontificate of Walcher, when Aldwin came into this province and monastic life began to revive in it.[92]

So under the bishop's protection they led a placid and quiet monastic life. He loved them with all his heart like a benign father, and he often deigned to visit them himself, and generously to give them whatever they lacked. He had decided that, if the period of his life were to be of longer duration, he too would become a monk, and would establish a dwelling of monks around the holy body of the blessed Cuthbert. For which reason he laid the foundations and began to construct buildings for monks at Durham, on the site which they now occupy. But alas! he was prevented by death, and was unable to complete what he had decided upon—this was finished by his successor as will be explained subsequently.[93]

23. Bishop Walcher was so zealous that not only did he not permit [(lxxxii)] any of the possessions of the church to suffer harm, but he also increased them by acquiring through the king's gift a distinguished place, namely Waltham with its noble church, which is noted for its

---

[91] See above, p. 203 n. 80.

[92] This is presumably calculated from the arrival of the Viking Great Army in 866 (ASC, *s.a.*). For the date of Aldwin's arrival, see above, p. 201 n. 75.

[93] For the possibility that Walcher's building work in the claustral buildings survives partially in the present east range south of the chapter house and in the vaulted undercroft of the east end of the south range, see K. W. Markuson, 'Recent investigations in the east range of the cathedral monastery, Durham', in Coldstream and Draper, *Medieval Art and Architecture at Durham Cathedral*, pp. 37–48, at 39–41, and W. St John Hope, 'Notes on recent excavations in the cloister of Durham Abbey', *Proceedings of the Society of Antiquaries*, 2nd series, xxii (1908–9), 416–24.

pollet, adquisiuit.[94] Comitatum quoque Northanhymbrorum, capto a rege comite Waltheof, ipse susceperat disponendum.[95] Et ille quidem per uite honestatem et morum sobrietatem atque mansuetudinem, omnium amore dignus erat; uerumtamen quoniam[a] suos licenter que uoluissent et hostiliter nonnulla facientes non refrenebat, indigenarum animos offendebat. Denique archidiaconus illius multa ex ornamentis [b]et pecunia ecclesie[b] auferens, consanguineis et amicis distribuerat. Milites quoque nimis[c] insolenter se in populo habentes, multos sepius uiolenter diripiebant, aliquos etiam ex maioribus natu interficiebant. Quorum prauitates episcopus cum negligeret et nulla censure pontificalis auctoritate coerceret, sicut Heli quondam propter culpas filiorum interiit, [d]sic et iste[d] propter peccata suorum una die cum illis prostratus occubuit.[96]

[lxxvi]   Sed[e] paulo ante illius[f] mortem, idem pene [g]miraculum in prouincia Northanhymbrorum[g] contigit, quod olim ibidem[h] euenisse Beda in *Historia Anglorum* describit, ut uidelicet quidam [i]de morte resurgeret[i] ad uitam.[97] Qui uocabulo Eadulfus[j] non longe a Dunhelmo in uilla que Reuenswurthe dicitur habitans,[98] in egritudinem decidit, qui Sabbato quidem iam die in noctem declinante mortuus est, sed mane ante [k]solis ortum[k] de morte reuiuiscens ac subito residens, omnes qui ad suas exequias assederant,[l] pauore nimio ac tremore[m] perculsos in fugam uertit.[n] Sed ille fugientes reuocans, 'Nolite,' inquit, 'timere. Vere a morte surrexi. Signo sancte crucis [o]uos et domum hanc signate.'[o] Quo

---

[a] quia *Fx Y*   [b-b] ecclesie et pecunias *Ca*   [c] om. *T*   [d-d] ille *Fx*; et sic iste *L*   [e] De quodam mortuo reuiuiscente et de hiis que predixit de dampnacione Waltheof et de morte Walkeri episcopi et suorum *rubric H*   [f] eius *Fx H Y* [g-g] in prouincia Northanhymbrorum miraculum (om. *H*) *Fx H Y*   [h] om. *H Y* [i-i] resurgeret de morte *Fx Y*   [j] Radulfus *Y*   [k-k] ortum solis *H* [l] ascenderant *H*; consederant *Fx Y*   [m] timore *D Fx H Y*   [n] conuertit *Fx Y* [o-o] uos et domum hanc armate *F;* signate uos et domum istam *Ca*

---

[94] Holy Cross, Waltham (Essex), was founded in the time of King Cnut (1017–35), and refounded for a dean and twelve secular priests in the time of Edward the Confessor (1042–66); see D. Knowles and R. N. Hadcock, *Medieval Religious Houses: England and Wales* (2nd edn.; London, 1971), p. 178. According to *CMD* (Craster, 'Red book', p. 528), William the Conqueror gave it on the occasion of his visit to Durham in 1072. It appears as a possession of the bishops of Durham in *Domesday Book*, but early in Henry I's reign it was in the hands of his queen Matilda; see Offler, *Episcopal Charters*, p. 23. Cf. *The Waltham Chronicle*, ed. and trans. L. Watkiss and M. Chibnall (OMT, 1994), p. xxvi.

[95] Waltheof, son of Earl Siward, became earl of Northumbria in 1072; in 1075 he was implicated in the revolt of Ralph, earl of Norfolk, and Roger, earl of Norfolk, for which he was arrested and then executed in May 1076 (on his career, see F. S. Scott, 'Earl Waltheof of Northumbria', *Archaeologia Aeliana*, 4th ser. xxx (1952), 149–213). Bishop Walcher,

congregation of canons.[94] After Earl Waltheof had been captured by the king, the bishop also received the rule of the earldom of Northumbria.[95] He was worthy of the love of all through the honesty of his life, and the sobriety and gentleness of his ways. However, because he did not restrain his men from freely doing what they wished and indeed doing several things of a hostile nature, he offended the native inhabitants. Further, his archdeacon took much of the money and many of the ornaments from the church, and distributed them among his relations and friends. The knights also behaved very arrogantly towards the people, robbing many with violence, and killing some, even some of the older people. When the bishop disregarded their wrong-doing and did not constrain them with the censure of his episcopal authority, he was one day struck down along with them and died because of their sins, just as Eli once died for the guilt of his sons.[96]

Shortly before his death, however, almost the same miracle [lxxvi] happened in the province of the Northumbrians which Bede described in his *History of the English* as having formerly happened there, that is a certain person rose from the dead to life.[97] This man, whose name was Eadwulf and who lived not far from Durham in a vill called Ravensworth,[98] fell ill and died at nightfall on the Sabbath, but in the morning before sunrise he revived from death and sat up suddenly; so that everyone who was sitting there mourning him was struck with great fear and trembling and took to flight. But as they fled he called them back, and said: 'Do not be afraid, for I have truly risen from the dead. Make the sign of the holy cross on yourselves

whose appointment as earl was very unusual, held the office until his murder in 1080 (below, pp. 216–19).

[96] The biblical reference is to Samuel 3 with a verbal echo of v. 13. *HReg, s.a.* 1080, somewhat more fully JW, *s.a.* 1080 (iii. 32–7), and in summary William of Malmesbury, *Gesta regum*, ed. Mynors *et al.*, i. 498–501, give a quite different account of the reasons for Walcher's killing. According to this, it was in revenge for the killing of a member of the Northumbrian house of Bamburgh called Liulf by Walcher's kinsman Gilbert, acting on the instigation of the bishop's chaplain Leobwine. The sources relaying this account are not of course independent of each other, but it seems unlikely that it was invented. *LDE's* failure to mention it may have arisen from the fact that it was still too politically sensitive to relate at the beginning of the 12th cent. On Leobwine, see below, p. 215 n. 100.

[97] This is presumably a reference to Bede's account of the vision of heaven and hell granted to Dryhthelm who lived near the river Tweed (Bede, *HE* v. 12). Like Eadwulf's vision related here, Dryhthelm's occupied a single night. For the context of these visions in vision literature, see P. Dinzelbacher, *Vision und Visionsliteratur im Mittelalter* (Stuttgart, 1981), pp. 16, 142.

[98] Ravensworth is in fact just to the south-west of Gateshead (NZ 231 578).

dicto, innumera mox multitudo auicularum de exteriori ede per ostium erumpens, totam domum in qua sederunt repleuit, que *nimia importunitate* huc atque illuc uolitantes, ipsis pene oculis intuentium se ingerebant. Currens ergo diaconus quem presbiter ad ecclesiam rediens ibi dimiserat, aqua benedicta ipsos et domum respersit, nec mora omnis*b* illa monstruosa uolucrum multitudo ut fumus ex oculis disparuit. Is autem, qui de morte surrexerat, multa de beatitudine iustorum*c* et de pena dampnatorum que de corpore ductus uiderat retulit. Denique aliquos quos ante nouerat, cum beatis in sedibus florigeris letantes se recognouisse dicebat; quibusdam quos adhuc presens uita retinebat, gehennalis tormenti eternos cruciatus iam paratos nuntiabat. Horum unus Waltheof habebatur, qui postea cedis episcopi auctor fuerat,[99] de quo ille que uiderat referens:

'Ve,' inquit, 'ue illi! in ipsius infernalis camini medio preparata est ei mansio. Sedile ferreum eterno igne ignitum eum expectat, quod stridentibus undique flammis, multo fragore inextinguibiles iugiter scintillas*d* crepitat. Stant hinc et inde cum catenis ferreis horribiles ministri, spiritus uidelicet*e* maligni in illam sedem Waltheofum iamiamque suscepturi, et in eterni ignis incendium atrocius*f*miserum uinculis*f* insolubilibus coarturi.'

His dictis, ubinam episcopus et archidiaconus eius cum suis essent, requisiuit.[100] Cui cum dictum esset in Dunhelmo, *g*ille respondens,*g* 'Omnes,' inquit, 'illi iam perierunt. Episcopus iam defecit, suique omnes qui nunc extolluntur superbia, iam non esse reputati sunt.' At hi qui assederant, scientes episcopum cum suis omnibus incolumem, putabant illum hec non sana mente dicere. Quos iterum alloquens, 'Ego,' ait,*h* 'sanum sapio, atque hoc signo an uera sint que dico probare poteritis. Si ante uel post proximam feriam terciam mortuus fuero, scitote uniuersa*i* esse falsa que a me audistis. Sin autem in ipsa feria*j* moriar, uera me locutum procul dubio noueritis.' Itaque

a–a importunitate nimia L *b* om. Fx Y *c* beatorum H *d* ins. over line Fx Y *e* scilicet H; om. Y (ins. over line Fx) *f–f* uinculis miserum H *g–g* om. Fx Y *h* inquit Fx Y *i* omnia H *j* feria tercia F

---

[99] The name Waltheof suggests that this person was a member of the house of Bamburgh, of which it was a family name; he cannot otherwise be identified with certainty, although Cospatric, son of Earl Uhtred, had a son of this name (*DPSA* (Arnold, *Sym. Op.* ii. 383). *LDE* disagrees here with the account of the earls of Northumbria in *HReg, s.a.* 1072 (ibid. ii. 197–8), according to which the leader of Walcher's killers was Eadwulf Rus, a grandson (cf. *DPSA*; ibid., ii. 383) of Cospatric, son of Earl Uhtred; and he was soon afterwards killed by a woman and buried in Jedburgh

and on this house.' When he had said this, an innumerable multitude of little birds flocked through the door from the outside of the building, and filled the whole house in which they sat, flying with great boldness hither and thither, and almost bumping into the eyes of those who were watching. The deacon, who had been sent there by the priest when he went back to the church, ran and sprinkled the people and the house with holy water. At once the monstrous multitude of birds vanished before their eyes like smoke. The man who had arisen from the dead, however, told them many things concerning the blessedness of the just and the punishments of the damned which he had seen when he had been separated from his body. Further, he said that some whom he had previously known he had recognized amongst the blessed rejoicing in the flowery places; while to certain others who were still alive he foretold that the eternal tortures and torments were prepared for them in hell. One of these was Waltheof, who afterwards was the perpetrator of the bishop's death,[99] and this is what he said he had seen of him:

'Woe, woe to him! In the middle of the infernal oven a dwelling has been prepared for him. An iron seat made red-hot with eternal fire is prepared for him; all around flames hiss, and with a terrible noise the seat constantly throws up unquenchable sparks. On either side stand fearsome attendants with iron chains, evil spirits waiting to receive Waltheof in that seat, and to bind the wretched man pitilessly with indissoluble bonds in the conflagration of the eternal fire.'

After saying this, he asked where the bishop and the archdeacon were with their household.[100] When he was told they were in Durham, he responded: 'They have all perished now. The bishop has now died, and all his men who are now raised up in arrogance are reckoned to be no more.' Those who were sitting round knew that the bishop was safe with all his household, and thought that the man was not speaking with sound mind. He addressed them again: 'I know myself to be quite sane, and by this sign you will be able to prove whether what I say is true. If I die before or after next Tuesday, you will know that everything you have heard from me has been false; but if I die on that day itself, you will know that what I have spoken is

(Roxburghs.), whence his remains were ejected by Prior Turgot. For a genealogical table of the house of Bamburgh, see W. Page, 'Some remarks on the Northumbrian palatinates and regalities', *Archaeologia*, li (1888), 143–54, at p. 155.

[100] For the possibility that this unnamed archdeacon was Leobwine the chaplain, who was (according to *HReg* and John of Worcester, above p. 215 n. 100) instrumental in the events leading to Walcher's death, see Offler, 'Early archdeacons', pp. 191–2.

instante feria tercia ille defunctus est, nec multo post repentina episcopi et suorum omnium interfectione ea que ille predixerat uera esse manifestius rerum effectus edocuit. Sed et ille miserabilis, cui tanta *a*gehenne tormenta*a* iam *b*preparata uiderat,*b* scilicet Waltheof, post impiam tanti pontificis occisionem, et ipse a sue uxoris fratre penas inferni subiturus occiditur.

[lxxvii 24. Vt*c* autem qualiter nefanda episcopi cedes peracta sit ex ordine
(lxxxiii)] retexatur, statuto die quo et hi scilicet milites antistitis qui fecerant iniurias*d* et qui passi fuerant in pacem redirent et concordiam, episcopus ipse cum suis ad locum qui Ad Caput Capre*e* dicitur conuenit, cui qui ultra Tinam habitauerant uniuersi natu maiores cum infinita totius populi multitudine, in pessimum adunati consilium occurrerunt.[101] Declinans episcopus tumultum, ecclesiolam ipsius loci*f* intrauit, ubi conuocatis ad se populi primatibus de utriusque partis utilitate ac mutua amicitia tractauit.

Quo facto, episcopo cum paucissimis*g* suorum in ecclesia remanente, omnes qui aduocati*h* fuerant quasi consilio locuturi egrediuntur; et post paululum clamore tumultuantis turbe exorto, fit subito sine ullo humanitatis*i* respectu miserabilis*j* ubique*k* cedes hominum. Alii nanque milites episcopi sparsim per loca sedentes uel iacentes utpote nichil mali suspicantes, repente circundantes interficiunt. Alii ascendentes ecclesiam incendunt, alii euaginatis gladiis et uibrantibus hastis conglobatim ad hostium stantes, neminem uiuum exire permittunt. Nam qui intus erant cum iam uim flammarum sustinere non possent, humiliter peccata confessi percepta benedictione cum iam egrederentur, in ipso egressu mox trucidabantur.

Vltimus omnium restabat*l* episcopus, grauiores ipsa morte sustinens*m* in corde dolores. Intolerabile illi fuit quod suos cum presbiteris et diaconibus ante se uidit extinctos, sciebat quod nec sibi manus hostium parceret. *n*Inter hec*n* diuersa mortis pena coartatur, ut quam magis eligat ipse nesciat. Ignis eum ad arma hostium fugere compellebat, arma repellebant ad ignem. Mors dilata, fuerat ei grauior pena. Leuamentum doloris uidebatur

---

a–a tormenta gehenne L   *b–b* predixerat F   *c* Walkerus episcopus occiditur apud Gatesheued *rubric H*; Walcherus episcopus cum suis clericis occiditur (apud Capud Capre iuxta Nouum Castrum *add.* T; apud Capud Capre iuxta Nouum Castellum *add.* V) *rubric Fx T V Y*   *d* iniuriam Fx Y   *e* anglice Gatisheuid *in marg.* (s.xiv) Y   *f* om. T   *g* paucis Fx (corr. in marg.) Y   *h* uocati H   *i* humilitatis D   *j* mirabilis D   *k* ubi Ca (signe de renvoi in marg.)   *l* restat H   *m* ferens F   *n–n* Igitur hac Fx H Y

beyond doubt the truth.' When Tuesday came he died, and not long afterwards the unexpected murder of the bishop and all his household showed clearly by this course of events that what the man had predicted was true. But that miserable Waltheof for whom he had seen such torments of hell prepared, after the impious killing of so great a bishop was himself killed by his wife's brother and went to suffer the infernal punishments.

24. Let us now disclose in due order how the evil death of the bishop [lxxvii came about. On the day which had been agreed for the bishop's (lxxxiii)] knights who had done the injuries and those who had suffered them to be reconciled in peace and concord, the bishop and his men came to the place called Gateshead, where all the elders who lived beyond the Tyne with a great multitude of the whole people brought together by the worst advice were also assembled.[101] The bishop avoided the commotion by entering a small church in that place. There he summoned to him the chief men of the people, and discussed with them the common benefit and mutual friendship of both parties.

After this the bishop remained in the church with a very few of his men, while those who had been called together went outside as if to hold discussions; and after a short time a shout went up from the vociferous crowd and suddenly men were being massacred on all sides without mercy. For some surrounded and killed the bishop's knights without warning, who were sitting or lying here and there suspecting no mischief. Others climbed up the church and set fire to it, while others drawing their swords or brandishing their spears stood massed at the door permitting no one to come out alive. For those who were inside, since they could not bear the force of the flames, humbly confessed their sins, received blessing, and went out to be cut down at once as soon as they crossed the threshold.

Last of all remained the bishop, suffering in his heart worse pangs than death itself. It was intolerable for him that he had seen his men as well as his priests and deacons murdered before his eyes, and he knew that the hand of his enemies would not spare him. Surrounded by death in different shapes, he did not know which to choose. The fire was forcing him to cast himself on to the weapons of his enemies, the weapons were forcing him back to the fire. The longer death was delayed, the worse would be the torment. Anything that brought

---

[101] On the river Tyne as the boundary between the jurisdiction of the bishops of Durham and that of the earls of Northumbria, see above, p. 202 n. 77.

ferre, quicquid mortem *citius posset* inferre. Cum ergo seuientium
flammarum uires iam ulterius ferre nequiuisset, precibus Deo animam
commendans ad hostium processit, factoque digitis e contra signo
crucis cum iam pallio quo erat indutus oculos et caput uelaret, in ipso
ostio heu! proh dolor! lanceis confoditur, cui etiam mortuo crebra
gladiis uulnera infliguntur. Tanta nanque fuerat eorum bestialis
crudelitas, ut nec eo mortuo satiari potuisset.[102]

Hec detestanda omnibus cedes antistitis, pridie Idus Maii feria
quinta ante Rogationes facta est, peractis in episcopatu suo[b] nouem
annis et duobus mensibus.[103] Cuius occisione audita, fratres Gyr-
wensis monasterii ascendentes nauiculam ad locum nauigarunt,[c] et
[d]corpus patris sui[d] et antistitis uix propter uulnerum frequentiam
agnitum et[e] penitus omni tegmine spoliatum, cum graui luctu
impositum naui ad monasterium detulerunt; quod[f] Dunhelmum
inde perlatum, non eo quo pontificem decebat funeris obsequio
sepulture est traditum. [g]Tota nanque[g] urbe discursantes illius inter-
fectores furebant, statim enim post illam abhominandam cedem illo
aduenerant, ut expugnato castello homines episcopi qui supererant
perimerent. At his uiriliter se defendentibus, illi non sine suorum[h]
detrimento[i] frustrato labore oppugnantes fatigabantur. Quarto die
obsidionis abscedentes per diuersa disperguntur, et uniuersi quos
nefaria[j] cedes antistitis Deo et hominibus detestabiles fecerat, aut
uaria clade consumuntur, aut relictis domibus et possessionibus
incertis[k] profugi sedibus exules uagantur.

Nec mora ea que gesta fuerant fama ubique diuulgante, Odo
Baiocensis episcopus, qui tunc a rege secundus fuerat,[l] et multi
cum eo primates regni cum multa armatorum manu Dunhelmum
uenerunt, et dum mortem episcopi ulciscerentur terram pene totam[m]
in solitudinem redegerunt.[104] Miseros[n] indigenas, qui sua confisi

a–a posset citius *Fx H Y*   *b* om. *Fx H*   *c* nauigant *Fx H Y*
d–d patris sui *H*; patris sui corpus *Fx Y* (corpus *ins. over line Y*)   *e* om. *Fx Y*
f in *add. H Y*   *g–g* Tanta ergo *T*   *h* om. *H*   *i* om. *L*   *j* nefanda
Ca   *k* in terris *T*   *l* erat *Fx H*   *m* om. *Fx H Y*   *n* et *add. Fx*

---

[102] The sources listed on p. 213 n. 96 supply further details about the circumstances of
Walcher's death, notably the information that his assailants were seeking to kill his
chaplain Leobwine, whose refusal to leave the church led to Walcher himself going out to
his death.

[103] JW iii. 32–3 also dates the killing to 14 May. In the Durham obituaries it is entered
twice under 14 May (Piper, 'Lists', pp. 188, 195). Easter was 12 April in 1080, so the
Minor Rogations (i.e. the Monday, Tuesday, and Wednesday before Ascension Day)
would have begun on Monday 18 May.

[104] Odo, bishop of Bayeux (1049/50–97) and half brother of William the Conqueror,
was given the earldom of Kent after the Conquest and was one of the most powerful men

death quickly seemed also to promise relief for his anguish. So when he was able no longer to bear the heat of the raging flames, he commended his soul with prayers to God, and went to the door, making the sign of the cross with his fingers and covering his eyes and head with the pall he was wearing. Alas! alas! on the very threshold he was pierced through and through with spears, and many sword wounds were even inflicted on his dead body. So intense was the bestial cruelty of his murderers that they were not satisfied just to have killed him.[102]

This murder of the bishop, a crime abominable to everyone, was committed on 14 May, the Thursday before Rogationtide, when he had been bishop for nine years and two months.[103] When the brothers of the monastery of Jarrow heard of his murder, they boarded a boat and sailed to Gateshead. In deep mourning, they took up the body of their father the bishop, almost stripped of clothing and hardly recognizable from the number of wounds, placed it on a boat, and conveyed it to their monastery. Thence it was taken to Durham for burial. The funeral rites fell short of the bishop's due, for his murderers were raging through the town. They had come immediately after the abominable killing aiming to capture the castle and kill all the bishop's surviving men. But the latter stoutly defended themselves, so that the insurgents lost some of their men and were exhausted by their fruitless assault. On the fourth day of the siege they went away and dispersed to various places. All whom the evil killing of the bishop had made detestable to God and to men were either overtaken by death in various forms, or left their homes and their possessions and wandered as homeless fugitives and exiles.

When news of what had been done spread far and wide, Bishop Odo of Bayeux, who was then second only to the king, came to Durham with many of the leading men of the kingdom and a large force of armed men; and in avenging the death of the bishop virtually laid the land waste.[104] They ordered many of the wretched

in England until the confiscation of his English lands, first in 1082, and then definitively in 1088 (D. Bates, 'The character and career of Odo, bishop of Bayeux (1049/50–1097)', *Speculum*, l (1975), 1–20). Regarding the expedition described here, JW iii. 36–7 states only: 'Ob quorum detestande necis uindictam, rex Willemus eodem anno deuastauit Northymbriam', but *HReg*, s.a. 1080 (Arnold, *Sym. Op.* ii. 210–11), perhaps following *LDE*, adds to these words 'misso illuc Odone Baiocensi episcopo cum multa militari manu'. The description of Odo as 'then second only to the king' is probably a reference to Odo's exercise of vice-regal authority in the years 1077–80, during William I's only extended absence from the kingdom, although the basis of this authority was only informal (F. West, *The Justiciarship in England 1066–1232* (Cambridge, 1966), pp. 4–6).

innocentia domi resederant, plerosque ut^a noxios aut decollari aut membrorum detruncatione preceperunt debilitari. Nonnullis ut salutem et uitam pretio redimerent, crimen falso imponebatur. Quedam etiam ex ornamentis ecclesie, inter que et baculum pastoralem materia et arte mirandam ^b(erat enim de saphiro^b factus), prefatus episcopus abstulit, qui posito in castello militum presidio ^cprotinus abscessit.^{c 105}

^a om. Fx Y   ^{b–b} de saphiro erat enim T   ^{c–c} abscessit protinus T

---

[105] The castle was of course Durham Castle, built in 1072 (*HReg, s.a.* 1072 (Arnold, *Sym. Op.* ii. 199–200), and see p. 322 n. 106). Fx, L, and Y here insert *De miraculis* c. 8 with the heading 'lxxxiiii Quomodo quidam furtum quod in monasterio eius penetrauerat (perpetruerat Y) ipse perdidit uitam sicque ibidem miserabiliter interiit.' The chapter

inhabitants who, relying on their innocence had stayed at home, to be beheaded as criminals or mutilated by the amputation of limbs. Several were falsely accused of crimes, to make them redeem their lives and purchase their safety with money. Bishop Odo also took away certain ornaments from the church, including a pastoral staff of wonderful substance and workmanship (for it was made of sapphire). This was put in the castle under the guard of the soldiers and soon disappeared.[105]

relates how after the murder of Bishop Walcher a Norman soldier, deceiving the monks by a show of piety, stole property which had been placed in the monastery for safety, but went mad as a result. In C, a 14th-cent. marginal notes read: 'deficit capitulum' and 'Hic deficit capitulum'. T has a 14th-cent. note at the bottom of the page (fo. 50[r]: 'Hic deficit capitulum lxxiiii, Quomodo quidam furtum et cetera').

⟨Liber quartus⟩

I. Transactis*a* post occisionem Walcheri episcopi sex mensibus et decem diebus, anno imperii Willelmi quinto decimo, abbas monasterii sancti *b*martyris Vincentii*b* Willelmus ab ipso rege electus, episcopatum Dunhelmensis ecclesie quintas Idus Nouembris suscepit regendum;[1] ordinatio uero*c* illius aliquanto post (id est tertias Nonas Ianuarii), uidelicet in octauis sancti Iohannis euangeliste die dominica presente rege et episcopis totius Anglie astantibus ab archiepiscopo Eboracensi Thoma solenniter est adimpleta.[2]

Hic quidem Willelmus in ipso sue iuuentutis tempore, cum esset *d*de clero*d* Baiocensis ecclesie, in monasterium sancti Carilefi patrem iam multo ante monachum effectum secutus,[3] suscepto habitu monachico in monastici ordinis obseruantia singulariter pre ceteris amore ac studio strenuus habebatur, ideoque ad superiores gradus paulatim ascendens promouebatur. Primo enim prior claustri, deinde secundus ab abbate (maior scilicet prior) constituitur,[4] inde ad uicinum prefati martyris monasterium abbas eligitur.[5] Nec multo post nominatus rex, quia eius industriam in rebus sepe difficillimis

---

a Transactis *with large decorated initial C F;* Willelmus de Sancto Karilefo (monachus *add. T*) factus est Dunelmensis episcopus (episcopus Dunelmie *Fx T Y*) *rubric Fx H T Y*   *b–b* Vincentii martyris *H*   *c om. H*   *d–d om F*

---

[1] William I was king of England 1066–87. Since Walcher died on 14 May 1080, the period of 6 months and 10 days said to have elapsed between his murder and the election of William of Saint-Calais on 9 Nov. has to be understood as a period of 178 days (i.e. 6 months of 28 days + 10); see Offler, *DIV*, p. 73 n. 3. The date 9 Nov. is also given by *HReg*, *s.a.* 1080 (Arnold, *Sym. Op.* i. 211), and repeated by Offler, *DIV*, p. 73.

[2] Although *HReg*, *s.a.* 1081 (*Arnold, Sym. Op.* ii. 211), gives 2 Jan. (*.iv. Nonas Ianuarii*), and JW iii. 38–9, gives 5 Jan. (*nonas Ianuarii*), *LDE*'s date, which is repeated by Offler, *DIV* (p. 73), is certainly correct: 3 Jan. is the Octave of St John and it was a Sunday in 1081. Offler, *DIV*, states that the council took place at Gloucester, presumably deriving its information from *HReg*, loc. cit. These sources provide the only precise dating for this council which is mentioned in the *Acta Lanfranci* and William of Malmesbury's *De antiquitate Glastoniensis ecclesie;* the former text explains that Archbishop Thomas of York (1070–1100) had to be assisted in the consecration by Archbishop Lanfranc of Canterbury (1070–89) and his suffragans because the Scottish bishops, York's own suffragans, were disqualified from doing so. See *Councils and Synods with other Documents relating to the English Church*, i. *A.D. 871–1204*, part ii, *1066–1204*, ed. D. Whitelock, M. Brett, and C. N. L. Brooke (Oxford, 1981), pp. 629–32, and *Two of the Saxon Chronicles Parallel*, ed. J. Earle and C. Plummer (2 vols., Oxford, 1892–9), i. 289–90.

[3] The words 'of the clergy' (*de clero*) have been written in C by the scribe identified with Symeon over an erasure of two or three words (Rollason, 'Erasures', pp. 155–6). *LDE*'s is the only known account of William of Saint-Calais's early career. See

1. In the fifth year of King William's reign, when six months and ten [lxxviii
days had passed since the killing of Bishop Walcher, William, abbot [lxxxv)]
of the monastery of St Vincent the Martyr, was elected by the king
himself, and became bishop of Durham on 9 November.[1] His
ordination, however, took place some time later, being solemnly
performed by Archbishop Thomas of York on Sunday 3 January,
the Octave of St John the Evangelist, in the presence of the king and
the bishops of all England.[2]

In his youth, while this William had been one of the clergy of the
church of Bayeux, he entered the monastery of St Calais, following in
the footsteps of his father who had become a monk there long before.[3]
After William had received the monastic habit, he showed himself
more vigorous than any of the others in observing the monastic
ordinances with love and diligence, so that he was gradually promoted
to higher offices. First he was made claustral prior, then great prior
(second only to the abbot),[4] then he was elected abbot of the
neighbouring monastery of St Vincent the Martyr.[5] Not long afterwards King William (as we have said) promoted him to the bishopric
by God's ordinance, because his assiduity had been proven, often in

L. Guilloreau, 'Guillaume de Saint-Calais, évêque de Durham, (. . .?-1096)', *Revue
historique et archéologique du Maine*, lxxiv (1913), 209–32, at pp. 209–13; H. S. Offler,
'William of Saint-Calais, first Norman bishop of Durham', *Transactions of the Architectural
and Archaeological Society of Durham and Northumberland*, x (1950), 258–79 (repr. Offler,
North of the Tees, no. v); and W. M. Aird, 'An absent friend: the career of William of St
Calais', in Rollason, *Anglo-Norman Durham*, pp. 287–9. Aird doubts the force of
Guilloreau's suggestion that William was from the Bessin and he does not believe that
Odo had much influence on his career (p. 287). Saint-Calais is in the county of Maine. See
L. H. Cottineau, *Répertoire topo-bibliographique des abbayes et prieurés* (2 vols., Macon,
1935–7), ii, cols. 2625–6. Nothing else is known of William's father, although his mother's
name, Ascelina, is preserved as an obit alongside the bishop's own in DCL, B.IV.24 (Piper,
'Lists', p. 189). For evidence that William was devoted to the patron saint of the monastery
of Saint-Calais throughout his career, see Aird, op. cit., pp. 287–8.

[4] The roles of the prior and claustral prior, the former called 'great' in relation to the
latter, are described in some detail in *Monastic Constitutions*, ed. Knowles, pp. 75–7, and
see p. 76 n.

[5] This monastery was in Le Mans (Cottineau, *Répertoire topo-bibliographique*, ii. cols.
1730–1). William is recorded in the cartulary as having defended the abbey's rights to a
mill and as having acknowledged the gift to it of some houses and vineyards made under
the auspices of William the Conqueror; see *Cartulaire de l'Abbaye de Saint Vincent du
Mans, premier cartulaire*, ed. R. Charles and M. d'Elbenne (Le Mans, 1886–1913), nos. 99,
100, 621; see also nos. 474, 567, and 787, where the death of William's predecessor as abbot
is dated to 1078.

probatam habuit,[6] etiam[a] ad episcopatum (sicut iam dictum est) ordinante Deo promouit. Erat enim pontificali ministerio satis idoneus, ecclesiasticis et secularibus litteris nobiliter eruditus, in diuinis et humanis rebus multum industrius, morum honestate ita compositus, ut per id temporis nemo in hac ei putaretur esse preferendus. Inerat [b]illi etiam[b] tanta ingenii subtilitas, ut non facile quis occurreret qui profundius consilium inueniret. Cum gratia sapientie, multa ei suppetebat facultas eloquentie. Erat et[c] memorie tam[d] tenacis, ut in hoc etiam nimium[e] esset admirabilis. Strenuitate sua atque prudentia non solum ad predicti regis Anglorum et ad[f] regis Francorum, sed etiam ad pape apostolici[g] notitiam peruenerat et gratiam.[7] Gratum erat illis uirum talem interdum[h] suscipere, eloquenter simul et sapienter loquentem audire. Cibo ac[i] potu satis[j] erat sobrius, uestimentis semper mediocribus usus, fide catholicus, corpore castus. Et quoniam magne familiaritatis locum[k] apud regem habuerat, monasteriorum et ecclesiarum libertatem in quantum potuit defendere semper[l] ac tueri curabat.[8]

[(lxxxvi)] **2.** Igitur[m] sedem episcopatus sancti Cuthberti gratia [n]Dei adeptus,[n] terram illius pene desolatam inuenit, locumque quem sacri corporis sui presentia illustrat, negligentiori quam eius deceret sanctitatem seruitio despicabiliter destitutum conspexit.[9] Nam neque sui ordinis

---

[a] om. T   [b-b] etiam illi Fx Y   [c] enim Fx L; etiam V   [d] om. F
[e] nimis F   [f] om. T   [g] om. F   [h] om. H   [i] et F   [j] simul T
[k] om. H   [l] om. H   [m] De merore (Meror Fx T V) W. (Willelmi Fx T V)
Dunelmi episcopi rubric Fx T V Y   [n-n] adeptus Dei Fx L Y

---

[6] Maine was a troubled border region between Normandy and Anjou, control of which was frequently in dispute between the rulers of those duchies; see e.g. Douglas, *William the Conqueror*, pp. 405–6, and J. Le Patourel, *The Norman Empire* (Oxford, 1976), pp. 16–18. The 'difficult matters' referred to may have been to do with this, perhaps in connection with diplomatic services he had performed there and in Anjou and France, and with William the Conqueror's dispute with his eldest son Robert (see Offler, *Transactions of the Architectural and Archaeological Society of Durham and Northumberland*, x (1950), 262; F. Barlow, *The English Church 1066–1154* (London, 1979), p. 64; and Aird, in Rollason, *Anglo-Norman Durham*, p. 289).

[7] King Philip I of France (1060–1108) and Pope Gregory VII (1073–85).

[8] Recent palaeographical research has demonstrated that William of Saint-Calais's familiarity with William the Conqueror extended to his being put in overall charge of the Domesday Survey: see P. Chaplais, 'William of St Calais and the Domesday Survey', *Domesday Studies*, ed. J. C. Holt (Woodbridge, 1987), pp. 65–77.

[9] The desolation of the see was presumably the result of Odo of Bayeux's ravaging following Walcher's murder (see above, pp. 218–19). The statement about the inadequacy of the canons is not altogether consistent with statements above about their reform under the supervision of Walcher (see above, pp. 194–7). With the minimum alterations needed

⟨Book iv⟩

very difficult affairs.[6] He was indeed well suited to the episcopal office, nobly educated in ecclesiastical and secular literature, very zealous in divine and human affairs, possessed of moral honesty, so that at that time no one could have been considered to surpass him in this. He had such subtlety of mind that it was not easy to find anyone who would give sounder advice. He was possessed of wisdom and well-equipped with eloquence; and his memory was so tenacious that in this too he was greatly to be admired. By his vigour and prudence he came to the notice and favour not only of the aforementioned king of the English and the king of France, but also to that of the apostolic pope.[7] It was a pleasure for these persons to receive such a man and to hear him speaking eloquently and wisely. He was moderate in eating and drinking, he wore always simple clothes, and he was catholic in his faith and chaste in his body. Because he had a position of great familiarity with the king, he took pains always to guard and defend as far as he could the liberty of churches and monasteries.[8]

2. So when William had by the grace of God received the see of St Cuthbert, he found the saint's land virtually desolate, and he perceived that the place which the saint renders illustrious by the presence of his body was shamefully destitute and provided with a degree of service inappropriate to his sanctity.[9] For he found neither [(lxxxvi)]

to convert it into an account in the first person, this entire chapter was taken exactly as it appears in C and used as the preamble for the purported diploma of Bishop William of Saint-Calais concerning the foundation and endowment of the monastery of Durham which was entered in the *Liber Vitae*, fos. 49–50, probably soon after the completion of *LDE* (printed and discussed, Offler, *Episcopal Charters*, no. 3, pp. 6–15). The remainder of the diploma is made up of a purported record of the grant by Saint-Calais to the monks of Billingham (NZ 457 223), Aycliffe (NZ 282 222), Jarrow (NZ 339 653), Monkwearmouth (NZ 407 589), Rainton (NZ 32 46), North and South Pittington (NZ 32 43), Monk Hesleden (NZ 44 38), Dalton (NZ 408 481), Merrington (NZ 26 31), Shincliffe (NZ 29 40), and Elvet on the east of Durham City (NZ 275 419), in Co. Durham; Willington (NZ 31 67), Wallsend (NZ 29 66), Lindisfarne (NU 126 417), and Fenham (NU 086 408), Norham (NU 900 472), and Shoreswood (NU 941 465), north of the Tyne; and various possessions in Nottinghamshire, Lincolnshire, and the City of York. In line with *LDE*'s account below, the grant mentions King William and Queen Matilda and also Pope Gregory VII. Offler noted that, although it is possible that *LDE* was drawing on a genuine diploma, the text in *Liber Vitae* is derived from it and is formally spurious. Nevertheless, it was probably entered into that book soon after the completion of *LDE* and is therefore an early document, probably representing 'pretty fairly what the monastery could have claimed to have acquired by the time of Bishop William's death in 1096' (Offler, *Episcopal Charters*, p. 9). For criticisms of detail of this statement and for the view that this charter should be regarded as a *pancarte* or summary charter, see D. Bates, 'The forged charters of William the Conqueror and Bishop William of Saint-Calais', Rollason, *Anglo-Norman Durham*, pp. 111–24, at 112–13. This document in the *Liber Vitae* was itself used to

[See p. 226 for n. 9 cont.]

ibi monachos, neque regulares repperiuit[a] canonicos.[10] Vnde [b]graui
merore[b] confectus, Deum et sanctum Cuthbertum sedulo et suppliciter rogauit, ut sibi ad emendandum que minus conuenientia[c]
uiderat, consulendo succurrerent, et succurrendo perficerent. Igitur
senes et prudentiores totius episcopii[d] homines[11] qualiter in initio
apud sanctum ageretur Cuthbertum ab illo exquisiti, sedem illius
episcopalem in insula Lindisfarnensi fuisse, monachosque tam uiuo
quam ibidem sepulto uenerabiliter[e] seruisse responderunt, quorum
quoque assertioni uite illius libellus et *Ecclesiastica Gentis Anglorum*
concordat *Hystoria*.[12] Longo dehinc tempore transacto, crudelis
barbarorum manus non hunc solum (ut supra dictum est) sed et
alia circunquaque loca uastantes, nobilem illius cenobii cetum ausu
sacrilego neci tradiderunt. Sed non impune. Nam omnes in breui,
iusta Dei uindicta terribiliter percussi, a temporalibus[f] ad eterna
cruciandi tormenta sunt prerepti.[13]

His ergo perceptis, pristinum ad illius sacrum corpus restaurare
pertractans seruitium, ne [g]quis que sui[g] solius molimine fecisset
irritanda putaret, regis Willelmi et coniugis sue Mathildis regine, et
Landfranci Cantuariensis archiepiscopi consilium petiuit. Rex statim
ut ex omni parte tam utilis consilii roboraretur[h] consensus, ad papam
Gregorium tam de his eum[i] consulturum, quam de aliis que
mandauerat sibi locuturum [j]eum misit.[j][14] Cui cum de beati patris[k]
Cuthberti[l] sanctitate quedam licet pauca dixisset, illius per omnia
sibi[m] placuit consilium, ut uidelicet monachos quos in duobus

    [a] reperit *Fx H L Y*   [b-b] merore graui *Fx L Y*   [c] conuenientius *Y*
[d] episcopatus *Fx L Y*; *altered to* episcopatus *T*   [e] *om.* H L Y; *ins. above line* Fx
[f] temporibus *V*   [g-g] sui quis que *T*   [h] laboraretur *Fx L Y*   [i] *om. Fx H*
L Y   [j-j] emisit *Fx L*   [k] *om. Ca (signe de renvoi in marg.)*   [l] *om. V*
[m] *om. H*

fabricate a further charter incorporating claims relating to Carlisle and Teviotdale and
elsewhere and to the rights of the prior and monks (Offler, *Episcopal Charters*, no. 3a, but
for the dating, see now Bates, in Rollason, *Anglo-Norman Durham*, p. 115).

[10] *LDE* presumably means that the reform of the clerks carried out by Walcher (above,
pp. 194–7) had either not been a success or had been swept away after his murder.

[11] The identity of these men is puzzling. An episcopal synod may be envisaged, such as
seems to be represented by the (probably authentic) witness list to the spurious
confirmation of Tynemouth to the prior and monks of Durham by William of Saint-
Calais (Offler, *Episcopal Charters*, no. *5). This included the priests of the churches of
Hexham, Tynemouth, Sedgefield, Bedlington, Chester-le-Street, Auckland, Aycliffe,
Egglescliffe, and Brancepeth, most or all of which are thought to have been ancient
foundations.

[12] The 'little book about his life' must be Bede, *V. Cuth.*, a copy of which was certainly
at Durham when Saint-Calais arrived, and is now preserved as CCCC 183 (see e.g.

monks of his own order, nor regular canons.[10] For this reason he was afflicted with great sorrow, and he humbly and sedulously beseeched God and St Cuthbert that they should aid him with their counsel as to how to put right what he saw to be quite unsuitable, and that they should also aid him to carry this through. So he asked the older and wiser men of the whole bishopric[11] how matters had been arranged in the time of St Cuthbert, when the church was founded, and they replied that his episcopal see had been on the island of Lindisfarne, and that monks had reverently served him there both while he was alive and when he was in his grave. What they asserted tallied with the little book about his life and with the *Ecclesiastical History of the English People*.[12] A long time after this a host of cruel barbarians had devastated not only Lindisfarne (as was said above) but also other places round about, and with sacrilegious audacity had put to death the noble community of that monastery. But not with impunity! For before long the just vengeance of God had smitten all of them fearfully, and they had been snatched from this life to be consigned to eternal tortures and torments.[13]

When the bishop had learned all this, he considered in his mind how to restore to the saint's sacred body the service which it had formerly enjoyed; and so that no one might deem things offensive that he had done solely on his own initiative, he consulted King William, his wife Queen Mathilda, and Lanfranc, archbishop of Canterbury. So that support for so valuable a scheme should be enlisted from every quarter, the king at once sent him to Pope Gregory to consult the pontiff about this as as well as to discuss with him other matters which the king had commanded him to raise.[14] When the bishop had told the pope just a little about the sanctity of the blessed father Cuthbert, the pope approved his scheme in every way, that is that the communities of monks which he had found at

Keynes, in *Learning and Literature*, ed. Lapidge and Gneuss, pp. 143–201, at 181–5). The other text was Bede, *HE*, an item in one of the manuscripts presented by Saint-Calais himself to Durham and now DCL, B.II.35. See A. J. Piper, 'The historical interests of the Durham monks', Rollason, *Symeon*, pp. 301–32, at 310–11.

[13] The cross-reference is to pp. 86–7, 88–9, above.

[14] The exact date of this visit and the nature of the 'other matters' are not known. It may have been soon after his consecration, for Gregory VII (1073–85) faced armed opposition at Rome from the Emperor Henry IV from 21 May to June 1081, although he does not seem to have been wholly preoccupied with his struggle with the emperor thereafter; see e.g., H. E. J. Cowdrey, *Pope Gregory VII, 1073–1085* (Oxford, 1998), pp. 213–15. William of Saint-Calais was present at a legal suit in Normandy on 15 Sept. 1082, and may then have been returning from Rome (*Regesta Regum Anglo-Normannorum: The Acta of William I 1066–1087*, ed. D. Bates (Oxford, 1998), no. 264; cf. no. 253).

episcopatus locis Wiramuthe et Gyrwe inuenerat, in unum coram
sancto illius corpore congregaret, quia episcopatus paruitas ad tria
monachorum cenobia non sufficeret.[15] Hoc quoque apostolica
deuotissime[a] confirmando auctoritate, suas per memoratum episcopum litteras[b] regi Willelmo et Landfranco archipresuli[c] direxit,
suam ex parte Domini et sancti Petri benedictionem illis omnibusque huiusmodi propositum adiuuare conantibus largiens, eos
uero si qui nisu contrario talia debilitare presumerent, perpetuo
eorundem ex parte anathemate nisi digna satisfactione resipiscerent,
feriens.[16]

Talem pape consensum cum rex audisset, non mediocriter gauisus,
sub testimonio Mathildis regine, Landfranci archiepiscopi, ceteror-
umque baronum suorum ad hoc peragendum licentiam dedit, immo
propere ut perageret episcopo precepit. Insuper etiam leges sancti
Cuthberti quas ipse coram sancto illius corpore sicut unquam
meliores sub aliquo priorum fuerant, fide sua sancierat, denuo tunc
renouando confirmauit.[17]

[lxxix
(lxxxvii)]
3. Anno[d] [e]ab Incarnatione Domini[e] millesimo octogesimo tercio, a
transitu uero patris Cuthberti trecentesimo nonagesimo septimo, ex
quo[f] autem ab Aldhuno episcopo incorruptum eiusdem patris corpus
in Dunhelmum est perlatum octogesimo nono, qui est annus regni
Willelmi duodeuicesimo, ex quo autem Aldwinus cum duobus sociis
in prouinciam Northanhymbrorum uenerat decimus, episcopatus
uero Willelmi tercius, septimas Kalendas Iunii, feria sexta,[18] memoratus episcopus monachos ex supradictis duobus monasteriis, uidelicet[g] apostolorum Petri et Pauli in Wiramuthe et in[h] Gyruum, simul

---

[a] om. H L Y; ins. over line Fx   [b] om. F   [c] archiepiscopo H
[d] Monachi in (om. T) Dunelmo conuenerunt rubric Fx H T Y; Monachi Dunelmensis
ecclesie rubric V   [e-e] Domini incarnatione T   [f] om. F   [g] scilicet H
[h] om. H

---

[15] These communities had been endowed by Bishop Walcher with lands belonging to
the church of Durham (see above, pp. 204–5, 208–11).
[16] The papal bull mentioned here may also be referred to in a privilege of Pope Calixtus
II for the prior and monks of Durham issued in 1123, which speaks of 'domini
predecessoris nostri felicis memorie Gregorii pape septimi preceptum' in connection
with the expulsion of the canons from Durham; see *Papsturkunden in England*, ed.
W. Holtzmann (3 vols., Berlin and Göttingen, 1930–52), ii. 138–40 (no. 5). The purported
bull of Gregory VII for Durham, the earliest copy of which is preserved in a late 12th-cent.
hand in DCL, A.II.16, is certainly a forgery of the end of the 12th cent. See Holtzmann,
Papsturkunde, ii. 132–6 (no. 2); and, for the discovery by Wilhelm Levison of the copy in
DCL, A.II.16, G. V. Scammell, *Hugh du Puiset, Bishop of Durham* (Cambridge, 1956),

two places in his bishopric, Wearmouth and Jarrow, should be amalgamated into one in the presence of the saint's holy body, because the bishopric was too small to support three communities of monks.[15] In order most solemnly to confirm this by apostolic authority, the pope sent by the hand of the bishop letters to King William and Archbishop Lanfranc, in which he gave his blessing on behalf of the Lord and St Peter to them and to all those who should strive to promote this scheme, but on behalf of the Lord and St Peter he imposed eternal anathema on any who should presume with perverse efforts to undermine such measures, unless they should desist and make due satisfaction.[16]

When the king heard that the pope had given his consent in this way, he rejoiced greatly and with Queen Mathilda, Archbishop Lanfranc, and his barons as witnesses he granted permission for this scheme to be put into effect, indeed he ordered the bishop to do so speedily. In addition, he also renewed and confirmed afresh the laws of St Cuthbert, which he himself had in the presence of the saint's holy body sanctioned with his oath more unequivocally than they had ever been under any of his predecessors.[17]

3. In the year of Our Lord's Incarnation 1083, the 397th year from [lxxix the death of father Cuthbert, the eighty-ninth from when Bishop (lxxxvii)] Ealdhun brought the undecayed body of the same father to Durham, that is the eighteenth year of King William, the tenth since Aldwin came into the province of the Northumbrians with two companions, the third year of William's episcopate, on Friday 26 May[18] the aforementioned bishop joined together as one community the monks from the two monasteries of the apostles Peter and Paul, respectively at Wearmouth and Jarrow, and brought

pp. 304–5. For a view sceptical of Gregory's involvement in the reform of Durham, see Foster, in Rollason, *Anglo-Norman Durham*, p. 61.

[17] For King William I's oath at Cuthbert's tomb, see above, pp. 198–201. No documents purporting to be either the grant of permission by the king or the confirmation of the laws have survived. The inflated version of the grant of lands and privileges by Saint-Calais (Offler, *Episcopal Charters*, no. *3a; *Regesta I*, ed. Davis, no. 148) purports to have been made at a council at London in 1082 in the presence of the king and Archbishop Lanfranc; but this document was not fabricated until the late 12th cent. so *LDE* cannot have been referring to it (Bates, in Rollason, *Anglo-Norman Durham*).

[18] Note the elaborateness of the dating clause which is consistent with dates given earlier for the death of Cuthbert (687), the arrival of Ealdhun in Durham (995), and the election of Bishop William of Saint-Calais (1080). It confirms a date of 1074 for the arrival of Aldwin in Northumbria (above, p. 201, n. 75). See Jäschke, in Rollason, *Symeon*, pp. 57, 59–60.

congregatos *numero uiginti tres* in Dunhelmum perduxit;[19] quibus
tercio die post (id est ipso die sancto Pentecostes) in ecclesiam sancti
Cuthberti perductis, apostolici pape iussionem per auctoritatem
beati Petri apostolorum principis, factam atque excellentissimi
regis Willelmi uoluntatem populis qui conuenerant manifestauit.
Quo facto, beatissime Dei genitrici Marie et sanctissimo *suo patrono*
Cuthberto monachos commendans, ecclesiam illis et illos ecclesie
contradidit. Denique mox inter ipsa sacre misse solennia secundum
morem illos monachicum propositum profitentes et in eodem loco
stabilitatem promittentes benedixit, et ad sacrum sanctissimi patris
Cuthberti corpus inseparabiliter astrinxit.

Eos uero qui prius inibi habitauerant, nomen tantum canonicorum
habentes, sed in nullo canonicorum regulam sequentes, precepit ut si
in ipsa ecclesia residere uellent, deinceps in monachico proposito cum
monachis uitam agerent. At illi de ecclesia exire quam taliter ingredi
maluerunt, preter unum uidelicet decanum illorum,[d] cui a filio
monacho uix ut monachus fieret persuaderi poterat.[e][20]

a–a om. C Ca D Fx H L T V Y   *b–b* sancti Petri principis apostolorum Ca
c–c patrono suo T   *d* eorum Fx H L Y   *e* propter quod dicitur quod prebende
de Aukeland, Derlington, Norton, Esington (Ekington Fx; Egington L) facte fuerunt
tantum pro illis canonicis ex prouisione domini pape ut haberent unde uiuerent suo
perpetuo *add.* Fx L Y

---

[19] Two part-lines have been erased here in C. The words 'numero uiginti' are visible
under ultra-violet light and these are followed by two minims. It is not possible to establish
whether there was originally a third minim. The erasure may perhaps have been due to
disputes about how many of the monks of Durham had originally come from Jarrow and
Monkwearmouth (Rollason, 'Erasures', p. 154). The implication of the next sentence in
the text is that there were new recruits to the priory at once.

[20] C has here a space (probably an erasure) of fourteen lines to the bottom of fo. 80ʳ and an
erasure of six lines at the top of fo. 80ᵛ. No text is recoverable by any means. At this point,
Fx, L, and Y read 'according to which it is said that the prebends of Auckland, Darlington,
Norton, and Easington were created solely for those canons by provision of the lord pope, so
that they should have in perpetuity the wherewithal to live'. A late 16th-cent. archaicizing
hand has inserted these words (with *Ekington* as in Fx and L) on lines 3–7 of the erasure on
fo. 80ᵛ of C. T has a late 14th- or early 15th-cent. addition at the bottom of the page (fo.52ʳ)
keyed to the text by a cross in a circle: 'propter quod dicitur pro prebende de Auklande,
Derlyngton et Norton facte fuerant dm (?) pro illis canonicis ex prouisione domine pape ut
haberent unde uiuerent pro perpetuo'. Norton, Auckland, and Darlington were collegiate
churches of the diocese of Durham, and Norton still possesses the remains of a cruciform
church, probably of late 11th-cent. date, which E. Cambridge has suggested might have been
the church built there for the canons expelled from Durham (Rollason, *Anglo-Norman
Durham*, pp. 145–8; see also Rollason, in *England in the Eleventh Century*, ed. Hicks, pp. 183–
98, at n. 37 and refs. therein). Easington may also have been collegiate, since there are
references to portions having been granted there in the 13th cent. (an arrangment which had
come to an end by 1235; M. G. Snape pers. comm., citing *Rotuli litterarum patentium in Turri
Londinensi asservati*, i. *1201–1216*, ed. T. D. Hardy (London, 1835), p. 104, *Calendar of*

them, twenty-three in number, to Durham.[19] On the third day after this (that is on the holy day of Pentecost itself) he led them into the church of St Cuthbert, and he made known to the people congregated there the command of the apostolic pope by authority of the blessed Peter, prince of the apostles, and the actions and wishes of the most excellent King William. When this had been done, the bishop commended the monks to the most blessed mother of God, Mary, and to the most holy patron, Cuthbert, and he handed over the church to them and them to the church. Directly after this, in the course of celebrating mass he blessed as was customary those professing the monastic vocation and vowing to remain permanently in that place, and he bound them indissolubly to the sacred body of the most holy father Cuthbert.

The bishop ordered that those who had previously dwelt in the church, and who had been canons only by name since they in no way followed the rule of canons, should henceforth lead their lives with the monks and according to the monastic vocation if they wished to remain in the church. But they preferred to leave the church rather than to enter on those terms, except one who was their dean, and who was persuaded with difficulty by his son who was a monk that he also should become a monk.[20]

Patent Rolls, 1225–1232, p. 168, DCDCM, misc. ch. 5155). Y's account of the origins of these churches, tracing them to the expulsion of the canons from Durham, may not, however, be correct. Collation of Y and C shows that they are in other respects very close, so the note about the canons may be no more ancient than Y. Conclusions might easily have been drawn in 14th-cent. Durham about the origins of the churches in question, without there having been any basis in reality for these. For further discussion, see Rollason, 'Erasures', pp. 150–3, where the evidence relating to Easington was not taken into account.

On the standard of life of the pre-monastic community at Durham, see Rollason, in Hicks, *England in the Eleventh Century*, pp. 187–91. The dean was presumably the senior or vice-gerent of that community after the bishop, although elsewhere this title could be used for the head of a secular collegiate foundation (P. H. Hase, 'The mother churches of Hampshire', in *Minsters and Parish Churches*, ed. Blair, pp. 45–66, at 50, 52, 59–60). A dean called Leofwine was killed with Walcher in 1080 (Thorpe, *Fl. Wig.* ii. 16 (*s.a.* 1080)). Cf. the almost identical account in *HReg*, *s.a.* 1080 (Arnold, *Sym. Op.*ii. 210), where this dean is called Leobwine. On the probable confusion between Leofwine and this Leobwine, who was the bishop's chaplain and may have been his archdeacon, see Offler, 'Early archdeacons', pp. 191–2.

Doubt has been cast on the veracity of Symeon's account of the expulsion of the clerks by Aird, in Rollason, *Symeon*, pp. 35–40, and Aird, *Cuthbert*, pp. 126–31, 137–8. He argues that other histories do not note the expulsion of the clerks; that the analogy of Lanfranc's reform of Christ Church Canterbury would suggest that continuity of personnel was likely; that Symeon's handling of the pre-1083 community is inconsistent; and that some of the names of monks in the post-1083 community are the same as those of known pre-1083 clerks (see above, p. 163 n. 28). But none of his arguments is conclusive. See also Aird, 'Origins and Development', pp. 135–92.

Tribus ergo post monachorum professionem factam euolutis diebus, episcopus omnibus illis in unum conuocatis, communi consilio monasterii officia siue negotia his quos grauiores et prudentiores et ad hoc idoneos perspexit, cum magno Dei timore ac discretione distribuit. Et congruo quidem ordine a capite (id est ab altari) incipiens, cuidam illorum scilicet Leofwino uiro prudenti et Deum ualde timenti ecclesie curam et sancti Cuthberti corporis incorrupti ^acustodiam commisit,^a secretariumque constituit.[21] Deinde ^bAldwino quem pro insita illi prudentia et magne discretionis moderamine ac morum honestate ualde strenuum nouerat, intus et foris totius monasterii curam et dispensationem delegauit, et ut sine illius consilio uel prouidentia nil ageretur statuit.[22] Denique^b terrarum possessiones illorum ita a suis possessionibus segregauit, ut suas omnino ab episcopi seruitio et ab omni consuetudine liberas et quietas ad suum uictum et uestitum terras monachi possiderent. Antiqua enim ipsius ecclesie hoc^c exigit consuetudo, ut qui Deo coram sancti Cuthberti corpore ministrant, segregatas a terris episcopi suas habeant.[23] Atque ideo rex Willelmus et antea (sicut supra dictum est) et nunc cum monachi Dunhelmum uenissent, Billingham cum suis appendiciis ad uictum specialiter eorum qui in ipsa ecclesia Deo et sancto confessori ministrant, pro sua filiorumque salute donauit.[24] Episcopus quoque aliquantulum quidem terre monachis largitus est; uerumtamen ut sine indigentia ^det penuria^d Christo seruirent, sufficientes ad uictum illorum ac uestitum terras eis una cum rege ipse prouiderat^e et iamiamque daturus erat, sed ne id^f ad effectum

---

^{a–a} commisit custodiam *Fx L Y*   ^{b–b} *om. Fx (supplied in top margin by later hand) L Y*   ^c *om. H*   ^{d–d} *om. F*   ^e preuiderat *D H Y*   ^f *om. L*

[21] A Leofwin appears 23rd in the list of monks (above, pp. 6–7); and three monks of this name occur in the early 12th-cent. Durham obits (Piper, 'Lists', pp. 178, 192, 196, 201). It should be noted that Elfred, son of Westou, who seems to have had responsibility for St Cuthbert's relics earlier in the century, is termed in *LDE* 'custos ecclesie' (above, p. 162).

[22] *LDE*'s account makes it clear that the bishop appointed Prior Aldwin as he was later to do Prior Turgot. There is nothing here to give substance to the claims in the Durham forgeries of the late 12th cent. that the prior should be elected by the monks (cf. below p. 241 n. 34). On the other hand, *LDE*'s emphasis on the need for Aldwin's counsel and agreement may have helped to fuel the claims in those forgeries that the prior should have the first voice after the bishop. See Offler, *Episcopal Charters*, nos. *3a, *4, *4a, *4b, *7 for texts and comment; see also Scammell, *Puiset*, pp. 300–7, and for the dating, Bates, in Rollason, *Anglo-Norman Durham*, pp. 115–24.

Three days after the monks had made their profession, the bishop called them all together and by common counsel and with great discretion and fear of God he assigned the monastic offices and responsibilities to those he perceived as the most serious-minded, the most prudent, and the most suited to the tasks. Beginning appropriately from the head (that is from the altar) he committed the care of the church and the custody of the undecayed body of St Cuthbert to one of their number called Leofwin, a prudent man who greatly feared God, and made him sacristan.[21] Then he delegated the care and superintendence of the whole monastery within and without the cloister to Aldwin, whom he knew to be a man of great zeal in his natural wisdom, the moderation of his great discretion, and the honesty of his life, and he decreed that nothing should be done without Aldwin's counsel and foresight.[22] Then he segregated his own landed possessions from theirs, so that the monks should possess their lands for the purpose of their maintenance and clothing, entirely free and quit of episcopal service and of all customary exactions. This was made necessary by the ancient custom of this church that whoever should serve God there in the presence of the body of St Cuthbert should hold their lands segregated from those of the bishop.[23] As was said above, King William had previously granted Billingham with all its appurtenances specially for the maintenance of those serving God and the holy confessor in this church, and now when the monks came to Durham he renewed the grant for the salvation of himself and his sons.[24] The bishop himself also gave the monks a small portion of land; and so that they might serve Christ without indigence and penury, he had made provision with the king for a grant of sufficient land for their maintenance and clothing, and he was about to give this to them,

---

[23] *LDE*'s statement seems contradictory here: William of Saint-Calais had to segregate the lands, even though ancient custom was that they should be segregated. The most recent discussion of Durham, that of Crosby, *Bishop and Chapter*, pp. 132–51, argues that no definite division of lands was made before the time of Hugh of le Puiset (1153–95), and even after that the situation was unclear into the 13th cent.

[24] The cross-reference is to pp. 198–9, above. No document of William I relating to Billingham has survived, but there does survive a writ of William Rufus granting Billingham to St Cuthbert and his monks (Durham, Dean and Chapter Muniments, 1.1. Reg.7; facsimile in *Facsimiles of English Royal Writs to 1100*, ed. T. A. M. Bishop and P. Chaplais (Oxford, 1957), no. 8 (*Regesta I*, ed. Davis, no. 344)).

perueniret, primo regis ac[a] postea episcopi mors impedimento fuerat.[25]

[lxxx   4. Ecclesiam[b] [c]sane sancti Oswini[c] in Tinemuthe iamdudum [d]donante
(lxxxviii)]   Walchero episcopo cum comitatum regeret,[d] monachi cum adhuc
essent in Gyruum possederant,[26] unde etiam [e]ossa ipsius sancti[e] ad se
transferentes, in ecclesia sancti Pauli secum non paruo tempore
habuerunt, que postmodum ad priorem locum retulerunt.[27] Deinde
prefati antistitis Willelmi tempore comes Northanhymbrorum
Albrius hoc donum renouauit, ipsamque ecclesiam cum suo presbitero ecclesie sancti Cuthberti perpetuo possidendam adiecit.[28] Que

    [a] et H Y; om. Fx L   [b] Tinemuthe fuit possessio monachorum de Garue (Gerue
Y; Girue Fx; Jaroue V) rubric Fx H V Y; Tynemuthe fuit possessio de (truncated) rubric T
[c–c] sancti Oswini sane L Y; sane ins. over line Fx   [d–d] donantibus Northymbrie
comitibus C Ca D Fx H L T V Y   [e–e] ipsius sancti ossa Ca; Oswini add. H.

    [25] F. Barlow argued that there probably was segregation of lands before William of
Saint-Calais's time, drawing attention in particular to the grants specifically to the monks
of the estates of Billingham, Aycliffe, Monkwearmouth, Jarrow, and Hemingbrough in
Yorkshire (Durham Jurisdictional Peculiars (Oxford, 1950), pp. 5–6; see above, p. 225 n. 9).
Barlow's view is supported by the evidence of a parallel situation at Christ Church,
Canterbury, where it seems that there was segregation of lands before the Conquest (B. W.
Kissan, 'Lanfranc's alleged division of the lands between archbishop and community',
English Historical Review, liv (1939), 285–93, and E. John, 'The division of the mensa in
early English monasteries', Journal of Ecclesiastical History, vi (1955), 143–55). According
to Barlow, what happened was that William of Saint-Calais confirmed the existing grants
to the monks and to these were added Billingham and a small, unspecified grant from the
bishop himself. A wider scheme for division of lands between the bishop and the monks
was projected but not implemented at once. This delay cannot have been the result of
William of Saint-Calais's death which was neither sudden nor immediately after the
foundation of the priory; it must have resulted from the bishop's reluctance to envisage
such a division given his view of bishop and monks as a unified community, and perhaps
also from problems associated with such a division. In fact, a division was eventually made,
probably not before the time of Hugh of le Puiset (1153–95), and even then it was de facto
rather than de jure. The situation as regards free disposal of the monks' churches and the
sharing out of episcopal rights over them remained unresolved, thus opening the way for
disputes between the monks and the bishop which were fuelled by further claims on the
part of the monks and were only resolved by the agreement of 1229 known as Le Convenit
(Feodarium, ed. Greenwell pp. 212–17; Crosby, Bishop and Chapter, pp. 132–51). In this
connection should be noted LDE's statement above that the lands of the monks were to be
free from any service to the bishop and from any customs: the author was evidently very
sensitive to such stipulations. See also Aird, Cuthbert, pp. 145–7.
    [26] Tynemouth (NZ 374 695), which occupies a rocky promontory on the north side of
the mouth of Tyne, may have been an early monastery, although there is no evidence for
this aside from the discovery of the remains of a building of uncertain date and of a carved
cross of 9th-cent. date (Cramp, in Wilson, Archaeology of Anglo-Saxon England, pp. 217–
20, and Cramp, Corpus i. 226). On the burial of St Oswine there, see above, pp. 164–5
n. 31, and, for evidence that the Jarrow community supervised Tynemouth in the years
before 1083, see below, p. 235 n. 28.
    The attribution of the grant of Tynemouth to Bishop Walcher seems to be the original

when first the death of the king and then his own death prevented him from putting this into effect.[25]

4. While they were still at Jarrow, the monks had been in possession of the church of St Oswine at Tynemouth, which they had been given a long time ago by Bishop Walcher during his tenure of the earldom of Northumbria.[26] They had translated Oswine's relics from there and had kept them under their direct care in their own church of St Paul for a long time before returning them afterwards to their former resting place.[27] Later on, in Bishop William's time, Aubrey, earl of Northumbria renewed this gift, and granted in perpetuity the church itself and its priest to the church of St Cuthbert.[28] Since this had been

[lxxx (lxxxviii)]

sense of the words in C now erased and preserved only in F. C has almost a line erased, and the hand identified as that of Symeon has substituted 'by the earls of Northumbria' for the original text, apparently modifying 'donante' to 'donantibus'. The writing has had to be excessively spaced and there is still some blank space left. Under ultra-violet light the downstroke of the *g* of *regeret* is visible. On the historical context of the grant and of the alteration of the text of *LDE*, see Offler, *Episcopal Charters*, pp. 4–6. The grant must have been made between 1075, when Walcher became earl after Waltheof forfeited that position, and 1080 when the bishop was murdered (*HReg*, *s.a.* 1075 (Arnold, *Sym. Op*.ii. 207, and above pp. 212–13, 214–19). Tynemouth was a vill of the earl, so Walcher would have made the grant in that capacity. Offler argues that the reason for the alteration of the text was that, in their attempts to wrest Tynemouth back from St Albans (see below, pp. 236–7), the monks needed a better title than Walcher's grant, for the bishop's role as earl had been 'unprecedented, unsuccessful and ambiguous'. C was therefore altered to show the grant as having been made by unnamed earls. Possibly Earls Waltheof (1072–5) and Aubrey (1080) were meant. The latter appears in this connection below; the former was credited with the gift of Tynemouth in *HReg*, *s.a.* 1080, and in the possibly interpolated passage *s.a.* 1121 (Arnold, *Sym. Op*.ii. 209 and 260–1). For the appearance of Waltheof and Aubrey in the forged Durham charters, see below, n. 28.

[27] The discovery in 1065 with the agreement of Bishop Æthelwine of Durham of the relics of St Oswine at Tynemouth is described in *HReg*, *s.a.* 1065, and in the possibly interpolated passage *s.a.* 1121 (Arnold, *Sym. Op*.ii. 177 and 261), and also in *Vita Oswini*, where the body is said to have been found undecayed (*Miscellanea biographica*, ed. Raine, pp. 11–17). In this last text, which appears to emanate from Tynemouth after it had become a cell of St Albans, there is no mention of the monks of Jarrow holding Tynemouth or removing the relics of St Oswine.

[28] According to *HReg*, *s.a.* 1072 (Arnold, *Sym. Op*.ii. 199), Aubrey was made earl after Walcher's death in 1080 but was not effective in difficult affairs and returned home, implying that his tenure of the office was short. There is no reason to doubt that he confirmed the gift of Tynemouth to the monks of Jarrow, but the extant charters in which Waltheof makes the gift and Aubrey confirms it are all forgeries of the late 12th cent. That in the *Liber Vitae*, fo. 46ᵛ, is based for the first part of it on the *HReg* and then on the passage above in *LDE* from 'Vnde etiam ossa' to 'per tres annos possederunt', adding to it a phrase stating that Aubrey's confirmation was made 'after the monks had by papal authority been transferred to Durham'. *LDE*'s reference to a priest at Tynemouth should be compared with the statement in *HReg*, *s.a.* 1121 (Arnold, *Sym. Op*. ii. 260), that after the gift of Tynemouth the church was supervised by a monk of Jarrow together with a canon of the pre-monastic community at Durham (see also, above, p. 234 n. 25).

cum iam per quindecim annos uelut deserta sine tecto durasset, eam monachi culmine imposito renouarunt, et per tres annos possederunt.[29] *a*Cum uero postea Robertus de Mulbreio in comitatum Albrio successisset, propter inimicitias que inter episcopum et ipsum agitabantur, sancti Cuthberti monachos de ipsa ecclesia expulit, eamque Paulo abbati monasterii sancti Albani martyris tradidit. Qui uidelicet abbas a Dunhelmensibus monachis frequenter admonitus, rogatus et prohibitus ne aliena inuaderet, audire noluit, quin potius suos illuc ad habitandum misit. Quos non multo post ipse secutus, repente ibi infirmitate corripitur, et dum domum *b*redire temptaret*b* moritur. Ipse quoque comes postea in eadem ecclesia quam sancto Cuthberto abstulit, res omnes et honorem cum sui *corporis libertate* amisit.*a* [30]

5. At*c* uero*d* episcopus Willelmus nichil unquam de ecclesia auferebat, quin potius semper inferre, et multis eam ac preciosis ornamentorum speciebus studebat exornare. Iura quoque ecclesie, leges et priuilegia strenuitate sua atque*e* prudentia ita Deo adiuuante defendebat et conseruabat, ut eo uiuente nullius temeritate, nullius uiolentia infringi uel uiolari possent. Nam et quasdam terras de quibus semper inter episcopum Dunhelmensem et comitem Northanhymbrensium contentio fuerat, ita ecclesie liberas et quietas reliquit, ut deinceps aliquas ex his consuetudines preter episcopum exigere nemo uel*f* debeat uel possit, quod cartule

---

a–a om. *Fx L Y*   *b–b* temptaret redire *F*   *c* Capitulum rubric *V Y*; Qualiter Willelmus episcopus se habuit erga monachos rubric *T V (add. s. xiv ex.)*   *d* om. *L Y; ins. over line Fx*   *e* ac *Y*   *f* om. *Ca*

---

[29] Fx, L, and Y omit the remainder of this chapter and give instead *De miraculis* c. 13 (Arnold, *Sym. Op.* ii. 345–7), in Fx and Y with the heading 'Quomodo Paulus abbas et Robertus comes in loco quem sancto abstulerant iniurie penam (postea *Fx*) receperunt'. T has at the foot of the page (fo. 52ᵛ) in a late 14th- or early 15th-cent. hand: 'Hic deficit capitulum lxxxix, Quomodo Paulus et cetera'. The chapter describes how Mowbray, who had fallen into disfavour with the king, was captured by royal forces in Tynemouth church itself and thrown into prison where he subsequently died. Mowbray's crime was his revolt of 1095–6 (Freeman, *William Rufus*, ii. 36–48). If Tynemouth church had lost its roof in the course of the Norman depredations of 1072, as reported in *Vita Oswini*, c. 8 (*Miscellanea biographica*, ed. Raine, pp. 20–1), and was left for 15 years and then held by the monks of Jarrow for three, this would give 1090 as the date of the gift made by Robert de Mowbray, earl of Northumbria (1080/1 to 1095), which is also the date given by the 13th-cent. St Albans chronicler Matthew Paris, *Chronica maiora*, ed. H. R. Luard (7 vols., RS lvii, 1872–3), ii. 31; see Offler, *Episcopal Charters*, p. 5. The reasons for

more or less deserted and roofless for fifteen years, the monks restored it and put on a new roof, and held it for three years.[29] Afterwards, however, when Robert de Mowbray succeeded Aubrey in the earldom, he expelled the monks of St Cuthbert from that church on account of enmity which was stirred up between himself and the bishop, and he gave it to Paul, abbot of the monastery of St Alban the Martyr. Although the Durham monks frequently admonished this abbot and requested him not to trespass upon what did not belong to him, and forbade him from doing so, he refused to listen to them and instead sent his monks to live there. He followed them not long afterwards, but he was suddenly taken ill there and died while he was trying to get home. Also the earl himself in that very church which he had taken from St Cuthbert afterwards lost all his possessions, together with his honour and his freedom.[30]

5. Bishop William, however, never took anything from the church, rather he strove always to enrich it and to adorn it with many precious ornaments of all sorts. With God's help he defended and preserved the rights, laws, and privileges of the church, so that while he lived they could not be infringed or violated by the violence or temerity of anyone. Certain lands which had always been in dispute between the earl of Northumbria and the bishop of Durham he left to the church free and quit of all claim, so that thereafter no one except the bishop should or could exact any customary dues from these lands, as the

---

Mowbray's enmity towards William of Saint-Calais are not known for certain, but they may have been the land disputes described in the next chapter. It has been suggested that in 1095 the bishop may have allied with the earl in revolt against the king (Freeman, *William Rufus*, ii. 38). *De miraculis* c. 13 (Arnold, *Sym. Op.*ii. 345) says only that he was stirred up with hatred against the church of St Cuthbert. Paul was abbot of St Albans from 1077 to 1093.

[30] *HReg*, s.a. 1093 (Arnold, *Sym. Op.* ii. 221), records tersely in a passage, the other elements of which are taken from John of Worcester, 'Iste Paulus contra interdictum monachorum Dunelmensium ecclesiam de Tynemuthe, quam ipsi possederant, per uiolentiam Rodberti comitis ingressus, tactus ibidem infirmitate, rediens, in itinere in Seteringtun iuxta Eboracum moritur.' A summary account of the Tynemouth affair is given *s.a.* 1121 (Arnold, *Sym. Op.* ii. 260–2), which is the account of the Durham monks' legal bid to recover Tynemouth. Paul is said to have come to take possession of Tynemouth in the face of an express prohibition by Prior Turgot. See also *Liber Vitae*, fo. 46ᵛ. The story of Paul's death and Mowbray's downfall is told in *De miraculis* c. 13, of which the last three words are identical with the last three here (above, n. 29).

ecclesie ostendunt.[31] Monachos ipsos ut pater dulcissimus filios carissimos amplectebatur, protegebat, fouebat, ac summa discretione regebat. Siue enim arguebat siue blandiebatur, amabilis omnibus illis erat, quia illius neque districtio rigida, neque mansuetudo soluta. Ita ex altero alterum temperabat, ut seueritas illius iocunda, et iocunditas esset seuera. Nimium eos diligens, nimium ab eis diligebatur. *a*Ad sui habitus reuerentiam, et ad ordinis obseruantiam precipue illos hortabatur.*a* Hoc presens uerbo, hoc absens missis sepius ad eos litteris agere curabat. Hanc illius diligentiam, hoc studium testantur etiam ille que in illius memoriam seruantur in hac ecclesia sacre admonitionis littere, quas cum regiis impeditus negotiis uenire non posset, ipse ad eos direxerat, quarum hic aliquas inserere congruum uidetur.

[lxxxi (xc)] 6. Guillelmus*b* *c*Dunhelmensis episcopus*c* suis in Christo fratribus et filiis Dunhelmensibus cenobitis, salutem et uiuificam benedictionem. Non credo uos discredere quantum michi displiceat quod uobiscum ut deceret morari non ualeo.*d* Sed qualicumque*e* modo uel loco peccando laborem, mens tamen in uobis assidue delectata quiescit. Precor ergo ut et uos tribulationes nostras *f*mente cotidie*f* uideatis, et imbecillitatem meam deuotis orationibus et elemosinis caritatiue et sine fastidio sustentetis. Hoc autem precipiendo precor, et precando precipio, ut in amorem ordinis uestri feruendo crescatis, et ordinem pro nulla necessitate uel causa declinare permittatis, et nulli parcatis in ordine. In ecclesia uero non properando sed licenter et honeste psalmos et cetera decantetis. Confessiones uestras frequenter priori faciatis, conuentus firmiter et absque ulla retentione ab omnibus teneatur, preter egrotos et eos qui exterioribus negotiis sunt regulariter deputati. Et quia presens uobis que deberem dicere non

a–a om. T   *b* Epistola Willelmi episcopi ad monachos Dunelmenses *rubric Fx H T V Y; collated with DCL, B. IV. 24, fo. 74r (siglum B. IV. 24)*   *c–c* episcopus Dunelmensis L   *d* possum Ca   *e* qualique T; qualicunque B. IV. 24   *f–f* cotidie mente Fx L Y

---

[31] An agreement between William of Saint-Calais and Robert de Mowbray concerning Aycliffe and other vills is preserved as Durham, Dean and Chapter Muniments, 1.1. Reg. 17 (printed *Feodarium*, ed. Greenwell, appendix, pp. lxxxii–lxxxiii, and *Regesta Regum Anglo-Normannorum, 1066–1154*, i. *Regesta Willelmi Conquestoris et Willelmi Rufi, 1066–1100*, ed. H. W. C. Davis (Oxford, 1913), no. 349). Preserved on a late 12th-cent. roll, the agreement dates, if authentic, to 1094, pointing to a conciliation between earl and bishop very shortly after the former's appropriation of Tynemouth (Offler, *Episcopal Charters*, pp. 10–11). It gives the lands in question as Aycliffe (NZ 282 222) and, in its parish, Ricknall (NZ 306 244), Woodham (NZ 287 268), Heworth (NZ 293 233), Brafferton (NZ

charters of the church show.[31] As the kindest of fathers cherishes his dearest sons, so he protected, cared for, and with utmost discretion governed the monks themselves. Whether censuring or praising them, he was amiable to them all, because his sternness was not rigid nor his gentleness lax, so that he tempered one with the other, making his severity jocund and his jocundity severe. He loved them greatly, and was greatly loved by them in return. He exhorted each of them above all to revere the habit they wore and to observe the monastic order. When he was present he took pains to do this by word of mouth, when absent by sending frequent letters to them. This diligence and effort of his is attested to by the letters of pious admonition which are preserved in this church in memory of him, and which he sent to them when he was prevented by the king's affairs from coming himself. It seems appropriate to insert one here.

6. William, bishop of Durham, to the monks of Durham, his brothers [lxxxi (xc)] in Christ and his sons, greeting and salvation-giving blessing! I am sure you will not doubt how much it displeases me that I am not able to stay with you as I should; but in whatever way or in whatever place I may labour in this sinful world my mind takes constant delight in you and so finds rest. I ask therefore that you should daily keep our tribulations in your minds, and that you should charitably and without aversion sustain me in my weakness with devout prayers and alms. I ask this as I command it, and I command it as I ask it, that you should increase in fervent love of your order, and that you should not permit that order to decline by any necessity or for any cause, and that you should spare no one in your order its rigours. In the church you should chant the Psalms *et cetera* not in haste but freely and decently. You should make confession frequently to the prior, and chapter should be attended rigorously by all with no holding back, except for the sick and those who are officially assigned to outside business. Because I am not able to say to you what I should were I

295 211), Newhouse (? NZ 259 209), Preston-le-Skerne (NZ 311 244), and Ketton (31 20); Claxton (NZ 477 282) in Greatham parish, Chilton (NZ 28 29) in Merrington parish, Stainton (NZ 071 186), Winston-on-Tees (NZ 143 168), and Westwick (NZ 072 155) in Gainford parish, Wolviston (NZ 455 258) in Billingham parish, *Esmidebrok*, and Killerby (NZ 192 199) in Heighington parish (A. J. Piper, pers. comm.). For the identifications with modern place-names, see also Mawer, *Place-names*. The dispute, which concerned mediatized regalian rights, had its origins in the grants made by Bishop Ealdhun as a dowry for his daughter Ecgfrida (Arnold, *Sym. Op.* i. 215; Aird, *Cuthbert*, pp. 162–3). Aycliffe appears in the 1464 inventory of Durham priory lands (*Feodarium*, ed. Greenwell, pp. 160–1).

ualeo, litteras istas unaquaque septimana semel*a* in capitulo recitate, ut et hec firmius teneatis, et me in his litteris loquentem audiendo, Deo diligentius commendetis. Et quia caritas operit multitudinem peccatorum, non solum peregrinis et hospitibus sed omnibus omnino gentibus ueram facite caritatem. Per hec et per alia bona opera faciat uos et hic sane temporaliter uiuere, et perennem*b* gloriam eternaliter possidere, qui uiuit et regnat Deus per immortalia *c*secula seculorum.*c*[32]

[lxxxii 7. Anno*d* Dominice Incarnationis millesimo octogesimo septimo,
(xci)] quarto anno aduentus monachorum in Dunhelmum pene transacto, uenerandus prior Aldwinus pridie Idus*e* Aprilis *f*terminum uite*f* presentis habuit, *g*quarto decimo anno*g* ex quo primum in Northanhymbrorum prouinciam uenerat.[33] De cuius obitu episcopus cum fratribus multum contristatus indoluit, quia erat uir bonus et modestus, prudentia et consilio ecclesie ualde necessarius, et in quocunque negotio ne Deum offenderet*h* *i*maxime sollicitus.*i* Cuius memoriam ut in suis orationibus monachi Dunhelmenses indesinenter agant, ipse meritis suis omnino exigit, quem preuium*j* in ipsam prouinciam ducem habuerunt, ubi exemplo illius*k* et magisterio habitantes Christo seruire ceperunt. In cuius*l* locum iure prioratus discipulum illius*m* uidelicet Turgotum communi fratrum consilio episcopus surrogauit, et totius monasterii curam intus et foris cum Dei timore illum agere imperauit.[34]

[lxxxiii Eodem*n* anno quo Aldwinus est defunctus, rex Willelmus cum
(xcii)] adhuc de uicesimo secundo *o*regni eius anno*o* quinque septimane restarent, quintas*p* Idus Septembris moriens, Willelmo filio reliquit imperium.[35]

---

a *om.* F   *b* perhennem *DCL, MS B. IV. 24*   *c–c* seculorum secula *D;* seculorum secula Amen *Fx L Y*   *d* Obiit Alduuinus primus prior Dunelmie *rubric Fx H T V Y*   *e* Kalendas *H*   *f–f* uite terminum *H*   *g–g* anno quarto decimo *Ca*   *h* negotio *add. Ca*   *i–i* sollicitus maxime *Fx (with tranposition marks) L Y*   *j* primum *Fx*   *k* eius *Fx L Y*   *l* huius *Fx L Y*   *m* eius *Fx L Y*   *n* Obiit Willelmus primus rex Anglorum *rubric Fx H T V Y*   *o–o* anno eius regni *Fx L*   *p* quinta *F*

---

[32] Aside from some trivial scribal variants, the text of this letter in *LDE* is identical to a free-standing copy of it in DCL, B. IV. 24, fo. 74*r*. Since that manuscript was almost certainly the cantor's book, it seems very likely that the copy of the letter in it was actually used for reading aloud in the way which *LDE* describes. On the scribe of this copy, see Gullick, in Rollason, *Anglo-Norman Durham*, pp. 95, 97. On the letter as an

present, read out this letter once a week in the chapter, so that you may adhere more firmly to these precepts, and in listening to me speaking in this letter you may commend yourselves to God more diligently. Because charity transcends a multitude of sins, be truly charitable not only to pilgrims and guests but to any people whatsoever. Through these and other good works God, who lives and reigns for ever and ever, will see to it that you live righteously in this world and achieve eternal glory in the next.[32]

7. In the year of Our Lord's Incarnation 1087, when the fourth year [lxxxii since the coming of the monks to Durham had barely passed, the (xci)] venerable Prior Aldwin reached the end of this life on 12 April, in the fourteenth year since he had first come into the kingdom of the Northumbrians.[33] The bishop and the monks were much saddened by his death and lamented, because he was a good and modest man, one of whom the church had great need for his prudence and counsel, and very conscientious in all things lest he offend God. His merits require that the monks of Durham should preserve his memory ceaselessly in their prayers, for he it was who had first led them into that kingdom, and it was by his example and teaching that they had begun to live there and to serve Christ. By common counsel of the brothers the bishop rightly appointed Turgot his disciple in his place as prior, and ordered him to direct the care of the entire monastery within and without in a God-fearing way.[34]

In the same year that Aldwin died, King William, when there still [lxxxiii remained to him five weeks of the twenty-second year of his reign, (xcii)] died on 9 September and left his realm to his son William.[35]

example of Symeon's use of pre-existing sources, see Meehan, in Rollason, *Symeon*, p. 129.

[33] Aldwin's death is recorded in *HReg s.a.* 1087 (Arnold, *Sym. Op.* ii. 213), in a passage added to one taken from JW. For the date of Aldwin's arrival in Northumbria, see above, p. 201 n. 75. The date of his death is also given against 11 Apr. in Durham obituaries, but since these are entered in the margins of the martyrology, it is likely that 12 Apr. was meant (Piper, 'Lists', p. 193, and see *Heads of Religious Houses*, p. 43).

[34] In view of the later claims by the monks that the prior should be elected by the convent, *LDE*'s certainty that the bishop appointed Turgot as he had done Aldwin before him is noteworthy, although perhaps the reference to the 'common counsel of the brothers' provided material for subsequent development (see above, p. 232, n. 22). Turgot's accession as prior and tenure of the office for twenty years less twelve days is recorded in the account of his life in *HReg s.a.* 1074 (Arnold, *Sym. Op.* ii. 204).

[35] The year was 1087. Cf. the formulation of the date in JW *s.a.* (iii. 46–7), and *HReg s.a.* (Arnold, *Sym. Op.* ii. 214): 'postquam uiginti annis, mensibus decem, et uiginti octo diebus genti Anglorum prefuit, quinta iduum Septembrium'.

[lxxxiv
(xciii)] 8. Huius*a* sicut et antea patris amicitiis antistes prefatus adiunctus, familiariter ei ad tempus adherebat, unde etiam Aluertonam cum suis appendiciis rex illi donabat.*b 36* Post non multum uero tempus*c* per aliorum machinamenta orta inter ipsos dissensione, episcopus ab episcopatu pulsus ultra mare secessit, quem comes Normannorum non ut*d* exulem sed ut patrem suscipiens, in magno honore per tres annos quibus ibi moratus est habuit.*37*

Ita monachi Dunhelmenses sui antistitis destituti solacio, cum multa se aduersa passuros formidarent, nec ab aliquo refouendos*e* sperarent, ita e contrario Deo per sancti Cuthberti merita se miserante protegebantur, ut nulla eis aduersitas noceret, et ipsum regem erga se satis*f* humanum inuenirent. Licet enim in alia monasteria et ecclesias ferocius ageret, ipsis tamen non solum nichil auferebat, sed etiam de suo dabat, et ab iniuriis malignorum sicut pater defendebat. Sed et priori ad se uenienti humiliter assurgens benigne illum suscepit, et ita per omnia sub se quemadmodum sub episcopo curam ecclesie cum omni*g* libertate agere precepit.*38* Hoc tempore refectorium quale hodie cernitur, monachi edificauerunt.*39* Tercio anno expulsionis episcopi, cum homines regis quoddam in Normannia castellum tenentes obsiderentur et iamiamque capiendi essent, eos episcopus a periculo liberauit, et consilio suo ut obsidio solueretur effecit. Vnde rex placatus, uniuersa que *h*in Anglia prius habuerat*h* ei restituit.*40* At

---

a Cuius *Y*; Willelmus episcopus (Dunhelmensis *add.* Fx T V Y) expulsus est ab Anglia (ab Anglia expulsus est *Fx V*; ab Anglia *om. T*) *rubric* Fx H T V Y   *b* donauit *Ca Fx L Y*   *c* temporis *Fx L*   *d* om. Fx H L Y   *e* se *add.* L Y   *f* om. H   *g* om. L   *h–h* prius habuit in Anglia *H*; prius habuit *Fx* (in Anglia *ins. over line*) L Y

36 It is not clear whether *LDE* means that the grant here referred to was made before William of Saint-Calais's banishment in Dec. 1088 (as suggested by *Early Yorkshire Charters II*, ed. Farrer, p. 266 (no. 927)), or whether the grant might have been made after Saint-Calais's return in 1091 and the phrase 'not long afterwards' simply refers to after William II's accession (Offler, *Episcopal Charters*, p. 51). No charter of William II relating to Northallerton has survived; and the purported *notitia* of the grant printed by Farrer, loc. cit., and in Raine, *Scriptores tres*, appendix, p. ccccxxv, is only an extract from the 15th-cent. *Libellus de exordio* of Prior Wessington (cf. Craster, 'Red Book', esp. p. 505). The most detailed account of the grant is a note in a 12th-cent. hand in *Liber Vitae*, fo. 50ᵛ–51ʳ, printed by Farrer, op. cit., pp. 269–72 (no. 931). No charter of William II exists or seems ever to have existed; and it appears that, although Northallerton was frequently confirmed to the convent in the course of the 12th cent., the monks felt the need at the end of the century to fabricate a charter of William of Saint-Calais which purports to record the grant of Allertonshire, including Northallerton itself, to the prior and monks of Durham in the presence of and by order of King William II.

37 *LDE*'s partisan attitude towards Saint-Calais is notable here. The bishop had in fact joined Odo of Bayeux's revolt in 1088, 'doing as Judas did to our Lord' as ASC, *s.a.* 1087 (*recte* 1088), puts it. See Offler, *DIV* and nn.

8. Bishop William was joined in friendship to the new King William [lxxxiv as he had been to his father, and for a time he remained on familiar (xciii)] terms with him, so that the king even gave him Northallerton with all its appurtenances.[36] Not long afterwards, however, dissension arose between them as a result of the machinations of others, and the bishop was expelled from his bishopric and went overseas, where the Duke of the Normans received him not as an exile but as a father, and held him in great honour for the three years that he remained there.[37]

So when the monks of Durham, deprived of the comfort of their bishop, feared that they would suffer many adversities without hope that anyone would take care of them, contrary to these fears they were protected by God, who had mercy on them because of the merits of St Cuthbert, so that no adversity harmed them, and they found the king himself reasonably kindly towards them. For although in other monasteries and churches he behaved more harshly, he not only took nothing from them, but even gave them of his own, and as his father had done he defended them from the injuries of the malevolent. Rising humbly when the prior came to him, he received him kindly, and commanded him in all things to attend to the care of the church in complete liberty under himself as he would have done under the bishop.[38] At this time the monks built the refectory as it appears today.[39] In the third year of the bishop's exile, when the king's men holding a certain castle in Normandy were being besieged and were on the point of being captured, the bishop freed them from danger, and through his counsel he caused the siege to be lifted. This so pleased the king that he restored to the bishop all his former possessions in England.[40] The bishop did not

---

[38] The position of Prior Turgot as vicegerent during the bishop's absence may have been significant in increasing the importance of the prior and the priory; see Aird, in Rollason, *Anglo-Norman Durham*, pp. 292–4.

[39] St John Hope, *Proceedings of the Society of Antiquaries*, 2nd ser. xxii (1908–9), p. 418, who notes that, since the refectory they had been using up to that time must presumably have been that built by Bishop Walcher, the construction of the new one must be seen as the first move in the rebuilding campaign which included the cathedral itself.

[40] The siege in question may have been that described in ASC, *s.a.* 1090, in the course of which William Rufus bribed King Philip of France to desert the cause of Robert Curthose. Offler suggested that Saint-Calais may have regained Rufus's favour by acting as his agent in dealings with Philip (*Transactions of the Architectural and Archaeological Society of Durham and Northumberland*, x (1950) 258–79, at p. 273, n. 46). The restitution to William of Saint-Calais presumably followed from the stipulation in the ensuing peace treaty that those who had lost their lands in England as a result of supporting Robert Curthose should recover them (JW, *s.a.* 1091 (iii. 58–9). For the royal writ restoring him, see H. H. E. Craster, 'A contemporary record of the pontificate of Ranulf Flambard', *Archaeologia Aeliana*, ser. 4 vii (1930), 33–56, at pp. 35–6.

ille nequaquam uacuus rediit, sed non pauca ex auro et argento sacra altaris uasa et diuersa ornamenta, sed et libros plurimos ad ecclesiam premittere curauit.[41]

[lxxxv] Nec[a] multo post [b]ecclesiam nonagesimo octauo anno[b] ex quo ab Aldhuno fundata fuerat, destrui precepit, et sequenti anno positis fundamentis nobiliori satis et maiori opere aliam construere cepit.[42]

[(xciv)] Est[c] autem incepta millesimo nonagesimo[d] tercio Dominice Incarnationis anno, pontificatus autem Willelmi tercio decimo, ex quo autem [e]monachi in Dunhelmum conuenerant[e] undecimo, tertias Idus Augusti, feria quinta.[43] Eo enim die episcopus et qui post eum [f]secundus erat[f] in ecclesia prior Turgotus cum ceteris fratribus primos in fundamento lapides posuerunt. Nam paulo ante (id est quartas Kalendas Augusti, feria sexta) idem episcopus et prior facta cum fratribus oratione ac data benedictione fundamentum ceperant fodere.[44] Igitur monachis suas officinas edificantibus, suis episcopus sumptibus ecclesie opus faciebat.[45]

Quo tempore memoratum priorem Turgotum ante totius episcopatus populos producens, uices suas etiam super illos ei iniunxit, ut

---

[a] Noua ecclesia in Dunelmo incoata est *rubric* H ecclesiam H L Y; ecclesiam *add. over line* Fx inchoata est *rubric* Fx T V Y   [d] lxxx H Dunelmum T V   [f-f] erat secundus Fx L Y

[b-b] nonagesimo octauo anno   [c] Noua ecclesia in Dunhelmo   [e-e] conuenerant monachi in

---

[41] According to *HReg*, s.a. 1091 (Arnold, *Sym. Op.* ii. 218), William was restored on 11 Sept. 1091 in the course of William Rufus's march against Malcolm, king of Scotland. The books referred to may have been those listed as having been given by Saint-Calais in a late 11th-cent. hand in the front of the Carilef Bible, DCL, MS A.II.4. See e.g. C. H. Turner, 'The earliest list of Durham MSS', *Journal of Theological Studies*, xix (1917–18), 121–32, and Piper, in Rollason, *Symeon*, pp. 310–11; for a facsimile of the list, see New Palaeographical Society, *Facsimiles of Ancient Manuscripts, etc.*, ed. E. M. Thompson *et al.* (2nd ser., London, 1913–30), pl. 17. According to *De miraculis* c. 10 (Arnold, *Sym. Op.* ii. 340–1), William of Saint-Calais's return coincided with the lifting of a threat to Durham posed by the presence of the hostile armies of King Malcolm III of Scotland and King William II of England.

[42] M. G. Snape suggests that *LDE*'s words may mean simply that the demolition of the old cathedral was ordered but not carried out in 1093; see 'Documentary evidence for the building of Durham Cathedral and its monastic buildings', *Medieval Art and Architecture at Durham Cathedral*, ed. Coldstream and Draper, pp. 20–36, at 21. Demolition of the existing church before at least the east end of the new one was finished would certainly have been an unusual procedure, and it has been assumed that, as at Winchester, the new church was built alongside Ealdhun's church; St John Hope, *Proceedings of the Society of Antiquaries*, xxii (1909), 417–24, argued that Ealdhun's church was below the south aisle and north part of the cloisters of the present church, while E. Cambridge argues that it lies entirely beneath the present cloister (Briggs *et al.*, *Archaeologia Aeliana*, 5th ser. xi (1983), 91–5. See also R. N. Bailey, E. Cambridge, and H. D. Briggs, *Dowsing and Church Archaeology* (Wimborne, 1988), pp. 42–4).

return empty-handed, but took care to send on ahead of him to the church many sacred altar vessels of gold and silver, various ornaments, and also many books.[41]

Not long afterwards, in the ninety-eighth year since it had been founded by Ealdhun, the bishop ordered the church to be demolished and after he had laid the foundations in the following year, he began to construct another on a nobler and grander scale.[42] [lxxxv]

This was begun on Thursday 11 August in the year 1093 of the Lord's Incarnation, the thirteenth of William's time as bishop, the eleventh since he had brought together the monks at Durham.[43] On that day the bishop and Prior Turgot, who was second in authority to him in the church, with the other brothers laid the first stones in the foundations. Shortly before (that is on Friday 29 July) the bishop and prior after saying prayers with the brothers and giving their blessing had begun to dig the foundations.[44] While the monks were responsible for building the monastic buildings, the bishop carried out the work on the church at his own expense.[45] [(xciv)]

At the same time he led Prior Turgot before the people of the whole bishopric and enjoined him to be his representative over them,

---

[43] The text from this sentence onwards to the end of the chapter forms the basis of a reworking of the account of the beginning of the cathedral and Turgot's appointment entered in an early 12th-cent. hand in *Liber Vitae*, fo. 46ᵛ.

[44] Note *LDE*'s designation in this passage of Turgot as second in command to the bishop; the same words are used in Offler, *DIV*, p. 100. Turgot's position had possibly been enhanced during Saint-Calais's exile (above, n. 38). The laying of the foundation stones is recounted in identical words in Offler, *DIV* (loc. cit.) with the addition of the sentence 'aderat ibi tunc et rex Scottorum Malcolmus, qui una cum eis in fundamento lapides cooperabatur'. The presence of Malcolm III is also mentioned in *HReg*, *s.a.* 1093 (Arnold, *Sym. Op.* ii. 220), repeated by *Chronicle of Melrose*, ed. Anderson, p. 29. Malcolm's presence is not, however, mentioned in *Liber Vitae*, fo. 46ᵛ. It has been doubted, especially as he was killed by the Northumbrians later in the year. V. Wall, however, argues that its omission from *LDE*'s account and its derivative in *Liber Vitae* was simply the result of that text's prime interest being in the position of Turgot as archdeacon, an interest still more strongly represented in *Liber Vitae*. She connects Malcolm's interest with his close association with Durham, represented e.g. by other entries in the *Liber Vitae*, and she suggests that he was present in Sept. 1093 en route to a meeting with William Rufus at Gloucester. See V. Wall, 'Malcolm III and the foundation of Durham Cathedral', Rollason, *Anglo-Norman Durham*, pp. 325–37. For further discussion, see Aird, *Cuthbert*, pp. 238–40.

[45] The author of the continuation beginning *Tribus dehinc annis ecclesia uacante pastore* recalls this arrangement only to note that it collapsed on Saint-Calais's death, leaving the monks to meet most of the costs of the construction of the church (below, pp. 266–7). The purpose of this passage in *LDE* may have been precisely to remind Flambard of the commitment which his predecessor had made on his behalf. Later bishops, however, were not backward in devoting resources to the embellishment of the cathedral; see A. J. Piper, 'The cathedral and its monastic community', *Durham Cathedral: A Celebration*, ed. D. Pocock (Durham, 1993), pp. 95–102, at 96–7.

scilicet per archidiaconatus officium, Christianitatis curam per totum ageret episcopatum, ita statuens ut quicumque illi successores fuerint in prioratu, similiter succedant et*a* in archidiaconatu.[46] Quod non*b* sine auctoritate uel exemplo fecit. Legitur enim in *Vita sancti Cuthberti* quod beatus Boisilus cum esset prepositus monasterii*c* de monasterio *d*frequenter exire et populo predicare*d* consueuit. Cui defuncto discipulus eius *e*beatus scilicet*e* Cuthbertus successit in prepositi (id est prioris) officium. Nam qui nunc prior, a beato Benedicto prepositus monasterii appellatur. Secutus ergo exemplum magistri pater Cuthbertus, sepissime propter animarum lucra de monasterio egredi solebat *ut sepe ebdomada integra, aliquando duabus uel tribus, nonnunquam etiam*f* mense pleno domum non rediret, sed demoratus in montanis plebem rusticam uerbo predicationis simul et exemplo uirtutis ad celestia uocaret.*g*47* Quapropter memoratus antistes ita constituisse dinoscitur, ut quicunque sancti Cuthberti in ipsius ecclesia successores in prioratu fuerint, etiam in predicationis officium curam agentes Christianitatis eidem succedant.*h*

9. Quo*i* tempore quidam militum episcopi uocabulo Boso*j* infirmitate correptus, ad extrema peruenisse uisus est, permodicum *k*enim ore et naribus trahens flatum*k* per tres dies raptus ab humanis rebus quasi mortuus sine ullo*l* sensu permansit, sed tercio die contra hoc quod sperari poterat, ad presentia rediit. Dicebat itaque *m*multa se*m* uidisse, nec tamen que illa fuerint donec, sicut iussus fuerat, priori retulisset, cuiquam indicare uolebat. Recuperata ergo sanitate, concitus ad illum uenit, secretum ab omnibus loquendi cum eo locum petiit. Vbi proiectis uestibus uirgas manu gestans nudus ad eius uestigia procidit, cum lacrimis exclamans, 'Ad te,' inquit, 'uenire, tibi iussus sum

---

a om. Fx H *b om. Ca (signe de renvoi in marg.)* *c om. Fx H L Y*
d–d exire et populo frequenter predicare *Fx Y*; exire et populo predicare frequenter *L*
e–e scilicet *om. F*; scilicet beatus *Fx L Y* *f om. H* *g* uocabat *F* *h* et cetera *add. L.* *i* Visio Bosonis *rubric Fx H T V Y* *j over erasure C*
k–k om. H *l* et *add. Fx L Y* *m–m* se multa *Fx L Y*

---

[46] *Liber Vitae*, fo. 46*v*, states that Aldwin had also been archdeacon, for after the words 'populos producens' it adds 'sicut et ante Alduinum priorem eius predecessor fuerat'. William of Malmesbury (*De gestis pontificum*, ed. Hamilton, pp. 273–4) stated that William of Saint-Calais conferred on the prior 'ut in toto episcopatu decanus et uicedominus esset', and he believed that Turgot's exercise of his powers led to Ranulf Flambard having him appointed bishop of St Andrews. Aird, *Cuthbert*, p. 152, suggests that Turgot had already been exercising the functions of archdeacon as a result of the bishop's exile. On Turgot's activities after his appointment as archdeacon, see Offler, 'Early archdeacons', p. 194. After Turgot, the convent only in fact claimed the right for the prior to have archdiaconal rights in the convent's own churches; see Barlow, *Durham Peculiars*, pp. 12–13. On monastic

so that through the office of archdeacon he should exercise pastoral care in all things throughout the bishopric, and he decreed that whoever might succeed him as prior should similarly assume the office of archdeacon.[46] He did not make this decree without valid authority and precedent. For we read in the *Life of St Cuthbert* that when the blessed Boisil was provost of a monastery, he was accustomed to go out from that monastery frequently and to preach to the people. After his death his disciple the blessed Cuthbert succeeded him in the office of provost (which means prior, for the person nowadays called prior was formerly called provost by the blessed Benedict). Father Cuthbert followed the example of his master, and was accustomed to go out of the monastery very frequently for the purpose of winning souls, so that often he would not come home for a whole week, sometimes for two or three, occasionally even for a month; but instead he would remain in the mountains, calling the country people to heaven by the words of his preaching and the example of his virtue.[47] Because of this Bishop William is known to have resolved that whoever should be St Cuthbert's successors as prior in this church should also succeed him both in preaching and in pastoral care.

9. At this time a certain knight of the bishop's called Boso was taken ill, and seemed to have come to his last hour. With only slight breathing coming from his mouth and nostrils, he was for three days taken from human affairs and remained unconscious as if dead, but on the third day he exceeded any possible hopes for him and regained consciousness. He said that he had seen many things, but he would not tell anyone what they were until he had related them to the prior, as he had been ordered to do. As soon as he had regained his health, he came in haste to the prior, and asked for a place where he might speak to him in private away from all the others. There he threw off his clothes and flung himself down naked at his feet, carrying rods in his hands and exclaiming with tears: 'I have been ordered to come to

[lxxxvi
(xcv)]

archdeacons at Bury St Edmunds, St Albans, Glastonbury, and Westminster, see J. Sayers, 'Monastic Archdeacons', *Church and Government in the Middle Ages: Essays presented to C. R. Cheney on his 70th Birthday*, ed. C. N. L. Brooke, D. E. Luscombe, G. H. Martin, and D. Owen (Cambridge, 1976), pp. 177–203.

[47] The account of Cuthbert's preaching is taken verbatim (italicized in the Latin text) from Bede, *V. Cuth.* c. 9; the word *prepositus* is translated as 'prior' by Colgrave but here rendered *provost*. The use of *prepositus* in c. 60 of the Rule of St Benedict is a peculiarity of the Durham copy in DCL, B.IV.24 (Piper, in Rollason, *Anglo-Norman Durham*, pp. 80–1, n. 8).

peccata confiteri, et meam deinceps que tamen ^{a}longa non^a erit uitam tuo imperio ordinare. Suscipe queso penitentem, et plagis uerberum medelam adhibe meorum uulneribus criminum, ut districtum Dei merear euadere iudicium.' Itaque multo cum gemitu peccata confessus est susceptaque penitentia, talia cepit narrare: 'Ductore,' inquit, 'preeunte per horrenda simul et amena loca sequebar. Erant omnes ^{b}huius ecclesie^b monachi quodam in loco congregati, ante quos multum ex sese^c splendoris emittens ueneranda crux portabatur, quam omnes uestiti ordinata ^{d}solenniter ^{e}sicut solent^d processione incedentes et cantantes sequebantur. Omnes in directum nusquam declinantes incedebant preter duos, qui a recti ordinis linea aliquantulum exorbitabant. Ibant autem omnes contra oppositum sibi immense^f altitudinis murum, in quo nec ostium nec fenestra ^{g}ulla uidebatur.^{g} Cogitante me ac mirante cur illo^h tenderent ubi aditus nullus patebat, ecce repente nescio qualiter ^{i}omnes intra murum erant.^{i} Ego autem foris remanens, huc illucque respexi si alicubi introspicere possem, et inuenta fenestrella, contemplatus sum per illam campum latissimum et uernantium flosculorum mira uarietate pulcherrimum, ex quibus admirandi suauitas odoris emanabat. Interrogatus a ductore meo si eos quos ibi uidi agnoscerem, aio etiam, "Monachos nostros hic recognosco." Et ille, "Dicito," inquit, "priori ut eos ad animarum suarum salutem diligentius hortetur, illos uero duos, quos ab ordine suo declinare uidisti, nominatim illi^j ostende. Re enim uera non parum a uia rectitudinis aberrant, quibus ^{k}magna incumbit^k necessitas, ut peccata sua purius confessi, emendatiorem uitam ducere festinent. Hucusque etenim puram ac^l rectam peccatorum suorum confessionem nunquam fecerant."

'Inde ductus, aspexi per campum latissimum totius ^{m}huius prouincie^m indigenas congregatos, qui equis admodum pinguibus sedentes et longas sicut soliti sunt hastas portantes, earumque collisione magnum facientes strepitum, multa ferebantur superbia. Is ergo qui me ducebat, an istos recognoscerem inquisiuit. Cui dum illum ^{n}atque illum^n et postremo uniuersos me recognoscere respondissem, "Omnes," ait, "isti iam^o in proximo peribunt." Nec mora omnis illa multitudo uelut fumus ex oculis euanuit. Quo facto, multo maiori quam priores superbia secuti sunt Francigene, qui et ipsi frementibus

you and confess my sins to you, and henceforth to order my life, which will not be long, according to your commands. I beg you to accept me as a penitent, and through the blows of these rods to bring healing to the wounds made by my crimes, that I may be worthy to escape the stern justice of God.' So with many sighs he confessed his sins, and after receiving penance he began to tell his story: 'I followed my guide through places which were frightful and places which were pleasant. All the monks of this church were gathered together in a certain place. Before them was carried a resplendent and venerable cross, which they all followed vested and in solemn procession, chanting as they walked as was their custom. They all advanced straight ahead without ever deviating, except for two who turned aside a little from the line of the true order. All went towards a wall of immense height which stood across their way and in which there seemed to be neither door nor window. As I considered and marvelled that they should be going where there seemed no way through, suddenly—I do not know how—all were inside the wall. But I remained outside, and looking this way and that to find a way of seeing in, I found a small window through which I saw a wide plain beautiful with the blooming of a marvellous variety of flowers, which gave off a scent of wonderful sweetness. Asked by my guide if I knew those whom I saw there, I replied: "I recognize here our monks." He said: "Tell this to the prior, that he should exhort them more diligently to the salvation of their souls, and name to him the two whom you saw turn aside from their order. Truly they are wandering not a little from the way of righteousness, so that there is a pressing necessity for them to confess their sins more fully, and to hasten to lead a more perfect life. For up to now they have never made complete and proper confession of their sins."

Led on from there, I saw on the wide plain the native inhabitants of this province gathered together. Much puffed up with arrogance, they were mounted on well-fed horses, carrying long lances as is their custom, and making a great noise by clashing them together. He who was leading me asked if I recognized them. When I replied that I knew such a one and such another and at length that I recognized them all, he said, "All these men will shortly perish." At once all that multitude vanished like smoke before my eyes. After this there followed the Frenchmen, who were much more arrogant than those

ʲ ei *Fx H*   *ᵏ⁻ᵏ* incumbit magna *Fx H L Y*   *ˡ* et *Fx H L*   *ᵐ⁻ᵐ* prouincie
huius *H*   *ⁿ⁻ⁿ* om. *H;* illum *om. F*   *ᵒ* om. *H*

equis subuecti et uniuerso*a* armorum genere induti, equorum frementium sonitu et armorum collisione immanem late faciebant tumultum; sed post paululum,*b* cum omni ipsorum gloria uelut subito terre hiatu absorti, nusquam comparuerunt. Deinde per extensum aliquot miliariis campum innumeram feminarum multitudinem*c* intueor, quarum tantam turbam dum admirarer, eas presbiterorum uxores esse a ductore meo didici. "Has," inquit, "miserabiles et illos qui ad sacrificandum Deo consecrati sunt, nec tamen illecebris carnalibus inuolui metuerunt, ue sempiternum et gehennalium flammarum atrocissimus expectat cruciatus."

'Inde in loco uaste ac*d* tetre solitudinis, magna altitudine domum totam*e* ex ferro fabrefactam aspexi, cuius ianua dum sepius aperiretur sepiusque clauderetur, ecce subito episcopus Willelmus efferens caput, ubinam Gosfridus monachus esset a me quesiuit.*f* [48] "Hic enim,"*g* inquit, "hic ad placitum mecum*h* adesse deberet." Hunc nanque episcopus*i* procuratorem sui episcopatus constituerat. Tunc is a quo ducebar me alloquens, "Certo," inquit, "scias episcopum citissime finem uite habiturum. Ille quoque quem ipse nominauit, tametsi aliquanto tardius eum moriendo sequetur. Tu quoniam adhuc licet breui tempore in mundo uiuere debes, ut iram Dei euadas, confessione peccatorum facta uitam secundum quod prior tibi ostenderit corrige, eique uniuersa que tibi sunt ostensa ne dubites manifestare." '

Hec et alia quamplura predictus miles se audisse et uidisse retulit, que quam uera sint paulo post et episcopi et aliorum multorum quos iam finiendos prenuntiauerat, mors secuta testimonium perhibet. Duo quoque illi qui ab ordine processionis deuiare uisi sunt fratres, eius uerbis fidem prebent, quorum uitam prior subtiliter discutiens, hoc quod miles de illis occulte audierat, uerum esse ipse inuenit.[49]

10. Dum*j* ergo uisionis sue ordinem iubente priore miles episcopo retulisset, ille talia contremiscens uehementer expauit, atque studiosius deinceps sue salutis curam gerere cepit, largiores uidelicet

---

a uniuersorum *Y*   *b* paulum *Ca*   *c* om. *Y; ins. over line Fx L*   *d* et *H Y*   *e* om. *F*   *f* inquisiuit *L*   *g* om. *H L Y; ins. over line Fx*   *h* meum *Ca*   *i* om. *Ca*   *j* Cum *F Fx H L Y*; Capitulum *rubric Fx L V Y*

---

48 This name is not found in the list of monks in *LDE* (above, pp. 6–15), but it is found in the list in *Liber Vitae*, in which it is interlined in a contemporary hand immediately after Turgot's name (Piper, 'Lists', 169–70, 178).

who had come before, and who were also riding spirited horses and were loaded with all manner of arms and making a monstrous tumult with the din of their snorting horses and the clashing of their weapons. After a little while, however, they and all their splendour were nowhere to be seen as if they had been swallowed by a sudden opening of the earth. Then over several miles of the plain I saw an innumerable multitude of women, and while I was marvelling at such a crowd of them I learned from my guide that these were the wives of priests. "Eternal woe and the atrocious torment of the flames of hell," he said, "awaits these miserable women and those who were consecrated for offering sacrifice to God but yet were not afraid to involve themselves in the lascivious affairs of the flesh."

Then in a vast and foul desert I saw a house of great height entirely made out of iron, the door of which was very frequently being opened and closed. Suddenly Bishop William put his head out and asked of me where the monk Gosfrid was.[48] "He should be with me here at the trial," he said. Now the bishop had appointed this man procurator of his bishopric. Then he who was leading me said to me: "Know for certain that the end of the bishop's life will soon come. The man also whom he has named will shortly afterwards follow him in death. Because you must continue living in the world although only for a short time, you must confess your sins and amend your life as the prior will show you so that you may escape the anger of God, and you must not hesitate to make known to him everything which has been revealed to you." '

These and many other things the knight related that he had heard or seen. Witness to their truth was provided by the fact that the bishop and many others who he had said were near their end did indeed die soon afterwards. Also those two brothers who were seen to deviate from the order of the procession also demonstrated the trustworthiness of his words, for the prior carefully examined their lives and found to be true what the knight had secretly heard about them.[49]

10. When at the prior's command the knight recounted his vision to the bishop, the latter trembled in great fear, and began thenceforth to take greater care of the health of his soul, being more generous in

---

[49] Nothing further is known of Boso. On the context of this vision account, which should be compared with the Vision of Orm, see Dinzelbacher, *Vision und Visionsliteratur*, esp. pp. 215–16.

elemosinas faciendo, prolixius et intentius orando, nullius negotii gratia priuata orationum cotidianarum statuta pretermittendo. Et quidem multo ante suum obitum tempore non parum infirmabatur, uerum ipso die natiuitatis Dominice apud Windelesoram acriori correptus dolore,[50] grauissime per octo dies letali morbo fatigabatur. Interim multi ad illum*a* uenerunt, alii ut in sua necessitate ipsius consilium quererent, erat enim magni consilii, nonnulli ut uexatum infirmitate, pie uisitationis uerbo consolarentur. Quod maxime *b*uenerabilis Cantuariensis*b* ecclesie archiepiscopus Anselmus fecit, cuius secreto colloquio*c* de salute anime ille diu potitus, consolationis et benedictionis gratiam se ab eo*d* percepisse gratulabatur.[51] Tanta infirmitate uexatus, nequaquam tamen longiorem uitam plus quam mortem quesiuit, sed hoc Deum intentius*e* *f*est deprecatus,*f* ut quod sibi *g*sciret magis*g* expedire, scilicet uel*h* diutius uiuere uel tunc uitam finire, id sibi dignaretur concedere. Die autem octauo quo Circuncisio *i*Dominica celebratur,*i* cum iam instante uespera irrecusabilem mortis sententiam iamiamque adesse sentiret, ea que fidelium morientium salus exposcit sibi postulans, uenerande memorie *j*Eboracensi archiepiscopo Thoma*j* cum Walkelino Wintoniensi et Iohanne Bathanensi episcopo*k* multum deuote officium administrante*l* ipse, catholicam confitens fidem, percepit.[52] Quibus et se et filios suos uidelicet huius ecclesie monachos quos multum*m* semper*n* dilexerat, fouendos et protegendos *o*quam maxime*o* commendare studebat.

Iacente illo atque sue euocationis horam expectante, episcopis inuicem de loco sepulture illius*p* conferentibus id*q* conueniens uidebatur, ut in ipsa sancti Cuthberti ecclesia eius corpus iure sepeliri

---

a eum Fx L T   *b–b* Cantuariensis uenerabilis H   *c* consilio T   *d* ipso L H Y   *e* om. H; attentius Fx L Y   *f–f* deprecatus est Ca H   *g–g* magis sciret H   *h* om. H   *i–i* celebratur Dominica Fx L; Dominica om. Y   *j–j* Eboracensi om. Y; ins. over line Fx; archiepiscopo Eboracensi L with Thoma om.   *k* episcopis Y   *l* ministratur Y   *m* om. H   *n* om. L Y; ins. over line Fx   *o–o* om. F   *p* eius H; sue Fx L Y   *q* quod add. Fx L Y

---

[50] According to William of Malmesbury (*De gestis pontificum*, ed. Hamilton, p. 273), discord had arisen between the bishop and the king, so that Rufus had summoned Saint-Calais to the Christmas assembly (Malmesbury locates it at Gloucester, but Windsor is probably correct), refusing to believe Saint-Calais's excuse that he was ill. Freeman, *William Rufus*, ii. 38, suggested that Saint-Calais may have been involved in Robert de Mowbray's revolt.

[51] The mention of Anselm, archbishop of Canterbury (1093–1109), is notable since, according to Eadmer, *Historia nouorum in Anglia*, ed. Martin Rule (RS 81; 1884), pp. 59–62, Saint-Calais had been prominent in attacking Anselm at the Council of Rockingham in 1095. Eadmer's work was apparently written shortly after 1109 and thus very soon after the completion of *LDE*. The reference here to Anselm's visit to Saint-Calais on his death-bed

alms-giving, praying at greater length and more intently, and not setting aside on account of any business the periods reserved for daily prayer in private. He was in fact quite ill for a long time before his death, but he was seized with more severe pain on Christmas day at Windsor,[50] and was sorely afflicted for eight days with a mortal illness. In that time many visited him, some out of the necessity to seek his advice for he was wise in counsel, many that they might console him, vexed as he was with infirmity, with pious words. Above all the venerable archbishop of Canterbury, Anselm, came to console him and talked privately to him for a long time about the salvation of his soul, and the bishop rejoiced to have received from him the grace of blessing and consolation.[51] Vexed by such infirmity he by no means sought to live longer in preference to dying, but he fervently begged this of God, that whatever he knew would best release him, whether he should live longer or should finish his life, he should deign to grant it to him. When on the evening of the eighth day, the day on which the Circumcision of Our Lord is celebrated, he felt the irreversible sentence of death on him, and he asked for those rites which the salvation of those dying in the faith demands, he made profession of the catholic faith and received the last office which was very devoutly celebrated by Thomas, archbishop of York of revered memory, with Walkelin, bishop of Winchester, and John, bishop of Bath.[52] To these men he committed himself and his children, or in other words the monks of this church whom he had always loved greatly, and he endeavoured as much as he could to commend them to the care and protection of these prelates.

Whilst he was lying there waiting for the hour of his summons, the bishops were deliberating on the place where he should be buried, and it seemed to them most fitting that his body should by rights be buried in St Cuthbert's church itself, since he had always devoted all

---

may have been designed to undermine just the sort of picture of Saint-Calais's unscrupulousness at Rockingham which Eadmer was to paint. Eadmer's accusations, which included attributing to Saint-Calais the ambition to supplant Anselm as archbishop and the advice that force should be used to prevent him appealing to the pope, must have been very hurtful to the Durham monks, and Offler even suggested that their publication in the *Historia nouorum* might have been the motive for the fabrication of the *De iniusta uexacione* (H. S. Offler, 'The tractate *De iniusta uexacione Willelmi episcopi primi*', *English Historical Review*, lxvi (1951), 320–41, at pp. 339–41) (repr. Offler, *North of the Tees*, no. vi)).

[52] Thomas, archbishop of York (1070–1100); Walkelin, bishop of Winchester (1070–98); and John, bishop of Wells (1088–1090) and then bishop of Bath, to which the see was transferred in 1090 from then until 1122.

deberet,[a] qui ad ipsum confessoris et episcopi sacrum corpus congregatione monachorum stabilita ut dignum et placitum Deo seruitium ibidem[b] iugiter fieret, quam maxime semper sollicitus fuerat. Quod contra ille clamans, hoc fieri multum prohibuit, 'Absit,' inquiens,[c] 'absit ut sancti Cuthberti ecclesie consuetudo, que ab antiquis temporibus tam sollicite hactenus seruabatur, mei corporis causa soluatur. Nunquam enim in loco[d] quo eius incorruptum corpus requiescit, alicuius defuncti corpus non solum non sepeliri, sed nec ad horam inferri licuit.' Placuit ergo illis ut in capitulo tumulari deberet, quatinus in loco quo fratres cotidie congregarentur,[e] uiso eius sepulchro carissimi patris memoria in eorum cordibus cotidie renouaretur.[53]

Interea ille acrius dolore coactus in mortem pallescere cepit. Itaque[f] instante hora gallicantus, quartas Nonas Ianuarii, feria quarta, uite terminum habuit.[54] Cuius corpus pontificalibus secundum morem uestimentis obuolutum fratres, qui cum eo fuerant, Dunhelmum transtulerunt, quod occurrentes monachi et clerus omnisque populus cum merore multo et planctu susceptum usque in ecclesiam sancti Michelis deportauerunt.[55]

[lxxxvii (xcvi)] Ibi[g] nanque prima nocte a clero et populo[h] exequie illius agebantur, mane autem facto ad se monachi corpus transferentes, ipsum diem cum nocte secuta in precibus et psalmorum decantationibus peruigiles transegerunt, atque sequenti die (hoc est sextas decimas Kalendas Februarii) in loco quem (ut supra [i]dictum est[i]) episcopi prouiderant, congruo cum[j] honore sepulture tradiderunt.

Quorum[k] ex tanti patris amissione quantus meror, quantus luctus [l]quantusque fuerit fletus,[l] puto hinc melius taceatur, quam supra id

---

[a] uideret Fx (corr. in marg.) L Y   [b] om. H L Y; ins. over line Fx   [c] inquit H Y   [d] in add. Ca Y   [e] congregantur Ca   [f] iamque Ca F D H T   [g] Obiit Willelmus primus Dunelmensis episcopus rubric Fx T V Y   [h] a populo F   [i-i] diximus Fx H L Y   [j] om. Fx L H Y   [k] Obiit Willelmus primus Dunelmensis episcopus rubric H   [l-l] quantus fletus fuerit T

---

[53] When the chapter house was excavated in 1874, three grave slabs were recovered inscribed respectively with the names of William of Saint-Calais's successors Ranulf Flambard, William of Sainte-Barbe, and Geoffrey Rufus, but no trace of William of Saint-Calais's own grave seems to have survived. See J. T. Fowler, 'An account of excavations made on the site of the chapter house of Durham Cathedral in 1874', Archaeologia, xlv (1880), 385–404, and id., 'Excavations on the site of the chapter house of Durham abbey', Transactions of the Architectural and Archaeological Society of Durham and Northumberland, ii (1869–79), 235–70, at pp. 240–1. It is possible that the chapter house as excavated had not been constructed by 1096, and that LDE is referrring to a different structure.

[54] 2 Jan. was indeed a Wednesday in 1096, and LDE is therefore preferable to JW iii.

his efforts to ensuring that the holy body of that bishop and confessor should have a continual service worthy and pleasing to God performed by the congregation of monks which he had established there. He protested against this, however, and earnestly forbade it. 'By no means,' he said, 'by no means let my dead body be the occasion of the customs of St Cuthbert's church being broken, which have been so carefully preserved from ancient times up to the present. Not only has it never been permitted for anyone to be buried in the place where his undecayed body rests, but even for a corpse to be brought there for a time has never been allowed.' They decided therefore that he should be interred in the chapter house, since the brethren would assemble there daily and the sight of their beloved father's tomb would daily renew his memory in their hearts.[53]

Meanwhile the bishop's illness grew more severe and he began to grow pale in death; and so he ended his life just before daybreak on Wednesday 2 January.[54] His body was wrapped in episcopal vestments as is customary, and the brethren who were with him took it to Durham. The monks, the clergy, all the people came to meet it, received it with much grief and lamenting, and carried it into the church of St Michael.[55]

There its obsequies were performed the first night by the clergy and people, but in the morning the monks took the body and passed that day and the following night praying, singing psalms, and keeping vigil. On the following day, that is 16 January, they buried it with due honour in the place which the bishops (as stated above) had designated.

I think it is better to be silent here about the greatness of their grief for the loss of such a father, and about how much they lamented and wept, rather than that it should be said that this surpasses what is

[lxxxvii (xcvi)]

82–3, which gives 1 Jan. 1096, but incorrectly states that it was a Wednesday. *HReg*, *s.a.* 1096 (Arnold, *Sym. Op.* ii. 226), gives 2 Jan. but as Monday (*feria ii*), which is surely an error for Wednesday (*feria iiii*). See *Alf*, p. 458. *LDE*'s calculation from the date of William of Saint-Calais's consecration is presumably on the basis of months of 28 days.

[55] L here inserts the text of *DIV* (Offler, *DIV*) in the original hand as c. xcvi (fos. 66ʳ– 74ᵛ). In C the words 'acrius . . . deportauerunt' are the beginning of an inserted quire written in the hand of William Claxton who has then added *DIV* (above, pp. xix, xxii). The reference to St Michael's church is problematic. The churches of medieval Durham are known to have been dedicated as follows: St Oswald, St Nicholas in the market-place, St Margaret in Crossgate (a chapel until the 14th cent.), St Giles in Gilesgate (not founded until 1112), and St Mary le Bow and St Mary the Less in the castle bailey. *LDE* is the only record of a church dedicated to St Michael; unless one of the churches listed later changed its dedication, the only remaining possibility is the chapel of Durham castle itself, which had certainly been constructed by this time (Ulrich Fischer, pers. comm.; see also Cambridge, in Rollason, *Anglo-Norman Durham*, pp. 153–6).

quod cuiquam credibile sit, aliquid dicatur. Nullus enim ut reor tunc inter illos erat, qui non illius uitam si fieri posset, sua morte redimere uellet. Defunctus est autem millesimo nonagesimo sexto*a* Dominice Incarnationis anno, cum iam in episcopatu quindecim annos et duos menses minus tribus diebus peregisset, *b*quando et*b* tercius decimus ex quo in Dunhelmum *c*congregati fuerant monachi*c* annus agebatur.*d*

a vii F   *b–b* quod est Fx *(corr. in marg.)* L   *c–c* monachi congregati fuerant F

credible to anyone. I believe, however, that there was not one among them who would not have redeemed the bishop's life with his own if he could have done so. The bishop died in the year of Our Lord's Incarnation 1096, when he had been bishop for three days less than fifteen years and two months, and in the thirteenth year after the monks had been brought together in Durham.

[d] Explicit historia Simeonis *rubric Ca*

APPENDIX A

Summary beginning 'Regnante apud Northanymbros'

Regnante[1] apud Northanymbros Christianissimo[a] rege et postea martyre Oswaldo, uir eximie sanctitatis Aidanus, primus in regno eiusdem regis uerbum fidei predicans, primus Lindisfarnensis siue Dunelmensis[b] ecclesie [c]fuit episcopus,[c] sedemque episcopalem simul et monachicam ut uenerabilis presbiter et monachus Beda in Historia Anglorum attestatur, in ipsa ecclesia habitationem iubente rege prefato et cooperante instituit anno ab incarnatione Domini sescentesimo tricesimo quinto. Ex hac ecclesia omnes ecclesie et monasteria prouincie Berniciorum sumpserunt exordium. Regio enim Northanymbrorum in duas diuiditur prouincias, Deirorum scilicet et Berniciorum. Permansit autem in prefata ecclesia monachorum congregatio nobilis et religiosa, per ducentos et quadraginta annos.[2]

Exinde crudelis barbarorum manus innumeris nauibus in Angliam transuecta, omnia quaqua uersum depopulans, etiam reges qui tunc [d]plures erant[d] Anglorum, inter quos et Edmundum[e] martyrem gloriosum interfecit. Northanymbrorum autem prouincias atrocius deuastans, omnes ecclesias,[f] omnia monasteria ferro et incendio[g] deleuit, adeo ut nullum pene Christianitatis signum post se discedens reliquerit. Vix episcopus suprascripte ecclesie Æardulfus,[h] cum incorrupto sancti Cuthberti confessoris corpore fugiens, euasit mortem cum paucis. Porro monachi qui loci reuerentia confidentes remanserant de ecclesia extracti, alii in mare ab hostibus summersi, alii captiui abducti, alii detruncati, alii aliis tormentis miserabiliter

[a] Christiano *T*   [b] Dunolmensis *Fx throughout*   [c-c] episcopus fuit *Fx*
[d-d] erant plures *T*   [e] Ædmundum *D*   [f] omnes prouincias *add. T*
[g] igne *T*   [h] Eardulphus *Fx L T*

[1] Ca has a contemporary rubric: 'Incipit prefatio reuerendi Symeonis monachi et precentoris ecclesie sancti Cuthberti Dunelmi in historia de exordio Christianitatis et religionis tocius Northumbrie de fide et origine sancti Oswaldi regis et martiris et de predicatione sancti Aidani episcopi.' C, Fx, and L have in early modern archaicizing hands (in C probably that of William Claxton) the heading, 'Breue summarium seu descriptio status ecclesie Lindisfernensis et Dunelmi a tempore Aidani usque ad Willelmum (Wilhelm *L*) Karilephe'. On the dating and character of this text, which probably belongs

While[1] Oswald, that most Christian king and afterwards also martyr, was ruling over the Northumbrians, Aidan, a man of exceptional sanctity and the first to preach the word of faith in Oswald's kingdom, was the first bishop of the church of Lindisfarne or Durham. As the venerable priest and monk Bede attests in his *History of the English*, he founded in that church in the year of Our Lord 635, by the order of the king and with his co-operation, at one and the same time an episcopal see and a dwelling for monks. It was from this church that all the churches and monasteries of the kingdom of the Bernicians took their origin. For the region of the Northumbrians is divided into two provinces, namely that of the Deirans and that of the Bernicians. A noble and religious congregation of monks remained in the aforesaid church for two hundred and forty years.[2]

At the end of that period, a cruel force of barbarians crossed to England in innumerable ships and devastated everything everywhere, even killing kings (of which the English had many at that time)— amongst them the glorious martyr Edmund. Indeed they devastated the provinces of the Northumbrians so atrociously and destroyed all the churches and monasteries with fire and sword, that when they departed they left behind them hardly a sign of Christianity. The bishop of the aforesaid church, Eardwulf, barely escaped death when with a few companions he fled with the undecayed body of the holy confessor Cuthbert. Moreover, the monks who had placed their trust in the holy character of the place and had remained were dragged from the church and some were drowned in the sea by the enemy, some led off into captivity, some beheaded, some miserably afflicted

to the second quarter of the 12th cent., see above, pp. lxvi–lxvii. A comparison between it and *LDE* suggests that the attitudes of the monks of Durham towards their predecessors, the clerks, had hardened since the composition of *LDE* (Foster, in Rollason, *Anglo-Norman Durham*, pp. 53–65; Aird, *Cuthbert*, pp. 108–11).

[2] The account in this paragraph is a plain summary of *LDE* (above, pp. 16–23); the period of 240 years corresponds to that from the foundation of Lindisfarne in 635 (above, pp. 20–1 and n. 10) and the departure of the community of St Cuthbert from Lindisfarne in 875 (above, pp. 102–3).

affecti,[a] omnes simul interierunt. Tali modo monachica congregatio defecit apud corpus sancti Cuthberti.[3]

Porro iam memoratus episcopus et post eum aliquot sui successores, dominantibus per multos annos in prouincia barbaris, cum sacri corporis thesauro incertis huc illucque sedibus uagabantur, nusquam ante faciem barbarorum et gladii imminentis habentes requiem, donec pace reddita et facta diuinitus reuelatione, in Dunelmum[b] ubi nunc requiescit perlatum sit.[c][4] Peremptis autem[d] ut dictum est memorate ecclesie monachis, paruuli qui inter illos[e] nutriebantur et instituebantur sub disciplina diligenter, quoquo modo euadentes manus hostium, corpus quidem sancti confessoris comitati sunt, sed tradita sibi districtione paulatim postposita, ecclesiasticam disciplinam odio habuerunt, remissioris uite illecebras secuti. Nec erat qui eos sub ecclesiastica censura coerceret, utpote cultura Dei destructis monasteriis et ecclesiis pene deficiente. Seculariter itaque omnino uiuentes, carni et sanguini inseruiebant, filios et filias generantes. Quorum posteri per successionem in ecclesia Dunelmensi fuerunt, nimis remisse uiuentes, nec ullam nisi carnalem uitam quam ducebant scientes, nec scire uolentes. Clerici uocabantur, sed nec habitu, nec conuersatione clericatum pretendebant.[5] Ordinem psalmorum in canendis horis secundum regulam sancti Benedicti institutum tenuerunt, hoc solum a primis institutoribus monachorum per paternam traditionem sibi transmissum seruantes.[6]

At Willelmo maiore regnum Anglie adepto, cum ecclesiarum et monasteriorum recalesceret religio, Walcherus de clero Leodiensis[f] ecclesie in presulatum ecclesie Dunelmensis sullimatur, uir natu nobilis, sed prudentia et honestate nobilior. Videns in ecclesia nec sui ordinis clericos nec monachos, grauiter indoluit, quippe quos nec ad emendatiorem uitam, nec ad mores ecclesiasticos corrigibiles inuenit.[7] Relegens autem hystoriam Anglorum et uitam sancti

---

[a] afflicti T   [b] Dunolmum Fx throughout   [c] est D   [d] om. D
[e] eos Fx   [f] Laodensis Fx

[3] This account of Viking attacks is a very compressed version of LDE (above, pp. 94–101), except that the killing of the monks in LDE relates to the raid on Lindisfarne in 793 (above, pp. 86–9) rather than to the activities of Halfdan. This text's claim that all the monks were killed differs from Symeon's account and may be intended further to denigrate the post-875 religious community (Aird, Cuthbert, p. 109).

[4] LDE's account is above, pp. 100–3, 144–7; the present text omits any mention of the community's residence at Chester-le-Street (above, pp. 122–43).

[5] The foregoing condemnation of the pre-1083 clerks of the community of St Cuthbert finds no real parallel in LDE, which does not even make it clear that they were married (above, pp. lxxxii–lxxxiii).

by other torments—all perished forthwith. In this way the monastic congregation around the body of St Cuthbert came to an end.[3]

However, while for many years the barbarians held sway in the province, Bishop Eardwulf and after him several of his successors wandered hither and thither with the treasure that was the sacred body, having no fixed home and never finding rest in the face of the barbarians and the constant threat of the sword, until, when peace had returned and a divine revelation had been received, the body was carried to Durham where it rests today.[4] When, as was described previously, the monks of the aforesaid church had been killed, the boys who were being cared for and diligently instructed in monastic discipline amongst them somehow escaped from the hand of the enemy and stayed with the body of the holy confessor; but little by little they set aside the strict way of life which had been handed on to them, and they began to hate ecclesiastical discipline and to yield to the allurements of a laxer life. There was no one to coerce them with the censure of the church since, now that the worship of God had almost ceased with the destruction of the churches and monasteries, they lived entirely secular lives, devoted to flesh and blood and begetting sons and daughters. Their descendants succeeded hereditarily to their place in the church of Durham, living in a very remiss way, and neither knowing nor wishing to know any other way of life than the carnal one which they led. They were called clerks but neither in their dress nor their manner of life could they lay claim to the clerical office.[5] In singing psalms for the various services, they kept the order prescribed by the Rule of St Benedict,[6] but this was the only thing handed down to them by their fathers from the first founders of monastic life which they did keep.

When William I took possession of the kingdom of England and the religious life of the churches and monasteries was reviving, Walcher, a cleric of the church of Liège, was raised to the see of Durham. He was a man noble by birth but nobler still in his prudence and integrity. When he saw that the members of his church were neither clerics of his own order nor monks, he was greatly grieved, especially as he found that they could not be persuaded either to improve their lives or to adhere to ecclesiastical norms.[7] But reading again the *History of the English* and the *Life of*

---

[6] Cf., above, pp. 102–5, 195–7.

[7] This account is also much more hostile to the clerks than *LDE* (above, pp. 194–7).

Cuthberti, que utraque uenerabilis Beda composuit, repperit monachorum congregationem a primo ipsius ecclesie presule Aidano et Osuualdo rege (ut supradictum est) ibidem locatam, et ante presulatum sancti*a* Cuthberti et post ad corpus ipsius Deo deseruisse donec (sicut dictum est) hostilis impietas eam funditus extinxisset. Cogitans ergo antiquum in ecclesia restaurare seruitium, Deum orauit, ut actiones suas aspirando preueniret, et adiuuando prosequeretur.[8]

Nec *b*multo post*b* quidam spiritu pauperes monachi, in australibus Anglie partibus*c* diuinitus commoniti,*d* ut Deo seruituri in prouincia Northanymbrorum peregrinarentur, ad episcopum uenerunt Walcherum, rogabantque ut in suo eis episcopatu ubi possent habitare, et si quos forte ualerent seruituros Deo sibi liceret aggregare.*e* Letior solito fit episcopus, eosque quasi a Deo sibi missos dulciter amplectitur, et reddita Deo gratiarum actione, benignissime suscipit.*f* Mittensque illos in Giruum et Wiramuthe, duo sui episcopatus loca, ubi sanctorum quondam fuerant habitationes, ibi precepit interim manere, sibique quos possent in Dei famulatum associare, donec processu temporis et maturo consilio constructis habitaculis, eos monachos monachi simul et episcopi Cuthberti corpori uicinius adiungeret. Fecerunt ut iusserat, et reedificantes *g*destructa sanctorum*g* habitacula, exemplo uite et doctrina nonnullis profuerent,*h* ut mundo abrenuntiantes, eos propositi sui*i* comites haberent. Exultat *j*in his uehementer*j* episcopus, quoniam per hos sperabat sacre religionis augmentum, ubi pene totius honestatis et pietatis inuenerat defectum. Interim circa parietes Dunelmensis ecclesie iactis fundamentis cepit edificare habitacula monachorum habitationi congrua, sed priusquam ea perficeret, crudeli suorum manibus morte preuentus est.[9]

Cui succedens in episcopatu*k* Guillelmus, uir (ut omnes qui eum nouerant attestantur) magne prudentie et consilii, locum ecclesiastica et monastica destitutum obseruatione ingemuit. Reuoluens et

---

a om. *T*   *b-b* post multum *T*   *c* om. *T*   *d* conuersi *Fx*
e congregare *Fx* with uel aggregare add. above line   *f* suscepit *T*
g-g sanctorum *T;* sanctorum destructa *D*   *h* profuerant *T*   *i* om. *T*
j-j uehementer in hiis *D*   *k* episcopatum *Ca D Fx*

---

[8] This account of Walcher's approach reads like *LDE*'s treatment of William of Saint-Calais.

[9] Above, pp. 210–11, 212–13, 214–19; note the very negative treatment of the state of Christianity in the region pre-1083.

St Cuthbert, both composed by the venerable Bede, he discovered that a congregation of monks, established in this church by its first bishop, Aidan, and by King Oswald (as we related earlier on) had served God before St Cuthbert's time as bishop, and had continued to do so after his death, gathered around his body, until (as we have described) they were completely wiped out by a godless enemy. As he was considering how to restore the former service of God in his church, he prayed to God that He might go before him in favouring his actions and bestow His help on him.[8]

Not long afterwards in the southern parts of England certain monks who were devoted to spiritual poverty were divinely urged that they should become pilgrims in the province of the Northumbrians in order to serve God there. They came to Bishop Walcher and asked that they might be given somewhere in his diocese where they could live and that he might allow them to gather together others, if they should be able, to serve God with them. This made the bishop more joyful than he had been accustomed to be; he embraced them delightedly as if they had been sent from God and, after giving thanks to God, he received them with great benevolence. He sent them to Jarrow and Wearmouth, two places in his diocese where there had formerly been habitations of the saints, and ordered them to remain there for the time being and associate with themselves in the service of God any others that they could, until in the fullness of time and after full consideration he might construct dwellings for them and join these monks more closely to the body of Cuthbert, who was at one and the same time both monk and bishop. They did as they were commanded and, rebuilding the habitations of the saints which had been destroyed, the example of their life and their doctrine were of such benefit to several persons that they gave up the world and associated themselves with the monks in their intentions. The bishop rejoiced greatly in these things, because he hoped through these monks to achieve an increase in holy religion, where he had found an almost complete lack of honesty and piety. Meanwhile, having laid the foundations around the walls of the church of Durham, he began to construct buildings suitable for monks to occupy, but he was prevented from finishing these by a cruel death at the hands of his own men.[9]

He was succeeded as bishop by William, a man (as all who knew him attest) of great prudence and excellent counsel, who was sorrowed that the place was destitute of ecclesiastical and monastic

ipse antiquorum scripta, ecclesiam illam a monachis uidelicet Aidano monacho *et pontifice,* et a monachis quos secum adduxerat, in primis fundatam repperit et perfectam, sed a paganis monachos interficientibus primeua seruitute destitutam. Itaque decreuit Deo auctore antiqua restaurare, queque predecessor suus[b] inceperat, ad effectum perducere. Alloquitur primo illos quos in ecclesia inuenerat, ut uel clerici regulares uel monachi fierent, ut quouis ordine disciplinati uitam ducerent. Sed quoniam durum eis erat assueta relinquere, et in[c] ueteri mente noua meditari, neutrum admiserunt. Episcopus regi magno Guillelmo uniuersa replicans, et que in libris scripta de ecclesia sepedicta,[d] et que nunc in ea inuenerat, mox ab ipso rege ad beate recordationis Gregorium septimum papam[e] mittitur, tam de his eum consulturus quam de aliis que sibi mandauerat. Cui cum de beati patris Cuthberti sanctitate quedam licet pauca dixisset, illius per omnia sibi placuit[f] consilium, ut uidelicet monachos quos in duobus episcopatus locis Guiramuthe et Girwe inuenerat, in unum coram sancto illius corpore congregaret, quia episcopatus paruitas ad tria monachorum cenobia non sufficeret. Hoc quoque apostolica confirmando auctoritate, regi, archiepiscopis et episcopis Anglie, suam super hoc uoluntatem remandauit et consensum. Vnde rex ualde gauisus, assidentibus[g] totius regni primatibus precepit ut rem quantocius ad effectum perduceret episcopus. Quod [h]factum est.[h] Euocatis[i] nanque de predictis locis monachis,[j] qui iam spiritu sancto filios Dei qui erant dispersi in unum congregante plures commanebant,[k] Dunelmum transtulit, ubi morum suorum sic[l] est consuetudo conuersionem profitentes, et stabilitatem, tam presentes quam successores eorum inseparabiliter beati Cuthberti corpori astrinxit. Sicque ad illud monachice conuersationis ordinem non nouum instituit, sed antiquum Deo renouante restituit.[10]

[a-a] *om.* T   [b] *add. later* T   [c] *modo* L   [d] supradicta T
[e] *erased* D   [f] *add. later* T   [g] assistentibus *Ca*   [h-h] est factum T
[i] Euocatos C D   [j] monachos D   [k] commendabant D T   [l] sicut Ca
Fx L

---

[10] Above, pp. 226–31. Note the tone of the last sentence, which seems to dismiss as worthless the history of the community of St Cuthbert between its departure from Lindisfarne in 875 and the introduction of Benedictine monks at Durham in 1083.

observance. He too considered in his mind the ancient writings and found that this church had originally been founded and completed by monks, that is by Aidan, who was both monk and bishop, and the monks whom he had brought with him, but that when these monks had been killed by the heathens it had been robbed of the service it had originally rendered to God. So, through the inspiration of God, he decided to restore the old order and to bring to completion what his predecessor had begun. First of all, he addressed those whom he had found in his church, that they might become regular clerics or monks, and lead their lives in a disciplined way in one or other of these orders. But because it was hard for them to leave accustomed things and to consider new matters in their old frame of mind, they would consent to neither. The bishop explained all this to the great king William, and everything which he had found written in books about the church we have mentioned so often and also what he had presently found in it, and the king soon sent him to Pope Gregory VII of blessed memory so that he should consult him both about these matters and also about others which he had entrusted to him. When the bishop had spoken but a few words to him about the sanctity of the blessed father Cuthbert, the pope agreed in all respects with the advice that the monks who were to be found in two places in the diocese, Wearmouth and Jarrow, should be united in one congregation around the saint's holy body, for the diocese was too small to be able to support three communities of monks. In order to confirm this with apostolic authority, the pope notified the king, archbishops and bishops of England of his will and consent relating to this matter. The king rejoiced greatly at this and, with the great men of the whole realm sitting around him, he ordered that the bishop should give effect to his plans as quickly as possible. This was done. For he summoned from the aforementioned places the monks (who were now numerous, for the Holy Spirit had been gathering together the sons of God who had previously been dispersed) and transferred them to Durham, where, as they bore witness (as was the custom of their way of life) to their conversion and stability, he inseparably bound both them and their successors to the body of the blessed Cuthbert. Thus he did not establish there a new order of monastic life, but rather he re-established an ancient one which God was renewing.[10]

APPENDIX B

Continuation beginning 'Tribus dehinc annis'

1. *ᵃ Tribus dehincᵃ* annis ecclesia uacante pastore, trecentas annuatim libras rex Willelmusᵇ in suum de episcopatu transtulit erarium.¹ A monachis uero nil accipiens, immo largus et beneficus, nil oppressionis et iniurie illis a quoquam irrogari permisit. Euolutis de quarto anno ab obitu episcopi quinque mensibus, rexᶜ dedit episcopatum Rannulfo,² qui propter quandam apud regem excellentiam singulariter nominabatur capellanus regis. Fuerat autem primo cum Mauricio Lundoniensi episcopo, sed, propter decaniam sibi ablatam orto discidio, spe altioris loci se transtulit ad regem. Nec eum fefellit spes. Admixtus enim causis regalium negotiorum, cum esset acrioris ingeniiᵈ et promptioris lingue, breuiᵉ in tantum excreuit, ut adepta apud regem familaritas totius ᶠAnglie potentesᶠ et natu quosqueᵍ nobiliores illum superferret.³ Totius nanque regni procurator constitutus, interdum insolentius accepta abutens potestate, cum negotiis regis pertinacius insisteretʰ plures offendere parui pendebat.⁴ Que res multorum ei inuidiam et odium contraxerat. Crebris accusationibus

---

ᵃ⁻ᵃ *coloured capitals C; large decorated initial C D Ca T; De Ranulfo episcopo rubric C (late med.); De periculo quod Ranulfus Flambard euasit rubric Fx T V Y* ᵇ W *above line C;* secundus *add. Fx L H Y* ᶜ Willelmus *above line C Ca D L Y* ᵈ negocii *T* ᵉ in breui *Fx H L Y* ᶠ⁻ᶠ Anglie *above line Y;* potentes Anglie *Fx L* ᵍ quoque *H* ʰ existeret *Fx Y; om. L*

---

¹ The king was William II (Rufus, 1087–1100); the custodian was Ranulf Flambard, later bishop of Durham (1099–1128); and the vacancy occurred from the death of William of Saint-Calais on 1 Jan. 1096 (above, pp. 252–7) to the accession of Flambard (below, n. 2). If the figure of £300 given here, for which there is no corroboration, is correct, it shows that royal exactions were considerably less than those made in the next vacancy (1128–30), when Henry I derived £648 18s from the see annually. See M. Howell, *Regalian Right in Medieval England* (London, 1962), pp. 25–9, and F. Barlow, *William Rufus* (London, 1983), pp. 237–8. The passage implies that in 1096 a *de facto* separation existed between property appropriated to the monks and that to the bishopric (Howell, *Regalian Right*, pp. 15–16, and above, p. 234 n. 25).

² Ranulf Flambard was nominated bishop of Durham at the Whitsun court (29 May) 1099, almost exactly three years and five months after the death of William of Saint-Calais on 1 Jan. 1096, and he was consecrated on 5 June (ASC E, *s.a.*; JW iii. 82–3, 90–1).

³ The details of Ranulf's early career are unclear. The Continuation seems to imply that

1. While the church was lacking a pastor for three years after this, [lxxxviii the king transferred £300 annually from the bishopric to his (xcvii)] treasury.[1] From the monks, however, he took nothing, but he was instead generous and benign, permitting no one to oppress them or to inflict injuries on them. When five months had passed of the fourth year since the bishop's death, the king gave the bishopric to Ranulf,[2] who had been specially nominated royal chaplain on account of some pre-eminence he enjoyed with the king. He had first of all been with Maurice, bishop of London, but, when discord had arisen over the post of dean which had been taken from him, he transferred his service to the king in the hope of promotion. Nor did this hope deceive him. Once he had involved himself in the king's affairs, because of his sharp intellect and ready tongue, he advanced so rapidly that the familiarity he acquired with the king placed him above the powerful men of all England, even those of the most noble birth.[3] When he had been made procurator of the whole realm, he used the power he had received so insolently, that when he was pressing the king's business most pertinaciously, he thought nothing of offending many people.[4] This aroused the ill-will and hatred of many against him. They tried to cloud over the clear sky of the

he was in the service of Maurice, bishop of London (1085/6–1107), which he left to place himself at the service of William Rufus. It is the only source for Ranulf's quarrel with Maurice, which is not implausible since Ranulf never in fact became dean of St Paul's even though his association with that church might have led him to expect such a position (Barlow, *William Rufus*, p. 203). Barlow (ibid., pp. 194–5) and R. W. Southern (*Medieval Humanism* (Oxford, 1970), pp. 183–205, at 187) prefer to believe that Ranulf left Maurice's service after the latter became bishop of London. In fact, the Continuation may well have been reliably informed by Ranulf himself, and its account is not really inconsistent with that of *Hugh the Chanter*, ed Johnson *et. al.*, pp. 10–11. According to this source, Ranulf was in summer 1086 'a chaplain and keeper of the king's seal under Maurice the chancellor, afterwards bishop of London', although the date may in reality have been 1085 (Fryde, *Handbook of British Chronology*, p. 83).

[4] Ranulf's position has been much debated. Cf. the statements that he was 'summus regiarum procurator opum et iusticiarius' (Orderic Vitalis, *Ecclesiastical History*, ed. Chibnall, iii. 310), and 'totius regni procurator' (*De gestis pontificum*, ed. Hamilton, p. 274). The most recent discussions are Barlow, *William Rufus*, pp. 193 and 200–2, and J. O. Prestwich, 'The career of Ranulf Flambard', in Rollason, *Anglo-Norman Durham*, pp. 299–310.

serenum animi regalis ei obnubilare, et locum familiaritatis conabantur interrumpere. Sed cum hic*a* casso labore deficerent, dolis circumuentum etiam extinguere machinabantur.[5]

[lxxxviii (H)] Quidam*b* Geroldus, aliorum*c* (ut dicitur) audacia simul et dolo armatus, ascensa *d*cum paucis nauicula,*d* conuenit capellanum Lundonie, suppliciter orans, ut ad dominum suum Mauricium episcopum infirmantem quantocius properaret, qui in uilla sua super ripam Tamesi fluminis extremum pene spiritum agens,[6] illius magnopere desideraret colloquium. In argumentum ueritatis dixit*e* se nauiculam a domino missam adduxisse, qua ad illum uelocius transueheretur. Ille, nil mali suspicatus, cum paucis suorum intrauit nauem, quam Geroldus*f* recto per alueum fluminis cursu ad mare dirigebat. Querente capellano, cur*g* tam diu nauigantes nusquam diuerterent ad littora, fingebant portum paulo*h* longius abesse, ubi aptior esset de nauicula egressus in terram. Interea prospiciens maiorem *i*medio in flumine*i* nauem anchoris stabilitam, quasi suum (ut sibi uidebatur) operiri*j* aduentum, ilico maligne deceptionis intellexit molimina. Quid plura? In nauem suspectam transponitur, numerosiorem armatorum manum habentem. Iam nulla uspiam euadendi spes. Ipse anulum quem digito gestabat, et notarius suus sigillum illius, medium proiecerunt*k* in flumen,*l* ne per hec ubique locorum per Angliam cognita, simulata precepta hostibus decipientibus transmissa, rerum perturbarent statum.[7] Tunc et homines sui emittuntur in terram, ualido prius sacramento obligati, ut nulli mortalium quicquam de abducto domino*m* dicerent. Iam nauis relicto flumine alta maris ingreditur, et suspensis uelis prospero aliquamdiu cursu uersus meridiem dirigitur. Interea remotius in prora sedente capellano, de genere mortis illius*n* fit inter nautas conspiratio. Eliguntur duo filii Belial, qui eum uel*o* in fluctus proicerent, uel fracto fustibus cerebro enecarent; habituri pretium sceleris optimas, quibus tunc

a huic *Fx H L Y*   *b* De periculo quod Radulphus Flambard euasit *rubric H*   *c corr. from* aliquorum *Fx;* aliquorum *L Y*   *d–d* nauicula cum paucis *Fx L Y*   *e om. L*   *f om. H L Y; above line Fx*   *g* quare *H L Y;* quare *with* uel cur *above line Fx*   *h add. above line Fx; om. L Y*   *i–i* in flumine medio *H;* in medio fluminis *Fx L Y*   *j* operire *V*   *k* proiecit *Fx L*   *l corr. from* flumine *Fx;* flumine *H L Y*   *m* suo *add. Fx H L T*   *n om. T*   *o om. T*

[5] The following anecdote is found only in the Continuation, and may have derived from Ranulf's own oral reminiscences at Durham. The date at which the incident described is supposed to have occurred is uncertain, although it must have been after 1085/6 when Maurice became bishop (see above, n. 3), and the Continuation certainly regards it as having taken place in the reign of William Rufus. Nevertheless, Southern assigned it for no

king's good-will towards him with frequent accusations, and to dislodge him from his position of familiarity. But when they had laboured at this in vain, they plotted to ensnare him with treachery and so to eliminate him.[5]

A certain Gerold, fortified (it is said) with the audacity of others as well as with guile, boarded a boat with a few men, and came to the chaplain in London, humbly begging him that he should hasten as quickly as possible to his lord Bishop Maurice who was ill, indeed almost breathing his last, at his manor on the banks of the river Thames,[6] and who greatly desired to have a talk with him. To add verisimilitude to this he said that he had come in the boat that his lord bishop had sent, in which he might the more rapidly be brought to him. Suspecting no foul play, Flambard embarked on the vessel with a few of his men, and Gerold steered it on a straight course down the river towards the sea. When the chaplain asked why they were sailing so long without landing at any point, a pretence was made that there was not far off a port which was very suitable for disembarkation. Then he saw a larger vessel lying at anchor in the river and (as it seemed to him) awaiting his arrival, and he perceived at once the workings of this malign deception. What more is there to say? He was put aboard this suspicious ship, on which there was a more numerous force of armed men. There was no hope of escape. He took the ring which he wore on his finger, and his notary took his master's seal, and they threw them into the middle of the river, so that their enemies should not be able to send forged writs deceitfully throughout England where the ring and the seal were known, and so disturb the peace of the state.[7] Then Flambard's men were put on shore, having first been bound by a great oath not to say anything to anyone living as to what had become of their abducted master. Then the ship left the river and entered the open sea; with its sails set, it made for a time a prosperous voyage southwards. Meanwhile the chaplain sat apart in the prow, and the sailors hatched a conspiracy amongst themselves as to what the manner of his death should be. They chose two sons of Belial who were either to throw him into the sea, or were to kill him by breaking his skull with cudgels; as the reward for this crime, they were to have the extremely fine clothes

[lxxxviii (H)]

---

obvious reason to 1085–7 (*Medieval Humanism*, p. 187). See Barlow, *William Rufus*, p. 198 n. 159.

[6] Stepney (Barlow, *William Rufus*, p. 198 n. 160, citing *Domesday Book*, i, fo. 127b–d, where Stepney is the only manor of the bishop of London downstream from London).

[7] Barlow, *William Rufus*, p. 198 n. 161, raises the possibility that the seal in question was a copy of the king's 'great' seal.

indutus fuerat, uestes. Quorum alter cum, negante altero, mantellum *illius sibi* uellet sortiri, protracta inde contentio, intentam[b] uiro distulit mortem.

Iamque die altero fauens ad uotum cesserat nauigatio, cum ecce uentus turbinis a meridie surgens totum a profundis sinibus conturbauit[c] mare, noxque repentina obduxit caligine celum. Iactatur hinc et inde procellis carina, iam non gubernaculo, sed uentis obediens et fluctibus. Nec ulterius procedere, nec litora ualebat[d] attingere. Iam rudentibus ruptis fractoque malo, non tam ferebatur aquis, quam ipsa ferebat aquas. Nichil certius quam mortem expectabant. Sola hec quantulacunque maris erat licentia, ut unde uenerat nauis rediret. Quo repellentibus eam undis, deliberata est in Rannulfum mortis sententia, ne euadens illatas ulciscatur iniurias. Porro quidam[e] secundus in naui a Geroldo tantum exhorrens scelus, repente astans, uultuque tristi et lacrimis suffuso, 'Proh dolor!' inquit, 'Rannulfe, iam morieris nostro scelere pessimo. Sed si michi ueniam dederis praue conspirationis, hic tui defensor astabo, tue uel uite uel mortis comes.' Tunc ille, sicut magnanimus semper erat in periculis, ingenti clamore uociferans, 'Quid tu,' inquit, 'Gerolde, cogitas? Quid de[f] nobis machinaris? Homo meus es, fidem michi debes; hanc uiolare non tibi cedet in prosperum. Resipisce et a pernitie facti ad quod intendis, animum reuoca. Quin potius accipe profuturum tibi per omne tempus uite tue consilium. Pete quantum uolueris. Ego sum qui plura petitis[g] prestare potero; et ne discredas promissis, ecce manu affirmo quod polliceor.' Ille non tam promissis illectus, quam potentia uiri exterritus, consensit; eductumque de naui iam in portum repulsa honorifico in sua domo, que litori prominebat, procurauit apparatu. Sed nequaquam credulus promissorum, fuge presidium iniens, eterno disparuit exilio. Rannulfus uero[h] accitis undecunque militibus, multa armatorum manu grandique strepitu deducitur Lundoniam, omnibus in stuporem uersis, ut quem fama diuulgauerat extinctum, subito quasi rediuiuus regalium negotiorum

---

a–a sibi illius *H*   [b] intentatam *Ca Fx H L T V (altered to* intentam*)* *Y*
[c] perturbauit *Fx L Y*   [d] ualebant *Fx H L Y*   [e] quidem *T*   [f] ne *Fx (corr. to* de*)* *Y*   [g] quam petis *Fx L Y*   [h] om. *H Y; over line Fx*

which he was wearing. One of them wanted to choose his mantle for himself, which the other denied him; so there was a protracted dispute, by which Flambard's intended death was delayed.

Now on the next day the sailing conditions favourable to their wishes had come to an end, for a whirlwind rose up from the south, making the sea angry from its very depths, and suddenly night covered the sky with darkness. The vessel was tossed hither and thither in the storm, responsive not to the rudder but to the wind and the waves. It was possible neither to sail on farther, nor to reach the shore. Now with the rigging torn and the mast broken, the ship was not so much carried on the water as carrying water in itself. They expected nothing more certainly than death. The only freedom of any sort which the sea allowed was that the ship should return whence it had come. With the waves driving the ship back, it was decided that the sentence of death should be carried out on Ranulf, lest he should escape and avenge the injuries done to him. A certain man, however, who was second-in-command to Gerold in the ship, was so horrified by the crime that he suddenly rose to his feet, his face grief-stricken and covered in tears, and said: 'Alas, Ranulf, now you are to die by our most evil crime. But if you will give me your pardon for my part in this evil conspiracy, here I will stand as your defender and your companion in life or death.' Then Ranulf, who always showed great spirit in the face of danger, shouted out in a loud voice: 'What are you thinking of, Gerold? What are you plotting against us? You are my man and you owe me fealty, which you will not be allowed to violate and still prosper. Come to your senses, and draw back your mind from the evil of the act which your are planning to commit. Accept instead this piece of advice which will stand you in good stead for the whole course of your future life. Ask of me however much you will. I am the sort of man who will give you more the more you ask; and so that you may not doubt my promises, here is my hand in confirmation of what I promise.' Gerold consented to this, not so much because he was won over by the promises as because he was terrified of Ranulf's forcefulness. As the ship had now been driven into port, Gerold disembarked him and honourably provided him with apparel in his own house, which overlooked the shore. Placing no credence at all in Ranulf's promises, however, he took refuge in flight, and went into permanent exile. For his part, Ranulf summoned soldiers from everywhere, and was escorted to London with a large armed guard and a great deal of noise. Everyone was astonished that a man who had been rumoured to be dead should suddenly appear as if brought

executor resideret. Acceptior dehinc regi, omnes inuidorum conatus cassauit; ita undique circumspectus, ut nullorum rege uiuo*ᵃ* pateret*ᵇ* insidiis.

Anno ab Incarnatione Domini millesimo nongentesimo nono, nonas Iunii, octauas Pentecostes, suscepto episcopatu consecratus est in ecclesia Sancti Pauli Lundonie, a Toma maiore Eboracensi archiepiscopo, sine ulla exactione professionis, sicut et*ᶜ* Willelmus quondam*ᵈ* predecessor ipsius.*ᵉ* [8] Post annum autem *ᶠ*et tres eoque amplius*ᶠ* menses accepti episcopatus rege in uenatu sagitta interfecto,[9] cirumuentus ab insidiantibus episcopus iussu Henrici, qui fratri successerat, octodecimas kalendas Septembris capitur, diligentique custodia in Turre Lundoniensi artatur.[10] Sed non multo post, scilicet*ᵍ* tertias nonas Februarii, magna calliditatis arte et suorum clandestino auxilio fugiens noctu, omnem sese terra marique persequentium elusit diligentiam.[11]

Veniens ergo Normanniam honorifice a duce Roberto fratre regis susceptus est, a quo Luxouiensem*ʰ* ecclesiam, que tunc *ⁱ*episcopo uacabat*ⁱ*, ad sui suorumque comitum subsidia accepit.*ʲ* [12] Post non multum temporis cum duce prefato armis cum fratre congressuro, multa classe reuehitur*ᵏ* in Angliam, ubi strenuis mediatoribus, pace inter fratres reformata, utriusque partis transfugis ex conditione pacis liber in sua permittitur reditus.[13] Inter quos et Rannulfus episcopium

---

ᵃ om. L   *ᵇ* pareret D Fx L Y (over correction)   *ᶜ* om. H   *ᵈ* om. Fx H L Y   *ᵉ* illius T V   *ᶠ⁻ᶠ* eoque amplius et tres Fx L Y   *ᵍ* om. V *ʰ* Lixoniensem H; Sixouiensem Fx (corr. to Luxouiensem) L   *ⁱ⁻ⁱ* uacabat episcopo T *ʲ* suscepit H T   *ᵏ* reuertitur L

---

[8] For the date, see above, p. 266 n. 2. Thomas of Bayeux was archbishop of York (1070–1100). On the avoidance of obedience to York, see H. S. Offler, 'Ranulf Flambard as bishop of Durham (1099–1128)', *Durham University Journal*, lxiv (1971), 14–25, at p. 18 (repr. Offler, *North of the Tees*, no. VII). For the royal writ confirming the grant of the bishopric to Ranulf, see Craster, *Archaeologia Aeliana*, ser. 4 vii (1930), 39–40.

[9] As William Rufus died on 2 Aug. 1100, this was in fact one year and two months after Ranulf's consecration on 5 June 1099.

[10] ASC, *s.a.* 1100, mentions Ranulf's imprisonment in the Tower. Orderic Vitalis (*Ecclesiastical History*, ed. Chibnall, v. 310–11), says that he was imprisoned 'as an incorrigible plunderer of the country', and on account of the many injuries he had inflicted on Henry and his subjects. According to Anselm, he was imprisoned for failing to pay the taxes he had collected for the king (*S. Anselmi Cantuariensis Archiepiscopi Opera Omnia*, ed. F. S. Schmitt (6 vols., Edinburgh, 1946–51), iv. 113).

[11] For details of Ranulf's escape, which was effected by means of a rope smuggled in a flagon of wine, see Orderic Vitalis, *Ecclesiastical History*, ed. Chibnall, v. 312–13. See also *William of Malmesbury, Gesta Regum*, ed. Mynors, c. 394.2; ASC E, *s.a.* 1101; *Henry of Huntingdon, Historia Anglorum*, ed. Greenway, vii. 23; and JW iii. 96–7. For a letter of

back to life, and resume his post as executor of royal affairs. More favoured from then on by the king, he was able to nullify all the efforts of his enemies; and he was so much on his guard everywhere, that while the king was alive no one could ensnare him.

In the year of Our Lord's incarnation 1099, on 5 June, the octave of Pentecost, he was consecrated to the bishopric, which he had accepted, in St Paul's Church, London, by Thomas, the great archbishop of York, without there being exacted from him any profession of obedience, just as had formerly been the case with his predecessor William.[8] One year and more than three months after he had accepted the bishopric, however, the king was killed by an arrow while hunting,[9] and the bishop, who was surrounded by those seeking to trap him, was arrested on 15 August by order of Henry, who had succeeded his brother, and held in close confinement in the Tower of London.[10] But not long afterwards, on 3 February in fact, he escaped at night by means of his own great cunning and the clandestine assistance of his men, and he eluded on land and sea the diligence of his pursuers.[11]

When he came to Normandy he was received with honour by the king's brother Duke Robert, and from him he received for the support of himself and his companions the church of Lisieux, which was then without a bishop.[12] Not long afterwards he was brought back to England by a great fleet, along with the duke who was bent on a clash of arms with his brother. There peace was re-established between the brothers by vigorous mediators, and it was a condition of peace that fugitives on both sides should be allowed to return to their own.[13] Amongst them Ranulf did indeed receive his

Pope Paschal ordering Ranulf to clear himself of the charges against him, see Craster, *Archaeologia Aeliana*, ser. 4 vii (1930), 41–2.

[12] Robert Curthose, the eldest son of William the Conqueror and duke of Normandy (1087–1106), had returned from the Holy Land in 1100, following the death of William Rufus, to mount an invasion of England against his brother, Henry I (1100–35). Orderic Vitalis (*Ecclesiastical History*, ed. Chibnall, v. 312–13) confirms that Ranulf was 'given refuge by the duke', and even states that he was 'placed in a position of authority in Normandy' ('Normannie prefectus est'). The situation with regard to the see of Lisieux, however, was more complex than the Continuation states. After the death of Bishop Gilbert in Aug. 1101, Ranulf had his brother Fulcher consecrated in his place in June 1102. After the latter's death, Ranulf intruded two of his sons aged about 12 on condition that should the elder die, the younger would succeed. Only in 1107 was an appropriate bishop, John of Séez, appointed to the see. See Orderic Vitalis, *Ecclesiastical History*, ed. Chibnall, v. 320–3 and 322 nn. 3–4.

[13] The treaty was the so-called 'Treaty of Alton' 1101 (Le Patourel, *Norman Empire*, p. 185 and n. 3, p. 186).

quidem recepit;*a* uerum gratiam regis licet magnis et continuis muneribus ad plenum sibi redintegrare nequaquam ualuit.[14] Sed ut hanc qualitercunque uel simulaticiam mereretur, aggrauauit manum super episcopatum, immoderatius inde exigens pecunias, quibus et regis et eius familiarium sibi emeret gratiam. Qua de causa fragili fretus iuuamine, sue dioceseos*b* appenditia (scilicet Carleol et Teuietedale) reuocare nequibat, que illo exulante, cum ecclesia non haberet defensorem, *c*ad suas quidam episcoporum*c* applicauerant.[15] Rex etiam ipse *d*odio ipsius*d* cartam ecclesie discindi et annichilari preceperat, quam ad confirmationem possessionum ecclesie a rege Willelmo impetrauerat.

[lxxxix (xcviii)] 2. Ceterum*e* inerat ei episcopo magnanimitas, quam quondam procurator regni contraxerat ex potentia, ut in conuentu procerum, uel primus, uel cum primis semper contenderet esse, et inter honorificos*f* honoris locum magnificentius obtineret, uastiori *g*sepius clamore et uultu minaci,*g* magis simulare indignationem quam exhibere. Ad hec facunda*h* ei uerborum inuentio, qua*i* seriis admiscens iocularia, dubios ueri et falsi suspendit auditores. Motus animi quoque*j* interdum leuis, nec diutius iram retinens, nec leticiam, ex altero in alterum permutari facilis.

Inter hec plurimum circa suos eminebat beneficiis. Iura libertatis episcopii*k* secundum uires contra extraneos defendebat. Circa opus ecclesie modo intentius modo remissius agebatur, sicut illi ex oblatione altaris uel cimiterii uel suppetebat pecunia uel deficiebat. His nanque sumptibus nauem ecclesie, circumductis parietibus, ad

---

a suscepit *corr. to* recepit *Ca*   *b* dioceses *H*   *c–c* quidam episcoporum *Fx H L Y*; quidam episcoporum ad suas dioceses *Fx H L Y*   *d–d om. H Y; over line Fx*
e De moribus Ranulphi (Dunelmensis *Fx Y*) episcopi *rubric Fx H Y (after* defensorem *above)*   *f* honorificatos *Fx L Y; corr. to* honorificos *Fx*   *g–g* semper uultuque minaci clamore *T (with late transposition marks)*   *h* facienda *H;* facundia *Y*
i quam *Ca V*   *j om. H Y*   *k* episcopi *V*

---

[14] On the date of the restitution: see Orderic Vitalis, *Ecclesiastical History*, ed. Chibnall, v. 322 n. 2, and Offler, *Durham University Journal*, lxiv (1971), 15. For documents relating to the restitution, including a safe-conduct for Ranulf Flambard, see Craster, *Archaeologia Aeliana*, ser. 4 vii (1930), 43–50. Offler noted (p. 16) that Ranulf's failure to involve himself in national affairs meant that he was 'free to concentrate his attention on Durham'.

[15] Durham's claim to exercise ecclesiastical rights over Carlisle and Teviotdale was included in a forged charter of William of Saint-Calais dating from the second half of the 12th cent. (Offler, *Episcopal Charters*, no. *3a (p. 16)). Although probably disputed by the

bishopric; although he continually made large gifts, however, he was by no means able fully to restore himself in the king's favour.[14] But so that he might deserve it or at least a semblance of it, he increased the weight of his hand on the bishopric, demanding money from it immoderately, so that he could use this to buy the favour of the king and his courtiers. Because of this the assistance he relied on was weak, and he was unable to regain the two appendages of his diocese (namely Carlisle and Teviotdale), which certain bishops had appropriated, while Ranulf had been in exile and the church had had no protector.[15] Out of hatred for him, the king had ordered the charter, which Ranulf had obtained from King William in confirmation of the possessions of the church, to be torn up and annulled.

2. In other respects, this bishop had in him a great spirit, which he had derived from the power he had enjoyed when he had formerly been procurator of the kingdom, so that in any gathering of great men he always strove to be either the first of them or to be amongst the first, and he obtained a magnificent place of honour amongst those who were honoured. With his immensely loud voice and his threatening looks, he simulated indignation rather than showing it in reality. With the eloquent inventiveness of his words, in which he mixed the jocular with the serious, he left his listeners in doubt as to what was true and what false. His mood was also sometimes capricious, so that neither his anger nor his merriment would last long, but he would change easily from one to the other.

[lxxxix (xcviii)]

Amongst all this, he was very notable in the benefits he bestowed on his people. As far as his strength allowed he defended the rights of his bishopric against outsiders. Towards the building of the church he acted at times more assiduously and at others with more remissness, depending on whether offerings made at the altar or dues from the cemetery were available to him or lacking. For having taken possession of these, he erected the walls of the nave of the

Scots in the case of Teviotdale as early as the mid-1070s (above, p. 209 n. 87), the claim, based perhaps on the traditions recorded in *HSC* cc. 4, 9, received some recognition in the late 11th cent. Two writs of King William II (dated 1092 × 5 and 1096 × 9; *Regesta regum anglo-normannorum, 1066–1154*, i, ed. Davis, nos. 463, 478), and one of Archbishop Thomas I of York (dated 1092 × 5) confirm that the spiritual jurisdiction and ecclesiastical administration of Carlisle pertained to Durham; and a letter of the same archbishop confirm Durham's right to supply chrism to Teviotdale. See Craster, *Archaeologia Aeliana*, 4th ser. vii (1930), 33–56, at 37–9, for the documents; and, further, id., *English Historical Review*, lxix (1954), 180–1. For Carlisle, see Summerson, *Medieval Carlisle*, i. 31, 34.

sui usque testudinem[a] erexerat.[b][16] Porro predecessor illius, qui opus inchoauit, id decernendo[c] statuerat, ut episcopus ex suo ecclesiam, monachi uero suas[d] ex [e]ecclesie collectis[e] facerent officinas. Quod illo cadente cecidit. Monachi enim omissis officinarum edificationibus, operi ecclesie insistunt, quam usque nauem Rannulfus iam[f] factam inuenit.[17] Addidit[g] etiam ornamentis ecclesie dorsalia, pallia, cappas, casulas, tunicas quoque et dalmaticas; angustias[h] curie monachorum porrecto in longum et latum spacio dilatauit.[18] Pauperibus modo rogatus, modo ultroneus larga manu fuit beneficus. Vrbem, licet hanc natura munierit, muro ipse reddidit[i] fortiorem et augustiorem. A cancello ecclesie[j] ad arcem usque castelli producta murum construxit longitudine.[19] Locum inter ecclesiam et castellum, quem multa [k]occupauerant habitacula,[k] in patentis campi redegit planitiem, ne uel ex sordibus contaminatio, uel ex ignibus ecclesiam attingerent pericula.[20] Diuersas Wiri fluminis ripas continuauit, structo de lapide magni operis ponte arcuato.[21] Condidit castellum in excelso prerupte rupis super Tuedam flumen, ut inde latronum incursus inhiberet et Scottorum irruptiones. Ibi enim utpote in confinio regni Anglorum et Scottorum, creber predantibus ante patebat excursus, nullo ibidem, quo huiusmodi impetus repellerentur,[l] presidio locato.[22]

Taliter impulsu quodam inpatiente otii de opere transibat ad opus,

---

[a] celsitudinem *Fx H L Y; corr. to* testitudinem *Fx*   [b] erexit *Fx L Y*
[c] *probably corr. from* discernendo *C;* discernendo *Fx H L Y*   [d] *om. Y; above line Fx*
[e]–[e] collectis ecclesie *H*   [f] iam eam *T*   [g] addit *Ca*   [h] angustias quoque *V*
[i] reddit *Ca*   [j] *om. H; above line Y*   [k]–[k] habitacula occupauerant *H*
[l] repelleretur *Ca Fx H L V Y*

[16] The word *testudo* is unusual but presumably means the vault, which was a stone rib-vault (J. Bilson. 'Durham cathedral: the chronology of its vaults', *Archaeological Journal*, lxxix (1922), 157–8; and D. Rollason, 'Durham Cathedral 1093–1193: sources and history', *Engineering a Cathedral: Proceedings of the Conference 'Engineering a Cathedral' held at Durham Cathedral on 9–11 Sept. 1993 as Part of the 900th Anniversary Celebrations of Durham Cathedral*, ed. M. Jackson (London, 1993), pp. 1–15, at 9).

[17] The east end of the church was sufficiently complete by 1104 for the body of St Cuthbert to be translated into it. See *De miraculis* c. 7, Raine, *Cuth. virt.* cc. 40–3, and *De gestis pontificum*, ed. Hamilton, pp. 275–6.

[18] *Curia* is here translated to mean the whole monastic precinct, although it is not impossible that it refers to the cloister of the cathedral, which was indeed enlarged, presumably when the nave was constructed. See Hope, *Proceedings of the Society of Antiquaries*, xxii (1909), 417–24.

[19] According to Offler, *Durham University Journal*, lxiv (1971), 20, a portion of this wall was exposed in Bailey Court, Durham, and it is marked on the map published by W. T. Jones, 'The walls and towers of Durham', *Durham University Journal*, xxii (1921), 273–8, after p. 278.

[20] The area referred to is the present Palace Green, which is indeed a level space.

church up to its vault.[16] His predecessor, however, who began the
construction, had laid it down as a decision that the bishop should
pay for the church from his own resources, and the monks should
pay for the monastic buildings out of what they had collected from
the church. On his death, however, this arrangement collapsed. For
the monks neglected the monastic buildings and concentrated on the
construction of the church, which Ranulf consequently found built
as far as the nave.[17] He also added to the ornaments of the church
dorsals, palls, copes, chasubles, tunics, and dalmatics; and he
extended the cramped precinct of the monks by a considerable
distance widthways and lengthways.[18] He was beneficent to the poor
with a generous hand, sometimes when he was asked, sometimes
spontaneously. Although the city was naturally fortified, he made it
stronger and more majestic with a wall. From the chancel of the
church to the stronghold of the castle he constructed a wall of great
length.[19] The space between the church and the castle, which had
been occupied by many dwellings, he made as flat and open as a
field, so that the church should be affected neither by the contam-
ination of their filth, nor the danger of fires.[20] He joined the two
banks of the river Wear with a stone bridge, a major construction
supported on arches.[21] He built a castle on the summit of a steep cliff
overlooking the river Tweed, in order to discourage attacks by
bandits and invasions by the Scots. For that place had previously
been often exposed to the inroads of raiders, since it lay on the
border of the kingdoms of the English and the Scots, and since no
garrison had been stationed there which could in any way repel such
attacks.[22]

He was so impulsive and impatient of leisure that he moved on
from task to task, thinking nothing of what he had achieved,

Archaeological evidence supporting the claim that the area was artificially levelled is
summarized by Carver, in *Medieval Art and Architecture at Durham Cathedral*, ed.
Coldstream and Draper, pp. 13–19, at 15–16.

[21] Early modern archaizing hands have added to the margins of C, Fx, and L a note
identifying the bridge with Framwellgate Bridge ('Nouus pons in Framwelgayt'), an
identification which is generally accepted (*VCH Durham*, iii. 11).

[22] The words 'Castellum de Norham' have been added to the margins of C, Fx, and L
in the same way as the note regarding Framwellgate Bridge (above n. 21). For the situation
and early history of Norham, see above, pp. 92–3 n. 33. On the castle, see C. H. H. Blair
and H. L. Honeyman, *Norham Castle, Northumberland* (London, 1966), and P. Dixon and
P. Marshall, 'The great tower in the twelfth century: the case of Norham Castle',
Archaeological Journal, cl (1993), 410–32. On the importance of Norham's construction
for the history of the Scottish border, see G. W. S. Barrow, 'The Anglo-Scottish border',
Northern History, iv (1966), 21–42, at p. 40.

nil reputans factum, nisi factis noua [a]iam facienda[a] succederent. Viuacis animi et uegeti fuit corporis, in eodem incolumitatis statu usque biennium ante mortem perdurans. Abhinc enim et salus ei paulatim languescere, et acumen sensus cepit retundi. Aggrauatus tandem letali morbo, ortu dierum canicularum in lectum decidit, eorundemque occasu moriens occidit.[23] Assederant egrotanti assidue maiores ecclesie, exortantes ut preoccuparet faciem Domini in confessione, et faceret sibi amicos de mammona iniquitatis, atque quibus deberet iusta cuique persolueret. Dehinc fit inter pauperes et debitores distributio pecunie. Sed quicquid[b] debitoribus, quicquid pecuniarum alicubi uel distributum fuerat, uel repositum, nisi quantum ecclesie quedam et pauperes acceperant, totum rex post obitum episcopi per exactores in suos thesauros recolligi iussit. [c]Vno ferme antequam moreretur mense, se in ecclesiam iussit[c] transportari; ubi residens contra altare, ex profundo [d]cordis erumpens[d] in gemitum, circumstantibus modo[e] clericis, et[f] pluribus episcopii hominibus, cepit altius penitere malorum que gesserat contra ecclesiam, scilicet quod eius pristinam libertatem redegerit in seruitutem, quod ingenuas illius consuetudines et terras quasdam abstulerit. 'Et hoc,'[g] inquit, 'non coactus inopia feci:[h] sed cupiditate illectus; plus uolui illis[i] nocere, quam potui. Nunc autem et[j] libertatem quam inueni, et quecumque abstuli reddo, ut michi peccatorum meorum penitenti [k]ueniam indulgeat[k] Deus.' Dehinc[l] per anulum altari impositum omnia restituit ecclesie[m] ablata, cartaque [n]sua et[n] sigillo confirmauit[o] restituta.[24]

[xc (H)] Obiit[p] autem peractis in episcopatu uiginti nouem annis et tribus mensibus et septem diebus. Eo autem[q] defuncto committitur episcopatus duobus[r] baronibus, uidelicet Iohanni de Amundauilla et

[a–a] facienda iam *Fx L T (above line) Y* [b] *om. H* [c–c] *add. at foot of page in contemp. hand T* [d–d] prerumpens corde *H* [e] monachis *Fx L Y; altered to* monachis *D* [f] populis *add. H* [g] hec *L* [h] *om. L; above line Fx* [i] *om. Fx H L Y* [j] *om. Fx H L Y* [k–k] ueniam *above line C T;* indulgeat ueniam *Fx L Y* [l] Obiit Radulphus episcopus *rubric H* [m] *om. L Y; above line Fx* [n–n] *om. L Y; above line Fx* [o] confirmante *Y* [p] Obiit Ranulphus anno .dccxxviii. in translatione sancti Cuthberti *contemp. marginal note Fx* [q] *om. H* [r] *om. L Y; above line Fx*

[23] 5 Sept. 1128 according to *HReg*, *s.a.* 1128 (Arnold, *Sym. Op.* ii. 283). According to the *Oxford English Dictionary, Second Edition, on Compact Disc* (Oxford, 1992), *s.u.* 'canicular', the dog-days are 'the days immediately preceding and following the heliacal (in modern times, according to some, the cosmical) rising of the dog-star (either Sirius or Procyon), which is about the 11th of August'. The period in question was considered the hottest and most unhealthy time of the year.

[24] Two charters describing these restitutions and mentioning the ring have survived; see Offler, *Episcopal Charters*, nos. 24 and 25 (pp. 107–11, 112–14). The first hands of the

concerned only that new tasks should take the place of those already
accomplished. Lively in mind and vigorous in body, he remained in
that same state of good health until two years before his death. From
then on his health began gradually to decline, and the sharpness of his
mind to become blunted. Afflicted at length by terminal illness, he
took to his bed at the beginning of the dog-days, and he died when
they came to an end.[23] Around his death-bed the elders of the church
sat in assiduous attendance, exhorting him to prepare for himself
through confession a place in the sight of the Lord, to use the riches
gained by his iniquity to make friends for himself, and to repay what
he justly owed to whomever he owed it. As a result his money was
divided amongst the poor and debtors. But after the bishop's death
the king ordered his tax-gatherers to collect into his treasury whatever
money had been repaid to debtors or distributed or repaid in any
quarter, except what had been received by certain churches or the
poor. About a month before he died, he ordered that he should be
carried into the church, where he sat facing the altar. With only clerks
and many men of the bishopric standing round him, he began to sigh
from the bottom of his heart, and to repent deeply of all the evil
which he had committed against the church, namely that he had
reduced her former liberty into servitude, and had taken away her
free customs and certain of her lands. 'And I did this,' he said, 'not
because I was forced by want, but because I was seduced by greed; I
wished to injure them more than I was able. Now, however, I restore
the liberty which I found, and whatever I have taken away, so that
God may grant to me as a penitent forgiveness of my sins.' Then by
placing his ring on the altar he restored to the church everything he
had taken away, and confirmed these restitutions by his charter under
his seal.[24]

When he died he had completed twenty-nine years, three months,   [xc (H)]
and seven days as bishop. After his death the bishopric was entrusted
to two barons, namely John of Amundeville and Geoffrey the Elder

continuation in C and Ca end here. In Ca the rest of the column is left blank and at the
beginning of the next folio another 12th-cent. hand has entered the following paragraph:
'Anno Dominice incarnationis millesimo centesimo uicesimo nono Rannulphus episcopus
Dunelmensis moritur, episcopatus sui anno uicesimo nono, regni regis Henrici uicesimo
octauo. Eo defuncto committitur episcopatus Dunelmensis duobus baronibus ad opus regis
censum colligentibus. Vacauitque episcopatus per quinquennium. Eo tempore nauis
ecclesie Dunelmensis monachis operi instantibus peracta est.' This is in place of the
paragraph in other manuscripts beginning 'Obiit autem peractis' and ending 'instantibus
peracta est', to which its last sentence and some phrases are identical. Ca then resumes as
in the other manuscripts but in a third 12th-cent. hand.

Gaufrido seniori[a] Esscotland,[25] ad opus regis censum colligentibus.
Vacauitque episcopatus per quinquennium excepto uno mense.[26] Eo
tempore nauis [b]ecclesie Dunelmensis[b] monachis operi instantibus
peracta est.

[xc (xcix)] 3. Anno[c] [d]Dominice incarnationis[d] millesimo centesimo tricesimo
tertio in episcopum[e] Dunelmensem eligitur Gaufridus regis Henrici[f]
cancellarius, qui Rufus dicebatur, [g]consecratusque est[g] Eboraci a
Turstino [h]archiepiscopo Eboracensi.[h][27] Cuius anno tercio rex Henricus moritur, anno Dominice incarnationis [i]millesimo centesimo
tricesimo quinto.[i] Cui mox[j] in regnum nepos ipsius regis ex sorore
Stephanus successit, qui laboriosissime[k] regnum Anglorum undeui-
ginti annis [l]exceptis duobus mensibus et septem diebus[l] tenuit,
dissidentibus inter se primatibus tocius regni. Dissensionis autem
causa hec erat: quod tempore regis Henrici, regnum filie[m] iurauer-
ant, que dudum imperatrix Alamannorum ea tempestate comiti
Andegauensium matrimonio copulata erat. Hac de causa Dauid
rex Scottorum et comites quique[n] Anglie a rege Stephano dissentientes,[o] dum sibi inuicem aduersantur, iniquis quibusque malitie
exercende facultatem tribuerunt, ut maior pars regni desolata
relinqueretur.[28]

Episcopus sane Gaufridus, primo episcopatus sui tempore,[p][29]
libertates et consuetudines tam ecclesie quam monachis more predecessorum suorum indulsit, et priori ecclesie quecumque uel patrum
ecclesie auctoritas, uel comprobata[q] seruauerat antiquitas et prisca

---

[a] *om. L Y; above line Fx*   [b-b] Dunelmensis ecclesie *Fx L Y*   [c] *large
decorated initial C D;* De electione Gaufridi Dunelmensis episcopi *rubric Fx T V Y*
[d-d] incarnationis Dominice *T;* Dominice *om. V*   [e] episcopatum *Fx H L Y*
[f] *om. Ca*   [g-g] consecratus *Ca*   [h-h] Eboracensi archiepiscopo *Fx L
T Y;* consecratus est uiii Idus Augusti eodem anno *contemp. marginal note Fx*
[i-i] millesimo centesimo tricesimo sexto *over alteration Ca*   [j] *om. T*
[k] laboriose *Fx L Y*   [l-l] *om. Ca*   [m] filie ipsius regis *Ca*   [n] quinque *Fx
L Y*   [o] dissidentes *with* uel dissentientes *above line Ca Fx;* dissidentes *L Y;*
desidentes *H*   [p] deprauatus a quibusdam seuerius cum monachis agere compellitur.
Sed non multo post in se reuersus *add. Ca*   [q] probata *Ca*

---

[25] John II of Amundeville had probably succeeded his father, John I of Amundeville, a
Norman tenant of the bishop of Durham in Lincolnshire, not long before Ranulf
Flambard's death (Offler, *Episcopal Charters*, pp. 77); Aird, *Cuthbert*, p. 209, notes that
a royal writ addressed to him shows that Henry I considered him the chief official in
Durham. Geoffrey Escolland witnesses Durham documents of the period 1099–1131, and
may have been succeeded by a son of the same name (Offler, *Charters*, p. 80, citing nos. 12,
18, and *Feodarium*, ed. W. Greenwell, p. 56 n.; see also Aird, *Cuthbert*, pp. 209, 217–18). It

Escolland,[25] who were to collect the dues on behalf of the king. The bishopric was vacant for five years all but a month.[26] In that time, the nave of the church of Durham was completed thanks to the monks urging the work forward.

3. In the year of Our Lord's incarnation 1133 Geoffrey, surnamed [xc (xcix)] Rufus, King Henry's chancellor, was elected bishop of Durham, and he was consecrated at York by Thurstan, archbishop of York.[27] In his third year, King Henry died, in the year of Our Lord's incarnation 1135. He was shortly afterwards succeeded in the kingdom by his nephew, his sister's son Stephen, who ruled the kingdom of England with great labour for nineteen years all but two months and seven days, during which time the magnates of the whole realm were quarrelling with each other. The cause of this dissension was that in the time of King Henry they had sworn to render the kingdom to his daughter, who had formerly been empress of the Germans, but who was at that time married to the duke of Anjou. Because of this David, king of Scots, and certain of the counts of England withdrew their support from King Stephen, and while they were fighting among themselves they gave certain evil people the opportunity to make mischief, so that the greater part of the kingdom was left desolate.[28]

Now, in the early part of his tenure of the bishopric, Geoffrey[29] granted to the church as well as to the monks their liberties and customs just as his predecessors had done, and he conceded benignly to the church's prior everything which had been reserved to him by the authority of the fathers of the church, or by proven antiquity and former custom. In his time the monks' chapter-house

was his son Robert I of Amundeville who was involved in supporting William of Sainte-Barbe (below, pp. 304–5).

[26] That is from the death of Ranulf Flambard (5 Sept. 1128) to the enthronement of Geoffrey Rufus (6 Aug. 1133); see J. Le Neve, *Fasti Ecclesiae Anglicanae 1066–1300*, ii (London, 1971), pp. 29–31.

[27] Geoffrey Rufus was consecrated and enthroned on 6 Aug. 1133; see Le Neve, *Fasti Ecclesiae Anglicanae*, ii. 30. Thurstan was archbishop of York (1119–40).

[28] On Stephen's reign, see R. H. C. Davis, *King Stephen 1135–1154* (3rd edn., London, 1990); E. King, 'The anarchy of King Stephen's reign', *Transactions of the Royal Historical Society*, 5th ser. xxxiv (1984), 133–53; and *The Anarchy of King Stephen's Reign*, ed. E. King (Oxford, 1994).

[29] Words added here by Ca, which were copied into the margin of C in an early modern archaizing hand, may be translated: 'Geoffrey was corrupted by certain people and compelled to act very severely towards the monks. But soon afterwards he came to himself and granted . . .' Geoffrey's surviving *acta* show that he made modest grants to the priory (Aird, *Cuthbert*, p. 179; Offler, *Charters*, nos. 28–9).

[xci (c)] consuetudo, benigne concessit. Ipsius*a* tempore capitulum monachorum*b* consummatum est.[30] Moriens*c* uero*d* ornamenta ecclesie non mediocria contulit. Sed in ipsius obitu contigit ecclesiam grauissimas tempestatum procellas incurrere.

[xcii (ci)] **4.** Erat*e* enim quidam*f* regis Scotie[31] cancellarius, *g*uidelicet*h* Willelmus Cumin,*g* iampridem *i*eiusdem Gaufridi*i* ante*j* episcopatum clericus,*k*[32] siquidem et ante*l* ab annis adolescentie*m* educauerat;[33] qui paululum ante obitum eiusdem*n* Dunelmensis*o* ueniens, et cum eo familiariter conuersatus, cum finem episcopi*p* appropinquare cerneret, familiares quosque clericos, castellanos etiam sibi fide uel sacramentis associat, ut mortuo episcopo eidem *q*castellum traderent et*q* committerent.[34] Totum autem consilium suum tam priori quam archidiaconibus ecclesie summopere celabat; et maturato rursus*r* itinere ad regem Scotie reuertitur, quasi ipsius adiumento*s* episcopatum Dunelmensem adepturus. Defunctus est autem eo absente episcopus die Rogationum secunda, feria scilicet tercia;[35] et nocte sequente, quia cadauer eius aliter teneri non potuit, exinteratus atque sale conditus est. Statimque pro celanda morte ipsius castelli introitus etiam ipsis archidiaconibus et priori iuxta solitum eum uisitare uolentibus interclusus est, et mors eius celata usque sextam feriam. Cum uero uersaretur in ore omnium sermo mortis eius, tradiderunt sepeliendum feria sexta quasi recenter mortuum; et sabbato sepultus est.[36]

[xciii (cii)] **5.** Dominica*t* sequente rediit Willelmus in castellum; et*u* quasi auctoritate regis Scotie munitus, quem ad suam factionem iam

---

a De capitulo *in marg. (late hand C);* De obitu Gaufridi episcopi Dunelmensis *(add. in contemp. hand* et factione W. Comin) *H*   *b* quale hodie cernitur inchoatum et *add. Ca*   *c* Obiit Gaufridus episcopus *rubric Fx T V Y*   *d* Gaufridus *add. Fx L Y*   *e* De factione (factis *T V*) Willelmi Comyn *rubric Fx T V Y*   *f* clericus *add. Ca*   *g-g om. Ca*   *h* scilicet *Fx L Y*   *i-i* eidem *Ca*   *j* ante et *Fx L Y*   *k* notus et a secretis *for* clericus *Ca*   *l* eum *Ca V*   *m* adolescentie eum *Fx H L Y*   *n* eiusdem episcopi *Fx H L Y*   *o* Dunelmum *Ca*   *p om. T*   *q-q* traderent et *om. Ca;* traderent castellum et *T*   *r* rursum *Fx L Y*   *s* adiuuamento *Fx L Y*   *t* Barones episcopatus Dunelmensis consenserunt Willelmo Comin *rubric Fx T V Y*   *u* ex *Y; om. Fx L*

---

[30] Markuson, *Medieval Art and Architecture at Durham Cathedral*, ed. Coldstream and Draper, p. 39.

[31] David I was king of Scots (1124–53).

[32] For the following account, reference should be made to Young, *Cumin*, and A. Young, 'The bishopric of Durham in Stephen's reign', Rollason, *Anglo-Norman Durham*, pp. 353–68; and the text should be compared with the work of John of Hexham (Arnold, *Sym. Op.*

was completed.[30] On his death-bed he gave not inconsiderable [xci (c)]
ornaments to the church. But through his death it happened that
the church was engulfed in great storms and tempests.

4. For there was a certain chancellor of the King of Scotland[31] called [xcii (ci)]
William Cumin who had previously been Geoffrey's cleric before he
became bishop.[32] Indeed even before that he had been educated by
him from his adolescence.[33] Shortly before the death of this same
bishop of Durham, he came and had familiar converse with him.
Seeing the bishop's end approaching, he made certain of the clerks of
the bishop's household and also the keepers of the castle swear fealty
to him and also oaths that they would hand over the castle into his
keeping after the bishop's death.[34] He completely concealed his whole
plan, however, from the prior and archdeacons of the cathedral, and
he quickly made the return journey to the King of Scots, seemingly so
that he could have his assistance in obtaining the bishopric of
Durham. While he was away, however, the bishop died on the
second day of Rogations, a Wednesday;[35] and the following night,
because it was not possible to keep his corpse in any other way, it was
disembowelled and preserved in salt. In order to conceal the bishop's
death, the entrance to the castle was at once closed even to the
archdeacons and the prior themselves when they wished to make their
customary visits to the bishop, and his death was kept secret until the
Saturday. But when news of it was on everyone's lips, he was finally
handed over for burial on the Saturday as if he had just died, and was
actually buried on the Sunday.[36]

5. On the following Sunday William returned to the castle, and, as [xciii (cii)]
it were armed with the authority of the King of Scotland, whom he
had now won over to his faction, he began to dispose of everything

ii. 309–17) and Laurence of Durham (*Dialogi Laurentii Dunelmensis monachi ac prioris*, ed.
J. Raine (SS lxx; Durham, 1870)).

[33] William Cumin's origins are obscure; the name is first found in a document of *c.*1121
in which he appears as a clerk in the English chancery and continues to occur in witness
lists to royal charters through the period (1123–33) when Geoffrey Rufus was chancellor of
England. John of Hexham's description of him as an *alumnus* of Geoffrey's (Arnold, *Sym.
Op.* ii. 309) probably does not mean that he was a relative, although it implies a close
relationship. On the above, see Young, *Cumin*, pp. 2–6. Cumin had become Chancellor of
Scotland by *c.*1136.

[34] From this point on the continuation in Ca diverges from that in other manuscripts
and is printed below (pp. 310–23).

[35] 6 May 1141.

[36] Cf. the similar account by John of Hexham (Arnold, *Sym. Op.* ii. 309).

inclinauerat, cepit quasi *ª*sua omnia*ª* disponere, singulisque et sepe communiter omnibus uerba faciens, quosdam illiciens*ᵇ* promissis, *ᶜ*alios attrahens blanditiis,*ᶜ* omnes autem exquisitis circumueniens astutiis, omnia pro posse et supra posse agebat, ut presumpta sibi permaneret potestas. Nec multus erat labor ut sibi barones adiungeret, qui prius pene expetitus est ab eis quam expeteret, tum timore eius preuentis, tum calliditate circumuenientis.*ᵈ* Infecit autem et unum archidiaconum malitie sue uenenis ut sibi assentiret.³⁷ Hec autem omnia in abscondito, in tenebris, et in umbra mortis; donec, adueniente rege Scotie, ³⁸ palam *ᵉ*sermo de his*ᵉ* fieret a baronibus qui regem comitabantur, Eustachio scilicet,*ᶠ* ³⁹ Rodberto de Brus,⁴⁰ Bernardo de Bailol,⁴¹ Hugone de Moreuile.⁴² Isti nanque in eius factionem facile adducti non minus spe commodi quam promissione lucri, singuli singillatim modo priori,⁴⁴ modo *ᵍ*archidiacono Rannulfo,*ᵍ* oportune, importune*ʰ* ⁴³ insistebant, promissis illicientes, minis terrentes, ut eum in episcopum eligerent. Responsum *ⁱ*eis est,*ⁱ* non posse hoc fieri tam inordinata electione, contra canonum iura et sanctorum patrum decreta, inconsulto domino legato Henrico, Wintoniensi episcopo,⁴⁵ matre quoque*ʲ* ecclesia,⁴⁶ neque die statuto, neque personis*ᵏ* religiosis ad tale negotium euocatis. Cum autem omnia facerent, et nichil efficerent, loquela tandem*ˡ* eo modo finita est, ut mitterentur ad curiam a capitulo legati cum rege Scotie, qui per ipsum regem, legatum et imperatricem requirerent,⁴⁷ quatinus ecclesie suam libertatem confirmarent, ut liberam et canonicam electionem facere possent. Missi ad hoc negotium non quos elegit

ᵃ⁻ᵃ omnia sua *Fx L Y*   *ᵇ* alliciens *Fx (corr. in marg.) H L Y*   *ᶜ⁻ᶜ* om. H; ins. as corr. Y; Quod barones episcopatus consenserunt Willelmo Cumin *rubric H* *ᵈ* preuenientis *Fx (corr. in marg.) H L Y*   *ᵉ⁻ᵉ* de his sermo *Fx H L Y*   *ᶠ* om. H; scilicet et *H L Y*   *ᵍ⁻ᵍ* Rannulfo archidiacono *Fx L Y*   *ʰ* om. H *ⁱ⁻ⁱ* est eis *C (with transposition marks) Fx L V T Y*   *ʲ* om. H   *ᵏ* uiris *T* *ˡ* tamen *Fx L Y*

---

³⁷ This was Robert, the other archdeacon being Ranulf, nephew of Ranulf Flambard (Offler, 'Early archdeacons', p. 202; Arnold, *Sym. Op.*, ii. 312).

³⁸ As described by John of Hexham (Arnold, *Sym. Op.* ii. 309): 'diuertensque ad Dunelmum receptus est in oppidum, precipitque omnia arbitrio imperatricis reseruari, Willelmum Cumin rerum gerendarum curam interim gerere'.

³⁹ Eustace fitz John, lord of Alnwick (Northumberland) and Malton (Yorks.) with strong English and Scottish royal connections (Young, *Cumin*, pp. 12–13).

⁴⁰ He held extensive estates in Yorkshire and Cleveland and also in Annandale (Young, *Cumin*, p. 12).

⁴¹ Lord of Bywell (Northumberland) and Gainford (Co. Durham) (Young, *Cumin*, pp. 13–14).

⁴² Constable of Scotland by 1140, this man held extensive lands in Scotland, and his family had lands in the honour of Huntingdon (Young, *Cumin*, p. 12).

as if it were his own. He talked to people individually and often together, enticing some with illicit promises, luring others with flattery, getting round everyone with his exquisite astuteness, and doing everything within his means and beyond his means to ensure that the power he had presumed to take on himself should remain in his hands. He did not have much trouble winning over the barons to his side, and he obtained what he wanted from them almost before he asked for it, for they were prevented from resisting both by fear of him and by his cunning in outmanoeuvring them. He also corrupted one of the archdeacons with the poison of his malice so that he won his assent.[37] All this was done hugger mugger, in the darkness, in the shadow of death, until the King of Scotland arrived[38] and it was talked openly of by the barons who accompanied the king, that is Eustace,[39] Robert Bruce,[40] Bernard of Balliol,[41] and Hugh of Morville.[42] For these were easily won over to Cumin's faction, no less by hope of advancement than by the promise of riches, and 'in season and out of season',[43] they brought pressure individually and separately, sometimes on the prior,[44] sometimes on the archdeacon Ranulf, enticing them with promises and frightening them with threats to the end that they should elect Cumin bishop. The reply made to them was that such an irregular election could not take place in this way, against canon law and the decrees of the holy fathers, without consulting the lord legate Henry, bishop of Winchester,[45] and also the mother church,[46] nor without a day being appointed, nor without summoning religious persons to take part in such a proceeding. When Cumin's supporters had done everything and achieved nothing, an agreement was reached that the chapter should send messengers to court with the king of Scotland, and the messengers should through him ask the legate and the empress to confirm the liberty of the church, so that they might hold a free and canonical election.[47] The messengers sent on this mission were not those elected by the chapter,

---

[43] 2 Tim. 4: 2.

[44] Prior Roger (?1138–1149); see *Heads of Religious Houses*, p. 43.

[45] Henry of Blois, abbot of Glastonbury (1126–71), bishop of Winchester (1129–71), and papal legate in England (1139–43).

[46] Presumably York is meant, although that church in fact did not interfere in Cumin's usurpation (Young, *Cumin*, pp. 14–15).

[47] The empress was Matilda, eldest child of Henry I; married first to the Emperor Henry V (d. 1125), she contested the throne of England with Stephen after her father's death in 1135. The variant section of the Continuation in Ca states that Cumin himself went with King David to the court (below).

capitulum, sed quos aduersariorum factio coegit. Tum*a* tamen in die
sacro Pentecostes in capitulo,[48] qui mittebantur a priore sub adiur-
atione diuini nominis astricti sunt, ne ad curiam uenientes aliud
quererent quam id ad quod missi fuerant, liberam scilicet electionem,
neque quenquam nominarent, aut nominatum susciperent.

Ierunt cum*b* plures*c* de episcopatu barones, omnes ei consentientes;
et remansit custodia eius in castello. Sed ad curiam uenientes, non
inuenerunt tunc legatum; neque tamen cessabat eius factio conari
quod poterat. Requisierunt ergo imperatricem et barones et nuntii qui
uenerant, ut consuleret*d* ecclesie Dunelmensi de persona nominata,
scilicet de*e* Willelmo. Posita tamen res in respectum est usque legati
aduentum. Cui tamen Rannulfus archidiaconus futurorum precauens
totius rei ordinem litteris mandauerat. Veniens autem legatus ad
curiam, statim per barones imperatricis et eis*f* qui a Dunelmo
uenerant de Willelmo requisitus est. Veruntamen presciens rei
ordinem, ad tam inordinatum non potuit assensum inclinari; sed
rem examinans, prescriptam factionem inuenit, fauctoribusque ipsius
digna animaduersione interdixit, ne Willelmum in episcopum nisi
canonica electione susciperent. Ipsi quoque Willelmo interdixit
omnem ecclesiasticam communionem, si episcopatum susciperet,
nisi canonice promotus. Attamen in die Sancti Iohannis Baptiste[49]
paratus erat Willelmus ab imperatrice baculum et anulum recipere;*g*
et data *h*hec ei*h* essent, nisi facta a Lundoniensibus dissensione cum
omnibus suis discederet ipsa die a Lundonia imperatrix.[50]

Discessit quoque et*i* Willelmus cum ea, regem Scotie comitatus.
Rediit Dunelmum Rodbertus archidiaconus, et barones de episcopatu, ferentes litteras imperatricis directas ad capitulum; quarum
summa hec erat: quod uellet ecclesiam nostram de pastore consultam
esse, et nominatim de illo quem*j* archidiaconus nominaret, et quod de
illo uellet, et de alio omnino nollet. Quesitum est ergo quis hic esset,

---

a Cum *Fx L T Y*   *b* cum eo *Fx H L T V Y*   *c* quamplures *Fx H L Y*
d consulerent *Fx L T Y*   *e* om. *Fx H L Y*   *f* eos *Fx H L Y*
g suscipere *Fx L Y*   *h–h* ei hec *Fx L Y*   *i* om. *H L Y; above line Fx T*
j quem Robertus *Fx H L T Y*

---

[48] 18 May 1141.
[49] 24 June 1141.
[50] On the alienation of London from Matilda at a critical point in 1141 and on the
'ultimately disastrous' consequences for herself of her support for Cumin, see M. Chibnall,
The Empress Matilda, Queen Consort, Queen Mother and Lady of the English (Oxford, 1991),
pp. 102–5, 138–9. Chibnall doubts nevertheless that Matilda was really prepared to invest
Cumin with the ring and staff herself (p. 138). See also the vivid account of the London

but those whom their adversaries' faction had forced upon them. Nevertheless, on the holy day of Pentecost,[48] those who were being sent were adjured by the prior in the chapter in the name of God that, when they reached the court, they should request nothing but what they had been sent to obtain, that is a free election, and they should neither nominate anyone, nor accept any nomination.

Very many of the barons of the bishopric went, all supporting Cumin; and his garrison remained in the castle. But when the delegation reached the court it did not find the legate there, although this did not stop Cumin's faction from doing what they could. The barons and messengers who had come therefore asked the empress to consult the church of Durham about the person who had been nominated, that is William. Consideration of the matter, however, was deferred until the arrival of the legate. Foreseeing how things would turn out, the archdeacon Ranulf had sent letters to the legate explaining the whole matter to him. When the latter arrived at court, requests were at once made to him in respect of William by the barons of the empress and those barons who had come from Durham. As he had already learned the true state of affairs, however, he could not be induced to give his assent to such an irregular proceeding, but having examined the case he found Cumin's faction to be just as it had been described to him in writing, and he prohibited William's partisans with justified reproaches from accepting William as bishop except by canonical election. He also placed William under an interdict as regards all communion with the church if he accepted the bishopric without being canonically promoted to it. Nevertheless on St John the Baptist's day[49] William was to accept the staff and ring from the empress, and these would have been given to him had there not been an uprising by the Londoners and the empress and her followers left London on that very day.[50]

William also left with her, in the entourage of the king of Scotland. The archdeacon Robert returned to Durham, and so did the barons of the bishopric bearing letters for the chapter from the empress, the substance of which was this: that she wished our church of Durham to be consulted concerning its pastor, and by name concerning him whom the archdeacon would nominate, and that she wished this to be done for that person, and for absolutely no one else. When it was

episode in William of Malmesbury, *Historia Novella, The Contemporary History*, ed. E. King and K. R. Potter (OMT, 1998), pp. 96–8. Cf below, pp. 312–13.

responsumque[a] quia Willelmus. Obsessa uero imperatrice apud Wintoniam,[51] inter fugientes fuga dilapsus Willelmus circa festum Sancti Michaelis[52] Dunelmum uenit; ubi regem Scottorum ab eadem obsessione pridie reuersum inuenit, in monachorum curia hospitatum; et ipse quidem statim[b] castellum intrauit. Iterum[c] ergo obsecrationes, postulationes pro eo,[d] sed non gratiarum [e]actio erat;[e] quoniam neque prior uel[f] capitulum neque Rannulfus archidiaconus uerba patiebantur admitti. Post multa tandem relictus est Willelmus in castello a rege, quasi custos episcopatus sub manu imperatricis;[g] et plegius factus est ipse[h] rex inter munitionem et priorem fratresque[i] monasterii, ne sibi alterutrum dampnum quererent aut facerent.

Discedente autem,[j] disponebat[k] Willelmus, non ut custos sed sicut iam episcopus factus, dans etiam terras, et homagium omnium baronum preter solius Rogeri de Coyneriis[53] suscipiens; et burgenses sacramenta fidelitatis sibi facere compulit. Cum autem cotidie Rannulfus archidiaconus instaret, neque aliquo modo flectere[l] posset eum ad suum uelle, tandem de Dunelmo eum disturbauit, immo et[m] a toto episcopatu exulem reddidit. Non habens enim ubi secure se ageret, uix Eboracum effugit; diripiente Willelmo omnia que ipsius erant, et neque domibus parcente, quas effringere fecit, [n]et abstrahere[n] atque[o] destruere. Rannulfus uero[p] cum magna difficultate ad regem Anglie euasit, et querimonias harum rerum apud ipsum et apud[q] dominum legatum deposuit. Protulit ergo legatus in Willelmum[r] tanquam inuasorem anathematis iaculum, donec scilicet ecclesie satisfaceret, et Rannulfo ablata restitueret; et ecclesie Eboracensi per ipsum archidiaconum mandauit eandem in Willelmum[s] proferre sententiam. Sed audita sua dampnatione Willelmus parum aut nichil inde curabat.[t]

In quadragesima ueniente Dunelmum Hereberto abbate de Rokesburch,[u][54] quasi occasionem nactus, conuenit[v] Rogerum priorem

[a] responsumque est *Fx L T (above line)*   [b] *om. Fx H L Y*   [c] Interim *Fx L Y*   [d] erant *add. Fx L T (above line) Y*   [e-e] actiones *Fx L T Y*   [f] neque *Fx L Y*   [g] *om. L*   [h] *om. Fx H L Y*   [i] et fratres *Fx H L Y*   [j] autem rege *Fx H L T V Y*   [k] disposuit *Fx L Y;* disponit *D H*   [l] inflectere *Fx L Y*   [m] *om. Fx L Y*   [n-n] *om. Fx L Y*   [o] et *H*   [p] *om. H L Y; over line Fx*   [q] *om. Fx L Y*   [r] Willelmo *Fx L Y*   [s] Willelmo *Fx L Y*   [t] curauit *T*   [u] Kelkou *Fx L Y;* Kelchou *H;* Kelkowe *over erasure T*   [v] *om. L Y; over line Fx*

[51] Chibnall, op. cit., pp. 112–13, for the context of the siege.
[52] 29 Sept. 1141
[53] Lord of lands in County Durham (including Middleton) and in Yorkshire, he

asked whom this meant, the reply was that it meant William. Now the empress was besieged in Winchester,[51] and William took flight amongst the fugitives from the siege and came to Durham at about the feast of St Michael,[52] where he found the king of Scots, who had returned from the same siege the previous day, a guest in the monks' court. William at once entered the castle. Again pleas and applications were made on his behalf, but they received no thanks, because neither the prior nor the chapter nor the archdeacon Ranulf would allow these words to be received. At length, after a great deal of this, the king left William in possession of the castle, as it were the custodian of the bishopric on behalf of the empress, and the king made a pledge between the castle and the prior and brothers of the monastery that they should neither seek to inflict nor actually inflict harm on each other.

When the king left, however, William disposed of affairs not as the custodian of the see but as if he were already the bishop. He granted lands; he received the homage of all the barons except only Roger de Conyers;[53] and he compelled the burgesses to swear oaths of fealty to him. When the archdeacon Ranulf stood out against him every day, and he could by no means bend him to his will, at length he harried him out of Durham, or rather exiled him from the whole of the bishopric. There was nowhere where Ranulf could be safe, and he scarcely managed to flee to York. William destroyed everything of his, not even sparing the houses which he had broken into, looted and destroyed. With great difficulty Ranulf escaped to the king of England, and lodged complaints concerning these matters with the king and with the lord legate. The legate therefore placed William as an invader of the bishopric under the scourge of anathema, until he should have made amends to the Church, and until he should have restored to Ranulf what he had taken from him; and through this same archdeacon he commanded the church of York to publish this sentence on William. But when William heard his condemnation, he cared little or nothing for it.

During Lent there came to Durham Herbert, abbot of Roxburgh.[54] Presented with this opportunity, William secretly summoned Prior

apparently had responsibility for Durham Castle after Ranulf Flambard's death, and was probably constable (Young, *Cumin*, p. 18). On the importance of the family in 12th-cent. Durham, see Aird, *Cuthbert*, pp. 209–15.

[54] For Herbert, see A. O. Anderson, *Scottish Annals from English Chroniclers, A.D. 500 to 1286*, ed. M. O. Anderson (Stamford, 1991), p. 221 and n. 2. Young, *Cumin*, assumes that his intention was to have himself accepted as bishop (p. 18).

secrete solum coram ipso abbate, districte inquisitionem faciens si se habere uellet episcopum, ut super hoc certitudinem regi Scotie mandaret. Veruntamen nichil ab eo quod uolebat extorquere ualens, dimisso illo, *a*cantorem, secretarium,*a* celerarium, monasterii singulos singillatim euocans, eandem cum omnibus inquisitionem agebat,*b* neque aliquid proficiebat.

In eadem quadragesima uenit Dunelmum monachus quidam gyrouagus de ordine Cistrensium, et statim a Willelmo in familiaritatem admissus.*c* Post multam inter se collocutionem*d* dimissus est ab eo ad machinandum negotium, quod postea satis patuit. Transacto enim tempore rediit idem monachus; et falsas litteras quasi a domno apostolico transmissas Willelmo detulit, sigillum contrafactum habens ad similitudinem signaculi apostolici. Ipsas litteras Willelmus letabundus quibusdam*e* ex fratribus ostendit; in quibus significare uidebatur apostolicus gaudium sibi esse de ipsius electione, quam a populo Dei*f* canonice factam audierat; precepisse quoque se legato suo Henrico Wyntoniensi episcopo, ne amplius molestaret eum. Dimisit deinde monachum ad regem Scottorum euntem, quoniam ad ipsum quoque eiusmodi*g* litteras ferebat quasi ab apostolico missas,*h* in quibus continebatur quod maxime eum uelle nouerat, scilicet ut*i* Matildam imperatricem Henrici regis filiam adiuuaret, deinde ut Willelmum Dunelmensem electum manuteneret. Neque difficile fuit ei, ut regem deciperet tali machinatione, qui ubique in regno suo ipsas litteras transcribi iussit; et monacho donans palefridum, et donis aliis honorans, ad Willelmum remisit.*j* Tantam rerum fallaciam Ricardus abbas Mailrosensis experiens, zelo zelatus est pro domo Israel,[55] tam horrenda in ea machinari exhorrens, ipsumque pseudolegatum monachum cepit,*k* et omnem suam machinationem confiteri fecit, qualiter Willelmi opere et promissis hec*l* operari edoctus et instigatus sit.

Post obitum*m* Gaufridi episcopi secundo, mandatus est prior a legato per obedientiam et sub excommunicationis intentione presentiam suam sibi exhibere. Veruntamen circumclusus custodia Willelmi, cum aperte hoc facere non ualeret,*n* occulto*o* exitu manus

---

a–a secretarium cantorem *Fx L Y*   *b* faciebat *Fx L Y*   *c* est *add. Fx L T (in marg.) Y (above line)*   *d* collusionem *T*   *e* quibus *Fx (corr. in marg.) L Y*   *f* om. *Fx H L Y*   *g* eiusdemmodi *Fx H L Y*   *h* commissas *H*   *i* om. *Fx L Y*   *j* transmisit *T*   *k* om. *H*   *l* hoc *Fx L*   *m* uero *add. T*   *n* in *add. Fx H L T Y; in add. above line C*   *o* inculto *V;* inculto *corr. to* occulto *C D*

---

[55] Abbot of Melrose 1136–48; see Anderson, *Early Sources*, ii. 195; cf. Num. 25: 13.

Roger on his own into the presence of this abbot, and questioned him closely as to whether he was willing to accept him as bishop, so that he might communicate certainty about this to the king of Scotland. But William was not able to extort anything of what he wanted from the prior, and dismissing him from his presence he summoned in turn and on their own the cantor, the sacrist, and the cellarer of the monastery, and asked them all the same question; but he got nowhere.

During that same Lent there came to Durham a wandering monk of the Cistercian order, and at once William admitted him into familiarity with him. After there had been much discussion between them, William sent him away to carry out some scheming, the nature of which was afterwards only too apparent. For some time later the monk returned, and brought with him a false letter purportedly sent from the lord pope to William, and with attached to it a counterfeit seal made to resemble the papal seal. Delightedly William showed certain of the brothers this letter. In it the pope purportedly expressed his joy at William's election, which he had heard had been canonically carried out by God's people; and he stated that he had ordered his legate Henry, bishop of Winchester, not to molest William any further. Then he sent the monk off to go to the king of Scotland, so that he could take to him also a letter of the same sort claiming to have been sent by the pope, in which was contained what he knew the king badly wanted to know, namely that he should help the Empress Matilda, daughter of King Henry, and that he should next support William as the elected bishop of Durham. It was not difficult for him to deceive the king with such a trick. The king ordered this letter to be copied everywhere in his kingdom, and he gave the monk a palfrey, honoured him with other gifts, and sent him back to William. Abbot Richard of Melrose, however, had experience of such trickery in affairs. Fired with zeal for the house of Israel,[55] he was horrified that such horrendous things had been contrived against it, and he arrested this pseudo-legate monk and made him confess his fraud completely, how William had instructed him and instigated him to devote himself to this by his actions and by his promises.

In the second year after the death of Bishop Geoffrey, the legate commanded the prior on his obedience and on pain of excommunication to come into his presence. Hemmed in as he was by William's guards, the prior was unable to do this openly, so he escaped from his

eius euasit, et quod iubebatur impleuit.[56] Hoc agnoscens Willelmus, ab illo[a] iam tempore aduersus fratres relictos seuitiam suam exercuit, plurima eis mala faciens, et pluriora promittens. Portas ita custodiri fecit, ut neque nuntium mittere nec recipere monachi quoquomodo possent. Sepenumero[b] etiam[c] uictualia eis inferri prohibuit, et seruientibus eorum aditum ad eos interdixit. Sigillum capituli in potestate habens, ad quos uolebat [d]et quas uolebat[d] pro sua causa litteras mittebat. Inter hec castellum apud Aluertonam edificauit, quod suo nepoti Willelmo dono dedit, coniungens ei matrimonio neptem comitis de Albermarl ad manutenementum suum.[57]

Anno[e] post obitum domini[f] Gaufridi episcopi tertio redierunt a Roma nuntii, qui pro negotio ecclesie Dunelmensis missi ad domnum apostolicum [g]Innocentium[58] fuerant[g] a priore et archidiacono Rannulfo, deferentes epistolam, qua eidem priori et archidiacono ex auctoritate apostolica iubebatur, quatinus infra quadraginta dies postquam litteras ipsas[h] uidissent, pastorem sibi eligerent; et si in ecclesia Dunelmensi facere non possent, uel in matre ecclesia uel in aliqua uicina tam sanctum opus explerent. Statuta ergo[i] die ad electionem, et personis de episcopatu mandatis, res Willelmum non latuit; mittensque itinera omnia obsedit, uicinis quoque mandauit, ut transeuntes obseruarent et sibi asseruarent. Vnde factum est, ut quosdam quidem ipse caperet, quosdam in alia prouincia secundum mandatum eius capi contingeret. Quamobrem nonnullos eius[j] rei timor a cepto itinere reuocauit.

[xciv (ciii)]　6. Facta[k] est tamen, Deo iuuante, iuxta domini apostolici mandatum electio de uenerabili uiro Willelmo decano Eboracensi ecclesie, Dominica[l] media quadragesima.[m][59] Miseratque Willelmus signatas capituli litteras, quippe qui sigilli (ut dictum est) potestatem habebat, cum duobus clericis, quibus electio fieri prohiberetur;[n] sed non indigne talis legatio repulsam promeruit. Cum autem absens esset[o]

---

[a] om. L Y; over line Fx　　　[b] Sepeuero Fx H L V Y　　　[c] om. H　　　[d–d] om. V; et quod uolebat Fx H L Y　　　[e] large decorated initial C D; Capitulum rubric Fx Y; Willelmus de Sancta Barbara (Barba T) electus est ad episcopatum Dunelmensis ecclesie rubric T V　　　[f] om. Fx H L Y　　　[g–g] fuerant Innocentium Y　　　[h] om. L [i] autem Fx H L Y　　　[j] huius T　　　[k] Willelmus de Sancta Barbara electus est ad episcopatum Dunelmensem rubric Fx H Y　　　[l] om. H L V Y; above line Fx [m] quadragesima Fx L Y　　　[n] prohibetur Fx H L Y　　　[o] om. H; above line T Y

---

[56] Compare the variant section of the Continuation in Ca which differs significantly in its account of the reasons for and circumstances of this journey (below, pp. 312–13).

[57] William, earl of Aumale, was a powerful Yorkshire landowner, viewed by William

hands by means of a clandestine departure, and did what he was commanded to do.[56] When William found out about this, he inflicted his ferocity from that time onwards on the monks who remained, and he did much mischief to them, and threatened them with more. He ordered the gates to be guarded so that the monks might by no means send or receive messengers. Often he also prohibited food and drink from being taken in to them, and he denied their servants access to them. He had the seal of the chapter in his possession, and he sent whom he wanted and what letters he wanted on behalf of his cause. While this was happening he built a castle at Northallerton, which he gave to his nephew William, uniting him in marriage for his upkeep to the niece of the earl of Aumale.[57]

In the third year after the death of Bishop Geoffrey, there returned from Rome the messengers, whom the prior and Archdeacon Ranulf had sent to the lord pope Innocent[58] regarding the business of the church of Durham. They brought with them a letter, which commanded the prior and the archdeacon by papal authority to elect a pastor for themselves within forty days of receiving this letter; and if they were not able to fulfil this holy duty in the church of Durham they should do so in the mother church or in some other neighbouring church. A day was therefore fixed for the election, and persons were summoned from the bishopric, but this was not concealed from William. He ordered all the roads to be blocked, and people in neighbouring areas to observe and keep a close watch for him on anyone passing through. So it was that he himself captured some and some were captured in other districts on his orders. For fear of this, not a few were dissuaded from continuing the journey they had begun.

6. Nevertheless by the aid of God and according to the command [xciv (ciii)] of the lord pope the election was carried out of the venerable man William, dean of the church of York, on Sunday in the middle of Lent.[59] William Cumin had sent letters sealed with the chapter's seal, which (as we said) he had in his possession, with two clerks who were to prohibit the election from taking place, but such a legation justly received the rebuff which it deserved. Now William

of Newburgh as 'sub Stephano rex uerior' (Young, *Cumin*, p. 20; D. Nicholl, *Thurstan, Archbishop of York (1114–1140)* (York, 1964), p. 240, citing *Chronicles of the Reigns of Stephen, Henry II, and Richard I*, ed. R. Howlett (4 vols.; RS lxxxii; London, 1884–9), i. 103).   [58] Innocent II (1130–24 Sept. 1133).

[59] William of Sainte-Barbe (14 Mar. 1143–1152).

idem Willelmus, ad concilium quod tunc Lundonie celebrabatur^a profectus, et rem totam penitus ignoraret, obuiam factus est priori, et personis per quos eadem de ipso facta fuerat^b electio, apud Wintrintham super Humbre flumen ad Eboracum de concilio rediens. Ibi tunc prior et archidiaconus cum ceteris in ecclesia iterata denominatione, ipsum in electum ecclesie^c Dunelmensis episcopum confirmauerunt; nolentemque et maxime reluctantem ad altare traxerunt, 'Te Deum laudamus' cantantes.

[xciv (H)]   Sequente^d sancta festiuitate Pentecostes[60] reuerso de transmarinis ^epartibus legato,^e Wintoniam ^fcum eo profecti sunt,^f cum mandasset ei legatus in ui^g obedientie ad se uenire. Examinata ergo electione secundum domni apostolici mandata et sanctorum patrum decreta, regisque assensu quesito et accepto, sicut mandauerat domnus papa, sacratus est a legato Dominica ante festum natiuitatis Sancti^h Iohannis Baptiste,[61] et Eboracum rediit mane post festum ⁱapostolorum Petri et Pauli.ⁱ[62]

[xcv (civ)]   7. Miserat^j etiam ^kWillelmus nuntios cum litteris,^k quas signari fecerat sigillo capituli, per quos fieri prohiberetur consecratio ipsius electi. Veruntamen, audita consecratione ipsius,^l sue mentis angustias in fratres ecclesie effudit, multis modis eos uexans. Vexabat quoque ualde sacerdotes, quoscunque cessare a diuino ministerio pro sui excommunicatione credebat, contra sanctorum conciliorum decreta ut celebrarent diuina compellens; et sepeliri faciebat per suos homines qui relinquebantur insepulti a presbyteris.

Orta est interim^m inter ipsum etⁿ Rogerum de Coyneriis discordia, quoniam homagium et sacramenta non potuit ab ipso, sicut ceteri barones ei fecerant, extorquere. Cepit ergo Rogerus ad sui munimentum domum suam munire apud Biscoptun[63] ipsius Willelmi timore.^o Audito hoc,^p Willelmus multam manum ad locum occupandum misit; sed a spe cadens in semet recessit.

---

^a celebratur *V T*   ^b est *Fx (corr. in marg.) H L Y*   ^c *om. Fx H L Y*
^d De crudelitate Willelmi Cumin et de rebellione eius *rubric H*   ^{e–e} legato partibus *L*
^{f–f} profecti sunt cum eo *Fx L Y*   ^g uirtute *H*   ^h Beati *Fx L Y*   ^{i–i} Petri et Pauli apostolorum *H*   ^j De crudelitate Willelmi Comin, et de rebellione eius *rubric Fx T V Y*   ^{k–k} nuntios cum litteris Willelmus *Fx L Y*   ^l illius *Fx H L Y*   ^m iterum *H*   ⁿ *om. L Y; over line Fx V*   ^o add. *in top marg. somewhat later T*   ^p *om. L Y; over line Fx*

---

[60] 23 May 1143.
[61] The variant section of the Continuation in Ca emphasizes Henry of Blois's influence in winning the king's support (below, pp. 314–15).

the dean was away at a council which was being held in London, and knew nothing of the matter. The prior and those persons by whom the election had been carried out met him at Wintringham on the Humber as he was returning to York from the council. There the prior and the archdeacon with the others repeated the nomination in the church, and confirmed his election as bishop of the church of Durham. Unwillingly and very reluctantly indeed he was dragged to the altar while they chanted 'Te Deum laudamus'.

On the holy feast of Pentecost which followed,[60] the legate had returned from overseas, and they went to Winchester with him, since the legate had summoned the bishop on his obedience to come to him. The election was examined according to the mandates of the lord pope and the decrees of the holy fathers, and the king's assent was sought and received, as the lord pope had commanded, and the bishop was consecrated by the legate on the Sunday before the feast of St John the Baptist,[61] and he returned to York on the morning after the feast of the apostles Peter and Paul.[62] [xciv (H)]

7. William Cumin had sent messengers with a letter, which he had had sealed with the chapter's seal, through whom the consecration of the bishop elect was to be prohibited from taking place. When he heard that the consecration had actually been performed, however, he unleashed the anguish of his mind against the brothers of the church, and harassed them in many ways. He also seriously maltreated the priests. Contrary to the decrees of the holy councils, he compelled all those whom he believed to have ceased to exercise holy ministry on account of his excommunication to celebrate services; and he had those left unburied by the priests interred by his own men. [xcv (civ)]

Meanwhile discord arose between him and Roger de Conyers, because he could not extort from him homage and oaths of fealty, such as the other barons had done to him. So for fear of William, Roger began for his own protection to fortify his residence at Bishopton.[63] When William heard of this, he sent a strong force to occupy the place, but their hopes were not realised and they returned.

---

[62] 20 and 30 June 1143. The variant section of the Continuation in Ca states that he excommunicated those who had invaded his church (below, pp. 314–15).

[63] Near Stockton (Co. Durham; NZ 368 209), this is a substantial motte and bailey castle with a motte some 30 ft high (Young, *Cumin*, p. 21; N. McCord, *North-East History from the Air* (Chichester, 1991), pp. 38, 40; Young in Rollason, *Anglo-Norman Durham*, p. 360 and pl. 80).

Non multis post diebus, inuitatus a quibusdam, non tamen[a] multis, de episcopatu baronibus, infra episcopatum uenit episcopus post festum Assumptionis Sancte[b] Marie,[64] tractus magis a suis quam libenter ueniens. Susceptus est optabiliter a multis, qui ad eum relicto Willelmo confluebant; et apud Biscoptun paucis diebus perhendinans, horum homagium capiebat qui uoluntarie [c]id offerebant, nulli uim aliquam inferens, sed qui uoluntarie[c] ueniebant benigne suscipiens. Conduxerunt deinde[d] episcopum Dunelmum Rogerus de Coyneriis et barones qui ad eum confluxerant, ad munitionem sui militari manu muniti, sperantes uel ipsum Willelmum a malis suis penitere, uel eos qui cum eo fuerant ab ipso reuocare.

Multum[e] autem opinione decepti sunt. Non solum enim,[f] uti malorum penitens pacem non expetiit, sed neque nuntios pacis ad se missos tempore passus est, quibusdam non admissis, aliis effugatis, nonnullis minis et obprobriis fatigatis. Emittens denique quos secum habebat milites, appropinquantes muris episcopales [g]belli modo[g] reppulit. Vnde qui cum episcopo fuerant in se redeuntes, apud Sanctum Egidium,[65] que sic uocatur ecclesia, distante a muris[h] spacio,[i] cum ipso episcopo ea nocte manserunt. Mane autem facto, conglobatus Willelmus suorum satellitum pompa effractis ianuis in ecclesiam cum armatis[j] irrupit. Eratque uidere milites loricatos euaginatis gladiis inter altaria discurrere, arcuarios flentibus et orantibus monachis alios[k] intermisceri, alios[l] supra uerticem minari, omnem autem ecclesiam frementium atque tumultuantium uociferatione repleri. Et manus quidem a lesione monachorum uix abstinuerunt, cum tamen [m]eorum unum[m] iactu lapidis pene interemissent. Veruntamen custodiam militum et arcuariorum in ecclesia relinquentes ad modum castelli eam munierunt; et ueluti tripudiantes gaudio quod diuinitati contumeliam in loco pacis uiolatores, focos accendebant, nidores carnium quas coquebant pro thimiatum[n] odoribus adolentes,[66] pro uocibus cantantium uociferationes uigilantium cum sonitu cornium latius audiri faciebant.[67] Inter hec et contra

---

[a] om. H V; cum Fx L T (over line) Y   [b] om. L; beate Fx Y   [c–c] om. D Fx H L Y; add. in marg. (s. xvi with symbol used by William Claxton) Fx   [d] demum T [e] large decorated initial C D T; Capitulum, rubric V; Multi Fx L T (over alteration) Y [f] autem Fx L Y   [g–g] modo belli Fx L Y   [h] muris et T V   [i] qui add. T over line   [j] armis H   [k] om. Fx H L Y   [l] aliquos L   [m–m] unum eorum T   [n] thimiamatum Fx L T (over alteration from thimiatum) Y

---

[64] 15 Aug. 1143.

Not many days later, at the invitation of a few—but not many—barons of the bishopric, the new bishop came into his diocese after the feast of the Assumption of St Mary,[64] dragged there rather by his supporters than coming willingly. Many warmly received him, deserting William Cumin and flocking to the bishop. He stayed for a few days at Bishopton, receiving the homage of those who voluntarily offered it, applying force to no one, rather benignly receiving those who came to him voluntarily. Then Roger de Conyers and the other barons who had flocked to him conducted the bishop to Durham, defending him with military might, in the hope that either William Cumin would repent of his evils, or those who were with him might be dissuaded from continuing to support him.

They were, however, much disappointed in this expectation. For not only did Cumin not repent of his evils and sue for peace, but he would not even receive the messengers of peace sent to him at times, refusing admission to some, driving others away, and heaping threats and opprobrium on many. Then he sent out the knights he had with him and in warlike manner repelled the bishop's party which was approaching the walls. So those who were with the bishop withdrew, and spent the night with the bishop at St Giles, as the church is called, some distance from the walls.[65] In the morning, William Cumin, closely surrounded by his retinue of henchmen, broke down the doors of the cathedral, and burst in with armed men. There was to be seen the sight of mailed men with drawn swords charging between the altars. Some of the archers went in amongst the weeping and praying monks, some threatening them with blows to the head, and the whole cathedral was filled with roaring and shouting and tumult. Scarcely did they hold back from doing physical harm to the monks, since they nearly killed one of them with a blow from a stone. They left a guard of knights and archers in the cathedral and fortified it as if it were a castle; as if rejoicing that they had profaned this place of peace and abused God, they lit fires so that the smell of meat they were cooking rose up in place of the scent of incense,[66] and the cries of the watchmen and the sound of trumpets were to be heard in the place of the chanting of the choir.[67] While these things were going on,

---

[65] St Giles, Gilesgate (Co. Durham; NZ 285 427); see *VCH Durham*, iii. 11, 186–7.

[66] In C the original text breaks off and a 14th-cent. replacement leaf begins.

[67] The variant section of the Continuation in Ca gives a more detailed account of the atrocities of this phase and of the seizure of the cathedral (below, pp. 314–19).

episcopales[68] sepius prodeundo non sinebant eos moenibus appropinqare.

Occulte autem *a*Willelmus comiti Richmundie*a* [69] multum pecunie promittens mandauit, quatenus cum exercitu ueniens episcopum cum suis loco amoueret. Rem autem prenoscens episcopus, licet obsistere posse uideretur, ne uideretur effusione sanguinis *b*maculari causa*b* pietatis, ad Biscoptun cum suis discessit. Quem insequentes qui cum Willelmo erant, extremos agminis quos capere poterant misere trucidabant;*c* alios truncatis membris laniabant, quosdam mulctatos*d* carcerabant;*e* paucos, quos gladiis suis indignos credebant, per pecunie redemptionem dimittebant. Interim*f* quosdam monachorum, quos sibi contrarios credidit, de ecclesia eiecit. Exinde uesania Willelmi in dies augmentabatur, et modus iam crudelitatis non erat. Milites quidem*g* eius assidue prodeundo, et circa regionem omnem loca omnia cursando, quecunque inuenissent depredabantur, et neque nocte nec interdiu a depopulatione cessantes, quicquid rerum inuenissent passim diripiebant, alia comburendo,*h* alia diruendo, et quicquid in agris natum erat conterendo calcibus, aut depascendo delebant; perque terram cultam iter agendo faciebant eam*i* sterilem et uastitatis facie deformem uideri. Et ueluti post locustas silua cerni solet floribus et foliis spoliata, sic quacunque transibant solitudinem a tergo*j* relinquebant. Quoscunque enim magis perditos et in malitia famosos audiebat, adiungebat sibi; eratque inter eos certamen alius alium in nequitia superare; ut esset acceptior quicunque crudelior esset.

In hiis autem que fiebant horror quidem audire est, magis uero uidere miseria fuit. Neque enim solis rapinis et spoliationibus metiebantur audaciam; sed usque ad corporum laniationes atque cruciatus accedebant, non tamen*k* clam, siue per noctem, aut quoslibet homines, uerum luce, palam, nobiliores quosque*l* ad tormenta rapiendo. Plurimus autem erat ac uarius tormentorum modus; et quam dictu difficile, tam etiam auditu incredibile. Suspendebantur per domos in parietibus homines, in*m* transuersum medii

---

a–a comiti Willelmus de Richmundia *T*   *b–b* maculare causam *Fx (corr.) H L T;* maculari causam *Y*   *c* truciabant *T*   *d* uinculatos *D Fx H T Y* *e* incarcerebant *T*   *f* Iterum *Fx L Y*   *g* autem *H*   *h* et *add. T* *i* om. *H*   *j* a tergo *om. C*   *k* tantum *D*   *l* quousque *C Fx (corr. to* quousque) *L Y*   *m* per *D T*

---

[68] V breaks off here at the end of a gathering. A modern hand directs readers to another

they prevented the bishop's men[68] from approaching the walls by making frequent sallies.

Secretly William Cumin sent to the earl of Richmond,[69] promising him much money if he would come with an army and remove the bishop and his men. The bishop, however, had advance information of this and, although resistance seemed possible, he withdrew with his men to Bishopton so that his holy cause should not be seen to be stained with the shedding of blood. The men who were with William Cumin followed him, and those at the end of the bishop's column whom they were able to capture they mercilessly slaughtered. Others they mutilated by cutting off their limbs; others they stripped of their possessions and flung into prison. A few, whom they thought unworthy of their swords, they ransomed. Meanwhile, Cumin ejected from the cathedral certain of the monks whom he believed to be opposed to his cause. Then his savagery increased from day to day, and his cruelty knew no moderation. His soldiers went out assiduously and ranged over the whole region, plundering whatever they found, and never ceasing day and night from their harrying. Whatever they found as they passed they destroyed or burned, trampling under their hooves whatever was growing in the fields, and killing animals at pasture. Wherever they went, they made cultivated land seem sterile and unsightly like a desert. Just as we see a wood stripped of its flowers and leaves after the passage of locusts, so after they had passed through they left behind them desolation. Any men he heard to be damned and renowned for evil he enrolled in his party, and there was rivalry between them as to who should surpass his fellows in evil, and he who was the most cruel was the most popular.

If it is horrifying to hear of the things which they did, it was even more distressing to see them. They did not measure their audacity in plunder and ravaging only, but they went as far as bodily mutilation and torture, not even secretly nor at night, but some men they seized in broad daylight and openly, even dragging away and torturing men of nobler sort. The kinds of torment they inflicted were various and many, and as difficult to explain as they are incredible to hear about. They hung men from the walls of the houses with ropes tied tightly around the middle of their bodies, and great weights of mail or stones

volume in the Cottonian library, presumably T, which has at this point a parallel note referring to an imperfect copy in the same library.

[69] Alan of Brittany, earl of Richmond (1136–46).

corporis funibus coartatis, et collo atque pedibus immensis lori-
carum siue saxorum ponderibus alligatis;[a] pars utraque corporis
terre comprimebatur, neque tamen terram pressa tangebat. In huius
autem pena suspensi plures quam duodecim simul uisi sunt. Alios
autem alio stricto, per gelu fluminis alueo tempore hiemali dirupta
glacie cruciandos frigore[b] in aquam precipitauere,[c] et subinde
funibus extrahentes atque sepius immergentes, tante crudelitatis
spectaculo diros pascebant obtutus. Quorundam quoque per
medium parietis pedes emittentes, nudosque frigoribus nimiis[d]
opponebant, et interdum nocte tota sic cruciando relinquebant. Ad
hec accedebat genus illud supplicii exquisitum, quo simul compressa
in arctissimi loculi spatio membra collidebant; ubi supplicii antiquum genus noua transmutauit[e] crudelitas. Quomodo enim distensa
per eculeum crescebant olim membra ad supplicium, sic modo e
contra in se coartata minorabantur, et aliquando confracta interius
rumpebantur. Super hoc autem uinculorum immanitatem, carceris
feditatem, famis enormitatem quis explicare sufficiat? Sed ut multa
paucis absoluam, ubique per oppidum gemitus erat et plurima
mortis imago. Talibus quidem tormentorum generibus locus
semper honori habitus omnibus erat horrori,[f] et infernus quidem[g]
suppliciorum uocabatur.

Episcopus autem post festum Sancti Michaelis[70] propius Dunel-
mum accessit, et edificata ab hiis qui cum eo erant munitione in loco
qui Thornlaw[h] dicitur, ubi[i] commode[j] poterat, cum inopia uictitabat.
Verum in tantis malis cum extrema uastitas totius prouincie metuer-
etur, ad festum Sancti Andree per Eustachium filium Iohannis[71] et
Stephanum de Menyll[72] atque barones episcopatus treuge pacis cum
Willelmo composite sunt usque octauas Epiphanie;[73] promisitque
Willelmus malorum emendationem, sed fallaciter,[k] ut post patuit.
Satis enim demonstratus est in illum pro tempore meliora[l] simulasse;
quippe consumptis circumquaque, et quasi corrosis amaris eius
morsibus, que dare possent uel crudelitati eius materiam uel cupiditati predam; quatenus [m]forte si qui[m] tunc effugissent eius malitie
fauces, postmodum et liberius raperentur ad penas. Sacris autem

---

[a] illigatis *D H T*   [b] miseros *add. D Fx H T Y*   [c] precipitare *H*
[d] niueis *Fx*   [e] transmutabat *T*   [f] horror *Fx (corr. in marg.) H L Y*
[g] quidam *D Fx H L Y*   [h] Thornelawe *Fx H L T Y*   [i] ibi *D*
[j] quomodo *D T (corr. to* commode*)*   [k] faciliter *C (replacement leaf)*   [l] om. *T*
[m-m] si qui forte *D H T;* forte qui *Fx L*

attached to their neck and feet, so that both parts of the body were dragged down towards the ground without actually touching it. More than twelve men at a time were seen hung up in this form of torture. Others were tortured by the winter chill of the river, for the ice was broken and they were plunged into the water to be tortured by the cold, being repeatedly and rapidly submerged and withdrawn on ropes, so that the spectacle of such cruelty was dire indeed. As for others, their feet were left bare and protruding through the middle of a wall all night in the extreme cold to endure excruciating suffering. To this was added that exquisite form of torture in which all the members of the body were crushed and ground together in the very narrow space of a box, so that a new cruelty transformed an ancient form of torture. In a similar way limbs used to be stretched out in the torture of the rack, and then compressed and crushed together, so that they were often broken internally. Who is equal to describing the inhumanity of the shackles, the filth of the prison, the enormity of the starvation? To express many things in a few words, there were groans everywhere in the city, and many scenes of death. With torments like this a place accustomed to be held in honour became for all a place of horror, and was called indeed a hell of tortures.

Now after the feast of St Michael[70] the bishop came closer to Durham, and at Thornley, where it could conveniently be managed, the men who were with him built a fortification, where he supported himself in conditions of want. When among all these evils it was to be feared that the whole region would suffer total devastation, through the offices of Eustace fitz John,[71] Stephen of Meinil,[72] and the barons of the bishopric a truce was concluded with William Cumin on the feast of St Andrew to last until the octave of Epiphany.[73] William Cumin promised to make amends for his evil deeds, but he did this deceitfully as became clear afterwards. For he demonstrated clearly that under the circumstances he had only made a pretence of better behaviour towards the bishop. Now indeed he had consumed everything round about, and it was as if with his foul jaws he had gnawed whatever could provide an object for his cruelty or a prey for his greed. Any who had chanced to escape from the jaws of his malice, he later seized all the more easily to inflict sufferings on them. For even

[70] 29 Sept. 1143.

[71] He appears to have changed sides by this time (above, pp. 284–5).

[72] A member of the Yorkshire family of Meinil of Whorlton, who probably held land from the Balliols (Young, *Cumin*, p. 22, citing Offler, *Episcopal Charters*, p. 138).

[73] 30 Nov. 1143–13 Jan. 1144.

diebus Aduentus Domini quietus esse non poterat. Sed ab episcopatu modicum quiescens, in ^abarones uicinos^a atque in comitatum suam transtulit seuitiam, depopulando atque diripiendo omnia quecunque suos mittebat, et homines ad tormenta capiendo. Nocte quidem festiuitatis sancti Thome apostoli[74] Vmfridum de Thorp[75] in ^bdomo propria^b capiens, Dunelmum abduxit, et ad redemptionem posuit. Infra ^coctauum uero diem Natalis Dominici^c[76] in terra Bernardi de Bailol etiam strage hominum^d facta, ^emultam predam^e Dunelmum aduexit, et homines quos uiuos ceperat uariis tormentis affecit.

Infra terminum uero positarum treugarum uenit archiepiscopus Eboracensis[77] Dunelmum, et cum Willelmo agere cepit, quatinus se rebus deponeret et ^fad malorum^f penitudinem^g ueniret. Sperabatur-que tunc per archiepiscopum id effici posse, promittente Willelmo se consilium eius in omnibus secuturum. Reuerso autem de Eboraco episcopo, quo primum treugis positis abierat, ad colloquium utror-umque episcoporum extra oppidum Willelmus uenit. Presente quoque episcopo Carloliensi,[78] tandem per archiepiscopum treugas firme pacis dedit, et alterutrum accepit a baronibus episcopi, usque Sancti Iohannis Baptiste Natiuitatem;[79] ipse in castello^h interim mansurus, donec ad apostolicum mitteret episcopus, consilium de totaⁱ re quesiturus quid fieri oporteret. Interim haberet Willelmus tertiam partem de redditibus episcopatus inter Teysam et Tynam; ipso Willelmo palam reddente episcopo quicquid eius^j iuris esse deberet, infra burgum et extra, et quicquid ipse tenebat de episcopatu preter castellum. Hec conuentio per archiepiscopum firmata est, et a Willelmo atque baronibus episcopi utrimque^k affidata est teneri.

[xcvi (cv)] 8. Secessit^l autem episcopus exinde inchoante Quadragesima[80] in Northumbriam, relicto super negotia sua ^min episcopatu^m Hugone filio Pintonis dapifero suo;[81] et per totam Quadragesimam his que

---

^{a–a} uicinos barones *D H T*   ^{b–b} propria domo *T*   ^{c–c} uero octauum diem Dominici *T*   ^d om. *H*   ^{e–e} predam multam *H T*   ^{f–f} ad om. *H L;* malorum ad *Fx (corr. to* ad malorum*) Y*   ^g plenitudinem *L*   ^h castellum *Fx L Y*   ⁱ tanta *Fx H L Y*   ^j ei *Fx L Y*   ^k utrumque *C Y*   ^l De proditione Hugonis Puysun *rubric Fx T Y*; uel filius Pintonis *over line Fx*   ^{m–m} om. *H L Y; over line Fx*

---

[74] 21 Dec. 1143.

[75] Possibly a supporter or a tenant of Roger de Conyers (Young, *Cumin*, p. 35 n. 161).

[76] In C, the replacement leaf ends after *octauum* and the original text resumes (above, n. 66).

in the holy days of the Lord's Advent there was no peace. But for a while he left the bishopric in peace and transferred his savagery to the neighbouring barons and the earldom, ravaging and destroying wherever he sent his men, and capturing men for torture. On the night of the feast of St Thomas the Apostle[74] he captured Humphrey de Thorp[75] in his own home, brought him to Durham, and offered him for ransom. After the octave of Christmas[76] on the land of Bernard of Balliol he killed many men, and brought much plunder back to Durham; and those men whom he had captured alive he tortured in various ways.

After the end of the truce the Archbishop of York[77] came to Durham and began negotiate with William Cumin, urging him to withdraw from this business and to repent of his crimes. There were hopes that this could be achieved through the archbishop, for William Cumin promised to follow his counsel in everything. When Bishop William returned from York, where he had gone as soon as the truce was in place, William Cumin came to a meeting of both bishops outside the city. In the presence also of the bishop of Carlisle,[78] and through the archbishop's mediation, he conceded a truce until the Nativity of St John the Baptist, and he received the same in return from the bishop's barons.[79] Meanwhile he was to remain in the castle until the bishop should send to the pope to seek advice as to what should be done about the whole business. William Cumin was in the interim to have one third of the income of the bishopric between Tees and Tyne, and was to render publicly to Bishop William all the judicial rights which pertained to him, inside and outside the borough, and whatever he held of the bishopric apart from the castle. This agreement was confirmed by the archbishop, and on both sides William Cumin and the bishop's barons were sworn to uphold it.

8. The bishop went to Northumberland at the beginning of Lent,[80] [xcvi (cv)] leaving in charge of the affairs of his bishopric his steward, Hugh fitz Pinceon;[81] and for the whole of Lent he attended diligently to the

---

[77] William FitzHerbert, archbishop of York (1141–7, 1153–4).

[78] Æthelwulf, bishop of Carlisle (1133–57).

[79] 24 June 1144. The meaning of *alterutrum* is not clear here.

[80] 9 Feb. 1144.

[81] He inherited the office from his father Andreas Pinceon, Ranulf Flambard's steward; he held considerable estates, mostly in Lincolnshire (Aird, *Cuthbert*, pp. 219–20; Young, *Cumin*, p. 23).

fuerant episcopalis officii, tam dedicandis ecclesiis quam cimiteriis consecrandis, atque aliis agendis sollempnibus curiosus*a* inuigilabat. Nactus uero idem Hugo familiaritatem Willelmi, continuo in eum contumeliosus apparuit, qui sibi beneficiorum auctor extiterat, factus domini sui proditor, et perditis quibusque malitie exemplum.

[xcvi (H)] Comitatum*b* iniquitatis a Willelmo capiebat, primo quidem paruum, ampliorem autem proficiscens. Facile quidem mentiri paratus, mirusque fidem adhibere mendacio, et qui fallaciam uirtutem putaret; eaque aduersus dominum benignissimum usus est. Cuius patientia*c* supra quam satis erat expletus, satietatem suam tanquam fera belua in ipsum profudit, et tandem exuens se simulatione alter Trifon apparuit.[82]

Denique *d*reuerso in sua episcopo,*d* et apud Gyruum, que sic uocatur ecclesia, perhendinante, primum fraudibus et dolis eum circumuenire temptabat, omni*e* conatu affectans, quatinus ad loquelam contra Willelmum episcopus*f* iret, ubi certum erat Willelmi episcopi captionem moliri. Cauente autem hoc episcopo, non multo post malitie uenena, que aduersus eum occulte collecta sunt, *g*in apertum*g* effusa patuerunt. Seducto nanque quodam barone episcopi, Aschetino de Wirecestre,[83] et flexo ad hoc ut secum iret Dunelmum, tanquam*h* secum acturum de quibusdam ratiociniis*i* contra Willelmum de pactionibus premissis, aduenientem capi fecit a Willelmo, cum prius manu sua affidiasset nichil aduersi passurum. Et ille quidem uinculatus atque incarceratus est,*j* et tandem*k* *l*redemptionem positus.*l* Non*m* multo post Rodbertum de Amundauere,[84] sicut priorem, Willelmus cepit, ligauit, atque redemit. Deinde, sabbato post Ascensionem Domini,[85] primo mane, ad locum ubi erat episcopus nepos Willelmi, alter Willelmus, cum multa manu aduenit; et insultum faciens ad murum quo cingebatur ecclesia, hostiliter*n* ingressum moliebatur, ut episcopum cum suis captiuum abduceret. Pauci uero qui intus erant, nam plures in uilla sopori adhuc dediti erant, quoquo modo potuerunt se defendentes introitum inpugnantibus uetabant. Sed protegente

---

a curiosius *Fx H L Y*   *b* De prodicione Hugonis Pincun *rubric H*
c potentia *T*   *d-d* episcopo in sua reuerso *T*   *e* cum *Fx (corr. in marg.) L Y*
f om. *Fx (add. in marg.) L Y*   *g-g* aperte *Fx (corr. in marg.) L Y*   *h* om. *H;*
over line Y   *i* rationationibus *H*   *j* om. *H*   *k* ad *add. C (in marg.) Y*
l-l redemptioni positus *Fx H L Y*   *m* Nam *T*   *n* hostialiter *C*

---

[82] Tryphon was a usurper in the Seleucid Kingdom around 139 BC, who is referred to in
1 Macc. 14: 1.

things which pertain to the bishop's office, dedicating churches, consecrating churchyards, and carrying out other rites. Hugh, however, developed a familiarity with William Cumin, and at once he appeared contumacious to the one who had granted him benefices. In short he became a traitor to his lord, and a pattern of evil for depraved men. Companionship in iniquity he took from William, [xcvi (H)] small-scale at first, but progressing to become larger. He was prepared to lie easily, and he was remarkable in giving good faith to his falsehood. He regarded deceit as a virtue, and he made use of it against a lord who was so kind to him. When he had tried his lord's patience beyond all moderation, he discharged his excrement on himself like a wild beast, and at length stripped himself of his pretence and appeared like another Tryphon.[82]

So when the bishop had returned to his own estates and was staying at the church of Jarrow, Hugh first attempted to ensnare him with fraud and trickery, trying with all his might to persuade the bishop to go and make a speech against William Cumin, where the latter might with certainty effect his capture. The bishop, however, was on his guard against this, and not long afterwards the venom of malice, which had been secretly collected against him, was poured out openly. For he seduced one of the bishop's barons, Aschetin of Worcester,[83] and persuaded him to go with him to Durham, on the pretence that he would take action with him on various grounds against William Cumin relating to the pacts previously established; but when Aschetin arrived he had him captured by Cumin, even though he had before this personally sworn that nothing would happen to him. Chained and imprisoned, he was eventually put up for ransom. Not long afterwards Robert of Amundeville[84] was captured in the same way by William, bound, and ransomed. Then on the Sunday after Our Lord's Ascension,[85] first thing in the morning, William Cumin's nephew, who was also called William, came with a strong force to the place where the bishop was staying, shouted insults at the wall around the church, and tried to break in so that he and his men might take the bishop away captive. The few who were inside, for many were still asleep in the vill, tried as best they could to defend themselves and to deny entrance to the attackers.

---

[83] He had accounted for the farm of the bishop's Yorkshire manors in 1129–30, and had interests at Trimdon and Langdale in Co. Durham (Young, *Cumin*, p. 23).

[84] Holder of five fees of St Cuthbert's domain (Offler, *Charters*, p. 77).

[85] 7 May 1144.

Deo, cum a primo mane impugnantes usque[a] tertiam diei horam omni nisu institissent, spe frustrati in semet redierunt; spoliisque ablatis que ceperant extra murum, et equis abductis, Dunelmum reuersi sunt.

Episcopus autem opportunum sibi non esse uidens citra Tinam manere, uigilia Pentecosten[86] flumine transmeato, non multo post ad Lindisfarneam insulam perhendinaturus perrexit. Hugo filius Pintonis castellum de Tornlauu Willelmo prodidit, pactis inter eos firmatis de filia ipsius Hugonis cuidam nepoti Willelmi coniugio copulanda. Episcopus autem in comite [b]de Northumbria[b] spem habebat, qui et[c] scripto ei atque pacto firmauerat auxilio ei fore contra Willelmum, ut sedem intrare posset. Verum Willelmus, tempus redimens, comitem eludebat, treugas pacis cum eo componens usque post Assumptionem Sancte Marie.[87]

[xcvii] (cvi)] 9. Pridie[d] uero ante predictam festiuitatem Willelmus, coadunatis omnibus suis apud capellam[e] quandam Sancti Iohannis, de ipsa ecclesia castellum munire cepit, distante a Dunelmo eodem loco quasi lewgis quinque;[88] et operi quidem instanter instabat. Tres uero barones episcopi, Rogerus scilicet[f] de Coineriis, Gaufridus Escolland,[89] et Bertram de Bulemer,[90] sacrilegio cognito et profanatione diffamata,[g] eligentes magis pro sacris mori quam Dei iniurias non ultum inpergere, quanta potuerunt manu congregata, ad locum accesserunt, ut nefario operi impedimentum afferrent. Sed non eos sustinuerunt Willelmi adiutores. Quidam fuge se dederunt; alii uero se in ecclesia, que iam fossata propemodum tota cincta fuerat, se concluserunt; et super turrim stantes atque propugnacula[h] que fecerant, accedentes sagitando atque iaculando auertere conabantur, sed inaniter. Nam qui oppugnabant, neque quid paterentur[i] meditantes, nec quid pati possent metientes,[j] quidam eorum statim per fenestras irrepti,[k] alii super prophanos ignes immittentes, quoniam rei necessitas ita poscebat, citius quam sperabatur locum et sacrilegos

---

[a] ad *add. Fx H L Y*   [b–b] Northumbrie *Fx L Y*   [c] *om. Fx L Y*
[d] Castellum factum est de ecclesia Sancti Iohannis apud Merington *rubric H;* Quod castellum factum est de ecclesia Sancti Iohannis apud Meringtona, et de uindicta eorum qui hoc fecerunt *rubric Fx T Y*   [e] *om. Fx L Y*   [f] *om. Fx L Y*
[g] defamata *Fx L Y*   [h] per pugnacula *H;* per propugnacula *C D T (above line)*
[i] peterentur *H*   [j] nescientes *Fx L Y*   [k] erepti *Fx H L Y*

---

[86] 13 May 1144.
[87] 15 Aug. 1144.

Although the latter persisted from first thing in the morning until the third hour of the day with all their might, through the protection of God their hopes were frustrated and they withdrew. They took the spoils they had seized from outside the wall and also the horses, and they returned to Durham.

The bishop, however, seeing that it was not sensible for him to remain south of the Tyne, crossed the river on the vigil of Pentecost,[86] and soon afterwards reached Lindisfarne where he stayed. Hugh fitz Pinceon betrayed the castle of Thornley to William Cumin, a pact having been made between them that Hugh's daughter should be married to a certain nephew of William's. The bishop meanwhile placed his hope in the earl of Northumberland, to whom he had written and who had confirmed a pact with him that he would help him to regain his see against William Cumin. But the latter, buying time, deceived the earl and made a truce with him until the Assumption of St Mary.[87]

9. On the day before the aforesaid feast William gathered together all his men at a certain chapel of St John, and began to fortify it as a castle, the place being about five leagues from Durham,[88] and he was very assiduous in this task. Three of the bishop's barons, namely Roger de Conyers, Geoffrey Escolland,[89] and Bertram de Bulmer,[90] learning of this sacrilege and hearing rumours of the profanation, chose rather to die for the holy things than not to avenge injuries against God. So they assembled as strong a force as they could and advanced on the place, so that they might put a stop to the nefarious work. But William Cumin's helpers did not hold out against them. Some fled, and others shut themselves in the church, which was now almost entirely surrounded by a moat, and stood on the tower and the bulwarks which they had constructed, attempting in vain to turn back the attackers with spears and arrows. For the attackers were neither thinking of nor calculating what they might suffer. Some of them at once crawled in through the windows, others sending fire down on to the profane ones—as necessity demanded—captured both the place and the sacrilegious ones sooner than they could have hoped. Many

[xcvii (cvi)]

---

[88] Merrington (Co. Durham; NZ 262 315); see Arnold, *Sym. Op.* ii. 316, and Young, *Cumin*, p. 24.

[89] Lord of Seaham (Co. Durham), and possibly keeper of the temporalities of the bishopric after Ranulf Flambard's death (above, n. 25; Young, *Cumin* p. 24 and n. 171).

[90] He held an estate of five fees centred on Brancepeth (Co. Durham; NZ 223 377) (Young, *Cumin*, p. 24, Aird, *Cuthbert*, p. 215).

capiunt. Eorum uero*a* *b*flammis exusti sunt,*b* plures quoque captione abducti, Deo illis dignam reddente mercedem. Contigerat autem nepotem Willelmi, alterum Willelmum, prima die incepti operis illius infirmitate obprimi, siue hoc euentus, siue a Deo uindicta estimari debeat. Veruntamen inde sublatus, et nocte*c* Dunelmum delatus ex infirmitate in mentis uesaniam uenit, et aliquandiu misere uexatus expirauit. Quidam quoque cementarius, operi maligno propensius insistens, tempore quo locum ipsum capi contigit, in ipso inuentus opere repente insanire; et eductus a comitibus, antequam Dunelmum ueniret, masticans linguam suam mortuus est.

Congregato interim exercitu comes Henricus,[91] ducens secum episcopum, in prouinciam uenit, atque Dunelmum appropinquauit. Interea exeuntes Willelmi comites ignem hospitali apud*d* Sancti Egidii ecclesiam immiserunt, et uillam ad eam pertinentem totam concremauerunt. Partem quoque burgi, que ad monachorum ius pertinebat, igni tradiderunt. E uestigio comitis milites insecuti quod residuum erat*e* burgi incendio consumpserunt. Deinde comes ad Thornelaw cum exercitu uadens, reddentibus ei castellum Willelmi*f* custodibus, nequaquam id episcopo reddere uoluit, sed suos imposuit, qui terram, quam protegere debuerant, depredare ceperunt, et multa in episcopatu dampna fecerunt. Comes autem his actis in se rediit, et episcopus ad Nouum Castellum*g* perrexit. Ad eum locum non multo post rex Scotie uenit, tractus illic*h* a Willelmo, quod ei castellum tradere spoponderat. Veruntamen ad eius colloquium apud Gatesheuet ueniens spe frustratum reliquit; rediensque*i* Dunelmum, cum Rogero de Coyneriis pactiones*j* componere cepit.

[xcviii (cvii)] **10.** Quibus*k* tandem eo usque peruentum est, ut episcopus, non tam pactis credens quam a suis coactus, et multorum extrema necessitate compulsus, uersus Dunelmum ire perrexerit.*l* Iam*m* cum suis Rogerus de Coinneriis oppidum habebat, et Willelmus in monachorum curia episcopum expectabat.[92] Sic igitur*n* inopinabiliter rebus mutatis, episcopus in die festiuitatis Sancti Luce euangeliste[93] cum archiepiscopo Eboracensi et episcopo Carloliense

---

a plures *add. Fx L Y*   *b–b* exusti sunt flammis *Fx L Y*   *c* nocte tamen *T*
d om. *Fx L Y*   *e* ueteres *add. Fx above line*   *f* om. *T*   *g* Castrum *Fx*
h illuc *Fx L Y*   *i* rediens et *L Y*   *j* pactionem *H L Y*   *k* Willelmus de Sancta Barbara (Barba *T)* receptus est ad episcopatum Dunhelmie *rubric Fx T Y*   *l* perrexit *Fx L Y*   *m* Willelmus de Barbara receptus est in pace ad episcopatum Dunelmie *rubric H*   *n* om. *Fx (add. in marg.) L Y*

---

[91] Henry of Scotland, earl of Northumberland (1139–52).

were burned by the flames lighted by their attackers, many were led
away captive, and thus God rendered to them all their just reward. It
so happened that William Cumin's nephew, the other William, was
stricken by illness on the first day that that work was begun, and the
reader should judge whether this was an accident or the vengeance of
God. He was lifted up and taken by night to Durham, where his illness
changed into madness, and after a considerable while he died in great
distress. Also, when the place was captured, a certain mason, who had
been assiduous in this evil work, was found to have suddenly gone
mad while engaged on it. His companions set out to lead him to
Durham, but before he reached the city he bit out his tongue and died.

Earl Henry[91] now assembled an army, and bringing the bishop with
him he entered the province and approached Durham. Meanwhile
William Cumin's men came out and set fire to the hospital by the
church of St Giles, and burned down the whole of the vill attached to
it. They also committed to the flames part of the borough which was
under the jurisdiction of the monks. At once the earl's soldiers
followed after and destroyed what remained of the borough by fire.
Then the earl came with his army to Thornley, and William's
garrison handed over the castle to him; but he absolutely would not
return it to the bishop, entrusting it rather to his own men, who
began to ravage the land they were supposed to protect and to do
much damage to the bishopric. After all this had been done, the earl
withdrew to his own lands and the bishop travelled to Newcastle.
Soon afterwards the king of Scotland arrived there, persuaded to
come by William Cumin, because he had promised to hand over the
castle to him. But when he attended a meeting with him at Gateshead,
his hopes were frustrated and he returned to Durham to begin
drawing up pacts with Roger de Conyers.

10. So at length it came to this, that the bishop, not so much   [xcviii
believing in the pacts as forced to it by his men, and compelled by (cvii)]
extreme necessity, went towards Durham. Roger de Conyers was
then holding the city with his men, and William was waiting for the
bishop in the monks' precinct.[92] Thus the tables were unexpectedly
turned, and the bishop entered Durham with the Archbishop of York
and the Bishop of Carlisle on the feast of St Luke.[93] William Cumin

---

[92] The variant section of the Continuation in Ca (below, pp. 320–1) mentions the
surrender of Durham Castle to Roger de Conyers.
[93] 18 Oct. 1144.

Dunelmum intrauit. Cuius prostratus pedibus Willelmus, cum interrogante episcopo palam confiteretur nichil sibi aut*a* in pecunia aut in rebus aliis episcopum promisisse, sed de male actis quidem se penitere, gratis uero se castellum et omnia sua *b*episcopo dimittere,*b* ideoque se nudum ad ipsius pedes, et paratum ad satisfactionem de omnibus humiliter offerre. Ab episcopis, quantum ad eos pertinere poterat, salua reuerentia *c*domini apostolici,*d* ad initium penitentie susceptus est.*c* *e*Sacramento autem facto*e* coram ipsis episcopis, omnia que fecerat dampna singulis se redditurum promisit.[94]

Et sic post tam longum exilium, post tot uexationes, post multorum tam multa detrimenta, operante Deo consolationem suorum, in sede sua episcopus sollempniter *f*susceptus est.*f*

[Variant section of the Continuation beginning 'Tribus dehinc annis' found only in Ca (above, p. xxv, item 5)]

Eo igitur mortuo, ab eisdem extorsit, ut episcopus celaretur donec cum rege Scotie loqueretur, ut ipsius adiumento episcopatum acquireret. Proinde, quia cadauer aliter teneri non potuit, euisceratus est a suis episcopus, et a monachis absconditus, ne rem cogoscerent, a tertia feria usque ad sextam feriam. Tunc enim eodem a curia reuerso, prior et monachi admittuntur, castello iam ad uoluntatem ipsius disposito.[95]

Erat eo tempore maxima regni turbatio. Siquidem rex Stephanus dum comitem Cestrie in Lincolnia obsideret, idem comes furtim egreditur, et sociato sibi comite Gloecestrie ceterisque imperatricis fautoribus, ad urbem regreditur, ubi inter eos prelio facto rex milite

---

a uel L *b–b* dimittere episcopo T *c–c* domni pape humiliter penitenciam malefactorum suorum ab ipsis recepit Fx L Y (text as in C add. in marg. Fx L Y, in L by William Claxton) *d* pape H *e–e* Facto autem sacramento H *f–f* est susceptus H

---

[94] On Cumin's subsequent career, during which he was patronized by Theobald,

prostrated himself at his feet and, asked by the bishop, he openly
confessed that the bishop had never been promised anything either in
money or kind, but that he repented of his evil actions, that he would
freely hand over the castle and all his possessions to the bishop, and
therefore he lay naked at the bishop's feet, ready to make amends in
all humility. He was received into the first stages of penance by the
bishops, as far as they were able, saving the reverence of the lord
pope. He swore an oath in the presence of these bishops that he would
compensate everyone for the harm he had done.[94]

And thus after so a long an exile, after so many vexations, after
harm had been done to so many people, with God giving consolation
to his faithful, the bishop was solemnly received in his see.

[Variant section of the Continuation beginning 'Tribus dehinc annis' found only in Ca]

After the bishop's death, William Cumin extorted from them
[Bishop Geoffrey's household, clerks, and keepers of the castle] an
undertaking that the bishop's corpse would be concealed until he had
spoken with the king of Scots, so that he might obtain the bishopric
with the latter's help. So, because the corpse could not be kept in any
other way, the bishop's attendants disembowelled it and, lest they
should get to know of the bishop's death, it was hidden from the
monks from the Wednesday to the Saturday. Then when William
Cumin had returned from the court, the prior and monks were
admitted, the castle having by then been placed under his control.[95]

At that time there was a great disturbance in the kingdom. For
while King Stephen was besieging the earl of Chester in Lincoln, the
earl secretly escaped. He allied with the earl of Gloucester and other
supporters of the empress and returned to the city. In the ensuing

archbishop of Canterbury (1138–61), and regained some of his benefices in England, see
Arnold, *Sym. Op.* ii. 317, and Young, *Cumin*, pp. 26–7.
[95] By the bishop's nephew (below, pp. 316–17).

destitutus capitur, non tamen absque detrimento capientium. Erat siquidem robustus uiribus, et rebus bellicis eo tempore incomparabilis.[96] Eo igitur incarcerato, imperatrix (regis Henrici filia) cum magno fauore a Lundoniensibus excipitur. Quo comperto, rex Scotie Dauid ad curiam eiusdem proficiscitur, secum cancellarium suum ducens, qui precio ab eodem exegerat, ut eius causa erga imperatricem ageret. Iamque se Dunelmensem electum uocari uolebat, quod facile adulatoribus undecunque concurrentibus persuasum est. Denique in curia iam constitutus, tam a rege Scotie quam ceteris mediantibus tandem in assensum imperatrix inducitur. Factoque consensu, cum iamiamque se baculo episcopali ab imperatrice inuestiendum speraret, in ipsa curie coadunatione subito turba exoritur a regiis commota fautoribus, et imperatrix cum suis omnibus aufugit, Lundoniensium conspiratione comperta. Nec multo post, cum imperatrix Wintonie moraretur, ibidem a gente Lundoniensium obsidetur, qui reginam euocauerant, et ei Lundoniam tradiderant. Illic congressione facta a baronibus hinc inde pro partis utriusque fauore confluentibus, Rodbertus comes Gloecestrie capitur,[97] rex Scotie fugatur, ceteri quique huc illucque disperguntur. Hac uero captione contigit ut rex liber dimitteretur.

Rege Scotie repatriante, cancellarius predictus Dunelmi remansit per tres annos, quibus uacabat episcopatus, operibus pretendens quo respectu episcopatum desiderauit, nisi quantum eum spes honoris adipiscendi refrenabat. Multa in episcopatu cupiditatis, immo crudelitatis signa reliquit. Monachis tamen iocundus semper et affabilis erat, a quibus se promouendum sperabat. Sed eum sua spes fefellit. Secundo siquidem anno, ex consilio capituli prior ecclesie Eboracum proficiscitur, communicato primitus consilio, ut quem ipse cum maioribus ecclesie eligeret, ad hunc ceteri domi residentes animum intenderet, excommunicatis primitus ex sententia capituli Willelmi fautoribus.

Deinde uero legati Romam diriguntur, domino pape causam

---

[96] For the battle of Lincoln (1141), see Henry of Huntingdon, *Historia Anglorum*, ed. and trans. Greenway, pp. 724–39. The earl of Chester was Ranulf II (before 1100–53); the earl of Gloucester was Robert, illegitimate son of Henry I, earl of Gloucester (1122–47).

[97] The Empress Matilda was in Winchester to arrest Henry of Blois, bishop of Winchester, who fled to prepare himself for war. It was while Matilda's forces were besieging Henry's castle of Wolvesey in Winchester, that the empress's forces were surrounded. Robert of Gloucester fought a rearguard action at the ford of Stockbridge to allow her to escape; he was captured on 14 Sept. 1141 (Davis, *King Stephen*, pp. 59–60, and Rosalind Hill, 'The battle of Stockbridge 1141', *Studies in Medieval History presented to R. Allen Brown*, ed. Harper-Bill, pp. 173–7).

battle between them the king was deprived of the support of his troops and captured, not however without harm being done to those who captured him. For he was robust and strong, and at that time second to none in matters of warfare.[96] When he had been imprisoned, the empress (King Henry's daughter) was received with great favour by the citizens of London. When he learned of this, the king of Scots, David, travelled to her court, bringing with him his chancellor, who had obtained from him in exchange for money that he would urge his cause with the empress. For now he wanted to be called the elected bishop of Durham, which the admirers who flocked to him from all parts easily persuaded him that he was. Once he was established at the court, the empress was at length induced to assent to this as much by the king of Scots as by other mediators. When agreement had been reached and the chancellor was hoping that the empress would invest him at once with the episcopal staff, in the harmony of the court there arose a sudden uproar brought about by the king's supporters, and the empress and all her party fled, having discovered the conspiracy of the citizens of London. Not long afterwards, while the empress was staying at Winchester, she was besieged there by the citizens of London, who had summoned the queen to them, and had handed London over to her. At that place there was a clash of barons coming together from all parts and supporting both parties, and Robert, earl of Gloucester,[97] was captured, the king of Scots was put to flight, and certain others were scattered hither and thither. Through this capture it came about that the king was allowed to go free.

When the king of Scots returned to his own country, his chancellor remained at Durham for three years, during which time the bishopric was vacant. He showed by his deeds in what respect he desired the bishopric, except in so far as the hope of obtaining the honour held him back. He left many signs in the bishopric of his greed, or rather of his cruelty. He was always cheerful and affable to the monks, through whom he hoped that his cause would be advanced. But he was deceived in this hope. For in the second year, the prior of the church went to York on the advice of the chapter, having resolved with them first of all, that whomever he should elect with the elders of the church, those who stayed at home should fully support, after William's supporters had been excommunicated at the outset by sentence of the chapter.

Next legates were sent to Rome to explain their cause to the lord

indicaturi. A quo accepto eligendi quem uellent precepto, conuenientes in ecclesia Eboracensi, quia in Dunelmensi conuenire non poterant, conuocatis religiosis quibusdam de episcopatu personis, prior et eiusdem ecclesie archidiaconus, cum ceteris eiusdem ecclesie, decanum in episcopum eligunt, anno Dominice Incarnationis millesimo centesimo quadragesimo quarto.[98]

Erat eo tempore dominus Wintoniensis apostolice sedis legatus, cuius ope et consilio maxime innitebantur Dunelmenses contra inuasorem episcopatus. Qui et ab eodem pridem excommunicatus est cum fautoribus suis. Presentatum itaque sibi electum Dunelmensem suscepit honorifice, regemque fratrem suum scilicet ad assensum electionis inclinauit, et comitante gratia eiusdem debito cum honore consecrauit, septem episcopis astantibus, duodecimas Kalendas Iulii.

Consecratus uero Eboracum rediit, et in inuasores ecclesie sue sententiam excommunicationis propalauit. Mox uero quidam de baronibus episcopatus se eidem ut domino subdiderunt. E quibus Rogerus quidam de Coineriis continuo munitionem quandam in episcopatu firmauit, ubi, si opus esset, episcopus reciperetur ad sui suorumque tuitionem. Quo non multo post episcopus a suis uenire compellitur, si forte inuasores ecclesie resipiscere uoluissent. Nec interim uacabant castellani Dunelmenses quin predas ducerent, militibus qui ad episcopum confluebant occurrerent, et ad eum transeuntibus impedimento forent. Si qui uero locupletiores inde coniuncti fuissent, qui ad episcopum suum confugere uoluissent, tormentis continuo afficiebantur, donec se pecuniis redemissent. Fiebat itaque diebus singulis perscrutatio ingens, et quicunque ditior, calumpnie uicinior erat. Conducti enim ab inuasore milites pro libidine cuncta faciebant, et dum cupiditati modis omnibus satisfacere satagunt, pecunias singulorum tormentis et penis exquisitas extorquent. Miseranda tunc erat urbis facies, cum per domos singulas urbis tormenta innumera cerneres, tanquam si diuersorum temporum tiranni quique in unum confluxissent. Cerneres alios eculeis distendi, alios per uerenda sursum trahi, alios thecis paruissimis lapidibus substratis includi et pene quassari; alios uero in hieme ualidissima nudos extra domos uinciri, pedibus infra domos trunco inclusis. Inter hos et ipse qui castellum tradiderat, penis

---

[98] The correct date is 14 Mar. 1143 (above, p. 293 n. 59).

pope. Having received from him a precept allowing them to elect whomever they wished, they called a meeting in the church of York, because they could not do so in Durham, summoning to it certain religious persons from the bishopric, and the prior and the arch-deacon of the church of Durham, with others of that church. There they elected the dean [of York] to be bishop in the year of Our Lord's incarnation 1144.[98]

At that time, the Bishop of Winchester was the legate of the apostolic see, and the church of Durham relied heavily on his power and his advice in resisting him who had invaded the bishopric. First of all the legate excommunicated him along with his supporters. Then when the elected bishop of Durham was presented to him he received him with honour, and influenced his brother the king to assent to his election. Fortified with the king's favour, he consecrated him with the necessary honour in the presence of seven bishops on 20 June.

After his consecration he returned to York, and imposed a sentence of excommunication on those who had invaded his church. Soon indeed some of the barons of the bishopric submitted to him as their lord. One of them, a certain Roger de Conyers, at once established a fortification in the bishopric, where the bishop could be received, if necessary, for the safety of himself and his entourage. Not long afterwards the bishop was compelled by his supporters to come there, to see if the invaders of the church would come to their senses. Meanwhile those guarding Durham castle were not idle but rather engaged in plunder, and they confronted those knights who were flocking to the bishop, and hindered those people who were travelling to join him. If indeed any of the richer sort were amongst those wishing to flee to their bishop, they would at once torture them, until they paid them money to be released. Every day a great examination was made, and the more wealthy anyone was, the more likely they were to be maliciously accused. The knights under the command of the invader did everything according to their desires, and, while they were fully occupied satisfying in every way their cupidity, they extorted money from individuals by torments and punishments. Pitiable was the appearance of the city, when you might have seen innumerable scenes of torture in the various houses, as if the tyrants of all ages had all come together in one. Some were to be seen being stretched out on racks, others being dragged upwards by their genitals, others shut up in tiny chests placed under stones and almost battered to pieces, others indeed in the depth of winter bound naked outside their homes, with their feet and the trunks of their bodies under their houses. Amongst them was the bishop's

immanissimis ab eodem extinctus est, nepos scilicet episcopi, debitum sancto Cuthberto persoluens supplicium, qui inuasorem ipsius ecclesie infra castellum ad ipsius ecclesie detrimentum recepit.

Adiecit et hec inuasoris impietas, ut quoscunque monachos erga episcopum beniuolentiores ab ecclesia remoueret. Quod ex huiusmodi cepit occasione. Confluentibus enim ad episcopum undecunque militibus, siue spe lucri seu etiam ipsius episcopi exortationibus et reuerentia honestatis illius et religionis, erat enim et religione precipuus et precellens prudentia, a baronibus totius episcopatus inuitus compellitur uires experiri confluentium, si forte uel terrore humano cederet, qui diuino dedignabatur cedere. Subito igitur Dunelmi, astantes cum militum ualida manu, in proximo Dunelmi municipium firmare statuunt, unde cominus hostibus infra urbem constitutis congrederentur. Quod nec perficeretur, impedimento fuit comes de Richemund, qui mercede conductus ab ecclesie inuasore, egit nuntiis clandestinis ut episcopus abcederet: alioquin se superuenturum minabatur. Cessit episcopus, quia ei uires ad resistendum comiti non suppeterent, et alibi munitio a suis firmata est sexto ab urbe miliario. Vbi militibus congregatis per aliquantum temporis resedit, militibus cotidie ad urbem recurrentibus, et uires hostium infirmare certantibus. Nec multum proficere poterant, militibus Dunelmensibus occurrentibus, et satis superque strenue agentibus, qui quocunque diuertissent, uel superiores uel pares existebant.

Perseuerauit hec rerum turbatio inter episcopum Dunelmensem et episcopatus inuasorem per annum integrum et menses quatuor. Quibus completis, cum iam uirtus deficeret humana, nec spes aduersarios subigendi restaret, nisi ope et auxilio diuino, subito ostensione diuini miraculi terrentur aduersarii, unde sue uite metu et diuine terroris animaduersionis inuasa relinquere compelluntur. Dum enim, prioribus facinoribus noua cumulantes, super ecclesiam in honorem beati Iohannis euangeliste fabricatam castellum ad munimentum partis sue firmare satagunt, subito nepos eiusdem miles egregie uirtutis, in ipsa operis inchoatione, ultione diuina imminente et beati euangeliste, infirmitate correptus uix ad urbem

nephew who had handed over the castle. He was killed with unthinkable sufferings by the invader, and so he paid the penalty to St Cuthbert, for having received the invader of his church into the castle, to the detriment of the church itself.

This too was added to the impiousness of the invader, that he removed from the church whichever of the monks were the more well disposed towards the bishop. This happened in the following way. Knights assembled from all parts to support the bishop, either because they hoped for reward, or they were attracted by the exhortations of the bishop and by his reverend honesty and piety, for he was outstanding in his religious observance and distinguished for his prudence. Although he was unwilling, he was compelled by the barons of the whole bishopric to put to the test the strength of those rallying to him, to see whether the invader would cede to fear of human intervention, where he disdained to cede to fear of divine intervention. The Durham party therefore unexpectedly decided to take a stand with a strong force of troops and to establish a fortification near Durham, from which they could engage their enemies, who were established in the city, in close combat. They did not achieve this because they were prevented by the earl of Richmond, who was bribed by the invader of the church so that he intervened by secret messengers to cause the bishop to withdraw, threatening otherwise to come himself. The bishop gave in, because he did not have the forces at his disposal to resist the earl, and a fortification was established by his men at another place six miles from the city. There his troops were installed for some time, with soldiers going to the city everyday, and attempting to weaken their enemies' strength. They were not able to achieve much, for the troops from Durham came out to meet them and fought with more than sufficient strenuousness, so that wherever they went they found superior or at least equal forces confronting them.

This conflict between the bishop of Durham and the invader of the bishopric lasted for a whole year and four months. At the end of this time, when human strength was failing, and there was no longer hope of overcoming their enemies unless by the support and help of God, those enemies were unexpectedly terrified by the working of a divine miracle, as a result of which they were compelled to give up what they had invaded for fear of their lives and for terror of God's wrath. For when, adding fresh crimes to those formerly committed, they endeavoured to construct for the defence of their party a castle out of a church built in honour of St John the Evangelist, the invader's nephew, a distinguished knight, was at the very beginning of this work suddenly stricken with illness by the action of God's vengeance

reuertitur, ubi demonio traditus uexari cepit, quousque animam miserabiliter exhalaret. Alter etiam nepos eius iam pridem infirmitate subitanea diem clauserat ultimum. Nec multo post milites quique totius episcopatus cum baronibus congregati castellum illud quod super ecclesiam firmatum erat obsident: nec multo post, iniecto igne, obsessos quosdam igne conflagrarunt, quosdam ad deditionem compulerunt. Multi preterea ipsi inuasori familiarius adherentes, subitis intercepti casibus, utraque morte preuenti sunt. Ex his uero qui ecclesiam sancti Cuthberti uiolauerunt, pene nullus euasit, quin infra breue terminum pacis uiolate debitas sibi penas persoluerent.

Ecclesiam enim hac occasione uiolari contigit. Cum maiores totius episcopii, ipsum secum ducentes episcopum, urbi sicut premisimus uicinaretur, ut in proximo municipium facerent ad urbis obsidionem, quia ecclesia supra uallum*a* qua urbs cingitur collocata uidetur, metuentes ne forte clanculo milites in ecclesiam admitterentur, utpote monachis episcopo suo fauentibus, primo per alios monachos conuenit, ut suos in ecclesia custodes admitterent. Sed hoc monachis durissimum uidebatur, excommunicatis ecclesie delegare custodiam. Proinde se infra ecclesiam recipientes ualuas ecclesie claudunt, excommunicatis introitum interdicentes ecclesie, ipsi uero in oratione prosternuntur. Cum ecce sonitus aures eorum pulsat, militibus ianuas excidentibus. Alii uero, per scalas adeuntes fenestras, effractis fenestris introeunt, et ualuas sociis aperiunt. Deinde ecclesia duobus militibus ab ipso uiolatore committitur, monachis se infra officinas proprias cohibentibus, nec in ecclesia uel psallere presumentibus uel orare, propter excommunicatorum presentiam. Miseranda prorsus et deflenda rerum facies, ecclesiam illam celeberrimam in solitudinis uastitatem redactam, ut nec orandi monachis locus pateret, sed illius desolationem representaret, de qua scriptura commemorat: 'Et Ierusalem non inhabitatur, sed erat sicut deserta, nec erat qui ingrederetur et egrederetur de natis eius.'[99] Perseruerauit hec desolatio anno uno et ebdomadibus septem.

Denique, sinistris suorum euentibus territus, inuasor ecclesie cepit occasionem querere iram potius diuinam euadere, quam ecclesie

---

a uallem *Ca*

---

[99] 1 Macc. 3: 45.

and that of the blessed evangelist. Hardly had he been taken back to the city when he was delivered up to be tormented by a demon, until he breathed his last in misery. Another nephew of the invader had previously died from a sudden illness. Not long after this all the knights of the whole bishopric mustered with the barons and besieged the castle which had been constructed on that church. Soon they were able to set fire to it so that some of the besieged were burned in the fire, some were compelled to surrender. Meanwhile many of the closest adherents of the invader fell victim to various calamities, and were overtaken by death on all sides. Indeed, of those who profaned the cathedral of St Cuthbert, virtually none escaped, but rather they paid within a short term the penalty for the peace which they had violated.

The cathedral came to be profaned in the following circumstances. When, as we have described, the senior men of the whole bishopric came near the city leading the bishop with them, with the intention of constructing a fortification nearby from which to besiege the city, the enemies in the city feared that, because the cathedral was built above the rampart surrounding the city, it might happen that troops would be admitted secretly into the cathedral, seeing that the monks favoured the bishop. They therefore agreed first with some monks that their guards should be allowed into the cathedral. It appeared very hard to the monks, however, that the custody of the cathedral should be handed over to excommunicates. They therefore withdrew into the cathedral and shut the doors, denying entrance to the excommunicates, and prostrating themselves in prayer. Then a great noise assailed their ears as the soldiers broke down the doors. Indeed, some came in through the windows by means of ladders, breaking the windows so that they could get in and then opening the doors for their comrades. After that the profaner himself committed the cathedral to two knights. The monks kept themselves within their domestic buildings, and did not presume to sing psalms or to pray in the cathedral on account of the presence of excommunicates there. Everything seemed miserable and lamentable, with that most celebrated cathedral reduced to a desolation of solitude, so that it was not open to the prayers of the monks, but rather it represented that desolation of which it is written in the scriptures: 'Jerusalem was not inhabited, but was like a desert, and none of her sons either came in or went out.'[99] This desolation lasted for one year and seven weeks.

Then the invader of the church was terrified by the sinister events which befell his people, and he began to look for an opportunity rather to escape the wrath of God than to make amends to the church

quam leserat satisfacere. Veniente itaque in prouinciam illam archiepiscopo Eboracensi, eum mox ille excepit, et castellum cuidam ex baronibus, Rogerio scilicet de Coineriis in fidelitatem sancti Cuthberti seruandum commisit, ipse munitionem, quam dudum, ut premisimus, idem Rogerius firmauerat, ad sui suorumque tutitionem suscipiens. Taliter in sedem suam episcopus admittitur, et in statum pristinum redintegratur ecclesia, anno Dominice Incarnationis millesimo centesimo quadragesimo quarto, secundo anno consecrationis eiusdem episcopi Willelmi secundi.[100]

Nouem deinceps in episcopatu uixit annis, multa in episcopatu aduersa sustinens, tam propter regis Scotie exactiones non iustas, quam propter uicinorum latrocinia, et depredationes non tam crebras quam pene continuas. Ipsius temporibus dormitorium monachorum perfectum est.[101] Vixit in episcopatu annis nouem, mensibus quatuor, diebus quinque. Transiit Idus Decembris, tam annis plenus quam moribus;[102] uir et religione et prudentia plurimum laudabilis, posteris quoque imitabilis, in diuinis rebus a pueritia exercitatus, et ad officium episcopatus sufficienter idoneus; canitie quidem uenerabilis, sobrietate tamen uictus et uite continentia morumque grauitate uenerabilior.

Anno[a] Dominice incarnationis millesimo centesimo quinquagesimo quarto, anno regis Stephani octodecimo, papatus Eugenii nono, aduentus Anglorum in Angliam septingentesimo tertio, indictione prima, epacte uicesimo tertio, concurrentes tres, regularibus quintis, ciclo decennouenali uero quatuordecim, septuagesimo nono die post obitum Willelmi episcopi, undecimas Kalendas Februarii, electus est in episcopum Hugo, Eboracensis ecclesie thesaurarius et archidiaconus, conuenientibus quibusque religiosis personis totius episcopatus in capitulum Dunelmensem.[103] Qui regi Stephano presentatus suscipitur, electione capituli concessa, ordinatio tamen paululum remorata est, zelo domini Eboracensis archiepiscopi tunc Henrici, qui non solum electioni assensum non adhibuit, quin immo sententiam maledictionis in priorem et archidiaconum inconsulte intorsit. Quod tamen, quia et precipitanter et irrationabiliter nimis egerat, in

---

[a] De electione et ordinatione Hugonis episcopi, *rubric Ca*

[100] From this point on the Ca version introduces material not found in any other manuscript.

[101] The original eastern dormitory, over the chapter-house range.

[102] Both the calculation and the date are in error. William was elected on 14 Mar. 1143 and consecrated on 20 June 1143, dying on 14 Nov. 1152.

he had harmed. So when the archbishop of York came into that province, he at once received him, and committed the castle to one of the barons, namely Roger de Conyers, that he might have custody of it in fealty to St Cuthbert. He himself received that fortification which Roger had previously constructed, as we explained, for the protection of himself and his followers. In this way, the bishop was admitted to his bishopric, and the cathedral was restored to its pristine state, in the year of Our Lord's incarnation 1144, the second year of the consecration of Bishop William II.[100]

William was bishop for nine years, and he had to bear many adversities in that office, as much on account of the injust exactions of the king of Scotland, as on account of robberies committed by his neighbours, and of depredations which were not so much frequent as virtually continuous. In his time the monks' dormitory was completed.[101] He was bishop for nine years, four months, and five days. He died on 13 December, as old in years as in virtues.[102] He was a man exceedingly praiseworthy for his piety as well as for his wisdom, who should be imitated by those who come after him. He had been trained in divine things from boyhood, and he was well fitted for the office of bishop. Venerable in the whiteness of his head, he was all the more venerable in the sobriety of his diet, the restraint of his way of life, and the gravity of his manners.

In the year of Our Lord's incarnation 1154, the eighteenth year of King Stephen's reign, the ninth of the papacy of Eugenius, the seven hundred and third from the coming of the English to England, the first indiction, the twenty-third epact, the third concurrence, the fifth solar regular, the fourteenth of the decennovenal cycle, the seventy-ninth day after the death of Bishop William, 22 January, Hugh, treasurer and archdeacon of the church of York, was elected bishop, with religious persons from the whole of the diocese assembling for the purpose in the chapter of Durham.[103] He was presented to and received by King Stephen and the chapter's right of election was conceded; but the ordination was a little delayed by the zeal of the archbishop of York, who was then Henry, who not only declined to assent to the election, but instead ill-advisedly imposed a sentence of malediction on the prior and archdeacon. Because this had been done precipitately and very irrationally, however, it came to nothing. For

---

[103] The correct date is 22 Jan. 1153. For the errors in the dating criteria given here and for the possibility that their elaborateness connects Ca to Puiset himself, see B. Meehan, in Rollason, *Symeon*, p. 135.

irritum cessit; siquidem prior et archidiaconus, dominum papam tunc temporis Anastasium adeuntes, honorifice concessa et confirmata electione suscipiuntur, et ordinato a domino papa episcopo cum gaudio remearunt ad propria.[104]

Nactus episcopatum, ad munitionem sui suorumque castellum super Tuedam fluuium contra Scottorum irruptiones precepto regis edificauit, quod pridem a Ranulpho quondam Dunelmensi episcopo edificatum a Scottorum exercitu destructum fuerat.[105] Plura uero edificia in episcopatu fecit; necnon in ipsa urbe sedis sue, ueteribus destructis, noua et insignia fecit edificia.[106] In ecclesia sane sedis sue, in qua corpus beatissimi Cuthberti[a] requiescit, ornamenta multa dedit ecclesiam quoque insigni opere produxit, et tam longiorem quam clariorem reddidit, addito de longinquo marmore quo totum decoraretur edificium, multiplicatis insigni pictura fenestris uitreis circa altaria. Preterea uero quoddam feretrum nimis speciosum, auro purissimo et argento mundissimo optime fabricatum, lapidibusque pretiosis opere mirifico adornatum construxit, in quo uiri uenerabilis Bede presbiteri et Girwensis monachi ossa, cum multorum aliorum sanctorum reliquiis collocauit.[107]

---

[a] Churberti *Ca*

---

[104] Hugh of le Puiset was consecrated on 21 Dec. 1153 and enthroned on 2 May 1154. For the circumstances, see G. V. Scammell, *Hugh du Puiset, Bishop of Durham* (Oxford, 1956), pp. 12–21.

[105] See references given above, p. 92 n. 33.

[106] These included Elvet Bridge in Durham City, the rebuilt north range of Durham Castle, St Thomas's chapel, Grindon (co. Durham; NZ 395 256), and St Cuthbert's Church, Darlington. See *VCH Durham*, iii. 253; M. Leyland, 'The origins and development of Durham Castle', Rollason, *Anglo-Norman Durham*, pp. 407–24, at pp. 419–21; and J. A. Cunningham, 'Hugh of le Puiset and the church of St Cuthbert, Darlington', *Medieval Art and Architecture at Durham Cathedral*, ed. Draper and Coldstream, pp. 163–9.

the prior and the archdeacon went to the then lord pope Anastasius, who received and honourably allowed and confirmed the election. Ordained by the lord pope, the bishop joyfully returned to his own.[104]

Once in possession of the bishopric, he built by the king's order, for the protection of himself and his men, a castle on the river Tweed against the incursions of the Scots. This castle had originally been erected by Ranulf, formerly bishop of Durham, but it had been destroyed by the army of the Scots.[105] Hugh constructed various buildings in his bishopric, not least in his cathedral city, where he demolished old buildings and built new and distinguished ones.[106] Indeed, he gave many ornaments to his cathedral, itself, where the body of the most blessed Cuthbert rests, and he lengthened the cathedral itself with a distinguished construction, making it longer as well as lighter, bringing marble from distant parts with which the whole edifice was decorated, and increasing the number of windows around the altar which were glazed with distinction with painted glass. In addition, he had a certain very beautiful shrine superbly made of the purest gold and silver and adorned with precious stones set with wonderful workmanship. In this he placed the bones of the venerable Bede, priest and monk of Jarrow, together with the relics of many other saints.[107]

[107] Cf. the more detailed account by Geoffrey of Coldingham (Raine, *Scriptores tres,* p. 11), and see S. A. Harrison, 'Observations on the architecture of the Galilee Chapel', Rollason, *Anglo-Norman Durham,* pp. 213–34; and R. Halsey, 'The Galilee Chapel', *Medieval Art and Architecture at Durham Cathedral,* ed. Draper and Coldstream, pp. 59–73. The south-east door of the cloisters is almost certainly Puiset's work on stylistic grounds; for the possibility that the west towers are also his, see M. G. Jarrett and H. Mason, '"Greater and more splendid": some aspects of Romanesque Durham Cathedral', *Antiquaries Journal,* lxxv (1995), 189–233, at 223–7.

APPENDIX C

Lists of chapter-headings

D Fx H L T Y

Incipivnt capitvla ad inveniendvm qvod volveris in libro seqventi[1]

i. Quod omnes episcopi *ᵃLindisfarnenses siue Dunelmenses*ᵃ a sancto Aydano usque Walkerum*ᵇ* monachi fuerunt preter unum simoniacum Aldredum*ᶜ* nomine.

ii. Sanctus Cuthbertus factus est monachus.

iii. Quod episcopi et abbates simul in una eademque Lindisfarnense ecclesia fuerunt.

iv. Sanctus Beda doctor natus est in territorio Girwensi.

v. Quod unum monasterium erat in Weremutha et Girwa.

vi. A quibus doctoribus eruditus erat Beda.

vii. Quod*ᵈ* Wilfridus episcopus ab episcopatu totius*ᵉ* Northumbrie*ᶠ* expulsus est.

viii. Sanctus Cuthbertus ad episcopatum Hagustaldensem *ᵍest electus.*ᵍ

ix. Commutauerunt sedes Eata et Cuthbertus.

x. *ʰEgfridus rex anno consecracionis sancti Cuthberti occisus est Hʰ*

xi. Obiit sanctus Cuthbertus.

xii. Post undecim annos corpus sancti Cuthberti incorruptum inuentum est.

xiii. Ethelwaldus episcopus fecit crucem lapideam que adhuc cernitur in cimiterio Dunelmense .

ᵃ⁻ᵃ Lindisfarnensis siue Dunelmensis ecclesie *Fx L T* *ᵇ* episcopum *add. T Y* *ᶜ* uel Edredum *add. Fx (above line) T* *ᵈ* om. *Fx L T* *ᵉ* prouincie *add. D Fx L T Y* *ᶠ* Northanhymbrensium *T* *ᵍ⁻ᵍ* electus est *D T* *ʰ⁻ʰ* Quale exemplum uenerabilis Cuthbertus prebuit suis successoribus *D Fx L T Y*

---

[1] This list of chapter headings is found only in D, Fx, H, L, T, and Y. In D it is on an added quire of later date, so the earliest manuscript in which it is integral to the text is H. The following edition aims to represent the chapter list as found in H with the developments evident in the later manuscripts given in the notes. The rubric is found only in H, the central portion only legible with difficulty under ultraviolet light.

xiv. De genealogia Ceowulfi regis et omnium regum Northumbrie.

xv. Obiit Beda doctor.

xvi. De libris quos fecit Beda.

xvii. Ceowlfus rex*a* factus est monachus Lindisfarnensis.

xviii. Obiit Balterus anachorita de Tinningham.

xix. Eadbertus rex dimisso regno clericatum suscepit.

xx. Higbaldus factus est episcopus Lindisfarnensis.

xxi. Descripcio Lindisfarnensis insule.

xxii. Prima uastacio Lindisfarnensis insule a paganis.

xxiii. Ecclesia sancti Cuthberti in Norham edificata est.

xxiv. Carleol episcopatui Lindesfarnensi ecclesie subiacebat.

xxv. Secunda et extrema Lindisfarnensis insule uastacio sub Inguar et Hubba.

xxvi. De Osberto et Ella regibus qui Cretham et Billingham abstuler-unt sancto Cuthberto.

xxvii. Occiditur sanctus Eadmundus.

xxviii. De fuga Ardulphi episcopi cum corpore sancti Cuthberti *b*de insula Lindisfarnense.*b*

xxix. Quare mulieres non intrant in ecclesias sancti Cuthberti.

xxx. De septem uiris qui portabant feretrum sancti Cuthberti.*c*

xxxi (xxxii).[2] De fuga Ardulphi episcopi uersus Yberniam et de amissione texti ewangeliorum.

xxxii (xxxiii). Nomina quattuor uirorum principalium qui secuti sunt sanctum Cuthbertum.

xxxiii (xxxiv). Visio Hundredi.

xxxiv (xxxv). De inuentione texti ewangeliorum.

xxxv (xxxvi). De morte Alfdene.

xxxvi (xxxvii). De uisione Eadredi de Guthredo faciendo regem.

xxxvii (xxxviii). Sedes episcopalis*d* in Cunkacestre restauratur.

xxxviii (xxxix). De libertatibus et pace ecclesie*e* sancti Cuthberti a regibus Anglie*f* Elfredo et Guthredo statutis.

xxxix (xl). Scotti absorpti sunt apud Mundingedene.*g*

xl (xliii). Rainwald quidam rex paganus Northumbriam uastauit.

---

a *om. H*   *b–b* *om. H*   *c* et de Alfredo rege *add.* Fx L T Y; et de Alfredo rege cui sanctus Cuthbertus apparuit *add.* D; xxxi. Quomodo in peregrino habitu a ministro Elfredi panem diuisum Cuthbertus accepit *add.* Fx L T Y   *d* Dunelmensis *add.* Fx L T; Lindisfarnensis *add.* D Y   *e* *om.* L T   *f* Anglorum D Fx L T   *g* pugnantem contra eos Guthredo rege; xli. De priuilegiis Guthredi regis; xlii. De morte Elfredi (Egfridi Y) regis *add.* Fx L T Y

---

[2] From here on the number in brackets is the chapter-number given by Fx, L, T, and Y.

xli (xliv). De crudeli morte Onlafbal.

xlii (xlv). Sanctus Dunstanus natus est.

xliii (xlvi). Ethelstanus rex leges et libertates sancto Cuthberto confirmauit.

xliv (xlvii). Sexelm episcopus per sanctum Cuthbertum fugatus est.[a]

xlv (xlix). Aldunus episcopus cum corpore sancti Cuthberti fugam iniit.[b]

[c]xlvi. Corpus sancti Cuthberti Dunelmum delatum est.[c]

xlvii (l). Genealogia eorum qui corpus sancti Cuthberti Dunelmum portauerunt.[d]

xlviii (lii). De miraculis factis in ecclesia ubi sanctus Cuthbertus prius iacuit.[e]

xlix (liv). Aldunus episcopus quasdam uillas et terras quibusdam accomodauit que nunquam post ad ecclesiam redierunt.

l (lv). Populus Northanhimbrorum[f] apud Carrum interfectus est a Scottis.

li (lvi). De electione Eadmundi episcopi.

lii (lvii). De Alfredo larue.[g]

liii (lviii). De ossibus plurimorum sanctorum que Alfredus larue[h] de terra leuauit.

liv (lix). De reliquiis Bede doctoris.[i]

lv (lx). Cnut rex uenit ad sanctum Cuthbertum nudis pedibus.

lvi (lxi). Duncanus rex Scottorum Dunelmum obsedit set nichil proficiens[j] a suis in sua terra interfectus est.

lvii (lxii). De Eadredo symoniaco episcopo primo de ordine clericali.

lviii (lxiii). De Egelrico episcopo expulso sed postea per uim reconciliato.

lix (lxiv). De thesauro inuento apud Ceastre.[k]

lx (lxv). De Feochero presbitero cui in calice [l]pro sanguine[l] Christi [m]nigra species[m] apparuit.

lxi (lxvi). De Iudith comitissa et famula eius.[n]

lxii (lxviii). De serpente constringente collum cuiusdam.

lxiii (lxix). De denariis ardentibus in ore cuiusdam latronis.

[a] xlviii. De consecratione Alduni primi episcopi Dunelmensis *add. Fx L T Y*
[b] apud Rypon *add. Fx L T Y* [c-c] *om. Fx L T Y* [d] li. De consecratione (constructione *Y*) ecclesie Dunelmensis per Aldunum (per Aldunum *om. Y*) *add. Fx L T Y*
[e] liii. De dedicatione ecclesie Dunolm *add. Fx L T Y* [f] Northumbrie *T*
[g] *erased L;* filio Westou *add. above line Fx L T* [h] predictus *Fx; om. L* [i] et monachi de Jarrowe *Fx L Y (add. by later hand)* [j] postea *add. T Y* [k] et ab Egelrico episcopo asportato *add. D* [l-l] sanguinis *Fx L* [m-m] in nigra specie *Fx L T Y* [n] lxvii. Quomodo miles comitis Tosti Barcwith dum ianuas monasterii eius infringere cupit subito percussus interierit *add. Fx L T Y*

lxiv (lxx). De occisione Roberti Cumin apud Dunelmum.

lxv (lxxi). De nebula apud Aluertonam.

lxvi (lxxii). De fuga cum corpore sancti Cuthberti ad insulam Lindesfarnensem et de recessu maris.

lxvii (lxxiii). De morte Gillomichaelis.[a]

lxviii (lxxiv). Egelwinus episcopus cum thesauris ecclesie fugit.

lxix (lxxv). Walkerus factus est Dunelmensis episcopus.

lxx (lxxvi). Willelmus rex [b]de Dunelmo fugit[b] incredulus de incorruptione corporis sancti Cuthberti.

lxxi (lxxvii). De fugacione cuiusdam Ranulphi.

lxxii (lxxviii). De aduentu Aluuini monachi [c]sociorumque eius[c] in Northumbriam.

lxxiii (lxxix). Quod[h] habitacio monachorum [e]restauratur in Garue.[e]

[f]lxxiv. Alduuinus et Turgotus apud Mailros habitare ceperunt.[f]

lxxv. [g]Quod[h] habitacio monachorum apud Weremutham restauratur.[g]

[i]lxxvi. De quodam mortuo reuiuiscente et de hiis qui predixit de morte Walcheri episcopi et suorum.[i]

lxxvii (lxxxiii). Walkerus episcopus occiditur.[j]

lxxviii (lxxxv). Willelmus de Sancto Karilefo factus est [k]Dunelmensis episcopus.[k]

lxxix (lxxxvii). Monachi Weremute et Garue in Dunelmum conuenerunt et professionem fecerunt et ibidem remanserunt.

lxxx (lxxxviii) Tynemuthe fuit possessio monachorum de Gerue.[l]

lxxxi (xc). Epistola Willelmi Dunelmensis episcopi[m] [n]ad monachos Dunelmenses.[n]

lxxxii (xci). [o]Obiit Aldwinus primus prior Dunelmensis.[o]

lxxxiii (xcii). Obiit Willelmus primus rex Anglorum.

lxxxiiii (xciii). Willelmus episcopus Dunelmensis ab Anglia expulsus est.

---

[a] Gillonis Michaelis *Fx*   [b–b] fugit de Dunelmo *D*   [c–c] om. *T Y*
[d] om. *D L T Y*   [e–e] apud Girum et Wermuth restauratur *Fx;* apud Girum restauratur *L T*; apud Weremutam restauratur *Y*   [f–f] lxxx. Qualiter Aldwinus monachus cum Turgoto discipulo suo Gyruensem ecclesiam dereliquerunt *Fx L T Y*
[g–g] lxxxi. Turgotus factus est monachus de Wermuth *Fx L T Y*   [h] om. *D*
[i–i] lxxxii. De moribus Walcheri Dunolmensis episcopi et de uisione cuiusdam morientis *Fx L T Y*   [j] cum suis clericis add. *D;* cum suis clericis occiditur; lxxxiv. Quomodo quidam furtum quod in monasterio eius perpetrauerat cognouit et miserabiliter insania obiit (cognouit et miserabiliter insania obiit om. *Y*) *Fx L T Y*   [k–k] episcopus Dunelmensis; lxxxvi. De merore Willelmi episcopi Dunelmensi primi *Fx L T Y*
[l] lxxxix. Quomodo Paulus abbas et Robertus comes iniuriam pene receperunt add. *Fx L T Y*   [m] primi episcopi *L*   [n–n] om. *Fx L T Y*   [o–o] Aldwinus primus prior Dunelmensis obiit *D*

lxxxv (xciv). Noua ecclesia in Dunelmo inchoata est.

lxxxvi (xcv). Visio Bosonis.[a]

lxxxvii (xcvi). Obiit Willelmus Dunelmensis [b]episcopus primus.[b][3]

[CONTINUATION]

lxxxviii (xcvii). De periculo quod Randulphus[c] Flambard euasit.

lxxxix (xcviii). De moribus Randulphi[d] episcopi.

[e]xc (xcix). Obiit Randulphus episcopus Dunelmensis.[e]

[f]xci (c). Obiit Gaufridus episcopus Dunelmensis.[f][4]

xcii (ci). De factione Willelmi Cumin.[g]

xciii (cii). Barones episcopatus Dunelmensis [h]simul consenserunt Willelmo Cumin.[h]

xciv (ciii). Willelmus de Sancta Barbara electus est ad episcopatum Dunelmum.

xcv (civ). [i]De crudelitate Willelmi Cumin et de rebellione eius.[i]

xcvi (cv). De proditione Hugonis Pintun.[j]

xcvii (cvi). Quod castellum factum est de ecclesia sancti Iohannis apud[k] Merington [l]et de uindicta eorum qui hoc fecerunt.[l]

xcviii (cvii). Willelmus de Sancta Barbara receptus est in pace ad episcopatum[m] Dunelmensem.

Ca

INCIPIVNT CAPITVLA LIBRI PRIMI[5]

[i] De fide et origine sancti Oswaldi, et predicatione sancti Aidani, que sunt primitiua fundamenta ecclesie Dunelmi.

[ii] Quo anno beatus Oswaldus ecclesiam Lindisfarnensem fundauerit

---

[a] xcvi. De iniusta uexacione et obitu Willelmi primi episcopi Dunelmensis *add.* L
[b-b] primus rex Anglorum L   [c] Ranulf- *D throughout;* Ranulph- *Fx L T Y throughout*
[d] Dunelmi *add. Fx L T Y*   [e-e] De electione Gaufridi episcopi *Fx L T Y*
[f-f] *om.* H   [g] Comin *throughout D Fx L T Y;* et obitu Gaufridi episcopi *add.* H *in later hand*   [h-h] consenserunt Willelmo Comin D; Willelmo Comin consenserunt Fx L T Y   [i-i] De rebellione Willelmi Comin (Cumin D) et crudelitate ipsius D Fx L T Y   [j] Pinsun D Y; filii Pinconis dapiferi Willelmi de Sancta Barbara D Fx L T [k] de *Fx T Y;* in L   [l-l] *om. Fx L T Y*   [m] ecclesiam *Fx L T Y*

---

[3] This chapter is numbered 'xcvii' in L which, from this point on, is one number ahead of Fx, T, and Y.

[4] H's list omits this chapter so, from this point on, it has numbers one less than those of D's.

[5] This list of chapter-headings divided into four books is found only in Ca.

et quo de hoc seculo migrauerit et de presulatu Aidani et integritate brachii sancti Oswaldi.

[iii] De obitu sancti Aidani cuius anime exitus reuelatus est oculis beati Cuthberti et quo tempore Cuthbertus susceperit habitum monachi.

[iv] De Finano episcopo quomodo regem Merciorum baptizauerat et eis episcopum de suis ordinauerit et Ced ab eo consecratus quid fecerit.

[v] Qualiter Colmannus episcopatum dimiserit et episcopus Tudda obierit et sibi Eatam successurum impetrauit.

[vi] Quo tempore Eata episcopatum perceperit et beati Cuthberti conuersio facta sit et quanta spirituali perfectione uite sue pro- fectum instituerit.

[vii] Quando beatus Cuthbertus Lindisfarnensis ecclesie prioratum acceperit et qua dulcedine in anachoresi uixerit.

[viii] Quo tempore sanctus Beda natus sit et de monasterio illius et quanta scientia tunc in Anglia claruerit.

[ix] De electione sancti Cuthberti et quomodo de Farne eductus sit et ubi consecratus et que rex ei Egfridus eo die dederit.

[x] Qualiter in episcopatu sanctus Cuthbertus uixerit et quomodo de mundo emigrauerit et se ad Lindisfarnensem ecclesiam reduci permiserit.

[xi] Quomodo post undecim sepulture annos corpus eius incorruptum repertum sit et de Eadberto episcopo et Etheluuoldo qui uterque ei in anachoresi successit et qua etate Beda eius uitam scripserit.

[xii] De Etheluuoldo episcopo et cruce lapidea quam fecit.

[xiii] De Ceulfi regis prosapia et uita eius et pacientia.

[xiv] Quo euo uel tempore sanctus Beda obierit qualiter uixerit et quanta scripserit.

[xv] Epistola de transitu Bede et eius conuersatione.

Expliciunt capitula libri primi.

INCIPIVNT CAPITVLA LIBRI SECVNDI

[i] Quando et ubi Ceolfus rex monachus factus sit, et quanta secum dederit, et a quo apud Northam corpus illius delatum sit.

[ii] Qualiter quidam de regio genere ad pacem beati Cuthberti confugerit, et inde abstractus sit, et quomodo Kinewlf episcopus pro eo in carcere trusus sit, et de morte sancti Baltherii.

[iii] De industria et conuersione regis Edberti, et fratris eius presulatu, atque ipsius obitu.

[iv] De occisione regis Osulfi, et quo tempore Kinewlf episcopatum Higbaldo dimiserit et obierit, et quomodo uel ubi rex Elwoldus peremptus sit.

[v] De destructione ecclesie Lindisfarnensis et celeri ultione, et de Higbaldo, Egberto, et Egredo episcopis, et terris per illos acquisitis.

[vi] De secunda per Danos Lindisfarnensis ecclesie et Northymbrie depopulatione, et quo tempore, uel quare Eardulfus episcopus corpus sancti Cuthberti de insula tulerit, et quale seruitium deinceps celebratum sit a clericis.

[vii] Quare femine in ecclesia sancti Cuthberti non intrent, et de excessu sanctimonialium quondam de Coldingaham.

[viii] De femina que cimiterium sancti Cuthberti introiit, quam celeri uindicta punita sit.

[ix] Item de alia que per cimiterium cucurrit, qua morte seipsam extinxerit.

[x] De peste per Danos illata, et de septem portitoribus sancti Cuthberti, et de uisione regis Elfredi.

[xi] Quomodo corpus sancti Cuthberti ad Hyberniam transferri debuit, sed unda in sanguinem conuersa tempestate subita redactum sit.

[xii] De portitoribus sacri corporis ex diutino labore pertesis. Que nomina eis fuerint. Et qualiter equum, frenum, carrumque predicente sancto Cuthberto inuenerint, et textum euangeliorum in mare triduo demersum illesum receperint.

[xiii] Quomodo iussu sancti Cuthberti Guthredus sit rex effectus, et de donis eius, priuilegiis et largitionibus.

[xiv] Item de dignitatibus, et ecclesie priuilegiis.

[xv] Quid rex Elfredus moriens Edwardo filio suo preceperit.

[xvi] De episcopo Cutheardo, et quomodo Eadward monarchiam perceperit, et de Onlafbald, qualiter in limite ecclesie sancti Cuthberti interierit.

[xvii] De Tilredo episcopo, et de mandato regi Ethelstano per auum suum facto.

[xviii] De episcopo Wigredo, et quanta Ethelstanus rex sancto Cuthberto dedit, quando in Scotiam perrexit.

[xix] Quomodo sanctus Cuthbertus Sexelmum episcopum pepulit, et de terra sua fugauerit.

[xx] De morte Edmundi regis, et episcopatu Elsig.

Expliciunt capitula libri secundi.

INCIPIVNT CAPITVLA LIBRI TERTII

[i] Quomodo Aldunus corpus sancti Cuthberti in Rippun tulerit, et de Werdelau postea in Dunelmum uenerit, et de nominibus portitorum.

[ii] Qualiter locus ille habitabilis factus sit.

[iii] De contracta quadam sanata in loco ubi beati Cuthberti corpus requieuerat.

[iv] Quo tempore Aldunus episcopus ecclesiam in Dunelmo dedicauerit, et quot donariis a potentibus ditata sit.

[v] De Cnut rege, et oratione Alduni episcopi et morte.

[vi] Qualiter uoce ter de sepulcro sancti Cuthberti emissa, Eadmundus ipsius ecclesiae clericus ad episcopatum sit prouectus, et monachus factus.

[vii] De Elfredo presbitero quomodo in ecclesia sancti Cuthberti claruerit, et de capillo quem in igne posuit, et de reliquiis sacris pluribus quas beato Cuthberto reuelante in Dunelmum comportauit.

[viii] Quanta Cnut rex sancto Cuthberto dederit.

[ix] De obsessione Dunelmi et celeri uindicta regis et episcopi symoniaci et de Egelrico episcopo qui thesauros beati Cuthberti sustulit quomodo punitus sit.

[x] De presbitero nocte fornicante et in crastino missam celebrante quomodo particula corporis cum sanguine in nigredinem conuersam uiderit et percipiendo nimiam amaritudinem senserit.

[xi] Quomodo uxor Tosti comitis puellam in cimiterium beati Cuthberti miserit et mox infirmata in proximo obierit et de imaginibus deargentatis.

[xii] De quodam in campo obdormiente cuius collum serpens constrinxit sed in introitu ecclesiae sancti Cuthberti semper ab eo dissiliit qualiter liberatus fuit.

[xiii] De quodam ad sepulchrum in ore denarios furante qualiter sit punitus et restitutus.

[xiv] De donis Copsi comitis.

[xv] De Eaduuardo rege et W. et de Rodberto Cumin apud Dunelmum occiso et quomodo aque maris irrigue cesserint beati Cuthberti corpore ad insulam adueniente.

[xvi] De apparitione sancti Oswaldi et beati Cuthberti et subita morte Gillonis et ab eis predicta pena ultionis.

[xvii] De Egeluuino episcopo qui partem tesauri tulit quomodo reductus sit.

[xviii] De electione Walkeri episcopi sed tamen clerici.

[xix] De rege W. qui beati Cuthberti corpus an Dunelmo quiesceret explorare uoluit, qualiter punitus et fugatus sit.

[xx] Quomodo rex W. Ranulfum miserit ut terram sancti Cuthberti sub tributo redigeret sed beato Cuthberto uindicante furiosus sit effectus et restitutus et de priuilegiis W. regis.

[xxi] Qualiter Aldunus de Wincencumb cum duobus fratribus de Eouesham in Northymbriam aduenerint et quomodo ab episcopo Walkero suscepti sint et fructificauerint.

[xxii] De fratre ad Streneshalch pergente, et de fundamine aecclesiae beate Marie Eboraci, et quomodo Walkerus iterum Aldunum reuocauerit, et Weremuthe cum ceteris terris eis adiecerit.

[xxiii] De prouectu episcopi et suorum rapina feroci, et qualia tunc quidam de morte reuiuiscens de episcopo et ceteris multis uiderit et predixerit.

[xxiv] Qualiter episcopus Walkerus et ubi occisus atque sepultus sit, et quomodo pro eo uindicatum et ecclesia beati Cuthberti spoliata sit.

Expliciunt capitula libri tertii.

INCIPIVNT CAPITVLA LIBRI QVARTI

[i] Qualiter W. episcopus electus et sacratus sit, et quante uir scientie, probitatis et gratie fuerit.

[ii] Quomodo clericos de ecclesia beati Cuthberti eiecerit, et auctoritate pape et regis monachos prefatos introduxerit.

[iii] Quo die et tempore monachos Dunelmum duxerit et eos benedixerit et officia singula eis distribuerit.

[iv] De corpore sancti Osuui et de possessione ecclesiae de Tinemuthe et illius uiolenta ablatione.

[v] Quanta W. episcopus acquisierit et qualem se subditis exhibuerit.

[vi] Epistola W. episcopi ad monachos Dunelmenses.

[vii] De obitu prioris Alduni et successione Turgoti.

[viii] De exilio W. episcopi et quando posuerit fundamenta in Dunelmo noui monasterii.

[ix] Qualia Boso miles de cenobitis Dunelmensibus uiderit et quanta de obitu W. episcopi predixerit.

[x] Vbi idem episcopus obierit et quomodo Dunelmum corpus eius delatum sit.

INDEX OF MANUSCRIPTS CITED

INDEX OF QUOTATIONS AND ALLUSIONS

GENERAL INDEX

Where several monks of Durham of the same name occur in the text, especially in the lists on pp. 6–15, a single entry is given, indicating the number of monks of the name in question who are found (e.g. '(x4)' to indicate four monks of the same name).